सौन्दर्यलहरी

SAUNDARYALAHARĪ

(THE WAVE OF BEAUTY)

श्रीशङ्कराचार्यविरचिता

सौन्दर्यलहरी

SAUNDARYALAHARĪ

(THE WAVE OF BEAUTY)

OF

ŚRĪ ŚAṄKARA BHAGAVATPĀDĀCĀRYA

with the Commentary of Lakṣmīdhara

English Translation and Notes
by S.S. Sastri & T.R.S. Ayyangar

Revised & Critically Edited
By

DR N.C. PANDA
Reader in Sanskrit,
VVBIS & IS,
Panjab University,
Sadhu Ashram, Hoshiarpur.

BHARATIYA KALA PRAKASHAN
DELHI (INDIA)

Revised and Enlarged Edition : 2009
Edition : 2023
Revised Edition : 2025

Published by C.P. Gautam *for*
BHARATIYA KALA PRAKASHAN
3480/1, IInd Floor, Narang Colony, Tri Nagar,
Delhi - 110035, Mob.: 9811642997, 8595139625
E-mail : info@bkpbooks.com; sales.bkpbooks@gmail.com
Website: www.bkpbooks.com

ISBN : 978-81-8090-207-9

Laser Type Setting
Creative Graphics

Printed by :
G.S. Offset Printers
Delhi

Dedication

Dedicated
to
A true disciple of the Great Tāntric Scholar
Pt. Mahāmahopādhyāya Gopinath Kaviraj

Contents

शुभाशंसा

डॉ. नरसिंह चरण पण्डा महाभागस्य वेद-पुराण-दर्शन-काव्यादि विषयक वैदग्धं प्रख्यापयितुं तस्य सप्तदश-निबन्ध-सङ्ग्रहात्मकः Perspectives of Indian Thought इत्याख्यो ग्रन्थविशेष एवं पर्याप्त इति नास्ति संशीतिलेशः। किन्तु 'यावज्जीवमधीते विप्रः' इत्याभाणकं याथार्थ्यं प्रापयन्नयं विपश्चित्प्रवरः सम्प्रति तत्र भवद्भिराद्यशङ्कराचार्यपादैर्विरचितं सौन्दर्यलहरीति सुप्रसिद्धं स्तोत्रं लक्ष्मीधराख्यया व्याख्यया संवलितं पुनः सम्पाद्य प्रकाशयतीति महान् हर्षस्य विषयः।

स्तोत्रमिदं सर्वेष्वपि देवीस्तोत्रेष्वनन्यसाधारणत्वाच्छेखरायते स्वीयेनाद्वितीयेन वैशिष्ट्येनेति तद्विदः। अत एव नेकैर्व्याख्यानकलाकुशलैर्विद्वद्भिर्व्याख्यातमेत्स्तुतिदृष्ट्या काव्यदृष्ट्या यन्त्र-मन्त्र-तन्त्रानुष्ठानदृष्ट्या च, मैसूरविश्वविद्यालयस्य प्राच्यविद्या-संशोधनालयतः, ईश्वीये १९४५ तमे वर्षे प्रकाशितस्य सौन्दर्यलहरीति ग्रन्थस्य द्वितीयमुद्रणप्रस्तावनायामस्य त्रिंशतोऽप्यधिकानि व्याख्यानानि विद्यन्त इति विज्ञायते इति यल्लिखितमस्ति तेनापि भवत्यस्याविदिततरं महत्त्वम्।

स्तोत्रस्यास्य भाषा नितरां सहजा सुगमा प्राञ्जला चेति निदर्शनाय एकः श्लोकः अत्रोद्ध्रियते।

दृशा द्राघीयस्या दरदलितनीलोत्पलरुचा
दवीयांसं दीनं स्नपय कृपया मामपि शिवे।
अनेनायं धन्यो भवति न च ते हानिरियता
वने वा हर्म्ये वा समकरनिपातो हिमकरः।। सौ.ल. ५७।।

यद्यपि स्तुतिदृष्ट्या प्रतिपद्यमत्र विरचयितुः स्तवनकर्मनैपुण्यं सर्वविद्यावदातचेतसः परमौदार्यं च परिलक्ष्यत एव तथापि पद्यमेकमत्रोद्ध्रियते-

भवानि त्वं दासे मयि वितर दृष्टिं सकरुणां
इति स्तोतुं वाञ्छन्कथयति भवानि त्वमिति यः।

तदैव त्वं तस्मै दिशसि निजसायुज्यपदवीं
मुकुन्दब्रह्मेन्द्रस्फुटमकुटनीराजितपदाम्।। इति, सौ.ल. २२।।

काव्यदृशा सौन्दर्यलहरीति नामधेयमस्य याथार्थ्यं भजते, अत्र सर्वत्र कवे: काव्यरचनापाटवं सहृदयानां हृदयान्यावर्जयति। अस्य पद्येषु स्वाभाविकी पदशय्या, स्थाने भावनिवेश:, अकृत्रिमा अलङ्कारा:, प्रसादो गुण: वैदर्भी रीति: भक्तिभरित: शृङ्गाररसश्चेतिसर्वमपि काव्यं काव्यरसपिपासूनां तृत्यै सर्वथालमिति पद्यमेकमत्र दीयते–

स्मितज्योत्स्नाजालं तव वदनचन्द्रस्य पिबतां
चकोराणामासीदतिरसतया चञ्चुजडिमा।
अतस्ते शीतांशोरमृतलहरीमाम्लरुचय:
पिबन्ति स्वच्छन्दं निशि निशि भृशं काञ्जिकधिया।। सौ.ल. ६३।।

प्रतिश्लोकमस्य यन्त्र–मन्त्र–तन्त्रानुष्ठानविधिश्च तत्तद्व्याख्यातृभिरिहामुष्मिक–मनोरथसिद्धिकामानामुपकाराय तत्र–तत्र सम्यक् प्रतिपादित:। तदित्थं सौन्दर्यलहरी स्तोत्रमतिशेते सर्वाण्यप्यन्यानि देवीस्तोत्राणीति तद्विद:।

लक्ष्मीधराख्या व्याख्याप्यस्य स्तोत्रस्य किमप्यनन्यसाधारणवैशिष्ट्यं भजते, यतो हि–अत्र व्याख्यात्रा विपश्चिता श्लोकानुसारिपदानां व्याख्यानं तु कृतमेव सहैव अत्रेत्थं पदयोजनेत्युक्त्वा सर्वत्र श्लोकार्थ: स्फुटीकृत:। क्वचिच्चान्येषां व्याख्यातृणां मतान्यप्युपस्थापितानि। तथा तेषु तेषु श्लोकेषु निहितं तान्त्रिकरहस्यमपि युक्तिप्रमाणोपन्यासपुर:सरं व्याख्यातम्। अलङ्कारा अपि निरूपिता इति।

अस्माकं सुहृदा डा. नरसिंह चरण पण्डामहाभागेनास्य पुन: सम्पादनाय इमे बिन्दव: लक्षीकृता:–

1. सौन्दर्यलहरी श्लोक: (पाठभेद निर्देशपूर्वकम्)
2. रोमन–अक्षरेषु श्लोकच्छाया
3. लक्ष्मीधरव्याख्या
4. आङ्ग्लभाषायां व्याख्यानम्
5. परिशिष्टभागे च–

(क) शब्दसूची, (ख) अकारादि क्रमेण श्लोकसूची, (ग) अकारादिक्रमेण श्लोकपादसूची, (घ) प्रतिश्लोकमाश्रित्य यन्त्र–मन्त्रानुष्ठानविधि:, (ङ) सहायकग्रन्थसूची च।

विपश्चितानेन विभिन्नानि नव संस्करणान्यवलम्ब्य संस्करणमिदं सम्पाद्यते। पाठान्तराणि च सङ्केतपुरःसरं तत्रैव पृष्ठस्याधोभागे दत्तानीत्यस्य नावीन्यं वैशिष्ट्यं च। विद्वद्वर्योऽयं नितरां पटीयान् ग्रन्थसम्पादनकलायामित्यस्येदं सम्पादनकर्म दर्शं दर्शं प्रसीदतितराञ्चेतः। सौन्दर्यलहरीतिस्तोत्रस्यानुरागिणोऽपि कार्येणानेनोपकृता भविष्यन्तीति मे विश्वासः।

अन्ते च–

सोऽयं पण्डामहाभागो नृसिंहचरणः सुधीः।
सरस्वत्या निधेर्भूयः कुर्याद् वृद्धिं शतं समाः।।

इति कामये।

प्रो. जगदीशप्रसादः सेमवालः
अध्यक्षचरः, विश्वेश्वरानन्द विश्वबन्धु संस्कृत-
भारतभारती अनुशीलन संस्थानम्
पञ्जाब विश्वविद्यालयः, साधुआश्रमः,
होशियारपुरम्–१४६ ०२१, पञ्जाब।

Foreword

Ādi Śaṅkarācārya is credited with the authorship of *Bhāṣyas* (commentaries) on the three *Prasthānas* of the ancient Indian spiritual thought represented by the Upaniṣads, the *Bhagavadgītā* and the *Brahmasūtra*, written by Bādarāyaṇa Vyāsa. We discover in him through these *bhāṣyas*, a master dialectician well versed in the art of polemics convincingly refuting the metaphysical thought-projections of all rival schools of Indian philosophy, especially those of the Buddhists and the Mīmāṁsakas, then dominating the scene, thereby establishing his thesis, the doctrine of Advaitavāda.

He is also said to have composed a number of minor philosophical texts like *Vivekacūḍāmaṇi Upadeśasāhasrī, etc.* and devotional poems *(stotras)* like the *Dakṣiṇāmūrti-stotra,* the *Saundaryalaharī, Śivāṣṭaka-stotra, Śivapañcākṣara-stotra, Aparādha-bhañjana-stotra, Carpaṭapañjarikā-stotra,* the *Nirvāṇāṣṭaka,* etc. all filled with sublime spiritual thought and deep religious fervour. All these so called minor works and devotional poems reveal different facet in the personality of Ādi Śaṅkarācārya. This has led some well known scholars regarded as authorities on Śaṅkara's thought, to doubt the genuine of his authorship of devotional poems. They are of the view that devotional poems were composed later some other Śaṅkarācārya heading some Śaṅkara pīṭha.

Unfortunately these scholars appear to overlook the basic fact pertaining to transmission of spiritual wisdom by spiritual masters to their disciples. It was incumbant on the part of Ācārya to be always conscious of the capacity and inclination of the disciples and then give his discourse on spiritual subject, varying the style and content accordingly. Ādi Śaṅkarācārya wrote his *bhāṣyas,* on the three *Prasthānas* for the *Sannyāsī* disciples and minor works for the laity as they were more interested in their spiritual elevation than in listening to debates and logical refutation of opponents' views. Therefore, there is hardly any room for doubting the authenticity of Ādi Śaṅkarācārya's devotional poems. My revered teacher the late Mahāmahopādhyāya Gopinath Kaviraj expressed this opinion to me while shedding light on the contribution made by Ādi Śaṅkarācārya to ancient spiritual thought.

I am glad to find that Dr. Narasingha Charan Panda has taken up the re-publication of the *Saundaryalaharī* with the commentary of Lakṣmīdhara, the founder of the Śaṅkarācārya school, translated into English with notes by the late S.S. Sastri and T.R.S. Ayyangar, after thorough revision of the text and its translation, making it free from blemish.

I commend this edition to discerning readers.

Kolkata
1.3.2009

Prof. Debabrata Sen Sharma
Professor of Sanskrit (Retd.)

PREFACE

श्रुतिस्मृतिपुराणानामालयं करुणालयम्।
नमामि भगवत्पादशङ्करं लोकशङ्करम्।।

1. Ācārya Śaṅkara and his Literary Contribution :

Ācārya Śaṅkara is one of the greatest philosophers, India has ever produced and also the greatest exponent of Advaita Vedānta. He is worshipped as an incarnation of Lord Śiva.

Ācārya Śaṅkara's life is unique in more than one way. It is obvious that he performed numberless miracles. A Sanskrit Verse rightly says: When he was eight years old he had achieved mastery over the Vedas; at the twelve he had knowledge of all the *Śāstras;* by the time he was sixteen he had written his renowned commentary on the *Brahmasūtras;* and at thirty-two he become a sage and then departed from this world.

Ācārya Śaṅkara's vision of India regarding Hindu Philosophy is unique and outstanding. In a true sense he visualized the integrity of India. So he realized the need to establish *maṭhas* as centres to spread Vedic message not only to his contemporary society but to the generations to come. Hence, he established the Religious centres (*maṭhas*) in four corners of India with the intension of making the people of realize that India is spiritually and culturally one.

Śaṅkarācārya's philosophy was positive and optimistic. It is pertinent to note here that a number of critics declare his philosophy is not tenable to the thoughts those are being spread through these *maṭhas,* as he opines that the world is the creation of *Māyā,* i.e. illusion; and moreover, his philosophy advocates the *Nivṛtti* style of life, that is renunciation of *Karma*. But, in the context of his Advaitic thought, the world is accepted as the behavioural reality, i.e. *Vyāvahārikī-sattā*. So, in this context the social work as such was undertaken by this great exponent of Advaitic Philosophy.

The Indian people accepted his Advaitic Philosophy not because of his philosophic analysis, but due to his personality which was embodiment of Vedic *upāsanā*. It is clear from his simple devotional hymns sung in praise of a good number of Hindu gods, goddesses and other noble concepts. This wealth of *Stotra* literature had its wide impact on the *upāsanā* and *bhakti* trends prevailing in Hindu Vedic life.

The philosopher and the common man are equally benefitted by his simple, musical and sentimental style of devotional hymns as well as analytical exposition of philosophical concepts in his monumental commentaries of the *Brahmasūtras*, the *Upaniṣads* are the *Bhagavadgītā*. Śaṅkara's style of writing in lucid and deep. He explains the deep, mysterious and even highly complicated and tedious issues of Indian Philosophy with ease and understandable. We witness his sagacious erudition and analytical skill throughout his available works and commentaries. The works of Śaṅkarācārya have been divided into two main categories, *viz.* : (1) the Major works, and (2) the Minor works.

I. Major works of Śaṅkarācārya :

(A) Commentary on the *Principal Upaniṣads*

(B) Commentary on the *Bhagavadgītā*

(C) Commentary on the *Brahmasūtra*

The *Upaniṣads* representing the Veda *(śruti)*, the *Bhagavadgītā* representing the tradition *(smṛti)* and lastly the *Brahmasūtra*, that serves as the basis of literal exposition, are known *'prasthānatraya'* or the three basic works of Vedānta on which almost every great Ācāryas have commented. Ācārya Śaṅkara's exposition of these Vedāntic texts is monumental.

(A) Commentaries on the Upaniṣads : It is known that

Śaṅkarācārya was one of the most authentic and original interpreters of the Philosophy of the Upaniṣads. The main source of his philosophy was, by and large, the Upaniṣads. He has written commentary on the ten principal Upaniṣads, *viz., Īśa, Kena, Kaṭha, Praśna, Muṇḍaka, Māṇḍūkya, Taittirīya, Aitareya, Chāndogya* and *Bṛhadāraṇyaka.*

In addition to these, Śaṅkara might have commented upon the *Śvetāśvatara Upaniṣad, Nṛsiṁha Pūrvatāpanīya Upaniṣad, etc.,* as we frequently find references regarding this in the commentaries of these Upaniṣads written by the successors of Śaṅkarācārya. Śaṅkarā's commentaries on the Upaniṣads have the same excellence in the expression as found in his other works.

(B) Commentary on the *Bhagavadgītā* : The *Gītā* comes next to the Upaniṣads. It is given a status which is almost equal to that of Upaniṣads. It is regarded as a philosophical as well as religious treatise. Śaṅkarācārya describes *Gītā* as the quintessence of teaching of the entire Veda. Śaṅkara's commentary on *Gītā,* which starts from the eleventh verse of the second chapter, emphasises the role of knowledge responsible for causing liberation or *mukti.* The commentary with clear understanding of the conceptual meaning of the texts is quite evident of Śaṅkara's extensive knowledge, of his contemporary as well as previous schools of *Gītā* studies. He comments on the words and expressions of the text in the order, in which they occur in it, giving an introductory explanation and a concluding summary for each verse. While the commentators of *Gītā* propounded that the sole purpose of this religious text is to establish the theory of *Karman,* preached in Vedic lore to attain the liberation, but Śaṅkara's stress on the facts that *Gītā* intends to elucidate the theory of knowledge *(jñāna),* i.e. the knowledge of the Supreme.

(C) Commentary on the *Brahmasūtra* : The *Brahmasūtra* is originally written by Bādarāyaṇa Vyāsa. Ācārya Śaṅkara has commented upon his famous treatise, which is known as *Śārīrakabhāṣya*. There is no doubt that Śaṅkara's commentary is the masterly exposition of the *sūtras*.

II. Minor works of Śaṅkarācārya :

(A) In order to propagate the doctrine of Advaita Vedānta, he authored a number of works dealing with the problematic study of the particular concept of Advaitism for layman. These independent works in Sanskrit give the Advaitic viewpoint on the main concepts of Vedānta. Some of these famous works are as follows: (1) *Upadeśasāhasrī*, (2) *Vivekacūḍāmaṇi*, (3) *Ātmabodha*, (4) *Aparokṣānubhūti*, (5) *Pañcikaraṇam*, (6) *Vākyavṛtti*, (7) *Laghu-vākyavṛtti*, (8) *Prabodha Sudhākara*, (9) *Ṣaṭślokī*, (10) *Dośaślokī*, (11) *Svātmanirupaṇam*, (12) *Advaitānubhūti*, *etc.*

These *Stotras* are the fine examples of Śaṅkara's deep devotional feelings towards the Gods and Goddesses being worshipped by the Hindu people. The poetic aspect of Śaṅkara's philosophy is revealed in these *Stotras*. The use of appropriate metre and charming diction, evidently acknowledge the *kāvya-pratibhā* (poetic excellence) of Ācārya Śaṅkara.

(B) Bhakti *Stotras* of Śaṅkarācārya :

There are over 200 *Stotras* attributed to Ācārya Śaṅkara, but in fact, only a dozen or so can be original writing of Śaṅkara. Of these, the main *stotras* which can be ascribed to Śaṅkarācārya are as under :

(1) *Dakṣiṇāmūrti-stotra*, (2) *Carpaṭa-pañjarikā*, (3) *Ānanda-laharī*, (4) *Dvādaśapañjarikā*, (5) *Saptapadī*, (6) *Govindāṣṭaka*, and (7) *Viṣṇupadī-stotra*.

Thus, Śaṅkarācārya has fulfilled the need of intellectuals as well as common men by writing different books, commentaries and numerous devotional hymns.

(C) Works on Tantra :

There are two works on Tantra which are ascribed to Śaṅkarācārya, *viz. Saundaryalaharī* and *Prapañcasāra*.

2. *Saundaryalaharī* and its subject matter :

The *Saundaryalaharī* is universally recognized as an ancient and authoritative Tāntric work. The very title of this work '*Saundaryalaharī*' means, "the Wave of Beauty", that is praise of external and internal beauty of Mother Goddess. Both Divine Glory as well as human form of the Mother Goddess are considered to be the parts of her pearless beauty. Ācārya Śaṅkara has scaled the heights of his poetic imagination and sentimental rapture while singing the beautiful glory of the Mother Goddess. Among the hymns addressed to Goddess, the *Saundaryalaharī* occupies an unprecedented position. It deals with the forms of worship of Divine Śakti according to the ancient tradition of Samayācāra, which aims at and claims to be in perfect agreement with the Vedic teachings. *Saundaryalaharī* is a composition of one hundred verses (with three more verses found in various editions) in the famous Śikhariṇī metre. This great Tāntric text properly elaborates the various aspects of worship of the Divine Mother. However, it is one of the most inspiring devotional hymns which may help a *sādhaka* or devotee to obtain peace and final liberation.

Traditionally, this beautiful hymn is divided into two parts, known as *Ānandalaharī* and *Saundaryalaharī*. The first part of the work contains forty-one verses, which is widely known as *Ānandalaharī*. It mainly deals with the *Kuṇḍalinī-śakti* and the *Cakras* and other Tāntric subjects. The work contains the essence of *Śrīvidyā* in nutshell. *Śrīvidyā* means "that which confers unalloyed Bliss" in the union of Brahman and *Jīva*. In essence, it is a discipline of Brahmavidyā, extended to all persons including those not eligible to observe the Vedic rituals, without distinction of sex and caste. The first part of *Saundaryalaharī* chiefly deals with the most sacred *Śrīcakra*, which is called the abode of Śiva-Śakti and which forms the specific symbol of worship of the Goddess. The worship is done in the image of the Devī as well as in the *Śrīcakra*, otherwise known as *Śrīyantra*. In the worship of *Śriyantra* the personal and impersonal aspects of Brahman are harmonized. Ritual and meditation lead to the

Supreme Peace and Highest Bliss. The second part, *i.e.* the remaining verses of this text are devoted to the magnificent exposition of the charming beauty of Divine Mother, in the form of the Mother Goddess, from head to foot, in a highly poetical language and devotional fervour.

The *Śrīcakra* is considered as a complete representations of the spiritual union of Śiva and Śakti. It is engraved on metal-plates, to be drawn with sandal paste, vermillion or turmeric powder, on the bark of a tree called Bhūrja, on silk, or some other pure base; and is worshipped with sandal-paste, flowers, incense, lamp, food-offerings, lighting of camphor, *etc.* The *Rudrayāmala* describes the *Śrīcakra* as :

बिन्दुत्रिकोणवसुकोणदशारयुग्ममन्वस्त्रनागदलसंयुतषोडशारम्।
वृत्तत्रयं च धरणीसदनत्रयं च श्रीचक्रराजमुदितं परदेवतायाः।।

Lakṣmīdhara, the commentator of *Śaundaryalaharī,* quoted this verse in his commentary with a different reading of the second line as :

वृत्तत्रिभूपुरयुतं परितश्चतुर्द्वाः श्रीचक्रमेतदुदितं परदेवतायाः।

In support of the above verse he cites from the *Taittirīya Āraṇyaka* (1.31) as :

सतद्वाद्वारगमं ता। सꣳहार्यं नगरं तव।

The *Śrīcakra* consists of a *bindu* (central circle) *trikoṇa* (triangle), *aṣṭadala* (eight triangles), *antardaśāra* and *bahirdaśāra* (the pair of ten triangles), *aṣṭadala* (eight petals), *ṣoḍaśadala* (sixteen petals), and *bhūpuras* (three circles). So, *Śrīcakra* consists of nine *yonis* and forty-three triangles. In the nine *yonis,* five *Śakti cakras* and four *Śiva cakras* are enumerated. The five *Śakti cakras* are : *trikoṇa, aṣṭakoṇa, antardaśāra, bahirdaśāra* and *caturdaśāra.* The four *Śiva cakras* are : *bindu, aṣṭakoṇa, ṣoḍaśadala* and *bhūpura.* The nine *Śakti cakras* from *bindu* to *bhūpura* exemplify the creation of the microcosm and the macrocosm– the *jīva* and *prapañca.*

The *Śrīcakra* is one of the chief instruments of instruction of *Śrīvidyā* form of worship which comprising essentially the use of an esoteric fifteen syllable *mantra* representing the Supreme

Divine Power manifested as a form of the universe. In the *Lalitā Sahasranāma*, Devī Lalitā advises to the devotees to worship her in the *Śrīcakra*. She says : श्रीचक्रे मां समभ्यर्च्य जप्त्वा पञ्चदशाक्षरीम्। Thus, *Śrīcakra* is in every way considered as the highest symbol for the adoration of the Goddess, Tripurasundarī or Lalitā.

3. Commentaries and Expositions :

About thirty-five commentaries were written in different languages on *Saundaryalaharī*. Out of these commentaries, Lakṣmīdhara's *Lakṣmīdharā Ṭīkā*, Kaivalyāśrama's *Saubhāgyavardhanī*, Kāmeśvara Sūri's *Aruṇamodinī* Comm. and Rāmakavī's *Ḍiṇḍima* Comm. stand foremost. The other noticeable commentaries are : *Ānandagirīyā, Tātparyadīpinī, Padārthacandrikā, Gopālasundarī, Ānandalaharī Ṭīkā, etc.*

Since, Lakṣmīdhara's commentary is the oldest and most authentic exposition on *Saundaryalaharī*, I have opted it as reliable source for ascertaining the real meaning with exhaustive text variations, giving a full scope to the readers for selecting the appropriate text to discern the true spirit of the work as revealed by author himself.

Lakṣmīdhara accepted only one hundred verses of the text as the genuine composition of Śrī Śaṅkarācārya. But there are three more verses included in the text, accepted by some other commentators. Besides, most of the editions also contain 103 verses. So, I have included these three additional verses in this edition with the commentary of Kaivalyāśrama's *Saubhāgyavardhanī*.

In editing the text, I have mainly consulted the following works on *Saundaryalaharī*, published from different places, *viz* :

1. *Saundaryalaharī*, ed. and published by A. Kuppuswami, Woriyur, Tiruchirapalli-3, Ist edition, 1976.
2. *Saundaryalaharī*, ed. by N.S. Venkatanatha Charya, Oriental Research Institute, University of Mysore, Mysore, fourth edition, 1969.
3. *Saundaryalaharī*, tr. into English by S.S. Śāstrī and T.R.S. Ayyangar, the Theosophical Publishing House, Adyar, Madras, 2nd edition, 1948.

4. *Saundaryalaharī*, tr. into English by Swami Tapasyananda, Sri Ramakrishna Matha, Mylapore, Chennai, 1987.

5. *Saundaryalaharī*, Comm. and tr. into Hindi by Swami Vishnutirtha, Yogasri Peeth, Tihiri Gadwal, Rishikesh, 3rd reprint, 1970.

6. *Saundaryalaharī*, ed. with Tripura Sanskrit Comm. by Acharya Shri Charanatirtha Maharaj, Shri Bhubaneswari Peeth, Gondal, Saurashtra, Gujarat, 1961.

7. *Saundaryalaharī*, tr. into English by V.K. Subramanian, Motilal Banarsidass, Delhi, reprint edition, 1980.

4. Specific features of the Present Edition :

The present edition is being prepared on the basis of several published versions for the benefit of Indological Researchers and the common readers of Philosophy and Religion. The chief peculiarity of this edition is that it contains all variant readings of the texts (verses) and commentaries, available so far. The second specially of this work is to be noted here that it contains the revised English translation of S.S. Śāstrī and T.R.S. Ayyangar. Beside these, the commentary of Lakṣmīdhara, explanatory notes, transliteration of the verses, are some other unique features of this edition. In addition to these, this work is also furnished with several Indices, in which the diagrams of *Yantras* for each verse of the text, the mode of their worship, their *bīja-mantras* and *prayoga* (application), *etc.* have been given clearly. This material will enable the aspirant to achieve his desired goal, for which these *Yantras* are formulated.

Hope, this critically edited text of *Saundaryalaharī* with its authentic version will duly encourage the young Researchers to undertake the further Philosophical or conceptual study of this sacred hymn.

However, in presenting this new Revised edition of *Saundaryalaharī*, I humbly express my devotional joy into the lotus feet of the Divine Mother, being source of all inspiration and inexhaustible energy for me; and that I consider this effort as a result of Her Divine Grace; and that the discrepancies and errors crept in this edition are apparently due to my personal limits and ignorance.

5. Acknowledgements :

I am extremely grateful to my revered teacher Prof. Debabrata Sen Sharma, for contributing a scholarly 'Foreword' to this work. I am also extending my sincere regards and thanks to Prof. J.P. Semwal, for writing a few words in Sanskrit as *Śubhāśaṅsā* (Blessings) to this work. He has also thoroughly gone through the book with keen interest. I am indebted to him for his useful suggestions and illuminating guidance.

I acknowledge my heartfelt gratitude to Prof. Ghanshyam Uniyal, Prof. Krishna Murari Sharma and Prof. Surendra Mohan Mishra for their enlightening inspiration and scholarly suggestions to complete this work successfully.

I also owe sincere thanks to Prof. Shuk Dev Sharma, Hony. Professor, VVRI and Prof. Raghbir Singh, Chairman, Dept. of VVBIS & IS, Panjab University, Hoshiarpur, for their benevolent encouragement and invaluable suggestions.

I feel highly delighted in dedicating this book to my esteemed teacher Prof. Debabrata Sen Sharma, for his ingenuous affection and kind blessings.

I duly acknowledge the utmost co-operation extended by my wife Smt. Shraddhanjali Panda and lovely daughter Prajñā for providing me peaceful environment and true inspiring spirit.

I am also extending my sincere thanks to Shri Manmohan Kashyap, Computer Operator, Panjab University, Hoshiarpur, for his valuable co-operation.

Shri C.P. Gautam, publisher of Bharatiya Kala Prakashan, Delhi, deserves special mention here. Due to his personal interest and sincere efforts, the book has been brought out in time and also in beautiful form.

I owe an enormous debt of gratitude to all those Scholars, Institutions and Publishers, whose works / editions have helped me a lot in preparing this New Revised Edition.

Lastly, I pay my deep homage to the Divine Mother with whose grace all this endeavor as such is accomplished and resulted into this present form of *Brahma Yajña.*

सवित्रीभिर्वाचां शशिमणिशिलाभङ्गरुचिभि-
र्वशिन्याद्याभिस्त्वां सह जननि संचिन्तयति यः।
स कर्ता काव्यानां भवति महतां भङ्गिसुभगै-
र्वचोभिर्वाग्देवीवदनकमलामोदमधुरैः ॥

(सौन्दर्यलहरी, १७)

Guru Pūrṇimā
Dated : 7th July, 2009

Dr N.C. Panda
Reader in Sanskrit,
VVBIS & IS,
Panjab University,
Sadhu Ashram, Hoshiarpur.

Abbreviations

ई. उ.	:	ईश उपनिषद्
ऋ.	:	ऋग्वेद
कठ उ.	:	कठ उपनिषद्
तै. आ.	:	तैत्तिरीय आरण्यक
तै. उ.	:	तैत्तिरीय उपनिषद्
तै. ब्रा.	:	तैत्तिरीय ब्राह्मण
तै. सं.	:	तैत्तिरीय संहिता
बृ. उ.	:	बृहदारण्यक उपनिषद्

List of Transliterations

अ	:	a	क्	:	k	ध्	:	dh
आ	:	ā	ख्	:	kh	न्	:	n
इ	:	i	ग्	:	g	प्	:	p
ई	:	ī	घ्	:	gh	फ्	:	ph
उ	:	u	ङ्	:	ṅ	ब्	:	b
ऊ	:	ū	च्	:	c	भ्	:	bh
ऋ	:	ṛ	छ्	:	ch	म्	:	m
ॠ	:	ṝ	ज्	:	j	य्	:	y
ळ्	:	ḷ	झ्	:	jh	र्	:	r
लृ	:	lṛ	ञ्	:	ñ	ल्	:	l
लॄ	:	lṝ	ट्	:	ṭ	व्	:	v
ए	:	e	ठ्	:	ṭh	श्	:	ś
ऐ	:	ai	ड्	:	ḍ	ष्	:	ṣ
ओ	:	o	ढ्	:	ḍh	स्	:	s
औ	:	au	ण्	:	ṇ	ह्	:	h
ं	:	ṃ/ṁ	त्	:	t			
ः	:	ḥ	थ्	:	th			
			द्	:	d			

सौन्दर्यलहरीस्तोत्रविषयसूचनी

सौन्दर्यलहर्या विस्तृतविषयानुक्रमणिका

Introduction

The *Saundaryalaharī*, "the Wave of Beauty", eminently shares the characteristics of (i) a Poem displaying the finest touches of poetical fancy, (ii) a Stotra, Hymn in praise of the Goddess Tripurasundarī, (iii) a series of Mantras mystic formulae, to be used by the Upāsaka along with the corresponding Yantras, Diagrams, wherein the Devī is to be conceived as abiding, and (iv) an exposition of the Āgamas and Tantras, bearing on the worship of the Supreme Being in Its aspect of the Śakti, Creative Engery, known as the Śrī-vidyā, embodying the unerlying principles of Vaidika-dharma and as such having the sanction of the Vedas. In its first forty-one stanzas it encompasses the Ānandalaharī, "the Flood of the Blissfully Sublime". As the very names and the design of the two parts indicate, it points, in the one hand, to the way of approach to the *Paramātman*, attainable only through true spiritual devotion and knowledge of the real nature of the *Paramātman*, supplemented by the highest Yoga of *Nirvikalpasamādhi;* on the the other hand, it leads in effect to the merging of the *Jīvātman* of the *Upāsaka* into the non-differentiated Brahman, so exquisitely exponded in the Upaniṣads and other authoritative works dealing with the Monistic Ideal of the Vedānta, through the worship of the qualified Brahman, so well portrayed in Stotras, Āgamas, Tantras, Purāṇas and Karmakāṇḍa, thus typifying-*nirguṇopāsanā* through *saguṇopāsanā* in essence.

A unique feature of the Sanātana-dharma of the ancient Ṛṣis of this Puṇyabhūmi of ours, which has enabled this time-hallowed system of theirs to endure through the ages, consists in the fact that it is elastic and comprehends systems adapted to the capacity idiosyncrasy and stage of development attained by the various classes of persons owing allegiance to it, from individuals on the highest to the lowest rungs of the ladder of spiritual Evolution. The highest forms of worship envisaged by the Vedic Seers of yore stand far above the ken of the vast majority, for whose delectation suitable forms of worship of Viṣṇu, Śiva the Śakti and other Vedic deities have been elaborated by the large number of Āgamas, Tantras, Purāṇas, Itihāsas, *etc.*, all within the ambit of the Vedic ideal, and these have captured the imagination of these classes and continue to hold sway over their minds even to the present day.

One of such forms of worship is the Śrīvidyā, the worship of the Supreme Being in its feminine aspect of the Śakti, Creative Engery, which embraces two forms : (i) the Internal, meant for the more advanced, assuming the character of worship of the Supreme Being in the aspect of Śiva conjoint with the Śakti, at the various centres of energy of the human body, passing through various stages on to the highest, eschewing all rituals and ceremonies; and (ii) the External, intended for the less evolved, assuming the form of worshipping Yantras inscribed on the Bhūrja leaf, gold and other metallic plates, coloured linen or slabs, to the accompaniment of the repetition or particular Mantras made up of the Mātṛkās, with appropriate gestures, postures, facing of particular cardinal points, offerings of Dhūpa, Dīpa, Naivedya, *etc.*, all with a view to acquiring special pyschic powers, gratification of specific desires, *etc.*, of the Upāsaka. The former, known as the Samaya-mārga, is based on the Saṃhitās of the Śubhāgama-pañcaka, the works of five great Seers, and does not, in any way, run counter to Vedic principles. The latter, known as the Kaulamārga and dealt within the sixty-four Tantras, although primarily intended for the worship of the Devī, has, in course of time, afforded scope for the inclusion of vulgar practices (Vāmācāra) smacking of Kāpālika and Kṣapaṇaka usages, appealing to the venal side of human nature and excercising a demoralizing influnce on the votaries to an extent not countenanced by the Vedas. These unwholesome features of the Śākta cult began to weigh on the minds of high-souled reformers of the type of Śaṅkara-bhagavatpāda, who soon opened a crusade against such practices by expounding the sublime truths of the Samaya-mārga in their writings and preachings, with a view to uphold the beautiful methods of the Samaya doctrine and supplant the ugly features of the Kaulamārga. Hence, this work is appropriately called the Saundaryalaharī, the Flood of Beauty, washing out in its torrent the filth accumulted in the Kaula-mārga and restoring the purity of the Śrī-vidyā in relation to its external forms and ceremonies. In this laudable attempt he seems to have been ably served, in a later generation, by Lakṣmīdhara and Bhāskararāya, two celebrated scholars and stalwart mystics acquainted with the inner working of the worship of the Śrī-vidyā, in their commentaries on several works relating to it. Lakṣmīdhara's zeal for the preservation of the Samaya-mārga in all its purity and for the reform of the Kaulamārga is so great that he even steps beyond the province of a mere commentator and differs from the author of the original work in matters of detail, where he thinks his own personal experience of the recondite practices warrants him to do so.

Śrī Śaṅkara-bhagavatpāda is accredited as the author of the Saundaryalaharī[1] by Lakṣmīdhara, Bhāskararāya, Kaivalyā-śrama, Kameśvarasūri, Acyutānanda and a host of other commentators of the work. The author of the gloss, Sudhā-vidyotinī, on this work, however, ascribes it to his own father, Pravarasena, the son of Dramiḍa, a king of the Dramiḍa country, and says that on the strength of the information directly obtained from his father he wrote the said gloss. There are others who say that Śiva himself is the author of the Stotra, and yet other who maintain that it had its origin in the teeth of Lalitā, the Prime Śakti.[2] Those who ascribe it to Śaṅkara-bhagavat-

1. Vallabha-deva, who is assigned to the fifteenth century A.D., in his Su-bhāṣitāvalī, quotes the twenty-seventh stanza of this work, ascribing its authorship to Śrī Śaṅkara-bhagavatpāda.

2. There is yet another tradition about the prime source of this work. The story goes that Śaṅkara-bhagavatpāda,who is considered to be Īśvara incarnate, paid a visit to Kailāsa, clad in the robes of a mendicant, and took the Mantra-śāstra placed by the Devī on the throne of Īśvara.While he was about to leave Kailāsa along with the

pāda also aver that the Draviḍa-śiśu, referred to in stanza 75 of the work, is Śaṅkara himself, one of them, Kaivalyāśrama, even going to the extent of making a remark, in his gloss on one of the stanzas, that it is not found in the manuscripts of the Malaiyālam country, seeking thereby to fix the Malaiyālam country as the place of origin of the work and indirectly hinting that Śaṅkara-bhagavatpāda was a native of Malabar. The fact that there are as many as thirty-five glosses of this work known to be extant in various parts of India, of which only one attributes the authorship to a person other than Śaṅkara-bhagavatpāda, at least affords us greater proof of the genuineness of Śaṅkara-bhagavatpāda's authorship of this Stotra, than of several other stotras ascribed to him. Even if the reference to the Draviḍa-śiśu in the work be taken to point to some other person, whether it be Pravarasena, as is claimed by one of the commentaries, of Śrī Jñāna-saṃbandha, as is claimed by some chronologists, one noteworthy fact results out of this reference, *viz.*, that the Draviḍa-śiśu must either have been a contemporary of the author of this work or one belonging to a prior period. Till the identity and other antecedents of Pravarasena, king of the Draviḍa country, are fairly well established and his chronology fixed with a fair amount of accuracy, we are not warranted in drawing any inference therefrom relating to the genuineness of the claim put forward in his favour. As for Śrī Jñāna-saṃbandha, who is said to have flourished about 1,200 years ago, if the Draviḍa-śiśu under

spoil, Nandikeśvara, who was on duty hard by snatched the book from his hands. After grappling with him for a while, the Ācārya succeeded in retaining a portion of the book, which contained the first forty-one stanzas of the Saudaryalaharī, to which were added fifty-nine more stanzas composed later on by him to complete the work. All these traditions apart, any unsophisticated student of the Śrī-vidyā, after a thorough and close study of the literature bearing on it, is bound to arrive at the conclusion that this work of Śaṅkara gives a faithfil rendering of the views of his Parama-guru, Śrī Gauḍapādācārya as expounded by him in the Subhagodaya, in the first forty-one stanzas of this work for the delectation of the more advanced student, rounded off with a highly poetic adoration of the Devī, in the latter portion.

reference is to be taken to point to him, we have to infer that Śaṅkara-bhagavatpāda, to whom almost universally this work is attributed, must have flourished in the eighth century A.D, an inference which is supported by the view of European scholars that Śrī Śaṅkarācārya, the author of the Śārīraka-mīmāṃsā-bhāṣya, flourished between A.D. 788 and 820. If the opinion held by Indian scholars that Ādi Śaṅkara flourished in the sixth century B.C. should be adhered to and this work attributed to him, then the internal evidence afforded by the Draviḍa-śiśu will be perfectly useless,unless some other Draviḍa-śiśu answering to the description is dragged out of oblivion and presented to us as the one referred to by Śaṅkara-bhagavatpāda. We are loath to acquiesce in the view that Śaṅkara-bhagavatpāda sought to refer to himself as the Draviḍa-śiśu indicated in such vianglorious terms in the poem. We are therefore of opinion that the Draviḍa-śiśu referred to is Śrī Jñāna-sambandha and that this Stotra is the genuine work of Śrī-Śaṅkara-bhagavatpāda, who lived in the eighth century A.D.

In editing the text of the work, we have mainly followed the work published by the Government of Mysore as No. 11 of the Bibliotheca Sanskrita of the Government Oriental Library Series, after adopting suitable readings wherever we thought it necessary. The various readings gleaned from the commentaries of Lakṣmīdhara, Kaivalyāśrama, Kāmeśvarasūri and Arthur Avalon's edition of the Ānandalaharī have been given as foot-notes under the several stanzas, and we hope that they will afford an opportunity to the reader to appreciate the various shades of meaning sought to be read into the text. In the English rendering and the commentary of the stanzas we have largely drawn from the mine of information available in the commentaries mentioned above, the Malaiyālam commentary of Brahma-śrī Kaṇṭiyūr Mahādeva Śāstrin and the editions of the Ānandalaharī with English rendering, the notes and comments by Arthus Avalon and R. Ananta-kṛṣṇa Śāstrin.

We have added in the form of an appendix the Prayoga relating to each stanza, gleaned from several sources for the benefit of Upāsaka-readers and a preliminary note at the end of the first stanza as to the detailed procedure to be adopted for worship, common to all the stanzas.

The very essence of the Śrī-vidyā consists in its being availed of by its votaries to serve lofty and altruistic purposes. Hence, care should be always taken to see that it is not dethroned from its high pedestal, to serve ignoble and selfish ends.

॥ ॐ ॥

सौन्दर्यलहरी

Saundaryalaharī

The votaries of the Śakti, the Kuṇḍalinī, may be roughly divided into two classes: the Samayins or those who believe in the sameness of the Śakti and Śiva, and the Kaulas or those who worship the Kaulinī, the sleeping Kuṇḍalinī, *i.e.*, the Śakti, which resides in the *Mūlādhāra*, which is known as the Kula-plexus. The former believe in the rousing of the above Kuṇḍalinī, the grossest form of Cit, and its being worked up in successive stages, by Upāsanā, Tapas and Mantra-japa, through the six Cakras, which are the centres of Energy, on to the thousand-petalled lotus, wherein abide the *Śat* and the *Cit*, and where the unification of the *Jīvātman* with the Paramātman is to be effected. This form of worship is therefore exclusively internal. The Kaulas, on the other hand, worship the Kuṇḍalinī, even without rousing her from sleep and are satisfied with the attainment and enjoyment of purely temporal objects, believing, at the same time, that, with the rousing of the Kuṇḍalinī, they attain liberation. This form of worship is therefore mainly external. Mention may also be made, here, of some worshippers of the Śakti, who, in addition to attaching due importance to the external forms of worship of the Kaulas, try to rise higher, by making Upāsanā with Yantras, made of gold and other metals, awake the Kuṇḍalinī and even work her up as far as the *Anāhata* in the heart. Their worship may be characterized as partaking of both the external and internal forms. Śaṅkara-bhagavatpāda, the foremost exponent of the Samayācāra, extols Samayā, the Sādākhyā, the sixteenth digit of the Moon, in all her aspects, in the following hundred and three stanzas.

As, without a thorough grasp of the details of the formation of the *Śrī-cakra*, the full significance of the first, forty-one stanzas, which baffle even advanced student of Mantra-lore, cannot be adequately understood, a short description of the *Śrī-cakra* would be a fitting prelude to the elucidation attempted in the following pages.

The following construction is given by Kaivalyāśrama, a commentator of this work, for the building of the *Śrī-cakra* : Describe a circle, with an imaginary vertical line of a suitable length as its diameter. Divide the diameter into forty-eight equal parts and mark off the sixth, twelfth, seventeenth, twentieth, twenty-third, twenty-seventh, thirtieth thirty-sixth and forty-second divisions form the top. Draw nine chords, at right angles to the diameter, through the nine points makred off, and number them accordingly. Rub off 1/16th part of No. 1, 5/48ths of No. 2, 1/3rd of No. 4, 3/8ths of No. 5, 1/3rd of No. 6, 1/12th of No. 8, and 1/16th of No. 9, at both ends of each.[1] Draw triangles with lines, Nos. 1, 2, 4, 5, 6, 8, and 9 as bases and the middle points of Nos. 6, 9, 8, 7, 2, 1 and 3 respectively as their apexes. Draw also the two traingles with Nos. 3 and 7 as their bases and the lower and the upper extremities of the diameter as apexes respectively. Thus we get forth-three triangles pointing outwards, composed of one in the middle,

1. In the construction of the *Śrī-cakra* adopted by some worshippers, in actual practice, 1/12th of the chord No.2 is rubbed off on either side, instead of 5/48ths, as given by Kaivalyāśrama. Further, adopting 1/48th of the vertical diameter of the inmost circle as the unit, the positions of the several terms of the *Śrī-cakra* are also fixed as under : The height of the entire *Śrī-cakra* is ninety-six units, of which forty-eight are taken up by the inmost circle, leaving twenty-four units at the top and twenty-four at the bottom,. The eight-petalled and sixteen-petalled lotuses will touch the circles cutting the vertical diameter produced both-ways, at the eleventh and twentieth unit-distances from the upper and lower extremities of the diameter. Of the four remaining units, the three concentric circles lying beyond the sixteen-petalled lotus will take up one unit. The three units yet remaining, will mark the extremities of the three quadrangles forming the outermost boundary of the *Śrī-cakra*. By marking off forty-three units from either extremity of the outermost quadrangle, the intervening space of ten units should be rubbed off on the four sides of the three quadrangles forming the *Bhū-gṛha*. This will give the four gateways of the *Cakra*.

eight triangles around it, two sets of ten triangles around the eight triangles, one set about the other, and fourteen triangles around them. Then, by marking off eight points in the circumference equi-distant from one another, commencing from the upper extremity of the diameter and constructing one petal over each of them, is formed the eight-petalled lotus. Then, circumscribe a circle touching the outer extremity of the petals. Divide the circumference of the circle so described into sixteen equal divisions and draw symmetrically sixteen petals over them, as before. Then, circumscribe a circle round the sixteen-petalled lotus, as before, and enclose the second cricle so described in two concentric circles at equal distances from each other. Construct three squared about the outermost circle, with sides equidistant from each other, the innermost square not to touch the outermost circle. Marking off four doorways on the four sides, each equidistant from either extremities, rub off the interspaces. The figure thus formed in the *Śrī-cakra*. The centre of the circle is known as the *Bindu*. The five triangles with their apexes pointing downwards are indicative of the Śakti and the four with their apexes pointing uwards are of Śiva, according to the Vāmakeśvara-tantra, the recognized authority on *Śrī-vidyā*.

Lakṣmīdhara, a reputed commentator of this work, holds that, in the *Śrī-cakra,* the five triangles pointing upowards are of the Śakti and the four pointing downwards are of Śiva and speaks of the construction of the *Cakra,* as consisting of two different processes, the *Saṃhāra-krama,* from without inwards, and the *Sṛṣṭi-krama* from within outwards. The *Śrī-cakra* of the *Saṁhāra-krama* of Lakṣmīdhara can be obtained by turning the *Śri-cakra* recognized by the Vāmakeśvara-tantra upside down. This is given as the diagram relating to the twenty-second stanza. The *Śrī-cakra* of the *Sṛṣṭi-krama* is given as the diagram relating to the thirty-first stanza.

The mode of constructing the *Śrī-cakra,* in the *Sṛṣṭi-krama,* of the Samayins, according to him, is as follows : Draw an isosceles triangle with its apex pointing upwards and its base parallel to the bottom line of the sheet. Place the *Bindu,* a dot, a little above the base, in an imaginary vertical line bisecting the base. A little above the *Bindu,* draw a straight line parallel to the base, intersecting the sides of the original triangle. Draw an isosceles triangle with apex pointing upwards over this line. Draw a straight line through the apex of the first triangle, parallel to its base and construct an isosceles triangle on it, with apex pointing downwards, so that its sides may pass through the points of intersection of the base of the second triangle with the sides of the first triange. These two points, where three straight line intersect each other, are technically styled Marman-s, to distinguish them from the points of intersection of two straight lines, which are known as *Saṁdhis.* Thus, then, are formed the eight corner-triangles pointing outwards, which together are known as the *Aṣṭakoṇacakra.* By producing the topmost and the bottom-most of the three horizontal line both-ways and constructing two isosceles triangles, one of them with apex down and the other with apex up, so that the sides of the former may pass through the extremities of the bases of the two triangles pointing upwards and the sides of the latter triangle may pass through the extremities of the base of the original triangle pointing downwards. By producing the sides downwards, of the inner triangle with apex up and drawing a straight line parallel to the base, through the apex of the triangle pointing downwards, a new triangle is formed. Similarly, by producing the sides upwards, of the triangle with apex down and drawing a straight line parallel to the base, through the apex of the first outer triangle with apex up, another triangle is formed. At this stage are obtained ten corner-triangles pointing outwards, which together form what is known as the *Antardaśāra,* the inner ten-spoked, *Cakra.* Similarly, by producing the horizontal bases, drawing the arms of triangles at corner-points, so as to form Marmans and drawing straight lines parallel to the bases, through the apexes of triangles pointing up and down, the ten corner-triangles pointing outwards and known as the *Bahirdaśāra* or the outer ten-spoked *Cakra,* is formed. Again, by producing both-ways the bases at the top and the bottom of the *Antar-daśāra* and constructing isosceles triangles with apex down and apex up; and again by producing the sides of triangles whereby Marmans could be formed and drawing straight lines parallel to the bases, passing through the apexes of the freshly constructed triangles, the fourteen corner-triangles pointing outwards known as the *Catur-daśāra*, the fourteen-spoked *Cakra*, will be obtained. Thus, we get, in all, forty-three corner-triangles, including the inmost one, twenty-four *Saṃdhis* and eighteen *Marmans*. It may, however, be noted here, that Lakṣmīdhara commits an error in giving the number of Marmans as twenty-four and, quoting the Candra-jñānavidyā in this connection, seeks to reconcile the figure twenty-eight given therein, as of the Marmans, by pointing out that the eight-petalled lotus, the sixteen-petalled lotus, the three outermost circles and the three quadrangles may be treated as four Marmans, which, together with his twenty-four, would go to make up the twenty-eight Marmans of the Candra-jñānavidyā. This is apparently a laboured explanation, which, in trying to hide one fault, only results in making it two. A more ingenious attempt at reconciliation would have been, for him, to treat the six points of contact of the *Catur-daśāra* with the inmost circle also as Marmans. According to the Samayins, the four *Cakras* constituted by the *Bindu* (of the form of the *Śrī-cakra, viz.*, circular), the eight-pettalled lotus, the sixteen-petalled lotus and the quadrangular *Bhū-gṛha*, are of *Śiva*, which are interrelated with the *Tri-koṇa*, the *Aṣṭa-koṇa*, the dyas of *Daśa-koṇa's* and the *Caturdaśa-koṇa*, of the Śakti respectively, the *Bindu* of the quadrilateral standing apart from these. On the other hand, another set of Samayins hold that the eight-petalled lotus, the sixteen petalled lotus, the *Mekhalā-traya* (the triad of concentric circles), and the *Bhū-gṛha* (the three quadrialaterals) are the Śiva-cakras, and the *Tri-koṇa*, the *Aṣṭa-koṇa*, the dyad of *Daśa-koṇas*, and the *Catur-daśa-koṇa* are the five Śakti-cakras, and aver that the *Bindu* representing the Śiva-cakra s, when placed in the middle of the Śakti-cakras, would indicate the pervasive character of the Śiva-cakras in the Śakti-cakras. It has, however, to be noted that the Vāmakeśvara-tantra, while recognizing the *bindu* as a *Cakra*, does not do so in relation to the *Mekhalā-traya*, as will be seen from the enumeration of the *Cakras* according to it, which is as follows : "The *Bindu* in the middle, the triangle thereafter, the eight-spoked one thence, the two ten-spoked one there-about, the fourteen-spoked one about them, the eight-petalled lotus outside it, the sixteen-petalled lotus thereabout and last of all, the *Bhū-pura*, are named respectively the *Sarvānanda-maya* first, the *Sarva-siddhiprada* next, the *Sarva-roga-hara* thereafter, the *Sarva-rakṣā-kara* similarly, the *Sarvārtha-sādhaka-cakra*, the *Sarvasaubhāgya-dāyaka*, the *Sarva-saṃkṣobhana* the next one, the *Sarvāsā-paripūraka*, and lastly the *Trailokyamohana*—thus the nine with the nine names."

शिवः शक्त्या युक्तो यदि भवति शक्तः प्रभवितुं
न चेदेवं देवो न खलु कुशलः स्पन्दितुमपि।
अतस्त्वामाराध्यां हरिहरविरिञ्चादिभिरपि[1]
प्रणन्तुं स्तोतुं वा कथमकृतपुण्यः प्रभवति।।१।।

Śivaḥ śaktyā yukto yadi bhavati śaktaḥ prabhavituṃ
na ced evaṃ devo na khalu kuśalaḥ spanditum api/
Atastvām ārādhyāṃ hari-hara-viriñcādibhir api
praṇantuṃ stotuṃ vā katham akṛta-puṇyaḥ prabhavati//

Translation : Only if conjoint with the Śakti (Thyself), would Śiva earn the privilege to become overlord; otherwise the God is not able even to stir. While so, how dares one, who has acquired no merit, either to salute or to praise Thee, (O Goddess!) who art worthy of being adored even by Hari, Hara, Viriñca[2] and others?

लक्ष्मीधरं व्याख्या-

वन्दामहे महीयांसमंसलम्बिजटाभरम्।
यत्कङ्कणझणत्काररवः शब्दानुशासनम्।।
शेषाशेषोक्तिभूषाः कणचरणचणग्रन्थसौगन्ध्यजिघ्राः
भट्टोक्तिप्रौढिलीढा गुरुगुरुतरगीर्गुम्फशुम्भद्विजृम्भाः।
निश्शङ्काः शङ्करोक्तौ पशुपतिमतनिर्वाहकाः सांख्यसंख्याः
यस्य श्रीलोल्ललक्ष्मीधरविबुधमणेर्भान्ति वाचां निगुम्फाः[3] ।।
सोऽहं लक्ष्मीधरः प्राह टीकां लक्ष्मीधराभिधाम्।
एनां समाहितस्वान्ताः सेवन्तां सततं बुधाः।।

---

1. विरिञ्च्यादिभिरपि;
....विरंच्यादिभिरपि (Saurashtra edn).
2. *Viriñca* here means the creator *(sṛṣṭikartā)* of this universe. He is also known as Brahmā in our Indian tradition.
3. निगुम्भाः

स्यादेव मेऽलसतया मतिमान्द्यतो वा
दोषः क्वचित्क्वचिदथापि न कापि शङ्का।
नैसर्गिकी खलु गुणीकरणप्रवीणा
शक्तिः सदा विजयते[1] भुवि सज्जनानाम्।।

इह खलु शङ्करभगवत्पूज्यपादाः समयमततत्त्ववेदिनः समयाख्यां चन्द्रकलां श्लोकशतेन प्रस्तुवन्ति शिव इति। **शिवः** सर्वमङ्गलोपेतः सदाशिवतत्त्वम्। वश कान्तौ इत्यस्माद्धातोः शिवशब्दो निष्पन्नः। यथोक्तम्–

"हिसिधातोः सिंहशब्दो वशकान्तौ शिवः स्मृतः।
वर्णव्यत्ययतः सिद्धौ पश्यकः कश्यपो यथा।"

इति। 'वश कान्तौ' इत्ययं धातुः तुदादिः अदादिश्च संगृहीतः। तुदादेर्वशतेः दीप्तिरर्थः। कान्तिर्दीप्तिः। अदादेर्वष्टिरिति कामना अर्थः। इच्छाशक्त्याश्रयत्वात् ईश्वरस्य शिवत्वम्। वशति प्रकाशते स्वयं प्रकाश इति, यद्वा स्वस्मिन् प्रपञ्चं प्रकाशयतीति शिवः, यद्वा–'शीङ् स्वप्ने' इत्यस्माद्धातोः शिवशब्दो निष्पन्नः। स्वप्नं वाति क्षिपतीति शिवः, जाड्यरहितः, अविद्यानिर्मुक्त इत्यर्थः। यद्वा–स्वप्नमविद्यां वाति गच्छतीति शिवः, सादाख्यकलासंवलित इति यावत्। तस्यैव शिवशब्दवाच्यत्वं वक्ष्यते। तादृशः शिवः **शक्त्या** जगन्निर्माणशक्त्या **युक्तः** अवच्छिन्नः–अविद्यावच्छिन्नचैतन्यस्यैव ब्रह्मणः जगन्निर्माणे शक्तत्वात्। **यदि** भवति, भवति चेत्, तर्हि **शक्तः** समर्थः **प्रभवितुं** प्रपञ्चं निर्मातुम्। **न चेदेवं** शक्त्या युक्तो [2]न चेदित्यर्थः। दीव्यतीति **देवः** पूर्वोक्तः सदाशिवः। [3]**न खलु** निषेधसम्भावनायाम्। **स्पन्दितुमपि** चलितुमपि **कुशलः** समर्थः। निराकारस्य विभोराकाशतुल्यस्य स्पन्दनायोगादिति हृद्गतोऽर्थः।।

वाच्यार्थस्तु–शिवशक्त्योः जायापतिन्यायेन जायया शक्त्या युक्तश्चेत् प्रपञ्चरूप-सन्तानं निर्मातुं शक्नोति, तया वियुक्तश्चेन्न शक्नोतीति।।

आगमरहस्यार्थस्तु–[4]शिवशब्देन नवयोनिचक्रमध्ये चतुर्योन्यात्मकमर्धचक्रमुच्यते। शक्तिशब्देन अवशिष्टं पञ्चयोन्यात्मकमर्धचक्रमुच्यते। एवमर्धद्वयमिलितं नवयोन्यात्मकं चक्रं भवति। एतस्माच्चक्रादेव जगदुत्पत्तिस्थितिलया भवन्तीति पुरस्तान्निवेदयिष्यते। उक्तं च–

---

1. खलु।
2. न भवेदित्यर्थः।
3. न खलु निषेधसम्भावनयोः।
4. शिवशब्देन शिवयोः संबन्धि 'चतुर्भिः श्रीकण्ठैः' इति निरूपयिष्यमाणनवयोन्यात्मक-श्रीचक्रमध्ये–म.।

**"चतुर्भिः शिवचक्रैश्च शक्तिचक्रैश्च पञ्चभिः।
शिवशक्त्यात्मकं ज्ञेयं श्रीचक्रं शिवयोर्वपुः।।"**

इति। शिवशक्त्योर्मेलनं षड्विंशं सर्वतत्त्वातीतं तत्त्वान्तरमिति पुरस्तान्निवेदयिष्यते। तस्मान्मेलनादेव जगदुत्पत्तिस्थितिलयाः, न केवलादेवेति च वक्ष्यते। यथोक्तं वामकेश्वरमहातन्त्रे चतुश्शत्याम्–

**"परोऽपि शक्तिरहितः शक्त्या युक्तो भवेद्यदि।
सृष्टिस्थितिलयान् कर्तुमशक्तः शक्त एव हि।।"** इति।

एतच्च 'चतुर्भिः श्रीकण्ठैः'[1] इत्यादिश्लोकव्याख्यानावसरे निपुणतरमुपपादयिष्यामः।।

अतः तस्माद्धेतोः **त्वां** भवतीं, **आराध्यां** आराधयितुं पूजयितुमर्हां, **हरिहर-विरिञ्चादिभिः,** हरिर्विष्णुः, हरो रुद्रः, विरिञ्चो ब्रह्मा, आदिशब्देन इन्द्रादयः संगृह्यन्ते। ते च अधिकारपुरुषाः प्रपञ्चान्तः पातिनः। तैर्नमस्कार्यत्वं प्रपञ्चजनयित्र्याः भगवत्याः युक्तमेवेत्युक्तम् "अतस्त्वामाराध्याम्" इति, न तु आरोपस्तुतिरिति ध्येयम्। यद्वा–निगमा वा आदिशब्देन संगृह्यन्ते, निगमसेव्यत्वात् भगवत्याः। तदुत्तरत्र 'श्रुतीनां मूर्धान'[2] इत्यादौ स्फोर्यते। विरिञ्चशब्दः अकारान्तः। **अपिशब्दः** कथंशब्दार्थमुपस्करोति। **प्रणन्तुं** नमस्कर्तुम्। प्रशब्दः कायिकं वाचिकं मानसिकं च त्रिविधं नमस्कारमाह। **स्तोतुं वा,** केवलं स्तुतिमात्रमपि कर्तुं वेत्यर्थः। **अकृतपुण्यः**–पूर्वजन्मार्जिपुण्यनिचयः कृतपुण्यः, तदन्यः अकृतपुण्यः **प्रभवति** ईष्टे शक्तः।।

अत्रेत्थं पदयोजना–हे भगवति शिवो देवः शक्त्या युक्तो भवति यदि, तदा प्रभवितुं शक्तः। एवं न चेत्, स्पन्दितुमपि कुशलो न खलु। अतः हरिहरविरिञ्चादिभिरपि आराध्यां त्वाम् अकृतपुण्यः प्रणन्तुं स्तोतुं वा कथं प्रभवति।। १ ।।

Notes : In keeping with the time-hallowed tradition among great writers of Darśana literature, to forestall, in essence, the content of the entire work at the very beginning, the first stanza of this work may be said to contain the quintessence of the *Śrī-vidyā*, the worship of the Devī. Though liberation is the goal aimed at by all votaries of the *Śrī-vidyā*, still, in view of the various ways of appraoch, due to differences in temperament, idiosyncrasy, as well as their intellectual and spiritual advancement, there is room for the said goal being looked upon from various angles of vision.

1. ११ श्लोकः।
2. ८४ श्लोकः।

Kāmeśvarasūri, the talented commentator of this work, has, in his elaborate commentary of the first stanza, dealt with fourteen different aspects of Śiva and the Śakti, interpreting the stanza from the following points of view : (1) Vedānta, (2) Sāṁkhya, (3) The Chief Deity of *Śrī-vidyā*, (4) Significant Words, (5) Their Significance, (6) Genesis of Sounds, (7) The Yantra, (8) The Praṇava, (9) The Mātṛkā, the Saṁskṛta Alphabet, (10) Kādi-vidyā, (11) Hādi-vidyā, (12) The Pañcākṣarī, (13) The Guru, the Initiator, and (14) Candrakalā. In addition to the plain English rendering of the first stanza given above, the fourteen different aspects of Kāmeśvarasūri are also set forth in the form of fourteen different renderings hereunder :

1. Only when in conjunction with the Śakti, (the Māyā with the two-fold functions of Āvaraṇa—veiling the real, and Vikṣepa—showing the unreal, not independently however of the Brahman, which is Śiva) would Śiva (the auspicious, undefiled Bliss, *i.e.*, the Brahman, which is the Supreme Existence, Consciousness and Bliss, and becomes Īśvara when amalgamated with the Māyā) acquire the power to create, (sustain and destroy the elements, Ether, *etc.*, and the variants evolved out of them, as also to become one with them); otherwise the *Deva* (who indulges in the pastimes of creation, *etc.*,) becomes incapable even of stirring, (not to speak of engaging in the direction of such pastimes). While so, how dares one, who has not (purified his mind, by the accumulation of) virtuous deeds (through many a previous incarnation, has not studied intensively the Upaniṣadic lore and attained Self-realization, through the grace of his Guru and thereby been enabled to comprehend Thy real nature, by the removal of the cobwebs of illusion, which ensnare even the great), either to salute (by way of bidding adieu to Thee) or to extol (with a view to being spared Thy attentions) thee, (that hast endowed even Īśvara with such powers and that art proficient in rendering what is impossible, possible), (O *māyā*!) that art worthy of being served even by Hari (Viṣṇu, the sustainer), Hara (Rudra, the destroyer), Viriñca (Brahman, the creator) and others (of that type, subject to *Avidyā*)?

2. Only when in conjunction with the Śakti (Prakṛti] the blind creative Energy, endowed with the three properties : Sattva, Rajas and Tamas—Rhythm, Mobility and Inertia) would Śiva (the lame Puruṣa, called Īśvara, characterized by indifference and not capable

of acting independently (acquire the reputation of being the creator and enjoyer of the world. Should it be otherwise, the *Deva* (Īśvara) become totally incapable even of stirring, (much more so, of any action he is reputed to be the author of, as it is from the Prakṛti, in the presence of the Puruṣa, that the *Mahat, Ahaṁkāra, Tanmātras, etc.*, in their order, have had their origin). While it is so, how dares one who has not acquired Thy *Sattva-guṇa* (and hence, the proper knowledge derived from a study of Kapila's system, with the help of a Guru) to salute or to sing the priase (in some such manner as, "What shall I say of Thee, O crest-jewel of chaste women! that hast established Thy greatness, without in any way affecting Thy husband's, Thyself blind and He indifferent"), of Thee (O Goddess!) that art worthy of being served, even by Hari, Hara and Viriñca, (each one of them, by partaking of the *Sattva, Tamas* and *Rajas* respectively of Thy *guṇa-s*, in their work of sustenance, destruction and creation) and such others?

3. Only when frolicking with the Śakti (His consort, Haimavatī, seated on His lap) would Śiva (possessed of infinite auspicious qualities, from whom Bhava—the creator, *Mṛḍa*—the sustainer, and Hara—the destroyer, take their origin, who has His seat on Mount Kailāsa and in the inmost core of the *Śrī-cakra*) be capable of procreating (as His progeny, the entire universe, nourishing it and becoming its overlord); otherwise, the *Deva* (though self-effulgent) becomes powerless even of stirring; (much less would there be scope for Him to be credited with achievements, such as the burning of the three Puras, swallowing the virulent Halāhala and the like). While so, how dares one, (who cannot lay any claim to having worshipped at Thy lotus-feet during previous lives) either to make obeisance (by body, word of mouth and mind) before, or to glorify Thee (O Goddess!) that art served by Hari, Hara, Viriñca (and Īśvara, as the four legs of Thy couch, by Sadāśiva as Thy mattress, Mahendra as They spittoon and so on)?

4. Only when in conjunction with (what is implied by the word) 'Śakti', *viz.*, the letter 'E', the Guṇated combination of 'A' and 'I' in the inverse order, *i.e.*, 'I' and 'A'), does the word 'Śiva' acquire a form denoting a deity for the welfare of all the world; if not so, this word forfeits its luminosity and is turned into a mere sibilant and dento-labial stump, unpronounceable and meaningless. While so,

how dares one, who has acquired no merit, either to salute or to praise Thee, (*i.e.*, the vital letter 'E') that art muttered in prayer witht the word 'Śiva', by Hari, Hara, Viriñca (Brahmā) and others?

5. Only by the conjunction of the Śakti (the appropriate group of words in their proper sequence) would Śiva (the aggregate of their significance) acquire the quality of appealing to the hearts of wise men; otherwise the *Deva* (the mere thought, without the expression) will not serve his purpose in everyday life. While so, how dares one, who has acquired no merit, either to salute or to priase Thee, (that art inseparably yoked with thought-forms), O Goddess! that art worthy of being adored even by Hari, Hara, Viriñca and others (for that very reason)?

6. Only in conjunction with the Śakti, (the Parā-śakti, the essential basic principle of the Śabda-brahman, who, though one, is spoken of with different names by persons of different persuasions, *e.g*, as the Śakti by Śāktas, as the *Cit* by Śaivas, as the Kuṇḍalinī by Yogins, as the Prakṛti by Sāṁkhyas, as the Brahman by Vedāntins, as the Buddhi by Bauddhas, as the Mahāsattā by Jātivādins and as the absolute *Dravya* by Dravyavādins and who has assumed diverse forms ue to the conditions brought about by the Māyā-śakti dependent on her) would Śiva, (the Śabda-prapañca) acquire the power to manifest itself (in the Paśyantī, Madhyamā and Vaikharī stages; and while in the Madhyamā stage, to attain the form of Śabda and Artha and the interrelation between the two). Otherwise, (without the Parā-śakti) the *Deva*, the Śabda-brahman, could not be pronounced with the help of the palate and other vocal organs and thus not attain the Vaikharī stage. While so, how dares one, who has acquired no merit, either to salute or to praise Thee (that art the prime cause of the manifestation of the qualified Brahman and the unfolding of the phenomenal world), O Goddess! that art worthy of being abored even by Hari, Hara, Viriñca and other gods, (who have, at their command, the four stages of *Parā, Paśyantī, Madhyamā* and *Vaikharī)?*

7. Only of Śiva (the set of four triangles of the nine triangles of the *Śrī-cakra-yantra)* comes to be placed with the Śakti (the set of five remaining triangles of the same *Cakra*) of if Śiva (*viz.*, the *Bindu*, the point) gets inseparably connected with the Śakti *(viz.*, the *Tri-koṇa*, the triangle*)* (*i.e.*, on the bodies of the two thus coming together) would there be scope for the formation of the eight, the

two sets of ten and the fourteen *koṇas*, traingles pointing outwards, along with the eight-petalled and the sixteen-petalled lotuses and the two triads of circles and quarangels, as also for the creation, sustenance and destruction of the words. If neither of these is the case, the *Deva* (the aforesaid Śiva) would be incapable of affording scope for the formation of the different parts of the *Cakra* detailed above, or for its division into the creative, sustaining and destructive aspects, or for the three *Prastāra*-s into *Ku, Śa* and *La*, signifying the Earth, the golden Meru and Mount Kailāsa. while so, how dares one, who has acquired no merit, either to salute or to praise Thee, with an adequate knowledge of the Tantras, O venerable One! that art served by Hari—the Sun, Hara—the Fire, Viriñca—the Moon, (Vaśinī, *etc.*, Vāmā, *etc.*, and other Śaktis, as well as the fifty-one letters of eight groups of the Alphabet, seated in their respective seats as prescribed, in the *Cakra)?*

8. Only when brought into union with the Śakti, ('A') with (•), would Śiva (the dyad of 'U' and 'M') acquire the power of assuming the form of *Praṇava*, the embodied from of *Nāda, etc.*, assuming the stages of *Parā, Paśynatī, etc.*, wherefrom originate the *Svaras, Varṇas, Padas* and *Vākyas* galore. If not, the *Deva* (the dyad of 'U'and 'M') becomes utterly incapable of producing the *Praṇava*, becoming dumbfounded. While so, how dared one, who has acquired no merit, either to salute or to priase Thee (of the form of the *Praṇava*), O Goddess! that art worthy of being adored by Hari, Hara and Viriñca—as the deities of the components of the *praṇava;*, Agni, Vāyu and Sūrya—their Ṛṣi-s; *Gāyatrī, triṣṭubh* and *Jagatī*—their metres; *Rakta, Śukla* and *Kṛṣṇa*—their colours; *Jāgrat, Svapna* and *Suṣupti*—their states; Bhūmi, Antarikṣa and Svarga—their seats; Udātta, An-udātta and Svarita—their Svaras; *Ṛk, Yajus* and *Sāman*—their Vedas; Gārha-patya, Āhavanīya and Dakṣiṇa—their Agnis; Prāhṇa, Madhyāhna and Aparāhṇa—their *Kālas; Sattva, Rajas* and *Tamas*—their Guṇas; *Sṛṣṭi, Sthiti* and *Saṁhāra*—their functions : all these standing in the order appropriate to them?

9. Only in combination with the Śakti, (the group of sixteen vowels, representing the six Nityā-śaktis and the sixteen different modes of intonation), would Śiva, (the group of thirty-five consonants, taken individually and all of them taken collectively, representing the thirty-six Tattvas in all), acquire the power of generation the several Vedas, Purāṇas and other lore. Otherwise

the *Deva* would become unpronounceable and meaningless. While so, how dares one, who has acquired no merit, either to salute or to praise Thee, O Goddess! that art adored by hari, Hara, Viriñca and others, as the Alphabet made up of the vital vowels and consonants and all that they go to make up?

10. Śiva, (the syllable '*Ka*'), only when placed in juxtaposition with the Śakti, (the syllable 'E'), pronounced separately thereafter, would take the form of the sacred fifteen-syllabled or the sixteen-syllabled Mantra. If the initial syllable 'Ka' is not so placed along with the syllable 'E', the *Deva*, (the syllable 'I', even though followed by) Kuśala, (the Pṛthvī-bīja, 'La'), is impotent by itself to form a Mantra. Then, by (the dyad of 'Ha-s' and the dyad of 'Sa-s', respectively represented by the Sun and the Moon, indicated by the word) Hari; by Hara, (the syllable 'Ka'); by Viriñca, (the syllable 'Ka'); (by the dyad of 'La-s', represented by) Ādi, (the foremost of the gods); (thus producing the two sets of five and three syllables, *viz.*, 'Ha Sa Ka Ha La' and 'Sa Ka La', which along with the foregoing set of four syllables, *viz.*, 'Ka E Ī La', constitute the three sets of twelve syllables in the aggregate); (and the three Hṛl-lekhā-s obtained from Hari-hara-vi-riṃ, in the following manner : the first 'Hrīṃ' from Hari-riṃ, the second from Hara-vi-riṃ, and the third from Hara-vi-rim, by suppressing the italicized and suitably combining them; thus getting the full-fledged Mantra, called the Pañca-daśākṣarī the fifteen-syllabled Mantra), with each of the three 'Hrīṃ-s' placed immediately after the three sets of syllables already obtained; by the suppression of the italicized in '*Śivaḥ*' with which the stanza begins) and the addition of 'riṃ', the last syllable so far dealt with, 'Śrīṃ*, the Bīja of Cādi, (Lakṣmī who took birth before the Moon, indicated by 'Ca'), which, together with and pervading through the foregoing fifteen syllables, forms the Ṣoḍaśākṣarī (the sixteen-syllabled Mantra). While so, how dare one, who has acquired no proficiency in Mantra-lore, either to salute or to praise Thee, O Goddess! that art of the form of Kādi-vidyā and that art meditated upon by Hari, Hara, Viriñca and others, as assuming fifteen or sixteen diverse forms of the fifteen or sixteen syllables pervading the entire universe?

11. Śiva, (the syllable 'Ha'), only when placed in juxtaposition with the Śakti, (the syllable 'Sa', thereafter), would take the form of the sacred fifteen-syllabled Mantra. If the initial syllable 'Ha' is not so placed along with the syllable 'Sa', the *Deva*, (the syllable

'Ka'), though followed by *Kuśala,* (the Pṛthvī-bīja, 'La'), turns out to be powerless by itself to form a Mantra. Thus the first set of four syllables 'Ha Sa Ka La' is obtained. Again 'Ha' (standing for Śiva), 'Sa' (for the Śakti) and 'Ka' (for the Deva), as before, and Kha-lu (the Ākāśa-bīja, 'Ha') and Ku-śa-la (the Pṛthvībīja, 'La') being placed thereafter, will yield the second set of five syllables, 'Ha Sa Ka Ha La'. Then, by Hari, (the syllable 'Sa', the Vāyu-bīja), Hara, (the syllable 'Ka') and Viriñca, (the syllable 'La', which precedes, in the order of the Alphabet, the letter 'Va',) is yielded the third set of the three syllables 'Sa Ka La'; by adding the syllable 'Hrīṃ' to each of the three sets, after deriving the three 'Hrīṃ-s' from Hari-Hara-vi-riṃ : the first 'Hrīṃ' from H*a*ri-*r*iṃ, the second from H*ara*-vi-*r*iṃ, and the third from H*ara*-vi-riṃ by suppressing the italicized the suitably combining them; the full Mantra called the Pañcadaśākṣari of the Hādi-vidyā, devoutly worshipped by Lopā-mudrā, is formed. While so, how dared one, who is unfit to worship Thee, no knowing They greatness, as described in the Dakṣiṇā-mūrti-saṁhitā, either to salute or to praise Thee?

12. (The crude form,) 'Śiva,' when under the influence of the Śakti, ('E' of the 'Ne' of Pāṇini technique, *i.e.*, the dative singular termination, by suppper-adding the indeclinable, *'Namaḥ'*, indicated by the same Śakti), would be capable of being formed into the Pañcākṣari-mantra, *viz.*, *'Śivāya namaḥ'*. If not, the *Deva* (the crude form 'Śiva' is incapable of being pronounced as a Mantra, proclaiming the oneness of Śiva and Śivā. Therefore, how dares one, who has no merit either to salute or to praise Thee, O Goddess! that art of the form of the Pañcākṣari-mantra and so worshipped by Hari, Hara, Viriñca, and others?

13. Only when Śiva, (the Guru), in endowed with the Śakti (the accomplishments resulting from muttering the *Śrī-vidyā-mantra,* devotion to the Goddess of *Śrīvidyā, etc.,*), would the Śiṣya be able to give a good account of himself, with the grace of the Guru, who is the embodiment of Parameśvara. If his grace is not so accomplished, even the Śiṣya, though shining otherwise, becomes incapable of acquiring even the smallest capacity. Hence, how dares one, who has acquired no merit, either to salute or to praise Thee, O Goddess! the embodiment of the Guru-mūrti, that art worshipped as such by Hari, Hara, Viriñca and others, as, otherwise, it would not be possible for them to understand the esoteric significance of the Mantra?

14. Śiva, (the first digit of the waxing Moon, known as Darśā, which has the character of Śiva-tattva), only when conjoined with the Śakti, (the second digit of the same, known as *Dṛṣṭā* and of the character of Śaktitattva) would be able to acquire the quality of being seen and to be hailed, in the heavens. If not, the *Deva,* (the first digit), is incapable of shining and gladdening the hearts of the worlds, so as to conduce to its welfare, as also to add to the grace of the remaining lunar digits, Darśatā and others. Hence, how dares one, who has not accumulated religious merit in his previous incarnations, either to salute or to praise Thee, O Goddess! of the form of the eternal Candrakalā, (the sixteenth digit), that art worthy of being worshipped by Hari, Hara, Viriñca and others?

According to the Bhairava-yāmala, the *Bindu* of the *Tri-koṇa* and the three *Cakras* lying outside the *Caturdasāra, viz.*, the *Aṣṭa-dala,* the *Ṣoḍaśa-dala* and the *Bhū-gṛha,* these four are representative of Śiva; while the *Tri-koṇa,* the *Aṣṭa-koṇa,* the *Antar-daśāra,* the *Bahir-daśāra* and the *Catur-daśāra* and representative of the Śakti. Without their conjunction, the *Śrī-cakra,* which may be taken to signify the origin of the world, cannot be formed. In other words, the universe will cease to be, when there will be the Mahā-pralaya, the final dissolution. The Vāmakeśvara-tantra says that Śiva ceases to have either name or manifestation, without the Śakti. The Devī-bhāgavata avers that Śiva, deprived of the Kuṇḍalinī-śakti, is but Śava, a corpse. Acyutānanda, a commentator, remarks that the creative Engery of the Śakti, in her three-fold aspects of Icchā—Will, *Jñāna*—Wisdom, and *Kriyā*—Activity, is essential for Śiva, to accomplish anything; and Hari, Hara and Viriñca stand for 'A', 'U' and 'M' respectively, the constituents of the Praṇava-mantra and the other Devatā-s referred to by the word, '*Ādi*', are other Mantra-s. The *Praṇava* is the foremost *Mantra* of the Veda-s. Hence, it follows that the Śakti is fit to be worshipped with the *Praṇava* and the other Vedamantra-s. 'Haṃ', The *Bīja* of Śiva, when combined with '*Saḥ*', the *Bīja* of the Śakti, yields the Haṁsamantra, which helps one to realize the import of the Mahā-vākya, '*Tat tvam asi*', by reminding him of it, with its form 'So'ham'. Again, Haṁsa, the cosmic breath, which is made up of 'Haṁ' (Śiva), the outgoing breath, and 'Saḥ' (the Śakti), the ingoing breath, symbolizes creation in the form of Evolution and dissolution in the form of Involution. Śiva and the Śakti (consonants and vowels, contributing to make up Akṣaras (imperishables) remain as the Niṣ-kala-brahman, during the

Pralaya, as Para-śiva and Śāntā, (transcending the thirty-six Eternal Verities), in a state of quiescence. Or Śāntā's awakening and operating on Śiva as the Śakti, there is brought about the creation of the world.

From the combination of Śiva and the Śakti, Kaivalyāśrama derives the *Parā-prāsāda-mantra*—'Hsauḥ', and the An-uttara-mantra—'Aḥ', wherein 'H' and 'A' stand for Śiva, and 'Sauḥ' and the Visarga for the Śakti respectively. He also derives the Pāśādi-try-akṣarīmantra, made up of the traid of monosyllables, 'Āṃ Hrīṃ Kroṃ' 'Tvā "mā" *rādhyāṃ hari-hara-viriñcādibhir api*' of this stanza, construing it as—Thee (the Bhuvaneśvarī, Hrīṃ[1]) served (on one side) by 'Āṃ' (the Pāśa) and (on the other side) by Hari ('oṃ'), Hara ('R'), and Viriñca ('K'), in the reverse order *i.e.*, 'Kroṃ' (the Aṅkuśa).

The word *'Ādi'* in *'Hari-hara-viriñcādibhiḥ'* is wide enough to comprehend any number of Upāsaka-s with their characterstic ways of approaching the Goddess. So far as could be ascertained from Tantric literature, fifteen such Upāsaka-s with their characteristic Mantras are enumerated hereunder : (1) HARI—Ha Sa Ka La Hrīṃ, Ha Sa Ka Ha La Hrīṃ, Sa Ka La Hrīṃ, Sa Ha Ka La Hrīṃ] Sa Ha Ka Ha La Hrīṃ, Sa Ha Sa Ka La Hrīṃ.[1] (2) HARA—Ha Sa Ka La Hrīṃ, Ha Sa Ka Ha La Hrīṃ, Sa Ka La Hrīṃ, Ha Sa Ka La Ha Sa Ka Ha La Sa Ka La Hrīṃ. (3) VIRIÑCA—Ka E Ī La Hrīṃ, Ha Ka Ha La Hrīṃ, Ha Sa Ka La Hrīṃ. (4) MANU—Ka Ha E Ī La Hrīṃ, Ha Ka E Ī La Hrīṃ, Sa Ka E Ī La Hrīṃ. (5) CANDRA—Sa Ha Ka E I La Hrīṃ, Ha Sa Ka Ha E Ī La Hrīṃ, Ha Sa Ka E Ī La Hrīṃ (6) KUBERA—Ha Sa Ka E Ī La Hrīṃ, Ha Sa Ka Ha E Ī La Hrīṃ, Sa Ha Ka E Ī La Hrīṃ. (7) LOPĀ-MUDRĀ—Ha Sa Ka La Hrīṃ, Ha Sa Ka Ha La Hrīṃ, Sa Ka La Hrīṃ. (8) AGASTYA--Ka E Ī La Hrīṃ, Ha Sa Ka Ha La Hrīṃ, Sa Ha Sa Ka La Hrīṃ. (9) NANDIKEŚVARA—Sa E Ī La Hrīṃ, Sa Ha Ka Ha La Hrīṃ, Sa Ka La Hrīṃ. (10) SŪRYA—Ha Sa Ka La Hrīṃ, Sa Ha Ka La Hrīṃ, Sa Ka Ha La Hrīṃ. (11) SKANDA—Ha Sa Ka La Hrīṃ, Ha Sa Ka Sa Ka La Hrīṃ, Sa Ha Ka Ha La Hrīṃ. (12) MANMATHA—Ka E Ī La Hrīṃ, Ha Sa Ka Ha La Hrīṃ. Sa Ka La Hrīṃ. (13) ŚAKRA—Ka E Ī La Hrīṃ, Ha Ka Ha La Hrīṃ, Sa Ka Ha La Hrīṃ (?). (14) DURVĀSAS—Ha Sa Ka La Ha

1. The fourth and sixth Khaṇḍa-s of this *Vidyā* are, according to the Jñānārṇava-tantra, Sa E Ī La Hrīṃ and Sa Ka E Ī La Hrīṃ respectively, as construed by Kaivalyāśrama.

Sa Ka Ha La Sa Ka La Hrīṃ.[1] (15) YAMA— Ka Ha E Ī La Hrīṃ, Ha La E Ī La Hrīṃ, Sa Ka E I La Hrīṃ

According to a commentator, Śaṅkara-bhagavatpāda, although he has ostensibly framed the entire work on the basis of the *Pañcadaśākṣara,* is said to have not been entirely oblivious of the importance of the *Ṣoḍaśākṣarī*, as may be inferred from the fact that in composing the first half of the first stanza, he has significantly made use of sixteen distinct words. The same question is further dwelt upon at length under stanza the thirty second.

The *Saundaryalaharī*, in addition to dealing with the aspects of the Devī as the consort of Śiva, is also looked upon as a collection of Mantras possessed of considerable sanctity and merit. Each stanza has a Yantra with *Bījākṣara,* prescribed courses of worship, *japa* and a distinctive aim to be achieved by the practice of the *Mantra.*

The following general remarks may be offered regarding the worship of the Devī, (with the Yantra and the *Bījakṣara* of the respective stanzas and the prayer of the Devī, with the muttering of the respective stanzas sitting before the *Yantra,* attended with the Pañcopacāra and other observances as detailed below. As the *Yantras* are themselves considered to be possessed of *Caitanya,* they are generally inscribed on gold plates. The worship in the case of each *Yantra* is to last for a prescribed number of days, and the formalities prescribed for each *Yantra* should be scrupulously adhered to, on each of the days of worship. Such worship is credited with the bestowal of specific fruits. In the case of one who is a successful adept in the practice of any other Mantra, the fruit of worship of the Mahātripurasundarī with the muttering of these stanzas is easily accomplished. In the case of others, success depends on the faith and devotion brought to bear on the worship. It is considered reprehensible to put the efficacy of any Mantra to test. Should there be any delay or difficulty experienced by the worshipper, more devotion is the only sovereign remedy.

---

1. 'La Hrīṃ', the last two syllables of this Mantra are apparently taken to be 'Laharī' by Bhāskararāya, as will be seen from "Haḥ sūryaḥ saś" candraḥ, ko' gniḥ, tān eanti bhinattiti ha-sa-ka-hā; sā cā sā laharī ceti tathā, durvāso-vidyāyāṃ hakāra-rephayor vibhajyāpi pāṭhāt"in his Setubandha.

RULES OF OBSERVANCE[1]—I. *Ṛṣyādi* : For this Stotra of Śrī Saundaryalaharī, Govinda is the Ṛṣi (seer) ; *Anuṣṭubh* is the Chandas (metrical form); Śrī Mahātripura-sundarī is the Deity; '*Śivaḥ śaktryā yuktaḥ* (Śiva conjoint with the Śakti) is the *Bīja* : '*Suddhāsindhor madhye*' (In the middle of the ocean of nectar) is the Śakti : '*Japo jalpaḥ śilpam*' (All prattle is the muttering of thy prayer) is the Kīlaka. II. *Kara-nyāsa* : Hrāṃ, to the thumbs Namaḥ; Harīṃ, to the forefingers Svāhā; Hrūṃ, to the middle fingers Vaṣaṭ; Hraiṃ, to the ring-fingers Huṃ; Hrauṃ, to the little fingers Vauṣaṭ; Hraḥ, to the palms and the backs of the hands Phaṭ. III. *Aṅga-nyāsa* : Hrāṃ, to the heart Namaḥ; Hrīṃ, to the head Svāhā; Hrūṃ, to the tuft of hair Vaṣaṭ; Hraiṃ, to the armour Huṃ; Hrauṃ, to the three eyes Vauṣaṭ; Hraḥ, to the missile Phaṭ. IV. *Dhyāna* : My salutations to the deity that has conquered the colour of the Japā flower with her ruddy complexion, that carries in her hands the Pāśa (noose), the Aṅkuśa (goad), the bow and the arrows, that has copper-coloured eyes, and that wears the red garland as her special ornament, with her mouth filled with Tāmbūla, the Tripura-sundarī. V. *Pañcopacāra*, which should be performed as follows : Laṃ, to thee of the form of Pṛthivī (Earth), I offer Gandha (sandal paste); Haṃ, to thee of the form of Ākāśa (Ether), I offer flowers; Yaṃ, to thee of the form of Vāyu (Air), I offer Dhūpa (incense); Raṃ, to thee of the form of Vahni (Fire), I offer Dīpa (light offering); Vaṃ, to thee of the form of Jala (Water), I offer Naivedya (food offering). VI. *Japa* : the muttering of the respective stanzas for the requisite number of tiems. VII. The prescribed *Naivedya* (food offering).

The Yantra with Bījākṣara-s relating to each stanza is appended under each. Other particulars regarding (1) the inscription of the

---

1. **अनुष्ठानप्रकारः**–1. ऋष्यादिः–अस्य श्रीसौन्दर्यलहरीस्तोत्रस्य गोविन्द ऋषिः ; अनुष्टुप्छन्दः, श्रीमहात्रिपुरसुन्दरी देवता; 'शिवः शक्त्या युक्तः' इति बीजम् ; 'सुधासिन्धोर्मध्ये' इति शक्तिः; 'जपो जल्पः शिल्पम्' इति कीलकम्। 2. करन्यासः–ह्रां अङ्गुष्ठाभ्यां नमः; ह्रीं तर्जनीभ्यां स्वाहा ; ह्रूं मध्यमाभ्यां वषट् ; ह्रैं अनामिकाभ्यां हुं ; ह्रौं कनिष्ठिकाभ्यां वौषट् ; ह्रः करतलकरपृष्ठाभ्यां फट्। 3. अङ्गन्यासः–ह्रां हृदयाय नमः ; ह्रीं शिरसे स्वाहा; ह्रूं शिखायै वषट्, ह्रैं कवचाय हुं ;ह्रौं नेत्रत्रयाय वौषट् ; ह्रः अस्त्राय फट्। 4. ध्यानम्– "लौहित्यनिर्जित-जपाकुसुमानुरागां पाशाङ्कुशौ धनुरिषूनपि धारयन्तीम् ताम्रेक्षणामरुणमाल्यविशेषभूषां ताम्बूलपूरितमुखीं त्रिपुरां नमामि।। 5. पञ्चोपचारः–लं पृथिव्यात्मने गन्धं कल्पयामि; हं आकाशात्मने पुष्पं कल्पयामि ; यं वाय्वात्मने धूपं कल्पयामि। रं वह्न्यात्मने दीपं कल्पयामि; वं जलात्मने नैवेद्यं कल्पयामि।।

Yantra, (2) the number of days of worship, (3) the number of times for muttering the stanza, (4) particulars regarding Naivedya, (5) any other particulars and (6) the fruit of the *Japa*, are shown in a tabular statement as an Appendix at the end.

तनीयांसं पांसुं तव चरणपङ्केरुहभवं
विरिञ्चिः[1] संचिन्वन्विरचयति लोकानविकलम्।[2]
बहत्येनं शौरिः कथमपि सहस्रेण शिरसां
हरः संक्षुद्यैनं[3] भजति भसितोद्धूलनविधिम्[4]॥ २॥

Tanīyāṃsaṃ pāṃsuṃ tava caraṇa-paṅke-ruhabhavaṃ
viriñciḥ saṃcinvan viracayati lokān avikalam/
Vahatyenaṃ śauriḥ katham api sahasreṇa śirasāṃ
haraḥ saṃkṣudyainaṃ bhajati bhasitoddhūlanavidhim//

Translation : Viriñci, having gathered the tiniest speck of dust of Thy lotus-like feet, creates the worlds, leaving nothing to be desired; Śauri carries the same with much effort on his thousand heads; while Hara, pulverizing the same, smears (his body) with it, as though with ashes.

तनीयांसं अतिसूक्ष्मं, **पांसुं** रजःकणं, **तव** भवत्याः, देव्याः **चरणपङ्केरुहभवं** चरणौ पङ्केरुहे इव ताभ्यां भवं **विरिञ्चिः** ब्रह्मा–विरिञ्चिशब्द इकारान्तः, 'विरिञ्चिश्च विरिञ्चनः' इति अमरशेषे अभिधानात्। **संचिन्वन्** सम्पादयन्, भाण्डीकुर्वन्नित्यर्थः, **विरचयति** विविधान् करोति, **लोकान्**–लोक्यन्त इति लोकाः स्थावरजङ्गमात्मकप्रपञ्च इत्यर्थः। यद्वा–ऊर्ध्वलोकाः सप्त भूरादयः, अधोलोकाः सप्त अतलादयः, एवं [5]चतुर्दशलोकान्। **अविकलं** परस्परासङ्कीर्णं यथा भवति तथा। यद्वा–यावत्प्रलयमेषां वैकल्यं यथा न भवति यथा। **वहति** प्रापयति रक्षति **एनं** पांसुकणं चतुर्दशलोकात्मकतया अवस्थितम्। **शौरिः** शूरस्य यदोरपत्यं शौरिः बलभद्रः; तेन शेषो लक्ष्यते, शेषावतारत्वात् बलभद्रस्य। यद्वा–शृणाति हिनस्ति दशतीति शौरिः सर्पराजः, शेष इति यावत्। यद्वा–शौरिः विष्णुः। तथोक्तं चतुःशत्याम्–

---

1. विरंचि : (Saurashtra Edition)
2. लोकानविकलान् (Ānandagirīyā Comm.)
3. संक्षुभ्यैनं (Saurashtra Edn)
4. ०द्धूननविधिम्. (Rare reading)
5. चतुर्दशलोकाः तान्।

"शिंशुमारात्मना विष्णुः सप्तलोकानधः स्थितान्।
दध्रे शेषतया लोकान् भूरादीनूर्ध्वतः स्थितान्"।। इति।

शेषपक्षेऽपि शेष एव विष्णुः, रक्षणे विष्णोरेवाधिकारात्। **कथमपि** कथंचित्, **सहस्रेण शिरसाम्।** **हरः** अन्तकाले प्रपञ्चं हरतीति हरः, **संक्षुद्य** सम्यक् मर्दयित्वा, **एनं** चतुर्दशभुवनात्मकतया अवस्थितं पादरजःकणं, **भजति** सेवते, [1]उपदिहतीत्यर्थः। **भसितोद्धूलनविधिं** भसितेन उपदेहनं अङ्गरागकरणं, तस्य विधिः अनुष्ठानं तं तथोक्तम्।।

अत्रेत्थं पदयोजना–हे भगवति विरिञ्चिः तव चरणपङ्केरुहभवं तनीयांसं पांसुं सञ्चिन्वन् लोकान् अविकलं विरचयति। हे भगवति शौरिरेनं शिरसां सहस्रेण कथमपि वहति। हे भगवति एवं संक्षुद्य हरः भसितोद्धूलनविधिं भजति।।

अयं भावः–ब्रह्मविष्णुमहेश्वराणां प्रपञ्चविषयसृष्टिस्थितिलयकर्तृत्वं भगवत्याः पादाब्जरेणुमहिमायत्तमिति।। २।।

Notes : *Viriñci* the same as *Viriñcā* of the first stanza; both the words denote Brahman, the creator, *Speck of dust*—used in a collective sense, as otherwise the worlds could not ostensibly be created out of a single speck, nor would it require the thousand heads of Śauri to carry it with effort, nor would it be enough to smear the prodigious body of Hara with. *Thy lotus-like feet*—Thy : of Thee, the prime cause of all the worlds; hence the dust on her feet acquires all her virtues. According to Kaṇāda, the founder of the Vaiśeṣika school and Akṣa-pāda, the founder of the Nyāya school, the world is made up of the primary atoms of Earth, Water, Fire and Air, which, at the desire of Īśvara, arrange themselves, in the first instance, into Dvy-aṇukas, consisting of two atoms each, which, in their turn, arrange themselves into Try-aṇukas, consisting of three Dvyaṇuka-s each. It is on groups of these Try-aṇukas, that the cosmogony of these two schools is based. Such a conception of the order of creation should not be considered as a mere surmise of the poet, as it is the fact that the Paramāṇu (of the Devī's feet) is the prime-cause of the creation of the world, that forms the basis of their theory. *The worlds*—both animate and inanimate. The seven upper worlds : *Bhūr, Bhuvar, Suvar, Mahar, Jana, Tapas* and *Satya*, as also the seven nether worlds : *A-tala, Vi-tala, Su-tala, Rasā-tala,*

---

1. उपजीवतीत्यर्थः।

Talā-tala, Mahā-tala and *Pātāla* may also be meant. *Śauri*—Viṣṇu, the sustainer, who is said to be lifting the fourteen worlds, the nether seven in the form of Śiṃśumāra, a porpoise, and the upper seven as Śeṣa. Lakṣmī-dhara construes the word as Balabhadra, (the descendant of Śūra, the Yādava-chief) lifting the worlds in the form of Śeṣa. It may however be noted that, according to Amarasiṃha, Śauri is one of the recognized names of Viṣṇu and not of Balabhadara. *Hara*—Saṃhāra-rudra, the destroyer.

The greatness of the Devī is borne testimony to by the abject dependence of the creator, the sustainer and the destroyer of the worlds on the dust of her feet, for carrying out their respective avocations. It is further enhanced by the fact, that the single speck of her feet provides material for the creator to create all the worlds, with their various contents. The same speck calls forth great effort from Viṣṇu, the thousand-headed, to lift its weight with his myriads of heads, and the mighty Saṃhāra-rudra, with his prodigious form, has to reduce this tiny speck to ashes, by way of destroying the worlds, for the Bhasmasnāna. Again, as observed by Kaivalyāśrama, the ashes are but the residuum left by all the elements and their various transformations, after the application of his Saṃhāra-śakti by Rudra, with a view to smear his body with ashes, in conformity with the Mantra prescribed therefor. Further, the same commentator, fortified by Dattātreya's view, explains the esoteric significance of the speck of dust as follows : The Devī has four feet, named Śukla, Rakta, Miśra and Nirvāṇa, the first two resting on the two-petalled lotus of the *Āññā-cakra,* the third on the twelve-petalled lotus of the heart and the fourth on the thousand-petalled lotus of the, *Dvā-daśānta,* with Viṣṇu, Brahman, Rudra and Sadā-śiva as their respective deities, who, assuming their characteristic Guṇas—*Sattva, Rajas, Tamas* and *Guṇātītatva,* through the speck of dust resting on the four feet, occupy themselves in their respective avocations of creation, sustenance, destruction and bathing in the nectar of the region of the Moon in the thousand-petalled lotus. Kameśvarasūri, however, rebuts this view and points out that it runs counter to what Śaṅkara-bhagavatpāda would uphold, as everywhere in the entire work, he refers to only one pair of feet of the Devī, and that as such it is far-fetched, and adds that if it was meant merely to derive the three Guṇas of Hari, Viriñci and Hara, that could as well as attained by explaining that the speck of dust, being of variegated colours, partakes of the three Guṇas.

Kaivalyāśrama's view may, however, be reconciled by pointing out that this exposition is only esoteric and should not be taken to hold good to the very letter.

Excluding the thousand-petalled *Cakra,* reference has been made above to the two *Cakras, viz., Ājñā* and *An-āhata.* These, along with four others, are centres of phychic energy in the human body. They are : (1) *Mūlādhāra* of four petals, in the region lying two Aṅgulas above the anus : (2) *Svādhiṣṭhāna* of six petals, in the region of the genitals ; (3) *maṇi-pūra* of ten petals, in the region of the navel; (4) *An-āhata* of twelve petals, in the region of the heart; (5) *Viśuddhi* of sixteen petals, in the region of the throat ; and (6) *Ājñā* of two petals, in the region between the eyebrows. When meditating upon these *Cakras,* the four letters from 'Va' to 'Sa' should be thought of a resting on the four petals of the *Mūlādhāra,* the six letters from 'Ba' to 'La' on the six petals of the *Svādhiṣṭhāna,* the ten letters from 'Ḍa' to 'Pha' on the ten petals, of the *Maṇi-pūra,* the twelve letters from 'Ka' to 'Ṭha' on the twelve petals of the *Anāhata,* sixteen letters from 'A' to 'Visarga' on the sixteen petals of the *Viśuddhi,* and the two letters 'Ha' and 'Kṣa' on the two petals of the *Ājñā-cakra.*

तमेव पांसुं प्रस्तौति–

अविद्यानामन्तस्तिमिरमिहिरद्वीपनगरी[1]
जडानां चैतन्यस्तबकमकरन्दस्त्रुतिझरी[2] ।
दरिद्राणां चिन्तामणिगुणनिका जन्मजलधौ
निमग्नानां दंष्ट्रा मुररिपुवराहस्य भवती[3] ।। ३ ।।

Avidyānām antas-timira-mihira-dvīpa-nagarī
jaḍānāṃ caitanya-stabaka-makaranda-srutijharī/
Daridrāṇāṃ cintā-maṇi-guṇanikā janma-jaladhau
nimagnānāṃ daṃṣṭrā mura-ripu-varāhasya bhavatī.//

Translation : Thou art the island-city of the Suns, illumining the internal darkness of the ignorant; (Thou art) the stream, ever flowing with the honey of the cluster-of-flowers of consciousness, for the dull-witted; (Thou art) the Cintā-maṇi-duplicate (in bestowing their heart's desire) on the destitute; and the tusk of the Wild Boar (Avatāra) of Mura-ripu, in the case of those submerged in the Ocean of births (and deaths).

1. मिहिरोद्दीपनकरी, मिहिरोद्दीपनगरी ।
2. स्त्रुतिशिरा, स्त्रुतिसिरा, स्त्रुतिसृतिः, स्त्रुतिनदी ।
3. भवति (Tiruchirapalli & MLBD Editions).

एषः पांसुः **अविद्यानां** अविद्याविष्टचित्तानां, अज्ञानिनामित्यर्थः, न तु अविद्यमानविद्यानां, अविद्यायां भावरूपत्वात्। अर्शआदित्वात् अच्प्रत्ययः, अविद्यावन्तः अविद्या इति। यद्वा–अविद्याविष्टचित्ता अपि उपचारेण अविद्या इति। तेषां **अन्तस्तिमिरमिहिरद्वीपगनरी**–अन्तस्तिमिरं अन्तः स्थिताज्ञानम् अज्ञानस्य तिमितरत्वारोपणं आवरकत्वसाम्यात्–यथा बाह्यपदार्थानावृणोति तमः, तथा आन्तरपदार्थं आत्मानं आवृणोति अविद्या। तस्य तिमिरस्य मिहिरद्वीपनगरी, मिहिरस्य सूर्यस्य द्वीपः समुद्रमध्ये उदयप्रदेशः, तत्र नगरी पत्तनं, वासगृहमिति यावत्। **जडानां** मन्दानां दुर्मेधसां, **चैतन्यस्तबकमकरन्दस्रुतिझरी**–चेतनैव चैतन्यम्, स्वार्थे ष्यञ्, चेतना नाम आत्मगतपदार्थप्रबोधकारिणी चित्तविस्ताररूपा काचन शक्तिः, तदेव स्तबकः कल्पवृक्षपुष्पगुच्छः, तस्य मकरन्दः पुष्परसः, तस्य स्रुतिः स्रवणं निष्यन्दः, तस्य झरी प्रवाहः। **दरिद्राणां** दीनानां, **चिन्तामणिगुणनिका** चिन्तामणेः रत्नविशेषस्य गुणनिका गुणना आम्रेडनं, समूह इति यावत्। **जन्मजलधौ** जन्मैव संसार एवं जलधिः समुद्रः, संसारे समुद्रत्वारोपणं अपारत्वसाम्यात्। तत्र **निमग्नानां** नितरां उन्मज्जनरात्येिन मग्नानाम्। **दंष्ट्रा**–स्पष्टम्। **मुररिपुवराहस्य**, मुरो नाम दैत्यः, तस्य रिपुः विष्णुः, अयं मुररिपुशब्दः विशेषणवाच्यपि विशेष्यं विष्णुमेव कथयति, शब्दस्वाभाव्यात्। न चात्र पङ्कजादिपदवत् शक्तिसङ्कोचः, द्रव्यवाचकत्वादस्येति। तस्य वराहः अवतारविशेषः, तस्य तथोक्तस्य **भवति** वर्तते।।

अत्रेत्थं पदयोजना–हे भगवति तव[1] पादाब्जरेणुः एषः अविद्यानाम् अन्तस्तिमिरमिहिरद्वीपनगरी, जडानां चैतन्यस्तबकमरकन्दस्रुतिझरी, दरिद्राणां चिन्तामणिगुणनिका, जन्मजलधौ निमग्नानां मुररिपुवराहस्य दंष्ट्रा भवति।।

अत्र परिणामालङ्कारः, आरोप्यमाणस्य आरोपविषयात्मतया स्थितेः। तथा च मङ्खकसूत्रम्–'आरोप्यमाणस्य प्रकृतोपयोगित्वे परिणामः' इति। अस्यैवार्थः आरोप्यमाणस्य प्रकृतोपयोगित्वं आरोपविषयात्मतया स्थितिनिबन्धनमेवेति फलाभिप्रायेणोक्त इति। यद्वा–उल्लेखाङ्कारः, नगर्यादिरूपेण पांसोरुल्लेखनात्। रूपकं वा भवतु, प्रकृतोपयोगो न विवक्ष्यत इति।। ३।।

Notes : *Thou*—the rendering of the original word *'Bhavatī'*, stands for the Devī. With the reading *'Bhavati'*, meaning 'becomes', *'Pāṃsu'*, 'the speck of dust' of the previous stanza, will have to be understood as the subject. The island-city of the Suns—this may be taken to mean some imaginary island in the middle of the ocean,

1. भ्वत्पादाब्जरेणुः।

wherefrom the disc of the Sun apparently rises above the horizon. The implication is that the Sun of knowledge dispels the darkness of ignorance from the mind of the wordly-minded. As the internal darkness, accumulated during numberless previous births, is so intense as to occupy every nook and corner of the mind of the person harbouring it, one commentator is of the view that the Mihira, the Sun, refers to the twelve Āditya-s,[1] rising simultaneously with all their effulgence from their island-abode, so as to drive away even the smallest vestige of such darkness. The reading *'Timira-mihiroddīpana-karī'*, (in the Fem. gender) meaning 'causing the Sun of knowledge to manifest itself in all its glory,' if adopted, will not permit of *'Pāṃsu'* (Mas. gender) being taken as the subject, while it will make complete sense with the reading *'Bhavatī'*. *The ignorant*—not possessed of Vidyā, which may be construed as either *Devatā-jñāna* or *Ātma-jñāna, i.e.,* mere Karmathas, who indulge in the observance of Jyotiṣṭoma and other rituals according to the rules prescribed in the Karma-kāṇḍa; or those that are under the delusion that the world entirely depends on Brahman, Viṣṇu and Rudra, while in reality it hangs on the mercy of the Devī, whose dependants these three gods are. The cluster of flowers—*i.e.* all forms of consciousness. *Cintā-maṇi-duplicate*—Cintāmaṇi is the gem said to be in the possession of Indra and is credited with the power of bestowing whatever is thought of by its Upāsakas. Here the Devī is figuratively represented to be the duplicate of the gem with all its powers, as she is the embodiment of the Dāna-śakti. According to one commentator, *'Cintā-maṇi-guṇanikā'* means a rosary of Cintāmaṇi beads. *Mura-ripu*—Viṣṇu, the destroyer of Mura, a demon. The reference here is to the incarnation of Viṣṇu in the form of a Wild Boar, who is said to have lifted on his tusk the submerged worlds and rescued them after vanquishing Hiraṇyākṣa, his foe.

Kameśvarasūri takes the first line of the stanza to imply that the Devī dispels the darkness of ignorance pervading the minds of those that hold the view that *Avidyā* is the root-cause of the world, by imparting the true knowledge of Īśvara. He takes the second line to imply the dispelling of the ignorance of the Sāṃkhyas who

---

1. The twelve Ādityas are—(1) Dhātṛ, (2) Mitra, (3) Aryaman, (4) Rudra, (5) Varuṇa, (6) Sūrya, (7) Bhaga, (8) Vivasvat, (9) Pūṣan, (10) Savitṛ, (11) Tvaṣṭṛ, and (12) Viṣṇu.

believe that the *Jaḍa*, non-sentient Mūla-prakṛti, is the cause of the worlds, by the adoption of similar means. Again he takes the third line to imply that the Devī warns the Paramāṇu-vādins, who hold the primary atoms to be the cause of the world, to be more circumspect, should they be disposed to arrive at the correct theory. The last line implies, according to him, the questionable ways adopted by the least evolved persons immersed in satiating their carnal instincts and appetites in their everyday-life, and suggests the remedial measure of the precepts in the Mahābhārata and other works bearing on right conduct, as the means of saving them.

According to Kaivalyāśrama, this stanza is indicative of the deity of the Kāma-rāja-mātṛkā, who should be meditated upon, by all votaries to the *Śrīvidyā*, as effulgent with the radiance of myriads of morning Suns, holding in her four hands the rosary of crystal beads, the sugar cane-bow, Cupid's five arrows and the Holy Writ, as having three eyes and wearing the crescent-moon as her crest-jewel. He is also of opinion that the Vāgbhava-bīja, *'Aiṃ'* of the Tripurā, which occupies the forefront of the three Bījas, Vāg-bhava, Kāma-rāja, and Śakti, is indicated by the stanza, for the reason that *'Aiṃ'* is composed of *'A'*, the initial letter of the Ṛgveda, *'A'*, that of the Sāmaveda, and 'I', that of the Yajurveda, construed as follows : The initial letters of the Sāma-veda and the Yajur-veda combined go to form 'E', and with the initial letter of the Ṛgveda placed before and combined with it, would result in *'Ai'*, which, with the nasal Ardhamātrā of the Upaniṣads, becomes *'Aiṃ'*, the *Trayī-mayī-vidyā*, which has the virtues of dispelling *Avidyā*, ignorance, with the first 'A', of removing *Jaḍatva*, non-sentience, with the second 'A', and of bestowing one's heart's desires with 'I' and Kaivalya with the Ardhamātrā.

त्वदन्यः पाणिभ्यामभयवरदो दैवतगणः
त्वमेका नैवासि प्रकटितवराभीत्यभिनया।
भयात्त्रातुं दातुं फलमपि च वाञ्छासमधिकं
शरण्ये[1] लोकानां तव हि चरणावेव निपुणौ।।४।।

Tvadanyaḥ pāṇibhyām abhayavarado daivatagaṇas
tvaṃ ekā naivāsi prakaṭika-varābhīty-abhinayā/
Bhayāt trātuṃ dātuṃ phalam api ca vāñchāsamadhikaṃ
śaraṇye lokānāṃ tava hi caraṇāv eva nipuṇau.//

1. शरण्या (Saurashtra edn)

Translation : (O Goddess), who affordest shelter to all the (fugitive) worlds! The league of gods, save Thee, dispels fear and bestows boons with two hands. Indeed,Thou alone dost not demonstrate the boon-bestowing and fear-dispelling gestures (with Thy hands). For, Thy feet, by themselves, are proficient in affording immunity from fear and bestowing boons transcending (one's) desire.

त्वत् भवत्याः सकाशात्, **अन्यः** इतरः, **पाणिभ्यां** हस्ताभ्यां **अभयवरदः** अभयं भयराहित्यं, भयात्त्राणमिति यावत्, वरः इष्टार्थः, तौ ददातीति अभयवरदः, एकेन हस्तेन अभयदः अन्येन वरद इत्यर्थः। **दैवतगणः** देवता एव दैवतानि, विनयादित्वात् स्वार्थे अण्, 'स्वार्थिकाः प्रत्ययाः प्रकृतितो लिङ्गवचनान्यतिवर्तन्ते', यथा चेतनैव चैतन्यमिति। तेषां गणः इन्द्रादयः आदित्यादयश्च गणदेवताः। **त्वं** भवती, **एका** मुख्या, एकसंख्यासंख्येया वा, **नैवासि** न भवस्येव। **प्रकटितवराभीत्यभिनया**– प्रकटितः, प्रकाशितः, हस्ताभ्यामिति शेषः, वरः इष्टार्थः अभीतिः अभयं भयात् त्राणं, तयोरभिनयः अभिव्यञ्जनं यस्याः सा तथोक्ता। हस्ताभ्यां अभयवरप्रदानं सर्वदैवतसाधारणमिति अस्याः असाधारणं अभयवरप्रदानप्रकारमाह–**भयात् त्रातुं** संसाराद्रक्षितुं, **दातुं फलं** वाञ्छितार्थानुरूपं, **अपि च** समुच्चये, **वाञ्छासमधिकं** वाञ्छयाः कामनायाः सम्यगधिकं, कामितार्थादधिकमित्यर्थः। **शरण्ये** शरणार्हे **लोकानां** चतुर्दशभुवनानाम्। **तव** भवत्याः। **हिशब्दः** इत्यर्थे, इति संचिन्त्येत्यर्थः। **चरणौ** पादौ। एवकारः अवधारणे। **निपुणौ** समर्थौ।।

अत्रेत्थं पदयोजना–हे भगवति! लोकानां शरण्ये! त्वदन्यो दैवतगणः पाणिभ्यामभयवरदः। एका त्वं पाणिभ्यां प्रकटितवराभीत्यभिनया नैवासि हि। इति संचिन्त्य तव चरणावेव भयात्त्रातुं वाञ्छासमधिकं फलमपि च दातुं निपुणौ।।

अयं भावः–हस्ताभ्यामभयवरदानं सर्वसाधारणमिति कृत्वा त्वच्चरणावेव तादृशाभयवरप्रदाने स्वयमेव व्यापृतौ। अतस्तव न कर्तव्यं हस्ताभ्यामभयवरप्रदानं, प्रयोजनाभावात्, सर्वसाधारण्यप्रसङ्गात्, लोकैकशरण्यत्वव्याघाताच्चेत्युपदेश इति।।

अत्र व्यतिरेकालङ्कारः स्पष्टः। वाक्यलिङ्गकः काव्यलिङ्गालङ्कारोऽपि स्पष्टः। तयोरङ्गाङ्गिभावेन सङ्करः।।४।।

Notes : Who affordest shelter—*Śaraṇyā*, the Saṃskṛt equivalent, means 'who affords shelter'. It may also be taken to signify, 'who has the *Śrī-cakra* as her worthy (Śaraṇa) abode'. *All the fugitive worlds*—the worlds that have their origin in the feet of the Devī, seeking shelter at the very place of their origin; what is more, the very gods, who pose with their hands the dispelling of fear and the grainting of boons, themselves seek shelter at the Devī's feet. Thou alone dost not demonstrate—Evidently this refers to the fact that, wheareas the gods merely employ their hands for posing, the Devī, the unique Goddess that she is, even though she has four hands, engages them otherwise, in carrying the *Pāśa*, the *Aṅkuśa*, the sugar-cane-bow and arrows, and, at the same time, causes her feet to do not merely what the other gods profess to do, but even more in graining what her devotees seek at her hands. It is worthy of note that while some of the gods are capable of graining *Svarga-bhoga* and others *Mokṣa* alone, the Devī bestows on her votaries both the enjoyment of celestial pleasures and liberation. Gestures—the Abhayada-posture assumed by the right palm uplifted, as if to denote 'do not fear', and the Varada-posture with the left palm pointing downwards, as if to indicate readiness to give. The Bālā-*mantra* 'Aiṃ Klīṃ Sauḥ' is indicated by this stanza.

हरिस्त्वामाराध्य प्रणतजनसौभाग्यजननीं
पुरा नारी भूत्वा पुररिपुमपि[1] क्षोभमनयत्।
स्मरोऽपि त्वां नत्वा रतिनयनलेह्येन वपुषा
मुनीनामप्यन्तः प्रभवति हि मोहाय महताम्।।५।।

Haristvām ārādhya praṇata-jana-saubhāgya Jananīṃ
purā nārī bhūtvā pura-ripum api kṣobham anayat/
Smaro'pi tvāṃ natvā rati-nayana-lehyena vapuṣā
munīnām apy antaḥ prabhavati hi mohāya mahatām.//

Translation : Having adored Thee, the bestower of prosperity to those that make obeisance before Thee, Hari (Viṣṇu), of yore, assumed the form of a woman and fascinated even the destroyer of the (three) *Puras.* Smara (cupid) likewise, by worshipping Thee, is powerful enough to rouse the passion of even great sages, with a (charming) frame fit to be licked by Rati's eyes.

हरिः विष्णुः, **त्वां** भवतीं चक्ररूपिणीं विद्यारूपिणीं च **आराध्य** पूजयित्वा जपित्या ध्यात्वा च। अत एव त्रिपुरसुन्दरीप्रस्तारभेदेषु एकस्य प्रस्तारस्य ऋषिः विष्णुः। ऋषिर्नाम वेदस्थितो मन्त्रो येन दृष्टः स इति। अत एवाहुः 'दर्शनादृषिः' इति। इयं

1. स्मररिपुमपि।

पञ्चदशाक्षरी विद्या ऋग्वेदे आम्नाता 'चत्वार ईं बिभ्रति क्षेमयन्तः'[1] इत्यादौ। न चात्र ईंकारत्रयं, हृल्लेखात्रयस्यैव श्रुतत्त्वात्, इति वाच्यम्। षोडशकलात्मकस्य श्रीबीजस्य गुरुसम्प्रदायवशाद्विज्ञेयस्य स्थितत्वात् चतुर्णामींकाराणां सिद्धेः मूलविद्यायाः वेदस्थितत्वं सिद्धम्।

अत्र केचित्तु कुलसमयाचाराभिज्ञाः **'चत्वार ईं बिभ्रति क्षेमयन्तः'**[1] इत्यादिश्रुतिबोधिताश्चत्वार ईंकाराः ईकारेण सार्धं हृल्लेखात्रयमित्याहुः। तन्न, ईकारस्य ईंकारत्वोक्तेरयुक्तत्वात्, मूलविद्यायाः षोडशवर्णात्मकत्वात्, षोडशवर्णात्मकत्वं च षोडशनित्याप्रकृतिभूतत्वात् मूलविद्यायाः। एतच्च **'चतुष्षष्ट्या तन्त्रैः'**[2] इति **'शिवः शक्तिः कामः'**[3] इति च श्लोकद्वयव्याख्यानावसरे निपुणतरमुपपादयिष्यामः। किञ्चास्य मन्त्रस्य वेदमूलत्वं संज्ञानानुवाकेन[4] 'इयं वाव सरघा'[5] इत्यनुवाकेन च प्रतिपाद्यत इति वक्ष्यते।।

प्रकृतमनुसरामः–**प्रणतजनसौभाग्यजननीं,** प्रकर्षेण नताः प्रणताः कायिकवाचिकमानसिकनमस्कारवन्तः जनाः भक्तलोकाः, तेषां सौभाग्यस्य जननी प्रसवित्री तां ; **पुरा** पूर्वं **नारी** कान्ता **भूत्वा** नारीरूपं धृत्वा, **पुररिपुं** त्रिपुरान्तकम्। **अपिशब्दो** जितेन्द्रियत्वं संभावयति। **क्षोभं** मनोविकारं, **अनयत्** नयति स्म। 'गतिबुद्धि' इत्यादिसूत्रेण द्विकर्मकत्वम्। **स्मरोऽपि** मन्मथोऽपि। अपिशब्दः पूर्वोक्तविष्णुधर्मं समुच्चिनोति। यथा विष्णुर्भवन्मन्त्रस्य ऋषिः, एवं स्मरोऽपि। **त्वां** भवतीं, **नत्वा** शरणमुपगम्य, श्रीचक्रं सम्यगभ्यर्च्य, त्वन्मूलविद्यां सम्यगभ्यस्य, त्वत्प्रभावापन्नसत्त्वः **रतिनयनलेह्येन** रतेः स्वपत्न्याः नयनाभ्यां लेह्येन लेहनार्हेण, रतिनयनैकदृश्येनेत्यर्थः। यद्वा–रतिर्नाम अतिसुन्दरी, तस्याः नयनपेयेन इत्यतिसौन्दर्यं कामदेहस्येति। **वपुषा** देहेन। **मुनीनां** जितेन्द्रियाणाम्। **अपिशब्दः** संभावनायाम्। **अन्तः** अन्तरङ्गे चित्तवृत्तौ। **प्रभवति** समर्थः। **हि** प्रसिद्धौ। **मोहाय** शब्दादिविषयावाञ्छोत्पादनाय। **महतां** महात्मनाम्।

अत्रेत्थं पदयोजना–हे भगवति! प्रणतजनसौभाग्यजननीं त्वां हरिराराध्य पुरा नारी भूत्वा पुररिपुमपि क्षोभमनयत्। स्मरोऽपि त्वां नत्वा रतिनयनलेह्येन वपुषा महतां मुनीनामप्यन्तर्मोहाय प्रभवति हि।।

पुरा किल नारायणः स्त्रीरूपधारी कनकस्वामिनं प्रलोभ्य अवधीत्। तादृशं स्त्रीरूपं

---

1. ऋ० ५-४७-४।
2. ३१ श्लोक।
3. ३२ श्लोक।
4. तै०ब्रा० ३-१०-१।
5. तै०ब्रा० ३-१०-१०।

शम्भुना प्रार्थितः सन् तस्मै दर्शयित्वा तं व्यामोहयामासेति कथा अनुसन्धेया। मन्मथोऽपि सकलमुनिमनस्संक्षोभं कुर्वाणः प्रवर्तते। एतच्च वामकेश्वरमहातन्त्रे चतुःशत्यां निरूपितम्–

"एतामेव [1]पुराऽऽराध्य विद्यां त्रैलोक्यमोहिनीम्।
त्रैलोक्यं मोहयामास कामारिं भगवान् हरिः।।
कामदेवोऽपि देवेशीं[2] देवीं त्रिपुरसुन्दरीम्।
समाराध्याभवल्लोके सर्वसौभाग्यसुन्दरः।। इति"।।

अतश्च यत्र यत्र रतिमूलकं मनस्संक्षोभकरणं भवति तत्तद्भगवतीप्रसादलभ्यमिति वक्तुं कवेरयमारम्भः।।५।।

Notes: Adored Thee—meditated upon the Devī by worshipping her in the form of the *Śrī-cakra* and muttering the Vidyā, *viz.*, the Pañca-daśākṣarī, which is of her shape. There is a peculiar appropriateness in Viṣṇu worshipping the Devī, as he is the seer of the first Khaṇḍa of the Pañca-daśākṣarī, as well as the first Prastāra, made up of the Lopā-mudrā and the Nandikeśvara-vidyās, as mentioned in the Jñānārṇava-tantra. *Prosperity*—implies beauty of form, fine accomplishments, progeny, opulence, etc. *Of yore*—Lakṣmīdhara narrates the incident of Kanakasvāmin, whom Viṣṇu fascinated in the form of a beautiful damsel and eventually killed when requested by Śiva to appear before him in that form, Viṣṇu did so, with the result depicted in the stanza. Other commentators take it back to the days of the churning of the ocean by the Devas and the Dānavas for the extraction of nectar, when Viṣṇu is said to have appeared as Mohinī, whose beauty so enraptured the Dānavas that they were altogether deceived by Viṣṇu at the time of the distribution of the nectar and were thus rendered mortal. The rest of the story is as narrated by Lakṣmīdhara. This only enhanced the powers of the Devī, as, after all, Viṣṇu, as a true worshipper given to muttering constantly the syllable, 'Īṃ', denoting her Kāmakalā form, assumed her form, *i.e.*, that of the loveliest woman imaginable and attracted the attention of even

1. पुरा ध्यात्वा।
2. महात्रिपुरसुन्दरीम्।

Śiva, the saintliest among the gods and the destroyer of Manmatha. *Smara likewise*—likewise, *i.e.* with equal potency and in the same manner as Viṣṇu, Smara, Manmatha, who, along with his consort Ratī, is first worshipped at the entrance to the holy of holies at the time of worship of the Tripura-sundarī, is the seer of the Pañcadaśākṣarī of three Khaṇḍas, which, with the Śrī-bīja, 'Śrīṃ' as the fourth Khaṇḍa, becomes the Soḍaśākṣarī of the *Śrī-vidyā*, with the sixteen Nityās constituting the sixteen Kalās, which, again, with its four 'Īṃ-s', takes its origin from the Ṛgveda mantra, *'Catvāra Īṃ bibhrati kṣemayantaḥ'*. Those who attach greater sanctity to the Kādi-vidyā of fifteen syllables (than to the Hādi-vidyā of an equal number of syllables) hold that the former, by itself answers to the description of the Ṛgveda-mantra, as it contains four 'Ī-s'. But this construction of *'Catvāra Īṃ bibhrati'* is defective from the point of view of syntax and for the reason that the Mantra contains one 'Ī' and three 'Ī'm-s' and, with a view of conform to the requirement of the Vedic text, the three 'Ī-s' (of the Hrīṃ-s therein) are separated and, together with the 'Ī' of the Vidyā, are made to answer to the description of the Vedic text. On the other hand, the Mūla-vidyā of sixteen syllables, made up of four Khaṇḍas, each of them containing an 'Ī'm', is on all fours with the requirements of the Vedic text. This view is also supported by the Taittirīya-brāhmaṇa III, x, 1 and 10.

Acyutānanda derives from the stanza the Sādhya-siddhāsana-vidyā—'Hrīṃ, Klīṃ' Bleṃ', the fourth of the Catur-āsana-nyāsar in the following manner : 'H' and 'R' from 'Hariḥ'; 'Īṃ' from 'Jananīṃ' ; Klīṃ, the Kāma-bīja, as indicated by the word 'Smara'; 'V', (which is the same as 'B') from 'Vapuṣā'; 'Le' from 'Lehya', and 'Ṃ' from 'Munīnāṃ'.

यद्यपि पूर्वस्मिन् श्लोके भगवतीप्रसादासादितं मन्मथस्य प्रागल्भ्यमुक्तं, तथापि मन्मथस्य अनङ्गविद्यायां मन्मथप्रस्तारस्य ऋषित्वात् तदायत्तमति–प्रागल्भ्यमाह–

धनुः पौष्पं मौर्वी मधुकरमयी पञ्च विशिखा[1]
वसन्तः सामन्तो मलयमरुदायोधनरथः।
तथाऽप्येकः सर्वं हिमगिरिसुते कामपि कृपा-
मपाङ्गत्ते[2] लब्ध्वा जगदिदमनङ्गो विजयते।। ६ ।।

Dhanuḥ pauṣpaṃ maurvī madhu-kara-mayī pañca viśikhā
vasantaḥ sāmanto malaya-marud āyodhanarathaḥ.

---

1. विशिखाः 2. अपागांत्ते, अपांङ्गं ते।

Tathā 'pyekaḥ sarvaṃ hima-giri- sute kām api kṛpām
apāṅgāt te labdhvā jagad idam anaṅgo vijayate.//

Translation : O Daughter of the snow-capped Mountain! That Anaṅga, (whose) bow is of flowers, (whose) bow-string is of (a row of) bees (who has but) five arrows, (who has as) his feudatory, *Vasanta,* and the *Malaya*-breeze as his, war-chariot, (he), even though thus equipped, having obtained some grace from Thy side-glance, conquers all this world single-handed.

अत्र पद्ये यत्तदोरध्याहारः। उभयाध्याहारः सकलकविसमयसिद्धः। यथा रघुवंशे–'**वागर्थाविव सम्पृक्तौ**' इत्यत्र यौ सम्पृक्तौ तौ वन्दे इति। तथा 'ये नाम केचिदिह नः प्रथयन्त्यवज्ञाम्'[1] इत्यादौ य उत्पत्स्यते तं प्रत्येष यत्न इति। **धनुः** आयोधनसाधनं चापः **पौष्पं** पुष्पमयम्। पुष्पाणामतिमृदुलत्वात् स्पर्शासहत्वात् नमनाकर्षणादिचाप- कार्यानर्हत्वमिति तात्पर्यम्। **मौर्वी** शिञ्जिनी, **मधुकरमयी** मधुकरैः भ्रमरैः प्रचुरा, भ्रमरपङ्क्तिनिर्मितेत्यर्थः। परस्परासम्बद्धानां शिञ्जिनीत्वं न सङ्गच्छत इति तात्पर्यम्। **पञ्च** पञ्चसङ्ख्यासङ्ख्यया:, **विशिखाः** बाणाः। पञ्चानां विक्षेपणे तूष्णीम्भाव एव शरणमिति तात्पर्यम्। किञ्च–'**पञ्च विशिखाः**' इत्यनेन तद्विशिखानां प्रसूनात्मकत्व- प्रसिद्धेः विशिखकार्यकारित्वाभाव इति तात्पर्यम्। **वसन्तः** कालविशेषः, 'वसन्तो मधुमाधवौ इत्यभिधानात्। **सामन्तः** सचिवः। तस्य कालात्मकत्वात् साचिव्यकारित्वं न सङ्गच्छत इति तात्पर्यम्। **मलयमरुत्** दक्षिणानिलः **आयोधनरथः** आयोधनस्य युद्धस्य साधनं स्यन्दनः। मलयमरुतो मलये स्थितत्वात् न सार्वत्रिकत्वम्, सार्वत्रिकत्वेऽपि न सर्वदा सद्भावः, सर्वदा सद्भावेऽपि नीरूपत्वाद्रथकार्याकारित्वाभाव इति तात्पर्यम्। **तथापि** उक्तप्रकारे सार्वजनीने सिद्धेऽपि **एकः** असहायशूरः **सर्वं** सकलं प्रपञ्चम्। **हिमगिरिसुते** हिमप्रधानो गिरिः हिमगिरिः, शाकपार्थिवादित्वात्साधुः, तस्य सुता नन्दिनी, तस्याः सम्बुद्धिः। **कां** अनिर्वाच्याम्। **अपि** शब्दः सम्भावनायाम् **कृपां** अनुकम्पाम्। **अपाङ्गात्** कटाक्षात्, **ते** तव, **लब्ध्वा** प्राप्य। **जगत्** जङ्गमात्मकं लोकं, स्थावरात्मकस्याप्रसक्तेः। इदं परिदृश्यमानम्। **अनङ्गः** अङ्गरहितः। अत्र साधकस्यापि दौर्बल्यं सूचितम्। हस्ताभावादेव चापाकर्षणशरसन्धाने अप्यसम्भाविते। पादभावाच्च [2]रथादौ स्थितिरप्य- संभाविता। वक्त्रनयनाद्यभावात् वयस्येन मधुना सार्धं सम्भाषणसन्निरीक्षणसहासनादयः असम्भाव्या इति तात्पर्यम्। **विजयते**, 'विपराभ्यां जेः' इत्यात्मनेपदम्।।

1. मालतीमाधेव।
2. रथावस्थितिरपि।

अत्रेत्थं पदयोजना—हे हिमगिरिसुते! यस्यानङ्गस्य धनुः पौष्पं, मौर्वी मधुकरमयी, विशिखाः पञ्च, सामन्तो वसन्तः, आयोधनरथः मलयमरुत्, तथाऽपि सोऽनङ्गः, एकः ते अपाङ्गात् कामपि कृपां लब्ध्वा सर्वमिदं जगत् विजयते।।

अत्र विभावनालङ्कारः विजयसाधनाभावेऽपि विजयोत्पत्तेः। '**कारणेन विना कार्योत्पत्तिर्विभावना**' इति लक्षणम्।। ६।।

Notes : One phase of the greatness of Anaṅga, the formless Manmatha, due to the grace of the Devī and redounding to his credit, *i.e.* his subjugating the unconquerable will and rousing the passions of great sages, has been dealt with in the previous stanza. Yet another phase, which further enhances the greatness of this seer of the Prastāra called after him, is referred to in this stanza. *viz.*, though ill-equipped as a warrior, *i.e.*, with flimsy weapons., poor following and no armament worth the name, he has won the unique distinction of being the conqueror of the world, all due to the marvellous effect of the Devī's side-glance cast on him, as if to recompense him for the loss of his body, which was burnt to ashes by the fire from the third eye (the *Jñānacakṣus*) of Śiva, her Lord, when his Yoga was sought to be disturbed by Manmatha, in his attempt to rouse the passion of Śiva for his Mountain-bride, the Devī.

'Klīṃ', the Kāmabīja, is indicated by this stanza and could be derived therefrom in the following manner : 'K' from 'Kām apī', 'L' from 'Malaya', 'Ī' from 'Maurvī' and the Anusvāra from 'Pauṣpaṃ'.

'सुधासिन्धोर्मध्ये' इत्युत्तरश्लोकोपयोगितया समयिनां चतुर्विधैक्यानुसन्धानमहिम्ना मणिपूरे भगवत्या यादृशं स्फुरति रूपं तादृशं प्रस्तौति—

क्वणत्काञ्चीदामा करिकलभकुम्भस्तननता[1]
परिक्षीणा मध्ये परिणतशरच्चन्द्रवदना।
धनुर्बाणान्पाशं सृणिमपि दधाना करतलैः
पुरस्तादास्तां नः पुरमथितुराहोपुरुषिका।। ७।।

Kvaṇat-kāñcī-dāmā kari-kalabha-kumbha-stananatā
parikṣīṇā madhye pariṇata-śarac-candra-vadanā/
Dhanur bāṇān pāśaṃ sṛṇim api dadhānā karatalaiḥ
purastād āstāṃ naḥ pura-mathitur āho-puruṣikā.//

---

1. ०स्तनभरा.।

Translation : May the great Pride (incarnate) of the Vanquisher of the (three) Puras, with a jingling girdle, (slightly) bent (under the weight of) the breasts resembling the frontal globes of a young elephant, slim in the waist, with a face (bright) like the autumnal full-moon, and wielding a bow, arrows, a noose (rope) and a goad (*aṅkuśa)* with Her hands, stand forth before us!

क्वणत्काञ्चीदामा शिञ्जन्मणिमेखला। **करिकलभकुम्भस्तननता** करिकलभ-कुम्भतुल्याभ्यां स्तनाभ्यामीषन्नम्रमध्येत्यर्थः। **परिक्षीणा** कृशा, **मध्ये** अवलग्ने, तनुमध्येत्यर्थः। **परिणतशरच्चन्द्रवदना** परिणतः सम्पूर्णकलः शरदि शरत्काले चन्द्रः इन्दुः तद्वद्वदनं यस्याः सा। **धनुः** चापं, **बाणान्** पुष्पमयान्, **पाशं** दाम, **सृणिं** अङ्कुशम्। **अपिशब्दः** उक्तमेव समुच्चिनोति। **दधाना** बिभ्रती, **करतलैः** चतुर्भिः हस्ताम्बुजैः। **पुरस्तात्** हृदयकमले, मणिपूरान्निर्गत्येति शेषः। **आस्तां** उपविशतु। **नः** अस्माकम्। **पुरमथितुः** त्रिपुरान्तकस्य। यद्वा–पुराणि त्रीणि वर्णानि त्रिपुराबीजानि मथ्नाति, मथित्वा नवनीतं करोति यस्मिन् रुद्रयामले स **रुद्रः** पुरमथितेत्युच्यते। **आहोपुरुषिका**–अहोशब्द आश्चर्यवाची ; पुरुषशब्दस्य प्रत्यगात्मवाचिनः अहंशब्दवाच्यत्वं लक्ष्यते ; अतः अहो अहम्भावः आहोपुरुषिका, अहङ्कार इति यावत्। रुद्रस्याहङ्काररूपित्वं भगवत्याः 'शिवः शक्त्या'[1] इत्यादिश्लोकव्याख्याने प्रपञ्चितम्, प्रपञ्चयिष्यते च।।

अत्रेत्थं पदयोजना–क्वणत्काञ्चीदामा करिकलभकुम्भस्तननता मध्ये परिक्षीणा परिणतशरच्चन्द्रवदना धनुः बाणान् पाशं सृणिमपि करतलैः दधाना पुरमथितुराहो-पुरुषिका: नः पुरस्तादास्ताम्।।

अत्र यद्वक्तव्यं तत्तु 'तवाज्ञाचक्रस्थम्'[2] इत्यादिश्लोकषट्कव्याख्यानान्ते निपुणतर-मुपपादयिष्यते, तत्त एवावधार्यम्।।७।।

Notes : The great Pride (incarnate) of the Vanquisher of the (three) *Puras*—According to Ḍiṇḍima, a commentary, Śiva is very fond of worshipping in this form the Devī, to whom he is so devoted. *Āho-puruṣikā*—the Saṃskṛt equivalent of 'Pride', may be construed in two different ways : '*Aho*' is the interjection indicating surprise, 'Puruṣa' is the *Prayag-ātman*, which is the same as the 'Aham', 'I'. Hence, the abstract noun from the compound formed would mean 'the Pride incarnate', which, being of the redoubtable Mahādeva,

---

1. १ श्लोकः।
2. ३६ श्लोकः।

is the 'great Pride incarnate'; or 'Aho' means the 'Ātman', 'I', which with 'Puruṣa' would means, 'verily, I am the Puruṣa'; hence '*Āho-puruṣikā*', means 'the state of being such Puruṣa, possessed of the self-consciousness indicative of having the Śakti as his Devī.' *Pura-mathitṛ*—is the Śiva who is the vanquisher of the three Puras; this may also be construed as 'the extractor of the three syllables', forming the Tri-purā-bīja, '*Aiṃ Klīṃ Sauḥ*', which, according to the Rudrayāmala, the great god extracted as the essence, after churning the Saṃskṛt Alphabet therefor, even as one churns the curds for the extraction of butter. The coupling of the words '*Puramathituḥ*' and '*Āho-puruṣikā*', in a way, indicates the necessity for the worship of the two conjointly, so beautifully elaborated in the first stanza. Jingling—so as to be heard in the heart-lotus of the meditating Yogin. Wielding a bow, etc.—The Devī carries in her lower left arm the sugar-cane-bow with a string of bees, in her lower right arm the five arrows of Kamals, Raktakairava, Kahlāra, Indīvara and Sahakāra flowers; in her upper left arm the Pāśa, noose, shining like coral, and in her upper right arm the Aṅkuśa, goad, shining like the crescent. These weapons of the Devī are said to assume the Sthūla (gross), the Sūkṣma (Mantra-maya), and the Para (Vāsanā-maya) forms. The first of these has been indicated above. As for the subtle form assumed by them, the bow is of the form of the syllable 'Thaṃ', the five arrows of the forms of 'Drāṃ', 'Drīṃ', 'Drīṃ', 'Klīṃ', 'Blūṃ' and 'Saḥ', the Pāśa of 'Hrīṃ' and the Aṅkuśa of 'Kroṃ'. As for the Para-rūpa in the form of Vāsanā, the bow is the Manas, the five arrows are the five Tanmātras, sound, touch, *etc.*, passions constitute the Pāsa, while anger is the Aṅkuśa. Before us—*i.e.*, in our Hṛdaya-kamala; moving from the *Maṇi-pūra* on to the *An-āhata* of the heart-lotus, while we are in the act of meditating on the Devī. The resplendent form of the Devī is of three aspects, gross, subtle and of the form of Vāsanā. The Sthūla form has been described above; the Sūkṣma aspect is of the form of the Pañca-daśākṣari or the Ṣoḍaśākṣarī, as the case may be; and the Para aspect is the Kuṇḍalinī-śakti itself. The esoteric significance of this stanza is that Śiva, the Prakāśa, becomes conscious of himself, only when reflected in the Devī, the Vimarśāṃśa.

From this stanza is said to be derived the Vaśinībīja, 'Blūṃ',[1] thus : 'B' from the word 'Bāṇān', 'L' from '*Kara-talaiḥ*', 'U' from '*pura-mathituḥ*', and the *Bindu* from '*Āstāṃ*'.

1. The Vaśinī-bīja is represented to 'Rblūṃ' by the Vāmakeśvara-tantra, in which case the 'Rb' may be derived from 'Dhanur-bāṇān'.

सुधासिन्धोर्मध्ये सुरविटपिवाटीपरिवृते
मणिद्वीपे नीपोपवनवति चिन्तामणिगृहे।
शिवाऽऽकारे मञ्चे परमशिवपर्यङ्कनिलयां
भजन्ति त्वां धन्याः कतिचन चिदानन्दलहरीम्।।८।।

Śudhā-sindhor madhye sura-viṭapi-vāṭī-parivṛte
maṇi-dvīpe nīpopavana-vati cintā-maṇi-gṛhe/
Śivā kāre mañce parama-śiva-paryaṅka-nilayāṃ
bhajanti tvāṃ dhanyāḥ katicana cid-ānanda-laharīm//

Translation : Blessed are the few that serve Thee, the flood of Consciousness and Bliss, having, as Thy abode, the mattress of Paramaśiva, laid on the couch of the (multi-triangular) form of Śivā, in the mansion built of precious Cinntāmaṇi gems (stones), attached to the pleasure-gardent of Nīpa (*kadamba*) trees, in the island of gems, surrounded by an avenue of Kalpa trees and situated amidst the ocean of nectar.

सुधासिन्धोः अमृतसमुद्रस्य **मध्ये सुरविटपिवाटीपरिवृते** सुरविटपिनां कल्पवृक्षाणां वाटीभिः झम्पाभिः परवृते, **मणिद्वीपे** मणिमये अन्तरीपे, **नीपोपवनवति** नीपैः[1] कदम्बैः उपवनवति **चिन्तामणिगृहे** चिन्तामणिविरिचिते मन्दिरे **शिवाकारे** शिवात्मके शक्तिरूपे, त्रिकोणे इति यावत्, **मञ्चे** खट्वायां, **परमशिवपर्यङ्कनिलयां** परमशिव एव पर्यङ्कः तल्पं, तत्र निलयः अवस्थितिर्यस्याः तां, **भजन्ति** सेवन्ते, **त्वां** भवतीं, **धन्याः** त्वत्प्रसादवशात् कृतार्थाः, **कतिचन** विरलाः, **चिदानन्दलहरीं** चित् ज्ञानं, तदाकारः आनन्दः निरतिशयसुखं, तस्य लहरीं उत्सेकरूपाम्।।

अत्रेत्थं पदयोजना–हे भगवति! सुधासिन्धोः मध्ये सुरविटपिवाटीपरिवृते मणिद्वीपे नीपोपवनवति चिन्तामणिगृहे शिवाकारे मञ्चे परमशिवपर्यङ्कनिलयां त्वां चिदानन्दलहरीं कतिचन धन्याः भजन्ति।।

अत्रेदमनुसन्धेयम्–भगवत्पादाचार्याः समयमतपारदृश्वानः समयाचारप्रवणाः समयरूपां भगवतीं स्तुवन्ति। समयाचारो नाम आन्तरपूजारतिः। कुलाचारो नाम बाह्यपूजारतिरिति रहस्यम्। एतच्च '**तवाधारे मूले सह समयया**'[2] इत्यादिश्लोक-व्याख्यानावसरे निपुणतरमुपपादयिष्यामः। श्रीचक्रस्य वियच्चक्रमिति नामान्तरमस्ति वियच्चक्रत्वं तु वियत्पूज्यत्वात्। वियत्पूज्यत्वं द्विविधं, दहराकाशजं बाह्याकाशजं

1. नीपानां कदम्बानाम्।
2. ४१ श्लोकः।

चेति। बाह्याकाशजं नाम बाह्याकाशावकाशे पीठादौ भूर्जपत्रशुद्धपटहेमरजतादिपट्टतले लिखित्वा समाराधनम्। एतदेव कौलपूजेत्याहुर्वृद्धाः। तदुत्तरत्र स्फोर्यते। दहराकाशजं नाम हृदयाकाशावकाशे चक्रस्य पूजनम्। इदमेव समय–पूजेत्याहुः समयिनः। एतदप्युत्तरत्र स्फोर्यते। तत्र नवयोनिष्वधः–स्थितशिवात्मकयोनिचतुष्कस्योपरि ऊर्ध्वस्थितशक्त्यात्मयोनिपञ्चकाधःप्रदेशस्य बैन्दवस्थानस्य नाम सुधासिन्धुरिति।।

"बिन्दुस्थानं सुधासिन्धुः पञ्चयोन्यः सुरद्रुमाः।
तत्रैव नीपश्रेणी च तन्मध्ये मणिमण्डपम्।।
तत्र चिन्तामणिकृतं देव्या मन्दिरमुत्तमम्।
शिवात्मके महामञ्चे महेशानोपबर्हणे।।
अतिरम्यतरे तत्र कशिपुश्च सदाशिवः।
भृतकाश्च चतुष्पादा महेन्द्रश्च पतद्ग्रहः।।
तत्रास्ते परमेशानी महात्रिपुरसुन्दरी।
शिवार्कमण्डलं भित्त्वा द्रावयन्तीन्दुमण्डलम्।।
तदुद्भूतामृतस्यन्दिपरमानन्दनन्दिता ।
कुलयोषित्कुलं त्यक्त्वा परं वर्षणमेत्य सा।।"

इति भैरवयामळे वामकेश्वरमहातन्त्रे बहुरूपाष्टकविद्यायां कथितम्। 'देव्या मन्दिरमुत्तमम्' इत्यस्यार्थः–देवीमन्दिरं त्रयश्चत्वारिंशत्त्रिकोणात्मकं श्रीचक्रमुच्यते। अत उक्तं 'शिवाकारे मञ्चे' इति। त्रिकोणात्मकश्रीचक्रस्य बैन्दवस्थानं प्रत्यङ्गत्वात्, बैन्दवस्थानस्य प्रधानत्वात्, प्रधाने गुणस्यान्तर्भावात् तदन्तर्भाव उक्त इति रहस्यम्। 'भृतकाः' इत्यस्यार्थः–भृतकाः भृत्याः द्रुहिणहरिरुद्रेश्वराः। एतच्च **'गतास्ते मञ्चत्वं द्रुहिण'**[1] इत्यादिश्लोकव्याख्यानावसरे वक्ष्यते। 'शिवार्कमण्डलं भित्त्वा' इत्यस्यार्थः–शिवा नाम शक्तिः कुण्डलिनी अर्कमण्डलं हृत्कमलोपरि स्थितं भित्त्वा भिन्नं कृत्वा अवयुत्य आच्छाद्येत्यर्थः। अर्कमण्डलोपरि स्थितं ब्रह्मद्वारं पिधाय सहस्रकमलान्तस्स्थितमिन्दुमण्डलं दशति द्रावयति। अत एव कुलयोषित् कुण्डलिनीशक्तिः, कुलं कुलमार्गं सुषुम्नामार्गं, त्यक्त्वा तत्रैवेन्दुमण्डले आस्थाय, परं वर्षणं उत्कृष्टवर्षणं, द्विसप्ततिसहस्रनाडीषु प्रवर्षणं, कृत्वेति शेषः। सा कुण्डलिनी पुनः स्वस्थानमेत्य स्वाधिष्ठानं प्राप्य स्वपितीति तात्पर्यम्। शिवादीनां [2]मञ्चत्वोपधानत्वपतद्ग्रहत्वावस्थापन्नत्वं कामरूपत्वाद्देवानां अत्यन्तासन्नसेवार्थं घटते। इममेवार्थं संक्षेपेणोक्तवान् सदाशिवः–

---

1. ९२ श्लोकः।
2. मञ्चत्वोपपादनं पतद्ग्रहत्वाद्देवानाम्।

सुधाब्धौ नन्दनोद्याने रत्नमण्डपमध्यगाम्।
बालार्कमण्डलाभासां चतुर्बाहुं त्रिलोचनाम्।।
पाशाङ्कुशशरांश्चापं धारयन्तीं शिवां[1] श्रियम्।
ध्यात्वा च हृद्गतं[2] चक्रं व्रतस्थ: परमेश्वरीम्।।
पूर्वोक्तध्यानयोगेन चिन्तयन् [3]जपमाचरेत्।। इति।।

अनेन 'क्वणत्काञ्चीदामा' इति 'सुधासिन्धोर्मध्ये' इति च श्लोकद्वयमेकीकृत्य व्याख्यातमित्यवगन्तव्यम्।।

Notes : Blessed are the few—the few : those rare souls who, through worship, internal as well as external, of the Devī, their affinity to the Pañca-daśākṣarī, and the pure life that they lead during their last incarnate existence in this mundane world, are really blessed, for, they have discharged the duties incumbent upon human beings, preparatory to their being merged in the transcendent Existence, Consciousness and Bliss. *Serve Thee*—worship Thee in the *Śrī-cakra.* This stanza refers to the worship of the *Śrī-cakra* as the Viyac-cakra (Ethereal centre), worshipped externally as on the pedestal, with the symbol inscribed on a Bhūrja leaf, a piece of clean linen, gold or silver plate, as is the practice of the Kaulas, and internally in the ethereal space, Dahara, of the heart, as is the practice of the Samayins. The mode of worship indicated in this stanza is of the form of the Devī, as abiding in her mansion, the *Śrī-cakra,* dealing as it does with the special environment in which the Devī has to be meditated upon, herself assuming the special form depicted in the previous stanza, which only amplifies what is here indicated about the Devī. The description given here closely follows the account given in the Bhairava-yāmala, which represents the Devī, as abiding for ever as the Kuṇḍalinī-śakti, piercing the solar region of the Dahara, covering the Brahma-randhra inside the thousand-petalled lotus, liquifying the lunar region, and delighting in the flood of nectar flowing therefrom. The Kuṇḍalinī, abiding in the Kula-patha, the Suṣumnā path, leaves it to reach the *Sahasrāra* and, after filling the entire system of Nāḍī-s with the nectar above referred to, returns to her abode,[4] the

1. श्रये। 2. यन्त्रम्।
3. सञ्चिन्त्य ध्यानमाचरेत्।
4. The abode of the Kuṇḍalinī is fixed by some in the *Mūlādhāra,* and by others in the *Svādhiṣṭhāna.* Yet others hold that, when she is asleep.

Svādhiṣṭhāna, and sleeps therein. Ocean of nectar—stands for the Baindava-sthāna, the quadrilateral seat of the *Bindu,* which is the essential one and brings within its scope the forty-three triangles forming the *Śrī-cakra,* the mansion of the Devī. The five traingles pointing upwards may be said to represent the five rows of Kalpa trees forming a fence around the mansion. Of the form of Śivā—*i.e.,* 'E', multi-triangular, the *Śrī-cakra,* her abode, being made up of forty-three triangles. The couch—The Devī is said to recline on a couch made up of Brahman, Hari, Rudra and Īśvara as the four feet, occupying the South-east, South-west, North-west and North-east corners respectively, Sadā-Śiva as the plank, Para-śiva, the All-witness, transcending the three Guṇas, turned by the Devī's glance into the mattress, not to speak of the other gods serving other purposes, all because of their desire to serve the Goddess, they being capable of assuming any desired form, as they are Kāmarūpas.

This stanza is deftly enough made by Kameśvara-sūri to bear on 'the Ānandalaharī', the first part of this work, as follows : *Sura-viṭapi-vāṭī,* etc.—full of pilgrim resorts, such as Śrī-śaila and other abodes of the several gods reputed to bestow the heart's desires of pilgrims, very much like the Kalpa trees. *Maṇi-dvīpa* is to be understood as, 'wherein are various places specially fitted for meditation'; *Cintā-maṇi-gṛhā,* as: 'wherein there are temples studded with Cintā-maṇi gems'; *Sudhāsindhoḥ,* as meaning, 'from the Hīmālaya, the abode of white glaciers, to the southern ocean'; *Śivākāre mañce,* as: 'Mount Kailāsa, which is as white as crystal and thus resembles Śiva in aspect'; *Parama-śiva-paryaṅka-nilayām,* as: 'blessed by being placed on the lap of the divine couple, Pārvatī and Parama-śiva'; '*Cid-ānanda-laharīm,* as: "the work of the name of 'Ānandalaharī', expounding the purely Cit-aspect of the Śakti'. The story is that Śaṅkara-bhagavatpāda, the author of this work, after finishing it, took it all the way to Kailāsa, there to lay it at the feet of the divine couple and receive their approbation, but on reaching Kailāsa, to his wonder saw the couple being praised with the stanzas of the self-same Ānanda-laharī and in consequence drenched in the Bliss of Supreme Consciousness.

This stanza is capable of yet another interpretation, which is

She abides in the *Mūlādhāra,* and when awake, resorts to the *Svādhiṣṭhāna,* which literally means her 'own abode'.

this : "Blessed are the few that adore Thee, the Cid-ānandalaharī, who ever abidest in the *Anāhata* of the heart-lotus, situated midway between Sudhā, the *Mūlādhāra* (or the feet), on the one side, and the Moon in the crest ever filling the system of Nāḍīs with nectar, on the other, of the human body, adorable because it embraces in its form all the gods and contains the substitutes for the several reputed places of pilgrimage, uch as Śrī-śaila, in the crest, *etc.*, (or the heart-lotus, the seat of Cintā, thought, dependent on the Ātman and therefore lustrous), well-protected by the ten vital airs, *Prāṇa* and others (or the deitieis presiding over the ten organs of sense), studded with the *Mūlādhāra* and other centres of Energy, radiant like so many isles of gems and encasing within itself the *Jīva*, which is as expansive as a tree from top of bottom."

The expression *Parama-śiva-paryaṅka-nilayām'* suggests, by implication, the union of Parama-śiva, the *Bindu* with the Parā-śakti, the *Nāda*, in the *Oṁkāra*, the couch made up of 'A', 'U', 'M' and the Ardhamātrā, representing Brahman, Hari, Rudra and Īśvara. The name of the Devī, 'Pañca-brahmāsanasthitā,' as given in the Lalitāsahasranāma-stotra, is further illustrated by this stanza.

The Bīja of Kāmeśvarī, 'Klīṃ', and that of Mahā-preta, 'Hsauḥ' may be derived from this stanza.

महीं मूलाधारे कमपि मणिपूरे हुतवहं
स्थितं स्वाधिष्ठाने हृदि मरुतमाकाशमुपरि।
मनोऽपि भ्रूमध्ये सकलमपि भित्त्वा कुलपथं[1]
सहस्रारे पद्मे सह रहसि पत्या विहरसे[2]।।९।।

Mahīṃ mūlādhāre kam api maṇi-pūre huta-vahaṃ
sthitaṃ svādhiṣṭhāne hṛdi marutam ākāśam upari/
Mano'pi bhrū-madhye sakalam api bhittvā kula-pathaṃ
sahasrāre padme saha rahasi patyā viharase.//

Translation : Thou art diverting Thyself, in secrecy with Thy Lord, in the thousand-petalled lotus, having pierced through the Earth situated in the *Mūlādhāra,* the Water in the *Maṇi-pūra,* the Fire abiding in the *Svādhiṣṭhāna,* the Air in the Heart *(An-āhata),* the Ether above it is *the Viśuddhi* and Manas

1. जित्वा कुलपथं, भित्वा ऽऽ कुलपथं।
2. विहरसि।

(mind) between the eyebrows (*the Ājñā)* and thus broken through the entire *Kula*-path (six *cakras* and *suṣumnā).*

महीं पृथिवीतत्त्वं, **मूलाधारे** मूले गुदस्थाने सर्वाधारभूतं चक्रं मूलाधारभूतमिति, तस्मिन् मूलाधारे।

सर्वाधारा मही यस्मात् मूलाधारतया स्थिता।
तदभावे तु देहस्य पातः स्यादुद्गमोऽपि वा।।

इति रुद्ररहस्ये। पृथिवीतत्त्वात्मकस्य मूलाधारस्याभावे देह ऊर्ध्वं वा गच्छेत्, अधो वा पतेदित्यर्थः। **कं** उदकतत्त्वम्। **अपि**शब्दः स्वाधिष्ठोनोक्तवह्निं समुच्चिनोति। **मणिपूरे** मणिपूरचक्रे, यत्र स्थिता भगवती मणिभिः तत्प्रदेशं पूरयति, स देशो मणिपूरः। समयिनां आन्तरपूजावसरे तृतीयकमले नानाविधमणिगणखचितभूषणार्पणं देव्याः कर्तव्यमिति रहस्यम्। **हुतवहं** अग्नितत्त्वम्, **स्थितं** प्रतिष्ठितं, **स्वाधिष्ठाने** स्वाधिष्ठाननामके चक्रे, कुण्डलिन्याः भगवत्याः [1]स्वयमधिष्ठाय ग्रन्थिं कृत्वा अवस्थानं स्वाधिष्ठानम्। यथोक्तं योगदीपिकायाम्–

रुद्रग्रन्थिरयं शक्तेः स्वाधिष्ठानाग्रसीमनि।। इति।।

यद्यपि आधारचक्रस्योपरि स्वाधिष्ठानं वर्णनीयं, तथापि आकाशादितत्त्वोत्पत्तिक्रममवलम्ब्य व्युत्क्रमेण मणिपूरचक्रवर्णनं कृतमित्यनुसन्धेयम्। एतच्च '**तवाज्ञाचक्रस्थम्**'[2] इत्यादिश्लोकषट्कव्याख्यानावसरे सम्यगुपवर्णितम्। **हृदि** हृदयाकाशे अनाहतनामनि चक्रे, अनाहतनादस्थानत्वात् अनाहतनामास्य। **मरुतं** मरुतत्त्वम्, **आकाशं** आकाशतत्त्वम्, **उपरि** पूर्वोक्तानामुपरि विशुद्धिचक्रे, शुद्धस्फटिकसङ्काशत्वात् विशुद्धिनामास्य। **मनः** मनस्तत्त्वम्, **अपि**शब्दः उक्तसमुच्चयार्थः, **भ्रूमध्ये** भ्रुवोरन्तराले आज्ञाचक्रे, अत्र आङ् ईषदर्थः, ज्ञा ज्ञानम्, ईषत् ज्ञानं यत्र जायते साधकानां भगवतीविषयम्। ब्रह्मग्रन्थिभेदनातिव्यग्रतया भगवत्या आज्ञाचक्रे क्षणमात्रावस्थानात् साधकानां तटिल्लेखारूपेण अवभासनात् आज्ञाचक्रनामास्य। स्थितमिति लिङ्गव्यत्ययेन सर्वत्रानुषज्यते। **सकलं** सर्वम्, **अपिः** समुच्चये, **भित्त्वा** (हित्वा) **कुलपथं** सुषुम्णामार्गम्, **सहस्रारे** सहस्रदले, **पद्मे** कमले, **सह** मिलित्वा, **रहसि** एकान्ते, **पत्या** सदाशिवेन, **विहरसे** क्रीडसे।।

अत्रेत्थं पदयोजना–हे भगवति! मूलाधारे महीं, कं मणिपूरे हुतवहमपि, स्वाधिष्ठाने हुतवहमेव, हृदि मरुतं, आकाशमुपरि, मनोऽपि भ्रूमध्ये आकाशमपि, स्थितमिति

---

1. स्वेच्छयाधिष्ठाय।
2. ३६ श्लोक।

लिङ्गव्यत्ययेन सर्वत्रानुषज्यते। सकलं कुलपथमपि भित्त्वा सहस्रारे पद्मे रहसि पत्या सह विहरसे।।

अत्रेदमनुसन्धेयम्–मूलाधारस्वाधिष्ठानमणिपूरानाहतविशुद्ध्याज्ञात्मकानि षट् चक्राणि। एतानि पृथिव्यग्निजलपवनाकाशमनस्तत्त्वात्मकानि। तानि तत्त्वानि तेषु चक्रेषु तन्मात्रतयाऽवस्थितानि। तन्मात्रास्तु गन्धरूपरसस्पर्शशब्दात्मकाः। आज्ञाचक्रस्थितेन मनस्तत्त्वेन एकादशेन्द्रियगणः संगृहीतः। एवमेकविंशतितत्त्वानि प्रतिपादितानि। पत्या सह रहसि सहस्रपत्रे विहरसे इत्यनेन तत्त्वचतुष्टयं सूचितम्। तच्च मायाशुद्धविद्यामहेश्वर-सदाशिवात्मकं तत्त्वचतुष्टयम्। एवं मिलित्वा पञ्चविंशतितत्त्वानि [1]मायापर्यन्तानि मायया युक्तत्वात् प्राकृतानि। माया महेश्वरेण संयुक्ता सती तस्य जीवभावमापादयति। स जीवः प्राकृत एव। शुद्धविद्या तु सदाशिवेन युक्ता सती सादाख्या कलेति व्यवह्रियते। अतो भगवती चतुर्विंशतितत्त्वा[2]न्यतिक्रान्ता सदाशिवेन पञ्चविंशेन सार्धं विहरमाणा षड्विंशतत्त्वात्मतामापन्ना परमात्मेति गीयते। एतदुक्तं भवति–सादाख्या कला पञ्चविंशेन सदाशिवेन मिलिता षड्विंशा भवति, मेलनस्य तत्त्वान्तरत्वात्। न चोभयोर्मेलन-मुभयात्मकम्। तस्य तादात्म्यरूपत्वात् तत्त्वान्तरमेवेति रहस्यम्। यत्तु श्रुतिवाक्यं 'पञ्चविंश आत्मा भवति'[3] इति तत्तु सदाशिवतत्त्वप्रतिपादनपरम्, न मेलनपरमिति ध्येयम्।।

ननु बैन्दवस्थानं श्रीचक्रस्य मध्यस्थितं, शिवचक्राणां चतुर्णामुपरि शक्तिचक्राणां पञ्चानामधस्तादवस्थितत्वात्, सहस्रारपद्मस्य तु शिरस्थितत्वात् सर्वेषामुपरि वर्तमानत्वात् तस्य बैन्दवस्थानत्वं नोपपद्यत इति चेत्–

निशम्यतां भागवतमतरहस्यम्–

चतुर्भिः शिवचक्रैश्च शक्तिचक्रैश्च पञ्चभिः।
शिवशक्तिमयं ज्ञेयं श्रीचक्रं शिवयोर्वपुः।।

इत्यादौ शक्तिचक्राणि त्रिकोणाष्टकोणदशारद्वितयचतुर्दशकोणात्मकानि पञ्च चक्राणि। शिवचक्राणि तु अष्टदलषोडशदलमेखलात्रितयभूपुरत्रयात्मकानीति। अतः शक्तिचक्राणां बाह्यतः शिवचक्राणि। शिवस्य शक्तिबाह्यत्वायोगात् तानि शिवचक्राणि बिन्दुरूपेणाकृष्य शक्तिचक्रान्तरे स्थापितानि। अत एव बिन्दुः शिवचक्रचतुष्टयात्मकः शक्तिचक्रेषु पञ्चसु व्यश्नुवानः समाप्त इति शिवशक्त्योरैक्यमिति केचित्।।

अन्ये तु–बिन्दुत्रिकोणयोरैक्यं, अष्टकोणाष्टदलाम्बुजयोः, दशारयुग्मषोडश-

---

1. प्रतिपादितानि, तानीत्यधिकम्।
2. न्यतिक्रान्ता शिवेन।
3. तै०ब्रा० १-२-६।

दलाम्बुजयो:, चतुर्दशारभूपुरयोरैक्यम्, अनेन प्रकारेण शिवशक्त्योरैक्यमित्याहु:। अत्र बिन्दुशब्देन शिवचक्रचतुष्टयप्रतिनिधिभूतो वर्तुलाकारो लक्ष्यते, न तु चतुष्कोणमध्यवर्ती बिन्दु:। स तु सहस्रकमलान्तर्गत: आधारस्वाधिष्ठानदशदलप्रकृतिभूत: शिवशक्तिमेलनाविष्टतनु: सादाख्यं षड्विंशं तत्त्वम्। तेन सह नादबिन्दुकलानामैक्यं नास्ति, तस्य नादबिन्दुकलातीतत्वात्। एतच्च पुरस्तात्प्रपञ्चयिष्यते। अत एव सहस्रमलान्तर्गतचन्द्रमण्डलमध्यवर्ती सुधासिन्धुरेव भगवत्या विहरणस्थानमिति 'सहस्रारे पद्मे सह रहसि पत्या विहरसे' इति 'सुधासिन्धोर्मध्ये' इति च श्लोकद्वयस्यैक एवार्थ इति रहस्यम्। इममेवार्थं भैरवयामले चन्द्रज्ञानविद्यायां शिव आह पार्वतीम्–

चतुर्भि: शिवचक्रैश्च शक्तिचक्रैश्च पञ्चभि:।
नवचक्रैश्च संसिद्धं श्रीचक्रं शिवयोर्वपु:।।
त्रिकोणमष्टकोणं च दशकोणद्वयं तथा।
चतुर्दशारं चैतानि शक्तिचक्राणि पञ्च च।।
बिन्दुश्चाष्टदलं पद्मं पद्मं षोडशपत्रकम्।
चतुरश्रं च चत्वारि शिवचक्राण्यनुक्रमात्।।
त्रिकोणे बैन्दवं श्लिष्टं अष्टारेऽष्टदलाम्बुजम्।
दशारयो: षोडशारं भूगृहं भुवनाश्रके।।
शैवानामपि शक्तानां चक्राणां च परस्परम्।
अविनाभावसम्बन्धं को जानाति स चक्रवित्।।
त्रिकोणमष्टकोणं च दशकोणद्वयं तथा।
मनुकोणं चतुष्कोणं कोणचक्राणि षट् क्रमात्।।
मूलाधारं तथा स्वाधिष्ठानं च मणिपूरकम्।
अनाहतं विशुद्ध्याख्यमाज्ञाचक्रं विदुर्बुधा:।।
तवाधारस्वरूपाणि कोणचक्राणि पार्वति।
त्रिकोणरूपिणी शक्ति: बिन्दुरूपशिव: स्मृत:।।
अविनाभावसम्बन्ध: तस्माद्बिन्दुत्रिकोणयो:।। इति।।

इत: पूर्वम्–

अधोमुखं चतुष्कोणं शिवचक्रात्मकं विदु:।।

इत्यनुसारेण 'अधोमुखानि चत्वारि त्रिकोणानि शिवात्मकानि' इत्युक्ति: 'शिवचक्राणि बाह्यानि तद्रूपेणावस्थितानि' इत्येवंपरेति ध्येयम्।।

यद्वा–कौलमतानुसारेण अधोमुखानि चत्वारि त्रिकोणानि शिवात्मकानि ऊर्ध्वमुखानि

पञ्च त्रिकोणानि शक्त्यात्मकानि। कौलमते संहारक्रमेण लेखने नवत्रिकोणात्मकं श्रीचक्रम्। एतत्सर्वं '**चतुर्भिः श्रीकण्ठैः**'[1] इत्यादिश्लोकव्याख्यानावसरे वक्तव्यमपि 'सहस्रारे पद्मे सह रहसि पत्या विहरसे' इत्यत्रावश्यं वक्तव्यत्वात् उभयोपयोगितया अत्रैव किञ्चित्कथितम् विस्तरस्तु तत्रैवावधार्यः।। ९।।

Notes : This stanza contains in a nutshell the quintessence of the sublimest truth of the Vedānta and the Yoga systems in harmonious combination, in relation to the worship of the Devī, as the Kuṇḍalinī-Śakti of the Piṇḍāṇḍa, (Microcosm) and as the Triupurasundarī of the Brahmāṇḍa, (Mcrocosm). For a proper appreciation of the same, a short account of the Eternal Verities, according to the conception of the ancient Ṛṣis of India and their bearing on the Cosmogony of the Microcosm and the Macrocosm, will be found useful.

An Eternal Verity may be defined as that which gives scope for functioning to all order of creation, till their final dissolution. Some Tantras classify the Eternal Verities into three groups, the Ātma-tattvas, the Vidyātattvas and the Śiva-tattvas. Those comprised under the first group are characterized by *Jaḍatva*, non-sentience; those of the second group partake of *Jaḍatva* and Prakāśakatva, both non-sentience and sentience; and those of the third group are characterized by Prakāśakatva, sentience pure and simple, with absolute Consciousness standing above them all. According to the Kalpa-sūtras, twenty-four fall under the first group, seven under the second, and five under the third, and may be arranged as shown hereunder, with their characteristic properties : (1) *Pṛthivī*—Earth, possessed of solidity; (2) *Ap*—Water, possessed of fluidity; (3) *Tejas*—Fire, possessed of heat; (4) *Vāyu*—Air, of the character of perpetual motion; (5) *Ākāśa*—Ether, of the character of space; (6) *Gandha-tan-mātra*—Smell, in the form of subtle Earth; (7) *Rasa-tan-mātra*—Taste, in the form of subtle Water; (8) *Rūpa-tan-mātra*—Form, in the form of subtle Fire; (9) *Sparsa-tan-mātra*—Touch, in the form of subtle Air; (10) *Śabda-tanmātra*—Sound, in the form of subtle Ether; (11) *Śrotra*—the auditory sense that perceives sound; (12) *Tvac*—the tactile sense that perceives touch; (13) *Cakṣus*—the optic sense that perceives form; (14) *Jihvā*—the gustatory sense that perceives taste; (15) *Ghrāṇa*—the olfactory

1. ११ श्लोकः।

sense that perceives smell; (16) *Vāc*—speech, the motor organ of articulate expression; (17) *Pāṇi*—the hand, the motor organ of grasping and leaving; (18) *Pāda*—the foot, the motor organ of locomotion; (19) *Pāyu*—the motor organ of evacuation; (20) *Upastha*—the motor organ of generation and carnal pleasure; (21) *Manas*—The Mind, the inner sense that is attained, when Rajas, the mobility of misery, preponderates over Sattva and Tamas, the rhythm of happiness and the inertia of delusion, and which is the root of all volition; (22) *Buddhi*—the Intellect, the inner sense which is attained, when rhythm preponderates over mobility and inertia, and as such is at the root of all conviction (23) *Ahaṁkāra*—Egoism, the inner sense which is attained, when inertia preponderates over rhythm and mobility, and which is the root of all fancy, converging towards the self; (24) *Prakṛti*, otherwise known as the *Citta*—which is attained by the equipoised state of rhythm, mobility and inertia; (25) *Puruṣa* or the *Jīva* (of the Microcosm)—which, though full in itself, commands only to a limited extent the five powers detailed below; (26) *Kalā*—the Kriyā-śakti, the power to do all things, but to a limited extent, inhering in the *Jīva;* (27) *Avidyā,* also called *Vidyā*—the *Jñāna-śakti,* in a veiled form and thus limited in its operation, inherent in the *Jīva;* (28) *Rāga*—the *Icchā-śakti,* perpetual satisfaction, which operates only partially and is therefore limited in extent, inherent in the *Jīva;* (29) *Cit-śakti*—perpetuity inherent in the *Jīva,* when limited by the operation of the six changes denoted by 'exists', 'takes birth', 'grows', 'ripens', 'wanes', and 'perishes'; (30) *Niyati*—that which causes *Avidyā* to weil the Ānanda-śakti, absolute independence, inherent in the *Jīva;* (31) *Māyā*—the condition operating upon the Īśvara, causing it to look upon the phenomenal world as 'this', *i.e.*, an entity separate from itself (32) *Śuddha-vidyā*—the condition operating upon the Sadā-śiva, causing it to identity itself with the phenomenal world, with the impression, 'I am this'; (33) *Maheśvara*—that which is operated upon by the Māyā; (34) *Sadā-śiva*—that which is operated upon by the Śuddha-vidyā; (35) *Śakti*—the desire which is but the impression of the world to be created; (36) *Śiva*—the absolute non-differentiated existence, when conditioned by the Śakti.

Fifteen more are added to the number of Eternal Verities by some, by a process of further elaboration, thus making fifty-one in all, answering to the fifty-one letters of the Saṃskṛt Alphabet. The other fifteen are the seven Dhātus, humours, (1) *Tvac*—the external sheath of organs; (2) *Asṛj*—blood; (3) *Māṁsa*—flesh; (4) *Medas*—Fat; (5) *Asthi*—bone; (6) *Majjā*—marrow and (7) *Śukra*—semen, the five vital airs, (8) *Prāṇa,* (9) *Apāna,* (10) *Vyāna,* (11) *Udāna,* (12) *Samāna;* and the three Guṇas, (13) Rhythm, (14) Mobility and (15) Inertia. The five Elements, the five Tanmātras, the five organs of perception, the five organs of motor action, the Mind, the Māyā, the Śuddha-vidyā, the Maheśvara and Sadā-śiva are the twenty-five Eternal Verities from the Vedic standpoint, while the others are capable of being included in the twenty-five.

In this stanza, the Devī of the Macrocosm, in the form of her exact prototype, the Kuṇḍalinī of the Microcosm, is represented as having broken through the entire *Kula*-path containing the six *Cakras,* of psychic energy, indicative of the twenty-one Tattvas, to reach her Lord in the *Sahasrāra,* the habitat of the four remaining sentient Tattvas, there to divert herself in secrecy with her Lord. Even as Parama-śiva, in the absence of his conjunction with the Tripurasundarī, is powerless, so also the *Jīva,* without the operation of the Kuṇḍalinī, will be very much the same as a corpse. The vital force, which is inherent in every limb, muscle, nerve-centre and other physiological organs and which causes the entire frame to function, is but one aspect of the Kuṇḍalinī. It is the self-same vital force that is the root-cause of the functioning of the entire phenomenal world and could be comprehended only by those rare mortals who have gained mastery over it. It is upon this fundamental fact that the system of Yoga is based, as the *Prāṇāyāma,* or the control of this vital force, forms the bedrock of that system. If only the secret of control of this vital force and the human mind (psychic force), which is only a subtle variety of the vital force, should be mastered by any person, he may be said to have conquered the phenomenal world. No wonder the Yogin takes his stand uopn the *Prāṇāyāma* and *Mano-laya* for the successful accomplishment of the state of Samādhi, his goal. It is with that end in view that the Yogin concentrates his mind, controls the vital force and projects them towards the *Mūlādhāra,* the first psychic centre of energy, which results in the rousing of the Kuṇḍalinī, dormant with its form of three-and-a-half spirals coiled therein. Those that are proficient in the Yoga-śāstra hold that this machine of the human frame, which is controlled by the Kuṇḍalinī, contains Seventy-two Thousand Nāḍīs, the main ones among them, *e.g.*, the Suṣumnā, the Iḍā, the Piṅgalā, *etc.,* having distinct functions connected with the respiratory system allotted to them, and the other important Nāḍīs controlling the sensory and motor organs. The psychic energy requisite to control the various organs is said to abide in the six *Cakras* of the Suṣumnā-path, provided with the three stages, known as the Rudra, Viṣṇu, and Brahmagranthis (knots), which are respectively the regions of Fire, the Sun and the Moon, each of them situated at the end of a pair of these *Cakras*, in the order given above. In the case of ordinary mortals, their vital energy is wasted through the Iḍā and Piṅgalā, but in the case of the initiated, it is regulated in such a way that the Prāṇa, coursing through the Iḍā and Piṅgalā, and also the Apāna, are made to conserve the purpose of rousing the Kuṇḍalinī and sending her up to the *Brahma-randhra.*

All impulses, psychic and organic, may be classified as volitional cognitional and actional, corresponding to the Icchā, Jñāna, and Kriyā-śaktis of the Devī. These, when pertaining to the body, are attributable to the Kuṇḍalinī, while the corresponding cosmic impulses are attributable to the Tripurasundarī.

Thou—in the form of the Tri-pura-sundarī of the Macrocosm and the kuṇḍalinī of the Microcosm. Thy Lord—the Śiva of the Macrocosm and the *Jīva* of the Microcosm, bereft of Māyā, illusion. The thousand pettaled lotus—which is no other than the upper *Śrī-cakra,* the *Bindu* of which represents the Śiva and the *Jīva* bereft of Māyā, as the case may be. This is the final resort, the *Nirvāṇa* of the accomplished seeker, lying beyond the Kula-path, the *Suṣumnā-mārga,* which contains the six *Cakras* mentioned in the stanza, in the ascending order of subtlety, with the three Granthis in their appropriate places. the *Sahasrāra* is considered to be the inner *Śrī-cakra* to be meditated upon with all the fifty-one letters of the Saṁskṛt Alphabet. The view is taken by some that the *Bindu* has its position in the *Bindu* of the *Cakra* and the other fifty letters are to be arranged consecutively over the thousand petals, twenty times. Śuddha-vidyā in coalescence with Sadā-śiva is known as the *Sādākhyā* or the Paramātman, which may be characterized as the twenty-sixth Tattva, on the attainment of which is experienced Nirvāṇa or *Jīvanmukti.* It is this aspect that is referred to in this stanza as the diversion of the Devī in secrecy with her Lord. Having pierced through—*i.e.,* having got beyond, after overcoming and absorbing in her own form. The ascent and the descent of the

Kuṇḍalinī constituting the Kuṇḍalinī-yoga are said to form an Antar-yāga. The Earth situated in the *Mūlādhāra*—but for the *Mūlādhāra*, which partakes of the character of the Earth-element through its subtle form of Gandha-tanmātra, the body will become unstable with its equilibrium disturbed. This *Cakra* is no other than the *Trikoṇa* of the *Śrī-cakra.* Piercing through this element would mean conquering it. The Yogin who does so is said to attain the power of penetration through massive stone walls, etc. *Water in the Maṇipūra—Maṇi-pūra,* the interior of which the Devī is said to fill with gems; hence the practice among the Samayins of the offering of jewels studded with various kinds of gems, while meditating on her in this seat. Although the *Maṇipura* is the third in the order of the *Çakras,* it has been given the second place in the stanza to suit the order of the elements. This *Cakra* represents water in its *Rasatanmātra* form. Conquest of this by the Yogin is said to confer on him the next higher power of mastery, such as floating, walking, *etc.,* over water. The inner *Daśāra* of the *Śrī-ckara* is indicated by this. *The Fire in the Svādhiṣṭhāna*—where the Devī is said to take her stand in the form of Kuṇḍalinī, of her own accord, making the knot of Rudra-granthi thereon. *The fire,* in the form of the Rūpa-tanmātra. The conquest of this by the Yogin is credited with the bestowal of the power of fire-walking, etc. The *Aṣṭa-koṇa* of the *Śrī-cakra* is indicated by this. *The Air in the heart*—the Air, in the form of Sparśa-tanmātra. The heart signifies the *Anāhata-cakara* of the heart-lotus. The word *'Anāhata'* means the Nāda, sound, produced without impact in the recess of the heart; hence the name of the *Cakara.* The outer *Daśāra* of the *Śrī-cakra* is indicated by this. By the conquest of Air, the Yogin is said to attain the fleetness of wind, buoyancy, etc. *The Ether*—in the form of Śabda-tanmātra. *Above—i.e.,* 'above the heart', by which is meant the *Cakra* which is clear as crystal, *viz.,* the *Viśuddhi.* The *Catur-daśāra* of the *Śrī-cakra* is indicated by this. By the conquest of this the Yogin attains the power of traversing the ethereal regions. It may be noted here that Pūrṇānandasvāmin, the author of the Ṣaṭ-cakranirūpaṇa and other Tāntrikas are of the view that the elements, Earth, Water, Fire, Air and Ether have, as their corresponding Cakra-s, the *Mūlādhāra,* the *Svādhiṣṭhāna,* the *Maṇipūra,* the *Anāhata* and the *Viśuddhi,* which as will be seen from this stanza, is at variance with the view of Śaṅkara-bhagavatpāda, the author of this work, who has, in this respect, the support of the

Vāmakeśvara-tantra in his favour, as explained by Bhāskararāya in his *Setu-bandha.*[1] Further, the letters indicated by the Māheśvara-sūtras—"Ha Ya Va Raṭ" and "Laṇ", which enumerate the Bījas of the five elements in the order in which they were revealed by Maheśvara's Ḍamaru, when place in juxtaposition with the names of the five *Cakras,* in their natural order, from the upper to the nether, the names of the five elements corresponding to the respective Bījas, as also the names of the parts of the *Śrī-cakra* which they indicate, in the Saṁhāra-krama bear out, beyond doubt, the correctness of the author's view.[2] *Manas between the eyebrows*—Manas, which embraces within itself the five senses of perception and the five senses of motor action, *i.e.,* in all, eleven *tattvas.* 'Between the eyebrows' refers to the *Ājñā-cakra,* so called because it is at this stage that a speck of knowledge about the Devī dawns. As she is bent on breaking through the *Brahma-granthi* on the way to the *Sahasrāra,* she remains there only for a trice manifesting herself in the form of a streak of lightning. The *Catuṣ-koṇa, i.e.,* the *Bhū-gṛha* of the *Śrī-cakra,* is indicated by this. By conquering the mind, the Yogin is said to attain mystic powers, such as clairvoyance, clairaudience, telepathy, etc. The mystic-powers ascribed above, as resulting from the mastery of these *Cakras,* at the various stages, are really so many pitfalls to be avoided by the practitioner, as they are likely to lead him astray from his final goal of *Nirvāṇa.*

These six *Cakras* are but temporary stages or planes wherein the Kuṇḍalinī rests awhile, avowedly for mastering them, while the *Sahasrāra* is her permanent abode, whence the parctitioner should nto lose sight of his final goal, *Nirvāṇa,* beguiled by the temptations offered by the psychic powers attainable at the lower centres, but should lead the Kuṇḍalinī on to the *Sahasrāra,* there to

1. शाक्ते मूलाधारस्थचतुर्दले, शक्तिरूपायाः कुण्डलिन्याः ; स्थानत्वात्। वह्नौ स्वाधिष्ठानस्थषड्दले, तत्र वह्नेर्विद्यमानत्वात्। तदुक्तमाचार्यभगवत्पादैः–महीं मूलाधारे कमपि मणिपूरे हुतवहं स्थितं स्वाधिष्ठाने हृदि मरुतमाकाशमुपरीति।"

2.

Bīja	*Bhūta*	*Cakra*	*Part of Śrī-cakra*	*Presiding deity*
Haṃ	Ether	Viśuddhi	Catur-daśāra	Jīva
Yaṃ	Air	An-āhata	Bahir-daśāra	Rudra
Vaṃ	Water	Maṇi-pūra	Antar-daśāra	Viṣṇu
Raṃ	Fire	Svādhiṣṭhāna	Aṣṭa-koṇa	Brahmā
Laṃ	Earth	Mūlādhāra	Tri-koṇa	Gaṇeśa

effect her union with her Lord. Up to the moment of such blending the practitioner retains his individual consciousness and thereafter enters on the blissful state of *Nirvāṇa* as long as the Kuṇḍalinī rests in the *Sahasrāra* prior to her descent therefrom. The duration of her stay there depends on the strength of practice and the previous experience of the practitioner. Broken through the entire path of kula—and thus having transcended the twenty-one Tattvas from Pṛthivī to Manas, and the six *Cakras*, which, when taken together, would from the lower *Śrī-cakra.*

सुधाधाराऽऽसारैश्चरणयुगलान्तर्विगलितैः
प्रपञ्चं सिञ्चन्ती पुनरपि रसाम्नायमहसः[1] ।
अवाप्य स्वां भूमिं भुजगनिभमध्युष्टवलयं[2]
स्वमात्मानं कृत्वा स्वपिषि कुलकुण्डे कुहरिणि[3] ।। १० ।।

Sudhā-dhārā-sārais caraṇa-yugalāntar vigalitaiḥ
prapañcaṃ siñcantī punar api rasāmnāyamahasaḥ/
Avāpya svāṃ bhūmiṃ bhuja-ga-nibbham adhyuṣṭavalayaṃ
svam ātmānam kṛtvā svapiṣi kula-kuṇḍe kuhariṇi//

Translation : Having in-filled the pathway of the *Nāḍīs* with the streaming shower of nectar flowing from Thy pair of feet, having resumed Thine own position from out of the resplendent Lunar regions, and Thyself assuming the form of a serpent of three-and-a half coils, sleepest Thou in the hollow of the Kula-kuṇḍa, *i.e.*, the lotus-root like Mulādhāra.

सुधाया अमृतस्य **धाराणामासारैः** सम्पातैः। अत्रासारशब्द एव धारासम्पातवचन इति धाराशब्दसाहचर्यात् आसारशब्दः सम्पातमात्रवचन इति न पौनरुक्त्यम्। यद्वा–**सुधाया आधारभूता आसारा** धारासम्पाताः, तैः **चरणयुगलान्तर्विगलितैः** चरणयुगलस्य पादारविन्दद्वितयस्य अन्तर्विगलितैः मध्यप्रदेशात् स्रवद्भिः, **प्रपञ्चं** द्विसप्ततिसहस्रसङ्ख्याकनाडीमार्गं, **सिञ्चन्ती** सेक्त्री, **पुनरपि** सेचनानन्तरमपि, **रसाम्नायमहसः** चन्द्रसकाशात्, रसाम्नायमहश्शब्दो यामलेषु कलानिधौ प्रसिद्धः, रसस्य सुधाया आम्नायो गुणानामाधिक्यमिति यावत्, तदात्मकं महः कान्तिर्यस्य सः रसाम्नायमहा इति व्युत्पत्तेः। **अवाप्य** प्राप्य, **स्वां** स्वकीयां, **भूमिं** आधारचक्रं, **भुजगनिभं** सर्पसदृशं, **अध्युष्टवलयं** अधिष्ठितकुण्डलनाविशेषं, स्वं निजं **आत्मानं**

1. ०महसा। 2. अध्यष्टवलयं।
3. कुहरिणी।

कृत्वा धृत्वा स्वरूपमवलम्ब्य उषित्वा, **स्वपिषि** निद्रासि–**कुलकुण्डे** कुः पृथिवीतत्त्वं लीयते यत्र तत्कुलं आधारचक्रम्। लक्षणया सुषुम्णामार्गः कुलमित्युच्यते। अत एव कौलाः कुलपूजकाः आधारसेवका इति कौलत्वं तेषामिति रहस्यम्। एतदुत्तरत्र प्रस्फोर्यते। कुलमार्गस्य सुषम्णाया मूले यत्कुण्डं कमलकन्दाकारं आधारकन्दं तस्मिन् कुहरिणि, कमलकन्दमध्यस्थितछिद्रतुल्यं छिद्रं यस्य कुण्डस्य तत्तथोक्तम्। आधारकन्दमध्यस्थितसुषिरमध्ये बिसतन्तुनिभा तत्र कुण्डलिनी शक्तिः वर्तत इति तात्पर्यम्।।

अत्रेत्थं पदयोजना–हे भगवति! चरणयुगलान्तर्विगलितैः सुधाधासारैः प्रपञ्चं सिञ्चन्ती रसाम्नायमहसः सकाशात् स्वां भूमिं पुनरप्यवाप्य भुजगनिभमध्युष्टवलयं स्वमात्मानं कृत्वा कुहरिणि कुलकुण्डे स्वपिषि।।

अत्रेदमनुसन्धेयम्–शिरस्स्थितं चन्द्रमण्डलं सर्वयोगशास्त्रसिद्धम्। तत्तु समयिनां मते श्रीचक्रमेव। चन्द्रमण्डलस्य षोडशकलात्मकत्वात्, श्रीविद्यायाः प्रतिपदादिषोडशदिनेषु कलावृद्धिक्षययोः वक्ष्यमाणत्वात्, चन्द्रमण्डलमेतदेव। बाह्यस्थितमपि चन्द्रमण्डलं श्रीचक्रमेवेति सुभगोदयव्याख्याने निदर्शितम्। तत्तु महारहस्यम् अतश्च शिरस्थितसहस्रदलकमलान्तर्गतश्रीचक्रात्मकशशिबिम्बमध्यस्थितया भगवत्याश्चरणकमलनिर्णेजनजलैः सुधामयैः साधकस्य सकलशरीरं संप्लाव्य पुनः भुजङ्गरूपेण आधारकुण्डं प्रविश्य सुषुम्णामवष्टभ्य सा भगवती स्वपितीति। यथोक्तं वामकेश्वरमहातन्त्रे–

> भुजङ्गाकाररूपेण मूलाधारं समाश्रिता।
> शक्तिः कुण्डलिनी नाम बिसतन्तुनिभाऽऽशुभा।।

आशुभा क्षणप्रभा विद्युन्निभेत्यर्थः।

> मूलकन्दं फणाग्रेण दृष्ट्वा कमलकन्दवत्।
> मुखेन पुच्छं संगृह्य ब्रह्मरन्ध्रं समाश्रिता।।
> पद्मासनगतः स्वस्थो गुदमाकुञ्च्य साधकः।
> वायुमूर्ध्वगतिं कुर्वन् कुम्भकाविष्टमानसः।।
> वाय्वाघातवशादग्निः स्वाधिष्ठानगतो ज्वलन्।
> ज्वलनाघातपवनाघातैरुन्निद्रितोऽहिराट् ।।
> रुद्रग्रन्थिं ततो भित्त्वा विष्णुग्रन्थिं भिनत्त्यतः।
> ब्रह्मग्रन्थिं च भित्त्वैव कमलानि भिनत्ति षट्।।
> सहस्रकमले शक्तिः शिवेन सह मोदते।
> सा चावस्था परा ज्ञेया सैव निर्वृतिकारणम्।। इति।।

श्रुतिरपि भगवत्याः चरणाम्बुजसुधाधारासारैः प्रपञ्चसेचनं प्रतिपादयति। तथा हि–

लोकस्य द्वारमर्चिमत्पवित्रम्।
ज्योतिष्मद्भ्राजमानं महस्वत्।
अमृतस्य धारा बहुधा दोहमानम्।
चरणं नो लोके सुधितान् दधातु।।[1]

अस्यार्थः–लोकस्य स्वनिवासस्थानस्य सायुज्यस्य वा साष्ट्यादेर्वा ब्रह्मलोकादेर्वा द्वारं, तत्प्रापकमित्यर्थः। अर्चिमत् अर्चींषि मयूखाः अस्य सन्तीति अर्चिमत्, अर्चिष्मदित्यर्थः। छान्दसः सकारलोपः। मयूखाः किरणाः। पवित्रं स्वयमतिशुद्धम्, अन्यशुद्धिहेतुश्च। 'ज्योतिष्मद्भ्राजमानं महस्वत्' इत्याम्रेडनं अर्चिष्मत्स्तुत्यर्थम्। यद्वा–

[2]त्रिखण्डं मातृकाचक्रं सोमसूर्यानलात्मकम्।

इति वक्ष्यते। 'अर्चिष्मत्' इत्यनेन आग्नेयान्यर्चींष्यष्टोत्तरशतं कथ्यन्ते। 'ज्योतिष्मत्' इत्यनेन ऐन्दवानि षट्त्रिंशदुत्तरशतं ज्योतींषि निर्दिश्यन्ते। 'महस्वत्' इत्यनेन भानवीयानि षोडशोत्तरशतं महांसि किरणाः संगृह्यन्ते। एतच्च '**क्षितौ षट्पञ्चाशत्**'[3] इतिश्लोक-व्याख्यानावसरे निपुणतरमुपपादयिष्यामः। अमृतस्य धाराः सुधाप्रवाहान् बहुधा बहुप्रकारेण द्विसप्ततिसहस्रनाडीमार्गेषु दोहमानं किरत् चन्द्रमण्डलगतसुधाधाराप्रवाहान् स्वनिर्णेजनपवित्रितान् वर्षेदित्यर्थः। तच्चरणं, चरणशब्दो नपुंसकः, 'पदङ्घ्रिश्चरणोऽस्त्रियाम्' इत्यमरः। नः अस्मान् साधकान् लोके प्रपञ्चे सुधितान् तृप्तान्, यद्वा–सञ्जातबुद्धिप्रकाशान् सुधियः, कृत्वा दधातु पुष्णातु।।

नन्वयं मन्त्रः अपाघास्विष्टिषु याज्यात्वेनाम्नातः। मन्त्राणां समवेतार्थ[4]प्रकाशन-शीलत्वात्, 'चरणाय स्वाहा' इति [5]चतुर्थ्यर्थोपहितशब्दस्यैव देवतात्वात्, एतद्व्याख्यानं न सङ्गच्छत इति चेत्–

उच्यते–अत्राहुः भगवत्पादाः–

सिद्धमन्त्रं परित्यज्य भिक्षामटति दुर्मतिः।

इति। अयमाशयः–वेदस्य सकर्तृकत्वासिद्धेः फलदानसमर्थत्वेन सर्वविद्वदभिमतं वृद्धव्यवहारावसितशक्तिकं 'लोकस्य द्वारम्' इत्यादिविशेषणविशिष्टत्वार्हं भगवत्याश्चरणमेव 'चरणाय स्वाहा' इत्यत्र चरणशब्देनाभिधीयत इति।। १०।।

---

1. तै०ब्रा० ३-१-३२।
2. त्रिविधम्।
3. १४ श्लो०।
4. स्वस्वदेवता प्रकाशन।
5. चतुर्थ्यन्तोपहित।

Notes : The previous stanza read along with this is said to contain the Kuṇḍalinī-rahasya-sopāna, *i.e.*, the secret ladder used by the Kuṇḍalinī, both for ascent and descent. The former deals with the Unneya-bhūmikā, *i.e.*, the ascent from the *Mūlādhāra* to the *Sahasrāra*, which has been fully set forth already. In this, the Anvaya and the *Pratyāvṛtti-bhūmikās* are briefly touched upon. By 'Anvaya' is meant the aftermath, *viz.*, the in-filling, through the Suṣumnā, of all the Nāḍīs of the Samayin; by 'Pratyāvṛtti' is meant the descent of the Kuṇḍalinī back to her hollow in the *Mūlādhāra*, there to resume her sleep.

In-filled—as a result of the sprinkling of nectar. The pathway of the *Nāḍīs*—The original word *'Prapañca'* is interpreted as the *'Nāḍī-prapañca,' i.e.*, the system of the Nāḍīs comprising the seventy-two thousand, all of them interrelated and connected with the main Nāḍī, the Suṣumṇā, which passed through the six *Cakras* with their three Granthis. *From Thy pair of feet—i.e.*, from the intermediate space between them. The nectar that flows therefrom is said to be the water that has washed the Devī's feet, which, by filling the entire body of the practitioner through the Naḍīs, makes him realize the Supreme Bliss. Those that hold the view that the Devī has four Caraṇas, the Śukla, the Rakta, the Miśra and the *Nirvāṇa* would have the Śukla and the Rakta as the pair of feet referred to in this stanza, for the reason that it is these two that have the *Ājñā-cakra* of the middle of the eyebrows as their seat. *Lunar regions*—The word 'Rasāmnāya-mahas', occurring in Tāntric literature, refers to the Moon, as it literally means 'endowed with splendour issuing out of the exuberance of nectar.' The word is also construed as "light revealing the six[1] Āmnāyas, eastern, southern, western, northern, upoward and downward, embracing the Mind in the *Ājñā,* the ether in the *Viśuddhi,* the Air in the *Anāhata,* Water in the *Maṇi-pūra,* Fire in the *Svādhiṣṭhāna,* and Earth in the *Mūlādhāra."* If this meaning is adopted, the reading 'Rasāmnāya-mahasā' would be appropriate, when this part of the stanza would mean 'having resumed Thine own position along with the splendour of the six Āmnāyas, etc.' Thine own position—*viz.*, the *Mūlādhāra,* Devī assumes in the Microcosm. *Three-and-a-half coils*—the word 'Adhyuṣṭa' of the original has the accepted significance of 'three-and-a-half' and does

1. The conventional word *'Rasa'* in *'Rasāmnāya'* indicated six, *Rasas* being six in number.

not admit of any etymological explanation. Hollow of the kula-kuṇḍa—the knot-like form of the *Mūlādhāra,* where there is a hollow. In the case of the reading 'Kuhariṇī' (Nom. case) the meaning would be, "Thou, (the Kuṇḍalinī) who dwellest in the hollow." Here is said to abide the Kuṇḍalinī in the form of a fine lotus-fibre. Kula-kuṇḍa is also taken to indicate the *Tri-koṇa* in the pericarp of the four-petalled lotus of the *Mūlādhāra.* The Samayins treat the disc of the Moon in the crest, as well as the external one, as the *Śrī-cakra,* as, in their view, the *Śrī-cakra* of the *Śrī-vidyā* is itself a Moon of sixteen *Kalās.*

The Kuṇḍalinī, during her ascent through the Suṣumnā-path, breaks through the six *Cakras,* which, being absorbed invisible. As these have to be reproduced and made manifest once again, she does this, out of her own radiant form, on her return journey homeward, after sprinkling nectar over the Prapañca, which signifies the Microcosm as well as the Macrocosm, as represented by the six *Cakras.* By construing the word 'Rasāmnāya-mahas' as implying the 'Vidhāna', 'doing', and the '*Prakāśa*', 'manifestation', of the *Rasas,* the lotuses, this purpose is achieved. In this view the stanza may be rendered thus : "Having sprinkled the Prapañca (composed of the twenty-one Tattvas represented by the six *Cakras),* and again having produced and made them manifest, out of Thine own resplendent form, having resumed Thine own seat, Thyself assuming Thine own form, serpent-like with the three-and-a-half coils, Thou of the abode of the hollow of the *Mūlādhāra* sleepest (there)."

पूर्वश्लोके इन्दुमण्डलात्मकं श्रीचक्रमित्युक्तम्। तदेव श्रीचक्रमुपदिशति–

चतुर्भिः श्रीकण्ठैः शिवयुवतिभिः पञ्चभिरपि[1]
प्रभिन्नाभिः शंभोर्नवभिरपि[2] मूलप्रकृतिभिः।
[3]त्रयश्चत्वारिंशद्वसुदलकलाश्रत्रिवलय-[4]
त्रिरेखाभिः सार्धं तव शरणकोणाः[5] परिणताः।।११।।

Caturbhiḥ śrī-kaṇṭhaiḥ śiva-yuvatibhiḥ pañcabhir api
prabhinnābhiḥ śaṃbhor navabhir api mūlaprakṛtibhiḥ/

---

1. पञ्चभिरधः।
2. नवभिरिति।
3. चतुश्चत्वारिंशद्।
4. कलाब्जत्रिवलय ; कलास्रत्रिवलय।
5. चरणकोणाः ; भवनंकोणाः।

Trayaś-catvāriṃśad vasu-dala-kalāśra-tri-valaya
tri-rekhābhiḥ sārdhaṃ tava śaraṇa-koṇāḥ pariṇatāḥ//

Translation : The angles contained in what constitutes Thy mansion (the *Śrī-cakra*), which is built of the nine Mūla-prakṛtis (the basic triangles), *viz.*, the four *Śrī-kaṇṭhas* (with apex downward)) and the five *Śiva-yuvatis* (with apex upward), all lying apart from Śaṃbhu (the *Bindu*), along with a lotus of eight petals, one of sixteen petals, the three circles and the three lines, turn out to be forty-three or forty-four (in number).

चतुर्भिः चतुस्सङ्ख्यासङ्ख्येयैः, **श्रीकण्ठैः**—शृणाति हिनस्तीति श्रीः, विषं कण्ठे यस्यासौ श्रीकण्ठः हरः, ते कोणा अपि श्रीकण्ठाः, तादात्म्यात् तद्वद्व्यपदेशः, अत एव बहुवचनसिद्धिः। श्रीकण्ठात्मकैरित्यर्थः। **शिवयुवतिभिः** शक्तिभिः, पूर्ववद्बहुवचन-सिद्धिः। शक्त्यात्मकैरित्यर्थः। **पञ्चभिः। अपिशब्दो** भेदे, **प्रभिन्नाभिः** प्रकर्षेण भिन्नाभिः। प्रकर्षस्तु शिवशक्तिचक्रमध्ये बैन्दवस्थानस्य विद्यमानत्वात्, एतच्च समयमतेन सृष्टिक्रमेण पञ्चचक्रलेखने ज्ञेयम्। कौलमतेन संहारक्रमेण नवयोनिचित्रलेखेन ऊर्ध्वाधोमुखतया अवस्थितेः प्रभिन्नत्वं ज्ञेयम्। तेनोभयं पृथक्पृथक् स्थितमित्यर्थः। **शम्भोः** इति पञ्चमी, शम्भुशब्देन चत्वारः श्रीकण्ठाः उच्यन्ते **नवभिः** नवसङ्ख्यैः, **अपि**—शब्दो वक्ष्यमाणबाहुल्यं समुच्चिनोति। **मूलप्रकृतिभिः** प्रपञ्चस्य मूलकारणैः, अत एव तेषां योनिशब्देन व्यवहारः। नव योनयो नवधात्वात्मकाः। तथा चोक्तं कामिकायाम्—

त्वगसृङ्मांसमेदोस्थिधातवः शक्तिमूलकाः।
मज्जाशुक्लप्राणजीवधातवः शिवमूलकाः।।
नवधातुरयं देहो नवयोनिसमुद्भवः।[1]
दशमी योनिरेकैव[2] परा शक्तिस्तदीश्वरी।। इति।।

दशमी योनिः बैन्दवस्थानम्, तदीश्वरी तस्य देहस्येत्यर्थः।।

1. "जीवधातुर्नाम जीवाधिष्ठानत्वात् ओजोधातुरेव जीवधातुरित्युच्यते। तदुक्तं वाग्भटेन—रसादिशुक्रान्तानां धातूनां प्रसादश्रेष्ठो जीवाधारभूतो धातुः ओज इति" इत्ययमधिको व्याख्यानरूपः पाठ दृश्यते।
2. 'दशमो धातुरेकैव' इति पाठान्तरम्।

[1]एवं पिण्डाण्डमुत्पन्नं तद्वद्ब्रह्माण्डमुद्भभौ।
पञ्च भूतानि शाक्तानि मायादीनि शिवस्य तु।।
माया च शुद्धविद्या च महेश्वरसदाशिवौ।
पञ्चविंशतितत्त्वानि तत्रैवान्तर्भवन्ति ते।।

एकादशेन्द्रियाणि शब्दादितन्मात्राः तच्छब्देन परामृश्यन्ते।

शिवशक्त्यात्मकं विद्धि जगदेतच्चराचरम्।
चरं पिण्डाण्डं, अचरं ब्रह्माण्डमित्यर्थः।।
केचित्तु एकपञ्चाशत्तत्वान्याहुः। तथाहि–
पञ्च भूतानि तन्मात्रपञ्चकं चेन्द्रियाणि च।
ज्ञानेन्द्रियाणि पञ्चैव तथा कर्मेन्द्रियाणि च।।
त्वगादिधातवस्सप्त पञ्च प्राणादिवायवः।
मनश्चाहङ्कृतिः ख्यातिर्गुणाः प्रकृतिपूरुषौ।।
रागो विद्या कला चैव नियतिः काल एव च।
माया च शुद्धविद्या च महेश्वरसदाशिवौ।।
शक्तिश्च शिवतत्त्वं च तत्त्वानि क्रमशो विदुः।। इति।।

एतान्येकपञ्चाशत्तत्त्वानि वायवीयसंहितादिशैवपुराणेषु सर्वेषु प्रतिपादितानि। अस्यार्थः–पञ्च भूतानि पृथिव्यप्तेजोवाय्वाकाशात्मकानि कार्यकारणरूपेणावस्थितानि। गन्धादितन्मात्रपञ्चकं पृथिव्यादीनां कारणभूतम्। ज्ञानेन्द्रियाणि श्रोत्रत्वक्चक्षुर्जिह्वाघ्राणात्मकानि। कर्मेन्द्रियाणि वाक्पाणिपादपायूपस्थात्मकानि। धातवः त्वगसृङ्मांसमेदोस्थिमज्जाशुक्लानि। वायवः प्राणापानव्यानोदानसमानाः। मनः मननात्मिका शक्तिः। अहङ्कृतिः अहङ्कारजनिका शक्तिः। ख्यातिः ज्ञानम्। गुणाः सत्त्वरजस्तमांसि। प्रकृतिः मूलप्रकृतिः। पुरुषो जीवः। रागः इच्छा। विद्या शास्त्रजनितविकल्पज्ञानम्। कलाः षष्ट्युत्तरत्रिशतसङ्ख्याकाः। नियतिः नियामिका शक्तिः। कालः संहरणशक्तिः। माया ऐन्द्रजालिकादिज्ञानम्[2]। शुद्धविद्या मोचकज्ञानम्। महेश्वरः रजोगुणविष्टः सृष्टिकर्ता। सदाशिवः सृष्टिस्थितिकर्ता। शक्तिः महेश्वरसदाशिवयोः रक्षणसर्जनशक्तिः। चकारात् कालात्मिका[3] संहारिणीशक्तिश्च। शिवतत्त्वं शुद्धबुद्धमुक्तस्वरूपम्। एतेषु सर्वेषु तत्त्वेषु कतिचन तत्त्वानि कुत्रचिदन्तर्भवन्ति। त्वगादिसप्तधातवः भूतेष्वन्तर्भवन्ति।

1. एकं।
2. 'काद्यज्ञानं' इति च पाठः।
3. 'कालस्य संहारिणी' इति पाठान्तरम्।

प्राणादिवायवः वायावन्तर्भवन्ति। अतो भूतेष्वेव तेषामन्तर्भावः। अहङ्कारस्य मनस्यन्तर्भावः। ख्यातेर्विद्यायामन्तर्भावः। गुणानां प्रकृतावन्तर्भावः प्रकृतेस्तु शक्तावन्तर्भावः। पुरुषस्य महेश्वरेऽन्तर्भावः। कलायाः शुद्धविद्यायामन्तर्भावः। नियतेस्तु शक्तावेवान्तर्भावः। कालस्य महेश्वरे सदाशिवे चान्तर्भावः। शक्तेस्तु शुद्धविद्यायामन्तर्भावः। शिवतत्त्वस्य सदाशिवतत्त्वेऽन्तर्भावः। इति तत्त्वानि पञ्चविंशतिरेव। पञ्च भूतानि तन्मात्रपञ्चकं पञ्च ज्ञानेन्द्रियाणि पञ्च कर्मेन्द्रियाणि मनस्तत्त्वं मायाविशुद्धविद्यामहेश्वरसदाशिवात्मकानि चत्वारि। एतानि पञ्चविंशतितत्त्वानि सर्वसंमतानि; श्रुत्यनुगृहीतत्वात्। तथा च श्रुतिः '**पञ्चविंश आत्मा भवति**'[1] इति। अतश्च षट्त्रिंशत्तत्त्वानीत्यादितत्त्वविकल्पः श्रुत्यनुसारेण पञ्चविंशतितत्त्वपर इत्यनुसन्धेयम्। अतश्च सर्वतत्त्वातीतं शिवशक्तिसम्पुटम्। तस्मादेव जगदुत्पत्तिः। तदुक्तं सुभगोदये–

परोऽपि शक्तिरहितः शक्तः कर्तुं न किञ्चन।
शक्तः स्यात्परमेशानि शक्त्या युक्तो भवेद्यदि।। इति।।

अत्र बहु वक्तव्यमस्ति। तत्तु सुभगोदयव्याख्यानावसरे निपुणतरमुपपादितमस्माभिरिति अलमतिविस्तरेण। प्रकृतमनुसरामः।।

चतुश्चत्वारिंशत् एतत्संख्याभिः, वसुदलकलाश्रत्रिवलयत्रिरेखाभिः, वसवोऽष्टौ, तेन वसुशब्देन अष्टसंख्या लक्ष्यते। वसुदलं अष्टदलं, कलाश्रं–कलाः षोडश: तेन कलाशब्देन षोडशसंख्या लक्ष्यते। अश्रशब्देन दलं लक्ष्यते। अतः कलाश्रं षोडशदलमित्यर्थः। त्रिवलयं त्रयाणां वलयानां समाहारः त्रिवलयं, त्रिमेखलमित्यर्थः। त्रिरेखाः प्राकारवलयाकाररेखाः, भूपुरत्रयमित्यर्थः। एतच्च भूपुरत्रयं चतुर्दिक्षु द्वारयुक्तम्। तथाचोक्तम्।।

बिन्दुत्रिकोणवसुकोणदशारयुग्ममन्वश्रनागदलसंयुतषोडशारम्।
वृत्तत्रिभूपुरयुतं परितश्चतुर्द्वाः श्रीचक्रमेतदुदितं परदेवतायाः।।

इति। श्रुतिरपि–

स॒तद्वाऽट्टार॑गम॒ं ता। स॒ꣳहार्य॒ं नग॑र॒ं तव॑।।[2]

इति। अस्यार्थः–सतद्वा, चतुर्द्वारमित्यर्थः। छान्दसोऽवर्णलोपश्च। अट्टारगमं अट्टारैः प्राकारवलयैः त्रिभिः अगमं दुर्गमम्। ता तानीमानि भूतानि। भगवति! तव नगरं पुरं श्रीचक्रात्मकं संहार्यं संहारकमित्यर्थः। पृथिव्यादिमहेश्वरान्तानि तत्त्वानि तत्रैव लीयन्त इति तात्पर्यम्।।

1. तै०ब्रा० १-२-६।   2. तै०आ० १-३१।

केचिदेवं व्याचक्षते–संहार्यं संहारक्रमेण लेखनीयमिति। तन्न, कौलमत एवं संहारक्रमेण चक्रस्य लेखनीयत्वादिति। प्रकृतमनुसरामः–

ताभिः **सार्धं** सह, **तव** भवत्याः, **शरणकोणाः** शरणं गृहं बैन्दवं मन्दिरं, तच्च कोणाश्चेति द्वन्द्वसमासः। ततः कोणाश्चतुश्चत्वारिंशदित्यर्थः।।

ननु बिन्दुत्रिकोणेत्यादिक्रमेण त्रिकोणबिन्दुभ्यां योगे षट्चत्वारिंशत्कोणाः बिन्दुपरित्यागे पञ्चचत्वारिंशत्कोणा इति चेत्–

सत्यं, प्रस्तारवशात्, त्रिकोणस्याधस्स्थितं कोणद्वयमष्टकोणे अन्तर्गतम्। ततश्च कोणाः त्रिचत्वारिंशदेवेति।।

शरणेन सार्धं कोणा इति द्वन्द्वसमासगत्या व्याख्यानम्। यद्वा–त्रयश्चत्वारिंशदिति पाठान्तरम्। तत्र स्पष्ट एवार्थः। **परिणताः** परिणामं प्राप्ताः अयमर्थः–त्रिकोणाष्टकोण-दशकोणयुगलचतुर्दशकोणात्मकानि शक्तिचक्राणि। अष्टदलषोडशदलमेखलात्रयभूपुर-त्रयात्मकानि चत्वारि शिवचक्राणि। त्रिकोण वसुदलं वसुकोणे षोडशदलं दशारयुग्मे मेखलात्रितयं भुवनाश्रके भूगृहं अन्तर्भूतमिति परिणतमित्युच्यते। एतच्च पूर्वमेव प्रतिपादितम्।।

अत्रेत्थं पदयोजना–हे भगवति! चतुर्भिः श्रीकण्ठैः शम्भोः सकाशात्प्रभिन्नाभिः पञ्चभिः शिवयुवतिभिः नवभिरपि मूलप्रकृतिभिः तव शरणकोणाः वसुदलकलाश्र-त्रिवलयत्रिरेखाभिः सार्धं परिणताः सन्तः चतुश्चत्वारिंशदिति।।

अत्रेदमनुसन्धेयम्–अस्मिन् चक्रे अष्टाविंशतिमर्मस्थानानि। सन्धयस्तु चतुर्विंशतिः।।

ननु मर्माणि चतुर्विंशतिरेव, कथमष्टाविंशतिः?

द्विरेखासङ्गमस्थानं सन्धिरित्यभिधीयते।
त्रिरेखासङ्गमस्थानं मर्म मर्मविदो विदुः।। इति।।

उच्यते–अष्टदलषोडशदलामेखलात्रयभूपुरत्रयाणां शिवचक्राणां त्रिरेखासङ्गम-स्थानत्वाभावेऽपि वाचनिकी मर्मसंज्ञा। यथोक्तं चन्द्रज्ञानविद्यायाम्–

मन्वश्रद्विदशाराष्टकोणवृत्तचतुष्टयम् ।
अष्टाविंशतिमर्माणि चतुर्विंशतिसन्धयः।। इति।।

अस्यार्थः–चतुर्दशकोणे दशारयुग्मे अष्टकोणे च त्रिरेखासङ्गमस्थानगणनायां चतुर्विंशतिमर्मस्थानानि वृत्तचतुष्टयेन शिवचक्रात्मकेन सार्धं अष्टाविंशतिरिति।।

एतत्सर्वं चक्रलेखनाऽपरिज्ञाने ज्ञातुं दुश्शकमिति चक्रलेखनप्रकारो निरूप्यते। स च द्विप्रकारः, सृष्टिक्रमेण संहारक्रमेण चेति। संहारक्रमेण लेखनं कौलमार्ग एव। तथापि नवयोनिपरिज्ञानार्थं स प्रकारो निरूप्यते।।

संहारक्रमेण तावत्–वृत्तमालिख्य, वृत्तमध्ये नव रेखाः लिखित्वा, पश्चिमरेखा-प्रान्ताभ्यां त्रिकोणमुत्पाद्य, स्वापेक्षया षष्ठ्या रेखया योजयेत्। एवं प्राग्रेखाप्रान्ताभ्यां त्रिकोणमुत्पाद्य स्वापेक्षया सप्तम्या रेखया योजयेत्। पश्चिमद्वितीयरेखाप्रान्ताभ्यां त्रिकोणमुत्पाद्य स्वापेक्षया अष्टम्या योजयेत्। प्राग्द्वितीयरेखाप्रान्ताभ्यां त्रिकोणमुत्पाद्य स्वापेक्षया अष्टम्या योजयेत्। ततः प्राक्पश्चिमतृतीयरेखाप्रान्ताभ्यां षट्कोणमालिखेत्[1]। षट्कोणमध्यस्थितह्रस्वरेखात्रितये पश्चिमरेखाप्रान्ताभ्यां त्रिकोणमुत्पाद्य स्वापेक्षया पञ्चम्या योजयेत्। एवं प्राग्रेखाप्रान्ताभ्यां त्रिकोणमुत्पाद्य स्वापेक्षया पञ्चम्या योजयेत्। मध्यस्थितातिह्रस्वरेखाप्रान्ताभ्यां त्रिकोणमुत्पाद्य स्वापेक्षया तृतीयरेखया योजयेत्। एवं चतुर्विंशतिमर्माणि चतुर्विंशतिसन्धयः, नवयोनिचक्रम्। एतत् कौलमतरहस्यम्।।

सृष्टिक्रमस्तु समयमार्गः। स च निरूप्यते–आदौ त्रिकोणमालिख्य, मध्ये बिन्दुं निक्षिप्य, बिन्दोरुपरि त्रिकोणं [2]भित्त्वा त्रिकोणान्तरं प्रागग्रं विलिख्य, प्रथमत्रिकोणाग्रात् त्रिकोणान्तरं पश्चिमाभिमुखं विलिखेत्। एवं अष्टकोणचक्रमुत्पन्नम्। एतस्मादेव दशारमुत्पादयेत्। तद्यथा–अष्टकोणप्राक्पश्चिमरेखाप्रान्ताभ्यां षट्कोणमुत्पाद्य विदिग्गत-मर्मस्थानेभ्यः चतुर्भ्यः चतुरस्त्रिकोणानुत्पाद्य अष्टकोणगतयोनेरुपरि दक्षिणोत्तरायतरेखा ईशानाग्निकोणत्रिकोणेषु योजयेत्, एवं पश्चिमतो योजयेत्, दशारं भवति। एतस्मादेव दशारात् पुनः दशारान्तरं उक्तरीत्या उत्पादयेत्। एतस्मादेव दशाराच्चतुर्दशारमुत्पादयेत्। तद्यथा–प्रथमदशारपूर्वपश्चिमरेखाप्रान्ताभ्यां षट्कोणमुत्पादयेत्। षट्कोणगत-मर्मस्थानेभ्यः चतुर्भ्यः त्रिकोणचतुष्कमुत्पादयेत्। ततः उपरिस्थितमर्मचतुष्टयात् दशारन्यायेन त्रिकोणचतुष्कमुत्पाद्य प्राक्पश्चिमरेखा मेलयेत्। एवं त्रयश्चत्वारिंशत्कोणाः, चतुर्विंशतिसन्धयः, चतुर्विंशतिमर्माणि इत। एतत् समयमतरहस्यम्।। अस्मिन् चक्रे त्रिकोणमूर्ध्वमुखं लेखनीयम्। कौलचक्रे त्रिकोणमध्यगतो बिन्दुः। समयचक्रे चतुष्कोण[3]मध्यगतो बिन्दुः। कौलचक्रे कोणसंख्या नास्ति, नवत्रिकोणात्मकत्वात्। नवानां त्रिकोणानां मेलने मर्मसन्धय एवोत्पद्यन्त इति महद्रहस्यम्।।

उभयचक्रसाधारणमत ऊर्ध्वमष्टदलपद्मं, ततः षोडशदलपद्मं, ततः मेखलात्रितयम्, ततश्चतुर्द्वारयुक्तं भूपुरत्रितयम्, इति श्रीचक्रोद्धारो विज्ञातव्यः।।

---

1. 'षट्कोणमुत्पाद्य वृत्तेन योजयेत्' इति। 2. लिखित्वा०।
3. 'षट्कोण' इति क्वचित् पाठः।

अत्र मेरुप्रस्तारकैलासप्रस्तारभूप्रस्तारा: त्रय: सम्भवन्ति। मेरुप्रस्तारो नाम–नित्याषोडशतादात्म्यम्। कैलासप्रस्तारो नाम–मातृकातादात्म्यम्। भूप्रस्तारो नाम–वशिन्यादितादात्म्यम्। एतत्सर्वं '**चतुष्षष्ट्या तन्त्रैः**'[1] इत्यादिश्लोकव्याख्यानावसरे निपुणतरमुपपादयिष्याम:।।

अत्र रुद्रयामले विशेष उक्त:–

पृश्नयो नाम मुनय: सर्वे चक्रसमाश्रया:।
सेवमानाश्चक्रविद्यां देवगन्धर्वपूजिताम्।।
अग्नीषोमात्मकं चक्रमग्नीषोममयं जगत्।
अग्नावन्तर्बभौ भानु: अग्नीषोममयं स्मृतम्।।
त्रिखण्डं मातृका चक्रं सोमसूर्यानलात्मकम्।
त्रिकोणं बैन्दवं सौम्यमष्टकोणं च मिश्रकम्।।
चक्रं चन्द्रमयं चैव दशारद्वितयं तथा।
चतुर्दशारं वह्नेस्तु चतुश्चक्रं च भानुमत्।।
एतत्प्रसादादिन्द्राद्या वसवोऽष्टौ मरुद्गणा:।
ये ये समृद्धा लोकेऽस्मिन् त्रिपुराचक्रसेवका:।
पुरत्रयं च चक्रस्य सोमसूर्यानलात्मकम्।
महालक्ष्म्या: पुरं चक्रं तत्रैवास्ते सदाशिव:।। इति।।

इममेवार्थं श्रुतिरप्याह तैत्तिरीयके अरुणोपनिषदि '**इमा नुकं भुवना सीषधेम**'[2] इत्यारभ्य '**ऋषिभिरदात् पृश्निभि:**'[2] इत्यन्ता। अरुणोपनिषन्नाम–अरुणाया: भगवत्या: प्रतिपादिका उपनिषत्। '**भद्रं कर्णेभि:**,'[3] इत्यारभ्य '**तपस्वी पुण्यो भवति**'[3] इत्यन्ता अरुणोपनिषत् अरुणामेव प्रतिपादयति। इममर्थं दृष्टवान् अरुणकेतु: ऋषि:। श्रुत्यर्थस्तावत्–

इ॒मा नु॑क॒ं भुव॑ना सीषधेम।।

अस्यार्थ:–पृश्नयो नाम मुनय: परस्परं सङ्गिरन्ते। इमां चक्रविद्याम्। नुकं वितर्के। भुवना भुवनानि। सीषधेम अवगच्छाम:। चक्रविद्यामुपाश्रित्यैव भुवनान्यवतिष्ठन्त इति वितर्कयाम इत्यर्थ:। यद्वा–इमां चक्रविद्यां भुवना भुवनात्मतया सीषधेम नुकं, नु पृच्छायाम्। 'नु पृच्छायां वितर्के च' इत्यमर:[4] ।।

---

1. ३१ श्लो.। 2. तै०आ० १-२७। 3. तै०आ० १ प्रश्न:।
4. नु: पृच्छायाम्। भुवनात्मतया कं पृष्ट्वा अवगच्छाम इत्यर्थ:। 'नुपृच्छायां वितर्के च इत्यमर:–इति कार्वेटिनगरमुद्रितकोशे।

इन्द्रश्च विश्वे च देवाः।।

अस्य वाक्यस्यार्थः स्पष्ट एव। चक्रविद्यामुपाश्रित्यैव आसत इति शेषः।।

यज्ञं च नस्तन्वं च प्रजां च। आदित्यैरिन्द्रः सह सीषधातु।।

अस्यार्थः—यज्ञमग्निष्टोमादिकं नः अस्माकं तन्वं तनूं शरीरार्धं पत्नीमिति यावत्। प्रजां सन्तानम्। चकारात्सर्वास्सम्पदः। आदित्यैः मरुद्गणैः, सह इन्द्रः चक्रविद्योपासनात् प्राप्तपरमैश्वर्यः। इन्द्रश्चक्रविद्यामस्माकं उपदिश्य सीषधातु सम्पा(दयतु)दितवान्। प्राप्तकाले लोट्।।

आदित्यैरिन्द्रः सगणो मरुद्भिः। अस्माकं भूत्ववितां तनूनाम्।।

मन्त्रद्वयस्यार्थः—तनूनां पुत्रमित्रकलत्रादीनां अविता रक्षकः भूतु भवतीत्यर्थः। इन्द्र एवास्माकं योगक्षेमसम्पादक इति भावः।।

आप्लवस्व प्रप्लवस्व।।

पृश्नयश्चक्रविद्यां प्रस्तुवन्ति। आपादमस्तकं प्लवनं अमृतनिष्यन्दसेचनं कुरु। प्रकर्षेण प्लवनं द्विसप्ततिसहस्रनाडीमार्गेषु आसेचनं कुरु।।

आण्डीभव ज मा मुहुः।

आण्डी—पिण्डाण्डं ब्रह्माण्डं च, च्विप्रत्ययान्तः। भव पिण्डाण्डरूपेणास्मदीयेन ब्रह्माण्डरूपेण बाह्येन भवदीयेन प्राप्नुहि, भवत्सायुज्यं देहीत्यर्थः। ज अवगच्छ। मुहुर्मामवगच्छ, अनुगृहाणेत्यर्थः। 'अज गतौ' इति धातोः अकारलोपश्छान्दसः।।

सुखादींदुःखनिधनाम्।।

अस्यार्थः—सुखमत्ति अदयतीति सुखादि सुखसम्पादकः इन्दुः चन्द्रः, बैन्दवस्थानगतः। खनिधनां—खं बैन्दवस्थानमेव नितरां धनं यस्यास्सा ताम्। यद्वा—सुखादीं सुखप्रथमां सुखात्मिकाम्। दुःखस्य निधनं नाशो तत्रेति दुःखनिधनां, अविज्ञातदुःख- गन्धामित्यर्थः। यद्वा—सुखादीं शोभनेन खेन इन्द्रियेण मनसा आदीं आद्यां, मनोवेद्यामित्यर्थः। दुःखनिधनां दुःखानां दुष्टेन्द्रियाणां चक्षुरादीनां अगोचरामिति।।

प्रतिमुञ्चस्व स्वां पुरम्।।

स्वां भागवतीं पुरं देहं रेफान्तःशब्दः, प्रतिमुञ्चस्व अधितिष्ठ।।

मरीचयः स्वायंभुवाः।।

अस्यार्थः–स्वयं भगवत्याः सकाशात् भवा उत्पन्नाः मरीचयो मयूखाः। सर्वाणि भुवनानि आवृत्य वर्तन्त इति वाक्यशेषः। सूर्यचन्द्राग्नीनां प्रकाशकत्वं स्वायंभुवमरीचि-प्रसादादेवेति उत्तरत्र वक्ष्यते।।

ये शरीराण्यकल्पयन्।।

अस्यार्थः—ये मयूखाः षष्ट्युत्तरत्रिशतसङ्ख्याकाः शरीराणि कालात्मकानि षष्ट्युत्तरत्रिशतसङ्ख्याकानि दिनानि, तान्येव संवत्सरः, 'संवत्सरो वै प्रजापतिः'[1] इति श्रुतेः।।

ते तं देहं कल्पयन्तु।।

ते मरीचयः, ते तव भगवत्याः, देहं कल्पयन्तु देहमाश्रयन्तु। देहशब्देन देहावयवचरणमुच्यते। भवच्चरणोत्पन्ना इत्यर्थः।।

मा च ते ख्या स्म तीरिषत्।।

ते तव ख्या ख्यतिः ज्ञानं मा च तीरिषत् अस्मान् न जहातु, भवद्विषयज्ञानं अस्माकं सदा सिद्ध्यत्वित्यर्थः।।

इतः परं पृश्नयश्चक्रविद्यानुष्ठाने त्वरमाणाः परस्परं सङ्गिरन्ते–

उत्तिष्ठत मा स्वप्त। अग्निमिच्छध्वं भारताः।
राज्ञः सोमस्य तृप्तासः। सूर्येण सयुजोषसः।।

ऋचोऽयमर्थः—हे भारताः भायां भारूपायां ज्योतीरूपायां चक्रविद्यायामिति यावत्, रताः उपासनारताः। यद्वा—भारत्याः सरस्वत्याः श्रीविद्यायाः उपासकाः। सामान्यविहितप्रत्ययस्य विशेषवाचित्वात् भारता इति। उत्तिष्ठत उपासनोपक्रमं कुरुत। मा स्वप्त अप्रमत्ता भवत। अग्निमिच्छध्वं स्वाधिष्ठानगताग्निं प्रज्वलयत। राज्ञश्चन्द्रस्य। उमया सहितः सोमः। चन्द्रमण्डलान्तर्गतबैन्दवस्थानगतत्वात् देव्याः, चन्द्रस्य सोमशब्दवाच्यत्वसिद्धिः। तस्य चन्द्रस्य निष्यन्दैः तृप्तासः तृप्ताः। सूर्येण अनाहतचक्रविशुद्धिचक्रयोर्मध्ये स्थितेन सूर्येण, सयुजा अग्निचन्द्रयोर्मध्यवर्तिना इत्यर्थः। यद्वा—सूर्येण सयुजा राज्ञा तृप्तास इत्यन्वयः। कीदृशाः?—उषसः प्लुष्टमायामयक्लेशाः। यद्वा—उषसः उषः काले ध्यानरताः, तस्मिन् काल एव भगवतीनिदिध्यासनादेर्विहितत्वात्।।

इतःपरं पूजासामग्रीमुपदिशन्ति पृश्नयः–

युवा सुवासाः।

युवा दृढाङ्गः स्वस्थः। सुवासाः शुभ्रवस्त्रः। इदं शुभ्राभरणशुभ्रमाल्यादीनामुपलक्षकम्। एवंविधः सन् पूजयेदिति शेषः।।

---

1. तै०ब्रा० १-६-२।

श्रीचक्रस्य स्वरूपं तावदाहुः–

अष्टचक्रा नवद्वारा।।

अष्टकोण–दशकोणद्वितय–चतुर्दशकोण–अष्टपत्र–षोडशपत्र–त्रिवलय–त्रिरेखात्मकानि अष्टौ चक्राणि यस्याः सा अष्टाचक्रा। अत एव नवद्वारा नवसङ्ख्याकानि द्वाराणि त्रिकोणरूपाणि यस्याः सा नवद्वारा।।

देवानां पूरयोध्या।।

देवानामिन्द्रादीनां पूज्यत्वेन सम्बन्धिनी पूः श्रीविद्यानगरम्। यद्वा–दीव्यन्तीति देवाः पञ्चविंशतितत्त्वानि तेषां पूरधिष्ठानम्। यद्वा–सूर्यचन्द्राग्नीनां पूः, सोमसूर्यानलात्मकत्वात् श्रीचक्रस्य। तस्य पुरत्रयसमष्टिरूपत्वात् पूरित्येकवचनसिद्धिरिति ध्येयम्। अयोध्या असाध्या, मन्दभाग्यानामिति शेषः।।

तस्याँ हिरण्मयः कोशः। स्वर्गो लोको ज्योतिषाऽऽवृतः।।

अस्यार्थः—तस्यां पुरि श्रीचक्रमध्ये हिरण्मयः कोशः, सहस्रदलकमलकोश इत्यर्थः, बैन्दवस्थाने सहस्रदलकमलकोशस्य विद्यमानत्वात्। तस्य कोशस्य ज्योतिषा स्वर्गो लोकः आवृतः। ज्योतिर्लोकः स्वर्गलोक इत्यर्थः।।

अथ पृश्नयः चक्रविद्योपासनायाः फलमाहु :–

यो वै तां ब्रह्मणो वेद। अमृतेनावृतां पुरीम्।
तस्मै ब्रह्म च ब्रह्मा च। आयुः कीर्तिं प्रजां ददुः।।

अयमर्थः—ब्रह्मणः ब्रह्मस्वरूपायाः भगवत्याः तां पूर्वोक्तां अमृतेन आवृतां चन्द्रमण्डलगलत्पीयूषधारावृतां पुरीं श्रीचक्ररूपां त्रिपुरायाः पुरं यो वेद ज्ञानपूर्वकमर्चनं करोति तस्मै विदुषे अर्चकाय, ब्रह्म च ब्रह्मस्वरूपा भगवती, ब्रह्मा च ब्रह्मरूपो भगवान्। चकारद्वयं उभयोर्मेलनं समुच्चिनोति, मिलितयोरेव बैन्दवथाने सहस्रारे सुधासिन्धुमध्ये मणिद्वीपे चिन्तामणिगृहे निवासात्। एतौ उभौ आयुः जीवितं कीर्तिं यशः, प्रजां सन्तानं, ददुः दद्याताम् इत्यर्थः। 'व्यत्ययो बहुलम्' इति वचनव्यत्ययः।।

शिवशक्त्योः तत्रैव निवासमाहुः–

विभ्राजमानाँ हरिणीम्। यशसा संपरीवृताम्।
पुरँ हिरण्मयीं ब्रह्मा। विवेशापराजिता।।

ऋचोऽयमर्थः–विभ्राजमानां–अनन्तकोटिसंख्याककिरणैरिति शेषः, प्रकाशमानाम्। हरिणीं हिरण्यवर्णां, 'हिरण्यवर्णां हरिणीं'[1] इति श्रुतेः। यशसा कीर्त्या सम्यक्परिवृताम्,

1. श्रीसूक्ते।

ये ये लोके कीर्तिमन्तस्ते सर्वे भगवतीप्रसादसमासादितकीर्तिमन्त इत्यर्थः। तां बैन्दवीं पुरं चिन्तामणिगृहं, ब्रह्मा सदाशिवः, '**ब्रह्मा शिवो मे अस्तु सदाशिवोम्**'[1] इति श्रुतेः पुल्लिङ्गब्रह्मशब्दसदाशिवशब्दयोः एक एवार्थः प्रतीतः। विवेश अपराजिता सादाख्या चन्द्रकला विवेश। वाक्यद्वयेन उभयोः प्रवेशभेदप्रतिपादनं "बैन्दवे चिन्तामणिगृहे सदाशिवः सर्वदा सन्निहितः ; अपराजिता कुण्डलिनीशक्तिः षट्चक्राणि भित्त्वा भूयो भूयः प्रविशति" इतीममर्थं ज्ञापयितुम्।।

शिवशक्त्योः तस्मिन् चक्रे अवस्थितिप्रकारमाहुः–

पराङै॑त्य॑ज्याम॒यी। पराङे॑त्य॑नाश॒की।।

अस्यार्थः—पराङ् अधोमुखी [2]चक्ररूपिणी शिवशक्त्योर्मध्ये शक्तिः अज्यामयी [3]ज्यानिरहिता नाशरहिता नित्या दुःखरहिता आनन्दमयी इत्यर्थः। एति वर्तते। यद्वा–अज्यामयी, ज्या भूमिः तेन पञ्चभूतानि लक्ष्यन्ते, तन्मयी, न भवतीत्यज्यामयी, मनस्तत्त्वादिमयी, शिवचक्रात्मकचतुर्योन्यात्मिकेति यावत्, शिवयोनीनां बैन्दवस्थानादधः अवाङ्मुखतया अवस्थानात्। अनाशकी नाशरहिता शक्तिचक्रात्मकपञ्चयोन्यात्मिका। पराङ् अधोमुखी एति, शक्तियोनीनामपि शिवयोन्यपेक्षया अवाङ्मुखत्वात्। एवं शिवयोनिशक्तियोन्योः परस्परमवाङ्मुखत्वं चक्रलेखनक्रमादवगम्यते।।

विदुषः फलमाहुः–

इ॒ह चा॑मुत्र॑ चान्वे॒ति। वि॒द्वान् देवासु॒रानु॑भ॒यान्।।

दीव्यन्तीति देवाः एकादशेन्द्रियाणि। असुराः असवः प्राणाः प्राणादिपञ्चवायवः तान् रान्ति आददत इति पञ्च तन्मात्रा[4] उच्यन्ते। उभयान् उभयत्र देवासुरेषु अन्वितान् मायाशुद्धविद्यामहेश्वरसदाशिवान्। यो विद्वान् पञ्चविंशतितत्त्वजातं विदित्वा शिवशक्तिसम्पुटात्मकं पञ्चविंशतितत्त्वविलक्षणं षड्विंशतत्त्वं यस्तु वेत्ति स विद्वान् इह च इह लोके, पूजातारतम्यवशात्, अमुत्र च परलोके, सार्ष्टिसालोक्यसामीप्य-सारूप्यसायुज्यात्मिकया पञ्चविधया मुक्त्या अन्वेति युज्यते। साष्ट्यादिस्वरूपं सप्रपञ्चं पुरस्तात्[5] प्रपञ्च्यते।।

अथ देवासुरोभयज्ञानोपायमाहुः–

---

1. तै० उ० ४-२९।
2. चन्द्ररूपिणी।
3. ज्याविरहिता।
4. 'महदादयः' इत्यधिकः पाठः क्वचित् दृश्यते।
5. ९९ श्लोकव्याख्याने।

यत्कुमारी मन्द्रयते। यद्योषिद्यत्पतिव्रता।
अरिष्टं यत्किंच क्रियते। अग्निस्तदनुवेधति।।

अयमर्थः—कुण्डलिनीशक्तेरवस्थात्रयं विद्यते। यस्मिन् चक्रे कुमारी कौमारावस्थामापन्ना प्रथमं सुप्तोत्थिता मन्द्रयते मन्द्रस्वरं करोति, कुण्डलिन्याः सर्पात्मकत्वात्। सर्पो हि सुप्तोत्थाने मन्द्रस्वरं करोति, तद्वदित्यर्थः। यद्योषित् यस्मिन् चक्रे कुलयोषित् विष्णुग्रन्थिपर्यन्तं गत्वा, रातीति शेषः।

कुलयोषितं कुलं त्यक्त्वा राति विष्णोः प्रभेदने।

इति सनत्कुमारवचनात्। यत् यस्मिन् चक्रे पतिव्रता पत्या सदाशिवेन सार्धं सहस्रदलकमले विहरमाणा। रिष्टं शुभाभावं 'रिष्टं क्षेमे शुभाभावे' इत्यभिधानात्, तदन्यदरिष्टं शुभं, अमृतास्वादमित्यर्थः, यत्किञ्चित्क्रियते तत् स्वाधिष्ठानगतोऽग्निः अनुवेधति सहायं करोति। अतश्च अभ्यासवशात् वायुना अग्निं प्रज्वाल्य अग्निशिखानुविद्धविलीनचन्द्रमण्डलगलत्पीयूषधारानुभवे पञ्चविंशतितत्त्वातीता परमेश्वरी इति ज्ञातुं सुशकमित्युपदेशः।।

चक्रविद्योपासनं वर्णिनां आश्रमिणां ज्ञानिनामज्ञानिनां च फलदायकमित्यभिसन्धायाहुः—

अशृतासश्शृतासश्च। यज्वानो येऽप्ययज्वनः। स्वर्यन्तो नापेक्षन्ते।।

अयमर्थः—अशृतासः अपक्काः, अक्षपितान्तःकरणकल्मषा इत्यर्थः। शृतासश्च पक्काश्च—'आज्जसेरसुक्' इत्यसुगागमः, क्षपितान्तःकरणकल्मषा इत्यर्थः। यज्वानः यजनशीलाः त्रैवर्णिकाः आश्रमिणश्च। अयज्वनः यागरहिताः शूद्रादयः। '**तस्माच्छूद्रो यज्ञेऽनवक्लृप्तः**'[1] इति श्रुतिः त्रैवर्णिकैकनियताधिकारयज्ञशब्दवाच्याग्निष्टोमादिपरा। चक्रविद्योपासने शूद्राणामपि अधिकारचोदनात्, निषादस्थपतिवत् वैदिके कर्मण्यधिकारसिद्धेः न काचित् क्षतिः! यन्तः, इण् गतौ, चक्रविद्यामवगच्छन्तः स्वः स्वर्गं नापेक्षन्ते।।

चक्रविद्योपासनाव्यतिरेकेण देवतान्तरोपासनायामनिष्टमाहुः—

इन्द्रमग्निं च ये विदुः। सिकता इव संयन्ति।
रश्मिभिः समुदीरिताः। अस्माल्लोकादमुष्माच्च।।

अयमर्थः—सुरासुरमुख्यवन्दितचरणारविन्दायाः सर्वभूतान्तर्यामिन्याः सर्वव्यापिन्याः जगदुत्पत्तिस्थितिलयहेतोश्चक्रविद्याया अन्यत्वेन ये इन्द्रमग्निं, चकारात् यमादिलोक-

1. तै०सं० ७.१.१।

पालान् पृथिव्यादिसदाशिवान्ततत्त्वानि च, उपास्यत्वेन ये विदुः ते सिकता इव वालुकाकणा इव संयन्ति, परस्परं विरलाः भ्रष्टा भवेयुरित्यर्थः। किञ्च—रश्मिभिः यमपाशैः उत्तरप्रबन्धे 'अपेत वीत' इत्यादौ प्रतिपादितैः, समुदीरिताः संयता बद्धा भवेयुः इत्यर्थः। किञ्च—अस्माल्लोकात् अमुष्माल्लोकाच्च भ्रष्टा भवेयुरिति शेषः। अत एव श्रुत्यन्तरम्–

अन्धं तमः प्रविशन्ति येऽविद्यामुपासते।।[1]

अयमर्थः–अविद्यां विद्याविरुद्धां ज्ञानमार्गविरुद्धां इन्द्रादिसेवां **'वाचं धेनुमुपासीत'**[2] इत्येवमध्यारोपितसेवां च ये कुर्वते ते अविद्वांसः अन्धं तमः प्रविशन्ति अन्धतामिस्रं प्रविशन्तीत्यर्थः। चकारः प्रकरणसमाप्तिद्योतकः।।

ऋषिभिरदात् पृश्निभिः।।

पृश्निनामभिः ऋषिभिः एतत्सर्वमदात्, अदायि। कर्मणि लुङ्। छान्दसः कर्मणि प्रत्ययलोपः, कर्तृप्रत्ययव्यत्ययश्च। ऋषिभिः पृश्निभिरेवमुक्तमित्यर्थः। यद्वा–पृश्निभिः ऋषिभिः सहितः ऋषिसङ्घः एवमदात्, वाचमिति शेषः, उक्तवानित्यर्थः।। ११ ।।

Notes : The angles contained in what constitutes Thy mansion—*i.e.*, the angles of the *Śrī-cakra,* which forms the Devī's *Śaraṇa,* abode. The word 'angles' should be understood as the angels at the apex of the triangles pointing outwards in the *Śrī-cakra.* Other take it in the sense of 'triangles', probably with a view to avoid what they consider to be the contingency of having to reckon two more angles in taking the inmost triangle into account. There is no room, in our view, for any such contingency. In calculating the number of Koṇas in the *Śrī-cakra,* we should start with the initial triangle with which we began the design of the *Śrī-cakra* with which we began the design of the *Śrī-cakra* in *Sṛṣṭi-krama,* and not the inmost triangle, which was derived later on. As the angles at the base of the initial triangle form two of the corner angles of the *Aṣṭa-koṇa,* the angle pointing upwards alone has to be taken into account. *The nine Mūla-prakṛtis*—the nine root-cause of the *Śrī-cakra, i.e.,* the nine triangles having as their bases the nine horizontal lines drawn perpendicular to the diameter. They also signify the prime cause of *Prapañca, i.e.,* primordial matter, and are also appropriately called the nine Yonis, which are said to be of the form of the nine Dhātus

---

1. ई०उ० ९।
2. बृ०उ० ७-८-१।

which go to make up the body of the Microcosm. The five Dhātus, humours : Tvac, Asṛj, Māṁsa, Medas and Asthi, originate from the Śakti ; and Majjā, Śukla, Prāṇa and the *Jīva* of the Microcosm originate from Śiva ; while the five *Bhūtas*, the five *tanmātras*, the five *Jñānendriyas*, the five *Karmendriyas* and the *Manas* of the Macrocosm have their origin in the Śakti, and likewise Māyā, Śuddhavidyā, Maheśvara and Sadāśiva are from Śiva. Thus, it will be seen that the nine basic triangles, involving the twenty-five Tattvas, stand for the entire Microcosm and Macrocosm. 'Śrī-kaṇṭhas' and 'Śiva-yuvatis' are the traingles so designated. *Lying apart from Śaṁbhu*—'Śaṁbhu' stands for the *Bindu*, which lies in the quadrilateral and therefore apart from the nine triangles. The words Vasu and Kalā in Saṁskṛt are conventional for 8 and 16, and here denote the eight-petalled and the sixteen-petalled lotus respectively. The three circles and the three lines—in drawing the *Śrī-cakra* some describe only one circle in the place of the three *Mekhalās*, forgetting that the two already existing circles form the pericarps of the eight-petalled and the sixteen-petalled lotus. This is against the view of the majority. *The three lines*—the author of the Saundaryalaharī is not apparently of the view that four doorways, one on each side, should be provided for the quadrangular *Bhū-gṛha* of three lines, as, otherwise, he would have specifically made mention of them here. Although Vāmakeśvara-tantra and some others hold the view that the *Bhū-gṛha* has four doorways, still Bhāskararāya, in his Setu-bandha makes mention of the fact that the Yāmala is silent[1] about the doorways and Śaṅkara-bhagavatpāda in his Saundaryalaharī follows suit with the same view. Strangely enough, Lakṣmīdhara,[2] who strongly supports the view in favour of the doorways, quotes the selfsame authority in support of his view, taking care, however, to fabricate a reading of his own, convenient for his purpose. The word 'Dvāropānta' occurring in stanza *96 infra*, however seems to lend support to Lakṣmīdhara's view. Forty-three in number—comprising the vertical angle of the initial *Tri-koṇa*, the eight corner angles of the *Aṣṭa-koṇa* pointing outwards, the twenty corner angles of the internal and external *Daśāras* pointing outwards, and the fourteen corner angles of the *Caturdaśāra* pointing outwards are the forty-

---

1. बिन्दुत्रिकोणवसुकोणदशारयुग्ममन्वश्रनागदलसंयुतषोडशारम्।
   वृत्तत्रयं च धरणीसदनत्रयं च श्रीचक्रराजमुदितं परदेवतायाः।।
2. वृत्तत्रिभूपुरयुतं परितश्चतुर्द्वाः श्रीचक्रमेतदुदितं परदेवतायाः।

three *Koṇas* meant. The portions of the *Śrī-cakra* lying outside these angles are considered as merged in them, the *Aṣṭa-dala-padma* in the *Tri-koṇa, the Ṣoḍaśa-dala* in the *Aṣṭa-koṇa, Mekhalā-traya* in the two *Daśāras,* and the *Bhū-gṛha* in the *Catur-daśāra* respectively. Those who adopt the reading *'Catuś-catvāriṃśat'* understand the word *'Śaraṇa-koṇāḥ'* as "*bindu,* the abode of Śiva, and the angles and give their number as forty-four."

The *Śrī-cakra* (containing the fifty-one letters of the Alphabet), which is the Devī's abode, inside which is the abode of Lakṣmī, is construed as of the character of Soma, Sūrya and Anala. Some hold the view that it contains the three regions of the Moon, the Sun and Fire in the descending order in three distinct parts among the six *Cakras* forming part of it. Others maintain that it partakes of the character of each of the three, offering the following explanation : The forty-three angles of the *Śrī-cakra* are represented by the sixteen Kalās of the Moon and the twenty-seven stars in its Soma aspect; by the twelve Kalās, twelve Mūrtis, twelve Ṛṣis, the three Vedas and the four *Svaras* in its Sūrya aspect; and by the *Tri-koṇa* representing Agni, the *Aṣṭa-koṇa,* the eight Mūrtis of Agni, the *Antar-daśāra,* the ten Kalās, of Agni, the *Bahir-daśāra,* the ten Vibhūtis of Agni, the Viśva over which the three tongues representing the three Guṇas of Agni spread, made up of the fourteen worlds representing the *Catur-daśāra* in its Agni aspect. It may be pointed out in this connection that this stanza is considered by some as the Bahiryāga, the external sacrifice of the Upāsakas of the Devī, while the previous two stanzas deal with the Antaryāga, the internal sacrifice, as both of them culminate in the partaking, by the Upāsaka, of the Parāmṛta as *Havya.*

There are three ways in which the parts of the *Śrī-cakra* are viewed, as providing abodes for the deities, each one of them forming the basis of a distinct form of worship. They are known as the Meru, the Kailāsa, and the Bhū-prastāras.[1] The arrangement of

---

1. Umānanda-nātha, in his treatise named Nityotsava, which deals with the daily worship of the Devī, makes mention of the Bhū-prastāra and the Meru-prastāra only, leaving off the Kailāsa-prastāra, citing the Tantra-rāja as his authority. According to him the Bhū-prastāra has for its requisite a flat plate of gold four inches square and weighing six tolas, over which is worked-out in relief the *Śrī-cakra.* Meru-prastāra is spoken of as of three kinds : (a) The three Cakras

the sixteen Nityās according to the design of the *Meru-prastāra* is as follows : The sixteen Nityās, *viz.*, Mahātripura-sundarī, Kameśvarī, Bhaga-mālinī, Nitya-klinnā, Bheruṇḍā, Vahni-vāsinī, Mahā-vidyeśvarī, Śivadūtī, Tvaritā, Kula-sundarī, Nityā, Nīla-patākā, Vijayā, Sarva-maṅgalā, Jvālā-mālinikā and Cit-kalā are split into eight pairs, in the order above named. The fifty-one letters of the Alphabet are similarly divided into the following eight groups, *viz.*, *A-varga, Ka-varga, Ca-varga, Ṭa-varga, Ta-varga, Pa-varga, Ya-varga* and *Śa-varga*. The pairs of deities along with the groups of letters are then considered as having their places over the eight petals of the *Aṣṭa-dala-padma,* commencing from the petal pointing to the east, clockwise. Each petal thus comes to be identified with a distinct pair of deities and a group of letters. In the same manner, commencing from the angle pointing eastwards of the *Aṣṭa-koṇa,* the same pairs of deities and groups of letters should be considered as inherent in each corresponding angle of the *Aṣṭa-koṇa*. The same Nityās coupled with the sixteen vowels should be identified as having their place in the sixteen petals of the *Ṣoḍaśa-dala-padma* and as inherent in the *Dvi-daśāra*. The first two of the Nityās are considered to be of the form of the *Trikoṇa* and the *Bindu* respectively; the other fourteen Nityās are considered as inherent in the fourteen angles of the *Catur-daśāra*. This is how the Nityās are considered to inhere in the *Śrī-cakra*. The arrangement of the fifty-one Mātṛkās according to the design of the *Kailāsa-prastāra* is as follows : The sixteen vowels, the very life of the Alphabet, corresponding to the sixteen Niytās, are compressed into 'Aḥ' which is made up of the 'A' preceding the 'E' and the 'Visarga' derived from 'Sa' of the Pañca-daśākṣarī. This is assigned its place in the *Baindava-sthāna* and shuld be considered as also inhering there. The consonants, commencing from 'Ka' and ending with 'Ma', known as the 'Sparśa', with the three syllables 'Āṃ', 'Hrīṃ', 'Krīm' (the Pāśāṅkuśa-bījas), these twenty-eight should be considered as inherent in the angles of the *Aṣṭa-koṇa* and the two *Daśāras,* one

commencing from the Bhū-pura or Bhū-gṛha constituting the *Sṛṣṭi-cakras,* the next three constituting the *Sthiti-cakras* and the last three constituting the *Saṃhāra-cakras* are wrought in massive gold in three stages rising one above the other in the form of a pyramid : (b) the Bhū-pura as the first stage, the two lotuses as the second stage, and the six other *Cakras* as the third rising one above the other in the form of a pyramid ; and (c) the nine *Cakras* rising one above the other in nine stages.

letter in each angle, the remaining nine letters commencing from 'Ya', after duplication, should be considered as inherent in the fourteen angles of the *Carut-daśa-koṇa* and the four Śiva-cakras, one in each. This is how the Mātṛkās are considered to inhere in the *Śrī-cakra*. The arrangment of the deities consisting of Vaśinī and others, according to the design of the *Bhū-prastāra*, is as follows : The sixteen Nityās, split into eight pairs along with one of the eight deities, *viz.*, Vaśinī, Kameśvarī, Modinī, Vimalā, Aruṇā, Jayinī, Sarveśvarī and Kaulinī added to each pair, the eight groups of three deities each thus formed, should be considered as inherent in the eight *Cakras* lying beyond the *Bindu* and the *Tri-koṇa*, one in each. The Mahātripura-sundarī should be considered as inherent in the middle of the *Śrī-cakra;* the eight Vargas, the eight deities, Vaśinī, *etc.*, the remaining fifteen Nityās and the twelve Yoginīs, *viz.*, Vidyā-yoginī, Recikā-yoginī, Mocikā-yoginī, Amṛtā-yoginī, Dīpikā-yoginī, Jñāna-yoginī, Āpyāyanī-yoginī, Vyāpinī-yoginī, Medhā-yoginī, Vyoma-rūpā-yoginī, Siddhi-rūpā-yoginī and Lakṣmī-yogini, constituting forty-three in all, should be considered inherent in the forty-three angles of the *Śrī-cakra*, one in each. In the four door-ways, the four deities, *viz.*, Gandhākarṣinī, Rasākarṣiṇi, Rūpākarṣinī and Sparśākarṣiṇī, should be considered as inherent. This is how the Vaśinī, *etc.*, are considered to inhere in the *Śrī-cakra*. The worship of the *Śrī-cakra* as well as the successful accomplishment of the Yogic practice of rousing the Kuṇḍalinī and leading it to the *Sahasrāra*, thence back of the *Mūlādhāra*, by the Ṛṣis of yore is borne testimony to by the Taittirīyāraṇyaka, when it makes reference to the Pṛṣnis (Tait. I, 27).

त्वदीयं सौन्दर्यं तुहिनगिरिकन्ये तुलयितुं[1]
कवीन्द्राः कल्पन्तें कथमपि विरिञ्चि[2]प्रभृतयः।
[3]यदालोकौत्सुक्यादमरललना यान्ति मनसा
[4]तपोभिर्दुष्प्रापामपि गिरिशसायुज्यपदवीम्।। १२।।

Tvadīyaṃ saundaryaṃ tuhina-giri-kanye tulayituṃ
kavīndrāḥ kalpante katham api viriñci-prabhṛtayaḥ/
Yad-ālokautsukyād amara-lalanā yānti manasā
tapobhir duṣ-prāpām api giriśa-sāyujya-padavīm.//

---

1. कवयितुं।
2. विरंचि।
3. यदालोक्यौ.....।
4. पशूनाम्.।

Translation : O Daughter of the snow-capped Mountain! The foremost poets, such as Viriñci and others, are baulked in their attempt to find a suitable match for Thy extreme beauty, as (even) celestial damsels, in their eagerness to appreciate which, mentally attain at-one-ment with Śiva (Giriśa), which is hard to attain even by severe penance.

त्वदीयं तव सम्बन्धि त्वद्देहगतमित्यर्थः। **सौन्दर्यं** लावण्यम्। **तुहिनगिरिकन्ये** तुहिनप्रधानो गिरिः हिमाद्रिः तस्य कन्या पुत्री, तस्याः सम्बुद्धिः। **तुलयितुं** तुलया समीकर्तुम्। **कवीन्द्राः** विद्वच्छ्रेष्ठाः **कल्पन्ते** शक्नुवन्ति, **कथमपि** कथंचिदपि, न कल्पन्त इत्यर्थः। **विरिञ्चिप्रभृतयः** विरिञ्चः **ब्रह्मा** प्रभृतिर्येषां ते हरीन्द्रादयः। **यत्** यस्मात्कारणात् **आलोकौत्सुक्यात्** आलोके भवत्सौन्दर्यालोके यदौत्सुक्यं तस्मात्, ल्यब्लोपे पञ्चमी, औत्सुक्यमवलम्ब्य। यद्वा–निमित्तपञ्चमी। **अमरललनाः** देवयोषितः **यान्ति** प्राप्नुवन्ति, **मनसा** अन्तःकरणेन, **तपोभिः** तपस्याभिः कृच्छ्रचान्द्रायणादिभिः **दुष्प्रापां** प्राप्तुमशक्याम्, **अपिर्विरोधे गिरिशसायुज्यपदवीम्**।।

अत्रेत्थं पदयोजना—हे तुहिनगिरिकन्ये! त्वदीयं सौन्दर्यं तुलयितुं विरिञ्चिप्रभृतयः कवीन्द्राः कथमपि कल्पन्ते। यद्यस्मात्कारणात् अमरललनाः आलोकौत्सुक्यात् तपोभिः दुष्प्रापामपि गिरिशसायुज्यपदवीं मनसा यान्ति।।

अयमर्थः–वाणीपतिवाचस्पतिप्रभृतीनामपि त्वत्सौन्दर्यं सदृशान्तरं परिकल्प्य वर्णयितुमशक्यम्, त्वत्सदृशसुन्दरवस्त्वन्तराभावात्। ऊर्वशीतिलोत्तमादीनामप्सरसां त्वत्सौन्दर्यलेशतुलायामपि तत्कोटिप्रवेशो दूरत एवापास्तः। यतश्चाप्सरसः त्वत्सौन्दर्य-दर्शने पुम्भावं प्रार्थयमानाः पुरुषान्तरदुरधिगमे त्वत्सौन्दर्यवस्तुनि सदाशिवैकगम्ये दुर्लभसदाशिवसायुज्यमनोरथा वर्तन्त इति। स्वयमेवाप्सरसः स्वसौन्दर्ये जुगुप्सितवत्य इति भावः।।

अत्र अनन्वयालङ्कारो ध्वन्यते, लोके क्वापि तुल्यवस्तुनोऽसद्भावात् स्वस्य स्वयमेव तुल्यमिति प्रतीतेः।। १२।।

Notes : In this stanza the author extols, though indirectly, the Sāyujya, the state of at-one-ment brought about by the merger of Śiva and the Śakti, the presiding deity of the Ānandalaharī, after describing her abode, the *Śrī-cakra*, in the previous one.

The foremost poets—those that indulge in portraiture of the sublime and the beautiful, our of the flights of their fancy, with the aid of rhetorical devices. Brahman is here spoken of as one of the foremost poets, in fact the foremost among them, for the reason that he is the author of the most beautiful among created things, and any attempt made by a poet in this direction could but be a poor imitation of Brahman's artistic skill. Further the Vedas, which afford the sublimest examples of poesy, owe their origin to him. *Baulked*—because they do not command that power of mental analysis and expression which would enable them to draw a pen-picture of the Devīs beauty, at least in terms of equally beautiful objects. Their only possible resource in this respect would be the celestial nymphs. But these in their own estimate fall so far short of the Devī that, in their eagerness to have a look at her, they always think of Śiva, who alone has the privilege of enjoying the Devī's beauty at close quarters, and in their emulation become one with him. In the case of the reading *'Yadālokya'*—having seen which, 'Manasā'—with the mind, the meaning would be 'having meditated upon Thy beauty'. The celestial nymphs, by the sheer strength of such Dhyāna-yoga, attain that one-ness with Śiva, which is denied even to the greatest of sages. notwithstanding their severe austerities. There is another reading *'Paśūnām'* for *'tapobhiḥ'*—meaning 'by those who are *Paśus*' (animals), in that they do not follow the Tantras.

नरं वर्षीयासं नयनविरसं नर्मसु जडं
तवापाङ्गालोके पतितमनुधावन्ति शतशः।
गलद्वेणीबन्धाः कुचकलशविस्त्रस्तसिचया
हठात्त्रुट्यत्काञ्च्यो विगलितदुकूला युवतयः॥ १३॥

Naraṃ varṣīyāṃsaṃ nayana-virasaṃ narmasu jaḍaṃ
tavāpāṅgāloke patitam anudhāvanti śataśaḥ/
Galad-veṇī-bandhāḥ kuca-kalaśa-visrasta-sicayā
haṭhāt truṭyat-kāñcya vigalita-dukūlā yuvatayaḥ//

Translation : Damsels in hundred, with their locks dishevelled, their sarees flying of their figures, their girdles bursting asunder with force, their silk garment slipping down, run after a decrepit, ugly and impotent man, who falls within the range of Thy side-glances.

नरं मनुष्यमात्रं, **वर्षीयासम्** अतिवृद्धं, **नयनविरसम्** नयनाभ्यां विरसं काचकामिलपटलादिनेत्रदोषयुक्तम्, **नर्मसु जडं** नर्मसु रतिकलासु जडं अतिमूढम्, **तव** भवत्याः **अपाङ्गालोके** कटाक्षवीक्षणे, **पतितं** कटाक्षैकगोचरमित्यर्थः, **अनुधावन्ति**

अनुधावमाना: **शतश:** शतसङ्ख्याका:, शतशब्द: सङ्ख्यातीतोपलक्षक:, भूर्भुवस्स्व-र्लोकस्थिता: सर्वा इत्यर्थ:। **गलद्वेणीबन्धा:**, गलन्तो वेणीबन्धा यासां ता:; **कुचकलशविस्रस्तसिचया:** कुचकलशाभ्यां विस्रस्ता: शिथिला: सिचया: चेलाञ्चला यासां ता:, **हठात्त्रुट्यत्काञ्च्य:** हठात् शीघ्रं त्रुट्यन्त्य: गलन्त्य: काञ्च्यो रशनाकलापा: यासां ता:, **विगलितदुकूला:** स्रस्तनीवीबन्धा:, **युवतय:** तरुण्य:।।

अत्रेत्थं पदयोजना–हे भगवति! वर्षीयासं नयनविरसं नर्मसु जडं तवापाङ्गालोके पतितं नरं शतश: युवतय: गलद्वेणीबन्धा: कुचकलशविस्रस्तसिचया: हठात्त्रुट्य-त्काञ्च्य: विगलितदुकूला: सत्य: तादृशं नरं मदनमिति मत्वेति शेष:, अनुधावन्ति।।

एतादृशान् मादनप्रयोगान् **'मुखं बिन्दुं कृत्वा'**[1] इत्यादिश्लोकव्याख्यानावसरे निपुणतरमुपपादयिष्याम:।। १३।।

Notes : This stanza may be characterized as one wherein the poet's fancy has run riot, in extolling the potency of the Devī's side-glances. If any description, in the true classic style, of women unhinged by the influence of passion is to be attempted by the saintliest of poets, it is to be met with in this stanza.

Run after—madly follow in the wake of, in the belief that he is Madana incarnate. To the exquisitely beautiful side-glances of the Devī is attributed the virtue of converting even the most repulsive into the most attractive in this stanza, and the same feature is dwelt upon further in the eighteenth and nineteenth stanzas *infra*, the motif in all the three cases being to raise Kāma, the satisfaction of desire and passion, to the rank of one of the four *Puruṣārthas*, the ends and aims of human existence. This is what is known as the Mādana-prayoga.

क्षितौ षट्पञ्चाशद् द्विसमधिकपञ्चाशदुदके
हुताशे द्वाषष्टि[2]श्चतुरधिकपञ्चाशदनिले।[3]
दिवि द्वि:षट्त्रिंशन्मनसि च चतु:षष्टिरिति[4] ये
मयूखास्तेषामप्युपरि तव पादाम्बुजयुगम्।। १४।।

Kṣitau ṣaṭ-pañcāśad dvi-samadhika-pañcāśad udake
hutāśe dvā-ṣaṣṭiś catur-adhika-pañcāśad anile/
Divi dviḥ-ṣaṭ-triṃśan manasi ca catuḥ-ṣaṣṭir iti ye
mayūkhās teṣām apy upari tava pādāmbuja yugam.//

1. १९ श्लोक:।
2. द्वाषष्ठि।
3. .... पंचाशदनले।
4. चतु:षष्ठिरिति।

Translation : The pair of lotus-like feet is far above those says, *viz.*, the fifty-six (rays) of (the *Mūlādhāra*, of the character of) Earth, the fifty-two of (the *Maṇi-pūra*, of the character of) Water, the sixty-two of (the *Svādhiṣṭhāna* of the character of) Fire, the fifty-four of (the *An-āhata*, of the character of) Air, the seventy Ether, and the sixty-four of (the *Ājñā*, of the character of) the Mind.

क्षितौ पृथिवीतत्त्वयुक्ते मूलाधारे **षट्पञ्चाशत्** षडुत्तरपञ्चाशत्संख्याकाः, **द्विसमधिकपञ्चाशत्** द्वाभ्यां समधिकाः पञ्चाशत् **उदके** उदकतत्त्वयुक्ते मणिपूरस्थाने, **हुताशे** वह्नितत्त्वयुक्ते स्वाधिष्ठानचक्रे, **द्वाषष्टिः** द्वौ च षष्टिश्च द्वाषष्टिः। 'विभाषा चत्वारिंशत्प्रभृतौ सर्वेषाम्' इति सूत्रेण द्विशब्दादिकारस्य आकारः। **चतुरधिकपञ्चाशत्** चतुस्संख्यया अधिकाः पञ्चाशत्, **अनिले** वायुतत्त्वयुक्ते अनाहतचक्रे, **दिवि** आकाशतत्त्वयुक्ते विशुद्धिचक्रे **द्विष्षट्त्रिंशत्** द्विरावृत्तषट्त्रिंशत्संख्याकाः द्विसप्तति-सङ्ख्याका इत्यर्थः, **मनसि**[1] मनस्तत्त्वयुक्ते आज्ञाचक्रे, **चतुष्षष्टिः**। इति एवंप्रकारेण ये प्रसिद्धाः शास्त्रेषु आगमेषु, स्वासंवेद्यत्वेन च योगिनां प्रसिद्धाः **मयूखाः** सन्ति **तेषां** मयूखानां **अप्युपरि** सहस्रदलमध्यवर्तिचन्द्रबिम्बात्मके बैन्दवापरनामके सुधासिन्धौ, **तव** भवत्याः, **पादाम्बुजयुगं** वर्तते विद्यते। एवं समयसम्प्रदाय इति शेषः।।

अत्रेत्थं पदयोजना-हे भगवति! ये मयूखाः क्षितौ षट्पञ्चाशत्, उदके द्विसमधिकपञ्चाशत्, हुताशे द्वाषष्टिः, अनिले चतुरधिकपञ्चाशत्, दिवि द्विष्षट्त्रिंशत्, मनसि चतुष्षष्टिः, इति तेषामुपरि तव पादाम्बुजयुगं वर्तते इति शेषः।।

अत्र षट्पञ्चाशदित्यादिसङ्ख्याशब्दानां सङ्ख्येयपरत्वात् सङ्ख्येयानां मयूखानां बहुत्वेऽपि एकवचनान्तत्वमेव। यथा-

> विंशत्याद्याः सदैकत्वे सर्वाः सङ्ख्येयसङ्ख्ययोः।
> सङ्ख्यार्थे द्विबहुत्वे स्तः..........................।।

न तु संख्येये इति नियमात्। संख्येयानां मयूखानां नियमाप्रसक्तेः बहुवचनान्तत्वं सिद्धम्। अत्रेदं तत्त्वम्—षट्पञ्चाशदित्यादिसंख्यानां संख्येयविशेषणत्वेऽपि न शुक्लादिगुणतौल्यं, यथाऽऽह पदमञ्जरीकारः-'विंशत्यादयो गुणाः न शुक्लादिभिः गुणैः समानधर्माणो भवितुमर्हन्ति। विंशत्यादयो हि तावत् पृथक्त्वयोगिषु द्रव्येषु वर्तन्त इति व्यासज्यवृत्तयः, शुक्लादयस्तु प्रत्येकपर्यवसायिनः' इति। अत्रेदमति-रहस्यम्-संख्येयपराणां संख्याशब्दानां बहुवचने षट्पञ्चाशतो मयूखा इति प्राप्तौ

1. मनः शब्देन एकादशेन्द्रियाणां ग्रहणम्।

षट्त्रिंशदुत्तरशतोत्तरत्रिसहस्रसंख्याकाः भवेयुः। अतो विवक्षितार्थसिद्धिरिति नियमफलमिति।

अत्रेदमनुसन्धेयम्–आधारस्वाधिष्ठानमणिपूरानहतविशुद्ध्याज्ञाचक्रात्मकं श्रीचक्रं त्रिखण्डं सोमसूर्यानलात्मकम्। मूलाधारस्वाधिष्ठानचक्रद्वयमेकं खण्डम्। मणिपूरानाहतचक्रद्वयमेकं खण्डम्। विशुद्ध्याज्ञाचक्रद्वयमेकं खण्डम्। अत्र प्रथमखण्डोपरि अग्निस्थानम्। तदेव रुदग्रन्थिरित्युच्यते। द्वितीयखण्डोपरि सूर्यस्थानम्। तदेव विष्णुग्रन्थिरित्युच्यते। तृतीयखण्डोपरि चन्द्रस्थानम्। तदेव ब्रह्मग्रन्थिरित्युच्यते। 'सोमसूर्यानलात्मकं' इति अवरोहणक्रमेणावगन्तव्यम्। तत्र प्रथमखण्डोपरि स्थितो वह्निः स्वज्वालाभिः प्रथमखण्डमावृणोति। द्वितीयखण्डोपरि स्थितः सूर्यः स्वकीयैः किरणैः द्वितीयखण्डमावृणोति। तृतीयखण्डोपरि स्थितः चन्द्रः स्वकलाभिः तृतीयखण्डमावृणोति। आधारचक्रे महीतत्त्वात्मके वह्नेः षट्पञ्चाशज्ज्वालाः, मणिपूरके उदकतत्त्वात्मके स्वोपरिस्थिते द्विपञ्चाशज्ज्वालाः। एवमष्टोत्तरशतं वह्नेः ज्वालाः। सूर्यस्य अग्नितत्त्वात्मके स्वाधिष्ठाने द्वाषष्टिकिरणाः, अनिलतत्त्वात्मके अनाहतचक्रे चतुःपञ्चाशत्किरणाः। सूर्यकिरणानां मणिपूरं विहाय स्वाधिष्ठानप्रवेशः सूर्याग्न्योरेकत्वात्, सूर्यान्तर्भावादग्नेश्च। स्वाधिष्ठानमणिपूरयोस्तु सूर्याग्निस्थानयोः मध्ये अग्निस्थाने सूर्यप्रवेशः सूर्यस्थाने अग्निप्रवेशः जगद्दहनाग्निशामक[1]संवर्तमेघात्मकसूर्यकिरणजनितवर्षोत्पत्त्यर्थम्। एतत्तु **'तटित्वन्तं शक्त्या'**[2] इत्यादिश्लोकव्याख्यानावसरे निपुणतरमुपपादयिष्यामः। एवं सूर्यस्य षोडशोत्तरशतं किरणा भवन्ति। चन्द्रस्य कलाः वियत्तत्वात्मके विशुद्धिचक्रे द्विसप्ततिः, मनस्तत्त्वात्मके आज्ञाचक्रे चतुष्षष्टिः। एवं चन्द्रस्य षट्त्रिंशदुत्तरशतं कलाः भवन्ति। यथोक्तं भैरवयामळे भैरवाष्टकप्रस्तावे–

अष्टोत्तरशतं वह्नेः षोडशोत्तरकं रवेः।
षट्त्रिंशदुत्तरशतं चन्द्रस्य च विनिर्णयः।। इति।।

एवं सोमसूर्यानलाः पिण्डाण्डब्रह्माण्डे आवृत्य वर्तन्ते। पिण्डाण्डब्रह्माण्डयोरैक्यात् पिण्डाण्डवृतिरेव ब्रह्माण्डावृतिरिति रहस्यम्। एवं पिण्डाण्डमतीत्य[3] वर्तते सहस्रकमलम्। तच्च ज्योत्स्नामयो लोकः। तत्रत्यश्चन्द्रमा नित्यकलः। एतच्च **'तवाज्ञाचक्रस्थम्'**[4] इत्यादिश्लोकव्याख्यानावसरे निपुणतरमुपपादयिष्यामः। 'आज्ञाचक्रोपरि स्थितश्चन्द्रः'

---

1. 'नामक' इत्यपि पाठः।
2. ४० श्लोकः।
3. 'आवृत्य' इत्यपि पाठः।
4. ३६ श्लोकः।

इति यदुक्तं तत्तु चन्द्रकलावस्थानमात्रम्, न तु चन्द्रस्य स्थानमिति। यदुक्तं सुभगोदये–षोडशकलानां षोडशनित्यात्मकत्वात्, तासां प्रतिपदादिशुक्लपक्षकृष्णपक्षतिथ्यात्मकतया वृद्धिक्षयसद्भावात्, चन्द्रस्यापि सहस्रकमलगतस्य वृद्धिक्षयौ भवत एवेति, तत्तु चन्द्रमसः वृद्धिक्षयौ न भवतः, किन्तु षोडशनित्यात्मकाः षोडशचन्द्रकलाः[1] प्रतिपदादिपौर्णमास्यन्ततिथिप्रवर्तिकाः, तथैव कृष्णप्रतिपदमारभ्य अमावस्यान्त[2] तिथिप्रवर्तिकाः स्वात्मतिरोधानातिरोधानाभ्यामिति मन्त्रविद्रहस्यम्।।

इदमत्रानुसन्धेयम्–श्रीविद्यायाः चन्द्रकलाविद्यापरनामधेयायाः पञ्चदशतिथिरूपत्वात् षष्ट्युत्तरत्रिशतं मयूखाः दिवात्मकाः, तेन संवत्सरो लक्ष्यते। तस्य कालशक्त्यात्मकस्य संवत्सरस्य प्रजापतिरूपत्वात्, प्रजापतेः जगत्कर्तृत्वात्, मरीचीनां जगदुत्पत्तिस्थितिलयकरत्वम्। ते च मरीचयः अस्मिन् ब्रह्माण्डे पिण्डाण्डे च षष्ट्युत्तरत्रिशतसंख्याकाः। एवं अनन्तकोटिपिण्डाण्डब्रह्माण्डेषु। एवमेव प्रतिब्रह्माण्डं प्रतिपिण्डाण्डं षष्ट्युत्तरत्रिशतसंख्याकाः मयूखाः। अतश्चानन्तमयूखाः। ते च मयूखाः सूर्यचन्द्राग्निसम्पृक्ताः भगवतीपादारविन्दजन्मानः तान् तान् लोकान् प्रकाशयन्ति। **अयं च लो॒कस्य॑ द्वार॑मर्चि॒मत्प॒वित्र॑म्**'[3] इति श्रुत्या मयूखानां भगवतीपादारविन्दसम्भव उक्तः। तथैव च '**मरी॑चयस्स्वाय॒ंभुवाः**'[4] इति श्रुत्या तेषां मरीचीनां सृष्टिस्थितिलयकरत्वमुक्तम्। एतदुक्तं भवति–सूर्यचन्द्राग्नयः भगवतीपादारविन्दोद्भूतानन्तकोटिकिरणमध्ये कतिपयान् किरणानाहृत्य भगवतीप्रसादसमासादितजगत्प्रकाशनसामर्थ्यात् जगन्ति प्रकाशयन्तीति। अतश्च सर्वलोकातिक्रान्तं चन्द्रकलाचक्रं बैन्दवस्थानमिति। तत्र वर्तमानं चरणाम्बुजम्। अनेककोटिब्राह्मण्डपिण्डाण्डावच्छिन्नमयूखानां उपर्येव वर्तमानत्वात् 'तेषामप्युपरि तव पादाम्बुजं तर्तते' इति सिद्धानुवादः, न त्वारोपस्तुतिरित्यनुसन्धेयम्। यथोक्तं भैरवयामळे चन्द्रज्ञानविद्यायां गौरीं प्रति महेश्वरेण–

साधु साधु महाभागे पृष्टं त्रैलोक्यसुन्दरि।
गुह्याद्गुह्यतमं ज्ञानं न कुत्रापि प्रकाशितम्।।
कलाविद्या पराशक्तेः[5] श्रीचक्राकाररूपिणी।
तन्मध्ये बैन्दवस्थानं तत्रास्ते परमेश्वरी।।

---

1. 'चन्द्राः' इत्येव क्वचित्पाठः।
2. 'अमावास्याप्रभृति कृष्णप्रतिपदन्त'। इति बहुषु कोशेषु पाठः।
3. तै०ब्रा० ३-१२-३।
4. तै० आ० १-२७।
5. 'शक्तिः' इति च पाठः।

सदाशिवेन सम्पृक्ता सर्वतत्त्वातिगा सती।
चक्रं त्रिपुरसुन्दर्याः ब्रह्माण्डाकारमीश्वरि।।
पञ्चभूतात्मकं चैव तन्मात्रात्मकमेव च।
इन्द्रियात्मकमेवं च मनस्तत्त्वात्मकं तथा।।
मायादितत्त्वरूपं च तत्त्वातीतं च बैन्दवम्।
बैन्दवे जगदुत्पत्तिस्थितिसंहारकारिणी।
सदाशिवेन सम्पृक्ता तत्त्वातीता महेश्वरी।
ज्योतीरूपा पराकारा यस्या देहोद्भवाश्शिवे।।
किरणाश्च सहस्रं च द्विसहस्रं च लक्षकम्।
कोटिरर्बुदमेतेषां परा सङ्ख्या न विद्यते।।
तामेवानुप्रविश्यैव भाति लोकं चराचरम्।
यस्या देव्या महेशानि भासा सर्वं विभासते।
तद्भासा रहितं किञ्चित् न च यच्च प्रकाशते।
तस्याश्च शिवशक्तेश्च चिद्रूपायाश्चितिं विना।।
आन्ध्यमापद्यते नूनं जगदेतच्चराचरम्।
तेषामनन्तकोटीनां मयूखानां महेश्वरि।।
मध्ये षष्ट्युत्तरं तेऽमी त्रिशतं किरणाश्शिवे।
ब्रह्माण्डं व्यश्नुवानास्ते सोमसूर्यानलात्मना।।
अग्नेरष्टोत्तरशतं षोडशोत्तरकं रवेः।
षट्त्रिंशदुत्तरशतं चन्द्रस्य किरणाश्शिवे।।
ब्रह्माण्डं भासयन्तस्ते पिण्डाण्डमपि शाङ्करि।
दिवा सूर्यस्तथा रात्रौ सोमो वह्निश्च सन्ध्ययोः।।
प्रकाशयन्तः कालांस्ते तस्मात्कालात्मकास्त्रयः।
षष्ट्युत्तरं च त्रिशतं दिनान्येव च हायनम्।।
हायनात्मा महादेवः प्रजापतिरिति श्रुतिः।
प्रजापतिर्लोककर्ता मरीचिप्रमुखान् मुनीन्।।
[1]सृजन्त्येते लोकपालान् ते सर्वे लोकरक्षकाः।
संहारश्च हरायत्तः उत्पत्तिर्भवनिर्मिता।।
रक्षा तु मृडसंलग्ना सृष्टिस्थितिलये शिवः।
नियुक्तः परमेशान्या जगदेवं प्रवर्तते।। इति।।

1. सृजन्ति ते।

'तामेवानुप्रविश्य' इत्यादिना—'तमेव भान्तमनुभाति सर्वं तस्य भासा सर्वमिदं विभाति[1]' इति श्रुत्यर्थोऽनूदितः। अत्र बहु वक्तव्यमस्ति, तदुत्तरत्र सम्यङ्निरूपयिष्यामः।।

Notes : In this stanza and exalted nature of the Devī's pair of feet, resting on the *Sahasrāra*, is described in detail, with reference to the six *Cakras* below the *Sahasrāra*. The Mayūkhas referred to in this stanza may be understood from four different points of view. (1) They are rays effulging from Agni, Sūrya and Soma, having as their position the Rudra, Viṣṇu- and Brahmā- granthis, over contiguous pairs of the six *Cakras* in the ascending order, their number being three hundred and sixty in all. (2) They indicate the lunar year of 360 Tithis, each Tithi representing a digit of the Moon, with the six seasons, Vasanta, Grīṣma, Varṣā, Śarad, Hemanta and Śiśira, corresponding to the six *Cakras*, and the Devī's feet standing above them all as : *Nāda* and *Bindu*, being Kālāgocara (transcending all time). (3) The Mayūkhas may be taken to indicate the several Tattvas represented by the elements corresponding to the Cakras, in two sets, so that one set may be ascribed to the Śakti and the other to Śiva, the Devīs feet being Tattvātīta and therefore transcending them all. (4) The Mayūkhas may also be construed as the Mātṛkās or letters of the Alphabet grouped as follows : 1. The fifty letter of the Alphabet, 'Kṣa' being left out of account, and the Bīja's 'Aiṃ', 'Hrīṃ', 'Śrīṃ', 'Aiṃ', 'Klīṃ' and 'Sauḥ', indicative of Earth. 2. The fifty letters as above and the Bījas 'Sauṃ' and 'Śrīṃ', of Water. The fifty letters, the fourteenth letter repeated four times, the Bīja-s 'Haṃ' and 'Saḥ', repeated four times, of Fire. 4. The fifty letters and 'Yaṃ', 'Raṃ', 'La' and 'Vaṃ', of Air. 5. The first fourteen vowels repeated five times and the Bīja-s 'Aiṃ' and 'Hrīṃ', of Ether. 6. The sixteen vowels repeated four times, of the Manas. It is said that with the three hundred and sixty syllables thus arrived at, together with 'Haṃ' and 'Saḥ', the requisite Nyāsa should be performed in the six *Cakras*. (*Vide* : Introduction to *Serpent-Power*, by Arthur Avalon).

According to the first of these views each ray is given a distinct Āvaraṇa-devatā of its own. In this classification are involved two kinds of Tantras, the Pūrva and the Uttara, the first pertaining to the Śakti and hence known as Śākta and the second pertaining to

1. कठ० ५-२५।

Śiva and styled Śāṃbhava. From the conjunction of the non-differentiated All-Witness, Śiva with the Śakti for the creation of the world, there effulges a radiance, known as Parā, pervading from the *Brahma-randhra* to the *Ājñā* in the middle of the eyebrows. This is known as the deity presiding over the humour Majjā—marrow. By her are generated the five deities known as Icchā, Jñāna, Kriyā, Kuṇḍalinī and Mātṛkā, manifesting themselves respectively in the *Viśuddhi* of the throat, typifying Ether, in the *An-āhata* of the heart, typifying Air, in the *Maṇi-pūra* of the navel, typifying Water, in the *Svādhiṣṭhāna* of the genitals, typifying Fire, and in the *Mūlādhāra* of the region above the anus, typifying Earth, presiding over Tvac, Asṛj, Māṁsa, Medas and Asthi and making up the entire, creation, animate and inanimate. The number of rays pertaining to Agni and manifesting in the *Mūlādhāra* and the *Maṇipūra* enveloping the first Khaṇḍa is 108. The number of rays of the Sun manifesting in the *Svādhiṣṭhāna* and the *Anāhata* and enveloping the second Khaṇḍa is 116.[1] The number of rays of the Moon manifesting in the *Viśuddhi* and the *Ājñā* and enveloping the third Khaṇḍa is 136. It has to be observed that the Moon of this region with its fifteen waxing and waning Kalās is but a reflection of the full Moon with perpetaul Kalās which has its place in the middle of the *Sahasrāra.* Kaivalyāśrama gives the names of the 360 deities presiding over the Mayūkhas in the order of the groups given in this stanza. These names are mentioned in the footnote under stanzas 36-41.

These rays are also looked upon as representing the Eternal Verities in the following manner : The five Tanmātra-s, the five elements, the ten organs of perception and motor action, the four Antaḥ-karaṇa-s, Kalā, Prakṛti, Puruṣa and Mahat, twenty-eight in all, duplicated so as to represent the Śakti and Śiva, yield fifty-six

---

1. The Sun and Fire, it should be understood, are of identical nature. The Sun shines over the Svādhiṣṭhāna and the An-āhata which lies beyond the Maṇīpūra. Fire blazed forth in the Mūlādhāra and the Maṇipūra which lies beyond the Svādhiṣṭhāna. Thus, there is an interlacing of the two regions. This is explained thus : the rays of the Sun have the power of evaporating moisture, which is then condensed into clouds during the Mahā-pralaya. In the event of the Fire blazing forth to devastate the Microcosm as well as the Macrocosm, the tremendous downpour from the gathered Saṁvarta clouds will have the effect of quenching the flame and bringing it under control.

as pertaining to Earth. The five elements, the ten organs of perception and motor action, their ten distinctive functions and Manas, twenty-six in all, duplicated as above, yield fifty-two as of Water. The five elements, the five *tanmātras,* the ten organs of perception and motor action, their ten distinctive functions and Manas, thirty-one in all, duplicated as above, yield sixty-two as of Agni. The twenty-eight Tattvas of Earth, excluding Mahat therefrom, *i.e.,* the twenty-seven so obtained, when duplicated as above, yield fifty-four as of Vāyu. The thirty-six Tattvas of the Kalpasūtras (*vide* note under stanza 9) duplicated as above yield seventy-two as of Ether. The same Tattvas excluding the last four, *i.e.,* thirty-two, when duplicated, yield sixty-four as of the Manas. These rays are generated in the first instance from the Devī's feet and are thence derived by the Moon, the Sun and Fire, who worship at her feet, for the evolution of the world. The special qualities possessed by these rays are described in detail in Bhairava-yāmala. The *Śrī-vidyā* is otherwise known as the Candra-kalā-vidyā or the lore relating to the waxing and waning of the fifteen Kalās, represented by the fifteen Tithis of the Pūrva-and Aparapakṣas, which form the basis of calculating duration. The year, which is thus one aspect of the manifestation of the Kāla-śakti, is said to be Prajāpati, the creator. Hence, these rays are verily the cause of the creation, sustenance and dissolution of the universe, the Microcosm as well as the Macrocosm. As there are myriads of such Microcosms and Macrocosm affected by the Sun, the Moon and Fire, through whom are diffused these rays which originate from the Devī's feet, the Mayūkhas referred to are not merely three hundred and sixty, but infinite. It also follows that the Baindavasthāna of the Candrakalā-cakra, wherein the Devī reigns supreme and wherefrom these rays originate and manifest themselves, transcends all worlds for all time.

सारस्वतप्रयोगमाह–

शरज्ज्योत्स्नाशुभ्रां[1] शशियुतजटाजूटमकुटां[2]
वरत्रासत्राणस्फटिकघुटिका[3]पुस्तककराम्[4] ।

---

1. शरज्जोत्स्नाशुद्धां ।
2. मुकुटां ।
3. घटिका ; गुणिका ; गुटिका ।
4. पुस्तकधरां ।

सकृन्न त्वां[1] नत्वा कथमिव[2] सतां संनिदधते
मधुक्षीरद्राक्षामधुरिमधुरीणा भणितयः[3] ।। १५ ।।

Śaraj-jyotsnā-śubhrāṃ-śaśī-yuta-jaṭā-jūṭa-makuṭāṃ
vara-trāsa-trāṇa-sphaṭika-ghuṭikā-pustaka-karām/
Sakṛnna tvāṃ natvā katham iva satāṃ saṃnidadhate
madhu-kṣīra-drākṣā-madhurima-dhurīṇā bhaṇi-tayaḥ//

Translation : How will worlds, which are of the sweetness of honey, milk and grap-juice, not be in the command of such as have bowed even once to Thee, who art bright as the autumnal moon-beams, who hast as Thy crown the coiled plaited-hair with the (crescent) Moon on, and who holdest in Thy hand the boon-bestowing (and) the security-affording (postures), a rosary of crystal beads and a book?

शरज्ज्योत्स्नाशुद्धां—शरदि शरत्काले ज्योत्स्ना चन्द्रिका तद्वच्छुद्धां अतिशुभ्राम्। **शशियुतजटाजूटमकुटां**—शशिना चन्द्रेण युतो युक्तः जटा जूटो मकुटो यस्यास्तां, चन्द्रकलावंतसामित्यर्थः। **वरत्रासत्राणस्फटिकघटिकापुस्तककराम्**—वरः इष्टदान-मुद्रा, त्रासत्राणं अभयदानमुद्रा, स्फटिकघटिका स्फटिकपानपात्रम्। स्फटिकाक्षमालेति केचित्। तत्पक्षे स्फटिक-गुलिकेति[4] पाठः। पुस्तकं विद्यामुद्रा, पुस्तकं वा, एतैर्युक्तकराम्। शाकपार्थिवादित्वात् मध्यमपदलोपः। न तु स्फटिकघटिकापुस्तकानि करेषु यस्याः इति सप्तमीबहुब्रीहिः। 'प्रहरणादिभ्य उपसङ्ख्यानम्' इति तस्य प्रहरणादिभ्य एवेति नियतत्वात्। **सकृत्** एकवारम्, नकारो निषेधार्थः, त्वा त्वामित्यर्थः, **नत्वा** नमस्कारं कृत्वा **कथं** कथंचित्, इवेति वाक्यालङ्कारे, **सतां** कवीश्वराणाम्, **संनिदधते** संनिधानं प्राप्नुवन्ति। **मधुक्षीरद्राक्षामधुरिमधुरीणाः फणितयः**—मधु क्षौद्रं, क्षीरं पयः, द्राक्षा मृद्वीका, एतेषां मधुरिमा माधुर्यं, तत्र धुरीणाः **धुरं** वहन्तीति धुरीणाः अग्रेसराः तद्वन्मधुरा इत्यर्थः। फणितयः वाग्वैखर्यः।।

अत्रेत्थं पदयोजना—हे भगवति! शरज्ज्योत्स्नाशुद्धां शशियुतजटाजूटमकुटां वरत्रासत्राणास्फटिकघटिकापुस्तककरां त्वा सकृन्नत्वा सतां मधुक्षीरद्राक्षामधुरिमधुरीणाः फणितयः कथमिव न सन्निदधते।।

---

1. सकृन्नत्वा नत्वां ; सकृन्नत्वा नु त्वां।
2. कथमपि।
3. .....धुरीणाः फणितयः।
4. 'घुटिका' इत्यपि पाठः।

अयमर्थः–अत्र व्यतिरेकमुखेन सकृन्नमस्कारोऽपि कवित्वबीजभूतसंस्कारोत्पादकः। तदभावे प्रकारान्तरेण येन केनापि तद्वीजोत्पत्तिर्नास्तीति सूचितम्।। १५ ।।

Notes : Even as the miraculous effect of the Devī's side-glance has been adverted to in the thirteenth stanza, the marvellous powers inherent in approaching the Devī with the right kind of meditation and prayer are expounded in this and the six accompanying stanzas. In this stanza is described the greatness of meditation of the Sāttvika type on the Devī's form, through the Vāgbhava-kūṭa of the Pañcadaśākṣarī. *To Thee*—the Devī in the form of the Vāgbhava-kūṭa. Bowing even once to the Devī is credited with making the Upāsaka a great poet and attain all knowledge. The Devī is said to be in the form of Kriyā-śakti, when meditated upon as the source of poetic talents. This stanza and the next two are spoken of as referring to the Sārasvata-prayoga.

कवीन्द्राणां चेतःकमलवनबालातपरुचिं
भजन्ते ये सन्तः कतिचिदरुणामेव भवतीम्।
[1]**विरिञ्चिप्रेयस्यास्तरुणतरशृङ्गारलहरी–**
गभीराभिर्वाग्भिर्विदधति सतां रञ्जनममी[2]।। १६ ।।

Kavīndrāṇāṃ cetaḥ-kamala-vana-bālātaparuciṃ
bhajante ye santaḥ kati cid aruṇām eva bhavatīm/
Viriñci-preyasyās taruṇa-tara-śṛṅgāra-laharī—
gabhīrābhir vāgbhir vidadhati satāṃ rañjanam amī.//

Translation : Such rare, high-souled men, who worship Thee as Aruṇā, radiant as the morning sun-light, (causing) the lotus-like minds of great poets (to bloom), delight (the assembly of) wise men, with their diction, profound like the fresh flood of erotic sentiments flowing from Viriñci's beloved spouse, *i.e,* Sarasvatī, the goddess of learning.

कवीन्द्राणां कवीश्वराणाम्, **चेतःकमलवनबालातपरुचिं**–चेतांस्येव कमलानि पद्मानि, तेषां वनं षण्डं, तस्य बालातपरुचिः प्राभातिकारुणकान्तिः, तां **भजन्ते** सेवन्ते, **ये सन्तः** सत्पुरुषाः, **कतिचित्** विरलाः, **अरुणामेव** अरुणाख्यां अरुणवर्णां च, **भवतीं त्वां**, **विरिञ्चिप्रेयस्याः** विरिञ्चिः ब्रह्मा तस्य प्रेयस्याः प्रियायाः सरस्वत्याः,

1. विरिञ्चिप्रेयस्यास्तरलतर.....।
2. सभा रंजनममी।

तरुणतरशृङ्गारलहरीगभीराभिः तरुणतरे अतियौवने। यद्वा–तरुणतरश्चासौ शृङ्गारश्च तस्य लहरी उद्रिक्तप्रवाहः। यद्वा–लहरीशब्देन समुद्रस्य चन्द्रोदये यादृश उत्सेकः सः उच्यते। लहरीयुक्तगभीराभिः अतिगम्भीराभिरित्यर्थः। **वाग्भिः** वाग्विलासैः। **विदधति** कुर्वन्ति, **सतां** सभासदां, **रञ्जनं** हृदयानुरञ्जनम्, **अमी** सन्तः परामृश्यन्ते।।

अत्रेत्थं पदयोजना—हे भगवति! कवीन्द्राणां चेतःकमलवनबालातपरुचिं अरुणामेव भवतीं कतिचित् ये सन्तः भजन्ते, अमी सन्तःविरिञ्चिप्रेयस्याः तरुणतरशृङ्गारलहरी-गभीराभिः वाग्भिः सतां रञ्जनं विदधति।।

अयमर्थः–हृदयकमले भगवतीमरुणां ध्यायन्तः पुम्भावमापन्ना सरस्वतीव शृङ्गाररसप्रधानैः वाग्विलासैः सभारञ्जनं कुर्वन्ति। भगवत्याः मातृकात्मकत्वात् सरस्वतीरूपत्वेनैव सारस्वतप्रदत्वम्। अरुणवर्णध्यानमहिम्ना शृङ्गाररसप्राधान्येन वाग्विलासप्रवृत्तिरिति। यथोक्तं वामकेश्वरतन्त्रे–

अरुणाख्यां भगवतीं अरुणाभां विचिन्तयेत्।
पाशाङ्कुशधरां देवीं धनुर्बाणधरां शिवाम्।।
वरदाभयहस्तां च पुस्तकाक्षस्रगन्विताम्।
अष्टबाहुं त्रिनयनां खेलन्तीममृताम्बुधौ।।
स करोत्येव शृङ्गाररसास्वादनलम्पटान्।
सभासदः सदा सर्वान् साधकेन्द्रः सभास्थले।। इति।।

अत्र परम्परितं रूपकमलङ्कारः, बालतपरुचित्वारोपणस्य चेतसि कमलत्वारोपणस्य निमित्तत्वात्, 'रूपकहेतुरूपकं परम्परितम्' इति लक्षणात्।। १६।।

Notes : The gift of poesy, at the result of exclusive worship of the Devī as Aruṇā in the heart of the votary, is indicated in the stanza. The greatness of meditation of the Rājasic type on the Devī's form, through the Vāgbhava-kūṭa, is indicated in this stanza. Some are of opinion that, for the reason that there is reference in this stanza to erotic sentiment, the Deva as Icchā-śakti presiding over the Kāma-rāja kūṭa is indicated in this stanza. *Minds—i.e.,* hearts. Poets, who meditate on the Devī as Aruṇā in their heart-lotuses, becomes, as a result of the Devī's grace, so many Sarasvatīs for the nonce, and with the choice diction and command of erotic sentiments, characteristic only of the Goddess of Learning, delight the assembly of wise men; in other words, the Devī has the power of converting her votaries into as many Sarasvatīs.

सवित्रीभिर्वाचां शशिमणिशिलाभङ्गरुचिभिः–
र्वशिन्याद्याभिस्त्वां सह जननि संचिन्तयति यः।
स कर्ता काव्यानां भवति[1] महतां भङ्गिसुभगै–[2]
र्वचोभिर्वाग्देर्वीवदनकमलामोदमधुरैः ।।१७।।

Savitrībhir vācāṃ śaśi-maṇi-śilā-bhaṅga-rucibhir
vaśiny-ādyābhis tvāṃ saha janani saṃ-cintayati yaḥ/
Sa kartā kāvyānāṃ bhavati mahatāṃ bhaṅgi-subhagair
vacobhir vāg-devī-vadana-kamalāmoda-madhuraiḥ//

Translation : O Mother! whoever contemplates Thee along with the generators of speech, Vaśinī and others, who are resplendent like the freshly cut moon-stones, becomes the author of great Kāvyas (epics), replete with words erudite in style and sweet with the fragrance of the lotus-like mouth of the Goddess of Learning or speech, *i.e.*, Sarasvatī.

सवित्रीभिः जनयित्रीभिः, **वाचां** गिरां, **शशिमणिशिलाभङ्गरुचिभिः** चन्द्रकान्तमणिशकलतुल्यकान्तिभिः, दलितचन्द्रकान्तमणेः अतिधावल्यं लोकसिद्धम्। **वशिन्याद्याभिः** वशिनीप्रमुखाभिः। तद्गुणसंविज्ञानो बहुव्रीहिः–वशिनी आद्या यासां ताः शक्तयोऽष्टौ वशिन्याद्याः, योगिन्यो द्वादश, गन्धाकर्षिण्यादयश्चतस्रः, इति वशिन्याद्याः। अत्र एकस्य आद्यशब्दस्य लोपः–वशिन्याद्याद्या इत्यर्थः। वशिन्यष्टकं– वशिनी, कामेश्वरी, मोदिनी, विमला, अरुणा, जयिनी, सर्वेश्वरी, कौलिनी। एताभिः **त्वां** भवतीं, **सह** साकं, **जननि**! हे मातः! **सञ्चिन्तयति यः**, **सः**साधकः **कर्ता** रचयिता, **काव्यानां** प्रबन्धानां, **भवति** समर्थः प्रभवति। **महतां** महात्मनां कालिदास– प्रभृतीनां, **भङ्गिरुचिभिः** भङ्गीनां रेखाणां, रुचिभिः स्वादुभिः **वचोभिः** वाग्विलासैः, **वाग्देवीवदनकमलामोदमधुरैः** वाग्देव्या भारत्याः वदनकमले यः आमोदः परिमलः तेन मधुरैः अव्यक्तैः, पुंभावमापन्नायाः भारत्याः वाग्विलासाः इमे इत्येवं भ्रमजनकैरित्यर्थः।।

अत्रेत्थं पदयोजना–हे जननि! वाचां सवित्रीभिःशशिमणिशिलाभङ्गरुचिभिः 'वशिन्याद्याभिः सह त्वां यः सञ्चिन्तयति, सह महतां भङ्गिरुचिभिः वाग्देवीवदन- कमलामोदमधुरैः वचोभिः काव्यानां कर्ता भवति।।

---

1. कविताभंगि।
2. भङ्गिरुचिभिः।

अत्रेदमनुसन्धेयम्–'वशिन्याद्याभिः त्वां' इत्यत्र त्वामित्यनेन भगवत्याः स्वरूपमुक्तम्। भगवत्याः स्वरूपं तु पञ्चाशद्वर्णात्मिका मातृकैव। एतत्तु '**शिवं शक्तिः कामः**'[1] इत्यादिश्लोकव्याख्यानावसरे प्रपञ्चयिष्यते। सेयं पञ्चाशद्वर्णात्मिका मातृका अष्टवर्गात्मिका भवति। ते चाष्टवर्गाः अकचटतपयशादयः। अकारादयः षोडश स्वराः प्रथमवर्गः। कादयः पञ्च द्वितीयः। चादयः पञ्च तृतीयः। टादयः पञ्च चतुर्थः। तादयः पञ्च पञ्चमः। पादयः पञ्च षष्ठः। यादयश्चत्वारः सप्तमः। शादयः पञ्च अष्टमः। एवं अष्टवर्गात्मिका भगवती मातृका त्रिपुरसुन्दरी अकचटतपयशवर्गेषु यथाक्रमं वशिन्यादिशक्तिभिर्योजिता बिन्दुत्रिकोणात्मकशिवचक्रचतुष्टयवसुकोणदशारद्वितय-चतुर्दशकोणात्मकेषु अष्टसु चक्रेषु योजिता ध्याता सती काव्यकर्तृत्वसंपादिका। वशिन्याद्याभिरिति आदिशब्देन कामेश्वरीप्रभृतीनां अष्टानां सङ्ग्रहणं विद्यादिद्वादश-योगिनीसङ्ग्रहणं गन्धाकर्षिण्यादिचतुष्टयसङ्ग्रहणं कृतमित्युक्तं भवति। वशिन्यष्टक-मुक्तम्। योगिनीद्वादशकं तु–विद्यायोगिनी, रेचिकायोगिनी, मोचिकायोगिनी, अमृतायोगिनी, दिपिकायोगिनी, ज्ञानयोगिनी, आप्यायनीयोगिनी, व्यापिनीयोगिनी, मेधायोगिनी, व्योमरूपा योगिनी, सिद्धिरूपा योगिनी, लक्ष्मीयोगिनी। एवं द्वादशयोगिनीभिः सार्धं वशिन्याद्याष्टकं मिलित्वा विंशतिकलाः भवन्ति। ताः विंशतिकलाः शुद्धस्फटिकसङ्काशाः दशारयुग्मकोणेषु सञ्चिन्तनीयाः उक्तफलदाः। अयं च भूप्रस्तारभेदः। भूप्रस्तारः '**चतुष्षष्ट्या तन्त्रैः**'[2] इत्यादिश्लोकव्याख्यानावसरे निपुणतरं निरूप्यते। गन्धाकर्षिणी, रसाकर्षिणी, रूपाकर्षिणी स्पर्शाकर्षिणी च चतुर्द्वारेषु [3]योजिताः उक्तफलदाः। तथा च श्रुतिः–

गन्धद्वारां दुराधर्षां नित्यपुष्टां करीषिणीम्।
ईश्वरीं सर्वभूतानां तामिहोपह्वये श्रियम्।।[4]

अस्या अर्थः–गन्धद्वारां गन्धरसरूपस्पर्शाः गन्धशब्देन संगृहीताः, तेन गन्धाकर्षिण्यादयः अधिदेवताः संगृहीता भवन्ति–गन्धाकर्षिणी, रसाकर्षिणी, रूपाकर्षिणी, स्पर्शाकर्षिणी चेति। ताभिर्युक्तानि चतुर्द्वाराणि यस्यां सा गन्धद्वारा, तां गन्धद्वाराम्। दुराधर्षां दुष्प्रधर्षां, मन्दभाग्यानामिति शेषः। नित्यपुष्टां नित्यानन्दस्वरूपिणीम्, करीषिणीं गन्धाद्याकर्षिणीमित्यर्थः। यद्वा–करिभिः गजैः ईषिणीं परिवृताम्। ईश्वरीं अधिदेवतां सर्वभूतानाम्, तां इह चक्रे उपह्वये श्रियं श्रीविद्याम्। गन्धद्वारामिति गन्धाकर्षिणी–चतुष्कं वशिन्याद्यष्टकं योगिनीद्वादशकं संगृहीतम्। तथा च शंभुवचनम्–

1. ३२ श्लोकः।
2. ३१ श्लोकः।
3. याज्ञिकी उ० १।
4. ध्यातास्तत्तदुक्तफलदाः।

मातृकां वशिनीयुक्तां योगिनीभिः समन्विताम्।
गन्धाद्याकर्षिणीयुक्तां संस्मरेत् त्रिपुराम्बिकाम्।

अत्रेदमनुसन्धेयम्–वशिन्यादयः शक्तयः पञ्चाशद्वर्णात्मिका इत्युक्तम्। तत्र वशिनीशक्तिः स्वरात्मिका। स्वराः षोडश अकारादयः। तेषां स्वरूपं सनत्कुमारसंहितायां पञ्चशत्यामुक्तं संक्षेपेण कथ्यते–अकारात्मिका शक्तिः अष्टभुजा पाशाङ्कुशवराभय-पुस्तकाक्षमालाकमण्डलुव्याख्यामुद्राकरा। एवं आकाराद्यात्मिकाः शक्तयः शुभ्रवर्णाः। इयांस्तु विशेषः–अकारात्मिकायाः शक्तेः मण्डलं अशीतिलक्षयोजनायतम्। आकारस्य तद्द्विगुणम्। इकारस्य नवतिलक्षयोजनायतम्। ईकारस्य तद्द्विगुणम्। उकारस्य कोटियोजनपरिमितपरिणाहं मण्डलम्। ऊकारस्य तद्द्विगुणम्। ऋकारस्य पञ्चाशल्लक्ष-योजनपरिमितं मण्डलम्। तद्द्विगुणम् ॠकारस्य। तद्द्विगुणं लृकारलॄकारयोरपि। एवं एकारस्य सार्धकोटिपरिणाहं मण्डलम्। ऐकार–ओकार–औकाराणां सममेव एकारेण। बिन्दुविसर्गयोस्तु अकारद्विगुणं मण्डलम्। व्यञ्जनशक्तीनां अकारमण्डलादर्धं मण्डलम्। ताः शक्तयः पाशाङ्कुशाक्षमालाकमण्डलुधराः। अन्तस्थास्तु पाशाङ्कुशाभयवरकराः। ऊष्माणस्तु पाशाङ्कुशाक्षमालावरकराः। ळकारक्षकारौ पाशाङ्कुशैक्षवशरासनपुष्पबाण-युक्तकरौ। एताः शक्तयः पञ्चाशद्वर्णात्मिकाः।।

केचित्तु–स्वरात्मिकाः शक्तयः स्फटिकाभाः। कादयो मावसानाः विद्रुमाभाः, यादयो नव पीतवर्णाः, क्षकारः अरुणवर्णः इति।।

अपरे तु–अकारादयो धूम्रवर्णाः, ककारादयः ठान्ताः सिन्दूरवर्णाः, डादिफान्ताः गौरवर्णाः, बादिलान्ताः अरुणवर्णाः, वादिसान्ताः कनकवर्णाः,[1] हक्षौ तटिदाभौ, ळकारस्तु लकार एवान्तर्भूतः, इति वदन्ति। इदमेवास्मन्मतं भगवत्पादाचार्याणामपि सम्मतम्। एतत्सर्वं सुभगोदयव्याख्यानावसरे चन्द्रकलायां सम्यङ्निरूपितमस्माभिः।। १७।।

Notes : The Upāsanā of the Devī in the form of Aruṇā was credited, in the previous stanza, with the bestowal of the gift of fluency. In this stanza persistence in the same meditation, but of the Sāttvika type, is said to turn the votary into a reputed author of epic poems.

Generators of speech, Vaśinī and others—the eight deities, Vaśini and others of the *Sarva-ro-ga-hara-cakra,* whose names and relationship with the *Śrī-cakra* have been dealt with under stanza. 11. They are said to preside over the eight groups of the letters of the Alphabet, A-, Ka-, Ca-, Ṭa-, Ta-, Pa-, Ya-, and Śa-vargas. They

---

1. "हक्षयोस्तु पादौ सादौ वा अन्तर्भाव," इत्यधिकः पाठः

are, according to the Āgama-s, of the colour of bright crystal. Their respective seats have been already noted in explaining the Bhū-prastāra. The twelve Yoginī-s and the four guardians of the door ways of the *Bhū-gṛha* are also implies by *'Vaśinī* and others'. Some say that the vowels are of crystal white colour, the letters Ka to Ma of the colour of coral, the nine letters from Ya, yellow, and Kṣa, red. Others hold that the vowels are of the colour of smoke, letters from ka to Ṭha of vermilion, from Ḍa to Pha white, from Ba to La which includes La scarlet, from Va to Sa of the colour of gold, and Ha and Kṣa of the colour of lighning. Lakṣmīdhara holds that the latter is the view held by the author. This verse is said to refer to the fruit to meditation on the Devī in the form of the Jñāna-śakti presiding over the Śaktikūṭa.

तनुच्छयाभिस्ते[1] तरुणतरणिश्रीधरणिभि–[2]
र्दिवं सर्वामुर्वीमरुणिमनिमग्नां[3] स्मरति यः।
भवन्त्यस्य त्रस्यद्वनहरिणशालीननयनाः
सहोर्वश्या वश्याः कति कति न[4] गीर्वाणगणिकाः।। १८।।

Tanuc-chāyābhis te taruṇa-taraṇi-śrī-dharaṇibhir
divaṃ sarvām urvīm aruṇima-nimagnāṃ smarati yaḥ/
Bhavanty asya trasya-vana-hariṇa-śālīna-nayanāḥ
sahorvaśyā vaśyāḥ kati kati na gīrvāṇa-gaṇikāḥ.//

Translation : How many among the celestial courtesans, inclusive of Urvaśī, with the shy eyes of the timid wild deer, would not be caught in the clutches of him, who conceived the entire Heaven and Earth submerged in the red radiance caused by the lustrous graces of Thy body, forming, as it were, the abodes of the splendour (rays) of the rising Sun.

तनुच्छयाभिः तनोः देहस्य छायाभिः कान्तिभिः, ते भवत्याः, **तरुणतरणि-श्रीसरणिभिः** तरुणतरणिः बालसूर्यः, तस्य श्रीः शोभा, तस्या इव सरणिः मार्गः–सौभाग्यमिति यावत्–यासां ताभिः, **दिवं** आकाशं, **सर्वां उर्वीं** कृत्स्नां भूमिं, रोदःप्रदेशमित्यर्थः। **अरुणिमनि** आरुण्ये, **मग्नां** अत्यरुणामिति यावत्। यद्वा–**अरुणिमनिमग्नां** नितरां मग्नाम्। यथोक्तं **शम्भुना–**

1. तेऽतरुण।
2. तरुणतरणिश्रीसरणिभि।
3. ....मरुणमणिमग्नाम् .... मरुणिमनि मग्नां।
4. कतिकतिन, कतिकति न।

यावकाब्धौ निमग्नां यो दिवं भूमिं विचिन्तयेत्।
तस्य सर्वा वशं याताः त्रैलोक्यवनिता द्रुतम्[1]।। इति।।

अतश्च अरुणिमशब्देन यावकाब्धिर्लक्ष्यते, यावकाब्धिमध्यस्थितामित्यर्थः। **स्मरति** चिन्तयति, **यः** साधकः, **भवन्ति, अस्य** साधकस्य, **त्रस्यद्वनहरिणशालीननयनाः** त्रस्यन्तो वनहरिणाः–वन (हरिण) शब्दः स्वच्छन्दचारित्वलक्षणया अतित्रासं लक्षयति–तेषामिव शालीने ह्रीणे, अतिसुन्दरे इति यावत् नयने यासां ताः तथोक्ताः **सह** साकम्, **ऊर्वशी** नाम देवगणिका तया **वश्याः** वशङ्गताः **कतिकति** आभीक्ष्ण्ये द्विरुक्तिः। **नः** निषेधे। **गीर्वाणगणिकाः** देववाराङ्गनाः।।

अत्रेत्थं पदयोजना–हे भगवति! तरुणतरणिश्रीसरणिभिः ते तनुच्छायाभिः सर्वां दिवं उर्वीं च अरुणिमनि मग्नां यः स्मरति अस्य त्रस्यद्वनहरिणशालीननयनाः गीर्वाणगणिकाः ऊर्वश्या सह कतिकति न वश्या भवन्ति? सर्वा अप्सरसो वश्या भवन्तीत्यर्थः।। १८।।

Notes : This stanza deals with the power bestowed by meditation on the Devī presiding over the Kāma-rāja-kūṭa in the form of Icchā-śakti. *With shy eyes of the timid deer*—the deer express their shyness and timidity with their tremulous eyes. Urvaśī and other celestial damsels, whose eyes are naturally steady and unwinking, because of their celestial birth, are so much filled with passion at the sight of the votary, that even their unwinking eyes betray restlessness, all on account of the *Devī's* grace. *Graces*—graceful features. *The abodes of splendour*—wherein the splendour abides.

मुखं बिन्दुं कृत्वा कुचयुगमधस्तस्य तदधो[2]
[3]हरार्धं ध्यायेद्यो हरमहिषि ते मन्मथकलाम्।
स सद्यः संक्षोभं नयति वनिता इत्यतिलघु[4]
त्रिलोकीमप्याशु भ्रमयति रवीन्दुस्तनयुगाम्।। १९।।

Mukhaṃ binduṃ kṛtvā kuca-yugam adhas tasya tad-adho
harārdhaṃ dhyāyed yo hara-mahiṣi te manmatha-kalām/
Sa sadyaḥ saṃkṣobhaṃ nayati vanitā ity ati-laghu
tri-lokīm apy āśu bhramayati ravīndu-stana-yugām.//

---

1. 'ध्रुवम्' इति पाठान्तरम्।
2. दधतः।
3. हकरार्धं ध्यायेद्धर.....।
4. वनितास्त्वित्यति लघु।

Translation : O Queen (Spouse) of Hara (Śiva)! It is but a trifle that one who contemplates Thy Manmatha-kalā, taking the *bindu* to be the face, what is there under to be the breasts, and still underneath to be one half of Hara (*i.e.*, a traingle), at once fascinates women (in general); (what is more) he very soon causes even Trilokī (the three worlds together) who has the Sun and the Moon as her breasts, to swirl.

मुखं वक्त्रं, **बिन्दुं** बिन्दुरूपं, **कृत्वा**, बिन्दुस्थाने मुखं ध्यात्वेत्यर्थः। **कुचयुगं** स्तनद्वयं, **अधः** अधस्तात्, **तस्य** मुखस्य। **तदधः** तस्य कुचयुगस्य अधःप्रदेशे, **हरार्धं** हरस्य अर्धं शक्तिः त्रिकोणं योनिरिति यावत्। **ध्यायेत्** चिन्तयेत्, **यः** साधकः। 'तत्र' इत्यध्याहार्यम्। **हरमहिषि!** हरस्य सदाशिवस्य महिषि जाये, **ते** भवत्याः, **मन्मथकलां** कामराजबीजम् **सः** साधकः, **सद्यः** तदानीमेव, **संक्षोभं** सर्वजगत्संक्षोभं चित्तविकारं, **नयति** प्रापयति, **वनिताः** स्त्रियः। इतिशब्दः क्रियाविशेषणद्योतकः। **अतिलघु** अतितुच्छम् **त्रिलोकीमपि** त्रिभुवनमपि, **आशु** शीघ्रं, **भ्रमयति रवीन्दुस्तनयुगां**—रवीन्दू सूर्यचन्द्रौ, तावेव स्तनौ, तयोः युगं यस्याः सा ताम्।।

अत्रेत्थं पदयोजना—हे हरमहिषि! मुखं बिन्दुं कृत्वा, तस्याधः कुचयुगं कृत्वा, तदधः हरार्धं कृत्वा, तत्र ते मन्मथकलां यः ध्यायेत् सः सद्यः वनिताः संक्षोभं नयतीति यत् तत् अतिलघु, किंतु रवीन्दुस्तनयुगां त्रिलोकीमपि आशु भ्रमयति।।

अत्र त्रिलोक्याः रवीन्दुस्तनयुगत्वविशेषणेन स्त्रीत्वारोपणं अयं मादनप्रयोगो वनितास्वेव प्रयोक्तव्य इति ज्ञापयितुम्।।

अत्रेदमनुसन्धेयम्—साधकः त्रिकोणे बिन्दुस्थाने साध्यायाः कान्तायाः वक्त्रं ध्यात्वा, तदधस्तात् तस्याः कुचयुगं ध्यात्वा, तत्कुचद्वयस्याधस्तात् तस्याः योनिं विचिन्त्य तत्र वक्त्रकुचद्वययोनिषु प्रधानाङ्गेषु मारबीजं सञ्चिन्त्य तया कान्तया आत्मनस्तादात्म्यं सम्पादयेत्। यथोक्तं चतुश्शत्याम्—

बिन्दुं सङ्कल्प्य वक्त्रं तु तदधस्तात्कुचद्वयम्।
तदधश्च हरार्धं तु चिन्तयेत्तदधोमुखम्।।
तत्र कामकलारूपामरुणां चिन्तयेदिह।
ततस्तेनैव रूपेण निजरूपं विचिन्तयेत्।। इति।।

एवं मादनप्रयोगाः अनेके सनत्कुमारसंहितायां सप्तशत्यामुक्ताः। अत्र कतिचन निरूप्यन्ते—

बिन्दौ तद्वक्त्रमारोप्य तदधो बाहुयुग्मकम्।
तदधः कुचयुग्मं तु तदधो योनिमेव च।।
एतेषु पञ्चस्थानेषु पञ्चबाणान्विचिन्तयेत्।।

पञ्चबाणबीजानि मुखे बाहुयुग्मे कुचमध्ये योनिमध्ये यथाक्रमं द्रां द्रीं क्लीं ब्लूं स इति चिन्तयेत् इत्यर्थः। अयं प्रयोगः कामराजप्रयोगसमय एव।।

त्रिकोणे बैन्दवस्थाने अधोवक्त्रं विचिन्तयेत्।
बिन्दोरुपरिभागे तु वक्त्रं सञ्चिन्त्य साधकः।।
तदुपर्येव वक्षोजद्वितयं संस्मरेद्बुधः।
तदुपर्येव योनिं च क्रमशो भुवनेश्वरीम्।।
श्रीविद्यां कामराजं च विन्यस्याशु विमोहयेत्।।

अयं प्रयोगः 'मुखं बिन्दुं कृत्वा' इति प्रयोगात् अतिशीघ्रकरः। अत्रापि पञ्चबाणप्रयोगः पूर्ववत्। एवमेतादृशमादनप्रयोगाः सनत्कुमारसंहितायां अवगन्तव्याः ग्रन्थविस्तरभयान्नोक्ताः।। १९।।

Notes : This staza, like the previous one, also affords an example of the Mādana-prayoga and deals with the fruit of meditation on the Devī, as Icchā-śakti presiding over the Kāmarāja-kūṭa, in virtue of which the votary acquires the power of fascinating women. Queen of Hara—*i.e.*, the Devī of the form of *Sac-cid-ānanda*, being the spouse of Hara, the Paramātman, who absorbs the entire universe unto Himself. This is also construed as the *Tri-koṇa*, which is the resort of the *bindu* in the form of Hara. *Thy Manmatha-kalā*—the Kāmakalā indicating Thee, *i.e.*, (1) 'Klīṃ', which, according to the Deva-nāgarī script, is made up of one *bindu* at the top, two *bindu*-like curves on either side of the 'K' thereunder and what is thereunder, *viz.*, the 'L'. (2) Bereft of the 'K' and 'L', this *Bīja* becomes the *Gupta-mahā-sārasvata-bīja, viz.*, 'Īm' which is made up of three *Bindu-s*, one above and two thereunder, the former indicating the Sun and the latter Fire and the Moon thereunder. (3) Which is of the form of 'E' *i.e.*, the Yoni, and (4) which is power in the form of the three Guṇas, *i.e.*, the Universe which is the product of the union of Śiva and the Śakti. Taking—*i.e.*, conceiving by the strength of meditation. One half of Hara—there is also another reading. 'Hakārārdham', meaning 'one half of Hakāra', which is the same as Hara. 'Hakarārdha' is capable of being construed in the following ways : (1) The upper half of 'Ha' being neglected, the lower half, which resembles 'E', is construed as the Yoni. (2) 'Ha' is Śiva and one half of Śiva will be Śivā, made up of Ś, I, V and Ā; eliding the consonants Ś and V, the other half 'I' and 'Ā', when combined, yields 'E', which is the Yoni. (3) 'Ha' stands for 'Ravi' and when half of it, *viz.*, the consonants 'R' and 'V' are elided, the resultant 'A' and 'I', when combined, yield 'E', the Yoni. According to Śrī-*krama*, the three *bindus* are : the first of Fire indicating *Rajas* and presided over by Brahman, is the face ; the second and third *bindus*, which are the Sun and the Moon, indicating *Sattva* and *Tamas*, presided over by Hari and Rudra, are the breasts. Below that, a subtle Cit-kalā, which is one half of 'Ha' with the upper half-neglected, and transcends all the three Guṇas, is the Yoni, *i.e.*, the transcends all the three Guṇas, is the Yoni, *i.e.*, the triangle connecting the three *Bindus*, indicating the three Guṇas, the characteristics of Brahman, Hari and Rudra. (4) 'Ha' is the 'Haṁsaḥ' and the one half of it, *viz.*, the consonants 'H' and 'S' being elided, the other half, 'Aṃ' and 'Aḥ', yield three *bindus*, which should be meditated upon as the Manmatha-kalā, *viz.*, 'E', the Yoni. (5) *Harārdham*—one half of Hara, *i.e.*, the Śakti, which means the Yoni. Besides these, there is also an esoteric significance, which should be received out of the mouth of the *Guru*. While the first half of the stanza extols the influence of the Devī on the votary with reference to women in general, the second half deals with the extraordinary infleunce which, through her grace, her votary has over the three worlds personified as the woman *par excellence*, and in virtue of which he becomes the lord of the three worlds, within the three Śaktis in harmony with his wishes. According to the Rudrayāmala, the Trilokī is said to assume the form of the Kāmarāja-kalā with the Sun and the Moon as her breasts. To swirl—by the extraordinary powers he commands as the true devotee of the Devī in the form of Icchā-śakti. Some hold the view that this verse speaks of *pañcamahāyāga*, esoterically, the union of the Kuṇḍalinī with Parama-śiva and of Maithuna on the material plane.

किरन्तीमङ्गेभ्यः किरणनिकुरुम्बामृतरसं
हृदि त्वामाधत्ते हिमकरशिलामूर्तिमिव यः।
स सर्पाणां दर्पं शमयति शकुन्ताधिप इव
[1]ज्वरप्लुष्टान्दृष्ट्या[2] सुखयति सुधाऽऽसारसिरया[3] ॥ २०॥

1. ज्वरप्लुष्टम्। 2. दृष्ट्वा।

3. सुधा ऽऽधारसिरया ; सुधाधारसया ; सुधासारशिरया।

Kirantīm aṅgebhyaḥ kiraṇa-nikurumbāmṛta-rasaṁ
hṛdi tvām ādhatte hima-kara-śilā-mūrtim iva yaḥ/
Sa sarpāṇāṁ darpaṁ śamayati śakuntādhipa iva
jvara-pluṣṭān dṛṣṭyā sukhayati sudhā-sāra-sirayā.//

Translation : He who contemplates Thee in his heart, who diffusest nectar in the form of beams from (Thy), limbs, as an image carved out of a moon-stone quells the pride of serpents, like the king of birds, and cures those afflicted with fever, with a look resembling the nectar-showering *Nāḍī*.

किरन्तीं वर्षन्तीं, **अङ्गेभ्यः** अवयवेभ्यः, **किरणनिकुरुम्बामृतरसं**-किरणानां मरीचीनां निकुरम्बः समूहः, तस्मादुत्पन्नः अमृतरसः तम्। **हृदि** हृदये, **त्वां** भवतीं, **आधत्ते** स्मरतीति यावत्। **हिमकरशिलामूर्तिं** हिमकरशिलायाः चन्द्रकान्तमणेः मूर्तिं पुत्तलिकां सालभञ्जिकां चन्द्रकान्तमणिनिर्मितदेहां, **इव यः** साधकः, **सः** साधकः, **सर्पाणां दर्पं शमयति शकुन्ताधिपः** शकुन्तानां पक्षिणां अधिपो गरुत्मान् इव। इवेति सम्भावनायाम्–गरुत्मदाकाराकारित्वमात्रं न भवति, अपि तु तत्कार्यकारित्वं सम्भावितमिति, गरुत्मान् भूत्वा, प्रत्यक्षो गरुत्मानिवेत्यर्थः। **ज्वरप्लुष्टान्** ज्वरेण प्लुष्टान् सन्तप्तान्, **दृष्ट्या** वीक्षणेन। अत्र दृष्टिप्रयोगः कथितः। **सुखयति** सुखिनः करोति। 'तत्करोति' इति णिचि 'णाविष्ठवत्प्रातिपदिकस्य' इति टिलोपः। एवं सुखयतीति रूपं सिद्धम्। **सुधाधारसिरया** सुधायाः आधारभूता सिरा अमृतस्यन्दिनी नाडी। यद्वा–सुधा धारात्मिका यस्यां सिरायामिति बहुव्रीहिः। 'स्त्रियाः पुंवत् भाषितपुंस्कात्' इत्यादिना पुंवद्भावः?। सुधाधारा चासौ सिरा च तया। सुधासारसिरयेति वा पाठःसुधासारात्मिका सिरा।।

अत्रेत्थं पदयोजना–हे दवि! यः साधकः अङ्गेभ्यः किरणनिकुरुम्बामृतरसं किरन्तीं हिमकरशिलामूर्तिमिव हृदि त्वां आधत्ते, सः शकुन्ताधिप इव दृष्ट्या सर्पाणां दर्पं शमयति। सुधाधारसिरया दृष्ट्या ज्वरप्लुष्टान् सुखयति।।

अनेन श्लोकेन गारुडप्रयोग उक्तः। तदुक्तं शतुश्शत्याम्–

षण्मासध्यानयोगेन जायते गरुडोपमः।
दृष्ट्या कर्षयते लोकं दृष्ट्यैव कुरुते वशम्।।
दृष्ट्या संक्षोभयेन्नारीं दृष्ट्यैव हरते विशम्।
दृष्ट्या चातुर्थिकादींश्च ज्वज्रान् नाशयते क्षणात्।।

चन्द्रकान्तशिलामूर्तिं चिन्तयित्वा विनाशयेत्।
तापज्वरानशेषांश्च शीघ्रं तार्क्ष्य इवापरः।।
गरुडध्यानयोगेन स्मरणान्नाशयेद्विषम्।। इति।।

अतश्च प्रातीतिकोऽन्वयः-यथा शकुन्ताधिपः सर्पाणां दर्पं शमयति एवं साधकेन्द्रः ज्वरप्लुष्टान् सुखयतीति-तिरस्कृत्य, साधकेन्द्रो ज्वरप्लुटन् सर्पाणां दर्पमपि शकुन्ताधिप इवेति आश्रित इति अनुसन्धेयः।। २०।।

Notes : Thee—who hast assumed the form of Amṛteśvarī. Quells the pride of serpents—at the very sight of the votary serpents are said to seek safe places of retreat, as, in virtue of the power acquired by him from meditation on the Devī, he appears to their eyes as Garutmat, the king of birds and the traditional vanquisher of serpents. The votary is thus indirectly an antidote to snake-bite. By 'fever' is meant any chronic disease, such as malaria, which afflicts mankind in general. Diseases are cured by the ordinary medical practitioner with the administration of drugs. But the votary of the Devī, through her grace, is endowed with the miraculous power of healing the afflicted by the mere casting of a look. Resembling the nectar-showering *Nāḍī*—*Nāḍī* referred to is the *Amṛta-nāḍī* recognized by the Yoginis, which, is filling the entire system of *Nāḍis* with nectar, fills the accomplished Yogin with the ecstasy of Bliss. This stanza refers to the special powers acquired by the Yogin, from worship of the Devī, wherewith even death could be conquered.

[1]तडिल्लेखातन्वीं तपनशशिवैश्वानरमयीं
निषण्णां [2]षण्णामप्युपरि कमलानां तव कलाम्।
महापद्माटव्यां मृदितमलमायेन[3] मनसा
महान्तः पश्यन्तो दधति परमाह्लादलहरीम्[4]।। २१।।

Taḍil-lekhā-tanvīṁ tapana-śaśi-vaiśvānara-mayīṁ
niṣaṇṇāṁ ṣaṇṇām apy upari kamalānāṁ tavakalām/
Mahā-padmāṭavyāṁ mṛdita-mala-māyena manasā
mahāntaḥ paśyanto dadhati paramāhlāda-la-harīm.//

Translation : Great men, who, with their minds bereft of

1. तटिल्लेखातन्वीं।
2. षण्णामुपरि।
3. मृदुतममममायेन।
4. परमानन्दलहरीम्।

impurity and illusion, look on Thy Kalā, slender as a streak of lightning, of the essence of the Sun, the Moon and Fire, and abiding in the great forest of lotuses, standing far above even the six lotuses, derive a flood of infinite Bliss.

तटिल्लेखा विद्युल्लेखा, तद्वत् **तन्वी** दीर्घसूक्ष्मा ज्योतिर्मयी क्षणप्रभा च ताम्। स्थिरसौदामिन्याः क्षणप्रभात्वम् आज्ञाचक्रे क्षणमात्रदर्शनात्। एतच्च आज्ञाशब्दार्थ-निरूपणावसरे पूर्वमेव प्रतिपादितम्। **तपनशशिवैश्वानरमयीं** सूर्यचन्द्रानलात्मिकाम्। एतच्च त्रिखण्डनिरूपणावसरे सम्यङ्निरूपितम्। **निषण्णां** आसीनाम्, **षण्णां** षट्सङ्ख्याकानाम्, **अपि** समुच्चये-ग्रन्थित्रयं ससुच्चिनोति। ग्रन्थित्रयस्यापि। **उपरि कमलानां** पद्मानाम्, षट्चक्राणां आधारस्वाधिष्ठानमणिपूरकानाहतविशुद्ध्याज्ञात्मकानां कमलस्वरूपत्वं पूर्वमेव निरूपितम्। **तव** भवत्याः, **कलां** सादाख्यां बैन्दवीकलाम्। **महापद्माटव्यां** महान्ति बहूनि पद्मानि पद्मदलानि सहस्रसंख्याकानि, तान्येव अटवी, तस्यां सहस्रदलकमलकर्णिकायामित्यर्थः। यद्वा–महापद्मं सहस्रदलकमलं, तदेव अटवी, तस्याम्। **मृदितमलमायेन** मृदिताः क्षपिताः, मलाः, कामादयः, मायाऽविद्या-ऽस्मिताहङ्कारादयः यस्य तनू तेन, **मनसा** अन्तःकरणेन, **महान्तः** योगीश्वराः, **पश्यन्तः** सादाख्यकलासुधाधारानिष्यन्दम् अनुभवन्तः, **दधति** अवरुन्धते। **परमाह्लादलहरीं** परमः निरतिशयः, आह्लादः सुखविशेषः, तस्य लहरीम् उद्रेकम् उद्रिक्तपरमानन्दं सादाख्यकलामृतानुभवजनितं, सर्वदा सम्पादयन्तीत्यर्थः।।

अत्रेत्थं पदयोजना–हे भगवति! तटिल्लेखातन्वीं तपनशशिवैश्वानरमयीं निषण्णां षणां कमलानामप्युपरि महापद्माटव्यां निषण्णां तव कलां मृदितमलमायेन मनसा पश्यन्तो महान्तः परमाह्लादलहरीं दधति।। २१ ।।

Notes : Bereft of impurity and illusion—with impurities such as carnal desire, volition, assumption, *etc.*, which are the result of illusion, completely attenuated. *Thy Kalā*—the Kalā known as Parā on the Devī in the form of Candra-kalā. This form is assumed by the Devī in the Baindava-sthāna of the *Sahasrāra*, when she is conjoined with Śiva. Streak of lightning—in the *Ājñā-cakra* and thereafter. *Essence of the Sun, etc.*—as without the Devī, the Sun, *etc.*, cannot exist. It may also be noted that the Sun, the Moon and Fire derive their luminosity, *etc.*, only through the Devī's grace. Great forest of lotuses—the thousand-petalled lotus in the *Dvādaśānta* is meant by this. In the case of the reading *'Mṛdutamam'*, the meaning would be 'without effort'. The meditation on the Kāma-kalā in the form of the Tri-pura-sundarī, the mother of Brahman,

Viṣṇu and Rudra, referred to in stanza 19, is said to be the Bāhya, or outer meditation. Stanza 21 is said to formulate the Ābhyantara, or inner meditation on the pure Citsvarūpa of the Devī, attainable only by the great. This form is very subtle, while the forms referred to previously are intended for votaries of lower capacities.

Meditation on the Devī along with the Mantra should be confined to the following eighteen seats of the liṅga-śarīra : the *Kulapadma, i.e.,* the Sahasrāra opening upwards from its place a little below the Mūlādhāra, the *Viṣu,* one of the two lotuses of eight and six petals respectively between the Kula-padma and the Mūlādhāra, the *Mūlādhāra,* the *Maṇipūra,* the *Svādhiṣṭhāna,* the *Anāhata,* the *Viśuddhi,* the *Lambikāgra,* the *Ājñā,* the *Indu,* the *Artha-candra,* the *Rodhinī,* the *Nāda,* the *Nādānta,* the *Śakti,* the *Vyāpikā,* the *Sa-manā* and the *Un-manā.* The fifteen syllables of the Pañca-daśākṣarī should be conceived as inherent in the first fifteen of these seats from below, one in each, and also every prior one of the fifteen syllables should be conceived as being dissolved in the immediately succeeding one, in order, the last of the fifteen being dissolved in the fire of the form of Yoni in the *Vyāpikā,* the Yoni conceived as in Īśvara of the form of the three *bindus,* Sūrya, Agni and Soma, and dissolved, the Sūrya in the Agni, the Agni in the Soma, in the *Samanā,* and the Some in the Sa-parārdha-kalā of the *Unmanā.* When all are dissolved, the Yogin, conceiving of the conjoint Śiva and the Śakti as his own Self, attains one-ness with the Śadāśiva tattva and becomes a *Jīvanmukta.*

भवानि त्वं दासे मयि वितर दृष्टिं सकरुणा-
मिति स्तोतुं वाञ्छन्कथयति भवानि[1] त्वमिति यः।
तदैव त्वं तस्मै दिशसि निजसायुज्यपदवीं
मुकुन्दब्रह्मेन्द्र[2]स्फुटमकुटनीराजितपदाम् ॥२२॥

Bhavāni tvaṁ dāse mayi vitara dṛṣṭiṁ sa-karuṇām
iti stotuṁ vāñchan kathayati bhavāni tvam ti yaḥ/
Tadaiva tvaṁ tasmai diśasi nija-sā-yujya-padaviṁ
mukunda-brahmendra-sphuṭa-makuṭa-nīrājita-padām.//

Translation : When one, desirous of earnestly beseeching Thee with the words, "O Bhavānī! mayest Thou cast Thy

1. भवानी।
2. स्फुट मुकुट।

merciful glance of me, Thy slave", pronounces the words, "*Bhavāni tvam*", (may I be Thou), that very moment, Thou bestowest on him the status identically Thine own, rendered lustrous by the brilliant crowns worn by Mukunda, Brahman and Indra.

हे **भवानि!** भवस्य पत्नि! **त्वं** भवती, **दासे मयि** दासभूते किङ्करे मयि, **वितर** देहि। **दृष्टिं** कटाक्षं, **सकरुणां** करुणायुक्तां, **इति** एवंप्रकारेण, **स्तोतुं** स्तोत्रं कर्तुं, **वाञ्छन्** इच्छन्, **कथयति** वदति। **भवानि त्वमिति** 'भवानि त्वं दासे मयि वितर दृष्टिं सकरुणाम्' इति वाक्यप्रतीकं 'भवानि त्वं' इत्येवं **यः** साधकः **तदैव** 'भवानि त्वम्' इति वाक्यैकदेशोच्चारणसमय एव, **त्वं** भवती **तस्मै** वाक्यैकदेशोच्चारकाय, **दिशसि** ददासि। **निजसायुज्यपदवीं** निजस्य आत्मनः सायुज्यपदवीं तादात्म्यम्। **मुकुन्दब्रह्मेन्द्रस्फुटमकुटनीराजितपदां** मुकुन्दो विष्णुः, ब्रह्मा द्रुहिणः, इन्द्रः आखण्डलः, तेषां स्फुटं यथा भवति तथा मकुटैः नीराजिते निराजनविधिक्रियाञ्चिते पदे पदाम्बुजे यस्यास्ताम्।।

अत्रेत्थं पदयोजना–हे भवानि! त्वं दासे मयि सकरुणां दृष्टिं वितरेति स्तोतुं वाञ्छन् भवानि त्वमिति यः कथयति तस्मै तदैव त्वं मुकुन्दब्रह्मेन्द्रस्फुटमकुटनीराजितपदां निजसायुज्यपदवीं दिशसि।।

अयमर्थः–'भवानि त्वं दासे मयि' इत्यादिवाक्यप्रतीके 'भवानि त्वं' इति पदद्वये 'भवानि' इति पदस्य लोडुत्तमपुरुषैकवचनान्तत्वमवगम्य तत्सामानाधिकरण्येन त्वं पदस्यान्वये महावाक्यप्रयोगोऽनेन साधकेन प्रयुक्त इति मत्वा महावाक्यफलं तादात्म्यं दिशति भगवती, जपहोमाद्युपासनाविधिभ्यः तादात्म्योपासनायाः सद्यः फलदायित्वात्–

अनिच्छयापि संस्पृष्टो दहत्येव हि पावकः।।

इति न्यायेन अविवक्षया प्रयुक्तमपि महावाक्यं फलदायकमिति, नापि अविमृश्यकारित्वं देव्या इति रहस्यम्।। २२।।

Notes : This stanza extols, by implication, the worship of the Devī, with the conception, by the worshipper, of his identity with her, in preference to the other form of worship, such as by the performance of Japa, Homa, *etc.*, as it is held, that the mere utterance of words, conveying the idea of the *Mahā-vākyas*, such as *'Tat tvam asi' etc.*, either intentionally or by accident, carries with it the full fruits attainable by the realization of their contents. The author of this work, after dealing with the *Antar-yāga* and *Bahir-yāga* methods of approach in the previous stanzas, deals with the potency of *Bhakti* or devotion in this stanza. *Bhakti* is held by a school of thought as leading to liberation in the form of Sā-lokya, reaching the abode of the Supreme Being, Sāmīpya, proximity to the Supreme Being, Sā-rūpya, becoming of the form of the Supreme Being, and Sā-yujya, At-one-ment with the Supreme Being. The liberation referred to here is Sā-yujya. Rendered lustrous—the implication is that Mukunda, Brahman and Indra hold the status referred to above in such high esteem, and so venerate it, as to perform Nīrājana (the waving of lights), as it were, before it, with their dazzling bright crowns serving the purposes of lights in the ceremony.

त्वया हृत्वा वामं वपुरपरितृप्तेन[1] मनसा
शरीरार्धं शंभोरपरमपि शङ्के हृतमभूत्।
[2]यदेतत्त्वद्रूपं सकलमरुणाभं त्रिनयनं
कुचाभ्यामानम्रं कुटिलशशिचूडालमकुटम्[3]।। २३।।

Tvayā hṛtvā vāmaṁ vapur a-paritṛptena manasā
śarīrādhaṁ śaṁbhor aparam api śaṅke hṛtam abhūt/
Yad etat tvad-rūpaṁ sakalam aruṇābhaṁ trinayanaṁ
kucābhyām ānamraṁ kuṭila-śaśi-cūḍāla-makuṭam//

Translation : I fancy that the other (half) as well, of Śaṁbhu's frame, has been absorbed by Thee, with Thy mind, not satisfied with having absorbed the left one; for, this, Thy form, is entirely of a red colour, has three eyes, is slightly bent with (the weight of) the breasts, and wears over its crown the Crescent-moon.

त्वया भवत्या, **हृत्वा** अपहृत्य, **वामं** वामार्धं, **वपुः** शरीरं, **अपरितृप्तेन** असन्तुष्टेन, **मनसा** अन्तःकरणेन, **शरीरार्धं शम्भोरपरमपि** दक्षिणमपि, **शङ्के** मन्ये, **हृतं** गृहीतं, **अभूत्। यत्** यस्मात् **एतत्** हृदयकमलान्तःप्रतिभासि, **त्वद्रूपं** तव शरीरं, **सकलं** कृत्स्नं वामदक्षिणभागात्मकं, **अरुणाभं** अरुणस्य प्रातःकालसूर्यस्याभेवाभा यस्य तत्। यद्वा–अरुणा रक्तवर्णा आभा प्रभा यस्य तत् अरुणाभम्। **त्रिनयनं** नयनत्रययुक्तं, **कुचाभ्यामानम्रं** स्तनाभ्यामीषन्नम्रं **कुटिलशशिचूडालमकुटं** कुटिलशशिना वक्रचन्द्रकलया चूडालं चूडावन्तं मकुटं यस्य तत्।।

---

1. ०तुष्टेन।
2. तथा हि त्वद्रूपं।
3. शशिचूडालमुकुटम्।

अत्रेत्थं पदयोजना–हे भगवति! शम्भोर्वामं वपुः त्वया हृत्वा अपरितृप्तेन मनसा अपरमपि शरीरार्धं हृतमभूदिति शङ्के; यत् एतत् त्वद्रूपं सकलमरुणाभं त्रिनयनं कुचाभ्यामानम्रं कुटिलशशिचूडालमकुटम्।।

अयमर्थः–भगवत्या शम्भोरेकस्मिन्नर्धे अपहृते अपरार्धस्याप्यपहार उत्प्रेक्ष्यते। यद्वा–उत्तरकौलसिद्धान्तप्रतिपादकोऽयं श्लोकः। उत्तरकौलसिद्धान्ते शक्तितत्त्वात् अन्यत् शिवतत्त्वं नास्ति। अतश्च शिवतत्त्वं शक्तितत्त्वे अन्तर्भूतमिति तदेव उपास्यमिति प्रस्तुतम्। एतच्च '**मनस्त्वं व्योम त्वम्**'[1] इति श्लोकव्याख्यानावसरे, **तवाधारे मूले**[2]' इति श्लोकव्याख्यानावसरे च निपुणतरमुपपादयिष्यामः।। २३।।

Notes : The theme of this stanza as of several others, is the complete union of Śiva with the Śakti. But the author accomplishes this purpose adroitly enough, by making use of the hermaphrodite form of *ardhanārīśvara,* in which Śiva is worshipped, wherein he occupies the right half, and Umā, his spouse, the left half. The distinct characteristic of Śiva are a pale-white colour, a crown with the crescent on and the three eyes. The Śakti is represented to have such a mastery over Śiva that, in the first instance, she gradually encroaches on his form and annexes one half of it, *viz.,* the left, wherein her characteristics, *viz.,* the colour of the rising Sun and her left breast replace Śiva's, while the third eye and the crown with the crescent on are shared in common. Not satisfied with this achievement of hers, she further encroaches on the right half of Śaṁbhu's form as well, and, having absorbed his entire form by eclipsing his colour and developing another breast, assumes the female-form, so well depicted in this stanza, thus showing beyond doubt that she has become more than one half of her Lord. This stanza may also be taken to support, by implication, the well-known doctrine of the Uttarakaulas, for whom there is no Śiva-tattva part from the Śakti-tattva, as the former stands absorbed in the latter.

जगत्सूते धाता हरिरवति रुद्रः क्षपयते[3]
तिरस्कुर्वन्नेतत्स्वमपि वपुरीशस्तिरयति[4]।
सदापूर्वः सर्वं तदिदमनुगृह्णाति च शिव-
स्तवाज्ञामालम्ब्य क्षणचलितयोर्भ्रूलतिकयोः[5]।। २४।।

1. ३५ श्लोकः।
2. ४१ श्लोकः।
3. रुद्रः क्षपयति।
4. पुनरीशस्तिरयति ; वपुरीशः स्थगयति।
5. क्षणवलितयोर्भ्रूलतिकयोः।

Jagat sūte dhātā harir avati rudraḥ kṣapayate
tiras-kurvann etat svam api vapur īśas tirayati/
Sadā-pūrvaḥ sarvaṁ tad idam anugṛhṇāti ca śivas
tavājñām ālambya kṣaṇa-calitayor bhrū-lati-kayoḥ.//

Translation : The Dhātṛ creates the world; Hari sustains it ; Rudra destroys it; making all this disappear, Īśa causes his own form to disappear as well ; while Sadāśiva, in pursuance of the mandate from Thy slightly-knit creeper-like eyebrows, blesses all this.

जगत् स्थावरजङ्गमात्मकं जगत्, **सूते** सृजति, **धाता** स्रष्टा। **हरिः** विष्णुः, **अवति** रक्षति। **रुद्रः क्षपयते** संहरति। धातृहरिरुद्राः सृष्टिस्थिति[1]लयाधिकारिणः। **तिरस्कुर्वन्** उपसंहरन्, **एतत्** धातृहरिरुद्रात्मकं त्रितयं, **स्वमपि** स्वकीयमपि, **वपुः** देहम्, **ईशः** महेश्वरतत्त्वं, **तिरयति** अन्तर्हितं करोति। ईश्वरः धातृहरिरुद्रान् आत्मन्यारोप्य स्वयमपि सदाशिवतत्त्वे अन्तर्भूत इत्यर्थः। अनेन ब्रह्माण्डप्रलय उक्तः। तदनन्तरं ब्रह्माण्डोत्पिपित्सा सदाशिवस्य जायते। तदानीमाह–सदापूर्व इति। सदाशब्दः पूर्वः यस्य शिवशब्दस्य सः **सदापूर्वः** शिवशब्दः। तेन सदा शिवशब्देन वाच्यवाचकयोः अभेदोपचारात् सदाशिवरूपं तत्त्वं उपचर्यते। सर्वं **तदिदं** पूर्वोक्तं धातृहरिरुद्रेशानात्मकं तत्त्वचतुष्टयं **अनुगृह्णाति**। चकारः शङ्काच्छेदे। **शिवः** सदाशिवः। कथमनुगृह्णातीत्याशङ्कायामाह– **तवाज्ञामालम्ब्य** इति। तव भवत्याः **क्षणचलितयोः भ्रूलतिकयोः** क्षणमात्रं चलितयोः, भ्रूलतिकाचलनेन विज्ञेयामाज्ञामालम्ब्येत्यर्थः। भवद्भ्रूविक्षेपमात्रेण धातृहरिरुद्रेशानात्मकं तत्त्वचतुष्टयमुत्पन्नं, भ्रकुटीकरणमात्रेण तद्विनष्टमिति अनेककोटिब्रह्माण्डानामुत्पादने संहरणे च त्वद्भ्रूविक्षेपमात्ररूपा शक्तिः साचिव्यं सदाशिवस्य करोतीति तात्पर्यम्।।

अत्रेत्थं पदयोजना–हे भगवति! धाता जगत् सूते। हरिः जगत् अवति। रुद्रः जगत् क्षपयते। ईशः एतत् तिरस्कुर्वन् स्वमपि वपुः तिरयति! सदापूर्वः शिवः सर्वं तदिदं तव क्षणचलितयोः भ्रूलतिकयोः आज्ञामालम्ब्य अनुगृह्णाति।। २४।।

Notes : The evolution and the involution of the Macrocosm preparatory to its creation once again, are indicated in this stanza. The world is in a state of evolution, through Brahman discharging his function of creating it and Viṣṇu discharging his function of sustaining it. Then commences the involution with the destruction of the world by Rudra, whereupon Īśvara causes the destroyed

---

1. लयकारिणः।

universe to disappear along with Brahman, Viṣṇu and Rudra, and himself disappears. During the process of involution, the lower *tattvas* merge into the higher *tattva*, Īśvara, who represents the lower *tattva-s* in their collective form and ceases to have an independent existence, after the process of involution is complete. There, then, remains Sadāśiva alone, who is the all-witness, and absorbs all the Tattvas including Īśvara in the Bīja-form within himself, and in his passive attitude implies his approval of the actions of the lower powers, who carry out the work of involution, in obedience to the pre-ordained laws of evolution and involution, himself standing changelss and eternal, preparatory to the creation of the universe once again, at the instance of the Devī, who conveys her mandate through the knitting of her eyebrows, as represented in this stanza. The implication is that the Devī is All-supreme and the five powers, through whom she carries out her mandates, are but her agents.

त्रयाणां देवानां त्रिगुणजनितानां[1] तव[2] शिवे
भवेत्पूजा पूजा तव चरणयोर्या विरचिता।
तथा हि [3]त्वत्पादोद्वहनमणिपीठस्य निकटे[4]
स्थिता ह्येते शश्वन्मुकुलितकरोत्तंसमकुटाः[5] ।। २५ ।।

Trayāṇāṁ devānāṁ tri-guṇa-janitānāṁ tava śive
bhavet pūjā pūjā tava caraṇayor yā viracitā/
Tathā hi tvat-pādodvahana-maṇi-pīṭhasya nikaṭe
sthitā hy ete śaśvan mukulita-karottaṁsa-makuṭāḥ//

Translation : O Spouse of Śiva! the homage rendered to Thy feet becomes by itself the homage rendered to the three gods born of Thy three *guṇas*. It is, therefore, meet that these (gods) ever stand by the jewelled seat on which Thy feet rest, with their folded hands adorning their crowns.

त्रयाणां देवानां धातृहरिरुद्राणामित्यर्थः। **त्रिगुणजनितानां** सत्वरजस्तमः-प्रभवानाम्, **तव** भवत्याः, हे **शिवे!** शिवमहिषि! **भवेत्** भवत्येव। प्राप्तकाले लिङ्। **पूजा** सपर्या, सैव **पूजा** नान्येति द्वितीयपूजाशब्दस्यार्थः। तव **चरणयोः या** पूजा **विरचिता** निर्मिता। युक्तं चैतदित्याह–**तथाहीत्यादिना। तथाहि** युक्तमेतत्।

1. त्रिगुणजनितानामपि शिवे।
2. परशिवे ; त्रिभुवने।
3. तत्पादोद्वहन।
4. निकटं।
5. समुकुटाः।

त्वत्पादोद्वहनमणिपीठस्य तव पादयोः उद्वहनार्थं यन्मणिपीठं परिकल्पितं तस्य **निकटे** उपसिंहासनसमीपे, **स्थिताः** वर्तन्ते स्म। **हि** यस्मात्, **एते** धातृहरिरुद्राः अधिकारिपुरुषाः, **शश्वत्** अनवरतं, **मुकुलितकरोत्तंसमकुटाः** मुकुलिताः कृताञ्जलयः करा एव उत्तंसाः तद्युक्ताः मकुट्यः येषां ते।।

अत्रेत्थं पदयोजना–हे शिवे! तव त्रिगुणजनितानां त्रयाणामपि देवानां तव चरणयोः या पूजा विरचिता भवेत् सैव पूजा। तथाहि त्वत्पादोद्वहनमणिपीठस्य निकटे हि यस्मात् मुकुलितकरोत्तंसमकुट्यः शश्वदेते स्थिताः।।

अयं भावः–भगवत्याः पादपीठसेवा पूजामात्रेण न लभ्यते, अपि तु भगवत्याः प्रसादवशादेवेति।। २५।।

Notes : This stanza implies that those who worship the Devī stand in no need of separately worshipping Brahmā, Viṣṇu and Rudra, who are but her agents, standing by her foot-stool, ever at her beck and call and in the act of adoring her.

विरिञ्चिः[1] पञ्चत्वं व्रजति हरिराप्नोति विरतिं
विनाशं कीनाशो भजति धनदो याति निधनम्।
[2]वितन्द्री माहेन्द्री विततिरपि संमीलतिदृशां[3]
महासंहारेऽस्मिन्विहरति[4] सति त्वत्पतिरसौ।। २६।।

Viriñciḥ pañcatvaṁ vrajati harir āpnoti viratiṁ
vināśaṁ kīnāśo bhajati dhana-do yāti nidhanam/
Vi-tandrī māhendrī vitatir api saṁmīlati dṛśāṁ
mahā-saṁhāre 'smin viharati sati tvat-patir asau.//

Translation : O Queen (Devī) of chastity! Viriñci goes back to the five elements ; Hari ceases to exist ; Kīnāśa (Yama) meets with destruction ; Kubera perishes; the array of the ever-wakeful eyes of Mahendra is also closed (for ever); in this great deluge, this Lord of Thine (alone) has His diversion.

विरिञ्चिः ब्रह्मा, **पञ्चत्वं** पञ्चभूतानां व्यष्टिरूपतां, मरणमिति यावत्, **व्रजति** याति। **हरिः** विष्णुः, **आप्नोति** प्राप्नोति, **विरतिं** उपरतिं, मरणमिति यावत्। **विनाशं** मृतिं, **कीनाशः** यमः **भजति**। **धनदः** कुबेरः, **निधनं** मरणं, **याति** प्राप्नोति। **वितन्द्री** विशेषेण तन्द्री प्रमीला जाड्यं यस्यास्सा, निद्राणेत्यर्थः, **मान्हेद्री** महेन्द्रस्येयं माहेन्द्री,

1. विरंचिः। 2. वितन्द्रा। 4. विलसति।
3. समीलितदृशा सम्मीलितदृशा; संमीलति दिशां।

चतुर्दशानां मनूनां इन्द्राणां **विततिरपि** सङ्कोऽपि, **सम्मीलितदृशा** सम्मीलिता दृशा दृष्टिर्यस्याः सा। 'हलन्तादपि टाबिष्यते' इति टाप्। यद्वा, सम्मीलितदृशा करणेन वितन्द्री माहेन्द्री। **महासंहारे** कल्पान्ते, **अस्मिन् विहरति** विशृङ्खलतया वर्तते। हे **सति!** पतिव्रते! **त्वत्पतिः** सदाशिवः हरः, **असौ** सहस्रदलकमले परिदृश्यमानः।

अत्रेत्थं पदयोजना–विरिञ्चिः पञ्चत्वं व्रजति। हरिः विरतिम् आप्नोति। कीनाशः विनाशं भजति। धनदः निधनं याति। माहेन्द्री विततिरपि सम्मीलितदृशा वितन्द्री। अस्मिन् महासंहारे सति! असौ त्वत्पतिः हरः विहरति।।

अयं भावः–सर्वेषामधिकारिपुरुषाणां [1]च संहारे ब्रह्माण्डभङ्गसमये तव पत्युर्यत् विहरणं तत् तव पातिव्रत्यमहिमायत्तमिति।। २६।।

Notes : This stanza extols the chastity of the Devī, in virtue of which her husband is not merely spared the general holocaust of gods, but strangely enough diverts himself amidst such weird environment. Viriñci, Hari, Kīnāśa (*i.e.*, Yama, the gods of death), Indra and other gods, who are *Amaras* according to tradition, meet with their death, during the Mahā-pralaya, but the Devī's Lord alone survives un-concerned.

जपो जल्पः शिल्पं सकलमपि मुद्राविरचना[2]
गतिः प्रादक्षिण्यक्रमणमशनाद्याहुतिविधिः[3]।
प्रणामः संवेशः सुखमखिलमात्मार्पणदशा[4]
सपर्यापर्यायस्तव भवतु यन्मे विलसितम्।। २७।।

Japo jalpaḥ śilpaṁ sakalam api mudrā-viracanā
gatiḥ prā-dakṣiṇya-kramaṇam aśanādy āhutividhiḥ/
Praṇāmaḥ saṁveśaḥ sukham akhilam ātmārparṇadaśā
saparyā-paryāyas tava bhavatu yan me vilasitam//

Translation : Whatever action it is of mine, may be taken (as intended) for Thy worship : (my) prattle, as muttering (Thy) prayer; the manifold forms of my manual work, as the Mudrās (gestures) employed in (Thy) worship; (my) loitering, as going round (Thee) clockwise; my taking nourishment, as offering

1. ईश्वराणामित्यधिकम्।
2. मुद्राविरचनम्।
3. प्रादक्षिण्यं भ्रमणमदनाद्याहुतिविधिः।
4. सुखमखिलमात्मार्पणदृशा ; ......आत्मार्पणदृशां।

oblations (to Thee); (my) lying down, as prostrating (before Thee); and (my) attending to all other comforts, as dedicating my entire self (to Thee).

जपः मन्त्रजपः, 'उपांशूच्चैर्वा क्रियते' इत्यादिभिश्चोदितः सः, **जल्पः** यादृच्छिकसल्लापः। **शिल्पं सकलमपि** हस्तविन्यासादिक्रियानिचयः, **मुद्राविरचना** मुद्राणां संक्षोभद्रावणाकर्षवश्योन्मादमहाङ्कुशखेचरीबीजयोनित्रिखण्डात्मकानां विरचना करणम्। **गतिः** यादृच्छिकगमनं **प्रादक्षिण्यक्रमणं** प्रदक्षिणक्रिया। **अशनादि** ओदनादियत्किञ्चित्पदार्थचर्वणम्, **आहुतिविधिः** आहुतीनां देवतोद्देशेन हविःप्रक्षेपणात्मकानां विधिः करणम्। **प्रणामः** नमस्कारः, **संवेशः** यादृच्छिकदण्डवल्लुठनम्, जल्पशिल्पव्यतिरेकेण अङ्गभङ्गनयनोन्मीलननिमीलनादिकं **च सुखं सुखकरं** वस्तु **अखिलं** समस्तं शब्दस्पर्शरूपरसगन्धादिकं **च सुखं सुखकरं** वस्तु **अखिलं** समस्तं शब्दस्पर्शरूपरसगन्धादिकं, **आत्मार्पणदृशा** आत्मार्पणबुद्ध्या, **सपर्यापर्यायः** सपर्या पूजा तस्याः पर्यायः रूपान्तरं, सपर्यैवेत्यर्थः, **तव** ते, **भवतु** भूयात्। **यत्** प्रसिद्धं, **मे** मम, **विलसितं** विलासः।।

अत्रेत्थं पदयोजनाः–हे भगवति! आत्मार्पणदृशा जपः जल्पः, सकलमपि शिल्पं मुद्राविरचना, गतिः प्रादक्षिण्यक्रमणं, अशनादि आहुतिविधिः, संवेशः प्रणामः, अखिलं सुखं मे यद्विलसितं च तव सपर्यापर्यायः भवतु।।

अयमर्थः–जल्पादीनां जपादिरूपता यथार्हं कल्पिता। एवं नयनोन्मीलननिमीलन-निमेषोन्मेषाङ्गभङ्गजृम्भादीनां यथार्हं सपर्यापर्यायता ऊह्या। शब्दादेः सुखकरस्य वस्तुनः षोडशोपचारव्यतिरेकेण आत्मार्पणबुद्ध्या त्याग एवं सपर्यापर्यायः, न तु स्वीकृतानाम्। यद्वा–शब्दादीनां यादृच्छिकसम्भवेन सुखप्रादुर्भावे तत्सुखं मच्छेषं न भवति किन्तु सदाशिवायेत्यर्पणं सपर्यापर्यायः।।

अत्रेदमनुसन्धेयम्–समयिनां मते समयस्य सादाख्यतत्त्वत्य सपर्या सहस्रदलकमल एव, न तु बाह्ये पीठादौ। ये ये समयिनो योगीश्वरा जीवन्मुक्ताः संसारयात्रामनुवर्तमानाः सादाख्यतत्त्वमनुचिन्तयन्तः आत्मैकप्रवणाः वर्तन्ते तेषां 'जपो जल्पश्शिल्पम्' इत्यादिना सपर्याप्रकारो निरूपितः। ये तु समयिनो योगीश्वराः विजने गुहान्तरे वा बद्धपद्मासनाः निगृहीतेन्द्रियाः सादाख्यतत्त्वध्यानैकनिष्ठाः वर्तन्ते तेषां वक्ष्यमाणचतुर्विधषड्विधै-क्यानुसन्धानमेव भगवत्याः सपर्येति अर्थादुक्तं भवति। अतश्च पक्षद्वयेऽपि बाह्यपूजायां तत्क्रियाकलापे च [1]तत्सम्पादनायां च क्लेशो नास्ति समयिनामिति रहस्यम्। यत्तु चन्द्रज्ञानविद्यायामुक्तम्–

---

1. तत्सम्पादनायासलेशो नास्ति।

सूर्यमण्डलमध्यस्थां देवीं त्रिपुरसुन्दरीम्।
पाशाङ्कुशधनुर्बाणान् धारयन्तीं प्रपूजयेत्।। इति।।

बाह्यपूजाप्रकारकथनं, तत्तु समयैकदेशिमतमिति पुरस्तात्प्रपञ्चयते।। २७।।

Notes : After descanting on the greatness of the Devī and the miraculous powers acquired by her votaries, as a result of meditating on her form with the appropriate Cakras, the author, in this stanza, deals with the manner in which a typical *Jīvanmukta* would worship the Devī, as prescribed in the Bhāvanopaniṣad. The worship of the Devī is of a two-fold character, *viz.*, exoteric (the lower form) and esoteric (the higher form). The former contains all the elements of prayer, gesture, circumambulation, oblation and prostration, as practised by the ordinary worshipper. The latter, which does not attach any importance to ceremonial forms, is referred to here as practised by the ever-hallowed *Jīvan-muktas.* The author so thoroughly identifies himself with this method that he uses the words 'of mine' significantly enough. Prattle—being made up of the Mātṛkās, which are divine, turns out to be prayer of some form, either mental or muttered or recited aloud. *Mudrās*—such as are used at the invocation of a deity and other connected rituals, which take the form of manual gestures. *Nourishment*—various kinds of solid and liquid food. This is considered as offering oblations to the Devī in the form of the Jāṭharāgni, vital energy in the belly. *Lying down*—includes sleep, turning one's limbs while in bed, *etc.* Lakṣmīdhara is of opinion that the worship of the Devī as the Sādākhyā-tattva in the *Sahasrāra*, and not the external kind, wherein the Devī is mounted on a pedestal, *etc.*, is meant by this stanza. Though Samayins have nothing to do with external forms, stillsothere is a class of Samayins who resort to the worship of the Devī in the middle of the solar disc, with Pāśa, Aṅkuśa, *etc.* in her arms, based on the authority of the *Candra-jñāna-vidyā.* This stanza contains the essence of the practice of *jñāna-yoga,* wherein all action is dedicated to the Paramātman here represented by the Tripurasundarī. In this sense every natural act and function without exception should be construed as an act of worship of the Devī.

'विरिञ्चिः पञ्चत्वम्' इति श्लोकेन यदुक्तं तदेव सोपस्करमाह–

सुधामप्यास्वाद्य[1] प्रतिभयजरामृत्युहरिणीं[2]
विपद्यन्ते विश्वे विधिशतमखाद्या दिविषदः।
करालं[3] यत्क्ष्वेलं[4] कवलितवतः[5] कालकलना
न शंभोस्तन्मूलं[6] तव जननि ताटङ्कमहिमा।। २८।।

Sudhām apy āsvādya pratibhaya-jarā-mṛtyu-hariṇīṁ
vipadyante viśve vidhi-śata-makhādyā diviṣadaḥ/
Karālaṁ yat kṣvelaṁ kavalitavataḥ kāla-kalanā
na śaṁbhos tan-mūlaṁ tava janani tāṭaṅka-mahimā//

Translation : O Mother! all the denizens of the celestial regions, such as Vidhi, Śata-makha and others, perish even after drinking nectar, which is reputed to confer immunity from terrible old age and death. If the period of life of Śaṁbhu, who has swallowed virulent poison, is beyond computation, it is all due to the peculiar virtue of Thy Tāṭaṅkas (ear-ornaments).

सुधां अमृतम्, **अपि** विरोधे, **आस्वाद्य** पीत्वा, **प्रतिभयजरामृत्युहरिणीं** प्रतिभयौ भयङ्करौ जरामृत्यू जरामरणे हरतीति प्रतिभयजरामृत्युहरिणी ताम्। **विपद्यन्ते** म्रियन्ते, **विश्वे** अखिलाः, **विधिशतमखाद्याः** विधिः ब्रह्मा, शतमखो देवेन्द्रः, तौ आद्यौ प्रभृतिभूतौ येषां ते, **दिविषदः** सुराः, **करालं** अत्युग्रं, **यत् क्ष्वेलं** विषं कालकूटं, **कवलितवतः** भक्षितवतः, **कालकलना** कालने अवसानकालेन कलना अवच्छेदः, मरणमिति यावत्, **न शम्भोः तन्मूलं** तस्य कालकलनाभावस्य मूलं कारणं **तव** भवत्याः, **जननि!** हे मातः! **ताटङ्कमहिमा** ताटङ्कस्य कर्णाभरणस्य सामर्थ्यम्।।

अत्रेत्थं पदयोजना–हे जननि! विश्वे विधिशतमखाद्याः दिविषदः प्रतिभयजरा–मृत्युहरिणीं सुधां आस्वाद्यापि विपद्यन्ते। करालं क्ष्वेलं कवलितवतः शम्भोः कालकलना नास्तीति यत् तन्मूलं तव ताटङ्कमहिमा।।

अयं भावः–यदि शम्भोरपि विपत्तिस्यात् ताटङ्कच्युतिः तर्हि स्यात्। ताटङ्कच्यावकत्वं कालस्य नास्ति, कालोत्पत्तिस्थितिलयानां ताटङ्कैकनियतत्वादिति देव्याः पातिव्रत्यमहिमा सर्वातिशायी इति।। २८।।

Notes : Having given some indication of the fruits attainable by a votary through Bhakti, devotion to the Devī, the author sets

---

1. प्रतिभव।
2. मृत्युहरणीं।
3. कराळं।
4. यत्क्ष्वेळं ; यत्क्ष्वेडं।
5. कबलितवतः, कबळिवतः।
6. शाम्भोः नूनं।

about, in this stanza, describing the marvelous powers excercised by the Devī's Tāṭaṅkas, through which alone eternal prosperity is vouchsafed to her devotees. Immunity from terrible old age and death—the apparent incongruity involved in conceiving of Brahma, Indra and other gods as perishing, in spite of their having drunk nectar, will vanish, if we take into account the fact that even the Devas meet with their dissolution at the time of the great deluge. Peculiar virtue of Thy Tāṭaṅkas—the word 'Tāṭaṅka' is understood by some as the Māṅgalya-sūtra, which it is the privilege of all Sumaṅgalīs, *i.e.*, women with their husbands alive, to wear around their necks. But the correct view is that the Tāṭaṅkas are ear-ornaments which are the outward symbols of Sumaṅgalīs, who are enjoined not to forsake their Tāṭaṅkas by any means, as their doing so would amount to their assuming the outward symbol of widowhood. In this view, the Devī's Tāṭaṅkas would lose their hold on her ears, only when Śaṁbhu could be overtaken by catastrophe, a contingency which is impossible, as the Devī's Tāṭaṅkas, whereon the very origin, duration and end of Kāla, *i.e.*, Time, depends. It is on this account that even the most virulent poison, which Śaṁbhu drank, had apparently no effect on him. So wonderful is the influence of the Devī on the longevity of her husband's life!

किरीटं वैरिञ्चं[1] परिहर पुरः कैटभभिदः
कठोरे कोटीरे स्खलसि जहि जम्भारिमकुटम्।[2]
प्रणम्रेष्वेतेषु प्रसभमुपयातस्य[3] भवनं
भवस्याभ्युत्थाने[4] तव परिजनोक्तिर्विजयते।। २९।।

Kirīṭaṁ vairiñcaṁ parihara puraḥ kaiṭabha-bhidaḥ
kaṭhore kotīre skhalasi jahi jambhāri-makuṭam/
Praṇamreṣv eteṣu prasabham upayātasya bhavanaṁ
bhavasyābhyutthāne tava parijanoktir vijayate.//

Translation : Glory to the words (of caution) of Thy servants : "Pray avoid the crown of Viriñci (lying) afore Thee!" "You will topple over the hard crest of the slayer of Kaiṭabha!" "Please keep off from the head-gear of the foe of Jambha!"—while all these three lay prostrate before Thee,—when, all of a

1. वैरिञ्च्यं ; वैरत्रं।
2. जम्भरिमुकुटम्।
3. प्रसभमभियातस्य।
4. हरस्याभ्युत्थाने।

sudden, Thou startedst to receive Bhava, who had comes to Thy abode!

किरीटं मकुटं, **वैरिञ्चं** विरिञ्चिसंबन्धि, **परिहर** दूरत एव कुरु, **पुरः** अग्रभागे। **कैटभभिदः** कैटभासुरं भिनत्तीति कैटभभित् तस्य विष्णोः, **कठोरे कोटीरे** मकुटाञ्चले, **स्खलसि**। अत्र काकुः अनुसन्धेया। **जहि** त्यज, **जम्भारिमकुटं** जम्भारेः इन्द्रस्य मकुटं किरीटम्। **प्रणम्रेषु** प्रकर्षेण दण्डवत् नतेषु **एतेषु** विरिञ्चिकैटभजिज्जम्भारिषु, **प्रसभं** अतिशीघ्रं ससंभ्रममित्यर्थः। **उपयातस्य** समागतस्य, **भवनं** मन्दिरं, **भवस्य** परमेश्वरस्य, **अभ्युत्थाने** अभिमुखोत्थितौ, **तव परिजनोक्तिः** सेवकानां वचनं, **विजयते** सर्वोत्कर्षेण वर्तते।।

अत्रेत्थं पदयोजना–हे भगवति! पुरः वैरिञ्चं किरीटं परिहर, कैटभमिदः कठोरे कोटीरे स्खलसि, जम्भारिमकुटं जहि, (इत्येवंरूपा) एतेषु प्रणम्रेषु सत्सु भवनमुपयातस्य भवस्य प्रसभं तवाभ्युत्थाने परिजनोक्तिर्विजयते। अत्र उदात्तालङ्कारः 'समृद्धिमद्वस्तु-वर्णनमुदात्तम्' इति लक्षणात्।। २९।।

Notes : Here is a touchingly graphic description of the reception accorded to her Lord by the Devī, while holding her court, surrounded by her maids-in-waiting and with the prostrate forms of Brahmā, Hari and Indra supplicating afore her, the maids administering here a timely warning, lest she should stumble on the crowns of the supplicating gods, in the warmth of her reception. *Keep off from the head-gear of the foe of Jambha*—the Saṁskrit verbal form *'Jahi'* is here used in the sense of *'Jahihi'*, (from the root *'hā'*, 'to abandon') and should not be construed as the Imperative second person singular of *'han'*, 'to kill', which would land us in an absurdity. To avoid this the reading *'Jahihīndrasya makuṭam'* may as well be suggested, but this would detract from the grandeur of the original.

स्वदेहोद्भूताभिर्घृणिभिरणिमाऽऽद्याभिरभितो[1]
[2]निषेव्ये नित्ये त्वामहमिति सदा भावयति यः।
किमाश्चर्यं तस्य त्रिनयनसमृद्धिं[3] **तृणयतो**[4]
महासंवर्ताग्निर्विरचयति नीराजनविधिम्।। ३०।।[5]

---

1. अभितोः ; अभितः।
2. निषेव्यां ; निषेवे।
3. त्रिभुवनसमृद्धिं।
4. तृणयतो ; तृणयतः।
5. This verse is printed (read) in the Saurashtra edition as verse No. 98.

Sva-dehodbhūtābhir ghṛṇibhir aṇimā-dyābhir abhito
niṣevye nitye tvām aham iti sadā bhāvayati yaḥ/
Kimāścaryaṁ tasya tri-nayana-samṛddhiṁ tṛṇayato
mahā-saṁvartāgnir viracayati nīrājana-vidhim//

Translation : (O Goddess) who art eternal and art served all around by the rays, Aṇimā and others emanating from Thine own frame! What is there to wonder at, if the Fire of the great Deluge should perform the ritual of waving lights before whosoever always conceives Thee as 'I am (Thou)', treating the wealth of Trinayana as mere straw?

स्वेदेहाद्भूताभिः स्वस्याः देहः स्वदेहः तस्मादुद्भूताभिः। अत्र देहशब्दो देहावयवं चरणं लक्षयति। **घृणिभिः** मयूखैः, मयूखानां चरणोद्भवत्वमुक्तं प्राक्। **अणिमाद्याभिः** अणिमागरिमेत्यादिभिः अष्टसिद्धिभिः, **अभितः** आवरणत्वेन अवस्थिताभिः[1] युक्तामिति शेषः। **निषेव्ये!** संसेव्ये! **नित्ये!** आद्यन्तरहिते! त्वामेतादृशीम्, **अहमिति** अहंभावनया, **सदा** सर्वकालं, **भावयति** ध्यानं करोति, **यः** साधकः, **किमाश्चर्यं** नास्त्याश्चर्यं, **तस्य** साधकस्य **त्रिनयसमृद्धिं** त्रीणि नयनानि मार्गाः [2]प्रापकाः सूर्यचन्द्राग्निरूपाः यस्य दर्शनायेति स त्रिनयनः। यद्वा– इडापिङ्गलासुषुम्नामार्गाः त्रयः तद्दर्शने उपाया इति त्रिनयनः सदाशिवः। यद्वा–त्रीणि नयनानि चक्षूंषि यस्य सः त्रिनयनः। क्षुभ्नादित्वात् णत्वाभावः। तस्य समृद्धिम् ऐश्वर्यं **तृणयतः** तृणीकुर्वतः, **महासंवर्ताग्निः** प्रलयकालग्निः **विरचयति** करोति। **नीराजनविधिं** नीराजनानुष्ठानम् [3]तस्य नीराजनक्रियायामवस्थितः प्रलयाग्निरपीत्यर्थः।।

अत्रेत्थं पदयोजना–हे नित्ये! निषेव्ये! स्वदेहोद्भूताभिः घृणिभिः अणिमाद्याभिः अभितोऽवस्थिताभिः[4] परिवृतां त्वां यः साधकः अहमिति सदा भावयति, त्रिनयनसमृद्धिं तृणयतः तस्य महासंवर्ताग्निः नीराजनविधिं विरचयतीत्यत्र किमाश्चर्यम्?

अयं भावः–अहमिति भावनया तादात्म्यसिद्धौ भगवत्याः तन्नीराजनविधिराश्चर्यकरो न भवतीति।। ३०।।

Notes : *Eternal*—that has neither beginning, nor end. *Rays*

1. 'नित्याभिः त्रिपुरसुन्दर्यादिभिः' इति प०शृ०-कोशयोः।
2. प्रकाराः।
3. तस्याम्।
4. 'नित्याभिश्च' इति प०शृ०-कोशयोः।

emanating from Thine own frame, i.e., the *Śrī-cakra* of nine parts, in the form of Āvaraṇa-devatās as detailed below : The three quadrangels of the Bhūgṛha, where-in abide the eight Siddhis—Aṇimā, Laghimā, Mahimā, Vaśitvā, Īśatvā, Prākāmya, Prāpti and Sarva-kāma-pradāyinī, in the first quadrangle; the eight Mātṛs—Brāhmī, Māheśvarī, Kaumārī, Vaiṣṇavī, Vārāhī, Māhendrī, Cāmuṇḍā and Mahā-lakṣmī, in the second quadrangle; the ten Mudrās—Sarva-saṁkṣobhiṇī, Sarva-vidrāviṇī, Sarvākarṣiṇī, Sarva-vaśaṁ-karī, Sarvonmādinī, Sarva-mahāṅkuśā, Sarva-khe-carī, Sarva-bīja, Sarva-yonī and Sarva-tri-khaṇḍā, in the third quadrangle; the sixteen Devatās—Kāmākarṣiṇī, Buddhy-ākarṣiṇī, Ahaṁkārākarṣiṇī, Śabdākarṣinī, Sparśākarṣiṇī, Rūpākarṣiṇī, Rasākarṣiṇī, Gandhākarṣiṇī, Cittākarṣiṇī, Dhairyākarṣiṇī, Smṛty-ākarṣiṇī, Nāmākarṣiṇī, Bijākarṣiṇī, Ātmākarṣiṇī, Amṛtākarṣiṇī and Śarīrākarṣiṇī, in the sixteen-petalled lotus; the eight Devatās—Anaṅga-kusumā, Anaṅga-mekhalā, Anaṅga-madanā, Anaṅga-madanāturā, Anaṅga-rekhā, Anaṅga-veginī, Anaṅgāṅkuśā and Anaṅga-mālinī, in the eight-petalled lotus : the fourteen Devatās—Sarvasaṁkṣobhiṇī, Sarvavidrāviṇī, Sarva-karṣiṇī, Sarvāhlādinī, Sarva-saṁmohanī, Sarva-stambhinī, Sarva-jṛmbhiṇī, Sarva-vaśaṁ-karī, Sarva-rañjanī, Sarvon-mādinī, Sarvārtha-sādhanī, Sarva-saṁpatti-pūraṇī, Sarva-mantra-mayī and Sarva-dvandva-kṣayaṁ-karī, in the *Catur-daśāra* ; the ten Devatās—Sarva-siddhi-prada, Sarva-saṁpat-pradā, Sarva-priyaṁ-karī, Sarva-maṅgala-kāriṇī, Sarva-kāma-pradā, Sarva-saubhāgya-dāyinī, Sarva-mṛtyu-praśamanī, Sarva-vighna-nivāriṇī, Sarvāṅga-sundarī and Sarva-duḥkha-vimocanī, in the *Bahir-daśāra;* the ten Devatās—Sarva-jñā, Sarva-śakti, Sarvaiśvarya-pradā, Sarva-jñānamayī, Sarva-vyādhi-vināśanī, Sarvādhāra-svarūpā, Sarva-pāpaharā, Sarvānandamayī, Sarva-rakṣā-sva-rūpiṇī and Sarvepsitaphala-pradā, in the *Antar-daśāra;* the eight Devatās,—Vaśinī, Kāmeśī, Modinī, Vimalā, Aruṇā, Jayinī, Sarveśī and Kaulinī, in the *Aṣṭa-koṇa;* the three Devatās—Kāmeśvarī, Vajreśī and Bhagamālā, in the *Tri-koṇa;* and the Tripura-sundarī in the middle. '*Frame*' is also taken by some to indicate the feet, the Mayūkhas sent out by which have been dealt with in stanza 14. This stanza represents the Yogin, who has attained one-ness with the Devī, as looking upon the untold wealth of Sadāśiva as a mere trifle, there being nothing else worthy of acquisition.

[1]चतुःषष्ट्या तन्त्रैः सकलमतिसंधाय[2] भुवनं
स्थितस्तत्तत्सिद्धिप्रसवपरतन्त्रैः[3] पशुपतिः।
पुनस्त्वन्निर्बन्धादखिलपुरुषार्थैकघटना-
स्वतन्त्रं ते तन्त्रं क्षितितलमवातीतरदिदम्।। ३१।।

Catuḥ-ṣaṣṭyā tantraiḥ sakalam atisaṁdhāya bhuvanaṁ
sthitas tat-tat-siddhi-prasava-para-tantraiḥ paśupatiḥ/
Punas tvan-nirbandhād akhila-puruṣārthaika-gha-ṭanā
sva-tantraṁ te tantraṁ kṣiti-talam avātītarad idam//

Translation : Paśupati, having deluded all the worlds with the sixty-four Tantras, which have as their sole purpose the conferring of the several *Śiddhis* attributed to each, has once again brought crown to this world, on account of Thy persuasion, Thy Tantra, which, of its own accord, would bring about the several ends and aims of human existence.

चतुष्षष्ट्या चतुष्षष्टिसङ्ख्याकैः महामायाशम्बरादिभिः, **तन्त्रैः** सिद्धान्तैः। अत्र चतुष्षष्टिशब्दस्य सङ्ख्येयपरत्वात् एकवचनान्तत्वम्। **सकलं** समस्तं, **अतिसंधाय** अपवाह्य वञ्चयित्वा, **भुवनं** प्रपञ्चं, **स्थितः** निवृत्तव्यापार; **तत्तत्सिद्धिप्रसवपरतन्त्रैः** ताश्च ताश्च सिद्धयः तत्तत्सिद्धयः चतुष्षष्टितन्त्रेषु एकस्मिन् एकस्मिन् तन्त्रे प्रयोजनभूताः एकैकसिद्धय इत्यर्थः, तासां प्रसवः उत्पत्तिः, तत्र परतन्त्रैः। यद्वा—तेषां तेषां सिद्धयः तत्तत्सिद्धयः, येषां येषां साधकानां स्वस्वाभिमताः सिद्धयः तासां प्रसवपरतन्त्रैः उत्पादकैकनियतैः। **पशुपतिः** पशूनां प्राणिनां पतिः, पश्यन्तीति पशवः **यद्वा**—इन्द्रियाण्येव पश्यन्तीति व्युत्पत्त्या पशवः, तान् पशून् पाति रक्षतीति पशुपतिः जीवः, शिव एव जीव इति पशुपतिः शिवः, **पुनः** भूयः, **त्वन्निर्बन्धात्** त्वया निर्बन्धः तस्मात्। चतुष्षष्टितन्त्रप्रतिपादित—सर्वसिद्धान्तरूपसकलपुरुषार्थसाधनभूततन्त्रान्तरोपदेशस्वीकारव्यग्रया देव्या भवत्या कृतो निर्बन्ध इति यावत्। यद्वा—त्वदिति भिन्नं पदं पञ्चम्यन्तम्। **अखिलपुरुषार्थैकघटनास्वतन्त्रम्** अखिलानां पुरुषार्थानां मुख्यत्वेन घटनायां स्वतन्त्रं स्वयमेव प्रधानं, **ते** भवत्याः, **तन्त्रं**, **क्षितितलं** भूतलं **अवातीतरत्।** तरतेर्णौ चङि रूपम्। गत्यर्थत्वात् 'गतिबुद्धि' इत्यादिसूत्रेण द्विकर्मकत्वम्। इदं वक्ष्यमाणम्।।

अत्रेत्थं पदयोजना—हे भगवति! पशुपतिः सकलं भुवनं तत्तत्सिद्धिप्रसवपरतन्त्रैः

---

1. चतुष्षष्ट्या ; चतुः षष्ट्या।
2. सकलमभिसंधाय।
3. पुनस्तत्तसिद्धिप्रसवपरतंत्रः ; प्रसभपरतन्त्रैः।

चतुष्षष्ट्या तन्त्रैः अतिसन्धाय सितः। पुनस्त्वन्निर्बन्धात् अखिलपुरुषार्थैकघटनास्वतन्त्रं ते तन्त्रमिदं क्षितितलमवातीतरत्।।

चतुष्षष्टितन्त्राणि चतुश्शत्याम्–

चतुष्षष्टिश्च तन्त्राणि मातृणामुत्तमानि च।
महामायाशम्बरं च योगिनीजालशम्बरम्।।
तत्त्वशम्बरकं चैव भैरवाष्टकमेव च।
बहुरूपाष्टकं चैव यामलाष्टकमेव च।।
चन्द्रज्ञानं मालिनी च महासंमोहनं तथा।
वामजुष्टं महादेवं वातुलं वातुलोत्तरम्।।
हृद्भेदं तन्त्रभेदं च गुह्ययन्त्रं च कामिकम्।
कलावादं कलासारं तथान्यत् कुब्जिकामतम्।।
तन्त्रोत्तरं च वीणाख्यं त्रोतलं त्रोतलोत्तरम्।
पञ्चामृतं रूपभेदं भूतोड्डामरमेव च।।
कुलसारं कुलोड्डीशं कुलचूडामणिं तथा।
सर्वज्ञानोत्तरं देव महाकालीमतं तथा।।
अरुणेशं [1]मोदिनीशं विकु[2]ण्ठेश्वरमेव च।
पूर्वपश्चिमदक्षं च उत्तरं च निरुत्तरम्[3]।।
विमलं विमलोत्थं च देवीमतमतः परम्।।

इत्येवं चतुष्षष्टितन्त्राणि पार्वतीं प्रति कथितानि। एतानि तन्त्राणि जगताम् अतिसन्धानकारणानि विनाशहेतुभूतानि, वैदिकमार्गदूरवर्तित्वात्। अत एवोक्तं भगवत्पादैः 'चतुष्षष्ट्या तन्त्रैः सकलमतिसन्धाय भुवनम्' सकल[4]–विद्वल्लोकप्रतारकाणि इमानि चतुष्षष्टितन्त्राणि इति। तथाहि–

---

1. मेदिनीशम्।
2. विकुण्डीश्वर।
3. महालक्ष्मीमतं चैव सिद्धयोगेश्वरीमतम्।
कुरूपिकामतं देवरूपिकामतमेव च।।
सर्ववीरमतं चैव विमलामतमुत्तमम्।
पूर्वपश्चिमदक्षं च उत्तरं च निरुत्तरम्।।
तन्त्रं वैशेषिकं ज्ञानं वीरावलि तथा परम्।
अरुणेशं मोहिनीशं विशुद्धेश्वरमेव च।।
इति वामकेश्वरतन्त्रपाठः।
4. इति वदद्भिः इत्यधिकम्।

महामायाशम्बरतन्त्रं मायाप्रपञ्चनिर्माणफलम्। मायाप्रपञ्चनिर्माणं नाम सर्वेषां चक्षुरादीनां अन्यथापदार्थग्रहणकारणं, यथा घटस्य पटाकरेण प्रतिभासनम्।।

योगिनीजालशम्बरम्–मायाप्रधानतन्त्रं शम्बरमित्युच्यते। तत्र तन्त्रे योगिनीनां जलदर्शनम्। तच्च श्मशानादिकुमार्गेण साध्यते।।

तत्त्वशम्बरम्–तत्त्वानां पृथिव्यादीनां शम्बरं महेन्द्रजालविद्या। महेन्द्रजालविद्यायां पृथिवीतत्त्वे उदकतत्त्वादीनि उदकतत्त्वं पृथिव्यादीनि तत्त्वानि एवमन्योन्यं प्रतिभासन्ते।।

भैरवाष्टकं नाम–सिद्धभैरव–वटुकभैरव–कङ्कालभैरव–कालभैरव–कालाग्निभैरव–योगिनीभैरव–महाभैरव–शक्तिभैरवप्रधानानि अष्टतन्त्राणि निध्याद्यैहिकफलसाधनान्यपि कापालिकमतत्वात् वैदिकमार्गदूराणि।।

बहुरूपाष्टकम्–शक्तेस्समुद्भूतानि रूपाणि ब्राह्मी, माहेश्वरी, कौमारी, वैष्णवी, वाराही, माहेन्द्री, चामुण्डा, शिवदूती चेत्यष्टौ रूपाणि। एतान्यवलम्ब्य प्रवृत्तानि तन्त्राणि अष्टौ, तेषां गणः अष्टकम्। एतदपि वेदमार्गदूरत्वात् हेयम्। अत्र श्रीविद्यायाः प्रसङ्गः बहुरूपाष्टकप्रस्तावे प्रसक्तानुप्रसक्त्या पातित इति न कश्चिद्दोषः।।

यमलाष्टकम्–यमलो नाम कामसिद्धान्तः?[1] तत्प्रतिपादकानि तन्त्राणि यामलान्यष्टौ। तेषां गणः यामलाष्टकम्। तदपि वैदिकमार्गदूरम्। यद्यपि चतुष्षष्टितन्त्राणां यमलत्वं लोकव्यवहारसिद्धम्; तत्तु अवैदिकत्वसाम्यात् उपचारादिति ध्येयम्।।

चन्द्रज्ञानम्–चन्द्रज्ञानविद्यायां षोडशनित्याप्रतिपादनम्। नित्याप्रतिपादकत्वेऽपि कापालिकमतान्तःपातित्वात् हेयमेव। उपादेयचन्द्रज्ञानविद्या चतुष्षष्टितन्त्रातीता।

मालिनीविद्या–समुद्रयानोपायहेतुः। सापि वैदिकमार्गदूरवर्तिनी।।

महासंमोहनम्–जाग्रतामपि निद्राहेतुः। सापि बालजिह्वाच्छेनादिकुमार्गेण साध्येति निषिद्धा।।

वामजुष्टमहादेवतन्त्रे–वामाचारप्रवर्तके इति हेये।।

वातुलं, वातुलोत्तरं, कामिकं च तन्त्रत्रयं कर्षणादिप्रतिष्ठान्तविधिप्रतिपादकम्। तस्मिन् तन्त्रत्रये कर्षणादिप्रतिष्ठान्ता विधयः एकदेशे प्रतिपादिताः। स चैकदेशो वैदिकमार्ग एव। अवशिष्टस्तु अवैदिकः।।

हृद्भेदतन्त्रं कापालिकमेव। यद्यपि हृद्भेदतन्त्रे षट्कमलभेदसहस्रार–प्रवेशौ प्रतिपादितौ, तथापि तस्मिन् तन्त्रे वामाचार एव प्रवृत्त इति कापालिकमेव तत्तन्त्रम्।।

---

1. यमला नाम कामसिद्धाम्बा। इति पाठः।।

तन्त्रभेद–गुह्यतन्त्रयो:–प्रकाशेन रहस्येन च परकृततन्त्राणां भेद इति तद्विद्यानुष्ठाने बहुहिंसाप्रसक्तेः तत्तन्त्रद्वयं वैदिकमार्गदूरम्।।

कलावादम्—कलानां चन्द्रकलानां वादः प्रतिपादनं यस्मिन् तन्त्रे तत् कलावादं वात्स्यायनादिकम्। यद्यपि कामपुरुषार्थत्वेऽपि कलाग्रहणमोक्षणदशस्थानग्रहण-चन्द्रकलारोपणादीनां कामपुरुषार्थे अनुपयोगात् परदारगमनादिनिषिद्धाचारोपदेशाच्च एकदेशे निषिद्धम्। यद्यपि निषिद्धांशः कापालिकतन्त्रं न भवति ; तथापि तत्र प्रवर्तमानः पुरुषः अवश्यं कापालिकाचारो भवतीति कापालिकत्वेन गणना तन्त्रस्य।।

कलासारम्–वर्णोत्कर्षविधिर्यत्र प्रवर्तते तत् कलासारं वामाचारप्रधानम्।।

कुब्जिकामतम्–घुटिकासिद्धिहेतुः। सोऽपि वामाचारप्रधान एव।।

तन्त्रोत्तरमते–रससिद्धिः।।

वीणाख्ये–वीणा नाम योगिनी। सा सिद्ध्यतीति वीणाख्यम्। सा वीणासंभोग-यक्षिणीति केचिदाहुः।।

त्रोतले–घुटिकाञ्जनपादुकासिद्धिः। घुटिका पानपात्रम्।।

त्रोतलोत्तरे–चतुष्षष्टिसहस्रसङ्ख्याकयक्षिणीनां दर्शनम्।।

पञ्चामृतम्–पञ्चानां पृथिव्यादीनां पिण्डाण्डे अमृतं यत्र मरणाभावः प्रतिपादितः तत् पञ्चामृतं तन्त्रम्। तदपि कापालिकमेव।।

रूपभेदादितन्त्रपञ्चकं मारणहेतुरिति अवैदिकम्।।

सर्वज्ञानादितन्त्रपञ्चकं कापालिकसिद्धान्तैकदेशिदिगम्बरमतमिति दूरत एव हेयम्।।

पूर्वादिदेवीमतपर्यन्तं दिगम्बरैकदेशक्षपणकमतमिति तत्ततोऽपि दूरत एव हेयम्।।

एवं चतुष्षष्टितन्त्राणि परिज्ञातॄणामपि वञ्चकानि। ऐहिकसिद्धिमात्रपरत्वात् वैदिकमार्गदूराणि। परिज्ञातारोपि ऐहिकफलापेक्षया तत्र कतिचन प्रवृत्ताः प्रतारिता एवेति रहस्यम्।।

ननु विप्रलिप्साद्याशयदोषरहितस्य भगवतः परमेश्वरस्य पशुपतेः कांश्चित्प्रति विप्रलम्भत्वं कथमिति चेत्–

मैवम्–परमेश्वरे परमकारुणिके विप्रलिप्साद्याशयदोषाः न सन्त्येव। किन्तु परमेश्वरः पशुपतिः ब्रह्मक्षत्रवैश्यशूद्रजातीयान् मूर्धा[1]वसिक्ताद्यनुलोमप्रतिलोमजातीया-नधिकृत्य तन्त्राणि निर्मितवान्। तत्र त्रैवर्णिकानां चन्द्रकलाविद्यासु वक्ष्यमाणास्वधिकारः।

1. मूर्धाभिषिक।

[1]शूद्रादीनां चतुष्षष्टितन्त्रेष्वधिकारः। एवमधिकारभेदमजानाना: अमीमांसका: व्यामुह्यन्ति। तेषामेवायं दोषः, न पशुपतेः परमेश्वरस्येति ध्येयम्।।

चन्द्रकलाविद्याष्टकं श्रीविद्याप्रतिपादकं तन्त्रं–चन्द्रकला, ज्योत्स्नावती कलानिधिः, कुलार्णवम्, कुलेश्वरी, भुवनेश्वरी, बार्हस्पत्यं, दूर्वासमतं चेति। अस्मिन् तन्त्राष्टके त्रैवर्णिकानां शूद्रादीनां च अधिकारोऽस्ति। तत्र ब्राह्मणादीनधिकृत्य सव्यमार्गेण प्रादक्षिण्येन सर्वोऽप्यनुष्ठानकलापः प्रतिपादितः। शूद्रादीनधिकृत्य अपसव्यमार्गेण वामाचारो निरूपितः।।

शुभागमतन्त्रपञ्चके वैदिकमार्गेण अनुष्ठानकलापो निरूपितः। अयं शुभागम-पञ्चकनिरूपितो मार्गः वसिष्ठसनकशुकसनन्दनसनत्कुमारैः पञ्चभिः मुनिभिः प्रदर्शितः। अयमेव समयाचार इति व्यवह्रियते। तथैवास्माभिरपि शुभागमपञ्चकानुसारेण समयमतमवलम्ब्यैव भगवत्पादमतमनुसृत्य व्याख्या रचिता। चन्द्रकलाविद्याष्टकं तु कुलसमयानुसारित्वेन मिश्रकमित्युच्यते विद्वद्भिः। चतुष्षष्टितन्त्राणि कुलमार्ग एव–

मिश्रकं कौलमार्गं च परित्याज्यं हि शाङ्करि।।

इति ईश्वरवचनात् मिश्रकमतं कौलमार्गं च परित्याज्यम्। कौलैः मृग्यते अवलम्ब्यत इति कौलमार्गः कौलमतम्। कर्मणि घञ्। अतश्च शुभागमपञ्चकमेव वैदिकैरादणीयम्। केवलसमयमार्गप्रदर्शनपरत्वात्। समयमार्गस्वरूपं तु '**तवाधारे मूले सह समयया**'[2] इत्यादिश्लोकव्याख्यानावसरे निपुणतरमुपादयिष्यामः।।

तत्र शुभागमपञ्चके षोडशनित्यानां प्रतिपादनं मूलविद्यायामन्तर्भावमङ्गीकृत्य अङ्गतया। चक्रविद्यायां अङ्गतयैवान्तर्भावः कथितः। अत एव चतुष्षष्टिविद्यान्तर्भूतायां चन्द्रज्ञानविद्यायां षोडशनित्याः प्रधानत्वेन प्रतिपादिता इति, तत्प्रतिपादकं तन्त्रं कौलमार्गः अयं तु समयमार्ग इति भेदः।।

अत्रेदमनुसन्धेयम्–शुभागमपञ्चकं नाम वासिष्ठसंहिता, सनकसंहिता, शुकसंहिता, सनन्दनसंहिता, सनत्कुमारसंहिता, इति पञ्च संहिताः शुभागमपञ्चकम्। तत्र वसिष्ठसंहितायां देवीं प्रति ईश्वरवचने वसिष्ठेन शक्तिर्बोधिता। यथा–

श्रृणु देवि प्रवक्ष्यामि नित्याषोडशकं तव[3]।
न कस्यचिन्मयाऽऽख्यातं सर्वतन्त्रेषु गोपितम्।।

---

1. शूद्राणां सङ्कीर्णानां च।
2. श्लोकः ४१।
3. 'षोडशकं नवम्' 'षोडशिकार्णवं तव' इत्यपि पाठान्तरे।

तत्रादौ प्रथमा नित्या महात्रिपुरसुन्दरी।
ततः कामेश्वरी नित्या नित्या च भगमालिनी।
नित्यक्लिन्ना तथा चैव भेरुण्डा वह्निवासिनी।
महा[1] विद्ये[वज्रे]श्वरी रौद्री त्वरिता कुलसुन्दरी।।
नित्या नीलपताका च विजया सर्वमङ्गला।
ज्वालामालिनि चिद्रूपाः एता नित्यास्तु षोडश।।
प्रतिपत्प्रभृतौ देव्याः पौर्णमास्यन्तमर्चयेत्।
एकादिवृद्ध्या हान्या च दर्शान्तं देवि विग्रहम्।।

एतच्च षोडशनित्यानां षोडशतिथ्यात्मकत्वम् उत्तरश्लोके निरूप्यते।।

इदानीं षोडशनित्यानां श्रीचक्रे अङ्गतया अन्तर्भावो निरूप्यते–षोडशनित्यास्तु अष्टवर्गात्मकतया अष्टदलपद्मे अष्टपत्रेषु स्थिताः यथाक्रमं अष्टकोणचक्रे प्रागादिकोण-मारभ्य एकैकस्मिन् कोणे द्विकंद्विकमन्तर्भूतम्। एवमष्टद्विकानि अष्टकोणेषु अन्तर्भूतानि। एता एव नित्याः षोडशस्वरात्मकतया षोडशदलपद्मे स्थिताः द्विदशारेऽन्तर्भूताः। एतासां नित्यानां मध्ये प्रथमं नित्याद्वयं त्रिकोणबिन्दुरूपेण स्थितम्। अवशिष्टास्तु चतुर्दश नित्याः मन्वश्रे अन्तर्भूताः मेखलात्रयभू पुरत्रये बैन्दवत्रिकोणयोरन्तर्भूते। एवं नित्यानां चक्रे अन्तर्भावः। इममेवान्तर्भावं मेरुप्रस्तारमाहुः। अत एव चन्द्रकलाविद्यायाः चक्रविद्यायाः सङ्गत्वं नित्यानां सिद्धम्।

सनन्दनसंहितायाम् ऋषीन् प्रति सनन्दनवचनम्–एतास्तु षोडशनित्याः चन्द्रकलायाः चक्रविद्याया अङ्गभूताः। एताश्च षोडशनित्याः स्वरात्मकाः पञ्चदशाक्षरीमन्त्रगत 'ए'कारादिभूत 'अ'कारविसर्गात्मक 'स' काराभ्यां सङ्गृहीताः जीवकलारूपाः बैन्दवस्थाने स्थापिताः तत्रैव अन्तर्भूताः। कादयो मावसानाः पाशाङ्कुशबीजयुक्तास्सन्तः अष्टारे दशकोणद्वये च अन्तर्भूताः। शिष्टास्तु यकारादयो नव वर्णाः द्विरावृत्त्या मन्वश्रे चतुर्दशकोणेषु चतुर्दश अन्तर्भूताः, शिष्टं वर्णचतुष्टयं शिवचक्र चतुष्टयेऽन्तर्भूतम्। इममेव कैलासप्रस्तारमाहुः। एवं नित्यानां चक्रविद्याया अङ्गत्वं प्रतिपादितम्।।

सनत्कुमारसंहितायामपि चक्रविद्यायां षोडशनित्यानां अङ्गत्वं प्रतिपादितम्। यथा सनत्कुमारवचनम्–श्रीचक्रस्याङ्गभूताः नित्याः वशिन्यादिभिः द्विकंद्विकं मेलयित्वा बैन्दवं त्रिकोणं विहाय अष्टसु कोणेष्वन्तर्भाव्याः। मध्ये त्रिपुरसुन्दरी अन्तर्भाव्या। अष्टवर्गास्तु अष्ट वशिन्यादयः, षोडश नित्याः, द्वादश योगिन्यः, चतस्रो गन्धाकर्षिण्यादयः–एवं चतुश्चत्वारिंशत्। अत्र एकां शक्तिं विहाय त्रयश्चत्वारिंशत्कोणेषु त्रयश्चत्वारिंशद्देवता

1. विश्वेश्वरी।

अन्तर्भाव्याः, एकां त्रिपुरसुन्दरीं बैन्दवस्थानादधस्तात्, गन्धाकर्षिण्यादयस्तु चतुर्द्वारेषु इति नित्यानां अङ्गत्वं प्रतिपादितम्। इममेव भूप्रस्तारमाहुः। अष्टानां वशिन्यादीनां द्वादशयोगिनीनां गन्धाकर्षिण्यादीनां नामधेयानि '**सवित्रीभिर्वाचाम्**'[1] इत्यादिश्लोक-व्याख्यानावसरे कथितानि ।। ३१ ।।

Notes : *Having deluded*—into accepting the *Śiddhis*, which stand far apart from the scripturally ordained path, and thus deceived them, they being incapable of distinguishing the spurious from the genuine. In this connection it may be observed that the so-called delusion, referred to above, is not the work of Paśupati, but is of the people's own making. According to Paśupati's design the Candra-kalā-vidyā comprised in the eight works, Candra-kalā, Jyotiṣ-matī, Kalā-nidhi, Kulārṇava, Kuleśvarī, Bhuvaneśvarī, Bārhas-patya and Durvāsa-mata, is meant for the exposition of the *Śrī-vidyā* to be followed by the twice-born by adopting the Savya (right) path, constituting the Samayācāra, and by other classes by adopting the Apa-savya (left) path, constituting the Vāmācāra, otherwise known as Kulācāra. As the Vidyā comprehends both the paths referred to above, it is also known as the Miśra or mixed path. Further, according to Paśupati's design, there are the sixty-four Tantras, which are intended exclusively for the Kaulas. As such, it will be seeen that no sort of differentiation between the various classes is aimed at in his design.[2] On the other hand, the difference is inherent in the classes themselves, due to difference of birth, which means breeding, mental equipment attained, and other consequential features. Paśupati, in his supreme mercy, has ordianed the two paths, the one more advanced and the other less, to suit the varying capacities of all classes. The sixty-four Tantras, if at all they prove defective, make no difference between the classes, as even wise men are as much subject to be drawn away by the worldly purposes attributed to the Tantras, to the exclusion of the attainment of the scriptural goal. *All the worlds*—Lakṣmīdhara and Kāmeśvarasuri take these words to indicate the low-born and the hybrid class, known as *Anu-loman* and *Prati-loman,* with an

---

1. १७ श्लोकः।
2. The Samayins also have works exclusively relating to their Ācāra. known as the Śubhāgama-pañcaka or the five Saṁhitā-s attributed to the sages Vasiṣṭha, Sanaka, Śuka, Sanandana and Sanat-kumāra.

admixture of aboriginal blood running in their veins, who are considered by them to be beyond the pale of the scriptural path, as, according to them, this path could be adopted only by the twice-born classes, because of their supposed high birth. Kaivalyāśrama adopts the reading '*Abhisaṁdhāya*', which means 'having attracted', along with '*Prasabha-para-tantraiḥ*', which means 'categorically asserting', and would construe the passage in some such way as follows : Paśupati, having attracted the people of the world to achieve one or other of the four aims of human existence, through the sixty-four Tantras, categorically asserting the several *Siddhis* attributed to each, has, at the persuasion of the Devī, brought down into this world a single Tantra, which would, by itself, enable them to achieve their several ends, thus incorporation the purposes served by the sixty-four Tantras.

With the sixty-four Tantras—the sixty-four Tantras are : (1) *Mahā-māyā-śambara*—having as its aim the deluding of the senses and the intellect. (2) *Yoginī-jāla-śambara*—legerdemain, involving the agency of Yoginīs, accomplished by resorting to the crematory and other ways of a repulsive nature and adopting questionable practices. (3) *Tantra-śambara*—by causing the lements to appear as though mutually transforming themselves. (4) *Siddha-bhairava, (5) Vaṭukabhairava,* (6) *Kaṅkāla-bhairava,* (7) *Kāla-bhairava,* (8) *Kālāgni-bhairava,* (9) *Yoginī-bhairava,* (10) *Mahā-bhairava,* (11) *Śakti-bhairava*—the eight Tantras having as their presiding deities the eight-fold aspects of Bhairava, which, although apparently serving some useful purpose to man, such as the finding of a treasuretrove. *etc.*, are considered objectionable, as they partake of Kāpālika doctrines. (12) *Brāhmī,* (13) *Māheśvarī,* (14) *Kaumārī,* (15) *Vaiṣṇavī,* (16) *Vārāhī,* (17) *Māheśvarī,* (18) *Cāmuṇḍā,* (19) *Śiva-dūtī*—the eight Tantras constituting the *Bahu-rūpāṣṭaka,* wherein importance is attached to the eight Śaktis. Even these are reprehensible, as they stray far away from the Vedic path, although they involve some knowledge of the Śrīvidyā incidentally, (20) *Brahmayāmala,* (21) *Viṣṇuyāmala,* (22) *Rudrayāmala,* (23) *Lakṣmīyāmala,* (24) *Umāyāmala,* (25) *Skandayāmala,* (26) *Gaṇeśayāmala,* (27) *Jayadrathayāmala*—the eight arts relating to Yāmalā, otherwise known as Kāma-siddhā, aiming at the gratificiation of several desires, which not having the sanction of the Vedas, are considered objectionable, so much so that even the sixty-four Tantras are sometimes spoken of collectively as Yāmala.

(28) *Candra-jñāna*—which expounds the sixteen Nityā-s and is however considered objectionable, as smacking of Kāpālika tenents. There is also a Tantra of the same name, which has nothing to do with any of the sixty-four Tantras herein mentioned. (29) *Mālinī-vidyā*—wherewith oceans could be crossed. (3) *Mahā-sammohana*—which brings on sleep in persons even during their waking state. As this involves the cutting of the tongues of a child to render the acquisition of such power possible, it is reprehensible. (31) *Vāma-juṣṭa,* (32) *Mahā-deva*—productive of awkward habits and tendencies, which may be characterized as Vāmācāra, filthy conduct. (33) *Vātula,* (34) *Vātulottara,* (35) *Kāmika*—incidentally expounding the rules relating to the procedure to be adopted for the several processes connected with the erection of temples, *etc.*, commencing from the withdrawal and ending with the establishment of powers, *etc.*, but involving features not countenanced by the Veda. (36) *Hṛdbheda-tantra*—which, though aiming of bursting through the six lotuses from Mūlādhāra onwards to the thousand-petalled one, falls within the province of the Kāpālika-tantra, as it has recourse to the adoption of Vāmācāra. (37) *Tantra-bheda,* (38) *Guhya-tantra*—which involve retaliatory processes, both overt and covert, aiming at the destruction of what has been achieved by other Tantras and the causation of severe pain to living beings, and as such are reprehensible. (39) *Kālā-vāda*—expounding the secrets relating to the digits of the Moon, such as are dealt with in Vātsyāyana's sexual science, which, though dealing with a very useful branch of knowledge, involves such objectionable features as the grasping and releasing of Kalās, the power of influencing the ten parts, the induction of the Candra-kalās and the countenancing of the wicked practice of alluring others' wives, and are on that account reprehensible. Although these have no direct bearing on the Kāpālika-tantra, still they amount, in effect, to such perverse doctrines that those who have recourse to such practices are bound to have more or less a leaning towards such views. (40) *Kalā-sāra*—which expounds the rules relating to the excellence of colour and is, as such, a Vāmācāra. (41) *Kuṇḍikā mata*—which deals with the attainment of marvellous powers by administering special pills. (42) *Matottara*—which deals with the conquest of quicksilver by special processes laying claim to alchemic and panaceal virtues. (43) *Vīṇākhya*—which deals with command over a Yakṣiṇī of that name, having influence over sexual virility.

(44) *Trotala*—dealing with magical tankards, collyria and sandals, the first credited with marvellous medicinal properties, the second with magical clairvoyant powers, and the third with mysterious powers of locomotion. (45) *Trotalottara*—credited with the power of bringing the sixty-four-thousand Yakṣiṇīs face to face. (46) *Pañcāmṛta*—dealing with the immortality inhering in the Piṇḍāṇḍa, microcosm of the five elements and the bestowal of such immortality on the votary of the Tantra. This is also of the Kāpālika type. (47) *Rūpa-bheda,* (48) *Bhūtoḍḍāmara,* (49) *Kula-sāra,* (50) *Kuloḍḍīśa,* (51) *Kula-cūḍāmaṇi*—all of which are credited with the power of bringing about death and are, as such, not recognized by the Veda. (52) *Sarva-jñānottara,* (53) *Mahākālī-mata,* (54) *Aruṇeśa,* (55) *Modinīśa,* (56) *Vikuṇṭheśvara*—the five Tantras, which have to be given up as they deal with the tenets of the Digambaras. (57) *Pūrvāmnāya,* (58) *Paścimāmnāya,* (59) *Dakṣiṇāmnāya,* (60) *Uttarāmnāya,* (61) *Nir-uttarāmnāya,* (62) *Vimala,* (63) *Vimalotta* and (64) *Devī-mata*—which have reference to the doctrines of the Kṣapaṇakas, and are as such to be discarded.

These are the sixty-four Tantras enumerated in the Vāmakeśvara-tantra, quoted by Lakṣmīdhara and explained by him. Bhāskararāya, the reputed commentator of the same treatise, however, differs from Lakṣmīdhara in the enumeration of the Tantras and treats (4 to 11) the *Bhairavāṣṭaka* as one Tantra, and (31 and 32) *Vāma-juṣṭa* and *Mahā-deva* as a single Tantra giving the name of *Mahocchuṣman* to it, and includes eight Tantras not enumerated by Lakṣmīdhara, *viz.*, (1) *Mahā-lakṣmī-mata,* (2) *Siddha-yogīśvarī-mata,* (3) *Ku-rūpikā-mata,* (4) *Deva-rūpikā-mata,* (5) *Sarva-vīra-mata,* (6) *Vimalā-mata,* (7) *Jñānārṇava* and (8) *Vīrāvalī* in the list. He also calls into question the view held by Lakṣmīdhara of considering the sixty-four Tantras as reprehensible and as upholding practices which have not the sanction of the Vedas, and avers that, as the Tantras have been recognized by the Vāmakeśvara-tantra and the Kalpa-sūtra as Śāstras, and as all Śāstras have the sanction of the Upaniṣads, Lakṣmīdhara's view is either coloured by prejudice or due to an imperfect understanding of the true import and utility of these Tantras. It may however be added in Lakṣmīdhara's defence that he pins his faith on a saying attributed to Īśvara, which he quotes to the effect that both the Miśra-and Kaula-paths are to be discarded. He therefore holds that the Samaya-mārga alone should be followed by the twice-born and that such is also the view of Śaṅkarabhagavatpāda.

Thy Tantra—taking 'Idam' as the attribute of the word 'Tantram', Lakṣmīdhara understands the words to imply, "this, *i.e.*, what immediately follows (in the text stanza), Thy Tantra". Bhāskararāya in his Setu-bandha, however, holds a different opinion, *viz.*, that by the words 'Thy Tantra' used in this stanza, the Vāmakeśvaratantra is meant, incidentally referring to the views held by others that it is the Jñānārṇava and yet others that it is the Tantrarāja; he refutes them for the reason, among others, that those Tantras themselves depend in certain respects upon the Vāmakeśvara-tantra for support. Evidently he takes the word 'Idam' as an attribute of 'Kṣititalam,' meaning 'this world'.

Acyutānanda, in his commentary on this stanza, alludes to the prevalent tradition that Śiva is in the habit of narrating Tantras to the Devī in Kailāsa, which Gaṇeśa records then and there, and after completion communicates to Maharṣis on Earth, and this practice continues for all time. Hence none of the Tantras could, according to the orthodox view referred to above, be considered unauthorized because of their later origin, as their validity will hold for all time. The commentator holds that whatever is established by the Purāṇas and the Āgamas should be held to be ever existence by the wise and not called into question from the point of view of the time of their origin, as they appear and disappear, according as they are revealed or withdrawn, and their importance lies entirely in the Siddhis to which they lead and the actual results flowing from them. 'Thy Tantra', which is significantly called 'Sva-tantra', is, in this view, the creation of the Lord and should not be confounded with the sixty-four Tantras.

It may be observed here that the authorities relied upon by the Samaya school, to which Lakṣmīdhara belongs, are alleged by them to be Mokṣaśāstras, or authorities inculcating the attainment of *Mokṣa* through the practice of the internal form of worship advocated by them. It is not however apparent on what authority this school of worship maintains that the Kaula form of worship does not lead to the attainment of *Mokṣa* and how, beyond the assertion that the Kaula practice of worshipping the Devī in the *Mūlādhara* is reprehensible, they seek to support it by quoting chapter and verse of any scriptural authority, which they hold as settling the question one way or the other.

अथ निखिलपुरुषार्थैकघटनास्वतन्त्रं भगवत्यास्तन्त्रं पशुपतिः क्षितितलमवातीतर-दित्युक्तं पूर्वश्लोके। तदेव तन्त्रं प्रस्तौति–

शिवः शक्तिः[1] कामः क्षितिरथ रविः शीतकिरणः[2]
स्मरो हंसः[3] शक्रस्तदनु च परामारहरयः।
अमी हृल्लेखाभिस्तिसृभिरवसानेषु घटिता[4]
भजन्ते वर्णास्ते तव जननि नामावयवताम्।। ३२।।

Śivaḥ śaktiḥ kāmaḥ kṣitir atha raviḥ śīta-kiraṇaḥ
smaro haṁsaḥ śakras tad-anu ca parā-māra harayaḥ/
Amī hṛl-lekhābhis tisṛbhir avasāneṣu ghaṭitā
bhajante varṇās te tava janani nāmāvayavatām//

Translation : O Mother! Śiva, Śakti, Kāma and Kṣiti; and then, Ravi, Śīra-kiraṇa, Smara, Haṁsa and Śakra ; and thereafter, Parā, Māra and Hari; these (three sets of) syllables, when conjoined severally at their ends with the three Hṛl-lekhās, become the components of Thy name.

शिवः ककारः। **शक्तिः** एकारः। **कामः** ईकारः। **क्षितिः** लकारः। **अथशब्दः** अवसानद्योतकः। **रविः** हकारः। **शीतकिरणः** सकारः। **स्मरः** ककारः। **हंसः** हकारः। **शक्रः** लकारः। **'तदनु च'** इति अवसानं द्योतयति। **परा** सकारः। **मारः** ककारः। **हरिः** लकारः। **अमी** द्वादश वर्णाः। **हृल्लेखाभिः** ह्रीङ्कारैः, **तिसृभिः** त्रित्वविशिष्टैः, **अवसानेषु** विरामस्थानेषु चतुष्कपञ्चकत्रिकाणामुपरि, **घटिताः** योजिताः, **भजन्ते** प्राप्नुवन्ति। **वर्णाः ते** पूर्वोक्ताः ककारादयः, तव भवत्याः, **जननि!** हे मातः! **नामावयवतां** नाम्नः त्रिपुरसुन्दरीमन्त्रस्य अवयवतां प्रतीकत्वम्।।

अत्रेत्थं पदयोजना–हे जननि! शिवः शक्तिः कामः क्षितिः अथ रविः शीतकिरणः स्वरः हंसः शक्रः तदनु च परामारहरयः इत्येते वर्णाः तिसृभिः हृल्लेखाभिः अवसानेषु घटिताः ते वर्णाः तव नामावयवतां भजन्ते।।

अत्रेदमनुसन्धेयम्–शिवः शक्तिः कामः क्षितिरिति वर्णचतुष्टयं आग्नेयं खण्डम्। रविः शीतकिरणः स्मरः हंसः शक्र इति वर्णपञ्चकं सौरं खण्डम्। उभयोः खण्डयोः मध्ये रुद्रग्रन्थिस्थानीयं हृल्लेखाबीजम्। परामारहरय इति वर्णत्रयेण सौम्यं खण्डं निरूपितम्। सौम्यसौरखण्डयोर्मध्ये विष्णुग्रन्थिस्थानीयं भुवनेश्वरीबीजम्। तुरीयमेकाक्षरं

1. शिवश्शक्तिः।
2. रविश्शीतकिरणः।
3. हंसश्शक्रस्तदनु।
4. घटिताः।

चन्द्रकलाखण्डम्। सौम्यचन्द्रकलाखण्डयोर्मध्ये ब्रह्मग्रन्थिस्थानीयं हल्लेखाबीजम्। चन्द्रकलाखण्डं तु गुरूपदेशवशादवगन्तव्यमिति न प्रकाशितम्। अत एव–

त्रिखण्डो मातृकामन्त्रः सोमसूर्यानलात्मकः।। इति।।

अवरोहक्रमेणेति शेषः। 'सोमसूर्यानलात्मकः' इत्येतावन्मात्रे वक्तव्ये त्रिखण्ड इत्युक्तिः ज्ञानशक्तीच्छाशक्तिक्रियाशक्त्यात्मकं खण्डत्रयमिति जाग्रत्स्वप्नसुषुप्त्यवस्था-त्रयात्मकं, विश्वतैजसप्राज्ञवृत्तित्रयात्मकम्, तमोरजस्सत्त्वगुणात्मकं इत्येवंपरा। एतच्च पुरस्तात्प्रपञ्चयिष्यामः।।

अत्र शिवश्शक्तिरित्यादिशब्दाः क्वचित् लक्षितलक्षणया क्वचित् लक्षणया ककारादिवर्णपराः। तथाहि त्रिपुरसुन्दरीमन्त्रस्य षोडशवर्णाः। ते च षोडश वर्णाः षोडशनित्यात्मतया स्थिताः। अत्र षोडश्याः कलायाः नित्यत्वव्यपदेशः चन्द्रकलात्व-रूपसाम्यात्। सा च परा कला चिदेकरसा। तस्याश्छाया विशुद्धिचक्रे षोडशारे कलात्मतया भ्रमतीति[1] रहस्यम्। सा प्रधानं प्रकृतिश्च। अस्या अङ्गभूताः पञ्चदश नित्या इति पूर्वश्लोके प्रतिपादितम्।।

यद्यपि ककारादयः श्रूयमाणाः पञ्चदश वर्णाः संप्रदायतो ज्ञातव्याः; एको वर्णः षोडशकलात्मकः [2]प्रधानभूत इति, यद्यपि षोडशी कला गुरुमुखादेव अवगन्तव्या; तथापि तस्या अप्रतिपादने व्याख्यानं सापेक्षमेव। अतोऽनुपादेयं स्यादेवेति सा कला निरूप्यते।

न च–

सच्छिष्यायोपदेष्टव्या गुरुभक्ताय सा कला।। इति।।

शिष्याणामेवोपदेष्टव्या नान्येषामिति वाच्यम्। ये तु मदीयं ग्रन्थं दृष्ट्वा तां कलां जानन्ति ते मच्छिष्या एवेत्यस्माकमनुग्रहः।।

ननु पादवन्दन–पादोपसङ्ग्रहण–हस्तमस्तकसंयोगादेः अङ्गकलापस्य शिष्यत्वा-पादकस्याभावे, कथं तेषु शिष्यत्वमिति चेत्–

सत्यम्, अस्मदीयग्रन्थं दृष्ट्वा षोडश्याः कलायाः स्वरूपं गुर्वन्तरमुखादेव जानतां शिष्यत्वं मास्तु। ये तु न जानन्ति गुरुमुखादपि तेषामुपदेशो न सम्भाव्यत एव, तदानीं गुर्वेकपरतन्त्रे अस्मिन् मन्त्रे "के वाऽस्माकं गुरवः?" इति जिज्ञासायामुदयमानायां

1. 'भ्राजतीति' इति पाठः।
2. प्रकृतिभूत इति।

तेषां जिज्ञासूनां वर्तमानानां वर्तिष्यमाणानां च वयमेव गुरव इति तेष्वनुग्रहः कृतोऽस्माभिः।।

षोडशी कला नाम शकार-रेफ-ईकार-बिन्द्वन्तो मन्त्रः। एतस्यैव बीजस्य नाम श्रीविद्येति। श्रीबीजात्मिका विद्या श्रीविद्येति रहस्यम्। एवं षोडशनित्यानां प्रकृतिभूताः ककारादयः। ताश्च षोडश नित्याः शुक्लप्रतिपदमारभ्य पौर्णमास्यन्ततिथिरूपाः, कृष्णपक्षप्रतिपदमारभ्य अमावास्यान्ततिथिरूपाः। एता एव चन्द्रकलाभिधानाः। चन्द्रकला एव प्रतिपदादितिथय इति सुप्रसिद्धम्। यथोक्तं ज्योतिश्शास्त्रे-

प्रतिपन्नाम विज्ञेया चन्द्रस्य प्रथमा कला।
द्वितीयाद्या द्वितीयाद्याः पक्षयोश्शुक्लकृष्णयोः।। इति।।

अयमर्थः-चन्द्रस्य प्रथमायाः कलायाः प्रतिपदिति नामधेयम्। सैव कलात्मिका सूर्यमण्डलान्निर्गता। कृष्णपक्षे तु सूर्यमण्डलं प्रविष्टा। एवं शुक्लपक्षे सूर्यमण्डलान्निर्गता द्वितीया कला द्वितीया तिथिः। कृष्णपक्षे तु सूर्यमण्डलं प्रविष्टा द्वितीया कला द्वितीया तिथिरिति। एवं सर्वत्र ऊहनीयम्। अतश्च पञ्चदशकलाव्यवधानं सूर्यचन्द्रयोर्यत्र सा पौर्णमासी। पञ्चदश्यां कलायां सूर्यचन्द्रयोरत्यन्तसंयोगः सा अमावास्येति ज्ञेयम्। अतः कौलमते चन्द्रकलात्मिकानां षोडशानां नित्यानां प्रतिदिनं एकस्या एवानुष्ठानम्। सर्वासां समयिमते। षोडश्याः कलायास्तु पञ्चदशस्वपि तिथिषु अनुष्ठानं सिद्धम्, पञ्चदशानां नित्यानां अत्रैव अन्तर्भावात्।।

अयं च सम्प्रदायक्रमः सम्यगुक्तोऽपि दुर्विज्ञेयं प्रमेयजातमिति विस्पष्टार्थं पुनरुच्यते। प्रतिपदि त्रिपुरसुन्दरीकला ध्येया। द्वितीयायां कामेश्वरीकला। तृतीयायां भगमालिनीकला। चतुर्थ्यां नित्यक्लिन्नाकला उपास्या। पञ्चम्यां भेरुण्डाख्या कला। षष्ठ्यां वह्निवासिनीकला। सप्तम्यां महा[1]विद्ये[वज्रे]श्वरीकला। अष्टम्यां रौद्रीकला। नवम्यां त्वरिताकला। दशम्यां कुलसुन्दरीकला। एकादश्यां नीलपताकाख्या कला। द्वादश्यां विजयाख्या कला। त्रयोदश्यां सर्वमङ्गलाख्या कला। चतुर्दश्यां ज्वालाख्या कला। पञ्चदश्यां मालिन्याख्या कला। सर्वासु तिथिषु चिद्रूपाख्या कला षोडशी उपास्या। प्रतिपदि या त्रिपुरसुन्दरी कथिता सा चिद्रूपात्मिका न भवति, चिद्रूपात्मिकायाः मूलविद्यायाः भिन्नत्वेन अनुष्ठानात्। मन्त्रभेदश्च-स मन्त्रः प्रतिपद्येव अनुष्ठेयो न द्वितीयायामिति। त्रिपुरसुन्दरीनित्यायाः नामसाम्यमित्यवगन्तव्यम्।।

एतासां षोडशनित्यानां चन्द्रकलात्मिकानां विशुद्धिचक्रं षोडशारं स्थानम्। तत्र

---

1. विश्वेश्वरीकला।

प्रागादिक्रमेण षोडश नित्याः तत्कोणेषु परिवर्तन्ते। तदधस्स्थितद्वादशारे संवित्कमले द्वादशसूर्यमण्डलानि प्रादक्षिण्यक्रमेण परिवर्तन्ते। तेषां द्वादशानां सूर्याणां द्वादशमासेषु अधिकारः।।

एतच्च सनत्कुमारसंहितायां श्लोकैः सप्तशत्या निरूपितं[1] संक्षेपेणोच्यते- सूर्यचन्द्रयोः देययानपितृयानात्मकेऽपिङ्गलानाडीमार्गेण अहोरात्रयोः सञ्चरणम्। चन्द्रस्तु वामनाडीमार्गेण सञ्चरन् द्विसप्ततिसहस्रनाडीमार्गं अमृतेन सिञ्चति। सूर्यस्तु दक्षिणनाडीमार्गेण सञ्चरन् तदुत्क्षिप्तान् अमृतबिन्दून् उपाहरति। यदा चन्द्रसूर्ययोः उभयोः आधारचक्रे समावेशः तदा अमावास्यातिथिरुत्पद्यते। कृष्णपक्षतिथयः ततः उत्पद्यन्ते। अत एव कुण्डलिनीशक्तिः आधारकुण्डे सूर्यकिरणसम्पर्कात् विलीनचन्द्रमण्डल- मध्यगलत्पीयूषपरिपूरिते स्वपिति। स्वापावस्थैव कृष्णपक्ष इत्युच्यते। योगी यदा समाहितचित्तः चन्द्रं चन्द्रस्थाने सूर्यं सूर्यस्थाने वायुना निरोद्धुं क्षमते तदा चन्द्रसूर्यौ निरुद्धौ अमृतसेचनतदाहरणयोः अशक्तौ। तदानीं वायुना प्रेरितेन स्वाधिष्ठानवह्निना शुष्कीभूते अमृतकुण्डे निराहारा कुण्डलिनी सुप्तोत्थिता सती सर्पवत् फूत्कारं कुर्वती ग्रन्थित्रयं भित्त्वा सहस्रदलकमलमध्यवर्ति चन्द्रमण्डलं दशति। तस्माद्गलत्पीयूषधाराः आज्ञाचक्रोपरिस्थितचन्द्रमण्डलं आप्लावयन्ति। तस्माद्गलिताभिः अमृतधाराभिः सर्वं देहमाप्लावयन्ति। ततश्च आज्ञाचक्रोपरिस्थितस्य चन्द्रमसः कलाः पञ्चदश नित्याः। ताः पञ्चदश तदधस्स्थितविशुद्धिचक्रमाश्रित्य परिवर्तन्ते। सहस्रदलकमलान्तस्स्थित- चन्द्रमण्डलं बैन्दवस्थानम्। तत्कला चिन्मयी आनन्दरूपा आत्मेति गीयते। सैव त्रिपुरसुन्दरी। एवं शुक्लपक्ष एव कुण्डलिनीप्रबोधः कर्तुं शक्यते योगीश्वराणां, न तु कृष्णपक्ष इति रहस्यम्। सर्वाः शुक्लपक्षतिथयः पौर्णमासीसंज्ञकाः। सर्वाः कृष्णपक्षतिथयस्तु अमावास्यायां अन्तर्भवन्ति। एकैवामावास्या कृष्णपक्ष इति गीयते। अत एव आधारं अन्धतामिस्रम्। स्वाधिष्ठानं तु सूर्यकिरणसम्पर्कात् मिश्रलोकः। मणिपूरस्तु अग्निस्थानत्वेऽपि तत्र स्थिते जले सूर्यकिरणप्रतिबिम्बात् मिश्रक एव लोकः। अनाहतं ज्योतिर्लोकः। एवं अनाहतचक्रपर्यन्तं ज्योतिस्तमोमिश्रको लोकः। विशुद्धिचक्रं चान्द्रो लोकः। आज्ञाचक्रं तु चन्द्रस्थानत्वात् सुधालोकः। अन्योर्लोकयोः सूर्यकिरणसम्पर्कात् ज्योत्स्ना नास्ति। सहस्रकमलं तु ज्योत्स्नामय एव लोकः। तत्र स्थितश्चन्द्रो नित्यकलायुक्तः। चन्द्रबिम्बं श्रीचक्रम्। कला सादाख्या। अतश्च त्रिकोणं आधारः, अष्टकोणं स्वाधिष्ठानम्, दशारं मणिपूरं, द्वितीयदशारं अनाहतं, चतुर्दशारं विशुद्धिचक्रम्, शिवचक्रचतुष्टयं आज्ञाचक्रं, बिन्दुस्थानं चतुरश्रं सहस्रकमलमिति

1. ततु संक्षेपेणोच्यते।

सिद्धम्। आज्ञाचक्रगतचन्द्रे पञ्चदश कलाः, षोडश्याः कलायाः प्रतिफलनं च। श्रीचक्ररूपचन्द्रबिम्बे एकैव कला, सा परमा कला। मिलित्वा षोडशकलाः। यथा–

> षोडशेन्दोः कला भानोः द्विर्द्वादश दशानले।
> सा पञ्चाशत्कला ज्ञेया मातृकाचक्ररूपिणी।। इति।।

एताः पञ्चाशत्कलाः पञ्चाशद्वर्णात्मिकाः पञ्चदशाक्षरीमन्त्रे अन्तर्भूताः। यथा–आदिमेन ककारेण अन्तिमो लकारः प्रत्याहृतः तन्मध्यवर्तिनां वर्णानां ग्राहकः। अयमेव लकारः एकारपर्ववर्तिना अकारेण प्रत्याहृतः पञ्चाशद्वर्णग्राहकः।।

ननु अनेनैव प्रत्याहारग्रहणेन पञ्चाशद्वर्णात्मकमातृकाग्रहणे किमर्थं ककारलकारयोः प्रत्याहारग्रहणप्रयासः?

उच्यते–ककारादिलकारान्तानां कलाशब्दवाच्यत्वं गौणम्, व्यञ्जनानां स्वरान् प्रति अङ्गत्वात्; कलानां स्वराणां प्रधानत्वमिति गुणप्रधानभावप्रदर्शनार्थं प्रत्याहारद्वयाश्रयणं कृतं सनकादिभिरिति ध्येयम्।।

चत्वारोऽनुस्वाराः बिन्दुलक्षकाः। तेन बिन्दुना तदुपरि प्रतीयमानो नादः सङ्गृहीतः। एवं नादबिन्दुकलात्मकं श्रीचक्रं त्रिखण्डमिति कथितम्। सादाख्या कला श्रीविद्यापरपर्याया नादबिन्दुकलातीता।

एताः षोडशनित्यासु अन्तर्भूताः। तथाहि–षोडश स्वराः, कादयः तान्ताः षोडश, थादयः सान्ताश्च षोडश। षोडशत्रिकं षोडशनित्यासु अन्तर्भूतम्। हकारः आकाशबीजं बैन्दवाकाशे निलीनम्। ळकारः अन्तस्थास्वन्तर्भूतोऽपि ककारेण प्रत्याहारार्थं पुनर्गृहीतः। क्षकारस्तु ककारषकारसमुदायरूपत्वात्। ककारादयः सान्ता द्विष्षोडश नित्यासु अन्तर्भूताः स्वरसहिताः।।

अकारेण प्रत्याहृतः क्षकारः अक्षमालेति गीयते। अतः क्षकारेण[1] सर्वा मातृकाः सङ्गृहीता भवन्ति। अत एव[2] अन्तिमखण्डे सकलह्रीमिति ककारलकरयोर्योगे कलाशब्दनिष्पत्तिः, कषयोर्योगे क्षकारनिष्पत्तिरिति, एवं मन्त्रेण सर्वा मातृकाः सङ्गृहीता इति तात्पर्यम्।।

अतश्च षोडशनित्यानां मन्त्रगतषोडशवर्णात्मकत्वं, षोडशवर्णानां पञ्चाशद्वर्णात्मकत्वं पञ्चाशद्वर्णानां सूर्यचन्द्राग्निकलात्मकत्वं, सूर्यचन्द्राग्निरूपेण त्रिखण्डत्वमिति ऐक्यचतुष्टयमनुसन्धेयम्।।[3]

1. 'अतः अज्ञ इति प्रत्याहरेण' अक्ष इति प्रत्याहारेण' इति पाठः।
2. अथवा इति पाठः।
3. 'विद्याचतुष्टय' इति पाठः।

एवं चक्रमन्त्रयोरपि। यथा ह्रीङ्कारत्रयं श्रीबीजं च शिवचक्रचतुष्टयात्मकत्रिकोणे बिन्दुरूपेण अन्तर्भूतम्। सकलेति वर्णत्रयेण सङ्गृहीतमातृका, अक्षमालात्मिका, मातृका उभयमपि यथायोगं चक्रे अन्तर्भूतम्। तथाहि–अन्तस्थाश्चत्वार:, ऊष्माणश्चत्वार:–एवमष्टौ वर्णा: अष्टकोणात्मका:। कादयो मावसाना: वर्गपञ्चमान् विहाय दशारयुग्मे अन्तर्भूता:। वर्गपञ्चमास्तु अनुस्वाररूपेण बिन्दावन्तर्भूता:। चतुर्दशारे चतुर्दश स्वरा अन्तर्भूता:। अनुस्वारविसर्गयो: बिन्दावन्तर्भाव:। इति चक्रमन्त्रयोरैक्यं सुभगोदयमतानुसारेण कथितम्।।

पूर्णोदयमतानुसारेण तु–सोमसूर्यानलात्मकतया चक्रस्य त्रिखण्डत्वम्। एवं मन्त्रस्यापि त्रिखण्डत्वं सुप्रसिद्धम्।[1] चन्द्रस्य कला: षोडश इन्दुखण्डे अन्तर्भूता:। स[2] च इन्दुखण्ड: इन्द्वात्मके यन्त्रखण्डेऽन्तर्भूत:। एवं भानो: चतुर्विंशतिकला: भानुखण्डेऽन्तर्भूता:। स च खण्ड: यन्त्रखण्डेऽन्तर्भूत:। एवमाग्नेया दशकला आग्नेयखण्डे अन्तर्भूता:। स च खण्ड: यन्त्रे आग्नेयखण्डे अन्तर्भवतीति कलायन्त्रमन्त्राणां ऐक्यमनुसन्धेयम्।।

सुभगोदये नित्यानां स्वरूपमुक्तम्–

दर्शाद्या: पूर्णिमान्ताश्च कला: पञ्चदशैव तु।
षोडशी तु कला ज्ञेया सच्चिदानन्दरूपिणी।। इति।।

अस्यार्थ:–दर्शाद्या: पूर्णिमान्ताश्च तिथय:। दर्शा नाम अमावास्यानन्तरभाविनी प्रतिपत्कला। तस्या ईषद्दर्शनात् दर्शा। दर्शा आद्या यासां ता:। पूर्णिमा अन्तो यासां ता:।।

दर्शा, दृष्टा, दर्शता, विश्वरूपा, सुदर्शना, आप्यायमाना, आप्यायमाना, आप्याया, सूनृता, इरा, आपूर्यमाणा, आपूर्यमाणा पूरयन्ती, पूर्णा, पौर्णमासी–एतानि नामधेयानि श्रुतिबोधितानि सङ्गृहीतानि 'दर्शाद्या: पूर्णिमान्ता:' इत्यनेन। एतासां स्वरूपं पुरस्तात् निवेदयिष्यते। दर्शादीनां पञ्चदशानां कलानां यथाक्रमं त्रिपुरसुन्दरीप्रभृतय: पञ्चदश नित्या: अधिदेवता:। षोडश्या: चिद्रूपात्मिकाया: कलाया: सादाख्यतत्त्वरूपत्वात् अधिदेवतान्तरं नास्ति। स्वयमेव सर्वस्य अधिदेवतेति ध्येयम्। एतासां नित्यानां अभिमानिनी देवता कामदेव: एक एव। अधिष्ठानदेवता कामेश्वरी एकैव। अतश्च मूलविद्यागतपञ्चदशवर्णानां दर्शादय: कला:, नित्या: कलाश्च, विग्रहान्तरमिति अनुसन्धेयम्। अत एव दर्शादिकलानां त्रिखण्डत्वं स्पष्टम्। दर्शा दृष्टा दर्शता विश्वरूपा

1. बैन्दव्य:।
2. सचायं खण्डद्वयात्मके।

सुदर्शना—एष आग्नेयः खण्डः। आप्यायमाना आप्यायमाना आप्याया सूनृता इरा—एष सौरः खण्डः। आपूर्यमाणा आपूर्यमाणा पूरयन्ती पूर्णा पौर्णमासीति—एष चान्द्रः खण्डः तृतीयो निरूपितः। एतासां कलानां नित्यात्वेन एक्यं सम्पाद्य प्रतिपदादौ उपासनाप्रकारः पूर्वमेव दिङ्मात्रं उदाहृतः। दर्शा कला शिवतत्त्वात्मिका। दृष्टा कला शक्तितत्त्वात्मिका। दर्शता कला मायातत्त्वात्मिका। विश्वरूपा कला शुद्धविद्यातत्त्वात्मिका। सुदर्शना कला जलतत्त्वात्मिका। एवं पञ्चतत्त्वात्मकं, खण्डं आग्नेयम्, अग्निरत्र अधिदेवता, कामदेवस्तु सर्वत्र अधिदेवता, कामेश्वरी सर्वत्र अधिष्ठात्रीत्युक्तम्। आप्यायमाना कला तेजस्तत्त्वात्मिका। आप्यायामाना कला वायुतत्त्वात्मिका। आप्याया कला मनस्तत्त्वात्मिका। सूनृता कला पृथिवीतत्त्वात्मिका। इरा कला आकाशतत्त्वात्मिका। आपूर्यमाणा कला विद्यातत्त्वात्मिका। एष सौरः खण्डो द्वितीयः। तत्र सूर्यो देवता। कामदेवस्तु सर्वत्र अधिदेवता। कामेश्वरी सर्वत्र अधिष्ठात्रीत्युक्तम्। आपूर्यमाणायाः कलायाः चन्द्रखण्डान्तस्स्थिताया अपि सौरखण्डे अन्तर्भावः। इराकलाप्रभेदत्वात् इराऽऽपूर्यमाणयोः ऐक्यमिति अनुसन्धेयम्। आपूर्यमाणा कला महेश्वरतत्त्वात्मिका। पूरयन्ती कला परतत्त्वात्मिका। पूर्णा कला आत्मतत्त्वात्मिका। पौर्णमासी कला सदाशिवतत्त्वात्मिका। एष सौम्यः खण्डः। सोमः अत्र अधिदवेता। कामदेवः सर्वत्र अधिदेवता। कामेश्वरी सर्वत्र अधिष्ठात्रीत्युक्तम्। नित्या कला सादाख्यतत्त्वात्मिका। एतास्तु विशुद्धिचक्रे षोडशारे प्रागादिक्रमेण षोडशदिक्षु परिभ्रमन्ति।।

तास्तु आज्ञाचक्रोपरिस्थितचन्द्रमण्डलस्य षोडश कलाः इति सुभगोदये यत् प्रपञ्चितं तत्तु—पञ्चदशकलानामेव षोडशारे परिभ्रमणं, षोडश्याः कलायाः सहस्रदलकमल एव अवस्थानं, तत्र अवस्थितायाः नित्यायाः कलायाः प्रभापटलं षोडशारे स्फुरति—इत्येवंपरमित्येव अनुसन्धेयम्।।

अयमर्थः—शिवः शक्तिः कामः क्षितिरिति शिवशब्देन शिवतत्त्वात्मिका दर्शाख्या कला त्रिपुरसुन्दरीनामधेया कथ्यते। तया तत्प्रकृतिभूतःककारे लक्ष्यते। एवं शक्तिशब्देन शक्तितत्त्वात्मिका या दृष्टा कला तया एकारो लक्ष्यते। काम इत्यनेन कामदेवत्या या दर्शता कला या ईकारो लक्ष्यते। क्षितिरित्यनेन "लकारः क्षितितत्त्वम्" इति शास्त्रान्तरप्रसिद्ध्या लकारो लक्ष्यते। रविरित्यनेन सूर्यखण्डात्मतया रविः हकारो लक्ष्यते। शीतकिरणः चन्द्रः। "सकारः चन्द्रबीजम्" इति शास्त्रान्तरप्रसिद्ध्या शीतकिरणशब्देन सकारो लक्ष्यते। स्मरशब्देन कामराजप्रकृतिभूतः ककारो लक्ष्यते। हंसः सूर्य हकाराधिपतिरितित्युक्तं प्राक्। शक्रः इन्द्रः। "लकारः इन्द्रबीजम्" इति शास्त्रान्तरप्रसिद्धेः शक्रशब्देन लकारो लक्ष्यते। परा चन्द्रकलेति चन्द्रबीजम् सकारो लक्ष्यते। मारः

कामराजबीजमिति तत्प्रकृतिभूतः ककारो लक्ष्यते। हरिः इन्द्रः लकारो लक्ष्यते। एवं मन्त्रगतवर्णानां ककारादीनां शिवादिपदानि लक्षकाणि, क्वचित् लक्षितलक्षकाणीति ध्येयम्।।

एवं पञ्चदशनित्यानां समुदायात्मकस्य मन्त्रस्य पञ्चदशतिथिषु अनुष्ठानं विहितम्। पृथक् नित्यानुष्ठानं तु प्रतिदिनं पृथक् नियतम्। एतच्च अतिरहस्यं गुरुमुखादेव अवगन्तव्यमपि शिष्यानुजिघृक्षया कथितम्। अतश्च इममेव अर्थं श्रुतिरप्याह–

दर्शाद्याः पूर्णिमान्ताश्च कलाः पञ्चदशैव तु।

इत्यत्र यत् बहु वक्तव्यं, तत्तु श्रुतिव्याख्यानावसरे निरूपयिष्यामः। तथा च तैत्तिरीयशाखायां काठके श्रूयते—'इयं वाव सरघा' इत्यनुवाकः[1]। तत्र षोडशनित्यात्मक-दिवसपरिज्ञाने फलं प्रतिपादितं, ज्ञानमात्रफलप्रतिपादकत्वात्। अनारभ्याधीतं अश्वमेधकाण्डानन्तरं 'संज्ञानं विज्ञानम्'[2] इति, तिथिप्रतिपादकवाक्यानां प्रकरणभेद एव। तस्य अनुवाकस्य ब्राह्मणम् 'इयं वाव सरघा' इति। एवम् उभयं मन्त्रब्राह्मणात्मकं अनारभ्याधीतं ज्ञानैकफलं वाक्यजातम्।।

[3]इयं वाव सरघा

अस्यार्थः–इयं चन्द्रकला सादाख्या सरघा सरघावत् मधुस्यन्दिनी अमृतस्यन्दिनीति श्रीचक्रात्मकचन्द्रस्य सारघात्वनिरूपणम्।।

[3]तस्या अग्निरेव सारघं मधु।

तस्याः सरघायाः अग्निरेव अग्निस्थानमेव बैन्दवं त्रिकोणं सारघं सरघोद्भूतं मधु, तस्यैव सुधासिन्धुरूपत्वात्।।

सारघस्य मधुनः उपचयापचयप्रकारमाह–

[3]या एताः पूर्वपक्षापरपक्षयो रात्रयः।

[4]एताः संज्ञानानुवाके कथिताः। पूर्वपक्षापरपक्षयोः शुक्लकृष्णपक्षयोः रात्रयः।।

[3]ता मधुकृतः।

ताः रात्रयः मधु कुर्वन्तीति मधुकृतः। रात्रिष्वेव मधुनः सङ्ग्रह इति लोकप्रसिद्धिः।

---

1. तैत्तिरीय ब्राह्मण, ३.१०.१०।
2. तै०ब्रा० ३.१०.१।
3. तै०ब्रा० ३.१०.१०।
4. यस्याः सुरघायाः इत्यधिकः।

रात्रावेव चन्द्रकलारूपायाः श्रीविद्यायाः अनुष्ठानं, न च दिवसे इति उपदेशः। पूर्वपक्षरात्रयः दर्शादिपौर्णमास्यन्ताः पूर्वं निरूपिताः। कृष्णपक्षरात्रिनामधेयानि तु–

[1]सुता सुन्वती प्रसुता सूयमानाऽभिषूयमाणा।
पीती प्रपा संपा तृप्तिस्तर्पयन्ती। कान्ता
काम्या कामजाताऽऽयुष्मती कामदुघा।।

एताः कृष्णपक्षरात्रयः। एतासां कृष्णपक्षरात्रीणां आधारचक्रे एव अमावास्यात्मकतया अवस्थानात्, समयिनां तत्र व्यवहाराभावात् शुक्लपक्षरात्रिष्वेव चन्द्रकलासञ्चारात्, तत्रैव कुण्डिलिनीप्रबोधात्, स्वरूपमात्रोद्देश एव कृतः। शुक्लपक्षरात्रीणामेव कलात्वम्। तत्स्वरूपं पूर्वमेव निरूपितम्।।

अत एव कुण्डलिनीप्रबोधो रात्रावेव, न दिवा, दिवसानां मधुनः स्रावकत्वादित्याह–

[2]यान्यहानि। ते मधुवृषाः।

मधु वर्षन्तीति मधुवृषाः। अत एव दिवा योगिनः कुण्डलिनीं (न) बोधयन्तीति, शुक्लकृष्णपक्षयोः दिवसानां नामानि नोक्तानि अप्रस्तुतत्वात्। तथापि वेदे फलश्रवणात्। उद्देशमात्रेण कथ्यन्ते। शुक्लपक्षदिवसनामानि–

सं[3]ज्ञानं विज्ञानं प्रज्ञानं जानदभिजानत्।
सङ्कल्पमानं प्रकल्पमानमुपकल्पमानमुपक्लृप्तं
क्लृप्तम्। श्रेयो वसीय आयत् संभूतं भूतम्।।

इति शुक्लपक्षदिवसनामानि। कृष्णपक्षदिवसनामानि तु–

[3]प्रस्तुतं विष्टुतꣳ सꣳस्तुतं कल्याणं विश्वरूपम्।
शुक्रममृतं तेजस्विः तेजः समिद्धम्। अरुणं
भानुमन्मरीचिमदभितपत्तपस्वत्।।

एतेषामुभयेषां शुक्लकृष्णपक्षाहोरात्राणां नामधेयानि [4]यो वेद तस्य फलमाह–

[5]स यो ह वा एता मधुकृतश्च मधुवृषाꣳश्च वेद।
कुर्वन्ति हास्यैता अग्नौ मधु। नास्येष्टापूर्तं धयन्ति।।

---

1. तै०ब्रा० ३.१०.१।
2. तै० ब्रा० ३-१०-१०।
3. तै०ब्रा० ३-१०-१।
4. तेषां वेदनस्य ; तेषां वेदस्य।
5. तै०ब्रा० ३-१०-१०।

सः यः एताः मधुकृतो रात्रीः मधुवृषान् दिवसान् पूर्वोक्तान् यो वेद अस्य वेत्तुः एताः अग्नौ बैन्दवस्थाने मधु सुधासिन्धुं कुर्वन्ति। अस्य इष्टापूर्तं वाञ्छितार्थपूर्तिं न धयन्ति न रिक्तीकुर्वन्ति।।

व्यतिरेके अनिष्टमाह–

[1]अथ यो न वेद। न हास्यैता अग्नौ मधु कुर्वन्ति।
धयन्त्यस्येष्टापूर्तम्।।

व्याख्यातप्रायमेतत्।।

अयमर्थः—चन्द्रकलाविद्यानुष्ठानं नाम मातृकामन्त्रयोरैक्यम्। मन्त्रचक्रयोरैक्यं, चक्रनित्ययोरैक्यं, नित्याप्रतिपदादिकलयोरैक्यमिति समयिमततत्त्वम्। एतदनुष्ठाने शुक्लपक्षकृष्णपक्षविवेकः, दिवसरात्रिविवेकश्च उपयुज्यते। दर्शादिपौणमास्यान्तास्वेव कलासु [2]चतुर्विधैक्यानुसन्धानं, न अमावास्यायाम्। कृष्णपक्षशब्दः अमावास्यापरः इत्युक्तं प्रागेव। अतश्च अमावास्यायामिव शुक्लपक्षदिवसेष्वपि न अनुष्ठानमिति ध्येयम्। एवं परिशेषवृत्त्या अमावास्यायाम् उपासनानिषेधः, न तु सर्वस्मिन् कृष्णपक्षे। अतश्च सर्वासु रात्रिषु अमावास्याव्यतिरिक्तासु उपासना, न सर्वेषु दिवसेषु इति गुरूपदेशवशात् ज्ञेयं रहस्यम्।।

अत उत्तरम्–

[3]यो ह वा अहोरात्राणां नामधेयानि वेद।
नाहोरात्रेष्वार्तिमार्छति। संज्ञानं विज्ञानं दर्शा
दृष्टेति। एतावनुवाकौ पूर्वपक्षस्याहोरात्राणां
नामधेयानि। प्रस्तुतं विष्टुतꣳसुता सुन्वतीति।
एतावनुवाकावपरपक्षस्याहोरात्राणां नामधेयानि।
नाहोरात्रेष्वार्तिमार्छति। य एवं वेद।।

इति वाक्यजातं पूर्वव्याख्ययैव व्याकृतम्। इतः परं वक्ष्यमाणं मुहूर्तार्धमास-घटिकादीनां कलानां नामधेयजातं तत्रैव अन्तर्भूतमिति तद्व्याख्यानेनैव व्याख्यातमिति अनुसन्धेयम्। अत एव संज्ञानानुवाकः 'इयं वाव सरघा' इत्यनुवाकश्च व्याकृतावेवेति अवगन्तव्यम्। यत्तु सावित्रप्रकाशके 'प्रजापतिर्देवानसृजत' इत्यनुवाके[3] 'स यदाह'

1. तै०ब्रा० ३-१०-१०। 2. चतुष्टयैक्यानुसन्धानम्?
3. तै०ब्रा० ३-१०-१०।

इत्यारभ्य 'जनको ह वैदेहः' इत्यन्तेन तिथ्यात्मकत्वं सवितुः प्रतिपादितम्, तत्तु सादाख्यतत्त्वात्मिकायाः चन्दकलाविद्यायाः श्रीविद्याऽपरनामधेयायाः पञ्चदश[1] तिथ्यात्मिकायाः प्रसादसमासादितसामर्थ्यं सवितुः, नान्यथेति प्रतिपादयितुं गौण्या वृत्त्या आह श्रुतिः। अत एव 'एष एव तत्।'[2] इति गौणवृत्त्याश्रयणं प्रकटीकृतम्। अत एतद्ग्रन्थकलापानन्तरवाक्यम्–

जनको ह वैदेहः। अहोरात्रैः समाजगाम[2]।।

इति आम्नातम्। जनकः उत्पादकः श्रीविद्यायाः ऋषिः। विदेह एव वैदेहः मन्मथः। अहोरात्रैः अहोरात्रात्मकैः पञ्चदशाक्षरीमन्त्रवर्णैः दर्शादिपूर्णिमान्तकलात्मकैः समाजगाम, तं मन्त्रं आहृतवानित्यर्थः। यस्तु मन्त्रं आहरति स ऋषिरित्युच्यते। अत एव अरुणोपनिषदि–

पुत्रो निरृत्या वैदेहः।[3]

निरृत्याः लक्ष्म्याः। यद्वा—अनिरृत्याः लक्ष्म्याः। पुत्रः वैदेहः मन्मथः।।

अचेता यश्च चेतनः।[3]

अनङ्गत्वादेव चेतोरहितः। चेतनश्च सर्वभूतान्तर्यामित्वात्।।

स तं मणिमविन्दत्।[3]

सः अनङ्गः तं प्रसिद्धं मणिं विद्यात्मकं रत्नम् अविन्दत् लब्धवान् अपश्यत्। असौ अनङ्ग अन्धोऽपि अपश्यदिति 'अन्धो मणिमविन्दित्'[3] इति वाक्यशेषबलात् लभ्यते। अत एव परचित्कलायाः विद्यायाः त्रिपुरसुन्दर्याः मन्मथः ऋषिरभूत्।।

सोऽनङ्गुलिरावयत्।[3]

स मन्मथः अनङ्गत्वादेव अनङ्गुलिः आवयत् असीव्यत्।।

सीवनानन्तरकृत्यमाह–

सोऽग्रीवः प्रत्यमुञ्चत्।[3]

सः मन्मथः अनङ्गत्वादेव अग्रीवः मणिसम्पादनफलं प्रत्यामोचनं अकरोत्, धृतवानित्वर्थः।।

विद्यारत्ने मणित्वारोपणस्य फलं धारणमेव न भवतीत्याह–

सोऽजिह्वो असश्चत।[4]

1. विद्यात्मिकायाः?
2. तै०ब्रा० ३-१०-९।
3. तै० आ० ११-१।
4. तै०आ० १-११।

सः अनङ्गः अनङ्गत्वादेव अजिह्वः जिह्वारहितः असश्चत अचोषत्, आस्वादितवानित्यर्थः।

एतदुक्तं भवति—अनङ्गः पूर्वं विद्यारत्नं पञ्चाशद्वर्णात्मकं षोडशनित्यात्मकं षोडशकलात्मकं नानावेदेषु नानास्मृतिषु नानापुराणेषु नानाविधागमेषु विप्रकीर्णं दृष्टवान्। तदनन्तरं विप्रकीर्णं इमं मन्त्रं दृष्ट्वा सीवनं कृतवान्। पञ्चाशद्वर्णान् त्रिधा विभज्य खण्डत्रयं कृत्वा त्रिपुरसुन्दर्यादिषोडशनित्याः तत्र अन्तर्भाव्य प्रतिपदादितिथीन् षोडश तत्रैव अन्तर्भाव्य, पञ्चदशवर्णात्मकं त्रिखण्डं कृत्वा, तत्र सोमसूर्यानलात्मकतया ब्रह्मविष्णुमहेश्वरात्मकतया सत्त्वरजस्तमस्तत्त्वव्यवस्थिततया जाग्रत्स्वप्न-सुषुप्त्यवस्थापन्नतया सृष्टिस्थितिलयहेतुभूततया निश्चित्य श्रीविद्यात्मके चतुर्थे खण्डे पञ्चदशकलानां अन्तर्भावं निश्चित्य भुवनेश्वरीप्रभृतीनां योगिनीविद्यानां नवानां त्रिकस्य त्रिकस्य एकैकह्रीङ्कारेण अन्तर्भावम् अङ्गीकृत्य, सर्वभूतात्मकं सर्वमन्त्रात्मकं सर्वतत्त्वात्मकं सर्वावस्थात्मकं सर्वदेवात्मकं सर्ववेदार्थात्मकं सर्वशब्दात्मकं सर्वशक्त्यात्मकं त्रिगुणात्मकं त्रिखण्डं त्रिगुणातीतं [1]सादाख्यापरपर्यायं षड्विंशशिवशक्तिसंपुटात्मकं निश्चित्य वर्णपञ्चदशकेन मूलविद्यां असीव्यत्। तदनन्तरं स्यूतं मन्त्रराजं [2]ग्रीवायां धृतवान् चिरकालं ध्यानयोगेन पूजितवान्। तदनन्तरं चन्द्रकलामृतास्वादं कृतवानिति सः मन्मथः ऋषिः अस्य मन्त्रस्येत्यर्थः।।

नैतमृषिं विदित्वा नगरं प्रविशेत्।[3]

एतम् ऋषिं मन्मथं विदित्वा नगरं श्रीचक्रात्मकं न प्रविशेत् ऋषिज्ञानपूर्वकं श्रीचक्रात्मकं नगरं न पूजयेत्, बाह्यपूजां न कुर्यादिति निषेधविधिः, बाह्यपूजायामेव ऋषिच्छन्दः प्रभृतिज्ञानपूर्वकत्वम्। आन्तरपूजायां तादात्म्यानुसन्धानात्मिकायां ऋष्यादिज्ञानं नास्त्येव। उपयोगस्तु दूरत एव। अतो वस्तुसिद्धऋष्यादिपर्युदासमुखेन श्रीचक्रस्य बाह्यपूजनं त्रैवर्णिकैः न कर्तव्यमिति नियम्यते। तदुक्तं सनत्कुमारसंहितायाम्—

बाह्यपूजा न कर्तव्या कर्तव्या बाह्यजातिभिः।
सा [4]क्षुद्रफलदा नृणाम् ऐहिकार्थैकसाधनात्।।
बाह्यपूजारतः कौलाः क्षपणाश्च कपालिकाः।
दिगम्बराश्चेतिहासा[5] वामकास्तन्त्रवादिनः।।

---

1. सादाख्यकलापर्यायम्।
2. गृहीत्वा।
3. तै०आ० १-११।
4. क्षुद्रधर्मदाः।
5. 'वीतावासा' इत्यपि कचित् दृश्यते।

आन्तराराधनपरा वैदिका ब्रह्मवादिनः।
जीवन्मुक्ताश्चरन्त्येते त्रिषु लोकेषु सर्वदा।। इति।।

कौलाः आधारचक्रपूजारताः। क्षपणकाः योषित्त्रिकोणपूजारताः। कापालिकाः दिगम्बराश्च उभयत्र निरताः। इतिहासाः[1] भैरवयामळप्रामाण्यवादिनः। वामकाः तन्त्रवादिनः इत्येके वदन्ति, वामकेश्वरतन्त्रप्रामाण्यवादिनः। केवलचक्रपूजकाः ते वेदबाह्या इत्यन्वयः। आन्तरपूजारताः ब्रह्मवादिनः शुभागमतत्त्ववेदिनः। शुभागमपञ्चकं पूर्वमेवोक्तम्। आन्तरपूजाप्रकारः पुरस्ताद्वक्ष्यते च।।

[2]यदि प्रविशेत्।

असंशये संशयोक्तिः 'यदि वेदाः प्रमाणं' इतिवत्। प्रविशेदेवेत्यर्थः।।

[2]मिथौ चरित्वा प्रविशेत्।

[3]मिथौ रहस्ये एकान्ते, चरित्वा अवगत्य। चर गतिभक्षणयोः। प्रविशेत्, आन्तरपूजां कुर्यादित्यर्थः। यद्वा–मिथौ मिथुनीभूतौ शिवौ, उभयोः मेलनं अवगत्य प्रविशेत् अनुसन्दधीतेति। पूर्वव्याख्यानेऽपि ऐकात्म्यानुसन्धाने सहायान्तरं न कर्तव्यम्। एकान्ते एव विद्या फलतीत्युपदेशः। तत्कथमित्याशङ्क्य दृष्टान्तेन दृढयति–

[2]तत्सम्भवस्य व्रतम्।

सम्भवो मन्मथः, चित्तजातत्वात्। तस्य व्रतं माहात्म्यं, सहायान्तरं तिरस्कृत्य एकाकिनैव रहस्ये स्त्रीपुरुषसंयोजनरूपम्। अतः मन्मथोपदिष्टमन्त्रानुष्ठानवतां तथैव तदनुष्ठानमिति गोप्येयं विद्येति तात्पर्यम्। द्वितीयव्याख्याने मन्मथो मिथनुं अवगत्य तस्मिन् मिथुने प्रविशति। एवं शिवशक्तिसंपुटम् अवगत्य साधकेन प्रवेष्टव्यमिति श्रुतेरर्थः। अतश्च 'पुत्रो निरृत्या वैदेहः,'[2] 'जनको ह वैदेहः'[4] इति च श्रुतिद्वयस्य वैदेहयोः उभयोः एकप्रत्यभिज्ञाविषयत्वात्, 'स यदाह'[4] इत्यादिवाक्यकदम्बकं प्रतिपदादि-तिथिरूपचन्द्रकलात्मिकायाः श्रीविद्यायाः प्रतिपादनद्वारा सवितुः तत्प्रसादजन्यं माहात्म्यं नान्यथेत्येवंपरमिति सर्वं अनवद्यम्।। ३२।।

Notes : The Tantra premised by the words 'Thy Tantra' in the previous stanza, as understood by Lakṣmīdhara, is further elaborated in this stanza, which may be termed as the coping stone

1. 'वीतावासा' इत्यपि कचित् दृश्यते।
2. तै०आ० १-११।
3. मिथौ=मिथ इत्यर्थः।
4. तै०ब्रा० ३-१०-९।

of the Samayins arch of worship. The Mantra itself, the Ṣoḍaśākṣarī, it is said, cannot be given out publicly, but should be imparted by the Guru to the devout pupil in secret. This may be inferred from the fact that the sixteenth syllable does not find a place in the description given in the stanza. Merely because the stanza makes mention of only fifteen syllables, it should not be understood that the Mantra indicated is the Pañca-daśākṣarī. The sixteenth syllable is the fourth Khaṇḍa of the Mantra and, like the fourth Pāda of the Gāyatrī, should be muttered only by adepts who are highly evolved spiritually, as only they could conceive with their minds the fourth Khaṇḍa, which is beyond the range of speech and thought and transcends all the Tattvas, being of the essence of pure consciousness. The stanza merely mentions fifteen conventional names indicative of syllables, which, when construed in the proper way, would yield the following result; Śiva is 'Ka'; Śakti represents 'E'; Kāma, 'Ī'; 'Kṣiti, 'La'; this is the first Khaṇḍa. Ravi is 'Ha'; Śīta-kiraṇa, 'Sa'; Smara, 'Ka'; Haṁsa, 'Ha'; and Śakra, 'La'; this is the second Khaṇda. Parā is 'Sa'; Māra, 'Ka'; and Hari, 'La'; this is the third Khaṇḍa. When the Hṛl-lekhā *i.e.*, 'Hrīṁ', is added to each of the three Khaṇḍas, the result is the Pañca-dasākṣarī-mantra. *Thy name*—by treating 'Nāma' of the last line as an indeclinable, the last words may be construed as 'verily become what constitutes Thee'. The chief component of the Mantra, *viz.*, the Ramā-bīja, when added on to the end, will convert the Pañcadaśākṣarī into the Ṣoḍaśākṣarī, which is really implied by the stanza. These sixteen syllables are the sixteen Candra-kalās or the fifteen Tithis of the lunar fortnight, and the sixteenth designated the Cit-kalā, with Tripurasundarī and other Nityās as their presiding deities. The first syllable 'Ka' with the last 'La' of the Pañcadaśākṣarī, make the Pratyāhāra, 'Kalā', implying all the Mātṛkās contained therein. Soma, Sūrya and Agni, which preside over the three Khaṇḍas of the Mantra, respectively indicate sixteen, twenty-four (by reduplication of the number indicated), and ten Kalās, thus making up fifty Kalās; these constitute the fifty Mātṛkās of the Devī, which are known by the Pratyāhāra Ākṣa (-mālā), made up of the 'A', occurring before 'E' of the first Khaṇḍa, and 'Kṣa', yielded by the 'Ka' and 'Sa' of the third Khaṇḍa.

Kāmeśvarasūri fully sets out the implications of the several conventional names occurring in the stanza, also in a different manner and as construed by him it would mean : O Mother of all the Devatās! Śiva—indicating Sadāśiva, and Bhava, Mṛḍa and Rudra taking their origin from him; Śaktī—indicating the Tripurasundarī and through her the sixteen Nityās including herself, as also other deities; Kāma—indicating Manas and through it, its functions, volition, *etc.*; Kṣiti—the Earth and through it the five elements; then, Ravi—known as Satya, the illuminator of all including the Earth, and through mutuall affinity the fire ; Śītakiraṇa—the Moon; Smara—his comrade; Haṁsa—Brahman, the creator; Śakra—the king of the gods; thereafter, the Parā-s—indicating other Śaktis; Māra—the Yama, who deals death to all; and Hari—Viṣṇu, who have respectively been assigned their seats from Kailāsa up to Vaikuṇṭha by Thee, the syllables indicated by the above along with the three Hṛl-lekhās or groups of the inner senses with the characteristics of Rhythm, Motion and Inertia, all these gods and the Mātṛkas reputed to be Thy form serve Thee.

The first four syllables of the Ṣodaśākṣarī constitute the first Khaṇḍa, relating to Agni, representing Kriyā-śakti, the Jāgrat state, the Viśva-vṛtti and Tamo-guṇa. The next five syllables consitute the second Khaṇḍa, relating to Sūrya, representing Icchā-śakti, the Svapna state, the Taijasa-vṛtti and Rajo-guṇa. The Hṛl-lekhā between the two represents the Rudra-granthi. The next three syllables constitute the third Khaṇḍa relating to Soma, representing Jñāna-śakti, the Suṣupti-state, the Prājña-vṛtti and Sattva-guṇa. The Hṛl-lekhā between the second and third Khaṇḍas represents the Viṣṇu-granthi. The fourth Khaṇḍa of one syllable, known as the Candra-kalā, which should be imparted by the Guru, is implied after the three aforesaid Khaṇḍas. The Hṛl-lekhā between the third and fourth Khaṇḍas represents the Brahma-granthi.

The sixteen syllables of the Mantra are to be looked upon as made up of the sixteen Nityās. The reason why the Parā-kalā, which is of the essence of pure consciousness, is known as Nityā is because of its resemblance to the sixteenth Kalā of the Moon of the *Sahasrāra*, reflected on the sixteenth petal of the sixteen-petalled lotus of the *Viśuddhi-cakra*. This alone is the essential and prime cause of the other fifteen, which are only its subordinate divisions. This sixteenth Kalā is 'S' plus 'r' plus 'ī' plus 'ṁ', from which the Vidyā itself derives its name of *Śrī-vidyā*. The sixteen syllables form the Prakṛtis of the sixteen Kalās or *Tithis* commencing from the *Śukla-pratipad* on to the *Pūrṇimā*, and similarly from *Kṛṣṇa-pratipad* on to the *Amā-*

vāsyā respectively, of the bright and dark lunar fortnights. *Pratipad,* the first Kalā, takes its origin from Sūrya in the bright fortnight and enters into it in the dark fortnight of the lunar month. Similarly, the other Kalās are to be understood to take their origin from and enter into the Sūrya to the bright and dark fortnights respectively. When there is an interval of fifteen Kalās between the Sun and the Moon, we have the full-moon, and when such interval vanishes, we have the new-moon. According to the Kaulācāra, the Nityā corresponding to the Kalā of every day should be worshipped. The Samayins on the other hand worship internally the sixteenth Kalā of the form of pure consciousness along with the Kalā of the day, every day. Although the sixteenth, known as the Cit-kalā, is sometimes given the name of 'Tripurasundarī' by which name the first Kalā is known, it should not be understood that the two Kalās are the same. The sixteen Nityās have their position on the sixteen petals of the *Viśuddhi-cakra* commencing from the petal pointing eastwards ; similarly, the twelve Ādityas have their position on the twelve petals of the *An-āhata* and excercise their influence over the twelve months of the yeart, one over each.

The influence of the Sun and the Moon over the human body and the part taken by them in helping the Yogin in the successful accomplishment of yoga may be summarized thus : The Sun and the Moon incessantly influence the Iḍā and Piṅgalā-nāḍids day and night. The Moon through the Iḍā in-fills all the Seventy-two-thousand Nāḍis with his nectar. The Sun is his turn gathers up the same nectar. As and when the Sun and the Moon have their conjunction in the Ādhāra-cakra, there is the new-moon, during which the Kuṇḍalinī has its sleep in the hollow of the *Mūlādhāra,* wherein is gathered the nectar flowing out of the lunar disc, melted in the presence of the rays of the Sun. Hence, its sleeping state is represented to be during the dark fornight. When the Yogin controls the passage of the Sun and Moon along with the vital air through the Nāḍis, by performing *Kumbhaka,* the Sun and the Moon being deprived of their functions of in-filling and gathering the nectar, the Amṛta-kuṇḍa in the *Mūlādhāra* gets dried up by the fire induced by the vital air, the Kuṇḍalinī becomes famished and is roused from sleep, as it were, with the Phūt-kāra of the snake, bursts through the three Granthis and bites the disc of the Moon in the middle of the thousand-petalled lotus. The shower of nectar flowing from the Moon drenches the lunar region of the *Ājñā-cakra,* and the whole body gets filled with nectar from the shower. Hence the fifteen Kalās of the Moon in the *Ājñā-cakra* then become Nityās, perpetually shining. These Kalās then reach and pervade the *Viśudhi-cakra.* The lunar disc in the middle of the thousand-petalled lotus is the *Baindava-sthāna.* That Kalā of the character of pure consciousness is said to be of the form of Bliss. That alone is the Tripurasundarī. Hence, follows the secret of the Yogin's successful accomplishment of rousing the Kuṇḍalinī only in the bright half of the lunar month. All the Tithis of the bright half are therefore known as the Full-moon, while the Tithis of the dark half inhere in the New-moon. Hence the *Mūlādhāra* is the region which is pitch dark. The *Svādhiṣṭhāna* being subject to the influence of the Sun and the Moon is a region of darkness and light mixed together, while the *Maṇipūra,* though essentially belonging to the region of Fire, is a region of darkness and light mixed together, owing to the reflection, in the water there, of the rays of the Sun. The *An-āhata* is the region of brightness. Thus, till the *An-āhata* is reached, the regions of the Cakras are either dark or of a mixed nature. The *Viśuddhi* lies in the region of the Moon. The *Ājñā,* being the seat of the Moon, is the region of nectar. As in these two regions there is the admixture of the Sun's rays, there is no Moon-light. The thousand-petalled lotus, on the other hand, is a region of Moon-light alone. The Moon there being possessed of the Nitya-kalā is perpetual, without waxing and waning. The disc of that Moon is the *Śrī-cakra,* while its Kalā is the Sādākhyā. The *Tri-koṇa* is the *Mūlādhāra.* The eight-spoked Cakra is the *Svādhiṣṭhāna.* The inner ten-spoked Cakra is the *Maṇipūra.* The outer ten-spoken *Cakra* is the *An-āhata.* The fourteen-spoked one is the *Viśuddhi.* The four triangles of Śiva constitute the *Ājñā-cakra.* The *Bindu-sthāna* in the quadrilateral is the thousand-petalled lotus. The Moon of the *Ājñā* has fifteen Kalās and contains the reflection of the sixteenth. In the disc of the Moon of the form of the *Śrī-cakra,* there is only one Kalā and that the Paramākalā. The three Anusvāras of the Pañca-daśākṣarī indicate the *Bindu* and, by implication, the *Nāda* thereof. Thus, the *Śrī-cakra* of the character of *Nāda, Bindu* and *Kalā* is also made up of three Khaṇḍas. The Sādākhyā, which is the same as the *Śrī-vidyā,* lies beyond the *Nāda, Bindu* and *Kalā.* The fifty kalās described above inhere in the sixteen Nityās as follow : The sixteen vowels, the sixteen consonants from 'Ka' to 'Ta', the sixteen consonants from 'Tha' to 'Sa', these inhere in the sixteen Nityās in triads. The *Akāśa-bīja* 'Ha', inheres in the

Ākāśa of the *Bindu* ; while *'Kṣa'*, which is composed of 'Ka' and 'Ṣa', inheres in the Nityās corresponding to its components. The sixteen Nityās being of the form of the sixteen syllables, the sixteen syllables being of the form of the fifty Mātṛkās, the fifty Mātṛkās being of the form of the Sun, the Moon and the Fire, which in their turn form the three Granthi's, thus the four kinds of harmonious relations become patent.

Similarly, the *Cakras* and the Mantras harmonize thus : The three Hrīṁs and Śrī-bīja inhere in the form of the *Bindu* of the *Tri-koṇa*, which represents the fourt Śiva-cakras. The letters comprised in the Pratyāhāras 'Kalā' and 'Akṣa' inhere in the *Śrī-cakra* as folows; the four semi-vowels and the four sibilants in the *Aṣṭa-koṇa;* the twenth letters from 'Ka' to 'Ma' the nasals excepted, in the two *Daśāras;* the nasal consonants through the *Anusvāra*, the *Anusvāra* and the *Visarga*, in the *Bindu;* and the remaining fourteen vowels, in the *Catur-daśāra*.

Even as the Mantra is composed of three Khaṇḍas, the *Cakra* may be looked upon from the aspects of Soma, Sūrya and Agni. The sixteen Kalās of the Moon inhere in the Indu-khaṇḍa of the Mantra, which in its turn inheres in the Indu-aspect of the Yantra. So also the twenty-four Kalās of the Sun inhere in the Saurakhaṇḍa of the Mantra, which inhere in the Solar aspect of the Yantra. Likewise, the ten Kalās of Agni inhere in the Agni-khaṇḍa of the Mantra, which inheres in the Agni aspect of the Yantra. Thus is the harmony between the Kalās of the Yantra and the Mantra.

The names of the sixteen Kalās as gathered from the Vedas are : Darśa, Dṛṣṭā, Darśatā, Viśva-rūpā, Sudarśanā, Āpyāyamānā, Āpyāyamānā, Āpyāyā, Sūnṛtā Irā, Āpūryamāṇā, Āpūryamāṇā, Pūrayantī, Pūrṇā, Paurṇamāsī and Cit-kalā. The deities that preside over them respectively are Tripurasundarī, Kāmeśvarī, Bhagamālinī, Nitya-klinnā, Bheruṇḍā, Vahni-vāsinī, Mahāvideśvarī, Śiva-dūtī, Tvaritā, Kulasundarī, Nityā, Nilapatākā, Vijayā, Sarvamaṅgalā, Jvālā-mālinikā and Cit-kalā. The Tattvas represented by them respectively are Śiva, Śakti, Māyā, Śuddha-vidyā, Jala, Tejas, Vāyu, Manas, Pṛthivī, Ākāśa, Vidyā, Maheśvara, Para-tattva Ātma-tattva, Sadāśiva-tattva and Sādākhyā-tattva. The Devatā influencing the entire group is Kāmadeva, while Kāmeśvarī presides over them all. Even as the sixteen syllables of the Mantra are divided into four Khaṇḍas, the Kalās may be divided in the same manner into four Khaṇḍas, with Agni, Sūrya, Soma and Sādakhyā as their presiding deities.

Kaivalyāśrama takes this stanza as indicating the Lopāmudrā-vidyā, the Bīja of all Mantras, in which case the first Khaṇḍa will have to be interpreted thus : 'Śiva' stands for 'Ha' 'Śakti' for 'Sa', 'Kāma' for 'Ka', and 'Kṣiti' for 'La', the other Khaṇḍas being understood as in the other case. He is also of opinion that the Trayodaśākṣarī-vidyā of Durvāsas could also be taken as indicated by this stanza, by dropping the first two Hṛl-lekhās of the Lopāmudrā-vidyā, generally known as Hādi-vidyā. According to the Ḍiṇḍima, this stanza contains the essence of the Vedas. It quotes from the Tripuratāpinī Upaniṣad in support of this view. Certain commentators not only take this stanza to refer to the Hādī-vidyā, but also state that the Mantra indicated is Ṣoḍaśākṣarī, which forms the basis of the Samaya form of worship, the sixteenth syllable not expressly mentioned having to be learnt from the *guru.*

स्मरं योनिं लक्ष्मीं त्रितयमिदमादौ[1] तव मनो
निधायैके नित्ये[2] निरवधिमहाभोगरसिकाः।
[3]भजन्ति त्वां चिन्तामणिगुणनिबद्धाक्षवलयाः[4]
[5]शिवाऽग्नौ [6]जुह्वन्तः सुरभिघृतधाराऽऽहुतिशतैः।। ३३।।

Smaraṁ yoniṁ lakṣmīṁ tri-tayam idam ādau tava manor
nidhāyaike nitye nir-avadhi-mahā-bhoga-rasikāḥ/
Bhajanti tvāṁ cintā-maṇi-guṇa-nibaddhākṣavalayāḥ
śivā'gnau juhvantaḥ surabhi-ghṛta-dhārā-" hutiśataiḥ//

Translation : O Goddess eternal! having placed this triad of Smara, Yoni and Lakṣmī before Thy Mantra, some (devotees of Thine), bent on the boundless enjoyment of Beatitude, worship Thee with rosaries strung with Cintāmaṇi beads, while offering hundreds of oblations with streams of Surabhi's ghee, in the purified fire of Śivā (triangle).

स्मरं कामराजं, **योनिं** भुवनेश्वरीं, **लक्ष्मीं** श्रीबीजम्, **इदं त्रितयं आदौ तव मनोः** मन्त्रस्य, **निधाय** संयोज्य, **एके** विरलाः समयिनः, **नित्ये!** आद्यन्तरहिते!

1. ०माद्ये।
2. चित्ते; चिन्ता।
3. जयन्ति ; जपन्ति।
4. बद्धाक्षरलयाः।
5. शिवाग्नौ।
6. जुह्वाना।

निरवधिमहाभोगरसिकाः अपरिच्छिन्ननित्यानुभवरसज्ञाः, परमयोगीश्वरा इति यावत्। **भजन्ति** सेवन्ते। **त्वां** भवतीं, सहस्रदलकमलात् अवरोप्य हृत्कमले संस्थाप्य तादृग्विधां **चिन्तामणिगुणनिबद्धाक्षवलयाः** चिन्तामणीनां गुणः गुणनं आम्रेडनं, समूह इति यावत्, तेन निबद्धो रचितः अक्षवलयः अक्षमालिका येषां ते। यद्वा–चिन्तामणय एव गुणनिबद्धाक्षाः सूत्ररचिताक्षाः पद्मबीजानि, तेषां वलयः मालिका येषां ते तथोक्ताः, **शिवाग्नौ** शिवा शक्तिः त्रिकोणमिति यावत्, तत्र संस्कृतः अग्निः शिवाग्निः। त्रिकोणे बैन्दवस्थाने स्वाधिष्ठानाग्निं अवयुत्य तत्र निक्षिप्य पाशाङ्कुशाभ्यां सन्निरुध्य भुवनेश्वर्या अवकुण्ठ्य अग्नेः जातकर्मादिषोडशसंस्काराः यत्र क्रियन्ते सः शिवाग्निरिति रहस्यमिति। अयमाशयः–त्रिकोणे बैन्दवस्थाने स्वाधिष्ठानाग्निं निक्षिप्येति। यद्यपि **बैन्दवस्थानं** चतुष्कोणं, तथापि पुरश्चरणात्मकक्रियायां संवित्कमले त्रिकोणं आरोप्य सहस्रकमलात् बैन्दवस्थानस्थां कामेश्वरीं अवरोप्य पुरश्चरणं कार्यमिति समयिमतरहस्यमिति आचार्याणां आशय इति। **जुह्वन्तः** सन्तर्पयन्तः, **सुरभिघृतधाराहुतिशतैः** सुरभिः कामगवी, तस्याः घृतम् आज्यं, तस्य धाराः, ताभिः आहुतयः हविःप्रक्षेपाः, तासां शतानि सहस्रं तैः।।

अत्रेत्थं पदयोजना–हे नित्ये! तव मनोः आदौ स्मरं योनिं लक्ष्मीम् इदं त्रितयं निधाय निरवधिमहाभोगरसिकाः एके चिन्तामणिगुणनिबद्धाक्षवलयाः शिवाग्नौ त्वां सुरभितघृतधाराहुतिशतैः जुह्वन्तः भजन्ति।।

अत्रेदं तत्त्वम्–समयिनां मन्त्रस्य पुरश्चरणं नास्ति। जपो नास्ति। बाह्यहोमोऽपि नास्ति। बाह्यपूजाविधयो न सन्त्येव। हृत्कमल एव सर्वं यावत् अनुष्ठेयम्। एतच्च **'जपो जल्पशिल्पम्'**[1] इत्यादिश्लोकव्याख्यानावसरे किञ्चिदुक्तम्। अवशिष्टं कृत्स्नं **'तवाज्ञाचक्रस्थम्'**[2] इत्यादि श्लोकषट्व्याख्यानावसरे निपुणतरमुपपादयिष्यामः।।

'तवाज्ञाचक्रस्थम्'[3] इत्यादिश्लोकषट्केन सामयिकं मतं निरूपयिष्यन् सप्रभेदं कौलमतं तदुपयोगितया निरूपयति। कौलमतं द्विविधं, पूर्वकौलम् उत्तरकौलं चेति।

Notes : This stanza ostensibly deals with the worship of the Devī by the Samayins, with all the external forms obtaining among Kaulas, while the next deals with the form of the Devī herself in the same strain. Stanza 35 clothes her in the aspect of pure matter, which is the basic principle of the doctrine of the Kaulas. The next six stanzas of the Ānandalaharī exclusively deal with the Samaya doctrine.

Starting with the Devī's Mantra, as given in the previous stanza,

---

1. २७ श्लोकः। 2. ३६ श्लोकः।
3. ३६ श्लोकः।

as the basis, this stanza deals with the procedure to be adopted by votaries desirous of achieving the special purposes of acquisition of power, wealth, beatitude, *etc.*, without having recourse to any external forms of worship or prayer. The device suggested herein is the placing before the Mantra of the triad of syllables represented by the conventional names, Smara, Yoni and Lakṣmī, which are capable of being interpreted in two ways : (1) 'Smara', meaning the Madanabīja—'Klīm'; 'Yoni', meaning the Bhuvaneśvarī-bīja—'Hrīṁ'; and 'Lakṣmī', meaning the Ramā-bīja—'Śrīṁ'. By placing these three before the Kādi-vidyā indicated by the previous stanza and meditating upon the Devī as of the form of the resultant Mantra, it is claimed that Mahā-bhoga, immense wealth and influence, is vouchsafed to the votary. 'Mahā-bhoga' may also be construed as 'final beatitude', the boundless enjoyment of which is the Yogin's goal. It is on this sense that our English rendering has been based. (2) By placing the trisyllable 'Ka E Ī', obtained from 'Smara' meaning—'Ka', 'Yoni' meaning—'E', and 'Lakṣmī' meaning—'Ī', in the place of 'Ha Sa Ka' of the Hādi-vidyā indicated by the previous stanza, the Mantra stands converted to Kādi-vidyā. The Hādi-vidyā is credited with the power of bestowing Liberation and is therefore considered superior to the Kādi-vidyā, which is credited only with the power of bestowing enjoyment of all forms, in this as well as in the other worlds.

There is also the reading *'Cintā-maṇi-guṇa-nibaddhā-kṣara-layāḥ'*, in which case the meaning would be—'and attain Liberation in the Akṣara, *viz.*, the Śabdabrahman, that is the Cit-kalā associated with the Guṇas–Sattva, Rajas and Tamas'. *Cintā-maṇi* is a gem to which is credited the virtue of bestowing all that is desired. As the Mātṛkās of the Devī have similar virtues, the word 'Cintā-maṇi-guṇa' may be taken to mean "the assemblage of Mātṛkās strung in the form of a rosary with 'Kṣa' serving as the Meru, the central bead, (which should not be crossed, while performing Japa)". *Surabhi* is the Kāma-dhenu, the celestial cow, granting all desires. *Surabhi* is also understood as meaning 'fragrant' and is said to indicate the fragrance of the current of nectar flowing in Go-loka, the abode of Viṣṇu. *On the Fire of Śivā (triangle)*—as the form of worship indicated her is entirely internal in accordance with the Samayācāra, the worshipper is enjoined to place the Agni of the *Svādhiṣṭhāna* in the *Baindava-sthāna,* which is the *Tri-koṇa,* and then conceive of the *Tri-koṇa* with the Agni as transposed upwards and, at the same time, the Devī of the thousand-petalled lotus as transposed downwards to the heart, and mentally perform offerings over the Fire as described in the stanza.

Kaivalyāśrama, who adopts the view that the Mantra indicated by the previous stanza is Hādi-vidyā and is turned to Kādi-vidyā by adopting the changes referred to in the first line, construes this stanza as describing the worship of the Devī in the following manner : Some devotees of Thine, with their external senses rendered devoid of their functions, by employing their minds in the investigation of the Bhāvārtha, Sampradāyārtha, Nigarbhārtha, Kaulikārtha, Rahasyārtha and Paramarahasyārtha of the Mantra,[1] with a view to the total annihilation of all previous impressions left on their minds relating to wordly attachment, which is so full of egotism and inimical to the attainment of the Paramātman, offer them as oblations of continuous streams of nectar-like ghee on the sacrificial Fire, effulgent with the radiance brought about by the mental attitude, 'I am Śiva', that refined alter-ego of the altruistic types. *'Juhvantaḥ'* is treated by some as the Present participle Nom. singular of 'Hu' 3rd conj. Parasm. 'to sacrifice'. But the correct form is *'Juhvataḥ'*; probably the form used is archaic. With a view to avoid the grammatical blunder some suggest the form 'Juhavānāḥ', which is equally open to the same objection, the root being only Parasmaipadin. To avoid this contingency, Kaivalyāśrama construes *'Juhv-antaḥ-surabhi-ghṛta-dhāra-huti-śataiḥ'*, as a single compound word meaning, "with hundreds of oblations of streams of fragrant ghee flowing out of the *Juhū*, the ladle." The same commentator understands the stanza as indicating Antaryāga and signifying : Some devotees, intent on offering the full oblation (*Pūrṇāhuti*), worship Thee, conceiving, with their minds, Thee, of the form of the Kuṇḍalinī, stretching from the *Mūlādhāra* to the *Brahmarandhra* in the form of the string of the fifty Mātṛkās, themselves assuming a firm posture, and offering the Pūrṇāhuti of a continuous stream of ghee of the form of Su-vāsanās, through the ladle of *Un-manī*, over the Fire of Śiva, with the mental attitude, 'I am Śiva'.

1. For a detailed exposition of the several meanings of this Mantra, the reader is referred to pp. 128-137 of the *Varivasyā-rahasya*, Vasanta Press Edition.

एतद्द्वितयं क्रमेण श्लोकद्वितयेनाह–

शरीरं त्वं शंभोः शशिमिहिरवक्षोरुहयुगं
तवात्मानं मन्ये भगवति [1]नवात्मानमनघम्।
अतः शेषः शेषीत्ययमुभयसाधारणतया
स्थितः संबन्धो वां समरसपरानन्दपरयोः[2]।। ३४।।

Śarīraṁ tvaṁ śaṁboḥ śaśi-mihira-vakṣo-ruha-yugaṁ
tavātmānaṁ manye bhagavati navātmānam an-agham/
Ataḥ śeṣaḥ śeṣīty ayam ubhaya-sādhāraṇatayā
sthitaḥ saṁbandho vāṁ sama-rasa-parānanda-parayoḥ//

Translation : O Glorious Goddess! Thou art the body of Śaṁbhu with the Sun and the Moon as the two breasts. I conceive Thy flawless frame to be *Navātman* (Śaṁbhu). Hence, the relationship of the essential and the accessory, in the case of Ye both, equipoised of Transcendent Bliss and Transcendent (Consciousness), stands even.

शरीरं देहः, **त्वं** भवती महाभैरवी, **शम्भोः** आनन्दभैरवस्य, **शशिमिहिर-वक्षोरुहयुगं** शशी चन्द्रः मिहिरः सूर्यः तावेव वक्षोरुहौ कुचौ तयोर्युगं युग्मं यस्य तत्। **तव** भवत्याः महाभैरव्याः, **आत्मानं** देहं, **मन्ये** जानामि। **भगवति!** भगः अस्या अस्तीति भगवती तस्याः सम्बुद्धिः।

उत्पत्तिं च विनाशं च भूतानामागतिं गतिम्।
वेत्ति विद्यामविद्यां च स वाच्यो भगवानिति।।

इति स्मरणात् उत्पत्यादिवेदनं भगः तद्वती भगवती। यद्वा–इन्दुकलाविद्यायाः नवयोन्यात्मकत्वात् नवयोनिमती भगवती। प्राशस्त्ये मतुप्। नवयोनिभिः प्रशस्तेत्यर्थः। **नवात्मानं**[3]–आनन्दभैरवम् नवव्यूहात्मकम्। आनन्दभैरवस्य नवव्यूहात्मकत्वं उपरिष्टात् वक्ष्यते। **अनघं** निर्दोषम्, **अतः** अस्माद्धेतोः, यतः कारणात् परानन्दपरयोः ऐक्यं तस्मादित्यर्थः। **शेषः** गुणभूतः अप्रधानम्, **शेषी** प्रधानम्, **इत्ययं** एवंप्रकारः, **उभयसाधारणतया** उभयोः भैरवीभैरवयोः साधारणतया साधारण्यात्, **स्थितिः** अवस्थितः, **सम्बन्धः** शेषशेषिभावरूपः, **वां युवयोः समरसपरानन्दपरयोः** समरसे सामरस्ययुक्ते परानन्दः आनन्दभैरवः परा आनन्दभैरवीरूपा चिच्छक्तिः कला, समरसे च ते परानन्दपरे च तयोः।।

1. भवात्मान०।
2. ०पदयोः।
3. आनन्दभैरवा नवव्यूहात्मतयोदाहृतः। आनन्दः।

अत्रेत्थं पदयोजना–हे भगवति! शम्भोस्त्वं शशिमिहिरवक्षोरुहयुगं शरीरं भवसीति शेषः। आनन्दभैरवस्य कालव्यूहान्तःपातित्वात् सूर्यचन्द्रयोः वक्षोरुहयुगत्वारोपणं युक्तम्। यद्वा–अयमन्वयः–हे भगवति! शशिमिहिरवक्षोरुहयुगं शरीरं शम्भोस्त्वमेव।

सूर्यचन्द्रौ स्तनौ देव्याः तावेव नयने स्मृतौ।
उभौ ताटङ्कयुगलमित्येषा वैदिकी श्रुतिः॥

इत्यनेन भगवत्याः शम्भुं प्रति शेषत्वमुक्तम्। हे भगवति! तवात्मानमनघं नवात्मानं मन्ये। अतः "शेषः शेषी" इत्ययं सम्बन्धः समरसपरानन्दपरयोः वां उभयसाधारणतया स्थितः॥

अत्रेदमनुसन्धेयम्–महाभैरवस्य नवात्मेति संज्ञा, नवव्यूहात्मकत्वात्। नव व्यूहास्तु–

कालव्यूहः कुलव्यूहो नामव्यूहस्तथैव च।
ज्ञानव्यूहस्तथा चित्तव्यूहः स्यात्तदनन्तरम्॥
नादव्यूहस्तथा बिन्दुव्यूहः स्यात्तदनन्तरम्।
कलाव्यूहस्तथा जीवव्यूहः स्यादिति ते नव॥

अस्यार्थः–

कालव्यूहो नाम–निमेषादिकल्पान्तावच्छिन्नकालसमुदायः कालव्यूहः। सूर्यचन्द्रयोरपि कालावच्छेदकतया कालव्यूहे अन्तर्भाव उक्तः॥

कुलव्यूहो नाम–नीलादिरूपव्यूहः।

नामव्यूहो नाम–संज्ञास्कन्धः॥

ज्ञानव्यूहो नाम–विज्ञानस्कन्धः। [1]भागव्यूह इति नामान्तरमस्ति। स च द्विविधः [2]सभागविभागभेदात्। [3]सभागो विकल्पः, [4]विभागो निर्विकल्पः॥

चित्तव्यूहो नाम–अहङ्कारपञ्चकस्कन्धः। अहङ्कारपञ्चकं नाम–अहङ्कारचित्तबुद्धि-महन्मनांसि॥

नादव्यूहो नाम–रागेच्छाकृतिप्रयत्नस्कन्धः। अनेन मातृकायाः परा पश्यन्ती मध्यमा वैखरी इति चत्वारि रूपाणि। परा नाम सान्तरोहरूपा। अन्तरे अन्तःकरणे ऊहेन तर्केण

1. भोगव्यूह इति।
2. सम्भोगविसम्भोगभेदात्।
3. सम्भोगो विकल्पः।
4. विसम्भोगो निर्विकल्पः।

सहितं रूपं यस्याः सा सान्तरोहरूपा। युक्तावस्थायामेव ज्ञातव्येत्यभिसन्धिः। यथोक्तं कामकलाविद्यायाम्–

या सान्तरोहरूपा परा[1] महेशी परा नाम।

पश्यन्ती नाम एषैव स्पष्टा उच्यते। यथोक्तं तत्रैव–

स्पष्टा[2] पश्यन्त्याख्या त्रिमातृका चक्रतां याता।।

त्रिमातृका त्रिखण्डयुक्ता मातृका पञ्चदशाक्षरी, तदात्मिका। सा च चक्रतां चक्रत्वं याता। त्रिखण्डात्मकचक्रैक्यं त्रिखण्डात्मकमातृकाया इति रहस्यम्। एतच्च पूर्वं बहुधा प्रपञ्चितम्। स्पष्टा युक्तावस्थायां अतिसूक्ष्मतया प्रतीता इत्यभिसन्धिः। मध्यमा नाम परापश्यन्त्योः उच्चानुच्चावस्थात्मिका। सा द्विविधा, वामादिव्यष्टिरूपा वामादिसमष्टिरूपा चेति। वामादिसमष्टिरूपा सूक्ष्मा ; वामादिव्यष्टिरूपा स्थूला। वामादयः शक्तयः–वामा, ज्येष्ठा, रौद्री, अम्बिका। एताश्चतस्रः शक्तयः श्रीचक्रान्तर्गताधोमुखचतुर्योन्यात्मिकाः। इच्छा, ज्ञानं, क्रिया, शान्ता, परा चेति पञ्च शक्तयः श्रीचक्रान्तर्गतोर्ध्वमुखशक्तियोन्यात्मिकाः। एताभिः शक्तिभिः नवव्यूहात्मिकाभिः भगवत्याः नवात्मत्वम् उच्यते। यथोक्तं तत्रैव–

एका परा तदन्या वामादिव्यष्टिमातृसृष्ट्यात्मा।
तेन नवात्मा माता जाता सा मध्यमाऽभिधानाभ्याम्।।
द्विविधा हि मध्यमा सा सूक्ष्मा स्थूलाकृतिः[3] स्थिरा सूक्ष्मा।
नवनादमयी स्थूला नववर्गात्मा तु भूतलिप्याख्या।।
आद्या कारणमन्या कार्यं त्वनयोर्यतस्ततो हेतोः।
सैवेयं न हि भेदस्तादात्म्यं[4] हेतुहेतुमदभीष्टम्।।

अस्यार्थः–एका परेति सत्वरजस्तमोगुणसाम्यरूपा। तदन्या पश्यन्ती अन्यतरगुणवैषम्यरूपेत्यर्थः। मध्यमा वामादिव्यष्टिरूपा स्थूलात्मिका। वामादयः शक्तयो बैन्दवस्थानस्य उभयत्र सम्पुटत्वेनावस्थिताः। अत एव एताः व्यूहशब्दवाच्यास्सत्यः नवात्मशब्देन व्यवह्रियन्ते। समष्टिरूपास्तु परायामन्तर्भूताः। तेन कारणेन माता मातृका नवात्मा जाता। सा मध्यमा अभिधानाभ्यां द्विविधा, हि यस्मात् सा मध्यमा सूक्ष्मा स्थूलाकृतिश्चेति द्विविधा। सूक्ष्मास्वरूपमाह–स्थिरेति। स्थैर्यावस्थायां युक्तावस्थायामेव

1. महेशी त्रिभाविता सैव।
2. पश्यन्त्यादित्रिमातृकाप्माच इति क्वचित्पाठो दृश्यते।
3. तथा, स्थिता।
4. हेतुहेतुमतोरिष्टम्, जनक जन्ययोरिष्टम्।

अवभास्या। नवनादमयीति–नव नादाः अकचटतपयशक्षाः। एते परस्परं भिन्नजातीयाः, स्वरकवर्गचवर्गटवर्गतवर्गपवर्गयवर्गशवर्गक्षवर्गाणां परस्परं भिन्नत्वेन प्रतीयमानत्वात्। तत्र प्रमाणमाह–भूतलिप्याख्येति। मिथ्याविज्ञेयमिथ्यारूपायाः लिपेः आख्यापकत्वं दर्पणप्रतिबिम्बस्य मुखज्ञापकत्वमिव न विरुध्यते। आद्या कारणमन्येति–आद्या सूक्ष्मरूपा मध्यमा कारणं स्थूलरूपायाः मध्यमायाः नववर्गात्मिकायाः। अनयोः कार्यकारणयोः यतस्ततो हेतोः सैवेयं सूक्ष्मैवेयं स्थूला। अतः स्थूलसूक्ष्मयोः ऐक्ये अभेदे विमर्शदशायामपि न कोऽपि हेतुरस्तीति तात्पर्येणोक्तम्–यतस्ततो हेतोरिति। तदेव प्रतिपादयति–न हि भेद इति। हेतुहेतुमदिति–हेतुहेतुमत्तादात्म्यम् अभीष्टमित्यन्वयः। सर्वत्र तादात्म्यं हेतुहेतुमद्व्यतिरेकेण नास्तीत्यर्थः। अतश्च मध्यमात्मिकायाः चिच्छक्तेः नवात्मता सिद्धा। रागेच्छाकृतिप्रयत्नानां कारणत्वेनागमेषु प्रसिद्धाः मायाशुद्धविद्यामहेश्वरसदाशिवाः रागादीनां तत्त्वभूताः सङ्गृहीताः। तैः परापश्यन्तीमध्यमावैखर्यः अधिष्ठानभूताः सङ्गृहीता इत्यवगन्तव्यम्।।

बिन्दुव्यूहो नाम–षट्चक्रसङ्घः।।

कलाव्यूहो नाम–पञ्चाशत्कलानां वर्णात्मिकानां सङ्घः।।

जीवव्यूहो नाम–भोक्तृस्कन्धः।।

एवं नवानां व्यूहानां भोक्तृभोग्यभोगरूपेणं त्रैविध्यम्। आत्मव्यूहस्य भोक्तृत्वेऽपि भोग्यभोगतादात्म्यात् [1]त्रैविध्यम्। एवं भोगव्यूहस्याप्यूह्यम्। अयमाशयः–आत्मव्यूहस्य भोक्तृत्वं, ज्ञानव्यूहस्य भोगत्वम्, कालव्यूहादीनां भोग्यत्वमेवेति आचार्याणां त्रैविध्यमभिप्रेतमिति। सर्वेषां व्यूहानां जीवव्यूहस्य सर्वत्र अन्वयादैक्यम्। कालव्यूहस्य अवच्छेदकत्वादैक्यम्। कुलनामव्यूहयोः निरूपकत्वादैक्यम्। ज्ञानव्यूहस्य बिन्दुव्यूहे तादात्म्यादैक्यम्। नादकलयोरैक्यात् नवव्यूहात्मकत्वं परमेश्वरस्य सिद्धमेव। अतो नवविधैक्यं भैरवीभैरवयोः ज्ञातव्यमिति कौलमतरहस्यम्। अत एव कौलाः [2]परमेश्वरं नवात्मेति व्यवहरन्ति। यथाहुः कौलाः–

नवव्यूहात्मको देवः परानन्दपरात्मकः।
नवात्मा भैरवो देवो भुक्तिमुक्तिप्रदायकः।।
परानन्दपराशक्तिः चिद्रूपाऽऽनन्दभैरवी।
तयोर्यदा सामरस्यं जगदुत्पद्यते तदा।।

---

1. अविरुद्धम्। एवं भोग्यव्यूहस्य भोगव्यूहस्याप्यूह्यम्।
2. परमेश्वरस्य नवात्मतेति।

इति दिङ्मात्रमुक्तम्। अवशिष्टं **'तवाधारे मूले'**[1] इत्यादौ निरूप्यते। अयं भाव:-आनन्दभैरवमहाभैरव्यो: परानन्दपरासंज्ञयो: तादात्म्ये सिद्धे नवात्मता द्वयो: समाना। अत: शेषशेषिभाव: आपेक्षिक:-यदा सृष्टिस्थितिलयेषु आनन्दभैरवस्य परानन्दसंज्ञिकस्य परचित्स्वरूपायाश्च महाभैरव्या: प्रयत्न: उत्पद्यते, तदा भैरवीप्राधान्यात् प्रधानं प्रकृतिशब्दवाच्या महाभैरवीति, तस्या: प्रधानत्वं शेषित्वं; आनन्दभैरवस्य अप्रधानत्वं गुणभाव: शेषत्वम्। यदा सर्वोपसंहारे प्रकृते: तन्मात्रावस्थितौ भैरव्या: स्वात्मनि अन्तर्भावात् भैरवस्य शेषित्वं तदा भैरव्या: शेषत्वमिति।। ३४।।

Notes : The Sun and the Moon—the Devī's breasts are referred to as these two heavenly bodies, which at the same time form part of Kāla, one of the nine aspects of Śiva. Hence, they form part of his frame. *Thy flawless frame*—which is not other than the *Śrī-cakra*, made up of the nine Yonis, the nine aspects of the Devī. *Navātman*—Śaṁbhu is characterized by the nine Vyūhas : Kāla, Kula, Nāman, Jñāna, Citta, Nāda, Bindu, Kalā and Jīva. *Kāla* designates duration, from the period taken by the twinkling of an eye up to the end of infinite Time. The Sun and the Moon are comprised hereunder. *Kula* comprehends blue, white and other colours. *Nāman* is conventional nomenclature, such as Ghaṭa, Paṭa and others. *Jñāna* is knowledge of the concrete and the abstract type. *Citta* is made up of Ahaṁ-kāra, Citta, Buddhi, Mahat and Manas. *Nāda* is made up of Parā, Paśyantī, Madhyamā and Vaikharī sounds. *Bindu* is made up of the six *Cakras*, the *Mūlādhāra* and others. *Kalā* comprises the fifty letters of the Alphabet. *Jīva* is the group of Jīvātmans, the enjoyers. The Devī is aslo characterized by the nine Vyūhas : Vāmā, Jyeṣṭhā, Raudrī and Ambikā, the four Yonis of the *Śrī-cakra* pointing downwards; and Icchā, Jñānā, Kriyā, Śāntā and Parā, the five Yonis of the same pointing upwards. Ānandabhairava who is Śaṁbhu of the form of Transcendent Bliss is said to be identical with Mahābhairavī, the Śakti of the form of Transcendent Consciousness. Hence, either of them is neither more nor less than the other. The two together form the whole. One cannot conceive of the one as separate from the other. Hence, the relationship of the essential and the accessory subsists mutually between them. While the functions of creation, sustenance and destruction are being discharged, the Devī's element predominates and Īśvara's subserves. After the Deluge, when those functions are in a state of quiescence, Īśvara's element prevails and the Devī's subserves.

1. ४१ श्लोक:।

Hence, the predominance and the subservience of the two are evenly matched. This stanza, in a way, indicates the oneness of Śiva and the Śakti as *Ādhāra* and *Ādheya*.

मनस्त्वं व्योम त्वं मरुदसि मरुत्सारथिरसि
त्वमापस्त्वं भूमिस्त्वयि परिणतायां न हि परम्।
त्वमेव स्वात्मानं परिणमयितुं विश्ववपुषा
चिदानन्दाकारं शिवयुवति[1] भावेन बिभृषे[2]।। ३५।।

Manas tvaṁ vyoma tvaṁ marud asi marutsārathir asi
tvam āpas tvaṁ bhūmis tvayi pariṇatāyāṁ na hi param/
Tvam eva svātmānaṁ pariṇamayituṁ, viśva-vapuṣā
cidānandākāraṁ śiva-yuvati bhāvena bibhṛṣe//

Translation : O youthful spouse of Śiva! Thou art the Mind, Thou the Ether, Thou the Air, Thou the Fire, Thou the Water, and Thou the Earth. When Thou has transformed Thyself (thus), there is nothig beyond. Thyself, with a view to manifesting Thyself in the form of the Universe, inwardly assumest the form of Consciousness and Bliss.

मनः मनस्तत्त्वं आज्ञाचक्रस्थितं त्वम् एव। **व्योम** आकाशतत्त्वं विशुद्धिचक्रान्तस्थितं त्वम् एव। **मरुत्** वायुतत्त्वं अनाहतनामकसंविच्चक्रान्तर्गतम्। **असि** इति त्वमित्यर्थे अव्ययम्। **मरुत्सारथिः** वायुसखः अग्नितत्त्वं स्वाधिष्ठानगतम्। **असि** इति पूर्ववत् अव्ययम्। **त्वम् आपः** अप्तत्त्वं मणिपूरान्तर्गतम्। त्वं **भूमिः** भूमितत्त्वं मूलाधारान्तर्गतम्। एवं रूपेण **त्वयि परिणतायां** परिणतिं तादात्म्यं गतायां, **न हि परं** इतः परं न किञ्चिदस्तीत्यर्थः। **त्वमेव स्वात्मानं** स्वस्वरूपं, **परिणमयितुं** परिणामवन्तं कर्तुं, **विश्ववपुषा** प्रपञ्चरूपेण **चिदानन्दाकारं** चिच्छक्तेः आनन्दभैरवस्य च आकारं, **शिवयुवति**! शिवयुवतिः हरपत्नी, युवतिशब्दात् 'सर्वतोऽक्तिन्नर्थादित्येके' इति ङीप्। तस्याः सम्बुद्धिः। **भावेन** चित्तेन, **बिभृषे**। यद्वा–**चिदानन्दाकारं** च ब्रह्मस्वरूपं शिवतत्त्वं, **शिवयुवतिभावेन** शिवस्य युवतिर्जाया तस्याः भावः तत्त्वं तेन।

अत्रेत्थं पदयोजना–हे भगवति! मनस्त्वं व्योम त्वं मरुदसि मरुत्सारथिरसि त्वमापस्त्वं भूमिः। त्वयि परिणतायां परं न हि। त्वमेव स्वात्मानं विश्ववपुषा परिणमयितुं शिवयुवति! भावेन चिदानन्दाकारं बिभृषे।।

---

1. हरयुवति ; हरमहिषि ; शिवमहिषि।
2. विमृषे।

अयमर्थः–'मनस्त्वं' इत्यादि 'भूमिः इत्यन्तेन पञ्चभूतात्मकः कार्यरूपः परिणामो विकारः उक्तः। 'त्वयि परिणतायाम्' इत्यनेन निर्विकारात्मकः कारणरूपेणावस्थिति-विशेषः प्रकृत्याः परिणामः उक्तः। 'न हि परम्' इत्यनेन अपरिणामिन्याः परिणामो नास्ति अनवस्थापत्तेः इति हि शब्दार्थः। तथोक्तं चतुश्शत्याम्–

शृणु देवि महाज्ञानं सर्वज्ञानोत्तमं प्रिये।
येन विज्ञानमात्रेण भवाब्धौ न निमज्जति।।
त्रिपुरा परमा शक्तिराद्या जाता महेश्वरि।
स्थूलसूक्ष्मविभागेन त्रैलोक्योत्पत्तिमातृका।।
कबलीकृतनिश्शेषतत्त्वग्रामस्वरूपिणी।
यस्यां परिणतायां तु न किञ्चित्परमिष्यते[1]।।

[2]अयमर्थः–कबलीकृतः आत्मन्यारोपितः कारणात्मतया अवस्थितः, यथा मृदि घट इव निश्शेषं यथा भवति तथा तत्त्वानां पञ्चतत्त्वानां ग्रामः समूहः कबलीकृतनिश्शेष-तत्त्वग्रामः, स एव स्वरूपं यस्यास्सा, कार्याणि कारणे उपसंहृत्य स्वयं कारणात्मना अवस्थितेत्यर्थः, सत्कार्यवादिनां मते कारणे कार्यस्यापि शक्तिरूपेण विद्यमानत्वात् इति। एतदुक्तं भवति—उत्तरकौलमते प्रधानमेव जगत्कर्तृ। प्रधानत्वादेव शेषभावो नास्ति, शिवस्याभावात्। तस्य परिणतिः पञ्चतत्त्वात्मिका। मनस्तत्त्वादिरूपेण प्रधानात्मिका शक्तिः परिणता। अतः मनःप्रभृतीनां शक्तिपरिणामः, तत्त्वानां स्वरूपपरिणामः। एवं प्रपञ्चं कार्यरूपं स्वस्यामारोप्य कारणरूपेण अवस्थिता। सा च [3]आधारकुण्डलिनीत्य-भिधीयते। इतःपरं यद्वक्तव्यमस्ति 'तदपि तवाधारे मूले'[4] इत्यादिश्लोकव्याख्यानावसरे निपुणतरमुपपादयिष्यामः।। ३५।।

Notes : With a view to demonstrating the Devīs being of the essence of the eight Mūrtis, the author extols her in this stanza from all points of view.

The Mind—the Yajamāna, one of the eight Mūrtis, the sacrificer, who makes up the resolve, 'I shall perform the sacrifice'. As the Moon is, according to a Vedic text, derived from the Mind, the word 'Mind' comprehends the Moon also. The Fire—owing to the close affinity subsisting between the Sun and Fire, the Sun is also

1. परिशिष्यते।
2. कबळीकृतनिश्शेषतत्त्वग्रामस्वरूपिणीत्यस्यायमर्थः।
3. आधारकुण्डे कुण्डलिनी।
4. ४१ श्लोकः।

comprehended by the term 'Fire'. Thus the Mind and the five elements, which the Devī is represented to be, cloths her with Aṣṭamūrtitva—the Aṣṭamūrtis constituting the Universe. Consciousness and Bliss—are the forms of the Brahman, which are interwoven with the eight forms related above. The esoteric significance of the tradition may be given as follows : O Goddess! thou art the Mind existing in the *Ājñā*, the Ether in the *Viśuddhi*, the Air in the *Anāhata*, the Fire in the *Svādhiṣṭhāna*, the Water in the *Maṇipūra*, and the Earth in the *Mūlādhāra*, all in their subtle forms. While thou art in this transformed state in the Microcosm, as Viśva, Taijasa and Prājña, as well as in the Macrocosm, as Virāj, Hiraṇyagarbha and Antaryāmin, with a view to assuming a gross form, thou, with the power of thy Icchā-śakti, assumest the forms of the Śakti, (*i.e.*, Cit), and Śiva, (*i.e.*, Ānanda), in this manner. This phenomenal world is essentially evolved out of the five elements and their subtle variants. The latter are only the other forms of the Devī. After the Deluge there remains only the Brahman, which is no other than Śiva and the Śakti combined. Śiva stands apart, all alone, with no functions of his own. The Śakti in combination with Śiva is the prime cause of the Universe. The Universe is the manifestation of the Śakti. Forms and names are transient, while the substance is eternal. It is this substance, the substratum below names and forms, which is operated upon by and evolved out of the Śakti.

From the accompaying table it will be seen that the Devī, who transcends all, manifests herself as the six Devas, with their six abodes, represented by the six Tattvas, which have, as their centres, the six *Cakras*, from a combination of which the entire Universe is made. The Devī, notwithstanding her gross and subtle transformation, remains the Cit, transcending all Tattvas, in combination with the Bliss of the Paramātman.

Tattvas	*Lokas*	*Devas*	*Cakras*
	Satya	Parā-śakti	Sahasrāra
Manas	Tapas	Śiva	Ājñā
Ākāśa	Jana	Sadā-śiva	Viśuddhi
Vāyu	Mahar	Maheśvara	Anāhata
Tejas	Svar	Rudra	Svādhiṣṭhāna
Ap	Bhuvar	Viṣṇu	Maṇipūra
Pṛthivī	Bhūr	Brahman	Mūlādhāra

According to the Uttara-kaula doctrine, the Parā-śakti which is the Pradhāna is the creator of the Universe. The Devī, being the Pradhāna, there is no need for her subservience to any other Tattva.

तवाज्ञाचक्रस्थं तपनशशिकोटिद्युतिधरं[1]
परं शम्भुं वन्दे परिमिलितपार्श्वं परचिता।
[2]यमाराध्यन्भक्त्या[3] रविशशिशुचनीनामविषये
[4]निरातङ्के लोको निवसति हि भालोकभवने[5]।। ३६।।

Tavājñā-cakra-sthaṁ tapana-śaśi-koṭi-dyuti-dharaṁ
paraṁ śaṁbhuṁ vande parimilita-pārśvaṁ paracitā/
Yam ārādhyan bhaktyā ravi-śaśi-śucīnām a-viṣaye
nir-ātaṅke loko nivasati hi bhā-loka-bhavane.//

Translation : I salute the Supreme Śaṁbhu, who stands in Thy *Ājñā-cakra,* who is effulgent with the radiance of myriads of Suns and Moons, whose (left) side is embraced by the Supreme Consciousness, and by worshipping whom, with all devotion, one takes abode in what luminous region, which transcends the reach of the Sun, the Moon and Fire, devoid of all agony.

तव त्वदीये, **आज्ञाचक्रस्थं** आज्ञाचक्रे स्थितं, **तपनशशिकोटिद्युतिधरं** तपनः सूर्यः शशी चन्द्रः तयोः कोटयः, अगिणतकोटिसङ्ख्याका इत्यर्थः, तासां द्युतिः कान्तिः तां धरतीति धरः, तं **परं शम्भुम्[6]**। पर इति संज्ञा शम्भोः। **परिमिलितपार्श्वं** परिमिलितौ पार्श्वौ दक्षिणोत्तरौ यस्य तम्। परा चासौ चिच्च **परचित्**। परशब्दः चित्संज्ञायां प्रसिद्धः। यं परचित्संवलितं परशिवं, **आराध्यन्** प्रसादयन् **भक्त्या** भजनप्रीत्या, **रविशशिशुचीनां** सूर्यचन्द्राग्नीनां **अविषये** अगोचरे, अत एव **निरालोके** आलोकरहिते, **अलोके** विजने एकान्ते, **निवसति,** त्वत्सायुज्यं प्राप्येति शेषः। **हिः** प्रसिद्धौ। **भालोकभुवने** ज्योत्स्नामये लोके सहस्रकमले।।

अत्रेत्थं पदयोजना–हे भगवति! तवाज्ञाचक्रस्थं तपनशशिकोटिद्युतिधरं परं शम्भुं

---

1. तपनशतकोटिद्युतिहरं।
2. यमाराद्धं ; यमाराध्य।
3. प्रेम्णा।
4. निरालोकेऽलोके ; सदालोके ; निजालोके ; निरलोके लोको।
5. भालोकभुवने ; सदालोकभवने ; सालोकभवने।
6. वन्देत्यधिकः ; वन्दे इत्यधिकः।

परचिता परिमिलितपार्श्वं वन्दे। यं भक्त्या आराध्यन् रविशशिशुचीनां अविषये निरालोके अलोके भालोकभुवने निवसति हि।।

अत्रेदमनुसन्धेयम्–'तवाज्ञाचक्रस्थम्' इति चक्रशब्देन साधकस्य भ्रूमध्यान्तरगत-श्रीचक्रान्तर्गतशिवचक्रचतुष्टयं कथ्यते। न तु द्विदलं पद्मं, तवेतिपदानन्वयादिति। एवमुत्तरत्राप्यूह्यम्। अत्र स्वाधिष्ठानाग्रे अग्निमण्डलं, अनाहतचक्राग्रे सूर्यमण्डलं, आज्ञाचक्राग्रे चन्द्रमण्डलमिति पूर्वमेव प्रतिपादितम्। अतश्च अग्निसूर्यचन्द्राणां [1]मयूखाः षष्ट्युत्तरत्रिशतसङ्ख्याकाः आधारचक्रप्रभृति आज्ञाचक्रपर्यन्तमेव विचरन्ति। एतदपि पूर्वमेव सम्यक् निरूपितम्। आज्ञाचक्रस्थितिचन्द्रात् अन्य एव सहस्रकमलस्थितश्चन्द्रः श्रीचक्रात्मकः नित्यकल इत्यपि पूर्वमेव सम्यक् निरूपितम्।। ३६।।

Notes : In the following six stanzas, the six *Cakras* of the Devī's form are dealt with, in the order of evolution, from the subtle to the gross, and the votary is represented to worship Śiva and the Śakti, as their presiding deities, in the manner in which they appear to him in the *Cakras.* Supreme Śaṁbhu—the name Para-śaṁbhu-nātha is given to this deity. In Thy *Ājñā-cakra*—(1) who is within the ambit of thy command, *i.e.*, ever at they command; or (2) standing in the *Ājñā-cakra* of two petals in the middle of thy eyebrows, or (3) in the Manas-tattva of thy form. Kāmeśvarasūri here observed as follows : If the question arises—how can there be the *Ājñā-cakra* in the form of the Devī, who has no special form of her own, the answer is that even though the real form of the Devī may not have the *Cakra,* still, in the form assumed by her in sport, there is the necessity for the *Cakras,* so as to enable her to meditate on her own form as combined with her Lords's. In this connection he criticizes the view held by Lakṣmīdhara, who interprets *'Tavājñā-cakra-stham'* as "the four Śiva-cakras of the *Śrī-cakra,* situated in the middle of the eyebrows of the practitioner", and "not the two petalled *Ājñā-cakra*", by pointing out that the word 'Tava' will in that case be meaningless or superfluous, and adds that *'Tava'* is absolutely necessary for the reason pointed out in connection with the necessity for assuming the *Cakras* in the Devīs form, and that it is the two-petalled lotus of the *Ājñā-cakra* that is really meant. This criticism will hold good in the case of the next five stanzas also.

The Supreme Consciousness—*i.e.*, the Devī of that form, to wit, thyself. She is given the name of Cit-parāmbā. *Which transcends the*

1. किरणः इत्यधिकः।

reach of—for, the Sun, the Moon and Fire are situated in the nether regions, *viz.*, the *An-āhata*, the *Ājñā* and the *Mūlādhāra* respectively, *i.e.*, for below the *Sahasrāra* which is the region of his quest. The Moon in the *Sahasrāra* being Nitya-kalā would not come under this description. *Luminous region*—the *Sahasrāra*, the abode of perpetual moonshine. In the case of the reading *'Nir-āloke'*, the meaning is 'where there is no light (of the kind known to us)', *Agony*—resulting from the cycles of births and deaths. The forms of the deities, Para-śaṁbhu-nātha and Cit-parāmbā, should be conceived of in the middle, and the sixty-four Mānasa-mayūkhas as surrounding them, when practising meditation as indicated in this stanza.[1] Some reverse the order of stanzas 36-41 in the ascending order of the *Cakras.*

विशुद्धौ ते शुद्धस्फटिकविशदं व्योमजनकं[2]
शिवं सेवे देवीमपि शिवसमानव्यवसिताम्[3]।
ययोः कान्त्या यान्त्या[4] शशिकिरणसारूप्यसरणिं[5]
विधूतान्तर्ध्वान्ता[6] विलसति चकोरीव जगती।। ३७।।

Viśuddhau te śuddha-sphaṭika-viśadaṁ vyomajanakaṁ
śivaṁ seve devīm api śiva-samāna-vyavasitām/

1. The sixty-four Mānasa-mayūkhas are : (1) Para, (2) Parā, (3) Bhara, (4) Bharā, (5) Cit, (6) Cit-parā, (7) Mahā-māyā, (8) Mahā-māyā-parā, (9) Sṛṣṭi, (10) Sṛṣṭi-parā, (11) Icchā, (12) Icchā-parā, (13) Sthiti, (14) Sthiti-parā, (15) Nirodha, (16) Nirodha-parā, (17) Mukti, (18) Mukti-parā, (19) Jñāna, (20) Jñāna-parā (21) Sat, (22) Satī-parā, (23) Asat, (24) Asati-parā, (25) Sad-asat, (26) Sadasati-parā, (27) Kriyā, (28) Kriyā-parā, (29) Ātman, (30) Ātma-parā, (31) Indriyāśraya, (32) Indriyāśraya-parā, (33) Go-cara, (34) Gocara-parā, (35) Loka-mukhya, (36) Loka-mukhyā-parā, (37) Vedavat (38) Vedavat-parā, (39) Saṁvid, (40) Saṁvit-parā, (41) Kuṇḍalinī, (42) Kuṇḍalinī-parā, (43) Sauṣumṇī, (44) Sauṣumṇī-parā, (45) Prāṇa-sūtra, (46) Prāṇa-sutra-parā, (47) Syanda, (48) Syanda-parā, (49) Mātṛkā, (50) Mātṛkā-parā, (51) Svarodbhava, (52) Svarodbhavā-parā, (53) Varṇa-ja, (54) Varṇa-ja-parā, (55) Śabda-ja, (56) Śabdajā-parā, (57) Varṇa-jñāta, (58) Varṇa-jñātā-parā, (59) Varga-ja, (60) Varga-jā-parā, (61) Saṁyoga-ja, (62) Saṁyoga-jā-parā, (63) Mantra-vigraha, and (64) Mantra-vigrahā-parā.
2. व्योमसदृशं।
3. शिव समानव्यसनिनीम् ; गिरिशसायुज्यपदवीम्।
4. यान्त्याः।
5. शशिकिरणसारूप्यसरणेः ; सरणिः ; सरणी।
6. विधूतान्तध्वान्ता।

Yayoḥ kāntyā yāntyā śaśi-kiraṇa-sārūpya-saraṇiṁ
vidhūtāntar-dhvāntā vilasati cakorīva jagatī//

Translation : I worship, in Thy *Viśuddhi cakra,* Śiva, clear as pure crystal and generating Vyoman, as also the Goddess, whose functions are the same as Śiva's; in virtue of the lustre of them both assuming equality of status with the moon-beams, the Universe, rid of its internal darkness, delights like a she-partridge, *i.e., Cakorī.*

विशुद्धौ विशुद्धिचक्रे **ते** भवत्या: **शुद्धस्फटिकविशदं** [1]त्रासरहितस्फटिकोपल-सदृशं अतिनिर्मलं **व्योमजनकं** व्योम्न: आकाशतत्त्वस्य जनकम् उत्पादकम्, '**तस्माद्वा एतस्मादात्मन आकाशस्संभूत:**'[2] इत्यादिश्रुते:। आज्ञाचक्रे आत्मतत्त्वात् उत्पन्नम् आकाशतत्त्वमित्यर्थ:। अत्र आत्मशब्दो मन:पर्यायवचन:। **शिवं** शिवतत्त्वं, **सेवे** उपासे। **देवीं** भगवतीम्, **अपिशब्द:** समुच्चये। **शिवसमानव्यवसितां** शिवेन समानं व्यवसितं व्यवसाय: प्रयत्न यस्या: तां, स्वयमपि शिव[3]शब्दवाच्येत्यर्थ:। **ययो:** शिवयो:, **कान्त्या:** प्रभाया:, **यान्त्या:** सरन्त्या:, **शशिकिरणसारूप्यसरणे:** चन्द्रकिरणसादृश्यमार्गात्, **विधूतान्तर्ध्वान्ता** विधूतं अन्तर्ध्वान्तं अज्ञानं यस्यास्सा, **विलसति** प्रकाशते। **चकोरीव** चकोरविहगीव, **जगती** त्रिलोकी।

अत्रेत्थं पदयोजना–हे भगवति! ते विशुद्धौ शुद्धस्फटिकविशदं व्योमजनकं शिवं। शिवसमानव्यवसितां देवीमपि सेवे; ययो: यान्त्या: शशिकिरणसारूप्यसरणे: कान्त्यास्सकाशात् जगती विधूतान्तर्ध्वान्ता चकोरीव विलसति।।

अयमर्थ:–यथा ज्योत्स्नापानेन चकोरी सन्तुष्टान्तरङ्गा, एवं शिवयो: ज्योत्स्नासदृश-प्रभाया: विधूतान्तर्ध्वान्त: सन्तुष्टान्तरङ्ग: साधकलोक: इति।।

अत्रेदमनुसन्धेयम्–विशुद्धिचक्रपूजायां सूर्यचन्द्रनिरोधात् षोडशारगतानां श्रीत्रिपुर-सुन्दरीप्रभृतीनां षोडशकलानां ज्योत्स्नाशोषणात् तच्चक्रस्थितयो: शिवयोरेव प्रभया ज्योत्स्नाकार्यमिति।। ३७।।

Notes : It may be observed here that, as in the worship of the *Viśuddhi-cakra* of the throat, there is obstruction caused by the practitioner in the functioning of the Sun and the Moon coursing through the Iḍā and Piṅgalā-nāḍīs and, as the sixteen Kalās,

1. त्रास: मण्यादिनिष्ठो दोष: इति मेदिनी।
2. तै० उ० २-१।
3. शिवतत्त्वं; शिवत्त्व।

represented by Tripurasundarī and other Nityās having their seats on the sixteen-petalled lotus of the *Viśuddhi-cakra,* lose their influence in consequence, it is the lustre of Śiva and the Śakti alone that serves the purpose of moonbeams in lighting up this region. The deities referred to in the stanza are given the names of Vyomeśvara and Vyomeśvarī and are to be meditated upon by the practitioner, as in the middle, surrounded by the seventy-two Nābhasa (Ethereal) Mayūkhas.[1] *Generating Vyoman*—being the prime cause of Ether, as borne out by the Śruti, 'From the Ātman is generated Ether'. *She-patridge*—the mystic quality of subsisting on moonbeams is traditionally ascribed to the *Cakora* bird. Some commentators take the Śiva indicated in this stanza as Ardhanārīśvara.

समुन्मीलत्संवित्कमलमकरन्दैकरसिकं
भजे हंसद्वन्द्वं किमपि महतां मानसचरम्।
यदालापादष्टादशगुणितविद्यापरिणति[2]
[3]र्यदादत्ते दोषाद् गुणमखिलमद्भ्यः[4] पय इव।। ३८ ।।

Samunmīlat-saṁvit-kamala-makarandaika-rasikaṁ
bhaje haṁsa-dvandvaṁ kim api mahatāṁ mānasa-caram/
Yad-ālāpād aṣṭā-daśa-guṇita-vidyā-pariṇatir
yad ādatte doṣād guṇam akhilam adbhyaḥ paya iva//

---

1. The seventy-two Nābhasa-mayūkhas are : (1) Hṛdaya, (2) Kaulikī, (3) Dhara, (4) Kāntā, (5) Bhoga, (6) Viśvā, (7) Bhava, (8) Yoginī, (9) Maha, (10) Brahma-sārā, (11) Śava, (12) Śabarī, (13) Drava, (14) Kālikā, (15) Rasa, (16) Juṣṭa-caṇḍāli, (17) Moha, (18) A-ghoreśi, (19) Mano-bhava, (20) Helā, (21) Keka, (22) Mahā-raktā, (23) Jñāna-guḥya, (24) Kubjikā, (25) Khara, (26) Ḍākinī, (27) Jvalana, (28) Śākinī, (29) Mahā-kula, (30) Lākinī, (31) Bhiyojjvala, (32) Kākinī, (33) Tejas, (34) Sākinī, (35) Mūrdhan, (36) Hākinī, (37) Vāmu, (38) Ṇapaghnī (?), (39) Kula, (40) Siṁhī (41) Saṁhāra, (42) Kulāmbikā, (43) Viśvaṁ-bhara, (44) Kāmā, (45) Kautila, (46) Kūna-mātā, (47) Gālava, (48) Kaṅkāti, (49) Vyoma, (50) Vyomā, (51) Śvasana, (52) Nādā, (53) Khe-cara, (54) Mahā-devī, (55) Bāhula, (56) Mahat-tarī, (57) Tāta, (58) Kuṇḍalinī, (59) Kulātīta, (60) Kuleśi, (61) Aja, (62) Īdhika, (63) An-anta, (64) Dipīkā, (65) Eṣa, (66) Recikā, (67) Śikhā, (68) Mocikā, (69) Parama, (70) Parā, (71) Para and (72) Cit.
2. परिणतिं।
3. समाधत्ते ; सदादत्ते ; सदाऽऽदत्ते।
4. गुणममलमद्भ्यः।

Translation : I worship that unique pair of swans (Śiva-Śakti), subsisting entirely on the honey of the blooming lotus of wisdom (the *Anāhata-cakra*) and gliding over the Mānasa of great minds; from whose mutual cackle, there results the exposition of the eighteen Vidyās, and which extracts all the good from the bad, even as it would, milk from the water (which dilutes it).

समुन्मीलत्संवित्कमलमकरन्दैकरसिकं समुन्मीलित् विकसत् संवित् ज्ञानं, तदेव कमलं, तत्र मकरन्दः, पुष्परसः, स चासौ एकश्च, न च एकशब्दस्य पूर्वनिपातः, 'विशेषणं विशेष्येण बहुलम्' इति परनिपातात्, यद्वा एकश्चासौ रसिकश्चेति एकरसिकः, मकरन्देन एकरसिकः इति पश्चात् समासः, तं तथोक्तम्। परमहंसस्वरूपयोः शिवयोः हंसत्वारोपणं संविदः कमलत्वारोपणे निमित्तम्। अतः संविदः कमलत्वे सिद्धे एकदेशरूपेण मकरन्देन चर्व्यमाणतैकप्रमाणो रस आरोप्यते। अत एव मकरन्दैकशब्दस्य तृतीयासमासः। **भजे** सेवे। **हंसद्वन्द्वं किमपि** अनिर्वाच्यम् इदन्तया निर्देष्टुं अशक्यं षड्विंश तत्त्वं शिवशक्तिसंपुटितं, **महतां** योगीश्वराणां, **मानसचरम्।** अत्र मानसशब्देन मनसि मानससरस्त्वं आरोप्यते, मानससरसि हंसानां नित्यवासात्। **यदालापात्** यस्य हंसद्वन्द्वस्य आलापात्, **अष्टादशगुणितविद्यापरिणतिः** अष्टादशविद्याः आलापरूपेण परिणता इत्यर्थः। **यत्** हंसद्वन्द्वं, **आदत्ते** गृह्णाति। **दोषात्**–ल्यब्लोपे पञ्चमी, दोषं अवयुत्य **गुणं** गुणशब्दो दोषाभावस्याप्युपलक्षकः, गुणवत् दोषभावस्यापि ग्राह्यत्वात्। **अखिलं**–समस्तं, **अद्भ्यः** उदकेभ्यः, **पय इव** दुग्धमिव।।

अत्रेत्थं पदयोजना–हे भगवति! [1]समुन्मीलत्संवित्कमलमकरन्दैकरसिकं महतां मानसचरं किमपि हंसद्वन्द्वं भजे; यदालापात् अष्टादशगुणितविद्यापरिणतिः, यत् दोषात् अखिलं गुणम् अद्भ्यः पय इव आदत्ते।।

अत्रेदमनुसन्धेयम्–संवित्कमलं अनाहतचक्रनामकमिति पूर्वमेवोक्तम्। उपासकाः [2]परमहंसमिथुनं संवित्कमले उपासते इति समयैकदेशिमतम्। अत एव महतां मानसचरमित्युक्तम्। भगवत्पादमतं तु–शिखिज्वालारूपः परमेश्वरः शिखिन्या स्वशक्त्या संवलितः अनाहतचक्रे दीपाङ्कुरवत् प्रतिभातीति। यथोक्तं भगवत्पादैः सुभगोदयव्याख्याने–

> शिखिज्वालारूपः समय इह सैवात्र समया।
> तयोस्सम्भेदो मे दिशतु हृदयाब्जैकनिलयः।।

इति। एतदेव अस्माकमपि अभिमतम्।। ३८।।

---

1. तवेत्यधिकः।
2. परमहंसाः हंसमिथुनम्।

Notes : *Pair of swans*—the *'Haṁ'* in *'Haṁsaḥ'* indicates the male-Śiva, and the *'Saḥ'* indicates the female-Śakti. Hence, the pair of syllables that make up the word, indicating Śiva and the Śakti combined, in compared to a *Haṁsa*-pair swimming in the minds of the great. Further, tradition ascribes to this bird the mystic property of separating the pure milk from the water with which it is adulterated. Hence, it is that the *Haṁsa*-pair is said to extract the good from the bad. The names of the couple of deities referred to are given as *Haṁśeśvara* and *Haṁseśvarī*. *Mānasa*—there is a pun on this word, implying Mānasa, the mind and also the lake of that name, far-famed for its swans. *Great minds*—some high-souled Samayins, who are adepts in the several stages of Yoga, are meant by this. *Mutual cackle*—when the two deities are in the waking state and when Rhythm predominates, their conversation assumes the form of the exposition of the Vedas and the Śāstras, through the Yogins in whose hearts they dwell; when Mobility predominates, it results in the appeasement of hunger, thirst, *etc.*, of the Yogins; similarly, with the preponderance of Inertia, anger, fear, *etc.*, are generated in the Yogins. The eighteen Vidyās are : (1) Śikṣā, (2) Kalpa, (3) Vyākaraṇa, (4) Nirukta, (5) Jyotiṣa, (6) Chandas, (7) Ṛk, (8) Yajus (9) Sāman, (10) Atharvan, (11) Pūrva-and Uttara-mīmāṁsā, (12) Nyāya, (13) Purāṇa, (14) Dharma-śāstra, (15) Āyur-veda, (16) Dhanur-veda, (17) Gāṁdharva and (18) Nīti-śāstra. There is also the reading *'Pariṇatiṁ samādhatte'*, when the meaning would be, "by constantly conversing about which (pair of swans) (the Sādhaka, practitioner) attains ripe mastery over the eighteen Vidyās and discriminates between good and bad, even as (the *Haṁsa*) would, between milk and water."

The worship indicated in this stanza, of the pair of swans in the heart-lotus, is followed by some Samayins. But Śaṅkarabhagavatpāda, as explained by him in his commentary on the Subhagodaya, is of the opinion that Śiva in the form of a flame, known as Śikhin, shines like a spout of light in the *Anāhatacakra*, in conjunction with the Devī of the name of Śikhinī. The deities Haṁseśvara and Haṁseśvarī should be meditated upon as in the middle of the Cakra surrounded by the fifty-four Vāyavya (Aerials) Mayūkhas.[1]

1. The fifty-four Vāyavya-mayūkhas are : (1) Khageśvara, (2) Bhadrā, (3) Kūrma, (4) Ādhārā, (5) Meṣa, (6) Kośā, (7) Mīna, (8) Mallikā,

तव स्वाधिष्ठाने हुतवहमधिष्ठाय निरतं[1]
तमीडे संवर्तं जननि[2] महतीं तां च समयाम्।
यदालोके लोकान्दहति महति क्रोधकलिते[3]
[4]दयार्द्रा यद्दृष्टिः शिशिरमुपचारं रचयति[5]।। ३९।।

Tava svādhiṣṭhāne huta-vaham adhiṣṭhāyaniratam
tam īḍe saṁvartaṁ janani mahatīṁ tāṁ ca samayām/
Yad-āloke lokān dahati mahati krodha-kalite
dayārdrā yad-dṛṣṭiḥ śiśiram upacāraṁ racayati//

Translation : O Mother! I glorify that Saṁvarta, who abides in Thy *Svādhiṣṭhāna-cakra,* presiding over Agni-*tattva,* and also that great Samayā, whose glance, glistening with pity, applies the chilling (soothing) process, when His mighty stare, pregnant with rage, consumes the worlds.

तव भवत्याः, **स्वाधिष्ठाने** स्वाधिष्ठानचक्रे, **हुतवहम्** अग्नितत्त्वं, **अधिष्ठाय,** आश्रित्य **निरतं,** अनवरतं **तं** प्रसिद्धं, **ईडे** स्तुवे, **संवर्तं** संवर्तनामकम् अग्निं, **जननि!** हे मातः! **महतीं** महच्छब्दवाच्यां, **तां** संवर्ताग्निरूपामित्यर्थः, **समयाम्। यदालोके** दर्शने, **लोकान्,** भूरादीन् **दहति** सति, **महति क्रोधकलिते, दयार्द्रा** कृपाविष्टा, **या दृष्टिः** आलोकः, **शिशिरं** शीतलं, **उपचारं रचयति।**

अत्रेत्थं पदयोजना–हे जननि! तव स्वाधिष्ठाने हुतवहं संवर्तमधिष्ठाय निरतं तं ईडे, समयां तां महतीं च ईडे। महति, क्रोधकलिते यदालोके लोकान् दहति सति या दयार्द्रा दृष्टिः शिशिरमुपचारं रचयति सा त्वदीया दृष्टिरिति शेषः।

अत्रेदमनुसन्धेयम्–स्वाधिष्ठानम् अग्नितत्त्वोत्पत्तिस्थितम्। तत्र उत्पन्नम् अग्निं

---

(9) Jñāna, (10) Vimalā, (11) Mahānanda, (12) Śarvarī, (13) Tivra, (14) Līlā, (15) Priya, (16) Kumudā, (17) Kālika, (18) Menakā, (19) Ḍāmara, (20) Ḍākinī, (321) Rāmara, (22) Rākinī, (23) Lāmara. (24) Lākinī, (25) Kāmara, (26) Kākini, (27) Sāmara, (28) Sākinī, (29) Hāmara, (30) Hākinī, (31) Ādhāreśa, (32) Rākā, (33) Cakriśa, (34) Bindu, (35) Kukura, (36) Kulā, (37) Mayaśriśa, (38) Kubjikā (39) Hṛdiśa, (40) Kāma-kalā, (41) Śirasa, (342) Kula-dipikā, (43) Śikheśa, (44) Sarveśā, (45) Varman, (46) Bahu-rūpā, (47) Aśaleśa, (48) Maha-tarī, (49) Para-guru, (50) Maṅgalā (51) Parādhi-guru, (52) Kośaṭā, (53) Pūjya-guru and (54) Rāmā.

1. नियतम्। 2. जननीं।
3. क्रोधकलिले। 4. दयार्द्रा या दृष्टिः ; दयार्द्राभिर्दृग्भिः ; दयार्द्रा दृष्टिस्ते।
5. रचयसि।

संवर्ताग्नितया आरोप्य तत्रैव महासंवर्ताग्निज्वालाकारशक्तिरूपतया अवस्थिता शक्तिः संभाव्या। ततः तयोः आलोकेन जगन्ति दग्धानि। तानि जगन्ति पुनः प्रसन्नायाः भगवत्या एव कृपारसपूरिता दृष्टिः मणिपूरप्रतिपादिता शिशिरोपचारं रचयतीति स्तुतिमात्रं, न वस्तुत इति।। ३९।।

Notes : The deities referred to are given the names of Saṁvarteśvara Samayāmbā and should be meditated upon by the practitioner, as in the middle, surrounded by sixty-two Taijasa (fiery) Mayūkhas.[1] Some commentators, by adopting the reading *'Yā dṛṣṭiḥ'*, and understanding *'Sā'*, make the glance as of the Devī in the *Maṇi-pūra* and thus make Samayā also participate in the burning of the world, when *'Yadāloke'* will have to be repeated twice, to comprehend the eye-glances of Samayā and Saṁvarta. The same is achieved by another reading, which is far better suited for the purpose, *viz.,* 'Dayārdrābhir' *dṛgbhiḥ śiśram upacāraṁ racayasi'*. In the regular order of the *Cakras,* from the *Ājñā* downwards, we should expect the *Maṇi-pūra* here. The author apparently follows the order of the Tattvas represented by the *Cakras,* in adopting the order of the stanzas.

तडित्वन्तं[1] शक्त्या तिमिरपरिपन्थिस्फुरणया
स्फुरन्नानारत्नाभरणपरिणद्धेन्द्रधनुषम् ।
[2]तव श्यामं मेघं कमपि[3] मणिपूरैकशरणं
निषेवे वर्षन्तं [4]हरमिहिरतप्तं त्रिभुवनम्।। ४०।।

---

1. The sixty-two Taijasa-mayūkhas are : (1) Parāpara, (2) Caṇḍeśvarā, (3) Parama, (4) Catuṣmatī, (5) Tat-para, (6) Guhya-kālī, (7) Apara, (8) Saṁvartā, (9) Cid-ānanda, (10) Nīla-kubjā, (11) A-ghora, (12) Gandhā, (13) Sama-rasa (14) Rasā, (15) Lalita, (16) Smarā, (17) Svaccha, (18) Sparśa, (19) Bhūteśvara, (20) Śabda, (21) Ānanda, (22) Ḍākinī, (23) Ālasya, (24) Ratnaḍākinī, (25) Prabhānanda, (26) Cakra-ḍākinī, (27) Yogānanda, (28) Padmā-ḍākini, (29) Atīta, (30) Kubja-ḍākinī, (31) Svāda, (32) Pracaṇḍa-ḍākinī, (33) Yogeśvara, (34) Caṇḍā, (35) Pīṭheśvara, (36) Kośalā, (37) Kula-koleśvara, (38) Pāvanī, (39) Kukṣeśvara, (40) Samayā, (41) Śrī-kaṇṭha, (42) Kāmā, (43) Ananta, (44) Revatī, (45) Saṁkara, (46) Jvālā, (47) Piṅgala, (48) Karāla, (49) Madākhya, (50) Kubjikā, (51) Karāla-rātri-guru, (52) Parā, (53) Siddha-guru, (54) Śānty-atitā, (55) Ratna-guru, (55) Śāntā, (57) Śiva-guru, (58) Vidyā, (59) Mela-guru, (60) pratiṣṭhā, (61) Samaya-guru and (62) Nivṛtti.
2. तडित्त्वन्तं; तटित्वन्तं
3. तमःश्यामं।
4. जननि।
5. स्मरमिहिरतप्तं।

Taḍitvantaṁ śaktyā timira-paripanthi-sphuraṇayā
sphuran-nānā-ratnābharaṇa-pariṇaddhendra-dhanuṣam/
Tava Śyāmaṁ meghaṁ kam api maṇi-pūraika-śaraṇaṁ
niṣeve varṣantaṁ hara-mihira-taptaṁ tri-bhuvanam//

Translation : I worship that redoubtable dark-blue cloud, abiding for ever in Thy *Maṇi-pūra,* endowed with brilliant lightning in the form of the Śakti, whose lustre controverts darkness, with a rainbow caused by the sparkling of variegated gems set in the jewels (of the Kuṇḍalinī), and showering rain over the worlds scroched by Hara (Fire) and Mihira (the Sun).

तटित्त्वन्तं तटित् सौदामिनी सा अस्यास्तीति तटित्वान् तं, **शक्त्या** तटिद्रूपया, **तिमिरपरिपन्थिस्फुरणया** तिमिरस्य मणिपूरगतस्य–मणिपूरचक्रं तामिस्रलोक इति प्रागुक्तः–तस्य परिपन्थि विरोधि स्फुरणं यस्यास्सा। अनेन स्थिरसौदामिनीत्वं भगवत्याः सूचितम्। इदमपि मेघस्य प्रावृषेण्यत्वसूचकं विशेषणम्। **स्फुरन्नानारत्नाभरण-परिणद्धेन्द्रधनुषं** स्फुरन्ति च तानि रत्नानि नानाविधानि तैः निर्मितानि आभरणानि भूषणानि तैः परिणद्धं निर्मितं इन्द्रधनुः यस्य तम्। 'वा संज्ञायाम्' इति नानङ्। नानाविधरत्नकान्तिसंवलिता स्थिरसौदामिनी इन्द्रचापभ्रान्तिं जनयतीति प्रावृषेण्यत्वे हेत्वन्तरम्। यथोक्तं सिद्धघुटिकायाम्–

मणिपूरैकवसतिः प्रावृषेण्यः सदाशिवः।
अम्बुदात्मतया भाति स्थिरसौदामिनी शिवा।। इति।।

तव भवत्याः, **श्यामं** श्यामवर्णं, **मेघं** मेघात्मना अवस्थितं पशुपतिं, **कमपि** इयत्तया निर्देष्टुमशक्यं, **मणिपूरैकशरणं** मणिपूरमेव एकं शरणं गृहं यस्य तम्। मणिशब्देन मणिधनुरुच्यते, मणिधनुस्स्वरूपत्वात् भगवत्याः, तया पूर्यते शरणं मणिपूरमिति रहस्यम्। **निषेवे** नितरां सेवे। **वर्षन्तं** वृष्टिं कुर्वन्तं **हरमिहिरतप्तं** हर एव मिहिरः सूर्यः महासंवर्ताग्निरिति यावत्, तेन तप्तं दग्धं **त्रिभुवनम्।।**

अत्रेत्थं पदयोजना–हे भगवति! तव मणिपूरैकशरणम् तिमिरपरिपन्थिस्फुरणया शक्त्या तटित्त्वन्तं स्फुरन्नानारत्नाभरणपरिणद्धेन्द्रधनुषं श्यामं हरमिहिरतप्तं त्रिभुवनं वर्षन्तं कमपि मेघं निषेवे।।

अत्रेदमनुसन्धेयम्–मणिपूरस्थाने जलतत्त्वं[1] उत्पन्नमिति प्राक् प्रतिपादितम्। तत्प्रकारः–सूर्यकिरणा एव अग्निसम्भिन्नाः मेघत्वमापन्नाः जलरूपेणेति मणिपूरस्य

1. मुख्यमुपत्नमिति।

आधारस्वाधिष्ठानयोर्मध्ये निवेशः। अनाहतोपरिस्थितसूर्यकिरणाः स्वाधिष्ठानाग्निना संवलिताः सन्तः मणिपूरं प्रविश्य जलत्वमापन्नाः तेन जलेन स्वाधिष्ठानाग्निना दग्धं जगत् आप्लावयन्तीति आगमरहस्यम्। अत्र 'स्फुरन्नानारत्नाभरणपरिणद्धेन्द्रधनुषम्' इत्यनेन मौर्वीरहितं धनुरित्याहुः आगमविदः। तच्च श्रूयते अरुणोपनिषदि—

तदिन्द्रधनुरित्यज्यम्। अभ्रवर्णेषु चक्षते।
एतदेव शंयोर्बार्हस्पत्यस्य। एतद्रुद्रस्य धनुः।[1]

इति। अस्यार्थः—रुद्रस्य मेघात्मकस्य धनुः अज्यं ज्यया मौर्व्या रहितमिति। अवशिष्टानि श्रुतिस्थपदानि सुभगोदयव्याख्याने व्याख्यातानि। एतत्सर्वं अरुणोपनिषदि **'योऽपां पुष्पम्'**[2] इत्यनुवाके 'योऽपाम्' इत्यारभ्य 'इमे वै लोका अप्सु प्रतिष्ठिताः' इत्यन्तेन प्रतिपादितम्। उदकात् चन्द्रोत्पत्तिः सूर्योत्पत्तिः अग्न्युत्पत्तिश्च दिवसानां चन्द्रकलात्मकानां तदंशानां नक्षत्राणां च उत्पत्तिः प्रतिपादिता। तदनन्तरं सम्मतित्वेन ऋगप्युक्ता—

तदेषाऽभ्युक्ता। अपाꣳ रसमुदयꣳ सन्।
सूर्ये शुक्रꣳसमाभृतम्। अपाꣳ रसस्य यो
रसः। तं वो गृह्णाम्युत्तमम्[3]**। इति।**

ऋचोऽयमर्थः—अपां रसम् उदयंसन्, योगीश्वराः प्राप्नुवन्नित्यर्थः। सूर्ये सूर्यमण्डले शुक्रम् अमृतं, समाभृतं सम्यक् आसमन्तात्पूरितम्। चन्द्रमण्डलगलत्पीयूषधाराभिरेव सूर्यस्य निर्वाह इत्यर्थः। अपां रसस्य पुष्परूपस्य चन्द्रमसः, यो रसः बैन्दवस्थानस्थितः[4] नित्यकलात्मकः, तं नित्यकलात्मकं रसं वः युष्मत्सकाशात्। उदकानां प्रस्तुतत्वात् वः इति उदकानामाभिमुख्यं मणिपूरे उदकमुत्पन्नमिति। ता आपः स्वाधिष्ठानाग्नेः उत्पादिकाः, आज्ञाचक्रस्थितस्य चन्द्रस्य उत्पादिकाः, अनाहतचक्रोपरिस्थितसूर्यस्यापि उत्पादिकाः, आज्ञाचक्रस्थितस्य चन्द्रस्य उत्पादिकाः, अनाहतचक्रोपरिस्थितसूर्यस्यापि उत्पादिकाः। अत उक्तं 'तं वो गृह्णाम्युत्तमम्' इति। तम् उत्तमं चन्द्रं सहस्रकमलस्थितं वः सकाशात् जानामीत्यर्थः।।

अस्मिन्नेव अनुवाके—

योऽप्सु नावं प्रतिष्ठितां वेद। प्रत्येव तिष्ठति।[5]

---

1. तै०आ० १-५।
2. तै०आ० १-२२।
3. तै० सं० १-५-११।
4. इत्युक्तकलात्मतया तं वो गृह्णाम्युत्तममित्यधिकम्।
5. तै० आ० १-२२।

इति श्रुतम्। अप्सु उदकतत्त्वात्मके मणिपूरे प्रतिष्ठितां नावं श्रीचक्रात्मिकाम्[1]।।

तथा च श्रुत्यन्तरम्–

सुत्रामाणं पृथिवीं द्यामनेहसं सुशर्माणमदितिं सुप्रणीतिम्। दैवीं नावं स्वरित्रामनागसमस्रवन्तीमारुहेमा स्वस्तये[2]।।

अस्या ऋचोऽयमर्थः–षुञ् अभिषवे। सुनोतीति सुत्रामा अग्निः अग्नितत्त्वं स्वाधिष्ठानगतमित्यर्थः, पृथिवीं मूलाधारस्थितां, द्यां गगनं विशुद्धिस्थितां, अनेहसं कालं मनस्तत्त्वं आज्ञाचक्रस्थितं, सुशर्माणं वायुतत्त्वं, अदितिम् अदित्यात्मकं जलतत्त्वं, सुप्रणीतिं सुमार्गे मोक्षे प्रणीतिं प्रकर्षेण नयन्तीम्। दैवीं देव्या इमां चक्रविद्यामित्यर्थः, नावं नौकां संसारसागरतरणोपायभूतां, स्वरित्रां सुदृढानि अरित्राणि लाङ्गलानि यस्याः सा तां, दुष्कर्मझञ्झापवनैः अचलमिति यावत्। अनागसं अस्रवन्तीं[4] स्वयं दृढां आरुहेम तत्प्रवणा भवेम तदेकनिरताः तदुपासनपदाः स्यामेत्यर्थः। स्वस्तये मोक्षाय, निरतिशयसुखावाप्त्य इति। अवशिष्टं श्रुतिजातं सुभगोदयव्याख्यानावसरे सम्यक् निरूपितमस्माभिः।। ४०।।

Notes : The names of the deities to be meditated upon in the *Maṇi-pūra-cakra* are said to be *Megheśvara* and *Saudāmanī.* They are also known as Amṛteśvara and Amṛteśvarī and are to be meditated upon by the practitioner as in the middle and surrounded by fifty-two Āpya (watery) Mayūkhas.[5] *Dark-blue-cloud*—the form assumed

---

1. वेद।
2. तै० सं० १-५-११।
3. स्थानस्थिताम्।
4. अस्रवन्तीं अरन्ध्राम्।
5. The fifty-two Āpya-mayūkhas are : (1) Sadyo-jāta, (2) Māyā, (3) Vāma-deva, (4) Śrī, (5) A-ghora, (6) Padmā, (7) Tat-puruṣa, (8) Ambikā, (9) An-anta, (10) Nivṛtti, (11) A-nātha, (12) Pratiṣṭhā, (13) Janāśrita, (14) Vidyā, (15) A-cintya, (16) Śāntā, (17) Śaśi-śekhara, (18) Umā, (19) Tīvra, (20) Gaṅgā, (21) Maṇi-vāha, (22) Sarasvatī, (23) Ambu-vāha, (24) Kamalā, (25) Tejo-dhiśa, (26) Pārvatī, (27) Vidyā-vāgīśvara, (28) Citrā, (29) Catur-vidheśvara, (30) Sukamalā, (31) Umā-gaṅgeśvara, (32) Mānmathā, (33) Kṛṣṇeśvara, (34) Śrīyā, (35) Śrī-kaṇṭha, (36) Layā, (37) An-anta, (38) Sati, (39) Śaṅkara, (40) Ratna-mekhalā, (41) Piṅgala, (42) Yaśovatī, (43) Sādhyākhya, (44) Haṁsānandā, (45) Para-divyaugha, (46) Vāmā, (47) Māra-divyaugha, (48) Jyeṣṭhā, (49) Piṭhaugha, (50) Raudrī, (51) Sarveśvara and (52) Sarva-mayī.

by Megheśvara. *Śakti*—known as Saudāmani. *Darkness*—of the *Maṇi-pūra* which is rendered into a region of light mixed with darkness, *i.e.*, Miśra-loka, by the light effulging from the Kuṇḍalinī-śakti. There is the traditional view held that the rays of the Sun from the *An-āhata*, conjointly with the heat-rays of the Fire of *Svādhiṣṭhāna*, convert the water of the *Maṇi-pūra* into clouds, which drench with their showers the world-conflagration caused by the *Svādhiṣṭāna*-Fire at the time of the Deluge. There is also the reading, *'Smara-mihira-taptam,'* which means, "consumed by the Sun of Desire". *'Hara-mihira'* is taken by some to indicate the twelve Ādityas, of the form of Hara, appearing at the Deluge to consume all the three worlds.

The following points called from Lakṣmīdhara's elaborate commentary on this stanza are noteworthy ; The Siddha ghuṭikā, a treatise on occultism, not known now to be extent, speaks of Sadā-śiva, manifesting himself in the *Maṇi-pūra* as a winter-cloud and shining there with his spouse of the form of resplendent lightning. A chapter in the Taittirīyāraṇyaka, wherein is given a detailed description of the origin of the Sun, Moon and Fire and also of the stars and other luminaries making days the nights, all from water, is quoted from. Therein the essence of water—nectar, is referred to as pervading the disc of the Sun, and the Yogin is represented as apostrophizing to the water of the *Maṇi-pūra*, asking for "the essence of that essence, which is of the highest order". The esssence of water is explained to be the Moon. From the Ap-tattva of the *Maṇi-pūra*, the Yogin desires to get at the Moon, the fountain source of all nectar, which, flowing from the lunar disc, passes on to the disc of the Sun, which is nourishes, as long as it flows. As the place of the Moon, the *Baindavasthāna*, is in the *Sahasrāra*, the esssence of the highest order is the nectar oozing out of the *Sahasrāra* and filling up all the Nāḍīs. A quotation from the Yajurveda (I, v, 11) deals with the crossing of the ocean of Saṁsāra in strongly built, well-designed and equipped boats, which could withstand the severest hurricanes and storms, wherewith the Yogin could attain Salvation. These boats are said to be comprised, in the *Śrī-vidyā*, one of the Fire in the *Svādhiṣṭhāna*, another of Earth in the *Mūlādhāra*, another of Ether in the *Viśūddhi*, another of Mind in the *Ājñā*, another of Air in the *An-āhata*, and yet another of Water in the *Maṇipūra*.

तवाधारे मूले सह समयया लास्यपरया
[1]नवात्मानं मन्ये[2] नवरसमहाताण्डवनटम्।
उभाभ्यामेताभ्यामुदयविधिमुद्दिश्य दयया[3]
सनाथाभ्यां जज्ञे जनकजननीमज्जगदिदम्।। ४१ ।।

Tavādhāre mūle saha samayayā lāsya-parayā
navātmānaṁ manye nava-rasa-mahā-tāṇḍava-naṭam/
Ubhābhyām etābhyām udaya-vidhim uddiśya dayayā
sanāthābhyāṁ jajñe janaka-jananī-maj-jagad idam.//

Translation : I conceive, in Thy *Mūlādhāra-cakra,* the Deity dancing the great Tāṇḍava, replete with the nine sentiments, along with Samayā intent upon Lāsya, as Navātman. This world came to own its father and mother in these two, with their manifest grace for the act of Creation.

तव भवत्याः, **आधारे** (आधारचक्रे)मूले मूलाधारचक्रे इत्यर्थः। **सह** साकं, **समयया** समयसंज्ञया, **लास्यपरया** लास्ये नृत्ये परं तात्पर्यं यस्याः तया। स्त्रीकर्तृकं नृत्यं लास्यमित्युच्यते। **नवात्मानं** आनन्दभैरवं, **मन्ये** जानामि। **नवरसमहाताण्डवनटं** नवभिः शृङ्गारादिभिः रसैः महत् अद्भुतं ताण्डवं–पुंकतृकं नृत्यं ताण्डवमित्युच्यते–तत्र नटं अभिनेतारम्। **उभाभ्याम् एताभ्याम्** [4]आनन्दभैरवीमहाभैरवाभ्याम्, **उदयविधिम्** [5]उत्पत्तिम् **उद्दिश्य**। कुत इत्याह–दययेति। दग्धलोकस्य पुनरुत्पादनिमित्तं **दयया सनाथाभ्यां** मिलिताभ्यां, **जज्ञे** उत्पन्नम्। **जनकजननीमत्** मातापितृमत्, **जगत्** प्रपञ्चम् इदं पूर्वोक्तम्। लास्यनाट्यसंविधानप्रतिपादनात् प्रकृतिपुरुषयोः दर्शने जगदुत्पत्तिः, लास्यनृत्तावसानमेव जगत्संहृतिरिति कौलसिद्धान्तः।।

अत्रेत्थं पदयोजना–हे भगवति! तव मूले आधारे लास्यपरया समयया सह नवरसमहाताण्डवनटं नवात्मानं मन्ये। उदयविधिमुद्दिश्य एताभ्याम् उभाभ्याम् दयया सनाथाभ्याम् **इदं** जगत् जनकजननीमत् जज्ञे ।।

अयं भावः–आधारस्वाधिष्ठानयोः तामिस्रलोकत्वात्, तत्र कौलानाम् अधिकारात्

1. शिवात्मानं, नटमभिनायकं ; भवात्मानं।
2. वन्दे।
3. उभयविधिं ; उभयमिदं।
4. आनन्दभैरवमहाभैरवीभ्यां पा०।
5. जगदुत्पत्तिमुद्दिश्य।

समयिनां आराधनाभावेऽपि स्वमतानुसारेण सहस्रकमले निषेव्यैव भगवती आधारस्वाधिष्ठानयोः सेव्येति महाभैरवी समयापदेन[1] उच्यत इति।।

अत्रेदमनुसन्धेयम्–आधारचक्रं त्रिकोणम्, आधारे बिन्दुः तिष्ठतीति च तावत् प्रसिद्धम्। अत्र कौलमते त्रिकोणमेव बिन्दुस्थानम्। स एव बिन्दुः तत्र आराध्यः। अत एव कौलाः त्रिकोणे बिन्दुं नित्यं समर्चयन्ति। तत् त्रिकोणं द्विविधं, श्रीचक्रान्तर्गत-नवयोनिमध्यवर्तिनी योनिः, सुन्दर्याः तरुण्याः प्रत्यक्षयोनिश्च। श्रीचक्रस्थितनवयोनि-मध्यगतयोनिं भूर्जहेमपट्टवस्त्रपीठादौ लिखितां पूर्वकौलाः पूजयन्ति। तरुण्याः प्रत्यक्षयोनिम् उत्तरकौलाः पूजयन्ति। उभयं योनिद्वयं बाह्यमेव न आन्तरम्। अतः तेषां आधारचक्रमेव पूज्यम्। तत्र स्थिता कुण्डलिनी शक्तिः कौलिनी इत्युच्यते। सैव उपास्या त्रिकोणपूजकानां इति रहस्यम्। एषा कुण्डलिनी शक्तिः बिन्दुरूपिणी निद्राणैव संपूज्या, तस्याः सदा निद्राणस्वाभाव्यात्। सा पूजा तामिस्रा। कुण्डलिनीप्रबोधो यदा स्यात्, तत्क्षणमेव मुक्तिः कौलानाम्। **अत एव क्षणमुक्ताः कौला इति व्यवहारः।**[2] तत्र सुरामांसमधुमत्स्यादिद्रव्यैः समाराधनं वामाचारप्रवृत्त्या। प्रत्यक्षत्रिकोणे बिन्दुस्थानं मन्मथच्छत्रं कृत्वा संपूजयन्ति, अधोमुखं त्रिकोणं अधोमुखमेव छत्रं पूजयन्ति। दिगम्बरक्षपणकादयस्तु स्त्रियं उत्तानां कृत्वा ऊर्ध्वं त्रिकोणं पूजयन्तीति रहस्यम्। अत्र बहु वक्तव्यमस्ति; तत्तु अवैदिकमार्गत्वात् स्मरणार्हमपि न भवति। तथापि दिङ्मात्रं निषेध्यत्वेन समयमतमार्गप्रदर्शनोपयोगितया उक्तमिति अलं विस्तरेण।।

अत्र समयिमतं निरूप्यते–त्रिकोणादि[3] षट्चक्रं आधारादिषट्चक्रात्मना परिणतमिति प्रागेव प्रतिपादितम्। तत्र श्रीचक्रे त्रिकोणं बैन्दवस्थानमिति तावत् सुप्रसिद्धम्। तत्र [4]त्रिकोणत्रयेण अष्टकोणनिर्माणे त्रिकोणादेव बिन्दुस्थानं भवति। तच्च चतुष्कोणमेव। तत्तु सहस्रकमलान्तर्गतं चन्द्रमण्डलमिति पूर्वमेव बहुधा प्रपञ्चितम्। एतत् चतुष्कोणमध्यं बैन्दवस्थानं 'सुधासिन्धुः' 'सरघा' इति बहुधा प्रपञ्चितं पूर्वमेव। एतत् चतुष्कोणमध्यं बिन्दुस्थानमिति बाह्यपूजा [5]तरुणीत्रिकोणपूजा च दूरत एव निरस्तेति ध्येयम्। अत एव समयिनां सहस्रकमले समयायाः समयस्य च शम्भोः पूजा। समया नाम–शम्भुना

1. 'पदेशेन' इति च पाठः।
2. "तस्मात् कौलानां त्रिकोणे आनन्दभैरवीमहाभैरवौ संपूज्यौ। साधकानां ताभ्यां तादात्म्येनावस्थानम्। अत एव कौलाः बिन्दुपूजावसरे भैरवाकारं दिगम्बरत्वमाश्रित्य समर्चयन्ति स्त्रीपुरुषाः" इति अधिकः पाठः केषुचित्कोशेषु।
3. चक्रात्मकम्।
4. कोणाष्टकोणनिर्माणे।
5. तरुणीपूजा।

साम्यं पञ्चविधं यातीति समया। [1]समयत्वं शम्भोरपि–पञ्चविधं साम्यं देव्या सह यातीति। अतः उभयोः समप्राधान्येनैव साम्यं विज्ञेयम्। पञ्चविधसाम्यं तु–अधिष्ठानसाम्यं, अवस्थानसाम्यं, अनुष्ठानसाम्यं, रूपसाम्यं, नामसाम्यं, चेति पञ्चविधं सम[2]–प्रधानयोरेव शिवयोः। यथा–'तवाधारे' इति अधिष्ठानसाम्यमुक्तम्, उभयोः आधारचक्रस्य अधिष्ठानरूपत्वात्। अनुष्ठानसाम्यं 'जनकजननीमज्जगदिदम्' इत्यनेन प्रतिपादितम्, उत्पादनक्रियायाम् उभयोः व्याप्रियमाणत्वात्। अवस्थानसाम्यं लास्यताण्डवशब्दाभ्यां प्रतिपादितम्। लास्यताण्डवयोः नृत्यरूपेण एकत्वम् उक्तं प्राक्। रूपसाम्यं तु आरुण्यं उभयोः तन्त्रान्तरसिद्धम्–

जपाकुसुमसङ्काशौ मदघूर्णितलोचनौ।
जगतः पितरौ वन्दे भैरवीभैरवात्मकौ।। इति।।

यद्वा–नवात्मानमिति रूपसाम्यं नामसाम्यं च प्रतिपदितमिति ध्येयम्। एवमेव इतरत्रापि ऊह्यम्। यथा–'तटित्त्वन्तम्' इत्यादौ तटित्त्वान् तटित्त्वती इति नामरूपसाम्ये। यद्यपि स्थिरसौदामिनीरूपायाः तटिद्रूपत्वात् तद्वत्त्वं नास्ति, तथापसौदामिन्याः स्थिरत्वमेव सर्वदा तटिद्युक्तत्वमिति तटित्वतीति उक्तिः युक्ता इति अनुसन्धेयम्। मणिपूरस्थानं अधिष्ठानमिति 'मणिपूरैकशरणं' इत्यनेन अधिष्ठानसाम्यमुक्तम्। 'स्फुरन्नानारत्नाभरणपरिणद्धेन्द्रधनुषम्' इत्यनेन 'वर्षन्तम्' इत्यनेन च प्रावृषेण्यत्वावस्थानसाम्यं प्रतिपादितम्'। 'तव स्वाधिष्ठाने' इत्यादिश्लोके 'स्वाधिष्ठाने' इत्यनेन अधिष्ठानसाम्यम् उक्तम्। 'महतीं' इत्यनेन महासंवर्तात्मकरूपनामसाम्ये प्रतिपादिते। स्वाधिष्ठानगताग्निसंश्रयणं अवस्थानसाम्यम्। लोकान् दहतीति अनुष्ठानसाम्यं प्रतिपादितम्। अनाहतचक्रे अनाहतम् अधिष्ठानमिति अधिष्ठानसाम्यमुक्तम्। हुतभुक्कणिकरूपतया रूपसाम्यं नामसाम्यं च। निवातदीपत्वोक्त्या अवस्थानसाम्यम्। वायुतत्त्वोत्पादकत्वं अनुष्ठानसाम्यमिति रहस्यम्। विशुद्धिचक्रं अधिष्ठानमिति अधिष्ठानसाम्यम् उक्तम्। 'शुद्धस्फटिकविशदम्' इत्यनेन रूपसाम्यं उक्तम्। 'व्योमजनकम् इत्यनेन अनुष्ठानसाम्यम् उक्तम्'। 'शिवं सेवे' इत्यनेन नामसाम्यम् 'शशिकिरणसारूप्यसरणेः' इत्यनेन अवस्थानसाम्यमिति। 'तवाज्ञाचक्रस्थम्' इत्यनेन अधिष्ठानसाम्यमुक्तम्। 'तपनशशिकोटिद्युतिधरं' इत्यनेन रूपसाम्यमुक्तम्। 'परं शम्भुम्' इत्यनेन नामसाम्यमुक्तम्। 'यमाराध्यन् भक्त्या' इत्यनेन अवस्थानसाम्यमुक्तम्। मुक्तिप्रदत्वमनुष्ठानसाम्यमिति साम्यपञ्चकं विज्ञेयम्। एतत् अतिरहस्यं शिष्यानुजिघृक्षया प्रकाशितम्।।

---

1. दूतीसमयस्य।

2. 'समययोः प्रधानयोः' इति च पाठः।

अतः समयपूजकाः समयिनः। तेषां षट्चक्रपूजा न नियता, अपि तु सहस्रकमल एव पूजा। सहस्रकमलपूजा नाम सहस्रकमलस्य बैन्दवस्थानत्वेन तन्मध्यगतचन्द्र-मण्डलस्य चतुरश्रात्मना, तन्मध्यबिन्दोः पञ्चविंशतितत्त्वातीतषड्विंशात्मकशिवशक्ति-मेलनरूपसादाख्यात्मना च अनुसन्धानम्। अत एव समयिमते बाह्याराधनं दूरत एव निरस्तम्। षोडशोपचाररूपपूजाङ्गकलापश्च ततोऽपि दूरत एव।।

तथा हि–आधारादिषट्चक्राणां त्रिकोणादिषट्चक्रत्वेन तादात्म्यम्, बिन्दुस्थानस्य चतुरश्र[1]सहस्रकमलत्वेन तादात्म्यं बिन्दुशिवयोस्तादात्म्यम्, एवं देवी[2]शिवयोस्तादात्म्य-मिति तादात्म्यत्रयम्। चक्रमन्त्रयोः ऐक्यं पूर्वमेवोक्तमिति, तेन सह चतुर्धा ऐक्यं समयिनां समयाराधनमिति महत् रहस्यम्।।

अत्र किंचित् उच्यते–समयिनां चतुर्विधैक्यानुसन्धानमेव भगवत्याः समाराधन-मित्येतत् सर्वसम्मतम्। केचित्तु षोढा ऐक्यमाहुः। यथा–नादबिन्दुकलातीतं भागवतं तत्त्वमिति सर्वागमरहस्यम्। नादः परापश्यन्तीमध्यमावैखरीरूपेण चतुर्विधः इति प्रागेवोक्तम्। परा त्रिकोणात्मिका, पश्यन्ती अष्टकोणचक्ररूपिणी, मध्यमा [3]द्विदशाररूपिणी, वैखरी चतुर्दशाररूपिणी। शिवचक्राणां अत्रैव अन्तर्भावः प्रतिपादित इति चतुश्चक्रात्मकं श्रीचक्रं नादशब्दवाच्यम्। बिन्दुर्नाम–षट्चक्राणि मूलाधारस्वाधिष्ठान-मणिपूरानाहतविशुद्ध्याज्ञात्मकानि बिन्दुशब्दवाच्यानि पूर्वमेव उक्तानि। कलाः पञ्चाशत्, षष्ट्युत्तरत्रिशतसङ्ख्यका वा। एवं नादबिन्दुकलातीता भगवतीति। सहस्रकमलं बिन्द्वतीतं बैन्दवस्थानात्मकं सुधासिन्ध्वपरपर्यायं सरघाशब्दवाच्यम्। नादातीतत्वं तु त्रिपुरसुन्दर्यादिशब्दाभिधेयम् 'दर्शा दृष्टा दर्शता' इत्याद्यपरपर्याय–'क ए ईलह्रीम्' इत्यादिमन्त्रवर्णनामक–पञ्चाशद्वर्णात्मक–षष्ट्युत्तरत्रिशतसङ्ख्यापरिगणितमहाकाला-त्मक–पञ्चदशकलातीता सादाख्या श्रीविद्यापरपर्याया चित्कलाशब्दवाच्या ब्रह्मविद्यापरपर्याया भगवती नादबिन्दुकलातीतं भागवतं तत्त्वमिति तत्त्वविद्रहस्यम्। अत्र नादबिन्दुकलानां परस्परैक्यानुसन्धानं षोढा भवतीति षोढा ऐक्यमाहुः। एवं भगवतीं षड्विधैक्येन सम्भाव्य पूजयित्वा सादाख्यायां विलीनो भवति। तदनन्तरं षड्विधैक्यानुसन्धानमहिम्ना गुरुकटाक्षसञ्जातमहावेधमहिम्ना च भगवती झडिति मूलाधारस्वाधिष्ठानात्मकचक्रद्वयं भित्त्वा मणिपूरे प्रत्यक्षं प्रतिभाति। महावेधप्रकारः–पूर्वं अभ्यासदशायां गुर्वेकपरतन्त्रः[4] महाविद्यां गुरुमुखादेव स्वीकृत्य ऋषिच्छन्दोदेवतापूर्वकं मूलमन्त्रस्य शुष्कजपं गुरूपदिष्टमार्गेण कुर्वन् आश्वयुजशुक्लपक्षे महानवमीशब्दाभिधे-

---

1. चतुरश्रस्य।
2. 'देह' इत्यपि पाठः।
3. मिश्रार इत्यपि पाठः।
4. तन्त्रमहा।

याष्टम्यां निशीथसमये गुरोः पदोपसङ्ग्रहणं कर्तव्यम्। तन्महिम्ना गुरोः तदानीं कर्तव्यहस्तमस्तकसंयोग–पुनर्मन्त्रोपदेश–षट्चक्रपूजाप्रकारोपदेश–षड्विधैक्यानुसन्धानोपदेश–वशात् महावेधः शैवः सादाख्यायाः प्रकाशरूपो जायते इति गुरु रहस्यम्। एवं महावेधे जाते भगवती मणिपूरे प्रत्यक्षा भवति सा समाराध्या। अर्ध्यपाद्यादिभूषणप्रतिपादनपर्यन्तं पूजाकलापं मणिपूरे निर्वर्त्य अनाहतमन्दिरं भगवतीं नीत्वा, धूपादिनैवेद्यहस्तप्रक्षालनान्तं कर्मकलापं तत्रैव समाप्य, विशुद्धौ भगवतीं सिंहासनासीनां सखीभिः सल्लापान् सम्भाषमाणां शुद्धस्फटिकसदृशैः मणिभिः पूजयेत्। शुद्धस्फटिकसदृशमणयो न मौक्तिकादयः, किंतु तदीयषोडशदलगतषोडशचन्द्रकला इति रहस्यम्। एवं संपूज्य आज्ञाचक्रं नीत्वा देवीं कामेश्वरीं नीराजनविधिभिः अनेकैः संप्रीणयेत्। अत एव उक्तं कर्णावतंसस्तुतौ मदीयायाम्–

आज्ञात्मकद्विदळपद्मगते तदानीं
विद्युन्निभे रविशशिप्रयतोत्कटाभे।
गण्डस्थलप्रतिफल[1]त्करदीपजाल–
कर्णावतंसकलिके कमलायताक्षि।। इति।

एवमाज्ञाचक्रे नीराजनविधिं कृत्वा संप्रीणयेत्। तदनन्तरं झडिति विद्युल्लतेव सहस्रकमलं अनुप्रविष्टा सुधालब्धौ पञ्चकल्पतरुच्छायायां मणिद्वीपे सरघामध्ये सदाशिवेन सार्धं विहरमाणा वर्तते। तदा तिरस्करिणीं प्रसार्य समीपे मन्दिरे स्वयं निवसेत्। यावत् भगवती विनिर्गता पुनः मूलाधारकुण्डं प्रविशति तावत्पर्यन्तं स्थातव्यमिति समयमततत्त्वरहस्यम्।।

अत्र शङ्करभगत्पादानां चतुर्विधैक्यानुसन्धानान्तरं मणिपूरे प्रत्यक्षायाः भगवत्याः स्वरूपं '**क्वणत्काञ्चीदामा**' इत्यादिध्यानप्रतिपादितं चतुर्भुजं धनुर्बाणपाशाङ्कुशयुक्त–रहस्यम्। तन्मतानुसारिणामपि तथैव प्रतिभाति भगवती।।

अस्माकं तु षड्विधैक्यानुसन्धानान्तरं मूलाधारद्विकं भित्त्वा मणिपूरे प्रसन्ना भगवती दशभुजा धनुर्बाणपाशाङ्कुशवरदाभयपुस्तकाक्षमालावीणाहस्ता। मन्मतैकदेशिनां पाशाङ्कुशपुण्ड्रेक्षुचापपुष्पबाणजपमालिकाशुकाभयवरदकरा करद्वयवक्षस्स्थलस्थापित–वीणा। उभयमस्माकं सम्मतमेव। कर्णावतंसस्तुतौ मदीयायाम्–

भवानि श्रीहस्तैर्वहसि फणिपाशं सृणिमधो
धनुः पौण्ड्रं पौष्पं शरमथ जपस्रक्शुकवरम्।
अथ द्वाभ्यां मुद्रामभयवरदानैकरसिके
क्वणद्वीणां द्वाभ्यामुरसि च कराभ्यां च बिभृषे।।

1. गण्डस्थलप्रतिगलत्करदीपजाल........।

समयिनां प्रत्यक्षं परिदृश्यमाना आस्ते भगवती। समयिनां सहस्रकमलपर्यन्तम् आन्तरपूजा कर्तव्या। सहस्रकमले तु तिरस्करिणीप्रसारणपर्यन्तं दर्शनमेव समाराधनम्। यदुक्तं सुभगोदये–

> **सूर्यमण्डलमध्यस्थां देवीं त्रिपुरसुन्दरीम्।**
> **पाशाङ्कुशधनुर्बाणहस्तां ध्यायेत्सुसाधकः।।**
> **त्रैलोक्यं मोहयेदाशु [1]वरनारीगणैर्युतम्।। इति।**

चर्चास्तोत्रेऽपि कालिदासकृते–

> **ये चिन्तयन्त्यरुणमण्डलमध्यवर्ति**
> **रूपं तवाम्ब नवयावकपङ्करम्यम्[2]।**
> **तेषां सदैव कुसुमायुधबाणभिन्न-**
> **वक्षस्स्थला मृगदृशो वशगा भवन्ति।। इति।**

अत्र समयिनां बाह्यपूजानिषेधात् सूर्यमण्डलान्तर्गतत्वेन पूजनं निषिद्धमित्याहुः। तत्र, ब्रह्माण्डस्थितपिण्डाण्डस्थितचन्द्रसूर्ययोः ऐक्यात् सूर्यस्य चन्द्रकलामृतनिष्यन्दवशात् उज्जीवनात्। यतः **'अपां रसमुदयंसन्'**[3] इत्यादिश्रुत्या प्रतिपादितमिति प्राक् प्रतिपादितम्, अतः चन्द्रकलाविद्यायाः सूर्यसम्पर्कात् तेजस्तिरोधानं स्यादिति केचन सङ्गिरन्ते ; तदपि अपास्तं वेदितव्यम्। अत एव पिण्डाण्डब्रह्माण्डचन्द्रयोरैक्यात् चन्द्रमण्डलान्तर्गतत्वेन चन्द्रकलाविद्यायाः पूजनं युज्यते। यत्तु पूर्वोक्तं चन्द्रबिम्बगतत्वेन देव्याः पूजननिषेधवचनं, तत्तु आन्तरचन्द्रस्य आज्ञाचक्रोपरिस्थितस्य सहस्र-कमलान्तर्गतचन्द्रकलामृतनिष्यन्दैः उज्जीवनमिति तत्र तस्याः पूजानिर्बन्धो नास्तीति, अत एव पिण्डाण्डब्रह्माण्डचन्द्रयोरैक्यात् ब्रह्माण्डस्थितचन्द्रमण्डलेऽपि पूजानिर्बन्धो नास्तीत्येवंपरम्।।

एवं हृदयकमल एव समाराधिता भगवती ऐहिकानि फलानि सर्वाणि ददाति। यदा वशिन्यादियुक्ता ध्याता सांरस्वतं ददाति। यावकरसाप्लुता ध्याता वशीकरणं ददाति। **'मुखं बिन्दुं कृत्वा'**[4] इत्यादिना ध्याता तादृशं फलं ददाति। हृदयकमले एव होमादिकं तर्पणादिकं च कार्यं ऐहिकफलसाधनमिति **'स्मरं योनिं लक्ष्मीम्'**[5] इत्यादिश्लोक-

---

1. नरनारीगणैः, शतं ; नरनारीमणैः, शतम्।
2. 'शोणम्' इत्यपि पाठः।
3. तै०आ० १-२२।
4. १९ श्लोकः।
5. ३३ श्लोकः।

व्याख्यानावसरे निपुणतरमुपपादितम्। अतः समयिनां ऐहिकामुष्मिकफलसाधनोपायः आन्तरपूजेति समयमततत्त्वम्।

अत्र भगवत्पादैः आधारकमलादिक्रमं विहाय आज्ञाचक्रादिक्रमेण अवरोहक्रमेण पूजाप्रकारः कथितः। अयमाशयः–'**आत्मन आकाशस्सम्भूतः। आकाशाद्वायुः। वायोरग्निः। अग्नेरापः। अद्भ्यः पृथिवी।**'[1] इति श्रौतक्रममवलम्ब्य अवरोहक्रम उक्तः। अत एव स्वाधिष्ठानानन्तरभाविनः मणिपूरस्य तदधःप्रदेशे निरूपणं युज्यते। आधारस्वाधिष्ठानानन्तरं मणिपूरकावस्थानमिति सर्वयोगशास्त्रसिद्धम्। तदपि संवर्ताग्निदग्धस्य जगतः उज्जीवनानन्तरं उत्पत्तिं वक्तुमित्यवगन्तव्यम्। एतच्च शुकसंहितायां '**शृणु देवि प्रवक्ष्यामि**' इत्यारभ्य एकनवतिश्लोकैः, श्रीचक्रस्य षट्चक्राणि प्रस्तुत्य '**इदानीं संप्रवक्ष्यामि**' इत्यारभ्य सार्धशत्या श्लोकैश्च सप्रपञ्चं प्रतिपादितम्। तत् तत एवावधार्यम्।।

न च '**ऊर्ध्वमूलमवाक्छाखं वृक्षं यो वेद संप्रति**'[2] इति श्रुतेः देहरूपवृक्षस्य शिर एव मूलं, करचरणाद्यवयवाश्शाखाः, अतश्च षट्कमलानां कदलीकुसुमोपमानां अधोमुखानाम् अवरोहक्रमेण कमलान्युक्तानीति तत्र पूजा सुकरेति तदानुगुण्येन भगवत्पादैरुक्तमिति वाच्यम्; तादात्म्यध्यानव्यतिरेकेण पूजायाः असंभवात्। संभवे वा श्रीचक्रगतत्रिकोणादिषट्चक्राणां अधोमुखत्वाभावात्,

"**मूलाधारस्थितामेव देवीं सुप्तां प्रबोधयेत्**" इति।

तत्रैव प्रबोधनियमात्, मूलाधारादिक्रमेणैव पूजा समयिनां कौलादीनां च [3]कार्येति परमगुरुमुखादेव अवगतं रहस्यम्। वामकेश्वरतन्त्रे आत्मपूजायां विशेष उक्तः–

पाशाङ्कुशौ तदीयौ तु रागद्वेषात्मकौ स्मृतौ।
शब्दस्पर्शादयो बाणाः मनस्तस्याभवद्धनुः।।
करणेन्द्रियचक्रस्थां देवीं संवित्स्वरूपिणीम्।
विश्वाहङ्कारपुष्पेण पूजयेत्सर्वसिद्धिभाक्।। इति।

[4]इयम् उपासनाविधिः क्रियात्मको नादरणीयः।। ४१ ।।

---

1. तै० उ० २-१।
2. तै० आ० १-११।
3. कायिकेति।
4. अयमुपासनाविधिः इति स्यात्।

Notes : The names of the deities to be meditated upon in this Cakra are Ādinaṭa and Lāśyeśvarī, surrounded by the fifty-six Pārthiva (Earthly) Mayūkhas.[1]

Samayā—the Devī that similarity with Śiva in Adhiṣṭhāna, Avasthāna, Anuṣṭhāna, Rūpa and Nāman. Similarly, the term 'Samaya', when applied to Śiva, should be construed as Īśvara who attains similarity with the Devī in the above respects. The doctrine relating to the worship of Samaya and Samayā is known as Samayāmata. When the Ādinaṭa and the Lāsyeśvarī, engaged in Tāṇḍava and Lāsya respectively, catch a glimpse of each other, the world is said to originate from them. When the Tāṇḍava and Lāsya cease, the world ceases to exist. This is the Kaula-doctrine. As the *Mūlādhāra* and the *Svādhiṣṭhāna* both belong to the region of darkness, the external worship of the Devī in those *Cakras* is countenanced exclusively by the Kaulas; even though the Samayins have nothing to do with such form of worship, still they may worship the Devī of the *Sahasrāra* mentally as having her place in these two gross *Cakras,* in keeping with their own doctrine. It is with a view to stressing this feature that the Devī has been designated significantly as Samayā in this and the previous stanza but one, which deal with the *Mūlādhāra* and the *Svādhiṣṭhāna,* which belong exclusively to the province of the Kaulas. According to the Kaulamārga, the *Bindu* is in the *Tri-koṇa* of the *Mūlādhāra.* Hence, the Kaulas worship the *Bindu* in the *Tri-koṇa* every day. That *Tri-koṇa* is of two kinds : one is situated in the middle of the nine Yogins of the *Śrī-cakra* and the other in the organ of a beautiful young woman. The Pūrva-kaulas worship the former painted or engraved in the Bhūrja leaf, gold plate, a piece of silk-cloth or on a platform.

1. The fifty-six Pārthiva-mayūkha-s are : (1) Uḍḍiśvara, (2) Uḍḍiśvarī, (3) Jaleśvara, (4) Jaleśvarī, (5) Pūrṇeśvara, (6) Pūrṇeśvarī, (7) Kāmeśvara, (8) Kāmeśvarī, (9) Śrī-kaṇṭha, (10) Gaganā, (11) An-anta, (12) Svarasā, (13) Śaṁ-kara, (14) Mati, (15) Piṅgalā, (16) Pātāla-devī, (17) Nāradākhya, (18) Nādā, (19) Ānanda, (20) Ḍākinī, (21) Ālasya, (22) Śākinī, (29) Pāda, (30) Hākinī, (31) Ādhāreśa, (32) Raktā, (33) Cakriśa, (34) Caṇḍā, (35) Kuraṅgiśa, (36) Karālā, (37) Madadhrīśa, (38) Mahocchuṣmā, (39) An-ādi-vimala, (40) Mātaṅgī, (41) Sarva-jña-vimala, (42) Pulindā, (43) Yoga-vimala, (44) Śambarī, (45) Siddha-vimala, (46) Vācāparā, (47) Samaya-vimala, (48) Kulālikā, (49) Mitreśa, (50) Kubjā (51) Uḍḍiśa, (52) Ladhvā, (53) Ṣasthiśa, (54) Kuleśvarī, (55) Caryādhiśa, and (56) Ajā.

The Uttara-kaulas worship the actual organ of the damsel. These are exclusively external in form and not internal, and as such their worship pertains only to the *Mūlādhāra-cakra*. The Kuṇḍalinī therein is known as Kaulinī. The worship of the *Tri-koṇa* pointing downwards therefore amounts to the worship of the Kaulinī of the form of *Bindu*. She is given to sleeping always and is therefore worshipped, while she is asleep. When she is roused from her sleep, that constitutes the Liberation for the Kaulas. She is propitiated with liquor, flesh, fish, *etc.*, mnemonically grouped as the *Pañca-makāras*. As these and the similarly degenerate practices of the Digambaras and kṣapaṇakas are not countenanced by the Vedas, they should be considered reprehensible.

According to the Samaya form, the six Cakras of the *Śrī-cakra* are identical with the six Cakras of the human body. The original *Tri-koṇa*, with which we began to design the *Ṣaṭ-koṇa* of the *Śrī-cakra*, is reputed to be the *Baindava-sthāna*. That is in effect a quadrilateral. We have already seen how this quadrilatera, which contains the *Baindava-sthāna*, is no other than the disc of the Moon in the thousand-petalled lotus. It is this *Baindava-sthāna* that is otherwise known as 'Sudhā-sindhu' and 'Saraghā'. Hence, neither the external worship of the *Baindava-sthāna* of the Pūrva-kaulas, nor the degenerate practices of the Uttara-kaulas can even be remotely meant by or associated with the Samaya form of worship of the *Tri-koṇa*. The worship of the Samaya-Samayā-conjunction in the *Sahasrāra* is alone the goal of the Samayins. The similarity between the Deva and the Devī in all the five respects is indicated in this stanza. The identity of abode is established by the words '*Tavādhāre*', meaning that the Deities have their abode in the *Mūlādhāra* of the Devī. The Lāsya or female-dance and the Tāṇḍava or male-dance, both being types of the same *Nṛtya*, their identity of *Avasthā* or condition is established. The words 'udaya-vidhim uddiśya' establish the identity of *Anuṣṭhāna* or occupation, both of them being intent on the same purpose, *viz.*, the creation of the world. The identities of form and name between the two are established by the word 'Navātman' occurring in this stanza, as further amplified by the same word occurring in stanza 34. Similarly, in the five other stanzas preceding this, wherein the two deities are conceived as placed in the middle of the other five *Cakras*, their identity in these five respects may be established from a careful examination of the stanzas.

For the Samayins the worship of the six *Cakras* is not essential, while that of the *Sahasrāra* is the *sine qua non* of their doctrine, which consists in the conceiving of the form of the disc of the Moon in the middle of the *Sahasrāra* as the quadrilateral, which is the seat of the *Bindu,* and the *Bindu* therein as the Sādākhyā transcending the twenty-five Tattvas, as it is the twenty-sixty Tattva of the form of the conjunction of the Śakti with Sadā-śiva. When the Samaya form of worship does not countenance external forms, it is needless to point out that observances, such as the sixteen kinds of Upacāras, are beyond the province of such worship. The identity between the six *Cakras* of the body, (such as the *Mūlādhāra* and others), with the six *Cakras* of the *Śrī-cakra,* (Such as *Tri-koṇa* and others), that between the quadrilateral containing the *Bindu* of the *Śrī-cakra* and the *Sahasrāra,* similarly that between the *Bindu* and Śiva, as also that between the *Śrī-cakra* in its entirety and the Pañca-daśākṣarī, these four kinds of identities are looked upon as forming the essential features of the Samaya form of worship.

Some are of the opinion that there are six kinds of identities. The Parā, one of the four divisions of *Nāda,* is of the form of the *Tri-koṇa* which does not contain the *Bindu.* Of the other three divisions of the *Nāda,* Paśyantī is of the form of the *Aṣṭa-koṇa* of the *Śrī-cakra;* while the Madhyamā is of the form of the two *Daśāras,* and the Vaikharī of the *Catur-daśāra.* The Śiva-cakras, consisting of the two lotuses, the *Mekhalātraya* and the *Bhū-gṛha,* are inherent in the Śakti-cakras detailed above. Hence, the *Śrī-cakra* is implied in the term *Nāda.* The six *Cakras, Mūlādhāra* and others of the body, are implied in the term *'Bindu'.* The *Kalās,* which may be taken either as fifty or three-hundred and sixty in number, and are comprehended in the five elements and the Manas-tattva, are far below the twenty-sixth Tattva. Hence, the Bhagavatī stands far above the *Nāda,* the *Bindu* and the *Kalā.* The *Sahasrāra* is beyond the *Bindu* of the six Cakras and is of the character of the *Baindava-sthāna,* the same as the *Sudhāsindhu* and described also as Saraghā in the Veda. The Tattva beyond the *Nāda* is the Sādākhyā the same as the *Śrī-vidyā* or the Brahma-vidyā and described by the term Cit-kalā, transcending the fifteen Kalās, Darśā, Dṛṣṭā, Darśatā and others, of the form of the fifteen syllables *'ka E Ī La Harīṁ'* and others, having as their names Tripurasundarī and others. The six identities referred to are the identities between the permutations of *Nāda, Bindu* and *Kalā,* taken two at a time. By worshipping the Devī with the conception of the six identities referred to above the practitioner becomes dissolved in the Sādākhyā-kalā. It is only after this, that, through the power acquired by meditation on the Devī, having in view the six identities, and the power of Mahā-vedha obtained, by the grace of the Guru, the Bhagavatī suddenly bursts through the *Mūlādhāra* and the *Svādhiṣṭhāna* centres of energy and manifests herself directly in the *Maṇi-pūra*. The manner in which the Mahā-vedha is acquired is as follows : Having at first, during the practising stage, got access to the Mahā-vidyā from the Guru in whose custody alone it is, and received instruction only from the mouth of the Guru, practising the mere muttering of the Mantra in the manner indicated by the Guru, he should at the hour of midnight, on the Aṣṭamī Tithi known as the Mahānavamī, in the bright half of the Āśva-yuja month, catch hold of the feet of his Guru. As a result of that, due to the contact of the Guru's hand placed on the crest of the disciple and the imparting once again by him of the Mantra, the procedure to be adopted for the worship of the six Cakras, and the manner in which the six kinds of identities are to be experienced by the disciple, there originates the power known as Śaiva-mahāvedha, whereby the practitioner realizes the manifestation of the Sādākhyā. When once the Mahā-vedha is generated in the practitioner, the Bhagavatī manifests herself in the *Maṇi-pūra*. Commencing from *Arghya, Pādya* and the like and till the offering of jewels set with gems, all the details of worship should be followed with due realization of the Kuṇḍalinī in the *Maṇi-pūra*, and the Devī should thence be transposed of the *Anāhata* chamber of the heart, where offerings, from Dhūpa onward till the offering of food and water for cleansing, should be made, and thereafter in the *Viśuddhi* she should be enthroned. While she is engaged in conversation with her comrades there, she should be worshipped with the crystal-like sixteen Kalās of the Moon there, as with so many gems and transposed to the *Ājñā-cakra*, where she, the Kameśvarī, should be propitiated by means of various kinds of waving of lights. Thereafter, suddently, like a streak of lightning, she flashes into the thousand-petalled lotus and, having entered that region, frolics in the company of Sadā-śiva, in the pleasure garden, under the shadow of the Kalpaka trees in Maṇi-dvīpa, in the middle of the ocean of nectar. Just then the screen should be dropped, and the practitioner should stand all alone till the Devī makes her exit therefrom on her way back to the *Mūlādhāra*.

The view of Śaṅkara-bhagavatpāda, as could be inferred from his description of the Devī in *'Kvaṇat-kāñcī-dā-mā'* (verse 7) and others is that the Devī manifests herself in the *Maṇipūra* of the practitioner after his realizing the four kinds of identity. The other view, that the manifestation is the result of the six kinds of identity being realized by the practitioner, is Lakṣmīdhara's.

Hence, the only means open to a Samayin to achieve his objects successful, in this as well as in the other world, is the internal form of worship and the internal form of worship alone.

एवं समयमतं सम्यक्प्रपञ्च्य समयायाः भगवत्याः किरीटप्रभृति पादान्तं वर्णयति–

गतैर्माणिक्यत्वं गगनमणिभिः सान्द्रघटितं
किरीटं ते हैमं हिमगिरिसुते कीर्तयति यः[1]।
[2]स नीडेयच्छयाच्छुरणशबलं[3] चन्द्रशकलं[4]
धनुः [5]शौनासीरं किमिति न निबन्धाति[6] धिषणाम्॥ ४२॥

Gatair māṇikya-tvaṁ gagana-maṇibhiḥ sāndra-ghaṭitaṁ
kirīṭaṁ te haimaṁ hima-giri-sute kīratyati yaḥ/
Sa nīḍeyac-chāyāc-churaṇa-śabalaṁ candra-śakalaṁ
dhanuḥ śaunāsīraṁ kim iti na nibadhnāti dhiṣaṇām//

Translation : O Daughter of the snow-capped Mountain! he who describes Thy crown of gold closely set with the (twelve) Suns, why will he not gain the impression that the crescent Moon (beside), variegated with the diffused lustre of the various gems embedded therein, is but Śunāśira's (Indra's) bow?

गतैः प्राप्तैः, **माणिक्यत्वं** रत्नभावं, **गगनमणिभिः** द्वादशादित्यैः। तेषाम् अत्यन्तसन्निकृष्टसेवार्थं भूषणगतमणित्वं युज्यते। **सान्द्रघटितं** सान्द्रं नीरन्ध्रं यथा भवति तथा घटितं खचितं, **किरीटं** मकुटं, **ते हैमं** हेम्नो विकारः, **हिमगिरिसुते!** हे पार्वति! **कीर्तयति** वर्णयति, यः, स कवीन्द्रः, **नीडेयच्छयाच्छुरणशबलं** नीडं गोलं तत्र खचितं नीडेयं रत्नजातं तस्य छाया तया छुरणेन व्यापनेन शबलं शबलवर्णं, **चन्द्रशकलं** चन्द्रखण्डं, **धनुः** कोदण्डं, **शौनासीरं** शुनासीरः इन्द्रः तस्य संबन्धि शौनासीरं, **किमिति न निबन्धाति धिषणां** बुद्धिम्॥

1. कः।
2. समीडे ; तमीडे ; समीपे।
3. स्फुरणशबलं ; छुरणपटलं ; छुरितशबलं ; छुरणशबला।
4. चन्द्रकलिका।
5. सौनासीरं।
6. किमिदमिति बध्नाति।

अत्रेत्थं पदयोजना–हे हिमगिरिसुते ! माणिक्यत्वं गतैः गगनमणिभिः सान्द्रघटितं हैमं ते किरीटं यः कीर्तयति सः नीडेयच्छायाच्छुरणशबलं चन्द्रशकलं शौनासीरं धनुरिति धिषणां किं न निबन्ध्नाति ।।

अयं भावः–किरीटवर्णनां कर्तुमुद्युञ्जानः कवीश्वरः तत्र स्थितां चन्द्ररेखां नानरत्नमणिकान्तिच्छुरितां दृष्ट्वा इन्द्रचापत्वेन कथं नाशङ्कते ? अवश्यं तस्य तच्छङ्का जायत एवेति ।।

अत्र उत्प्रेक्षालङ्कारः, चन्द्रशकलस्य इन्द्रचापत्वेनोत्प्रेक्षेणात् । यद्वा–अपह्नवालङ्कारः, इदं चन्द्रशकलं न भवति, अपि तु इन्द्रचाप इत्यपह्नवस्य प्रतिभानात् । यद्वा–सन्देहालङ्कारः, अयमिन्द्रचापः उत चन्द्रशकलमिति संशयात् । यद्वा–अतिशयोक्तिर-लङ्कारः, इन्दुशकलस्य इन्द्रचापत्वेन अध्यवसानात्; स्वधिषणां इन्द्रचापे किमिति न निबन्ध्नाति इति सामान्योक्तेः । एतेषां मध्ये एकस्य प्राधान्यं इतरस्योपसर्जनत्वमिति विनिगमकप्रमाणाभावात् सन्देहसङ्करः । (उत्प्रेक्षातिशयोक्ती स्पष्टे । अपह्नवस्तु तल्लिङ्गाभावादपि किमिति धिषणां न निबन्ध्नाति इत्यपह्नवोल्लेखस्य शक्यत्वात् । सन्दहेस्तु चन्द्रशकले दृष्टे इन्द्रचापस्य स्मृत्यारूढत्वात् उल्लेखयितुं शक्य एवेति सन्देहसङ्कर एव ज्यायान्) ।। ४२ ।।

Notes : Having thus far described the Bliss derived by meditation on the Devī in her various aspects, in detail, with a view to acquainting the worshippers, who are not fortunately circumstanced to meditate upon her in the requisite manner, with the grace and charms of her form, from head to foot, the author of this work has devoted for the purpose the rest of the stanzas composing it, known as the *Saundaryalaharī*, "the wave of beauty", as opposed to the *Ānandalaharī*, the prior portion of the work, so known because of the flood of spiritual Bliss wherein her votaries find themselves merged ongoing through it. However, this differentiation is not recognized by Lakṣmīdhara, Bhāskararāya, Kaivalyāśrama and other learned commentators, who call the entire work the *Saundaryalaharī*. With a view to singing the praises of the Devī, whose pair of feet stand far above the three hundred and sixty rays emanating from them (as described in stanza 14) the author sets about describing her form from her crown down to her toes. The twelve Suns—the original word *'Gagana-maṇibhiḥ'* literally means 'the sky-gems'; hence the Suns which are twelve in number. *Śunāsīra*—Indra. According to Kaivalyāśrama, the Kirīṭa-mantra *'Hiraṇya-kirīṭāya sahasrāditya-tejase namaḥ'*, "Salutation to the golden crown dazzling with the lustre of a thousand Suns", is derived from this stanza describing the Devīs crown.

धुनोतु ध्वान्तं नस्तुलितदलितेन्दीवरवनं
घनस्निग्धश्लक्ष्णं[1] चिकुरनिकुरुम्बं[2] तव शिवे।
यदीयं[3] सौरभ्यं सहजमुपलब्धुं सुमनसो
वसन्त्यस्मिन्मन्ये [4]वलमथनवाटीविटपिनाम्।। ४३।।

Dhunotu dhvāntaṁ nas tulity-dalitendīvara-vanaṁ
ghana-snigdha-ślakṣṇaṁ cikura-nikurumbaṁ tava śive/
Yadīyaṁ saurabhyaṁ sahajam upalabdhuṁ sumanaso
vasanty asmin manye vala-mathana-vāṭī-viṭa-pinām//

Translation : O Spouse of Śiva! may Thy lock of hair, which resembles an expanse of blue lilies in bloom and which is thick, shining and soft, drive away our (internal) darknes. I take it the flowers of the trees of the garden of the slayer of Vala, take up their abode in this (lock) (as though) to acquire its inherent fragrance.

धुनोतु अपनुदतु, **ध्वान्तम्** अन्तस्तिमिरं, **नः** अस्माकं, **तुलितदलितेन्दीवरवनं** तुलितं सदृशीकृतं दलितं भिन्नं, विकसितमित्यर्थः, इन्दीवराणां नीलोत्पलानां वनं यस्य। तत्। **घनस्निग्धश्लक्ष्णं** घनं सान्द्रं अविरलं स्निग्धं स्नेहयुक्तमिव स्थितं श्लक्ष्णं मृदु। एवमेतेषां विशेषणानां समासः। **चिकुरनिकुरुम्बं** चिकुराणां केशानां निकुरुम्बं समूहः केशपाशः धम्मिल्ल इत्यर्थः। **तव** भवत्याः, **शिवे**! भगवति! **यदीयं** यस्य धम्मिल्ल्स्य सम्बन्धि, **सौरभ्यं** परिमलं, **सहजं** स्वभावसिद्धं **उपलब्धुं** समाक्रष्टुं, **सुमनसः** पुष्पाणि, **वसन्ति** आसते। **अस्मिन्** धम्मिल्ले, **मन्ये** ध्रुवं, **वलमथन-वाटीविटपिनां** वलमथनः [5]बलारिः–वबयोरभेदोपचारः अनुप्रासार्थमङ्गीकृतः–तस्य वाटी उद्यानं तत्र विटपिनः कल्पवृक्षाः तेषाम्।।

अत्रेत्थं पदयोजना–हे शिवे! तुलितदलितेन्दीवरवनं घनस्निग्धश्लक्ष्णं तव चिकुरनिकुरुम्बं नः ध्वान्तं धुनोतु। यदीयं सहजं सौरभ्यं उपलब्धुं अस्मिन् वलमथनवाटीविटपिनां सुमनसः वसन्तीति मन्ये।।

1. घनं स्निग्धं श्लक्ष्णं ; घनस्निग्धं श्लक्ष्णं।
2. चिकुरनिकुरम्बं।
3. तदीयं।
4. बलमथनवाटी......।
5. बलारातिः, इन्द्र इति यावत्।

अत्र उत्प्रेक्षालङ्कारः, केशपाशवासनार्थमेव धृतायां कल्पवृक्षकुसुमानां अन्यथा-त्वेनोत्प्रेक्षणात्। तल्लक्षणम्–

सम्भावनमथोत्प्रेक्षा प्रकृतस्य परेण यत्।। इति।।

तुलितदलितेन्दीवरवनमित्यत्र उपमालङ्कारः। अनयोस्संसृष्टिः, तिलतण्डुलवत् संसृज्यमानत्वात्। क्षीरनीरवत् सम्बन्धः सङ्करः।।४३।।

Notes : The Devīs dark locks reflected on the heart of the meditating votary have the miraculous power of driving away the darkness therefrom. This enhances the greatness of the Devī to a remarkable extent. The slayer of Vala—Indra, who is reputed to have killed Balāsura. The form 'Vala', which, by the way, accentuates the effect of alliteration, is prevalent in South India, being the same as 'Bala'. The trees referred to are Kalpa trees and the garden is Nandana. Again, it is usual for women to wear flowers for adding fragrance to and enhancing the beauty of their locks; but in the case of the Devī, as the poet puts it, it is just the reverse.

[1]तनोतु क्षेमं नस्तव वदनसौन्दर्यलहरी-
परीवाहस्रोतः सरणिरिव सीमन्तसरणिः[2]।
वहन्ती सिन्दूरं प्रबलकबरीभारतिमिर-
[3]द्विषां बृन्दैर्बन्दीकृतमिव[4] नवीनार्ककिरणम्।।४४।।

Tanotu kṣemaṁ nas tava vadana-saundaryalaharī
parīvāha-srotaḥ-saraṇir iva sīmanta-saraṇiḥ/
Vahantī sindūraṁ prabala-kabarī-bhāra-timira
dviṣāṁ bṛndair bandī-kṛtam iva navīnārka-kiraṇam//

Translation : May the parting line of the hair over Thy forehead, which veril marks the track taken by the surging flood of beauty of Thy face and which bears the vermilion streak, resembling a beam of the newly rising Sun held in bondage by adversary hordes, *viz.*, the immensely powerful element of darkness in (the form of Thy) locks of hair, vouchsafe our welfare.

1. तनोत्विति पूर्वार्ध उत्तरार्धतया वहन्तीत्युत्तरार्धः पूर्वार्धतया च इतरपाठेषु दृश्यते।
2. सीमान्तसरणिः। (Ṛṣikeśa edn.)
3. त्विषां।
4. मन्दीकृतमिव।

तनोतु विस्तारयतु दिशत्वित्यर्थः। **क्षेमं** योगक्षेमात्मकं शुभं **नः** अस्माकं, **तव वदनसौन्दर्यलहरीपरीवाहस्त्रोतस्सरणिरिव**–इदमेकं पदम्, 'इवेन सह नित्यसमासो विभक्त्यलोपः पूर्वपदप्रकृतिस्वरत्वं च' इति नियमात्। वदनं मुखं तस्य सौन्दर्यस्य सुन्दरभावस्य लहरी उत्सेकः तस्य परीवाहः प्रवाहः 'उपसर्गस्य घञ्यमनुष्ये बहुलम्' इति परिशब्देकारस्य दीर्घः। तत्र स्रोतस्सरणिरिव स्रोतसः प्रवाहस्य सरणिरिव मार्ग इव स्थिता, **सीमन्तसरणिः** सीमन्ते धमिल्लमध्यप्रदेशे सरणिः सरण्याकाराकारिता रेखा, **वहन्ती** धारयन्ती, **सिन्दूरं** सिन्दूरपरागं, **प्रबलकबरीभारतिमिरद्विषां** प्रबलाः केशपाशात्मना लब्धजन्मतया प्रबलाः ते च ते कबरीभाराः, त एव केशपाशनिचया एव तिमिराणि तान्येव द्विषः शत्रवः तेषां, **वृन्दैः** समूहैः, **बन्दीकृतं** बन्दीग्रहणावरुद्धम्। **इव** इति संभावनायाम्। कविप्रौढोक्तिस्थले इवशब्दस्य संभावनैवार्थः, [1]अन्यत्र सादृश्यमिति विवेकः। **नवीनार्ककिरणं** नवीनः प्रातःकालीनः अर्कः सूर्यः तस्य किरणः तम्।।

अत्रेत्थं पदयोजना–हे भगवति! तव वदनसौन्दर्यलहरीपरीवाहस्त्रोतस्सरणिरिव स्थिता तव सीमन्तसरणिः प्रबलकबरीभारतिमिरद्विषां बृन्दैः बन्दीकृतं नवीनार्ककिरणमिव सिन्दूरं वहन्ती नः क्षेमं तनोतु।।

अत्र उत्प्रेक्षालङ्कारः; सीमन्तसरणेः स्रोतस्सरणित्वेनोत्प्रेक्षणात्। न चायमुपमालङ्कारः; स्वतस्सिद्धमनुपजीव्य कविप्रौढोक्तिमेवोपजीव्योत्थानात्। न च संभावनापरस्येवशब्दस्य समासविधानाभावात् उपमैवेति वाच्यम्। 'इवेन सह' इति मान्येनोभयार्थस्य इवशब्दस्य सग्रहणात् उभयत्रापि समासोऽस्तीति ध्येयम्। उत्तरार्धेऽप्युत्प्रेक्षालङ्कारः ; सिन्दूरस्य सूर्यकिरणात्मना संभावनात्। कबरीभारस्य तिमिरत्वारोपणात् रूपकालङ्कारोऽपि वर्तते। एवमनयोरङ्गाङ्गिभावेन सङ्करः ; संभावनां प्रति रूपकस्य निमित्तत्वात्।। ४४।।

Notes : The language is hyperbolical and presents poetic imagery of a high order. This stanza is also read with its former and latter halves changing places. Śrī Appayya Dīkṣita explains that while describing the Sīmanta line as the overflow of the flood of facial beauty it is the transcendence of the Devī's facial beauty that is intended to be suggested. Meditation on Devī's lovely Sīmanta as described in this verse delivers the devotee from ignorance, protects him from enemies and vouchsafes prosperity on him.

1. अर्थतः? इति पाठ।

अरालैः स्वाभाव्यादलिकलभसश्रीभिरलकैः[1]
[2]परीतं ते वक्त्रं परिहसति[3] पङ्केरुहरुचिम्।
दरस्मेरे यस्मिन्दशनरुचिकिञ्जल्करुचिरे
सुगन्धौ माद्यन्ति [4]स्मरदहनचक्षुर्मधुलिहः।।४५।।

Arālaiḥ svābhāvyād ali-kalabha-sa-śrībhir alakaiḥ
parītaṁ te vaktraṁ parihasati paṅke-ruha-rucim/
Dara-smere yasmin dasana-ruci-kiṅjalka-rucire
su-gandhau mādyanti smara-dahana-cakṣurmadhu-lihaḥ//

Translation : Surrounded by curly hair resembling (swarms of) young bees, Thy face scoffs at the beauty of the lotus-flower; in which face, smiling gently, rendered handsome by the filament-like brilliance of the teeth and endowed with fragrance, the bees of the eyes of Śiva, the Destroyer of Cupid.

अरालैः कुटिलैः, **स्वाभाव्यात्** स्वभावतः **अलिकलभसश्रीमिः** अलिकलभैः भ्रमरपोतैः सश्रीभिः समानाभैः। समासान्तविधेरनित्यत्वात् कप्रत्ययाभावः। **अलकैः** चूर्णकुन्तलैः, **परीतं** परितः इतं परीतं व्याप्तं **ते** तव, वक्त्रं **परिहसति,** तत्तुल्यं न भवतीत्यर्थः। **पङ्केरुहरुचिं** पङ्केरुहस्य कमलस्य रुचिं सौभाग्यं, **दरस्मेरे** दरमीषत् स्मेरो विकासः यस्य तादृशे, **यस्मिन् दशनरुचिकिञ्जल्करुचिरे** दशानानां दन्तानां रुचय एव किञ्जल्काः केसराः तैः रुचिरे सुभगे, **सुगन्धौ** सुपद्मगन्धौ, **माद्यन्ति** नन्दन्ति। **स्मरदहनचक्षुर्मधुलिहः** स्मरदहनस्य स्मरारेः ईश्वरस्य चक्षूंष्येव मधुलिहः भ्रमराः। जितमन्मथस्यापि वदनसौन्दर्यदर्शनं मादनहेतुरिति किमु वक्तव्यं त्वद्वदनसौन्दर्य-स्वरूपमिति भावः।।

अत्रेत्थं पदयोजना–हे भगवति! स्वाभाव्यादरालैः अलिकलभसश्रीभिः अलकैः परीतं ते वक्त्रं पङ्केरुहरुचिं परिहसति। दरस्मेरे दशनरुचिकिञ्जल्करुचिरे सुगन्धौ यस्मिन् स्मरदहनचक्षुर्मधुलिहः माद्यन्ति।।

अत्र उपमालङ्कारः, पङ्केरुहरुचिं परिहसतीत्यनेन वक्त्रस्य कमलसादृश्यप्रतीतेः। अलिकलभसश्रीभिरित्यत्र उपमालङ्कारः। अनयोरङ्गाङ्गिभावेन सङ्करः। दशनरुचि-

---

1. दलिकुलहसश्रीभि०।
2. परीतं चद्वक्रं तव हसति।
3. परिभवति।
4. स्मरमथन।

किञ्जल्करुचिरे इत्यत्र रूपकालङ्कारः, दशनरुचीनां किञ्जल्कत्वेनारोपणात्। स्मरदहन-चक्षुर्मधुलिहः इत्यत्र रूपकालङ्कारः ; चक्षुषां मधुलिट्त्वेनारोपणात्। अनयोरङ्गाङ्गिभावेन सङ्करः, सङ्करद्वयस्य संसृष्टिः।। ४५।।

Notes : The destroyer of Smara—Śiva. *Young bees—'Kalabha'* the Saṁskṛta word is generally used to signify the young one of an elephant. Here it is used to indicate the young one of a bee.

ललाटं लावण्यद्युतिविमलमाभाति तव यत्
द्वितीयं तन्मन्ये मकुटघटितं चन्द्रशकलम्[1]।
विपर्यासन्यासादुभयमपि[2] संभूय च[3] मिथः
[4]सुधालेपस्यूतिः परिणमति राकाहिमकरः।। ४६।।

Lalāṭaṁ lāvaṇya-dyuti-vimalam ābhāti tava yad
dvitīyaṁ tan manye makuṭa-ghaṭitaṁ candra-śakalam/
Viparyāsa-nyāsād ubhayam api saṁbhūya ca mithaḥ
sudhā-lepa-syūtiḥ pariṇamati rākā-hima-karaḥ//

Translation : I fancy, Thy forehead, which shines bright and clear in the effulgence of its beauty, is a second crescent fixed on to (Thy) crown. For, the two, by being placed invertedly (one above the other) and by blending together, turn out to be the Full-moon besmeared with the balm of nectar.

ललाटं, निटिलं, **लावण्यद्युतिविमलं** लावण्यं तारल्यमेव द्युतिर्ज्योत्स्ना तया विमलं स्निग्धं, **आभाति** आ सामन्ताद्भाति। **तव यत् द्वितीयं तत् मन्ये** शङ्के। **मकुटघटितं** किरीटकलितं **चन्द्रशकलं** चन्द्रार्धखण्डम्, **विपर्यासन्यासात्**—ललाटम् अवाक्कोणं वर्तते; चन्द्रशकलं ललाटस्योपरि ऊर्ध्वशृगं वर्तते; उभयोर्विपर्यासन्यासः शृङ्गचतुष्कसम्मेलनं, तस्मात् **उभयमपि** ललाटचन्द्रशकले, **संभूय** मिलित्वा, चकारोऽतिशयवाची। **मिथः** अन्योन्यं **सुधालेपस्यूतिः** सुधायाः अमृतस्य लेपः विलेपनं तस्य स्यूतिः सीवनं यस्य सः अमृतरससान्द्र इत्यर्थः। **परिणमति** तादूप्यं भजति, तदाकाराकारित इत्यर्थः। **राकाहिमकरः** राकायां पूर्णिमायां हिमकरश्चन्द्रः।।

अत्रेत्थं पदयोजना—हे भगवति ! तव यत् ललाटं लावण्यद्युतिविमलं आभाति तत्

1. मकुटशशिखण्डस्य शकलम्।
2. दुभयकृतसन्धानमिव तत्; उभयकृतसन्धानमयितः।
3. मिलितः।
4. सुधाऽऽलेपस्फूर्तिः।

मकुटघटितं द्वितीयं चन्द्रशकलं मन्ये। यद्यस्मात्कारणात् उभयमपि विपर्यासन्यासात् मिथः सम्भूय च सुधालेपस्यूतिः राकाहिमकरः परिणमति।।

पूर्णिमायां सम्पूर्णता चन्द्रस्य कथं भवेत्, किरीटे अर्धदेहाविष्टतया चन्द्रः परिदृश्यत इति पूर्णिमाचन्द्रं निमित्तीकृत्य ललाटमुत्प्रेक्ष्यते।।

अत्र उत्प्रेक्षालङ्कारः, ललाटस्य अर्धचन्द्रत्वेनात्प्रेक्षणात्। यद्वा-द्वितीयार्धे अतिशयोक्तिरलङ्कारः, राकाहिमकरस्य ललाटकिरीटघटितचन्द्ररेखाद्वितयनिर्माणा-सम्बन्धेऽपि सम्बन्धकथनात्। अत्र कविकल्पितवस्तुवृत्तसौन्दर्ययोरभेदाध्यवसायः। उत्प्रेक्षातिशयोक्त्योः अङ्गाङ्गिभावेन सङ्करः। '**अध्यवसायव्यापारप्राधान्ये उत्प्रेक्षा**' 'अध्यवसितप्राधान्ये त्वतिशयोक्तिः'। सूत्रद्वयस्यायमर्थः—'अध्यवसायविषयभूते अध्यवसानक्रियारूपस्य व्यापारस्य प्राधान्यं यत्र तत्रोत्प्रेक्षोत्थानम्। यदा अध्यवसाय-विषयभूते अध्यवसितस्यैव प्राधान्यं प्रतीयते, तदा अतिशयोक्तेरुत्थानम्। अध्यवसायो नाम—निश्चय-ज्ञानम्। तच्च कविप्रौढोक्तिसिद्धम्, न वास्तवम्। उत्प्रेक्षास्तु अध्यवसान-क्रियाप्राधान्यस्य द्योतकाः। 'मन्ये शङ्के ध्रुवम्' इत्येवमादयः स्वरूपोत्प्रेक्षाद्योतकाः। हेतूप्रेक्षायां हेतुरेव। फलोत्प्रेक्षायां फलमेव द्योतकम्। अत एव स्वरूपोत्प्रेक्षायां इवाद्यभावे हेतुफलयोरसम्भवात्, अतिशयोक्त्युत्प्रेक्षयोः भेदाभावात् सैवोत्प्रेक्षा अतिशयोक्तौ अन्तर्भूतेति दिङ्मात्रमुक्तम्।। ४६ ।।

Notes : *Besmeared with the balm of nectar*—there is a pun on the Saṁskṛt equivalent of this phrase which also means "cemented together with a coating of plaster". The idea is that the two crescents, by being placed in such a manner as to make their horns meet together, form themselves into the Full-moon, the flow of *Sudhā* from both of them completing the cementing process.

भ्रुवौ भुग्ने[1] किंचिद्भुवनभयभङ्गव्यसनिनि
त्वदीये नेत्राभ्यां मधुकररुचिभ्यां धृतगुणम्[2]।
धनुर्मन्ये सव्येतरकरगृहीतं रतिपतेः[3]
प्रकोष्ठे[4] मुष्टौ च स्थगयति निगूढान्तरमुमे[5]।। ४७।।

1. भ्रुवोर्मध्ये।
2. धृतगुणे ; धृतशरम्।
3. रतिपतिः।
4. प्रकोष्ठौ; प्रकोष्टे।
5. मिमे।

Bhruvau bhugne kiṁcid bhuvana-bhaya-bhaṅga-vyasanini
tvadīye netrābhyāṁ madhu-kara-rucibhyāṁ dhṛta-guṇam/
Dhanur manye savyetara-kara-gṛhītaṁ rati-pateḥ
prakoṣṭhe muṣṭau ca sthagayati nigūḍhāntaram ume//

Translation : O Umā, ever intent on the annihilation of the world's fear! I see in Thy slightly knitted pair of eye-brows the bow of Rati's consort, strung with Thy bee-like pair of eyes, and held (aloft) in his left hand with the middle part hidden, his wrist and clenched fist covering them.

भ्रुवौ भ्रूवल्ली, **भुग्ने** अवाक्छृङ्गतया वलयिते, **किंचित्** नात्यन्तं **भुवनभय-भङ्गव्यसनिनि!** भुवनानां जगतां भयस्य उपद्रवस्य भङ्गे नाशकरणे व्यसनं तदेकप्रवणता अस्या अस्तीति भुवनभयभङ्गव्यसनिनी तस्याः सम्बुद्धिः। **त्वदीये** भवत्संबन्धिन्यौ, **नेत्राभ्यां** अक्षिभ्यां, **मधुकररुचिभ्यां** मधुकराणां भ्रमराणामिव रुचिःशोभा ययोस्ताभ्यां मधुकराकाराकारिताभ्यामित्यर्थः। **धृतगुणं** धृतः सम्पादितः गुणः ज्यावल्ली यस्य तत्, **धनुः** चापं **मन्ये** शङ्के। **सव्येतरकरगृहीतं** सव्यो दक्षिणः तदितरो वामः स चासौ करश्च तेन गृहीतम्। सव्येतरशब्देन एकेनैव हस्तेन सर्वदा धृतम्, न तु बाणप्रयोगार्थमिति सूच्यते। **रतिपतेः** मन्मथस्य, **प्रकोष्ठे** मणिबन्धे, **मुष्टौ** अङ्गुलीनां ग्रन्थौ, अयं मुष्टिशब्दः अनुशासनवशात् स्त्रीलिङ्गोऽपि प्रयोगबाहुल्यात् पुल्लिङ्गतामापन्नः, गण्डूषशब्दवत्। यथा 'उदरं परिमाति मुष्टिना' इति नैषधे प्रयोगः। **स्थगयति** स्थगनं छादनं कुर्वति सति, **निगूढान्तरं** निगूढे अन्तरे मौर्विदण्डयोर्यस्य तत्, **उमे!** हे पार्वति।।

अत्रेत्थं पदयोजना–हे उमे! भुवनभयभङ्गव्यसनिनि। त्वदीये किञ्चिद्भुग्ने भ्रुवौ मधुकररुचिभ्यां नेत्राभ्यां धृतगुणं रतिपतेः सव्येतरकरगृहीतं प्रकोष्ठे मुष्टौ च स्थगयति सति निगूढान्तरं धनुर्मन्ये।।

अत्र भ्रुवौ धनुरिति रूपकम्, भ्रुवौः धनुरूपेण निरूपणात्। अत एव द्विवचनैक-वचनयोः सामानाधिकरण्यं भ्रुवौ धनुरिति।।

अयं भावः–विशेषणं चतुर्विधम्, व्यावर्तकविशेषणं, उपरञ्जकविशेषणं, उपलक्षणविशेषणं, उपधानविशेषणं चेति। तत्र व्यावर्तकविशेषणं नीलोत्पलमित्यादौ, तत्र नैल्यस्य श्वेतादिव्यावर्तकत्वात्। उपरञ्जकविशेषणं द्विविधम्–उपरञ्जनस्य आरोपविषयगोचरत्वेन, आरोप्यमाणगोचरत्वेन चेति। तत्र आरोपविषयगोचरत्वं **'मुखं चन्द्रः'** इत्यादौ। तत्र चन्द्रत्वेन मुखस्य उपरञ्जनम्। अत एव लिङ्गभेदेऽपि विशेषण-विशेष्यभावः सिद्धः। **'स तदुच्चकुचौ भवन्'** इति नैषधे। तत्र सः इति कलश एकः, द्वौ कुचौ, उभयोर्विशेषणविशेष्यभावः। आरोप्यमाणविशेषणं तु–'तिरस्करिण्यो जलदा

भवन्ति' अत्र आरोप्यमाणतिरस्करिणीत्वं आरोपविषयात्मतया स्थितम्। एतच्च पूर्वमेव निरूपितम्। उपलक्षणविशेषणम्–काकवद्देवदत्तगृहम्। पृथक् स्थिते(तिः) हि धर्मिणि उपलक्षणमिति उपलक्षणविदः। काकत्वादिजात्याविष्टस्यैव उपलक्षणत्वात् विशेषणतो भेदः। उपाधानविशेषणम्–'रक्तं स्फटिकम्' इति। धर्मात्मना उपाधायकत्वात् उपलक्षणतो भेदः। व्यावर्तकत्वात् नीलोत्पलादेर्व्यावृत्तिः।।

अत्रेदं तत्त्वम्–उपरञ्जकविशेषणस्थले–'मुखं चन्द्रः' 'कलशः स्तनौ' भ्रुवौ धनुः' इत्यादिस्थले–चन्द्रकलशाद्युपरञ्जकविशेषणानि आश्रितलिङ्गसङ्ख्यान्येव मुखादिकं स्तनादिकं च विशिंषन्तीति, न स्तनादेः मुखादेर्वा लिङ्गं सङ्ख्यां वा भजन्ते। नियतलिङ्गतया विशेष्यनिघ्नत्वाभावात् इतरेभ्यो विशेषणेभ्यो व्यावृत्तिः। मन्येशब्द-प्रयोगात् संभावनोत्थानात् उत्प्रेक्षालङ्कारोऽपि। अनयोः अनुसृष्टिः, अपृथक्स्थितयोः अलङ्कारयोः अङ्गाङ्गिभावात्। अपृथक्स्थितयोः अलङ्गारयोरङ्गाङ्गिभावोऽनुसर्जनम्, पृथक्स्थितयोस्तु सङ्करः इत्यालङ्कारिकरहस्यम्। अतिशयोक्तिरपि, भ्रूमध्यनासिका-मध्ययोः मुष्टिप्रकोष्ठस्थगितत्वेनाध्यवसानात्। अत्र नासिकायाः सव्येतरकरत्वे-नारोपणप्रतीतेः रूपकालङ्कारो ध्वन्यते। यद्वा–सव्येतरकरत्वेन नासिकायाः अध्यवसान-प्रतीतेः अतिशयोक्तिः। अनयोः सन्देहः सङ्करः।। ४७।।

Notes : The underlying idea is this : the Devī with her slightly knit eyebrows demonstrates, as it were, her sole purpose of dispelling fear from the hearts of her countless votaries, as, when she is in that posture, the eye-brows assume the form of a bow readily strung.

अहः सूते सव्यं तव नयनमर्कात्मकतया
त्रियामां वामं ते सृजति रजनीनायकतया।[1]
तृतीया [2]ते दृष्टिर्दरदलितहेमाम्बुजरुचिः[3]
समाधत्ते संध्यां दिवसनिशयोरन्तरचरीम्।। ४८।।

Ahaḥ sūte savyaṁ tava nayanam arkātmakatayā
tri-yāmāṁ vāmaṁ te sṛjati rajanī-nāyakatayā/
Tṛtīyā te dṛṣṭir dara-dalita-hemāmbuja-ruciḥ
samādhatte saṁdhyāṁ divasa-niśayor antara-carīm.//

Translation : Thy right eye, being of the form of the Sun, begets the Day, while Thy left (eye), of the form of the Moon,

1. रजनीनायकमयम्. रजनीनायकममुम्।
2. दृष्टिस्ते।
3. दरललितनीलाम्बुजरुचिः।

begets the Night; Thy third eye, which resembles a slightly blossomed gold-lotus, brings forth Twilight, which intervenes Day and Night.

अहः दिवसं **सूते** जनयति। **सव्यं** दक्षिणं, **तव नयनं** नेत्रं, **अर्कात्मकतया** सूर्यात्मकतया, **त्रियामां** रात्रिं **वामं** सव्येतरं, **ते** तव, **सृजति** सूते, [1]**रजनीनायकतया** चन्द्रात्मकतया। **तृतीया** निटिलस्थिता, **ते** तव, **दृष्टिः दरदलितहेमाम्बुजरुचिः** दरदलितमीषद्विकसितं हेमाम्बुजं [2]रक्ताम्बजुं तस्येव रुचिर्यस्याः सा, **समाधत्ते** सम्यगाधत्ते करोति, **दिवसनिशयोः** अहोरात्रयोः, **अन्तरचरीं** मध्यवर्तिनीं, **सन्ध्याम्** सायंप्रातरात्मकसन्ध्याकालद्वितयस्य अग्निहोत्रसाध्यत्वादिति भावः।।

अत्रेत्थं पदयोजना–हे भगवति! तव सव्यं नयनं अर्कात्मकतया अहः सूते वामं नयनं रजनीनायक[3]तया त्रियामां सृजति। ते तृतीया दृष्टिः दरदलितहेमाम्बुजरुचिः दिवसनिशयोः अन्तरचरीं सन्ध्यां समाधत्ते।।

अत्र सूर्यचन्द्राग्न्यात्मकनयनत्रयेण भगवत्याः [4]अवयवविशेषेण दिवसनिशा-सन्ध्यात्मककालत्रयोपलक्षितपक्षमासर्तुयुगकल्पादिकालोत्पत्तिकथनात् भगवत्याः कालावच्छेद्यत्वं दूरत एवापास्तमिति ध्वन्यते। इदमुत्तमं काव्यम्। मध्यमकाव्यता-प्रतीतिरपि, 'अर्कात्मतया' 'रजनीनायकमयम्' इति वाच्यमानत्वात्। दरदलितहेमाम्बुज-रुचिरित्यनेन अग्निनेत्रत्वं ध्वन्यते। अयमनुप्राणनात्मकः मध्यमोत्तमकाव्य-प्रयोजकध्वन्योः संसृष्टिः। संसृज्यमानं व्यङ्ग्यद्वयं प्रधानध्वनिना अङ्गाङ्गिभावेन सङ्कीर्यत इति दिक्।। ४८।।

Notes : This stanza, wherein the Devī's three eyes are said to bring forth day and night with the intervening twilight, may be said to indicate her character as transcending Kāla, all time, from day and night on to infinite time. Her being described as having three eyes indicates also her oneness with Īśvara, who is repute to have three eyes.

विशाला कल्याणी स्फुटरुचिरयोध्या कुवलयैः
कृपाधाराऽऽधारा[5] किमपि मधुरा भोगवतिका[6]।

---

1. रजनीनायकमयं चन्द्रात्मकम्।
2. सुवर्णकमलम्।
3. मयं सत् त्रियामां रात्रिम्।
4. अवयवरूपेण।
5. कृपाधाराधारा; कृपाधारापारा।
6. भोगलतिका; मधुराऽऽभोगवतिका।

अवन्ती दृष्टिस्ते बहुनगरविस्तारविजया[1]
ध्रुवं तत्तन्नामव्यवहरणयोग्या विजयते।। ४९।।

Viśalā kalyāṇī sphuṭa-rucir ayodhyā kuvalayaiḥ
kṛpā-dhārā-" dhārā kim api madhurā bhogavatikā/
Avantī dṛṣṭis te bahu-nagara-vistāra-vijayā
dhruvaṁ tat-tan-nāma-vyavaharaṇa-yogyā vijayate//

Translation : The glance of Thine eyes is all-comprehensive (Viśālā); spells prosperity (Kalyāṇī); serenely dazzles and (as such) cannot be faced in battle (A-yodhyā) by blue lilies; is the fountain-head of the stream of mercy (Dhārā); is superbly sweet (Madhurā); enjoys immence happiness (Bhogavatī); is the saviour (Avantī) (of the devoted); outrivals *in extenso* (Vijayā, nay) several (other) cities; and is indeed capable of being (appropriately) indicated by their respective names. All glory to it!

विशाला विपुला, **कल्याणी** मङ्गलात्मिका, **स्फुटरुचिः** प्रस्फुटकान्तिः, **अयोध्या** योद्धुमशक्या, **कुवलयैः** इन्दीवरैः, **कृपाधाराऽऽधारा** कृपाधाराणां करुणाप्रवाहाणां आधारभूता आधारशब्दस्य कर्मणि घञन्तत्वात् विशेष्यनिघ्नत्वेन रूपकत्वम्। **किमपि मधुरा** अव्यक्तमधुरा, **आभोगवतिका** आभोगः अन्तःपरिणाहः दैर्घ्यमिति यावत्। **अवन्ती** रक्षका, **दृष्टिः ते** नयनं **बहुनगरविस्तारविजया** बहूनां नगराणां विस्तारेण सामस्त्येन विजया स्फुरन्ती, **ध्रुवं** निश्चयः। **तत्तन्नामव्यवहरणयोग्या** तानि तानि च नामानि तत्तन्नामानि विशाला-कल्याणी-अयोध्या-धारा-मधुरा-भोगवती-अवन्ती-विजया-इत्यष्ट नगरनामानि, तैः तद्व्यवहरणं व्यवहारः तत्र योग्या, **विजयते** सर्वोत्कर्षेण वर्तते।।

अत्रेत्थं पदयोजना-हे भगवति! ते दृष्टिः विशाला कल्याणी स्फुटरुचिः कुवलयैः अयोध्या कृपाधाराऽऽधारा किमपि मधुरा आभोगवतिका अवन्ती बहुनगरविस्तारविजया तत्तन्नामव्यवहरणयोग्या ध्रुवं विजयते।।

अत्रेदमनुसन्धेयम्-विशालाप्रभृतयो विजयान्ताः अष्ट नगर्यः अष्ट दृष्टयश्च; विशाला नाम दृष्टिः अन्तर्विकासरूपा। कल्याणीदृष्टिर्विस्मिता। अयोध्यादृष्टिः स्मेरकनीनिका। धारादृष्टिः अलसा। मधुरादृष्टिः [2]वलिता। भोगवतीदृष्टिः स्निग्धा। अवन्तीदृष्टिः मुग्धा।

1. विजयात्।
2. विलसिता।

विजयादृष्टिः प्रान्तकनीनिका आकेकराख्या दृष्टिः। एता अष्ट दृष्टयः सर्वयोषित्समानाः। भगवत्यां तु विशेषः-एताः दृष्टयः यथाक्रमं संक्षोभाकर्षणद्रावणोन्मादवश्योच्चाटन-विद्वेषणमारणक्रियासु संभिन्नाः।।

एतदुक्तं भवति-भगवती यत्र प्रदेशे स्थित्वा अन्तर्विकासयुक्ततया विशालाख्यया दृष्ट्या जनसंक्षोभमकरोत् स देशो विशालानगरी। यत्र प्रदेशे स्थित्वा सा आकेकरया दृष्ट्या विजयाख्या शत्रुमारणमकरोत् स देशो विजयानगरी एवं मध्यवर्तिनानां षण्णां पुरां नामधेयान्यूह्यानि। यथोक्तं भगवत्पादैः-विशालाद्याः भगवत्याः दृष्टिविशेषाः संक्षोभादिकर्मसाधनभूताः अन्तर्विकासादिरूपाश्चेति सर्वमनवद्यमिति। एतदेव स्पष्टीकृतं तद्व्याख्याकारैः। तत् तत एव अवधार्यम्।। ४९।।

Notes : The glance of the Devī's eyes is said to be of an eight-fold character, each one of which is represented to indicate the name of a great city. These eight kinds of glances are common to all women. The glance known as Viśālā is said to bloom inward; that known as Kalyāṇī is said to be filled with surprise; the Ayodhyā-glance represents one with the expanded pupil; the Dhārāglance denotes idleness; the Madhurā-glance is that which shows a slight swirl; the Bhogavatī is the friendly one; Avantī is the one of an innocent nature; and Vijayā is the oblique one. The Devī's glances produce respectively the following effects : agitation, attraction, melting, infatuation, subjugation, exorcising, antagonizing and death-dealing.

कवीनां संदर्भस्तबकमकरन्दैकरसिकं[1]
कटाक्षव्याक्षेपभ्रमरकलभौ कर्णयुगलम्।
अमुञ्चन्तौ दृष्ट्वा तव नवरसास्वादतरला-
[2]वसूयासंसर्गादलिकनयनं किंचिदरुणम्[3] ।।५०।।

Kavīnāṁ saṁdarbha-stabaka-makarandaika-rasikaṁ
kaṭākṣa-vyākṣepa-bhramara-kalabhau karṇa-yugalam/
A-muñcantau dṛṣṭvā tava nava-rasāsvāda-taralāv
asūyā-saṁsargād alika-nayanaṁ kiṁcid aruṇam//

Translation : The (third) eye on Thy forehead is somewhat

1. मकरन्दैकभरितम्।
2. वसूयासंपर्कादलिकनयनं ; वसूयासन्दर्भादलिकनयनं।
3. किंस्विदरुणम्।

red, (as though) influenced by jealousy, seeing that Thy two young-bee-like obliquely-glancing (eyes), in their eagerness of swallow the nine Rasas (poetic sentiments), do not leave off Thy pair of ears, which chiefly delight in the honey of the cluster-of-flowers of poetic compositions.

कवीनां कवीश्वराणां, **सन्दर्भस्तबकमकरन्दैकरसिकं** सन्दर्भ: काव्यसन्दर्भ: स एव स्तबक: पुष्पगुच्छं तत्र मकरन्दे एकं मुख्यं रसिकं मुख्यरसिकं काव्यामृतास्वादैकरसिकमित्यर्थ:। **कटाक्षव्याक्षेपभ्रमरकलभौ** कटाक्षावेव व्याक्षेपौ व्याजौ ययोस्तौ, तौ च तौ भ्रमरकलभौ चेति समास:। भ्रमरकलभौ द्विरेफडिम्भौ। अत्र यद्यपि कलभशब्द: करिडिम्भवचन:, महाकविप्रयोगप्राचुर्यवशात् विशेषणसामान्यलक्षणौ भ्रमरकलभाविति। **कर्णयुगलं** कर्णयो: श्रवणयो: युग्मम्, **अमुञ्चन्तौ** रसास्वादलम्पटतया अत्यजन्तौ दृष्ट्वा, तृतीयस्य नयनस्य ऊर्ध्वस्थितत्वात्। **तव नवरसास्वादतरलौ** नवरसा: शृङ्गारादय: नवत्वसङ्ख्यायुक्ता: रसा: नवरसा: शाकपार्थिवादित्वादुत्तरपदलोप:; अन्यथा 'द्विगो:' इति ङीषि कृते नवरसी इति स्यात्। नवरसानामास्वादे भोगे तरलौ लम्पटौ, **असूयासंसर्गात्** असूया ईर्ष्या तस्या: संसर्ग: सम्बन्ध: तस्मात्, **अलिकनयनं** निटिलनेत्रं, **किञ्चिदरुणं** किञ्चित्कोपादिवारुणम्।।

अत्रेत्थं पदयोजना–हे भगवति! कवीनां सन्दर्भस्तबकमकरन्दैकरसिकं तव कर्णयुगलं कटाक्षव्याक्षेपभ्रमरकलभौ नवरसास्वादतरलौ अमुञ्चन्तौ दृष्ट्वा असूयासंसर्गात् अलिकनयनं किञ्चिदरुणम्।।

अयमर्थ :–नयनत्रयमध्ये द्वयोरमृतपाने सिद्धे एकस्य नयनस्य असूया युज्यते। आकर्णान्तनेत्रा भगवती इति वस्तुध्वनि:।।

अत्र अतिशयोक्तिरलङ्कार:; श्रवणयो:[1] काव्यामृतास्वादसबन्धाभावेऽपि सम्बन्ध-कथनात्। भ्रमरकलभावित्यत्र अपह्नवालङ्कार:। यद्वा–रूपकं, कटाक्षव्याक्षेप: कटाक्षात्मतया अवस्थितिरिति व्याख्येयम्। अतिशयोक्त्यन्तरमपि, भ्रमरकलभयो: मकरन्दास्वादासंबन्धेऽपि सम्बन्धकथनात्। कविकृतवस्तुकृतसौन्दर्ययोरभेदाध्यवसायात् अतिशयोक्त्योरनुप्राण्यानुप्राणकभाव: संबन्ध:। अपह्नवस्तु अङ्गाङ्गिभावेन सङ्कीर्ण:।।५०।।

Notes : Celestial and other bards sing the praises of the Devī with their choicest diction and always fill, as it were, her ears with the honey flowing from their composition. As her right and left eyes partake of it on account of their proximity to the ears, the

---

1. नेत्रयो: श्रवणगत इति कल्याणपुरमुद्रितकोशपाठ:।

third eye of the Devī is said to grow jealous of this and turn red in consequence.

**शिवे शृङ्गारार्द्रा तदितरजने[1] कुत्सनपरा
सरोषा गङ्गायां गिरिशचरिते[2] विस्मयवती।
हराहिभ्यो भीता सरसिरुहसौभाग्यजयिनी[3]
सखीषु स्मेरा ते मयि जननि[4] दृष्टिः सकरुणा।।५१।।**

*Śive śṛṅgārārdrā-tad-itara-jane kutsana-parā
sa-roṣā gaṅgāyāṁ giri-śa-carite vismaya-vatī/
Harāhibhyo bhītā sarasi-ruha-saubhāgya-jayinī
Sakhīṣu smerā te mayi jananai dṛṣṭiḥ sa-karuṇā//*

Translation : O Mother! Thy look is soft with love towards Śiva; scornful towards other folk; spiteful towards Gaṅgā; expressive of wonder of Giriśa's life-career; full of dread (when confronted) with the snakes (ornaments) of Hara; eclipses the beautiful colour of the lotus; smiles on Thy comrades; and is full of grace towards me.

शिवे सदाशिवे, **शृङ्गारार्द्रा** शृङ्गारेण शृङ्गाररसेन आर्द्रा आप्लुता, **तदितरजने** तस्मात् सदाशिवात् इतरजने तद्विषये **कुत्सनपरा** बीभत्सरसाविष्टा। अत्र कुत्सनं बीभत्सरसास्वादनजन्यान्तःकरणमुकुलीभावः कार्यकारणयोरभेदेन रसत्वेनोपचरितः। **सरोषा** रौद्ररसाविष्टा, रोषस्य स्थायिभावस्य रसत्वोक्तिरुपचारात्। **गङ्गायां** सपत्न्यामिति शेषः। **गिरिशचरिते** त्रिपुरविजयादौ, **विस्मयवती** अद्भुतरसाविष्टा, 'गिरिशनयने' इति पाठे तृतीयनयनेनैव मन्मथदहनम्, तादृशनयन एव इदानीं साकूतदर्शनमित्यद्भुतमिति ध्येयम्। **हराहिभ्यः** हरस्य परमेश्वरस्य अहिभ्यः सर्पेभ्यः, **भीता** भयरसाविष्टा, **सरसिरुहसौभाग्यजननी** सरसिरुहाणां सौभाग्यं रक्तिमा तस्य जननी उत्पादिका कोकनदकान्तिः, रक्तवर्णा वीररसाविष्टेत्यर्थः। अत्र अनुभावेन, नयनरक्तिम्ना वीररसो ध्वनितः। **सखीषु** वयस्यासु **स्मेरा** स्तब्धकनीनिका, अत्राप्यनुभावेन हास्यरसो ध्वन्यते। **ते** तव, **मयि जननि!** हे मातः! **दृष्टिः सकरुणा** करुणरसाविष्टा।।

अत्रेत्थं पदयोजना–हे जननि! ते दृष्टिः शिवे शृङ्गारार्द्रा, तदितरजने कुत्सनपरा,

1. तदितरमुखे।
2. गिरिशनयने।
3. सौभाग्यजननी।
4. जयति।

गङ्गायां सरोषा, [1]गिरिशचरिते विस्मयवती, हराहिभ्यो भीता, सरसिरुहसौभाग्यजननी, सखीषु स्मेरा, मयि सकरुणा।।

अत्र परस्परविरुद्धानां रसानां एकत्र नयने समावेशकथनात् विरोधालङ्कार:; अवस्थाभेदेन परिहारात् तस्य विरोधस्य आभासत्वम्। तल्लक्षणं विरोधाभासो विरोध:' इति। विक्रियाजनका एव रसा इति अष्टौ रसा:। भरतमते–

शान्तस्य निर्विकारत्वान्न शान्तं मेनिरे रसम्।

इति शान्तस्य रसत्वाभावात् अष्टावेव रसा: सङ्गृहीता:।।५१।।

Notes : Of the nine Rasas (sentiments), Śṛṅgāra (love), Bībhatsa (disgust), Raudra (passion), Adbhuta (wonder), Bhayānaka (terror), Vīra (heroism), Hāsya (mirth), Karuṇa (compassion), and Śānta (composure), all except the last one, find in the Devī's glance a resort, in the order mentioned in this stanza.

गते कर्णाभ्यर्णं गरुत[2] इव पक्ष्माणि दधती
पुरां भेत्तुश्चित्तप्रशमरसविद्रावणफले[3]।
इमे नेत्रे गोत्राधरपतिकुलोत्तंसकलिके
तवाकर्णाकृष्टस्मरशरविलासं कलयत:।।५२।।

Gate karṇābhyarṇaṁ garuta iva pakṣmāṇi dadhatī
purāṁ bhettuś citta-praśama-rasa-vidrāvaṇa-phale/
Ime netre gotrā-dhara-pati-kulottaṁsa-kalike
tavā-karṇākṛṣṭa-smara-śara-vilāsaṁ kalayataḥ//

Translation : O Crest-bud of the dynasty of the King of the Mountains! these two eyes of Thine, fringed with feather-like eyelashes, reaching Thine ears, and causing disturbance in the profound mental placidity of the Destroyer of the Cities (Śiva), play the part of Smara's arrows, drawn up to the ear.

गते प्राप्ते, **कर्णाभ्यर्णं** कर्णयो: समीपं, **गरुत** इव कङ्कपत्राणीव, **पक्ष्माणि दधती। पुरां** पुराणां **भेत्तु:** भेदकस्य, **चित्तप्रशमरसविद्रावण–फले** चित्ते अन्त:करणे प्रशमरस:[4] नैस्पृह्यमित्यर्थ:, तस्य विद्रावणं विनाशनं शृङ्गाररसोत्पादमिति यावत् तदेव

1. गिरिशनयनयोर्विस्मयवती।
2. गरुड।
3. फलम्।
4. शन्तररस इत्यधिक:।

फलं प्रयोजनं ययोस्ते चित्तप्रशमरसविद्रावणफले। अत्र फलशब्देन अध्यवसितेन अयोमयी बाणाग्रसूची कथ्यते। **इमे** हृदयाम्बुजे परिदृश्यमाने, **नेत्रे** नयने, **गोत्राधरपतिकुलोत्तंसकलिके!** गोत्रा भूमिः धरतीति धरः पचाद्यच्, गोत्रायाः धरो गोत्राधरः, अन्यथा गोत्रां धारयतीति विग्रहे कर्मण्यणि प्राप्तौ गोत्राधार इति स्यात्। अनेनैवाभिप्रायेण शक्तिधर इत्यत्र शक्तेः धरः शक्तिधरः इत्युक्तं क्षीरस्वामिना। गोत्राधरपतिः हिमवान् तस्य कुलोत्तंसकलिका कोरकः तस्याः सम्बुद्धिः। **तव** भवत्याः, **आकर्णाकृष्टस्मरशरविलासं** कर्णपर्यन्तमाकृष्टयोः स्मरशरयोः मन्मथबाणयोः विलासं सौभाग्यं **कलयतः** कुरुतः। लट्परस्मैपदद्विवचनान्तम्।।

अत्रेत्थं पदयोजना–हे गोत्राधरपतिकुलोत्तंसकलिके! तव इमे नेत्रे कर्णाभ्यर्णं गते पक्ष्माणि गरुत इव दधती पुरां भेत्तुः चित्तप्रशमरसविद्रावणफले आकर्णाकृष्टस्मरविलासं कलयतः।।

अयमर्थः–पञ्चबाणस्य स्त्रीणां कटाक्षः षष्ठो बाणः। पञ्चबाण इति प्रसिद्धिः प्राचुर्याभिप्रायेण। कटाक्षात्मकबाणो बाणपञ्चकतुल्य इति न षट्बाण इति व्यवहारः।।

अत्र निदर्शनालङ्कारः; स्मरशरविलाससदृशविलासकरणप्रतिभानात् प्रतिबिम्बाक्षेपात्।।५२।।

Notes : *Samara—i.e.,* Manmatha, the god of love. To him is ascribed the power of agitating the minds of his victims with his flower-arrows. The eyes of the Devī are here compared to Manmatha's arrows, her quarry being her Lord, Śiva. The poet significantly used the word *'Phala'*, with a pun on the word, as it means 'fruit' as well as 'an arrow-head'.

[1]बिभक्तत्रैवर्ण्यं [2]व्यतिकरितलीलाञ्जनतया[3]
विभाति त्वन्नेत्रत्रितयमिदमीशानदयिते।
पुनः स्त्रष्टुं देवान्द्रुहिणहरिरुद्रानुपरता-
न्रजः सत्त्वं बिभ्रत्तम इति[4] गुणानां त्रयमिव[5]।।५३।।

Vibhakta-trai-varṇyaṁ vyatikarita-līlāñjanatayā
vibhāti tvan-netra-tritayam idam īśāna-dayite/

---

1. त्रैवर्ण्यव्यतिकरित ; विविक्तत्रैवर्ण्यं।
2. व्यतिकलित।
3. नीलाम्बुजतया ; नीलाञ्जनतया ; नीलाम्बुजरुचा।
4. इव।
5. त्रयमिदम्।

Punaḥ sraṣṭuṁ devān druhiṇa-hari-rudrān uparatān
rajaḥ sattvaṁ bibhrat tama iti guṇānāṁ trayam iva.//

Translation : O Beloved of Īśāna! this triad of Thine eyes, displaying the three colours severally, smeared as it is with toilet-collyrium, shines out, as if possessing the triad of Guṇas—Rajas, Sattva and Tamas—so as to create once again the Devas—Druhiṇa, Hari and Rudra—when they cease to exist.

विभक्तत्रैवर्ण्यं विभक्तं परस्परासङ्कीर्णं त्रैवर्ण्यं त्रयो वर्णाः सितासितरक्ताः यस्येति बहुव्रीहिः, स्वार्थे ष्यञ्। महाभाग्यपुरुषाणां नयने रक्तरेखाः सन्ति, नयनगोलद्वयं श्वेतम्, यद्यपि कनीनिका नीला, तथापि तृतीयनयने कनीनिकायाः नैल्याभावात् इत्याह-**व्यतिकरितलीलाञ्जनतया** इति। व्यतिकरितं संवलितं लीलार्थं विलासार्थं धृतं अञ्जनं यस्य तत् तस्य भावस्तत्ता तया। तृतीयनयनगोलस्य श्वैत्यमङ्गीकृत्योक्तम्। **विभाति** विराजते। **त्वन्नेत्रत्रितयं** तव नेत्राणां त्रितयं, **इदं** परिदृश्यमानं, **ईशानदयिते** ईशानस्य महादेवस्य दयिता प्रेयसी तस्यास्सम्बुद्धिः, **पुनः स्रष्टुं** गतब्रह्माण्डानन्तरमस्मिन् ब्रह्माण्डे भूयो निर्मातुं, **देवान्** देवनधर्मयुक्तान्, [1]**द्रुहिणहरिरुद्रानुपरतान्** आत्मनि विलीनान्, **रजः** रजोगुणः, **सत्त्वं** सत्त्वगुणः, **बिभ्रत्** दधत्, **तमः** तमोगुणः, **इति** एवं **गुणानां** सत्त्वरजस्तमःसंज्ञिकानां, **त्रयं** त्रितयं, इव।।

अत्रेत्थं पदयोजना-हे ईशानदयिते! इदं त्वन्नेत्रत्रितयं व्यतिकरितलीलाञ्जनतया विभक्तत्रैवर्ण्यं उपरतान् द्रुहिणहरिरुद्रान् देवान् पुनः स्रष्टुं रजः सत्त्वं तम इति गुणानां त्रयमिव बिभ्रत् विभाति।।

अत्र सत्त्वगुण; श्वेतवर्णः रजोगुणो रक्तवर्णः तमोगुणो नीलवर्णः इति कविप्रसिद्धिः। तम इति निपातेनाप्यभिहिते कर्मणि न कर्मविभक्तिः; परिगणनस्य प्रायिकत्वादिति निपातेतिशब्देनाभिधानात् रजःसत्त्वतमःशब्दाः प्रथमान्ताः। यद्वा-द्वितीयान्ताः; निपाताभिधानस्य प्रायिकत्वात्। यथोक्तं वाग्भटेन-

हिंसा स्तेयान्यथाकामं पैशुन्यं पुरुषानृते।
संभिन्नालापव्यापादमभिध्यां दृग्विपर्ययम्।।
पापं कर्मेति दशधा कायवाङ्मनसैस्त्यजेत्। इति।

अत्र उत्प्रेक्षालङ्कारः, नयनगतस्य श्वेतरक्तनीलरेखात्रितयस्य सत्त्वरजस्तमोगुण-त्वेनोत्प्रेक्षणात्। अत्र भगवत्याः नयनाञ्जनदर्शनादेव सृष्टिस्थितिलया इति महानतिशतयो ध्वन्यत इत्यलङ्कारेण वस्तुध्वनिः।।५३।।

---

1. द्रुहिणहरिरुद्रान् ब्रह्मविष्णुमहेश्वरान् उपरतान्।

Notes : *The three colours*—red, white and dark, characteristic of the three Guṇas—Rajas, Sattva and Tamas respectively. *Create once again*—the allusion is to the tradition that the Trimūrti perish at the Great Deluge, when the universe has its involution, and are brought into existence once again after the Deluge, when the work of creation is undertaken by Śiva in conjunction with the Śakti.

पवित्रीकर्तुं नः पशुपतिपराधीनहृदये
[1]दयामित्रैर्नेत्रैररुणधवलश्यामरुचिभिः ।
नदः शोणो गङ्गा तपनतनयेति ध्रुवममुं
त्रयाणां तीर्थानामुपनयसि संभेदमनघम्[2] ।।५४।।

Pavitrī-kartuṁ naḥ paśu-pati-parādhīna-hṛdaye
dayā-mitrair netriar aruṇa-dhavala-śyāma-rucibhiḥ/
Nadaḥ śoṇo gaṅgā tapana-tanayeti dhruvam amuṁ
trayāṇāṁ tīrthānām upanayasi saṁbhedam an-agham//

Translation : O (Goddess) with a heart entirely devoted to Paśu-pati! Thou verily bringest about, with Thy merciful eyes, which are red, white and dark in colour, this hallowed (sin-washing) confluence of the three sacred streams of the rivers—Śoṇa, Gaṅgā and Tapana-tanayā (Yamunā), to sanctify us all.

एतदेव त्रैवर्ण्यं पुनरुत्प्रेक्ष्यते–**पवित्रीकर्तुं** अपवित्रान् पवित्रान् संपद्यमानान् कर्तुं 'अभूततद्भावे सम्पद्यकर्तरि च्विः'। **नः** अस्मान्, **पशुपतिपराधीनहृदये!** हरायत्तचित्ते! **दयामित्रैः** दयार्द्रैः, **नेत्रैः अरुणधवलश्यामरुचिभिः** प्रत्येकमिति शेषः। **नदः** [3]पुंप्रवाहः **शोणः** हिरण्यवाहः, स तु रक्तवर्णः, **गङ्गा** भागीरथी श्वेतवर्णा, **तपनतनया** कालिन्दी नीलवर्णा इति कविप्रसिद्धिः। **इति** एवं, **ध्रुवं** सत्यम्, **अमुं** परिदृश्यमानं, **त्रयाणां तीर्थानां** जलावताराणां, **संभेदं** नदीसङ्गमम्, **उपनयसि** संपादयसि। **अनघम्** अघापनोदकम्।।

अत्रेत्थं पदयोजना–हे पशुपतिपराधीनहृदये! दयामित्रैः अरुणधवलश्यामरुचिभिः नेत्रैः शोणो नदो गङ्गा तगनतनयेति त्रयाणां तीर्थानाम् अमुम् अनघं संभेदं नः पवित्रीकर्तुं उपनयसि ध्रुवम्। भक्तवत्सलत्वाद्देव्या इति भावः।।

अत्रोत्प्रेक्षालङ्कारः ; स्वभावसिद्धस्य नयनगतरेखात्रितयस्य सितासितरक्तवर्णात्मकस्य गङ्गायमुनाशोणसङ्गमत्वेनोत्प्रेक्षणात्।।५४।।

---

1. दयामिश्रैः।
2. संभेदमनघे।
3. पुण्यप्रवाहः।

Note : *Tapana-tanayā*—literally the daughter of the Sun, the Yamunā.

निमेषोन्मेषाभ्यां प्रलयमुदयं याति जगती[1]
तवेत्याहुः सन्तो धरणिधरराजन्यतनये।
त्वदुन्मेषाज्जातं जगदिदमशेषं प्रलयतः
परित्रातुं शङ्के परिहृतनिमेषास्तव दृशः।।५५।।

Nimeṣonmeṣābhyāṁ pralayam udayaṁ yāti jagatī
tavety āhuḥ santo dharaṇi-dhara-rājanya-tanaye/
Tvad-unmeṣāj jātaṁ jagad idam aśeṣaṁ pralayataḥ
paritrātuṁ śaṅke parihṛta-nimeṣās tava dṛśaḥ//

Translation : O Daughter of the King of the Mountains! the Sages say that the world has (its) dissolution and genesis with the closing and opening of Thine eyes. Methinks, Thine eyes are bereft of winking, with a view to save from dissolution this entire universe, which had its origin in the opening of Thine eyes.

निमेषो नाम पक्ष्मणां मुकुलीभावः, अत्र **उन्मेषो** नाम नयने पक्ष्मविकासः, ताभ्यां यथाक्रमं, **प्रलयं** संहारम् **उदयं** उद्भवं, **याति** प्राप्नोति। **जगती** जगत् **तव** भवत्याः, **इति** एवम्, **आहुः** ब्रुवते। 'ब्रुवः पञ्चानामादितः' इत्यादिना आहादेशः। **सन्तः** सत्पुरुषाः व्यासादयः। दृष्टिसृष्टिवादिमते ज्ञानव्यतिरेकेण ज्ञेयाभावात् निमेषोन्मेषाभ्यामित्युक्तेराञ्जस्यमिति ध्येयम्। **धरणिधरराजन्यतनये**! हिमाचलपुत्रिके! **त्वदुन्मेषात्** तव पक्ष्मस्पन्दात्, **जातं जगत्** भुवनम्, **इदं** परिदृश्यमानम् **अशेषं** कृत्स्नं, **प्रलयतः** महासंहारात्, **परित्रातुं** रक्षितुं, **शङ्के**[2]। **परिहृतनिमेषाः** तिरस्कृताक्षिस्पन्दाः, **तव दृशः** नयनानि।।

अत्रेत्थं पदयोजना–धरणिधरराजन्यतनये! तव निमेषोन्मेषाभ्यां जगती प्रलयमुदयं यातीति सन्तः आहुः। अतः त्वदुन्मेषात् जातं अशेषम् इदं जगत् प्रलयतः परित्रातुं तव दृशः परिहृतनिमेषाः इति शङ्के।।

अत्रोत्प्रेक्षालङ्कारः। देवतानामनिमेषत्वं स्वभावसिद्धम्; तच्च जगत्संरक्षणार्थमिति फलत्वेनोत्प्रेक्षणात् फलोत्प्रेक्षा। तत्र निमेषोन्मेषदशायां तौ जगदुत्पत्तिलयाविति देव्याः महिमा अवाङ्मनसगोचर इति वस्तु ध्वन्यते। अतः अलङ्कारेण वस्तुध्वनिः।।५५।।

1. जगति।
2. शङ्के मन्ये।

Notes : Here the Devī is represented to be ever wise awake, lest the universe should come to ruin, should she ever shut her eyes, thus demonstrating her concern, as the Divine Mother, for the welfare of her progeny, the world.

तवापर्णे कर्णेजपनयनपैशुन्यचकिता[1]
निलीयन्ते तोये नियतमनिमेषाः शफरिकाः।
इयं च श्रीर्बद्धच्छदपुटकवाटं[2] **कुवलयं**
जहाति प्रत्यूषे निशि च विघटय्य प्रविशति।।५६।।

Tavāparṇe karṇe-japa-nayana-paiśunya-cakitā
niliyante toye niyatam a-nimeṣāḥ śapharikāḥ/
Iyaṁ ca śrīr baddhac-chada-puṭa-kavāṭāṁ kuvalayaṁ
jahāti pratyūṣe niśi ca vighaṭayya praviśati//

Translation : O Aparṇā! the (glittering) Śapharikā fish ever hide themselves under water without winking, afraid of the tell-tale nature of Thine eyes, which are so close to Thine ears. The Goddess of Beauty, again, leaves the blue-lily at daybreak, when its doorlike petals close, and forces an entrance (into it) at nightfall.

तव भवत्याः, **अपर्णे!** पार्वति! **कर्णेजपनयनपैशुन्यचकिताः** कर्णेजपे कर्णसमीपं सदा गते नयने ताभ्यां यत्करिष्यमाणं पैशुन्यं पिशुनभावः, मर्मोद्घाटनं तस्माच्चकिताः, **निलीयन्ते** आकारगोपनेन स्थिताः इत्यर्थः। **तोये** उदके, **नियतं** निश्चयः, **अनिमेषाः** निमेषरहिताः **शफरिकाः** मीनयोषितः, **इयं च** परिदृश्यमाना नेत्रगता, श्रीः लक्ष्मीः, **बद्धच्छदपुटकवाटं** बद्धं संकलितं छदपुट एव कवाटं यस्य तत् कवाटसङ्घटितगृहमिव वर्तत इत्यर्थः। **कुवलयं** इन्दीवरं, **जहाति** त्यजति। **प्रत्यूषे** उषःकाले, **निशि च** रात्रौ च, **विघटय्य प्रविशति** संविशति।।

अत्रेत्थं पदयोजना–हे अपर्णे! तव कर्णेजपनयनपैशुन्यचकिताः शफरिकाः अनिमेषास्तोये निलीयन्ते नियतम्। किञ्च–इयं च श्रीः बद्धच्छदपुटकवाटं कुवलयं प्रत्यूषे जहाति निशि च तत् विघटय्य प्रविशति।।

अयमर्थः–लोके नेत्रसमं वस्तु शफरिका इन्दीवराणीति, एतद्द्वितयसमं नेत्रमिति च सुप्रसिद्धं उभयोः साम्यं, अत्र कविः–नेत्रसौभाग्यं शफरिकासु इन्दीवरेषु च वर्तते, तत्सौभाग्यमाहर्तुकामं नेत्रद्वयं तत्र पैशुन्यं करोतीममर्थम्वलम्ब्योत्प्रेक्षते।।

1. शून्यचकिता।
2. पुटकपाटं।

अत्र पूर्वार्धे उत्प्रेक्षालङ्कारः, शफरिकाणां जलाधिवासः, अनिमेषत्वं च स्वभावसिद्धम्, तदन्यथात्वेनोत्प्रेक्षणात्। द्वितीयार्धे अतिशयोक्तिः; नेत्रलक्ष्म्याः नेत्रं विहाय इन्दीवरेषु भक्त्यतिशयात् रात्रौ तद्रक्षणार्थं तदन्तर्भाववर्तित्वं, दिवा तद्विहाय नेत्रवर्तित्वं असंभवीति असंबन्धे संबन्धनिबन्धनात्। इन्दीवरस्य रात्रौ विकासः स्वभावसिद्धः, दिवा मुकुलीभावश्च। एतद्द्वयस्य लक्ष्मीकृतत्वासंबन्धेऽपि संबन्धकथनात् अतिशयोक्त्यन्तरम्। उभयोरनुसृष्टिः। अनुसृष्टिलक्षणं पूर्वमेवोक्तम्[1]। अत्र इन्दीवरस्य रात्रौ विकासः, नेत्रद्वयस्य दिवा विकासः। अतश्च दिवा लक्ष्मीः नेत्रे वसति, रात्रौ कुवलये। एवं लक्ष्मीः नक्तंदिवमुभयत्रैव चरति नान्यत्रेति। शफरीप्रभृतीनां लोके नेत्रोपमानवस्तूनां भगवतीनेत्रतुल्यता नास्तीति शफरिकाणामुदकमध्यविलीनत्वमेव युक्तमिति काव्यलिङ्गध्वनिरित्यलङ्कारध्वनिः।। ५६।।

Notes : The Devī's eyes resemble both the Śapharikā fish and the blue-lily. The poet weaves out of his imagination the situation so cleverly portrayed in this stanza. The aquatic asylum sought by the fish, which are ever awake, is said to be due to their fear, lest their rivals, the Devī's eyes, which are so close to her ears, should carry and tales against them. Similarly, the lilies lose their beauty at daybreak, when their petals close, and bloom with the fullness of their beauty of nightfall, when the Devī's eyes, being closed in sleep, would not outshine the beauty of the lilies.

दृशा द्राघीयस्या दरदलितनीलोत्पलरुचा[2]
दवीयांसं दीनं स्नपय कृपया मामपि शिवे।
अनेनायं[3] धन्यो भवति न च ते हानिरियता
वने वा हर्म्ये वा समकरनिपातो हिमकरः।। ५७।।

Dṛśā drāghīyasyā dara-dalita-nīlotpala-rucā
davīyāṁsaṁ dīnaṁ snapaya kṛpayā mām api śive/
Anenāyaṁ dhanyo bhavati na ca te hānir iyatā
vane vā harmye vā sama-kara-nipāto himakaraḥ//

Translation : O Spouse of Śiva! may Thou graciously bathe even me, who stands helpless at a far off distance, with Thy far-reaching glance, beautiful like the slightly blossomed blue-

---

1. ४७ श्लोकव्याख्यायाम्।
2. दरदलितनीलाम्बुजरुचा।
3. अनेनाहं।

lily. This (mortal) will derived the *summum bonum* of existence from such (action). By such action, no loss is after all sustained by Thee. The snow-beamed (Moon) sheds the selfsame lusture on a forest as well as a mansion.

दृशा कटाक्षदृष्ट्या, **द्राघीयस्या** दीर्घतरया, **दरदलितनीलोत्पलरुचा** दरदलितमीषद्विकसितं नीलोत्पलं इन्दीवरं तस्येव रुचिः कान्तिर्यस्याः तया, **दवीयांसं** दूरवर्तिनम्। दूरशब्दस्य **'स्थूलदूर'** इत्यादिना सूत्रेण यणो लोपः, पूर्ववर्णस्य गुणे कृते अवादेशे कृते सिद्धं रूपं दवीयानिति ईयसुन्प्रत्ययान्तम्। **दीनं** दरिद्रं, **स्नपय** स्नपनं कुरु। **कृपया** दयया, **मामपि** इतरजनसाधारण्यमपि शब्दार्थः। **शिवे!** मङ्गलात्मिके! **अनेन** एतावन्मात्रेण स्नपनेनापि, **अयं** जनः अहमित्यर्थः। **धन्यो** भवति कृतार्थो भवति। **न च ते** तव, **हानिः** द्रव्यनाशः **इयता** साधारणदर्शनमात्रेण, **वने वा** अरण्ये वा, **हर्म्ये प्रासादे वा, समकरनिपातः** समं तुल्यं यथा भवति तथा कराणां किरणानां निपातः व्यापनं यस्य स तथोक्तः। **हिमकरः** शीतरश्मिः।।

अत्रेत्थं पदयोजना–हे शिवे! द्राघीयस्या दरदलितनीलोत्पलरुचा दृशा दवीयांसं दीनं कृपया मामपि स्नपय अयम् अनेन धन्यो भवति। इयता ते हानिर्न च। तथा हि–हिमकरः वने वा हर्म्ये वा समकरनिपातो हि। स्वच्छान्तःकरणानां सर्वसाधारण्यं स्वभावसिद्धमिति भावः।।

अर्थान्तरन्यासोऽलङ्कारः; सामान्येन विशेषसमर्थनात्। सर्वसाधारण्यदर्शनं सर्वोत्कृष्टत्वे हेतुरिति नात्मीयतादर्शनापेक्षा अस्तीति ध्वनिः।।५७।।

Notes : The *Arthāntaranyāsa* in the last line may be noted. The votary appeals to the Devī to extend her glances, which are capable of being extended to an unlimited distance, to him also, as he stands separated by a very long distance from her holy presence.

अरालं ते पालीयुगलमगराजन्यतनये
न केषामाधत्ते[1] कुसुमशरकोदण्डकुतुकम्।
तिरश्चीनो यत्र श्रवणपथमुल्लङ्घ्य विलसन्-
अपाङ्गव्यासङ्गो दिशति शरसंधानधिषणाम्।।५८।।

Arālaṁ te pālī-yugalam aga-rājanya-tanaye
na keṣām ādhatte kusuma-śara-kodaṇḍa-kutukam/
Tiraścīno yatra śravaṇa-pathamullaṅghya vilasann-
apāṅga-vyāsaṅgo diśati śara-saṁdhāna-dhiṣaṇām//

1. केसामादत्ते।

Translation : O Daughter of the King of the Mountains! to whom would the arched pair of ridges (between Thine eyes and ears) not convey the grace of the bow of the flower-arrowed (god of love)? For, Thy long side-glance, directed across which (ridges) and reaching the vicinity of Thine ear, creates the impression of the mounting of an arrow (on the bow-string).

अरालं कुटिलं, **ते पालीयुगलं** कर्णयुगलनयनयुगलयोर्मध्यं, **अगराजन्यतनये!** नगेन्द्रतनये! **न केषामाधत्ते** सर्वेषां करोत्येव। **कुसुमशरकोदण्डकुतुकं** मन्मथचापसौभाग्यं, **तिरश्चीनः** तिर्यक्प्रसारितः, **यत्र** पालीयुगले, **श्रवणपथमुल्लङ्घ्य** कर्णान्तिकं प्राप्य, **विलसन्** स्फुरन्, **अपाङ्गव्यासङ्गः** अपाङ्गस्य कटाक्षस्य व्यासङ्गः दैर्घ्यं, **दिशति** करोति; **शरसन्धानधिषणां** शरसन्धानस्य बाणसंयोजनस्य धिषणां बुद्धिं तद्भ्रान्तिं संहितशरधिषणामिति यावत्।।

अत्रेत्थं पदयोजना–हे अगराजन्यतनये! ते पालीयुगलमरालं कुसुमशरकोदण्डकुतुकं केषां नाधत्ते। यद्यस्मात् यत्र तिरश्चीनः विलसन् अपाङ्गव्यासङ्गः श्रवणपथमुल्लङ्घ्य शरसन्धानधिषणां दिशति।।

अत्र भ्रान्तिमदलङ्कारः ; अपाङ्गे संहितशरभ्रान्तेरुत्थानात्। पालीयुगले कुसुमशर-कोदण्डबुद्धिः निश्चयात्मिका संशयपूर्विकेति सन्देहालङ्कार एव। अनयोरङ्गाङ्गिभावेन सङ्करः।। ५८।।

Notes : The negative interrogative of the first half of the stanza presupposes and affirmative reply. In the second half and oblique glance of the Devī is portrayed as the mounting of an arrow on the bow-string, the eye being compared to an arrow.

स्फुरद्गण्डाभोगप्रतिफलितताटङ्कयुगलं
चतुश्चक्रं मन्ये तव मुखमिदं मन्मथरथम्।[1]
यमारुह्य[2] **दुह्यत्यवनिरथमर्केन्दुचरणं**
महावीरो मारः प्रमथपतये सज्जितवते[3] **।। ५९।।**

Sphurad-gaṇḍābhoga-pratiphalita-tāṭaṅka-yugalaṁ
catuś-cakraṁ manye tava mukham idaṁ manmatha-ratham/
Yam āruhya druhyaty avani-ratham arkendu caraṇaṁ
mahā-vīro māraḥ pramatha-pataye sajjitavate//

1. मान्मथरथं। 2. यमाश्रित्य।
3. प्रमथपतये स्वं जितवते ; प्रमथपतयेऽश्वं जितवते।

Translation : This face of Thine, with the pair of Tāṭaṅkas (ear-ornaments) reflected on Thy glistening cheeks, I fancy to be the four-wheeled chariot of Manmatha, mounted on which, Māra, the valiant warrior that he is, confronts the Lord of the Pramatha (hosts) who (once) got ready (for battle, mounted on) the Earth-chariot with the Sun and the Moon as its two wheels.

स्फुरद्गण्डाभोगप्रतिफलितताटङ्कयुगलं स्फुरन्तौ च तौ गण्डाभोगौ च गण्डस्थले दर्पणवन्निर्मलावित्यर्थः। तत्र प्रतिफलितं ताटङ्कयुगलं यस्य सः तं **चतुश्चक्रं** चत्वारि चक्राणि रथचरणानि यस्य तं चतुश्चक्रं, **मन्ये** शङ्के। **तव** भवत्या, **मुखं** आस्यम्, इदं हृदयकमले परिदृश्यमानं, **मन्मथरथं** मदनस्य स्यन्दनं, **यं** रथम्, **आरुह्य** अधिष्ठाय, **दुह्यति** अपराध्यति विध्यतीति यावत्। **अवनिरथं**, भूमिरथं **अर्केन्दुचरणं** अर्केन्दू सूर्यचन्द्रौ तावेव चरणौ यस्य सः, **महावीरः** चतुश्चक्ररथारोहणमहिम्ना अप्रतिहतप्रतापः, **मारः** मन्मथः, **प्रमथपतये** त्रिपुरान्तकाय, **सज्जितवते** सज्जं कुर्वते सन्नद्धं कुर्वत इत्यर्थः।

अत्रेत्थं पदयोजना–हे भगवति ! तव इदं मुखं स्फुरद्गण्डाभोगप्रतिफलितताटङ्कयुगलं चतुश्चक्रं मन्मथरथं मन्ये। यमारुह्य मारः महावीरः सन् अवनिरथमर्केन्दुचरणं सज्जितवते प्रमथपतये द्रुह्यति। 'क्रुधद्रुहेर्ष्यासूयार्थानां यं प्रति कोपः' इति चतुर्थी।।

अत्र पूर्वार्धे उत्प्रेक्षालङ्कारः; भगवत्याः मुखस्य रथत्वेनोत्प्रेक्षणात्। द्वितीयार्धे आरोहणस्य महावीरत्वसम्पादकत्वकथनात् पदार्थहेतुकं काव्यलिङ्गमलङ्कारः। परमेश्वरस्य मन्मथेन सार्धं युद्धसन्नाहासंबन्धेऽपि संबन्धकथनादतिशयोक्तिः। काव्यलिङ्गातिशयोक्त्योरङ्गाङ्गिभावेन सङ्करः। उत्प्रेक्षायास्तु काव्यलिङ्गं प्रत्यनुप्राणकतैव, न संसृष्टिः, नापि सङ्करः इति ध्येयम्। पृथक्स्थित्या उपकारकमनुप्राणकम्। अपृथक्स्थित्या प्रयोजकम् उपसर्जनम्। पृथक्स्थित्या प्रयोजकमङ्गम्। एतद्विलक्षणं संसृष्टिरित्यालङ्कारिकमतरहस्यम्। एतच्च पूर्वमुक्तमपि स्पष्टार्थं पुनः प्रतिपादितमिति।।५९।।

Notes : The comparison of the Devī's face to a four-wheeled chariot is realistic, the face being the body of the chariot, and the two Tāṭaṅkas, ear-rings, suspended from the ear-lobes, and their reflected images cast on her cheeks forming the four chariot-wheels. The implication is that Manmatha, taking advantage of the beauty of the Devī's face, used it as his chariot and not only challenged the

1. तावेव।

redoubtable field-marshal of the Pramatha-gaṇas, who using the Earth itself as his chariot, mounted on Sun and the Moon as its wheels, once confronted the three Puras, but also vanquished him with the adventitious aid of the Devī's beauty. Kaivalyāśrama suggests that 'Āśriya' would be a better reading for 'Āruhya', remarking that it would be highly improper to conceive of Manmatha mounting on the Devī's countenance.

सरस्वत्याः सूक्तीरमृतलहरीकौशलहरीः
पिबन्त्याः शर्वाणि [1]श्रवणचुलुकाभ्यामविरलम्[2]।
चमत्कारश्लाघाचलितशिरसः कुण्डलगणो
[3]झणत्कारैस्तारैः प्रतिवचनमाचष्ट इव ते।।६०।।

Sarasvatyāḥ sūktīr amṛta-laharī-kauśala-harīḥ
pibantyāḥ śarvāṇi śravaṇa-culukābhyām aviralam/
Camatkāra-ślāghā-caita-śirasaḥ kuṇḍala-gaṇo
jhaṇat-kārais tāraiḥ prati-vacanam ācaṣṭa iva te//

Translation : O Consort of Śarva! while Thou hast been continuously drinking in, with the hollow of Thine outstretched ears, the sweet words of the goddess Sarasvatī, which keep far in the background the flood of nectar, and been shaking Thy head by way of appreciating the merit (of the composition), Thy various ear-ornaments echo in unison, as it were, with loud chimes.

सरस्वत्याः भारत्याः, **सूक्तीः** मधुरवचांसि, **अमृतलहरीकौशलहरीः**, अमृतलहर्याः सुधाप्रवाहोत्सेकस्य कौशलं सौभाग्यं हरन्तीति ताः। हरिशब्दः औणादिको निप्रत्ययान्तः, 'कृदिकारादक्तिनो वा ङीष् वक्तव्यः' इति ङीष्। **पिबन्त्याः** धयन्त्याः, **शर्वाणि!** शर्वस्य परमेश्वरस्य पत्नि! **श्रवणचुलुकाभ्यां** चुलुकं प्रसृत्यर्धं श्रवणे श्रोत्रे चुलुके ताभ्यां **अविरलं** यथा भवति तथा, सावधानेनेत्यर्थः। **चमत्कारश्लाघा-चलितशिरसः** चमदित्यव्ययमाश्चर्यानुकरणवाचि। कारशब्दः स्वरूपपरः। यद्वा–सुख-दुःखोद्भूतानन्दैः हठोत्थितचित्तविक्रिया चमत्करः ससीत्कारशरीरोल्लासनादिकृत्। चमत्कारश्लाघासु आश्चर्यानुकरणसन्दोहेषु चलितं शिरो यस्यास्तस्याः, **कुण्डलगणः**

1. श्रवणचषकाभ्यां।
2. मविरतम्।
3. रणत्कारैस्तारैः।

कर्णाभरणसमूहः, **झणत्कारैः** झणदित्यव्ययं भूषणरवानुकरणे। कारशब्दः स्वरूपवाची। झणत्कारैः **तारैः** अतिबहुलैः उच्चतरैः, **प्रतिवचनं** प्रतिशब्दम् अनुमोदवचनम्, **आचष्ट इव ते**।।

अत्रेत्थं पदयोजना–हे शर्वाणि! ते अमृतलहरीकौशलहरीः सूक्तीः श्रवणचुलुका-भ्यामविरलं पिबन्त्याः चमत्कारश्लाघाचलितशिरसः सरस्वत्याः कुण्डलगणः तारैः झणत्कारैः प्रतिवचनमाचष्ट इव।।

अत्र उत्तरार्धे उत्प्रेक्षालङ्कारः; झणत्काराणां प्रतिवचनत्वेन संभावनात्। पूर्वार्धे अतिशयोक्तिरलङ्कारः; सरस्वत्याः शिरःकम्पनसंबन्धाभावेऽपि संबन्धोक्तेरसंबन्धे-संबन्धनिबन्धनात्। उभयोरङ्गाङ्गिभावेन सङ्करः।। ६०।।

Notes : The sweet words of the goddess Sarasvatī—in praise of the Devī. The implication is that the goddess of learning, in her attempt to please her patron and win her approbation, had produced such an exquisitely beautiful composition, wherein she had risen to the exalted heights of the art of Poesy, her own field, as to have wrung from the Devī an appreciation indicated by the involuntary shaking of her head ; not merely that, but also the Devī's ear-ornaments, inanimate though they were, chimed in unison with their mistress's thoughts, as if touched by the description of their mistress's greatness.

Lakṣmīdhara construes the stanza in a different manner altogether, taking the sweet words as coming from the mouth of the Devī herself, on hearing which Sarasvatī, the goddess of learning, is so much over-powered by their grace, as to express her approbation by shaking her head, when her ear-ornaments also chime in unison. Lakṣmīdhara takes the last word 'Te' in the stanza as applying to 'Sūktīḥ', ignoring the proximity of the word, 'Sarasvatyāḥ', which immediately precedes it. While, therefore, the natural arrangement of the words in the stanza support our rendering given above, it must be admitted, in Lakṣmīdhara's defence, that the very design of the author in describing the Devī from head to foot, in the latter part of the poem lends support to Lakṣmīdhara's interpretation, as this stanza is ostensibly in praise of the 'Vāg-jharī', sweet flow of words of the Devī, and does not pertain to the proficiency of Sarasvatī in her art, as it is not germane to the topic of this part of the poem. Adopting the same line of argument, it may be noted that the position, assumed by the other commentators and followed by us in our rendering, is strengthened, as the description by the poet of the Devī's shaking of her head in appreciation of Sarasvatī's Vāg-jharī comes within the design adopted by the author in the latter part of the poem, such description being only of the Devī's face.

असौ नासावंशस्तुहिनगिरिवंशध्वजपटि
त्वदीयो नेदीयः[1] फलतु फलमस्माकमुचितम्।
[2]बहन्नन्तर्मुक्ताः [3]शिशिरतरनिश्वासघटिताः
समृद्ध्या [4]यस्तासां बहिरपि च मुक्तामणिधरः।।६१।।

Asau nāsā-vaṁśas tuhina-giri-vaṁśa-dhvaja-paṭī
tvadīyo nedīyaḥ phalatu phalam asmākamucitam/
Vahann antar muktāḥ śiśira-tara-niśvāsa-ghaṭitāḥ
samṛddhyā yas tāsāṁ bahir api ca muktā-maṇi-dharaḥ//

Translation : O Flag of the staff (dynasty) of the snow capped Mountain! may this, the bamboo of Thy nose, immediately bear us the cherished fruit. Bearing in its (hollow) interior pearls, kept in their places by Thy very cool breath, it wears a pearl outside also, there being an abundance of them (pearls therein).

असौ परिदृश्यमानः, **नासावंशः** नासा नासिका वंशः वंशदण्डः रूपकमेतत्। **तुहिनगिरिवंशध्वजपटि** तुहिनगिरेः हिमाचलस्य वंशस्य अन्वयस्य ध्वजपटि पताके! **त्वदीयः** भवदीयः, **नेदीयः** सन्निकृष्टतरं, **फलतु** निष्पादयतु। **फलम्** इष्टार्थं, **अस्माकं** मत्संबन्धिनां मम चेत्यर्थः। **उचितं** क्रियाविशेषणमेतत् यथेप्सितं **वहति** धारयति। **अन्तः** अभ्यन्तरे, **मुक्ताः** मुक्तामणीन् **शिशिरकणनिश्वासगलितं** शिशिरकरः चन्द्रः तस्य निश्वासो वामनाडीमार्गवायुः तेन गलितं सृतं, **समृद्ध्या** आधिक्येन, **यत्** यस्मात्कारणात्, **तासां** मुक्तानां, **बहिरपि च** बाह्यप्रदेशेऽपि नासिकाग्रवाम-भागेऽपीत्यर्थः। नासिकाकारितो वंशदण्डः **मुक्तामणिधरः** मुक्तामणिं धृतवान्। 'मुक्तामणिमधात्' इति सम्यक्पाठः।।

अत्रेत्थं पदयोजना–हे तुहिनगिरिवंशध्वजपटि! त्वदीयोऽसौ नासावंशः अस्माकं

1. नेदीयान्।
2. वहत्यन्तर्मुक्ताः।
3. शिशिरतरनिश्वासविदिताः; शिशिरकरनिश्वासगलितं; शिशिरतरनिश्वासजनिता; निश्वास गलिताः।
4. यत्तासां।

उचितं नेदीयः फलं फलतु। सः अन्तः मुक्ताः वहति। यद्यस्मात्कारणात् तासां समृद्ध्या शिशिरकरनिश्वासलगलितं बहिरपि च मुक्तामणिधरः।।

अत्र नासिकायाः वंशत्वारोपणात् रूपकम्। वंशत्वसाधकप्रतिपादकम् उत्तरार्धम्। वंशगर्भे मौक्तिकानि उद्भवन्तीति लोकशास्त्रमर्यादा। अतो नासावंशदण्डेऽपि अभ्यन्तरे मौक्तिकान्युद्भूतानि वर्तन्ते। नो चेन्नासादण्डस्य बहिः मुक्तामणिधरत्वं कथं सङ्घटत इत्यर्थापत्त्या वंशदण्डाकारो नासिकायाः समर्थित इति रूपकमेव सम्यक्।। ६१ ।।

Notes : Flag—Here is a clever metaphorical reference made by the poet to the devī, the daughter of Himavat, she being represented by implication as the flag conspicuously floating at the top of the dynasty of Himavat which is represented to be the bamboo-staff on which flag floats.

Staff—note the pun on the original word *'Vaṁśa'*, which means 'bamboo', as well as 'dynasty'. Here the Devī's nose is compared to the bamboo, which encloses a hollow within and which, according to the tradition obtaining among Saṁskṛt writers, is described as producing pearls. The cherished fruit—ostensibly the pearl of the bamboo, but really the *Kaivalya* sought from the Devī. The fact that the Devī's nose wears as an ornament a pearl outside, is taken advantage of by the poet, who represents it as one of the pearls in the hollow of the bamboo-like nose, cast by the exhaling breath of the Devī and forming an index, as it were, to the pearls inside. Lakṣmīdhara adopts the following reading : *"Vahaty antar muktāḥ śiśira-kara-niśvāsa-galitaṁ, samṛddhyā yat tāsāṁ bahir api ca muktā-maṇi-dharaḥ"*, and takes *'Śiśirakara'*, which means 'the Moon', as indicating the breath passing through the left (Iḍā) Nāḍī, wherein, according to Yoga-śāstra, the Moon functions. Then he construes the compound word *'Muktā-maṇi-dharaḥ'* as *'Muktā-maniṁ dhṛtavān'*, and not satisfied with this, suggests as a better reading, *'Muktā-maṇim adhāt'*. In that case the latter half would mean : "it bears pearls in its (hollow) interior and hence wears a pearl outside also, cast as it were by the lunar (left nostril) breath, there being an abundance of them (pearls therein)." Herein is reference to the South Indian custom of boring a hole through the left side of the nose of women, so as to attach an ornament with a pearl pendant.

प्रकृत्याऽऽरक्तायास्तव[1] सुदति दन्तच्छदरुचेः
[2]प्रवक्ष्ये सादृश्यं जनयतु फलं विद्रुमलता।

---

1. प्रकृत्या रक्तायास्तव। 2. परोक्षे।

[1]न बिम्बं [2]त्वद्बिम्बप्रतिफलनरागादरुणितं[3]
तुलामध्यारोढुं कथमिव न लज्जेत[4] कलया।।६२।।

Prakṛtyā" raktāyās tava sudati dantac-chada-ruceḥ
pravakṣye sādṛśyaṁ janayatu phalaṁ vidrumalatā/
Na bimbaṁ tvad-bimba-pratiphalana-rāgad aruṇitaṁ
tulām adhyāroḍhuṁ katham iva na lajjeta kalayā//

Translation : O (Goddess) with beautiful (rows of) teeth! I shall presently name what equal the lustre of Thy natrually red lips. Let the coral-creeper bear fruit. It is not the Bimba fruit. Having turned red because of the redness caused by the reflection of Thy form, how will it not feel ashamed to be weighed in the balance, even to the slightest extent?

प्रकृत्या स्वभावेन, **आरक्तायाः** आताम्रायाः, **तव सुदति** शोभनाः दन्ताः यस्याः तस्याः सम्बुद्धिः। **दन्तच्छदरुचेः** दन्तच्छदयोरोष्ठयोः रुचेः सौभाग्यस्य, **प्रवक्ष्ये** प्रकर्षेण कथये। **सादृश्यं** सदृशस्य भावः सादृश्यं, **जनयतु** उत्पादयतु। आशंसायां लोट्। विद्रुमस्य फलं यदि स्यात् तदा सदृशवस्तुसद्भावः न तु विद्रुममात्रं सदृशमिति। **फलं** पक्वफलं, पीतवर्णाभ्यो लताभ्यः उत्पन्नं फलं अतिरिक्तं, रक्तलतोत्पन्नस्य रक्तिमा किमु वक्तव्य इति तदेव सदृशमिति तात्पर्यम्। **विद्रुमलता** प्रवाललतिका। **न बिम्बं** बिम्बफलं **तद्बिम्बप्रतिफलनरागात्** तयोः दन्तच्छदयोः विम्बस्य प्रतिफलनं प्रतिबिम्बनं तेन रागः रक्तिमा तस्मात्। बिम्बफलमिति व्यवहारः अधरबिम्बप्रतिबिम्बप्रसादासादितः, अन्यथा तस्य बिम्बव्यवहारो न स्यात्। यथा स्फटिकादौ जपाकुसुमादेः प्रतिबिम्बवशादेव स्फटिकादीनां रक्तता एवं बिम्बफलस्यापीति। तद्बिम्बप्रतिफलनरागात्, **अरुणितं तुलामध्यारोढुं** तुलायां साम्यकथायां स्थातुं **कथमिव**। इवेति वाक्यालङ्कारे। **विलज्जेत** व्रीडेत, **कलया** लेशेन।।

अत्रेत्थं पदयोजना–हे सुदति! तव प्रकृत्या आरक्तायाः दन्तच्छदरुचेः सादृश्यं प्रवक्ष्ये। विद्रुमलता फलं जनयतु। बिम्बं पुनः तद्बिम्बप्रतिफलनरागादरुणितं कलयापि तुलामध्यारोढुं कथमिव न विलज्जेत। लज्जधातुरात्मनेपदी।।

अत्रातिशयोक्तिरलङ्कारः, यद्यर्थोक्तौ कल्पनात्। द्वितीयार्धे असम्बन्धे संबन्ध-

1. क्व बिम्बं।
2. तद्बिम्ब ; दृग्बिम्बः ; क्व बिम्ब।
3. भावदरुणितं ; लाभादरुणितं।
4. विलज्जेत।

निबन्धनातिशयोक्तिः, बिम्बप्रतिफलनासंबन्धेऽपि संबन्धकथनेनाभेदकथनात्। उभयोः संसृष्टिः।। ६२।।

Notes : Having described the nose of the Devī, the poet next proceeds to describe her lips, but finds himself baffled in calling to mind any object in nature, which, like the Devī's body, from head to foot, is of a naturally red colour and, at the same time, has a part redder still, corresponding to her lips. In the first flush, he lands on the coral creeper, which is of a similar hue, root and branch, and as he could not conceive of any part of it comparable to the Devī's lips, he fancies that, possibly, when the creeper bears fruit, the latter might be redder still and on that account resemble the Devī's lips. But as he has not heard of or seen the coral fruit, he pauses and is forced to say, 'let the coral-creeper bear fruit'. Then he lights on the Bimba fruit, as an alternative, but has to reject that also, for the reasons stated in the stanza. The reading *'Dṛg-bimba-pratiphalana'* means, "caused by the reflection of the Sun (one of the Devī's eyes) thereon", the underlying idea being apparently that the Bimba fruit has its colour turned to red, only as it ripens under the influence of the Sun's rays; while the reading *'Tad-bimba, etc.,'* means "caused by the reflection of the lips themselves', the word 'Tad' indicating 'Dantacchada', *i.e.*, lips. How will it not feel ashamed. *etc.*?—as the Bimba fruit does not make the slightest approach in point of colour to the Devī's lips, it is bound to feel ashamed at the very suggestion that it should stand such a comparison.

स्मितज्योत्स्नाजालं तव वदनचन्द्रस्य पिबतां
चकोराणामासीदतिरसतया चञ्चुजडिमा।
अतस्ते शीतांशोरमृतलहरीमाम्लरुचयः[1]
पिबन्ति स्वच्छन्दं निशि निशि भृशं काञ्जिकधिया।। ६३।।

Smita-jyotsnā-jālaṁ tava vadana-candrasya pibatāṁ
Cakorāṇām āsīd ati-rasatayā cañcu-jaḍimā/
Atas te śītāṁśor amṛta-laharīm āmla-rucayaḥ
pibanti svac-chandaṁ niśi niśi bhṛśaṁ kāñjikadhiyā//

Translation : There was satiety in the beaks (reached), owing to excessive sweetness, by the Cakora birds drinking the moonlight-like smile on Thy moon-like face. Hence, eager to

1. मम्लरुचयः ; भग्नरुचयः।

taste something sour, they freely drink, every night, ardently, the nectar flowing from the Moon, in the belief that it is gruel.

स्मितज्योत्स्नाजालं स्मितमीषद्धसितमेव ज्योत्स्ना तस्याः जालं वितानं, **तव वदनचन्द्रस्य** वदनमेव चन्द्रः तस्य **पिबतां** आस्वादयतां, **चकोराणां** पक्षिविशेषाणां **आसीत् अतिरसतया** अतिमाधुर्यात्, **चञ्चुजडिमा** जिह्वाजाड्यम्। **अतः** कारणात्, **ते** चकोराः, **शीतांशोः** चन्द्रस्य, **अमृतलहरीम्** अमृतस्य सुधायाः उत्सेकं ज्योत्स्नामृत-मित्यर्थः। **आम्लरुचयः** आम्ले अम्लरसे रुचिर्वाञ्छा येषां ते आम्लरुचयः, **पिबन्ति** भक्षयन्ति। **स्वच्छन्दं** यथेच्छं, **निशिनिशि** प्रतिनिशं ज्योत्स्नास्विति शेषः। **भृशं** अत्यर्थं, **काञ्जिकधिया** आरनालभ्रान्त्या।।

अत्रेत्थं पदयोजना–हे भगवति! तव वदनचन्द्रन्य स्मितज्योत्स्नाजालं पिबतां चकोराणां अतिरसतया चञ्चुजडिमा आसीत्, अतस्ते आम्लरुचयः शीतांशोरमृतलहरीं काञ्जिकधिया स्वच्छन्दं निशिनिशि भृशं पिबन्ति।।

अत्र अतिशयोक्तिरलङ्कारः चञ्चुजडिमनिबन्धनज्योत्स्नापानासम्बन्धेऽपि तत्सम्बन्धकथनात् अतिमधुरस्तन्यपानप्रसक्ताजिह्वाजाड्यनिबन्धनाम्लपिपासुभिः बालकैरभेदाध्यवसानस्य प्रतीतेः।। ६३।।

Notes : Something sour—by way of a change. Gruel—which resembles nectar in appearance.

अविश्रान्तं पत्युर्गुणगणकथाऽऽम्रेडनजपा[1]
[2]जपापुष्पच्छाया तव जननि जिह्वा जयति सा।
यदग्रासीनायाः स्फटिकदृषदच्छच्छविमयी[3]
सरस्वत्या मूर्तिः परिणमति माणिक्यवपुषा।। ६४।।

A-viśrāntaṁ patyur guṇa-gaṇa-kathā-" mreḍanajapā
japā-puṣpac-chāyā tava janani jihvā jayati sā/
Yad-agrāsīnāyāḥ sphaṭika-dṛṣad-acchac-chavimayī
sarasvatyā mūrtiḥ pariṇamati māṇikya-vapuṣā//

Translation : O Mother! glory to that tongue of Thine, which is of the colour of the Japā flower, and which unceasingly mutters players, reiterating the glorious achievements of Thy

---

1. म्रेडनजडा ; म्रेडनपरा।
2. जवापुष्पच्छाया।
3. च्छविरुचिः।

Lord, while the crystal-like, bright-white body of Sarasvatī seated at the tip (of Thy tongue) gets transformed into a ruby.

अविश्रान्तम् अनारतं, **पत्युः** सदाशिवस्य **गुणगणकथाम्रेडनजपा** गुणानां त्रिपुरविजयादीनां गणः समूहः तस्य कथा वृतान्तः तस्य आम्रेडनं द्विस्त्रिरुक्तिः तदेव जपो यस्यास्सा अनन्यमनस्केत्यर्थः। **जपापुष्पच्छाया** जपापुष्पं रक्तपुष्पीपुष्पं तस्य छायेव छाया कान्तिः यस्याः सा। **तव जननि!** हे मातः! **जिह्वा** रसना, **जयति** स्फुरति। **सा** तच्छब्दो वर्तिष्यमाणां प्रसिद्धिं परामृशति। **यदग्रासीनायाः** यस्या जिह्वायाः अग्रे आसीनायाः निषण्णायाः **स्फटिकदृषदच्छच्छविमयी** स्फटिकदृषदः स्फटिकोपलस्येव अच्छा छविः कान्तिः तया प्रचुरा। प्राचुर्यार्थे मयट्। स्फटिकधवलेत्यर्थः। **सरस्वत्याः** भारत्याः **मूर्तिः** स्वरूपं, **परिणमति** विकारमापद्यते, रूपान्तरं प्राप्नोतीति यावत्। **माणिक्यवपुषा** पद्मरागवपुषा।

अत्रेत्थं पदयोजना–हे जननि! तव सा जिह्वा अविश्रान्तं पत्युः गुणगणकथाम्रेडनजपा जपापुष्पच्छाया जयति, यद्ग्रासीनायाः सरस्वत्याः स्फटिकदृषदच्छच्छविमयी मूर्तिः माणिक्यवपुषा परिणमति। जिह्वायां रक्तत्वमात्रं न भवति। तटस्थानां रक्तीकरणे रक्तिम्नः शक्तिरपि। अत एव जयतीति प्रयुक्तम्।।

तद्गुणालङ्कारः 'तद्गुणः स्वगुणत्यागादन्योत्कृष्टगुणाहृतिः' इति लक्षणात्। देव्याः वदनाम्बुजे सर्वदा सरस्वती स्वमूर्त्या वसतीत्यागमरहस्यम्।। ६४।।

Notes : Ruby—as a result of the piece of crystal being set off against a red background.

रणे जित्वा [1]दैत्यानपहृतशिरस्त्रैः कवचिभि-
र्निवृत्तैश्चण्डांशत्रिपुरहरनिर्माल्यविमुखैः ।
[3]विशाखेन्द्रोपेन्द्रैः [4]शशिविशदकर्पूरशकला[5]
[6]विलीयन्ते मातस्तव वदनताम्बूलकबलाः[7]।। ६५।।

---

1. दैत्यानुपहृत ; न्परिहृत।
2. निवृत्तैश्चण्डीशत्रिपुर ; चण्डांशु ; चंन्द्रांशु।
3. विरिञ्चीन्द्रो।
4. शशिशिशिरकर्पूर।
5. शबला ; धवला।
6. विलुप्यन्ते ; विलिप्यन्ते।
7. वदनताम्बूलशकलाः ; कणिकाः।

Raṇe jitvā daityān apahṛta-śiras-traiḥ kavacibhir
nivṛttaiś caṇḍāṁśa-tri-pura-hara-nirmālya-vimukhaiḥ/
Viśākhendropendraiḥ śaśi-viśada-karpūra-śakalā
vilīyante mātas tava vadana-tāmbūla-kabalāḥ//

Translation : O Mother! the (chewed) betel-and-nut (mixed) with the powder of refined camphor radiant like the Moon, (spit) off Thy mouth, is eagerly set upon by Viśākha, Indra and Upendra, on their return after vanquishing the Daityas in battle, with their head-gear doffed and clad in armour, having given up the offal of Tripura-hara a falling to the share of Caṇḍa.

रणे युद्धे, **जित्वा** पराजितान् कृत्वा, **दैत्यान् अपहृतशिरस्त्रैः**[1] **कवचिभिः** वर्मयुक्तैः **निवृत्तैः** युद्धान्निवृत्तेः, **चण्डांशत्रिपुरनिर्माल्यविमुखैः** चण्डांशः चण्डभागः चण्डो नाम प्रमथः तस्य भागः स एव त्रिपुरहरस्य निर्माल्यं स्वीकृतावशिष्टं गन्धताम्बूलादि तत्र विमुखैः। 'हरनिर्माल्यं परित्याज्यम्' इत्यादिस्मृतयः चण्डांशरूपहरनिर्माल्य[2]-निषेधपरा इत्यवगन्तव्यमिति बोधयन्ति। **विशाखेन्द्रोपेन्द्रैः** विशाखः सेनानीः, युद्धेषु तस्यैव प्रामुख्यमित्यग्रे गणना, इन्द्रो महेन्द्रः उपेन्द्रः विष्णुः तेः **शशिविशदकर्पूरशकलाः** चन्द्रवद्विशदाः कर्पूरशकलाः घनसारखण्डाः येषां ते। **विलीयन्ते** विलयनं क्रियन्ते। **मातः!** हे जननि! **तव वदनताम्बूलकबलाः** वदननिर्गतास्ताम्बूलकबलाः।।

अत्रेत्थं पदयोजना–हे मातः! रणे दैत्यान् जित्वा अपहृतशिरस्त्रैः कवचिभिः निवृत्तैः चण्डांशत्रिपुरहरनिर्माल्यविमुखैः विशाखेन्द्रोपेन्द्रैः शशिविशदकर्पूरशकलाः तव वदनताम्बूलकबलाः विलीयन्ते।।

अयमर्थः–विशाखेन्द्रोपेन्द्राः दैत्यान् संहृत्य भगवत्याः कुमारं पुरस्कृत्य पादवन्दनार्थमागत्य शिरस्त्राण्यपहार्य पादोपसङ्ग्रहणमकुर्वन्। तदनन्तरं प्रसन्ना भगवती ईषत्खादितान् ताम्बूलकबलान् विततार। तद्गतकर्पूरशकलविलयनपर्यन्तं खादितवन्तः इत्युक्त्या एतादृशोऽनुग्रहः भगवत्याः कुमारस्वामिन्येव। इन्द्रादिष्वपि क्वाचित्क इत्यभिप्रायः।। ६५।।

Notes : *Viśākha*—Skanda, the commander-in-chief of the celestial army. *Upendra*—Viṣṇu, *Caṇḍa*—a devotee of Śiva,

1. अपहृतानि शिरोवेष्टनानि यैस्तैः स्वामिकार्यनिर्वर्तनानन्तरं सेवकानांराजसंमुखे प्रणामवेलयायां उष्णीषशिरस्त्रादिकं निर्मुच्य प्रणामः कर्तव्य इति परिपाटी; तां परिपाटीमाश्रित्याह–अपहृतशिरस्त्रैरिति।।

2. विशेषपरा।

worshipped as one of the Pañcamūrtis in Śiva shrines, whose privilege it is to claim as his the Nirmālya, what is thrown off, by his Lord. Skanda and his lieutenants, returning victorious from the battle-field, are represented here as sharing among themselves the chewed betel, nut and refined camphor spat out of the Devī's mouth, viewing it as a worthy meed for their trouble, after giving up to Caṇḍa the undisputed ownership of Śiva's offal. The doffing of the headgear is by way of showing their veneration for the Devī.

विपञ्च्या[1] गायन्ती[2] विविधमपदानं[3] पशुपते[4]-
स्त्वया ऽऽरब्धे वक्तुं चलितशिरसा[5] साधुवचने[6]।
तदीयैर्माधुर्यै[7]रपलपिततन्त्रीकलरवां
निजां वीणां[8] वाणी निचुलयति चोलेन[9] निभृतम्[10]॥ ६६॥

Vipañcyā gāyantī vividham apadānaṁ paśupatis
tvayā "rabdhe vaktuṃ calita-śirasā sādhuvacane/
Tadīyair mādhuryair apalapita-tantrī-kala-ravāṁ
nijāṁ vīṇāṁ vāṇī niculayati colena nibhṛtam//

Translation : *Vāṇī,* rendering upon the harp (songs recounting) the various past achievements of Paśupati, *i.e.,* Lord of creatures, quietly covers with is sheath her own instrument, the sweet notes of whose strings being far excelled by the soft melody of the words of praise with which Thou beganest, shaking Thy head, to applaud (her rendering).

विपञ्च्या वीणया, **गायन्ती** गानं कुर्वन्ती, **विविधं** अनेकप्रकारं त्रिपुरविजयदक्षयागध्वंसहालाहलधारणजलन्धरवधगजासुरवधादिकं, **अपदानं** वृत्तं कर्म, **पशुपतेः** ईश्वरस्य, **त्वया** भवत्या, **आरब्धे** उपक्रान्ते सति, **वक्तुं** निगदितुं, **चलितशिरसा**

1. विपंच्या।
2. गायन्त्या।
3. विविधमवदानं ; विविधमवदातं।
4. पुररिपो (is rarely accepted)
5. ललितवचसा ; स्खलितवचसा।
6. साधुवदने ; साधुवचनैः।
7. रुपहासित।
8. वार्णी।
9. चैलेन।
10. निभृताम्।

अन्तः सन्तोषवशात् स्वयं शिरःकम्पवत्या, **साधुवचने** मधुरवचने, **तदीयैः** तस्य वचनस्य सम्बन्धिभिः, **माधुर्यैः** माधुर्यगुणैः **अपलपिततन्त्रीकलरवाम्** अपलपिता अपहसिताः स्वकीयतन्त्रीकलरवाः यस्याः सा तां **निजां** स्वकीयां, **वीणां** विपञ्चीं, **वाणी** भारती, **निचुलयति** निचुलवर्ती करोति। निचुलः कूर्पासः। **चोलेन** चोलः कूर्पासविशेषः वीणाकूर्पासः। चोलेन निचुलवर्ती करोतीति सामान्यविशेषभावे, न पौनरुक्त्यम्। केचित्तु भोजमतावलम्बिन आहुः—चुलिधातुः तिरोधानवाचक इति। नितरां चुलयति अच्छादयतीत्यर्थः। **निभृतं** गूढं यथा भवति तथा।।

अत्रेत्थं पदयोजना–हे भगवति! पशुपतेः विविधं अपदानं विपञ्च्या गायन्ती त्वया वक्तुं चलितशिरसा साधुवचने आरब्धे सति तदीयैः माधुर्यैः अपलपिततन्त्रीकलरवां निजां वीणां वाणी चोलेन निचुलयति।

अत्रातिशयोक्तिरलङ्कारः, वीणायाः निचोलनासंबन्धेऽपि संबन्धकथनात्, यः पराजितो वैणिकः स्ववीणां चोलेन निचुलयति तेन सहाभेदाध्यवसायप्रतीतेः।। ६६।।

Notes : *Vāṇī*—Sarasvatī the Goddess of Learning. Paśupati—Lord Śiva. The sweet music of the Devī's words so far excelled the melodious notes produced by the delicate touches of Saravatī on her harp, that the latter, so well reputed as the finest player on the harp, the instrument ever associated with her name, quietly laid it aside the began to cover it with its sheath, as there was little chance of her making the feeblest approach even with her instrument to the Devī's melodious voice.

करग्रेण स्पृष्टं तुहिनगिरिणा वत्सलतया
गिरीशेनोदस्तं मुहुरधरपानाकुलतया।
करग्राह्यं शंभोर्मुखमुकुरवृन्तं गिरिसुते
कथंकारं ब्रूमस्तव [1]चिबुकमौपम्यरहितम्।। ६७।।

Karāgreṇa spṛṣṭaṁ tuhina-giriṇā vatsalatayā
girīśenodastaṁ muhur adhara-pānākulatayā/
Kara-grāhyaṁ śaṁbhor mukha-mukura-vṛntaṁ giri-sute
kathaṁ-kāraṁ brūmas tava cibukam aupamya-rahitam//

Translation : O Daughter of the Mountain! in what manner shall we describe Thy chin, touched by Himavat with the tips of his fingers by way of showing his affection towards his child,

---

1. चुबुकमौपम्यरहितम्।

raised often and often by the Lord of the Mount (Kailāsa) with eagerness to implant a kiss, fit to be fondly handled by Śaṁbhu, matchless and forming the base of Thy mirror-like face?

This stanza describes the chin of the Devī.

कराग्रेण अग्रकरेण, **स्पृष्टं** संमृष्टं, **तुहिनगिरिणा** हिमाद्रिणा जनकेन, **वत्सलतया** वात्सल्येन पित्रादीनां पुत्रादिषु प्रीतिः वात्सल्यशब्देनोच्यते। यथोक्तं सर्वज्ञसोमेश्वरेण— "पुत्रादौ वात्सल्यं, पत्न्यादौ प्रेम, शिष्यादावनुग्रहः, अग्रजादौ भक्तिः। अत्र आदिशब्देन गौणपुत्रगौणपत्नीगौणशिष्यगौणाग्रजाः गृह्यन्ते" इति। गौणपुत्रः पुत्रत्वेन कल्पितसंबन्धः न तु क्रीतादिः, तस्य पुत्रत्वात्। गौणपत्नी भुजिष्या। गौणशिष्यः शिष्यत्वेन कल्पितसंबन्ध एव न तु स्वीकृतमन्त्रग्रहणमात्रः। गौणाग्रजः कल्पितसंबन्धः न तु क्षेत्रजादिः। **गिरीशेन** शम्भुना, **उदस्तं** उन्नमितं, **मुहुः** अत्यर्थं, **अधरपानाकुलतया** अधरपानव्यग्रतया अतिप्रेम्णेत्यर्थः। **करग्राह्यं** करेण गृहीतुं योग्यं मुखावलोकनचुम्बनव्यग्रतया, **शम्भोः मुखमुकुरवृन्तं** मुखमेव मुकुरो दर्पणः तस्य वृन्तं तदाधारदण्डः तं **गिरिसुते!** हिमाद्रितनये! **कथंकारं** कथंकृत्वा **ब्रूमः** वर्णयामः। 'विभाषा कथमि लिङ्च' इति लिङर्थे संप्रधारणायां लट्। **तव** भवत्याः, **चुबुकं** अधराधःकर्णिकां, **औपम्यरहितं** उपमारहितम्। उपमाराहित्यं तु कमलकर्णिकादर्पणवृन्तोदयाद्रिशिखरशिलादीनां, शम्भुहिमगिरिकरोपलालनाजनितसौभाग्यातिशयाभावेन भगवतीचुबुकस्य तुलना नास्तीति।।

अत्रेत्थं पदयोजना–हे हिमगिरिसुते। तुहिनगिरिणा वत्सलतया कराग्रेण स्पृष्टं गिरीशेन अधरपानाकुलतया मुहुरुदस्तं शंभोः करग्राह्यं औपम्यरहितं तव मुखमुकुरवृन्तं चुबुकं कथंकारं ब्रूम इति।।

अत्रानन्वयालङ्कारो ध्वन्यते, सर्वोपमानिषेधेन स्वस्य स्वयमेव सदृशमित्यनन्वयालङ्कारप्रतीतेः।। ६७।।

भुजाश्लेषान्नित्यं पुरदमयितुः[1] कण्टकवती
तव ग्रीवा धत्ते मुखकमलनालश्रियमियम्।
स्वतः श्वेता कालागुरु[2]बहुलजम्बालमलिना
मृणालीलालित्यं वहति यदधो[3] हारलतिका।। ६८।।

---

1. पुरविजयिनः।
2. कालागरुबहुल ; कालागुरुबहल।
3. यदहो ; तदधो।

Bhujāśleṣān nityaṁ pura-damayituḥ kaṇṭaka-vatī
tava-grīvā dhatte mukha-kamala-nāla-śriyam iayam/
Svataḥ śvetā kālāguru-bahula-jambāla-malinā
mṛṇālī-lālityaṁ vahati yad-adho hāra-latikā//

Translation : This neck of Thine, horripilated often owing to the embrace of the vanquisher of the (three) Puras, assumes the aspect of the stalk Thy lotus-like face, for the reason that the pearl-necklace (worn) thereunder, itself white, but rendered dark owing to the profuse application of the black mud-like Aguru-paste, attains the beauty of the tender part of the lotus-stalk.

भुजाश्लेषात् भुजाभ्यामालिङ्गनात्, **नित्यं** सततं **पुरदमयितुः** पुरान्तकस्य, **कण्टकवती** सरोमाञ्चा, **तव ग्रीवा** कण्ठनालः, **धत्ते** दधति, **मुखकमलनालश्रियं** मुखमेव कमलं तस्य नालश्रियं दण्डसौभाग्यं, **इयं** ग्रीवा, **स्वतः श्वेता** स्वभावतः स्वच्छा, **कालागुरुबहुलजम्बालमलिना** कालो नीलवर्णः अगुरुः लघुकाष्ठं कृष्णगुरुरित्यर्थः तस्य बहुलः समृद्धः जम्बालः पङ्कः तेन मलिना मलीमसा, **मृणालीलालित्यं** बिसलतासौभाग्यं, **वहति** प्राप्नोति। यत् यस्मात्कारणात्, **अधः** अधःप्रदेशे, **हारलतिका** मुक्तावलिः।।

अत्रेत्थं पदयोजना–हे भगवति! तवेयं ग्रीवा पुरदमयितुः भुजाश्लेषात् नित्यं कण्टकवती मुखकमलनालश्रियं धत्ते, यत् अधः स्वतः श्वेता कालागुरुबहुल-जम्बालमलिना हारलतिका मृणालीलालित्यं वहति।।

पूर्वार्धे निदर्शनालङ्कारः, मुखकमलनालश्रियमित्यत्र श्रीसदृशी श्रीरिति प्रतिबिम्बा-क्षेपात्। रूपकमप्यलङ्कारः, मुखकमलमित्यत्र मुखे कमलत्वरूपणात्। अनयोरङ्गाङ्गि-भावेन सङ्करः। उत्तरार्धेऽपि निदर्शनालङ्कारः, मृणालीलालित्यमित्यत्र लालित्यसदृश-लालित्यमिति प्रतिबिम्बाक्षेपात्। उभयोरङ्गाङ्गिभावेन सङ्करः।। ६८।।

Notes : The Devī's face is the lotus, her horropilated neck is its stalk covered with horny processed, and the pearl necklace with the dark Aguru-paste is the tender part of the stalk embedded in the mud.

गले रेखास्तिस्रो गतिगमकगीतैकनिपुणे
[1]विवाहव्यानद्ध[2]प्रगुणगुणसंख्याप्रतिभुवः ।

1. विवादणयाख्यान।
2. त्रिगुणगुण।

विराजन्ते नानाविधमधुररागाकरभुवां[1]
त्रयाणां ग्रामाणां स्थितिनियमसीमान इव ते।।६९।।

Gale rekhās tisro gati-gamaka-gītaika-nipuṇe
vivāha-vyānaddha-praguṇa-guṇa-saṁkhyā-pratibhuvaḥ/
Virājante nānā-vidha-madhura-rāgākara-bhuvāṁ
trayāṇāṁ grāmāṇāṁ sthiti-niyama-sīmāna iva te.//

Translation : O unique Demonstrator of procedure, undulations and song! on Thy neck shine forth three lines, as though denoting the number of strings made of twisted threads auspiciously tied (round the neck) during (Thy) marriage forming as it were the boundaries demarcating the positions of the three *Grāmas,* which constitute the treasure-mine of the various kinds of melodious modes of Music.

गले कण्ठप्रदेशे, **रेखाः** भाग्यरेखाः, वलीरूपाः **तिस्रः**–

ललाटे च गले चैव मध्ये चापि वलित्रयम्।
स्त्रीपुंसयोरिदं ज्ञेयं महासौभाग्यसूचकम्।।

इति सामुद्रिकम्। **गतिगमकगीतैकनीपुणे!** गतिः सङ्गीतगतिः सङ्गीतस्य द्वे गती मार्गो देशी चेति। गमकः स्वस्य कम्पः–

स्वरस्य गमकः कम्पः स च पञ्चविधस्स्मृतः।

इति भरते। ते च पञ्चप्रकारास्तत्रैव ज्ञातव्याः। गीतं धातुमात्वात्मकं द्विविधम्।

वाङ्मातुरुच्यते गेयं धातुरित्यभिधीयते। इति।।

तत्र एका मुख्या चासौ निपुणा च तस्याः सम्बुद्धिः। **विवाहव्यानद्धप्रगुणगुण-सङ्ख्याप्रतिभुवः** विवाहे उद्वाहसमये व्यानद्धाः विशेषेण मङ्गलसूत्रबन्धनानन्तरं तत्समीपे आ समन्तात् कण्ठं कृत्स्नमावृत्य नद्धाः बद्धाः प्रगुणगुणाः बहुतन्तुनिर्मितसूत्राणि। तानि त्रीण्येव, यथोक्तं गृह्यकारैः–

माङ्गल्यतन्तुनानेन बध्वा मङ्गलसूत्रकम्।
वामहस्ते सरं बध्वा कण्ठे च त्रिसरं तथा।। इति।

इदं चानुष्ठानं देशतो व्यवस्थापितम्। अत एव क्वचिद्देशे मङ्गलसूत्रबन्धनं क्वचिद्देशे सरत्रयबन्धनं च क्वचिदुभयमपि नास्तीति। अस्य मतं सर्वत्रास्तीति। यद्वा–ग्रन्थकृतो देशे एतदुभयानुष्ठानं विद्यत एवेति ज्ञेयम्। प्रगुणगुणानां सङ्ख्या त्रित्वं तस्याः प्रतिभुवः। तथा प्रतिभूः उत्तमर्णस्य अधमर्णं ज्ञापयति एवं सङ्ख्यां ज्ञापयतीति प्रतिभुव इत्युक्तम्।

1. वागाकरभुवां।

सङ्ख्याज्ञापका: अस्मदाश्रयकण्ठे शंभुना पूर्वं भगवतीविवाहसमये सरत्रयमस्मिन् स्थले बद्धमिति द्रष्टृणां ज्ञापयति बलित्रयमिति भाव:। **विराजन्ते** अतितरां प्रकाशन्ते। **नानाविधमधुररागाकरभुवां** नानाविधा: अनेकप्रकारा: मधुरा: मनोरमा: रागा: तेषामाकरभुव:[1] खनिस्थानानि आश्रयभूता: तेषाम्।।

अयमर्थ:–[2]गीतय: पञ्च, तदुत्था: ग्रामरागा: त्रिंशत्, उपरागा: अष्टौ, रागास्तु विंशति:, जनकरागा: पञ्चदश, भाषारागा: षण्णवति:, विभाषारागा: विशंति:, आन्तरा भाषाश्च त्रय: इत्यादिकं रागाध्यायप्रतिपाद्यमत्रावगन्तव्यम्। ते च रागा: प्रसिद्धा:, मध्यमावतीमालवीश्रीभैरवीवङ्गालीवसन्ताधन्यासीदेश्यादिकं रागाङ्गम्। वेलावतीशुद्ध-वरालीपुन्नागवरालीनाट्यादिकं भाषाङ्गम्। रामक्रियादिकं क्रियाङ्गम्। प्रवीधी[3] धूर्जरीवरालीमलहरीप्रमुखं उपाङ्ग[4] च रागशब्देन सङ्गृहीतं इत्युक्तं नानाविधमधुर-रागाकरभुवाम् इति। **त्रयाणां ग्रामाणां** ग्रामशब्द: समूहवाचक: सर्वे स्वरा: त्रेधा संहता: षड्जग्रामो मध्यमग्रामो गान्धारग्राम: इति त्रेधा स्वरसंहति:। अत्र भूलोके ग्रामद्वयस्यैव प्रसर:। सप्तस्वराणामारोहावरोहक्रमेण मूर्छनाश्रयत्वम्। तच्च मन्द्रमध्यतारात्मना त्रेधा भवति। गान्धारग्रामस्य शरस्थानत्वान्मन्द्रादि-क्रमेणोपक्रमासंभवात् गान्धारग्रामो देवलोके प्रसृत:। यथोक्तं शार्ङ्गदेवेन–

ग्राम: स्वरसमूहस्स्यान्मूर्छनादेस्समाश्रय:।
तौ द्वौ धरातले स्यातां षड्जग्रामस्तथादिम:[5]।।
द्वितीयो मध्यमग्राम: तयोर्लक्षणमुच्यते।
क्रमात्स्वराणां सप्तानामरोहश्चावरोहणम्।।
मूर्छनेत्युच्यते ग्रामद्वये ता: सप्त सप्त च।। इति।।

एता: मूर्छना: शुद्धताना: इत्युच्यन्ते। अतश्च भगवत्या: कण्ठवलित्रयवर्णनायां ग्रामत्रयकथनं देवलोकव्यवहाराद्युज्यत इत्यनुसन्धेयम्। तेषां ग्रामाणां **स्थितिनियमसीमान:** स्थिते: अवस्थानस्य नियमार्थं परस्परं ग्रामाणां सङ्करो मा भूदिति तेषामन्ते रचिता: सीमान: सेतव **इव ते** तव।।

अत्रेत्थं पदयोजना–ते भगवति! गतिगमकगीतैकनिपुणे! ते गले तिस्रो रेखा: विवाहव्यानद्धप्रगुणगुणसङ्ख्याप्रतिभुव: नानाविधमधुररागाकरभुवां त्रयाणां ग्रामाणां स्थितिनियमसीमान इव विराजन्ते।।

---

1. स्वरस्थानानि।
2. गतय:।
3. द्रविडी।
4. उपरागम्।
5. तदादिम:।

पूर्वार्धे अनुमानालङ्कारः, रेखागतत्रित्वस्य मङ्गलसरत्रित्वानुमापकत्वात्। अनुमानस्य विच्छित्यात्मकत्वं लौकिकालङ्कारवैलक्षण्यादेव। तद्वैलक्षण्यं च पक्षधर्मतामात्रात् व्याप्त्यभाव एव, उभयसद्भावे लौकिकमेव स्यादिति रहस्यम्। विच्छित्तिरलौकिकी शोभा। उत्तरार्धे उत्प्रेक्षालङ्कारः, भगवत्याः कण्ठमध्यवर्तिस्वरग्रामत्रितयहेतुचिह्नतया वलित्रयस्य संभावनात्।। ६९।।

Notes : Procedure—differentiated as Mārga and Deśī, according to the Science of Music; the former is the original type known as Brahma-gītā, adopted when music came into vogue, while the latter represents the types adopted in the different Deśas or parts of the country. *Undulations*—due to variations in the modulation. *Song*—words set to music, *i.e.*, musical compositions. *Grāma-s*—musical scales, known as Ṣaḍja-Madhyama and Gāndhāra-grāmas, according as they commence from Ṣaḍja-, Madhyama- and Gāndhāra-*svaras.* The last Grāma is not in vogue in our world, while the second is recognized by some old writers to have been in vogue in their days. It is not, however, recognized now-a-days by modern exponents, such as Veṅkaṭa-makhin. Evidently all the three are known to celestial Music. Kaivalyāśrama makes mention of the Pañcama-grāma in the place of the Gāndhāra-grāma.

मृणालीमृद्वीनां तव भुजलतानां चतसृणां
चतुर्भिः सौन्दर्यं सरसिजभवः स्तौति वदनैः।
नखेभ्यः संत्रस्य[1]न्प्रथममथनादन्धकरिपो-
श्चतुर्णां शीर्षाणां[2] सममभयहस्तार्पणधिया।। ७०।।

Mṛṇālī-mṛdvīnāṁ tava bhuja-latānāṁ catasṛṇāṁ
caturbhiḥ saundaryaṁ sarasi-ja-bhavaḥ stauti vadanaiḥ/
Nakhebhyaḥ saṁtrasyan prathama-mathanād andhaka-ripos
caturṇāṁ śīrṣāṇāṁ samam abhaya-hastārpaṇa-dhiyā//

Translation : The lotus-born (Brahman) praises the beauty of Thy four creeper-like arms, with his four faces, afraid of the nails of the enemy of Andhaka, one of their fellows (the fifth head) having been once chopped off, in the belief that (the Devī's

1. प्रथमदमनात्; मदनमथनात्।
2. वक्त्राणां।
3. मभयदाना।

arms) would vouchsafe safety to his four (remaining) heads at the same time.

मृणाली बिसलता तद्वत् **मृद्वीनां** मृदूनां, 'वोतो गुणवचनात्' इति ङीप्। तव भवत्याः **भुजलतानां** बाहुलतानां **चतसृणां चतुर्भिः सौन्दर्यं** सौभाग्यं, **सरसिजभवो** ब्रह्मा, **स्तौति** प्रस्तौति। **वदनैः** वक्त्रैः, **नखेभ्यः** करजेभ्यः सकाशात्, **संत्रस्यन्** बिभ्यत् 'भीत्रार्थानां भयहेतुः' इत्यपादाने पञ्चमी। **प्रथममथनात्** पूर्वं मर्दितवतः। कर्तरि ल्युट्। यदाह वृत्तिकारः-'वोतो गुणवचनात्' इत्यत्र 'गुणमुक्तवान् गुणवचन' इति।

ब्रह्मणः पञ्चमशिरः नखाग्रेणाच्छिनद्धरः।

इति पुराणम्। तस्मात् प्रथममथनात्, **अन्धकरिपोः** सदाशिवस्य, **चतुर्णां शीर्षाणां** शिरसां, **समं** सकृदेव, **अभयहस्तार्पणधिया** अभयहस्तान्ग्रहीतुकाम इत्यर्थः।।

अत्रेत्थं पदयोजना-हे भगवति! तव मृणालीमृद्वीनां चतसृणां भुजलतानां सौन्दर्यं सरसिजभवः चतुर्भिर्वदनैः प्रथममथनात् अन्धकरिपोः नखेभ्यः संत्रस्यन् समं चतुर्णां शीर्षाणां अभयहस्तार्पणधिया स्तौति।।

काव्यलिङ्गमलङ्कारः, ब्रह्मैकनियतस्तोत्रस्य नखेभ्यः संत्रस्यन् इत्यादिना समर्थनात्। वाक्यार्थहेतुकं काव्यलिङ्गमिति ध्येयम्। भुजलतावर्णने ब्रह्मण एवाधिकारो नान्येषामिति काव्यलिङ्गेन ध्वन्यते वस्त्विति अलङ्कारेण वस्तुध्वनिः।। ७० ।।

Notes : Afraid of—and therefore seeking the Devī's grace, so as to ward off a similar contingency. *The enemy of Andhaka*—Śiva. The allusion is to the chopping off of the fifth head of Brahman by Parama-śiva. The story goes that Brahman had originally five heads like Paramaśiva and was vaunting, on that account, to have attained equality with the latter. Hence, to teach him a salutary lesson, Paramaśiva punished him thus and deprived him, once for all of the reason for such vainglory.

नखानामुद्योतैर्नवनलिनरागं[1] विहसतां
कराणां ते कान्तिं कथय कथयामः [2]कथमुमे।
[3]कयाचिद्वा साम्यं भजतु कलया[4] हन्त कमलं
[5]यदि क्रीडल्लक्ष्मीचरणतललाक्षा[6]ऽरुणदलम्।। ७१ ।।

---

1. नखानामुद्योतैः।
2. कथममी ; कथममुम्।
3. कदाचिद्वा।
4. विधया।
5. परिक्रीडल्लक्ष्मी।
6. लाक्षारसचणम्।

Nakhānām uddyotair nava-nalina-rāgaṁ vihasatām
karāṇāṁ te kāntiṁ kathaya kathayāmaḥ katham ume/
Kayācid vā sāmyaṁ bhajatu kalayā hanta kamalaṁ
yadi krīḍal-lakṣmī-cara-a-tala-lākṣā-' ruṇa-dalam//

Translation : O Umā! how shall we characterize the splendour of Thy hands which, with the lustre of their finger-nails, throw into the background the bright hue of the newly bloomed lotus? Pray tell us. In case the lotus (has) its petals turned red (from contact) with the lac-dye on the soles of Lakṣmī's feet playing upon it, then, by all means, let it (the lotus) somewhat resemble (Thy hands), as it cannot be helped.

नखानां नखराणां, **उद्योतैः** प्रभापटलैः, **नवनलिनरागं** प्रातर्विकसिताम्बुजकान्तिं, **विहसतां** अपलपतां, कराणां हस्तानां, **ते** तव, **कान्तिं** शोभां, **कथय** वद, **कथयामः** काव्यप्रबन्धं रचयामः, **कथं** केन प्रकारेण, **उमे!** पार्वति! **कयाचिद्वा** विधया। वेत्यसंशये संशयोक्तिः। केनापि प्रकारेण नास्तीत्यर्थः। **साम्यं** सादृश्यं, **भजतु** स्वीकरोतु **कलया** लेशेनापि **हन्त!** वाक्यारम्भे–

हन्त हर्षेऽनुकम्पायां वाक्यारम्भविषादयोः।।

इत्यमरः। **कमलं** पद्मम्, **यदि** संशये, तथापि सन्देह इत्यर्थः। क्रीडल्लक्ष्मी-चरणतललाक्षारसचणं क्रीडन्त्याः लक्ष्म्याः पद्मालयायाः चरणतलयोः लाक्षारसेन चणं वित्तं युक्तम्। 'तेन वित्तश्चुञ्चुप्चणपौ' इति चणप्।।

अत्रेत्थं पदयोजना–हे उमे! नखनामुद्योतैः नवनलिनरागं विहसतां ते कराणां कान्तिं कथं कथयामः कथय, कमलं कलयापि साम्यं कयाचिद्वा भजतु। हन्त कमलं क्रीडल्लक्ष्मीचरणतललाक्षारसचणं यदि तदा हि साम्यं भजत्विति। यद्वा कयाचिद्वा साम्यं भजतु विधयेति पाठः। तदा हन्त! कमलं कयाचिद्वा विधया साम्यं भजतु प्राप्नोतु इत्यन्वयः। तामेव विधामाह—यदि क्रीडल्लक्ष्मीचरणतललाक्षारसचणं तदा नान्यथेत्येकवाक्यतया अन्वयः।।

अत्रातिशयोक्तिरलङ्कारः, यद्यर्थोक्त्याऽतिशयकल्पनात्। पूर्वार्धे तद्गुणालङ्कारः, नखकान्तिभिरतिरक्तत्वात् कराणाम्। नवनलिनरागं विहसतामित्यत्र उपमालङ्कारः, उभयोस्संसृष्टिः, अपृथक्स्थित्या प्रयोजकत्वात् उभयोः संसृष्टिः।। ७१ ।।

Notes : The underlying ideal is that there is nothing comparable to the splendour of the Devī's hands, and if at all an approach is made to it by any thing, it is by the lotus flower. Even that is due to its having derived its hue from the lac-dye on Lakṣmī's feet playing upon it.

समं देवि स्कन्दद्विपवदनपीतं स्तनयुगं
तवेदं नः खेदं हरतु सततं प्रस्नुतमुखम्।
यदालोक्याशङ्काऽऽकुलितहृदयो[1] हासजनकः
स्वकुम्भौ हेरम्बः परिमृशति हस्तेन झटिति[2]।।७२।।

Samaṁ devi skanda-dvipa-vadana-pītaṁ stana-yugaṁ
tavedaṁ naḥ khedaṁ haratu satataṁ prasnutamukham/
Yad ālokyāśaṅkā-"kulita-hṛdayo hāsa-janakaḥ
sva-kumbhau herambaḥ parimṛśati hastena jhaṭ-iti//

Translation : O Goddess! may Thy breasts, ever flowing with milk and sucked simultaneously by Skanda and Dvipavadana—on seeing which Heramba, his mind distracted with doubt, suddenly touches his own pair of frontal globes with his hand, creating laughter—drive away our misery.

समं तुल्यकालं **देवि**! भगवति! **स्कन्दद्विपवदनपीतं स्कन्दः** कुमारः द्विपवदनो विनायकः ताभ्यां पीतं, **स्तनयुगं** कुचद्वन्द्वं **तव** भवत्याः, **इदं नः** अस्माकं, **खेदं** क्लेशं, **हरतु** अपनुदतु। **सततं** सर्वदा **प्रस्नुतमुखं** क्षीरस्राविमुखम्, **यत्** कुचद्वन्द्वं, **आलोक्य** विलोक्य, **आशङ्काकुलितहृदयः** आशङ्कायाः मदीयौ कुम्भौ अपहृतवतीत्याशङ्कायाः आकुलितं अवस्कन्दितं व्यग्रतरमित्यर्थः, तादृशं हृदयं मनो यस्य, **हासजनकः** मातापित्रोः (कुमारस्य च)। असौ बालिश इति प्रेम्णा हसितवन्तावित्यर्थः। **स्वस्य कुम्भौ** कुम्भस्थले, **हेरम्बः** विनायकः, **परिमृशति** परामृशति। विद्यते न वेति **हस्तेन** निमार्ष्टीत्यर्थः! **झडिति** शीघ्रम्।।

अत्रेत्थं पदयोजना–हे देवि! तव समं स्कन्दद्विपवदनपीतं इदं स्तनयुगं प्रस्नुतमुखं नः खेदं सततं हरतु, यत् आलोक्य आशङ्काकुलितहृदयः हेरम्बः हासजनकः हस्तेन झडिति स्वकुम्भौ परिमृशति।।

यस्याः पुत्रौ जगत्पूज्यपादौ विनायककुमारस्वामिनाविति देव्याः सर्वातिशायि माहात्म्यं इति प्रतीयते। देव्याः कुचकुम्भसाम्यं यदि स्यात्तदा विनायककुम्भयोरेव तौल्यमित्यतिशयोक्तिरपि प्रतीयते। विनायकः हस्तेन परिमृशतीत्यनेन विनायककुम्भयोस्तुल्यौ देवीकुचावेवेति उपमेयोपमापि ध्वन्यते। वस्त्वलङ्कारध्वनीनां एकव्यञ्जकानुप्रवेशेन सङ्करः।।७२।।

1. शङ्काकुलितहृदयो।
2. हस्तेन झडिति।

Notes : *Dvipa-vadana*—elephant-faced *i.e.,* Gaṇeśa. *Heramba*—is also Gaṇeśa. *Doubt*—as to whether he was sucking from the frontal globes of his own head or from his mother's breast. The confusion is due to the close similarity between the two pairs, to express which he scratches his head with his hand.

अमू ते वक्षोजावमृतरसमाणिक्यकुतुपौ[1]
न संदेहस्पन्दो नगपतिपताके मनसि नः।
पिबन्तौ तौ यस्मादविदितवधूसंगमरसौ[2]
कुमारावद्यापि द्विरदवदनक्रौञ्चदलनौ[3] **।।७३।।**

Amū te vakṣo-jāv amṛta-rasa-māṇikya-kutupau
na saṁdeha-spando naga-pati-patāke manasi naḥ/
Pibantau tau yasmād a-vidita-vadhū-saṁgama-rasau
kumārāv adyāpi dvi-rada-vadana-krauñca-dalanau//

Translation : O Emblem of the Lord of the Mountains! These two breasts of Thine are verily containers (chiselled out) of ruby and filled with nectar. There is not even the slightest doubt in our minds (about this). As Dvirada-vadana and Krauñca-dalana who drink (out of the two) are innocent of copulative pleasure, they are, even to-day, children.

अमू परिदृश्यमानौ, **ते** तव, **वक्षोजौ** कुचौ, **अमृतरसमाणिक्यकुतुपौ** अमृतरसस्य माणिक्यकुतुपौ अमृतरसपूरितमाणिक्यकुतुपावित्यर्थः। कुतुपशब्दो यद्यपि चर्मनिर्मित-घृततैलाद्याधारभूतघटसन्निभपात्रीवाचकः तथापि तस्याः भगवतीस्तनसादृश्यावगाहने अनधिकारात् तदर्थं माणिक्यरचितत्वमङ्गीकृतं कुतुपयोः। **न सन्देहस्पन्दः** सन्देहस्य स्पन्दनं लेशमात्रमिति यावत्। **नगपतिपताके! मनसि नः** अस्माकं, **पिबन्तौ तौ** माणिक्यकुतुपौ, **यस्मात्** कारणात्, **अविदितवधूसङ्गरसिकौ कुमारौ** शिशू भूत्वा, **अद्यापि** इदानीमपि श्लोकरचनाकालेऽपि, **द्विरदवदनक्रौञ्चदलनौ** द्विरदवदनो विनायकः क्रौञ्चदलनः क्रौञ्चाद्रिभेदनः कुमारस्वामी तौ।।

अत्रेत्थं पदयोजना– हे नगपतिपताके! अमू ते वक्षोजौ अमृतरसमाणिक्यकुतुपौ। अस्मिन्नर्थे नः मनसि सन्देहस्पन्दो नास्ति। यस्मात्तौ पिबन्तौ अविदितवधूसङ्गरसिकौ द्विरदवदनक्रौञ्चदलनौ अद्यापि कुमारौ भवतः।।

1. माणिक्यकलशौ।
2. ०वधूसङ्गरसिकौ।
3. क्रौञ्चदमनौ।

अत्र वाक्यार्थहेतुकं काव्यलिङ्गमलङ्कारः स्पष्ट एव। पूर्वपादे रूपकं वक्षोजयोः कुतुपत्वेनारोपणात्। यद्वा–निश्चयान्तस्सन्देहः इमौ वक्षोजौ उत कुतुपाविति सन्देहे कुतुपावेवेति निश्चयः, यतोऽमृतपानात् कुमारयोः शिशुत्वम्। स्तन्यपानमात्रात् शिशुत्वावस्थैवेति नियमो नास्ति, शैशवानन्तरं यौवनादेर[1]नुभूतत्वादिति। विनायककुमार-योस्तु सर्वदा शिशुत्वं अमृतपानवशादेवेति अमृतरसकुतुपसन्देहापनयने साधकं प्रमाणं द्वितीयार्धप्रमेयमिति सूक्तं निश्चयान्तस्सन्देह इति। 'कविकल्पितकोटिद्वयस्यावाच्यत्वं नास्ति' इति मङ्कुकः।। ७३।।

Notes : *Dvi-rada-vadana*—Gaṇeśa. *Krauñca-dalana*—the breaker of Krauñcādri, *i.e.*, Skanda. *Are, even to-day, children*—as both Gaṇeśa and Skanda, though long past the age of childhood, are ever in the enjoyment of the Bliss of the Brahman, the idea of copulative pleasure does not at all enter their minds, even though they are ever in the company of Siddhi-lakṣmī and Deva-senā, their respective consorts, and as such are verily children even to-day, being innocent of the worldly pleasure so often associated with the company of women.

वहत्यम्ब [2]स्तम्बेरमदनुजकुम्भप्रकृतिभिः
समारब्धां मुक्तामणिभिरमलां हारलतिकाम्।
कुचाभोगो बिम्बाधररुचिभिरन्तः शबलितां
प्रतापव्यामिश्रां[3] पुरदमयितुः कीर्त्तिमिव ते।। ७४।।

Vahaty amba stambe-rama-danu-ja-kumbha-pra-kṛtibhiḥ
samārabdhāṁ muktā-maṇbhir amalāṁ hāra-latikām/
Kucābhogo bimbādhara-rucibhir antaḥ śabalitāṁ
pratāpa-vyāmiśrāṁ pura-damayituḥ kīrttim iva te//

Translation : O Mother! the region of Thy breasts wears a creeper-like lucid garland, strung which pearls from the skull of Stambe-ramadanuja, its natural lustre variegated with the reflected lustre of Thy Bimba lips, (thus) resembling the fame of the vanquisher of the (three) Puras intermixed with his valour.

वहति दधति। **अम्ब!** मातः! **स्तम्बेरमदनुजकुम्भप्रकृतिभिः** स्तम्बेरमदनुजः

1. अनुभाव्यत्वादिति।
2. स्तम्बेरमवदनकुंभप्रकृतिभिः।
3. पुरविजयिनः।

गजासुरः तस्य कुम्भस्थलमेव प्रकृतिः जन्मभूमिः येषां तैः गजकुम्भेषु मुक्तामणय उद्भवन्ति। यथोक्तं सर्वज्ञसोमेश्वरेण–

गजकुम्भेषु वंशेषु फणासु जलदेषु च।
शुक्तिकायामिक्षुदण्डे षोढा मौक्तिकसंभवः।।
गजकुम्भे कर्बुराभाः वंशे रक्तसिताः स्मृताः।।
फणासु वासुकेरेव नीलवर्णा प्रकीर्तिताः।।
ज्योतिर्वर्णास्तु जलदे शुक्तिकायां सिताः स्मृताः।
इक्षुदण्डे पीतवर्णाः मणयो मौक्तिकाः स्मृताः।। इति।

गजकुम्भप्रकृतयो मौक्तिकमणयः कर्बुरवर्णाः, गजासुरकुम्भप्रकृतयस्तु विशेषत एवेति भावः। **समारब्धां** खचितां, **मुक्तामणिभिः** मौक्तिकैः, **अमलां** त्रासादिदोषरहितां न तु श्वेतां, गजकुम्भोद्भवानां कर्बुरत्वात्। **हारलतिकां** मुक्तावलिं, **कुचाभोगः** कुचमध्यप्रदेशः, **बिम्बाधररुचिभिः** बिम्बाकारोऽधरो बिम्बाधरः। शाकपार्थिवादित्वात्साधुः। बिम्बाधरस्य अधरबिम्बस्येव रुचिभिः, **अन्तश्शबलितां** सञ्जातचित्रवर्णाम्–

चित्रकिम्मीरकल्माषशबलैताश्च कर्बुरे।

इत्यमरः। अधरकान्तिसंवलिता शुक्तिमुक्तामणिमालिकेव भातीति भावः। **प्रतापव्यामिश्रां पुरदमयितुः** त्रिपुरान्तकस्य, **कीर्तिमिव ते** तव। प्रतापस्तु रक्तवर्णः कीर्तिस्तु श्वेतवर्णेति महाकविप्रसिद्धिः। अत एवास्य कवेः गजकुम्भोद्भवाः मणयः पाटलवर्णाः न शबलवर्णाः, अन्तश्शबलितामित्युक्तिरपि पाटलवर्णपरेत्यभिप्राय इत्यनुसन्धेयम्।।

अत्रेत्थं पदयोजना–हे अम्ब! ते कुचाभोगः स्तम्बेरमदनुजकुम्भप्रकृतिभिः मुक्तामणिभिः समारब्धाम् अमलां हारलतिकां बिम्बाधररुचिभिः अन्तः शबलितां प्रतापव्यामिश्रां पुरदमयितुः कीर्तिमिव वहति।।

अत्रोत्प्रेक्षालङ्कारः, हारलतिकायाः प्रतापसंवलितकीर्तित्वेन संभावनात्। बिम्बाधररुचिभिरित्यत्र उत्प्रेक्षा, स्वभावतो रक्तवर्णेषु बिम्बाधररुचिभिः संवलनादिवेति हेतारुत्प्रेक्षणात्। उभयोरनुप्राण्यानुप्राणकभावेन संबन्धः, अपृथक्स्थित्या उपत्कारकत्वात्।।७४।।

Notes : Skull of *Stambe-rama-danuja—i.e.,* of Gajāsura, a demon in the form of an elephant, said to have been vanquished by Śiva, who, to mark his victory over him, wore his hide as a garment. Pearls of various colours, according to tradition, are said to be found in the skull of an elephant, the hollow of a bamboo, the hood of a snake, the cloud, the sugarcane and the pearl-oyster. The pearls obtained from the skull of Gajāsura are worn by the Devī as a trophy round her neck. Again, fame is described by poets as of a white colour and valour of a red colour. Hence, the comparison between the pearl-necklace of the Devī tinged with the red lustre of her lips and the fame and valour of her Lord.

तव स्तन्यं मन्ये धरणिधरकन्ये[1] हृदयतः
[2]पयः पारावारः परिवहति सारस्वतमिव[3]।
दयावत्या[4] दत्तं [5]द्रविडशिशुरास्वाद्य तव यत्
कवीनां प्रौढानामजनि कमनीयः कवयिता।।७५।।

Tava stanyaṁ manye dharaṇi-dhara-kanye hṛdayataḥ
payaḥ-pārāvāraḥ parivahati sārasvatamiva/
Dayā-vatyā dattaṁ draviḍa-śiśur āsvādya tava yat
kavīnāṁ prauḍhānām ajani kamanīyaḥ kavayitā//

Translation : O Daughter of the Mountain! I fancy that the ocean of the milk of poesy rising out of Thy heart verily causes the milk of Thy breasts fo flow, on swallowing which (milk) given by Thee with grace, the Dravidan child became the poet-laureate among great poets.

तव स्तन्यं स्तनोद्भवं क्षीरं, **मन्ये** जानामि। [6]**धरणिधरकन्ये! हृदयतः** हृदयात्, **पयःपारावारः** क्षीरसमुद्रः। सुधाधारासारः इति वा पाठः। सुधायाः धाराणामासारः, सुधाप्रवाहः **परिवहति सारस्वतं** सरस्वतीमयमिव, स्तन्यस्य श्वेतवर्णत्वात् सरस्वतीमयत्वेनोत्प्रेक्षणम्, माधुर्यात्सुधारूपत्वेन च। **दयावत्या** प्रशस्तकृपायुक्तया, **दत्तं** स्तन्यं **द्रविलशिशुः** द्रविलजातिसमुद्भवः बालः एतत्स्तोत्रकर्ता **आस्वाद्य** पीत्वा, **तव यत्** कारणात्, **कवीनां** कवीश्वराणां **प्रौढानां** प्रगल्भानां मध्ये इति निर्धारणे षष्ठी। **अजनि** जातः। **कमनीयः** अतिरमणीयः, **कवयिता** कविः।।

1. तुहिनगिरिकन्ये।
2. स्वतः पारावारः ; सुधाधारासारः।
3. सारस्वत इव।
4. दयावृत्या।
5. द्रुहिणशिशुरास्वाद्य; द्रविलशिशुरास्वाद्य; द्रमिलशिशुरास्वाद्य; द्रविडशिशुरस्वाद्य।
6. तुहिनगिरिकन्ये।

अत्रेत्थं पदयोजना–हे धरणिधरकन्ये ! तव स्तन्यं हृदयतः उत्थितः सुधाधारासारः पयःपारावारः सारस्वतमिव परिवहतीति मन्ये। यद्यस्मात् दयावत्या त्वया दत्तं तव स्तन्यं द्रविलशिशुरास्वाद्य प्रौढानां कवीनां मध्ये कमनीयः कवयिता अजनि।

अत्रोत्प्रेक्षाद्वयं पदव्याख्यानावसरे कथितम्। उभयोः संसृष्टिः।।७५।।

Notes : Thy heart—the Devī's heart is here represented to contain the ocean of the milk of poesy, which ebbs and flows there. During spring-tide the milk of poesy over-flows and mixes with the milk of her breats. No wonder that the Dravidian child, nursed on such milk coupled with the Devī's grace, developed poetic talent of a high order.

Regarding the identity of the Infant Prodigy, the Draviḍa-śiśu here referred to, there are various versions. Lakṣmīdhara, Kaivalyāśrama and others maintain that the reference is to Śaṅkara-bhagavatpāda himself. The story is, according to Kaivalyāśrama, as follows : Śaṅkara's father, who was a pious devotee of the Devī, would never fail to visit the local temple every day and, after bathing the Devī with milk and making Pūjā, was in the habit of returning home with a small quantity of Nirmālya milk on which his little child was fed every day. When he had to be temporarily absent from his village, he left instructions with his wife that the Pūjā should be performed by her as usual during his absence. She was carrying out her husband's mandate, but as she had to keep aloof during her menstrual period, she directed her child, the infant Śaṅkara, to go to the temple and perform Pūjā in her stead. The child, in his simplicity, was under the impression that the milk was intended to be drunk by the Devī and felt surprised that the Devī would not partake of it. When at the importunity of the child, the Devī drank all the milk, he burst into tears and called upon her to return to him the usual quantity intended for his use. The Devī, out of compassion, suckled the child, whereupon it burst into rhapsodies of praise and returned home, singing songs which automatically came out of his mouth. Just then the child's father returned from his journey and greeted him with inexpressible joy. The Devī soon appeared to the father in a dream and prophesied a remarkable career for the child blessed by her breast-fedding.

Kāmeśvara-sūri, after narrating the above, gives another version of it, adding that version was current at Kāñcī and its neighbourhood in his days, In this version the father, who is very poor, is out on his begging excursion, while the mother is away fetching water from the river, and the child, suddenly waking in his cradle, cries for milk. Pārvatī and Parameśvara, who happen just then to pass way in their Ākāśayāna, hear the appealing cries of the infant and hie thither, when Pārvatī takes the child in her arms and suckles him out of compassion. The rest of the story is the same as the previous one.

There is yet another account given in the Malaiyāḷam edition of *Saundaryalaharī* by Kaṇṭiyūr Mahādeva Śāstrin, in his commentary on the forty-first stanza, *i.e.,* the last of the Ānandalaharī portion. According to this version, the entire work was of a Siddha of the name of Draviḍa-śiśu, who had it inscribed on the slopes of Mount Kailāsa, and when Śaṅkara-bhagavatpāda paid a visit to the Mount as a pilgrim and was reading the work, the Devī called the attention of the Siddha thereto and commanded him to wipe off the work as it contained profound secrets not to be revealed to mortals. Even before the Siddha carried out the said command, Śaṅkara was able to commit to memory forty-one stanzas at random out of the hundred. Before he could memorize the rest, the entire work had been cleanly wiped off by the Siddha. On his return home *Śaṅkara* wrote out from memory the forty-one stanzas, which now form the first part of the work, and composed the other stanzas requisite to make up the one hundred. The difference in the style and theme between the two parts is given out as a reason for credence being attached to this story of the authorship of the work. Draviḍaśiśu's marvellous powers of word-portraiture are ascribed in this story to his having been fed on the Devī's milk. Mahā-deva Śāstrin gives this story for what it is worth and does not express any opinion of his own on its authenticity.

Another commentator, the author of Sudhā-vidyotinī, says that the Dramiḍa-śiśu referred to is one Pravarasena, son of Dramiḍa, a Kṣattriya prince of the Dramiḍa country. This commentator, whose name cannot be traced, says that he is the son of Pravarasena and claims that the account given by him is authentic, as it is based on the direct testimony of the Dramiḍa-śiśu himself, *i.e.*, his father, the child of Dramiḍa. The story is that Dramiḍa, as soon as Pravarasena was born, was advised by his minister Śuka that the birth of the son was an evil portent for his family, and should the child be allowed to survive, he would lose his kingdom. The king ordered his men to abandon the child in the neighbouring hill-tracts. A tiger carried the child to its cavern and left him at its mouth taking him to be a bundle of gems. The child soon became reminiscent of his Yogic powers acquired during his previous birth and began to praise the Devī, who, taking pity on the child, nursed him. Some time thereafter the child was rescued by a party of hunters and restored to the throne.

Yet others look upon Śrī Jñāna-sambandha as the Draviḍa-śiśu. This is one of the four reputed Tamil Saints, (the others being Appa, Sundara, and Māṇikyavācaka) who are the authors of several hymns in praise of Śiva, and are almost deified throughout the Tamil country. Śrī Jñāna-sambandha is said to be a native of Shīyāli. His father, Śiva-pāda-hṛdaya, and his mother, Bhagavatī, were pious Brāhmaṇas, ever devoted to the worship of the God presiding over the local Śiva temple. By the Lord's grace a child was born to them after a long penance. One day, when this child was about three years old, he was taken to the temple-tank by Śiva-pāda-hṛdaya, who leaving him on the Ghat, went to bathe in the tank. The child, left alone in an unfamiliar environment, soon began to cry, calling out "Mother! Father!" This touched the heart of the Lord Śiva of the temple, who at once asked his spouse to take the child and feed him with her milk. The child was soon appeased and stood there with milk flowing out of his mouth. On noticing this, the father, who returned after bathing, questioned him as to who had suckled him. Whereupon the child burst forth with a song in praise of Śiva, and became later in life one of the recognized bards of Tamil Hymns. Śrī Jñāna-sambandha is said to have flourished about twelve centuries ago and was hence possibly a contemporary of Śaṅkara-bhagavatpāda.

It has to be noted, however, that the two stories narrated here, which have a direct bearing on Śaṅkara-bhagavatpāda as the Draviḍa-śiśu, are not borne out by any accounts of Śrī Śaṅkarācārya's life and times, and the fact that Śaṅkarācārya would not have given such a high testimonial to himself as indicated by the last line of the stanza, but would probably have couched a reference to his capacity as a poet in much milder language, militates against the position taken by Lakṣmīdhara and others.

हरक्रोधज्वालाऽऽवलिभिरवलीढेन[1] वपुषा
गभीरे ते नाभीसरसि कृतसङ्गो[2] मनसिजः।
समुत्तस्थौ तस्मादचलतनये धूमलतिका
जनस्तां जानीते [3]तव जननि रोमावलिरिति।। ७६ ।।

Hara-krodha-jvālā-" valibhir avalīḍhena vapuṣā
gabhīre te nābhī-sarasi kṛta-saṅgo manasi-jaḥ/
Samuttasthau tasmād acala-tanaye dhūma-latikā
janas tāṁ jānīte tava janani romāvalir iti.//

Translation : O Daughter of the Mountain! Manasi-ja drowned himself in the tank of Thy navel with his body enveloped in the flames caused by Hara's anger. Thence rose a creeper-like (column of) smoke. O Mother! the world takes it to be the line of down (above Thy navel).

हरस्य [4]**क्रोधज्वालावलिभिः अवलीढेन** आविष्टेन, **वपुषा गभीरे** निम्ने अत एव ते तव, **नाभीसरसि** नाभ्येव सरः तस्मिन्, **कृतसङ्गो मनसिजः** मन्मथः निमग्न इत्यर्थः। **समुत्तस्थौ** उदभूत्। **तस्मात्** नाभीसरसः **अचलतनये!** पार्वति! **धूमलतिका** धूमावलिः, अङ्गारप्रशमसमयोद्भवा। **जनः** लोकः, **तां** धूमलतिकां **जानीते** वर्णयति। **जननि!** मातः! **तव रोमावलिरिति** रोमराजिरिति।।

अत्रेत्थं पदयोजना–हे अचलतनये! मनसिजः हरक्रोधज्वालावलिभिः अवलीढेन वपुषा गभीरे ने नाभीसरसि कृतसङ्गः! तस्माद्धूमलतिका समुत्तस्थौ। हे जननि! तां जनः तव रोमावलिरिति जानीते।।

अत्रोत्प्रेक्षालङ्कारः रोमराजेः धूमलतिकात्वेनोत्प्रेक्षणात्। यद्वा जनस्तां जानीते इत्यनेन भ्रान्तिमान् प्रतीयते, रोमरेखादर्शनस्य धूमरेखाभ्रान्तिजनकत्वात्। यद्वा—अतिशयोक्तिः जनस्तां रोमावलिमध्यवस्यतीति प्रतीतेः। यद्वा—निश्चयान्तसन्देहः, तां रोमावलिरिति निश्चिनोतीति। एवं चतुर्णामलङ्काराणां जानीते इति पदादुत्थानात् एकवाचकानुप्रवेशेन सङ्करः।। ७६ ।।

Notes : *Manasija*—Manmatha, the god of love. Here the popular notion that flame, when quenched, will send up smoke, is effectively

1. हरक्रोधज्वालावलिभिः।
2. कृतवासो ; कृतरूपो ; मनु मग्नो।
3. जननि तव।
4. क्रोधाग्नेः।

made use of by the poet. The allusion is to the burning of Manmatha by Hara, when the former tried to rouse the passion of the latter.

यदेतत्कालिन्दीतनुतरतरङ्गाकृति शिवे
कृशे मध्ये किंचिज्जननि तव [1]यद्भाति [2]सुधियाम्।
विमर्दादन्योऽन्यं [3]कुचकलशयोरन्तरगतं
तनूभूतं व्योन प्रविशदिव नाभिं कुहरिणीम्।। ७७।।

Yad etat kālindī-tanu-tara-taraṅgākṛti śive
kṛśe madhye kiṁ cij janani tava yad bhāti sudhiyām/
Vimardād anyo'nyaṁ kuca-kalaśayor antara gataṁ
tanū-bhūtaṁ vyoma praviśad iva nābhiṁ kuhariṇīṁ//

Translation : O Spouse of Śiva, Mother (mine)! this something, assuming the form of the ripples of Kālindī (Yamunā) on Thy slim waist, appears to the enlightened (to be) the attenuated Ether intervening the two pot-like breasts, entering the hole of Thy navel, owing to the pressing against each of the two (breasts).

यतेतत् पुरः स्फुरत्। यच्छब्दस्य एतच्छब्दसहचरितस्य प्रसिद्धिवाचकत्वं नास्ति। अत एव पुनर्यच्छब्दोपादनम्। **कालिन्दीतनुतरतरङ्गाकृति** कालिन्द्याः यमुनायाः तनुतरतरङ्गः अतिसूक्ष्मतरङ्गः तस्याकृतिरिव आकृतिर्यस्य तत्। **शिवे!** भगवति! **कृशे** तनुनि, **मध्ये** अवलग्ने, **किञ्चित् जननि! तव यत् भाति** स्फुरति, **सुधियां** विदुषां, **विमर्दात्** सङ्घर्षात्, **अन्योन्यं** परस्परं, **कुचकलशयोः, अन्तरगतं** मध्यवर्ति, **तनूभूतं** सूक्ष्मभूतं, **व्योम** गगनं, **प्रविशदिव** प्रवेशं कुर्वदिव। नीलं नभः इत्याबालगोपाल-प्रसिद्धम्। गगनस्य नीलिमा च मूर्तत्वं च कविप्रसिद्धम्। **नाभिं कुहरिणीं** कुहरवतीम्।।

अत्रेत्थं पदयोजना—हे शिवे! जननि! तव कृशे मध्ये यदेतत्कालिन्दी-तनुतरतरङ्गाकृति किञ्चित् रोमावलिरूपं वस्तु सुधियां यद्भाति कुचकलशयोरन्तरगतं तनूभूतं व्योम अन्योन्यं विमर्दादेव कुहरिणीं नाभिं प्रविशदिव भाति। नीलं मूर्तं नभः कुचकलशविमर्दवशात् अधोभागे स्रस्तं नाभिपर्यन्तं जतुलतान्यायेनावतिष्ठते तद्रोमावलिं वदन्तीति भावः।।

अत्रोत्प्रेक्षालङ्कारः, रोमलतायाः गगनलतिकात्वेन सम्भावनात्। प्रथमपादे निदर्शना-लङ्कारः। तरङ्गाकृतीति बिम्बप्रतिबिम्बभावाक्षेपात्। अनयोस्संसृष्टिः।। ७७।।

---

1. तद्भाति ; तद्देवि गिरिशे।
2. सुधियः।
3. कुशकलशयोरन्तरगतं।

Notes : Something—the Romāvalī. *Kālindī*—the daughter of Mount Kalinda, *i.e.*, the Yamunā, whose water is represented to be of a dark colour. Ether—is also represented as dark in colour. This stanza also described the Romāvalī of the Devī. The Ether, when pressed, is represented as seeking shelter in the navel.

स्थिरो गङ्गाऽऽवर्तः[1] स्तनमुकुलरोमावलिलता-
[2]कलावालं कुण्डं कुसुमशरतेजोहुतभुजः।
रतेर्लीलाऽगारं किमपि तव [3]नाभिर्गिरिसुते
बिलद्वारं सिद्धेर्गिरिशनयनानां विजयते।।७८।।

Sthiro gaṅgā-"vartaḥ stana-mukula-romāvalilatā
kalāvālaṁ kuṇḍaṁ kusuma-śara-tejo-huta-bhujaḥ/
Rater līlā-"gāraṁ kim api tava nābhir giri-sute
bila-dvāraṁ siddher giri-śa-nayanānāṁ vijayate//

Translation : O Daughter of the Mountain! all glory to Thy navel (which may be characterized) in some such way (as) a motionless eddy of the Ganges; a trench for the growth of the creeper of the line of down, with the breasts as buds; the pit for maintaining the sacrificial Fire of the prowess of the flower-arrowed (Kusumaśara); the pleasure-bower of Rati; the mouth of the cavern for the attainment (of Yoga) by Giriśa's (Śiva's) eyes!

स्थिरः विनाशरहितः, **गङ्गावर्तः** गङ्गायाः अम्भसां भ्रमः, आवर्तस्य क्षणिकत्वात् तद्व्यतिरेकः स्थिर इति। **स्तनमुकुलरोमावलिलता कलावालं** स्तनावेव मुकुलौ पुष्पकोरकौ तयोः रोमावलिरेव लता आधारभूता, [4]जनयित्री तस्याः कला रेखा तस्याः आवालं आलवालम्। कुण्डं होमार्थं संपादितं वृत्तं अग्निस्थानं, **कुसुमचरतेजोहुतभुजः** कुसुमशरस्य मन्मथस्य तेजः दीप्तिरेव हुतभुक् वह्निः तस्य। **रतेः** मदनपत्न्याः, **लीलागारं** विलासगृहं तत्रैव सर्वदा मन्मथसद्भावात् तत्प्रेयसी तत्रैव वर्तत इति। **किमपि** अनिर्वाच्यं अतिसुन्दरमित्यर्थः। **तव नाभिः गिरिसुते!** पार्वति! **बिलद्वारं** गुहाद्वारं, **सिद्धेः** तपःसिद्धेः, **गिरिशनयनानां** सदाशिवचक्षुषां **विजयते** सर्वोत्कर्षेण स्फुरति।।

---

1. गंगावर्तः।
2. कुलावालं ; निजावालं ; जलावालं ; तलावालं।
3. नाभीति गिरिजे।
4. जगज्जननी तस्याः कुलाः किशोरः।

अत्रेत्थं पदयोजना–हे गिरिसुते! तव नाभिः स्थिरो गङ्गावर्तः स्तनमुकुलरोमावलिलताकलावालं कुसुमशरतेजोहुतभुजः कुण्डं रतेर्लीलागारं गिरिशनयनानां सिद्धेर्बिलद्वारं किमपि विजयते।।

अत्रोल्लेखालङ्कारः, एकस्या नाभेरनेकरीत्या उल्लेखात्। नायमतिशयोक्तिः, एकस्यानेकत्वोल्लेखनादेव। नाप्यतिशयोक्तिमाला, किमपीत्यध्यवसितुमशक्यत्वात् किमपीत्यनेन सार्धं मालात्वस्यानुचितत्वादिति रहस्यम्।।७८।।

Notes : The stanza gives a description of the Devī's navel, as assuming various aspects. *Kusuma-śara*—literally, the flower-arrowed, *i.e.*, Manmatha, the god of love. Mouth of the cavern—Yogins resort to secluded spots such as caverns of hills for practising Yoga and thereby attaining Bliss. The Devī's navel is compared to such a spot, resting in which, the eyes of Giriśa (as so many Yogins) seek to attain Bliss.

निसर्गक्षीणस्य स्तनतटभरेण क्लमजुषो
नमन्मूर्तेर्नाभौ[1] वलिषु च शनैस्त्रुट्यत[2] इव।
चिरं ते मध्यस्य त्रुटिततटिनीतीरतरुणा
[3]समावस्थास्थेम्नो भवतु कुशलं शैलतनये।।७९।।

Nisarga-kṣīṇasya stana-taṭa-bhareṇa klama-juṣo
naman-mūrter nābhau valiṣu ca śanais truṭyata iva/
Ciraṁ te madhyasya truṭita-taṭinī-tīra-taruṇā
samāvastha-sthemno bhavatu kuśalaṁ śailatanaye//

Translation : O Daughter of the Mountain! may safety be vouchsafes to Thy waist, which is by nature slim, which is in form as if about to give way in the region of the navel and the folds, and whose firmness is akin to that of a tree standing on the fragile bank of a river.

---

1. ....र्नारीलितक शनकै० ; र्नाभीवलिषु शनकै०।
The text 'नाभौ वलिषु' is accepted by almost all the commentators, *viz.*, Ḍinḍimabhāṣyam, Gopalasundarī, Ānandalaharīṭīkā, Padārthacandrikā, Tātparya Dīpinī, Ānandagirīyā, Aruṇamodinī, and Saubhāgyavardhanī. But Lakṣmīdharā comm. has not accepted this *pāṭha*.
2. शनकैस्त्रुट्यत।
3. समावस्था स्थेम्नो।

निसर्गक्षीणस्य स्वभावेन क्षीणस्यातिकृशस्य, **स्तनतटभरेण** स्तनतटयोः कुचतटयोः **भरेण, क्लमजुषः** क्लान्तिमतः **नमन्मूर्तेः नारीतिलक!** स्त्रीरत्नभूते! **शनकैः** स्तोकं, **त्रुट्यत इव** भिद्यमानस्येव, चिरं बहुकालं, **ते** तव, **मध्यस्य** अवलग्नस्य, **त्रुटिततटिनीतीरतरुणा** त्रुटिते भग्ने तटिन्याः वाहिन्याः तीरे तरुः वृक्षः तेन, समावस्थास्थेम्नः समायां तुल्यायां अवस्थायां स्थेमा स्थैर्यं यस्य तस्य, **भवतु** भूयात्। कुशलं क्षेमं त्रुटनाभावः, शैलतनये पार्वति!

अत्रेत्थं पदयोजना–हे शैलतनये! नारीतिलक! निसर्गक्षीणस्य स्तनतटभरेण क्लमजुषः नमन्मूर्तेः शनकैः त्रुट्यत इव त्रुटिततटिनीतीरतरुणा समावस्थास्थेम्नः ते मध्यस्य चिरं कुशलं भवतु।।

मध्यस्येत्येवमादिप्रयोगाः सहृदयहृदयाह्लादकारिणो महाकविशिक्षाभ्याससमासादिताः। एतादृशप्रयोगनिपुणः महाकविरित्युच्यते।।

अत्रोपमालङ्कारः, भग्ननदीकूलवर्तिमहीरुहशिखामूलिकासाम्यं मध्यस्येति।। ७९ ।।

Notes : Fragile bank—likely to give way at any moment, carrying the tree thereon along with it. The condition of the Devī's waist is similarly precarious, as it might apparently give way (owing to the weight of the two breasts above) at its weak spots, *viz.*, the navel and the folds. The optative form is significant, as the votary finds no one directly to appeal to.

[1]कुचौ सद्यः स्वि[2]द्यत्तटघटितकूर्पासभिदुरौ
कषन्तौ दोर्मूले[3] कनककलशाभौ कलयता[4]।
[5]तव त्रातुं [6]भङ्गादलमिति वलग्नं तनुभुवा
त्रिधा [7]नद्धं देवि त्रिवलि लवलीवल्लिभिरिव।। ८० ।।

Kucau sadyaḥ-svidyat-taṭa-ghaṭita-kūrpāsa-bhidurau
kaṣantau dor-mūle kanaka-kalaśābhau kalayatā
Tava trāruṁ bhaṅgād alam iti valagnaṁ tanubhuvā
tridhā naddhaṁ devi tri-vali lavalī-valibhir iva.//

Translation : O Goddess! Thy three-folded waist has been bound, as it were, by Tanu-bhū, three times over with the

1. कुचावेतौ।
2. सद्यस्तटतटित ; स्विद्यत्तटघटित।
3. दौर्मूलं।
4. कलयतः।
5. परित्रातुं।
6. भंगादुदरमविलग्नं ; भंगादबलमवलग्नं।
7. बद्धं।

Lavalī-creeper, with a view to save it from breaking, he having caused Thy two breasts which resemble pots of gold, to burst the garment covering their sides perspiring at that moment and to rub against the armpits.

कुचौ स्तनौ, **सद्यः** तदानीमेव, **स्विद्यत्तटघटितकूर्पासभिदुरौ** स्विद्यन्तौ स्वेदवन्तौ तटौ पार्श्वौ तयोर्घटितस्य कूर्पासस्य [1]भिदुरौ। 'कर्मकर्तरि कुरच्' इत्यत्र कर्तर्यपि कुरच्। रक्षितस्तु–'कर्मणि कर्तरि च कुरच्' इति व्याचष्टे। 'सद्यस्तनघटितकूर्पासभिदुरौ' इति पाठे सद्यस्तनं तदानीन्तनं नूतनत्वेन घटितं कूर्पासकं तस्य भिदुरौ। प्रतिक्षणं प्राणेश्वरस्य सदाशिवस्य रूपानुसन्धानेन उत्सिक्तावयवैर्भिद्यते सन्धिबन्धेषु कञ्चुलिकेति भावः। **कषन्तौ** निकषन्तौ **दोर्मूले** कक्षप्रान्तदेशे, **कनककलशाभौ** कनककलशयोर्हेम-कुम्भयोरिव आभा सौभाग्यं ययोस्तौ, **कलयता** रचयता निर्मिमाणेन, तव भवत्याः, **त्रातुं** रक्षितुं वलग्नमिति शेषः। यद्वा–प्रथमान्तस्य वलग्नशब्दस्य अत्र कर्मत्वेनान्वयः। **भङ्गात्** स्तनभरजनितात् **अलमिति** अलंशब्दोऽत्र वारणार्थः। भङ्गो मा भूदित्यर्थः। **वलग्नं** मध्यप्रदेशं, **तनुभुवा** मन्मथेन, **त्रिधा** त्रिप्रकारेण, **नद्धं** बद्धं, **देवि!** दीव्यन्ति! भगवति! **त्रिवलि** तिस्रो वलयो विभङ्गाः यस्य तत्। **लवलीवल्लिभिरिव** लवलीनां वल्लयः ताभिः। पीतवल्ली लवली, तत्पुष्पाणि श्वेतानि। अकारादिनिघण्टौ तु–लवलीत्युक्त्वा तल्लता वनकुलत्थलतेत्युक्तम्। यथात्रापि[2] स्वीकार्यम्। इवशब्दः संभावनायां, ध्रुवमित्यर्थः। इवशब्दस्य संभावनाद्योतकत्वमप्यस्तीति पूर्वमेवोक्तम्।।

अत्रेत्थं पदयोजना–हे देवि! सद्यः स्विद्यत्तटघटितकूर्पासभिदुरौ दोर्मूले कषन्तौ कनककलशाभौ कुचौ कलयता तनुभुवा भङ्गादलमिति वलग्नं त्रातुं त्रिवलि तव वलग्नं लवलीवल्लिभिः त्रिधा नद्धमिव।।

अत्र उत्प्रेक्षालङ्कारः, त्रिवलीनां लवलीवल्लीत्वेन संभावनात्। पूर्वार्धे अतिशयोक्तिरलङ्कारः, भगवत्याः कुचनिर्माणे मन्मथस्यैवाधिकारो न जरद्ब्रह्मण इति जरद्ब्रह्मनिर्माणसंबन्धेऽप्यसंबंधोक्त्या अभेदाध्यवसायः कविकृतवस्तुकृतयोः सौन्दर्य-योरेवेति। उभयोरङ्गाङ्गिभावेन सङ्करः। नन्वेवं कुचौ रचयता मन्मथेनेत्यनुवाद्य-विशेषणमहिम्ना मन्मथकर्तृत्वस्य सिद्धवदनुमानात्[3] कुचनिर्माणे वर्तमानसंबन्धाभावात् असंबन्धे संबन्धोक्तेरप्याञ्जस्यमेवेति चेत्–मैवम्; कुचौ कनककलशाभौ कलयतेति शतृप्रत्ययेन वर्तमानार्थेन कुचकरणस्य वर्तमानकालसंबन्धप्रतीतेरसंबन्धे संबन्धोक्ति-राञ्जसीति न वाच्यम्। भूतकालसम्बन्धेऽपि भूतकालक्रियावाचकाख्यातान्तधातुप्रयोगे युज्यते सम्बन्धेऽप्यसंबन्धकथनं न त्वनुवाद्यगतत्वेन सिद्धवदनुवादे।। ८०।।

1. भिदुरौ भेदकरौ।
2. यथारुचि।
3. सिद्धवदनुवादात्।

Notes : *Tanu-bhū*—Manmatha, the god of love. *Lavalī*—a wild creeper known for its enduring qualities. *To burst*—as a result of the surging passion. *Armpits*—encroaching upon them owing to increase in size.

गुरुत्वं विस्तारं क्षितिधरपतिः पार्वति निजा-
न्नितम्बादाच्छिद्य त्वयि [1]हरणरूपेण निदधे।
अतस्ते विस्तीर्णो गुरुरयमशेषां वसुमतीं
नितम्बप्राग्भारः स्थगयति लघुत्वं नयति च[2]॥८१॥

Gurutvaṁ vistāraṁ kṣiti-dhara-patiḥ pārvati nijān
nitambād ācchidya tvayi haraṇa-rūpeṇa nidadhe/
Atas te vistīrṇo gurur ayam aśeṣāṁ vasu-matīṁ
nitamba-prāg-bhāraḥ sthagayati laghutvaṁ nayati ca//

Translation : O Pārvatī! Thy father, the King of the Mountains bestowed on Thee, by way of dowry, heaviness and vastness taken out of his flanks. Hence, these, Thy prodigious hips, being (both) broad and heavy, hide from view the entire terrestrial world and make it light as well.

गुरुत्वं गौरवं, **विस्तारं** आयामपरिणाहं, **क्षितिधरपतिः** हिमवान्, **पार्वति!** शैलतनये! **निजात्** स्वकीयात्, **नितम्बात्** नितम्बप्रदेशात्, **आच्छिद्य** अवयुत्य, **त्वयि** भवत्यां, **हरणरूपेण** हरणात्मना, **निदधे** समर्पितवान्। हरणं नाम स्त्रीधनं–अध्यग्न्यध्यावाहनिकम्। यथोक्तं हारीतेन–

अध्यग्न्यध्यावाहनिकं हरणं स्त्रीधनं स्मृतम्। इति।

अस्यार्थः–अग्निमधिकृत्य दत्तमध्यग्नि विवाहसमये अग्निसमीपे पित्रादिभिर्यद्दत्तं तदध्यग्नि, विवाहानन्तरं वधूं गृहीत्वा स्वगृहं प्रतिजिगमिषावसरे पित्रादिर्भियद्दतं तदध्यावाहनिकमिति[3]। एतदुभयं हरणशब्दवाच्यमिति मन्वादिभिः स्मृतमिति। **अतः** तस्मात्कारणात्, **ते तव**, **विस्तीर्णः** आयामतः, **गुरुः** पृथुः, **अयं** परिदृश्यमानः, **अशेषां** कृत्स्नां, **वसुमतीं** पृथ्वीं **नितम्बप्राग्भारः** नितम्बस्य प्राग्भारः अतिशयः, **स्थगयति** छादयति। **लघुत्वं** लाघवं **नयति** प्रापयति **च**। चकारः[4] शङ्काच्छेदे अस्मिन्नर्थे न शङ्कितव्यमित्यर्थः॥

---

1. भरणरूपेण।
2. च नयति।
3. केचित्। अपरे–आहवनीयसमीपे यज्ञादौ पित्रादिभिर्यद्दत्तं–तदध्याहवनीयकमिति, इत्यधिकः पाठः।
4. शकारः।

अत्रेत्थं पदयोजना–हे पार्वति! क्षितिधरपति: गुरुत्वं विस्तारं निजात् नितम्बादाच्छिद्य त्वयि हरणरूपेण निदधे। अत: ते अयं नितम्बप्राग्भार: गुरु: विस्तीर्णस्सन् अशेषां वसुमतीं स्थगयति लघुत्वं नयति च।।

विस्तारेण स्थगनं गुरुत्वेन लाघवापादनमित्यर्थ:। प्रपञ्चे वसुमत्यामेव गुरुत्वविस्तारौ एकत्र स्थितौ तयोस्तिरस्करणमेकत्र स्थिताभ्यां गुरुत्वविस्ताराभ्यामेव विधेयमिति हिमाद्रिगतगुरुत्वविस्तारौ हिमाद्रे: भूधरत्वात् भूमिगतगुरुत्वविस्ताराभ्यामधिकाविति भावेन गृहीत्वा तत्तिरस्करणमिति क्षितिधरपति: अशेषां वसुमतीमिति च पदं प्रयुञ्जानस्य भाव:।।

अत्रातिशयोक्तिरलङ्कार:, हिमाद्रिगतगुरुत्वविस्तारयो: पार्वतीनितम्बगतगुरुत्व-विस्तारयोर्भेदेऽप्यभेदेनाध्यवसानात्। सेयं भेदे अभेदनिबन्धनादतिशयोक्ति-रलङ्कार:।। ८१ ।।

Notes : The King of the mountains—Himavān (Himālaya), the Devī's father. Hide from view—throw into the background.

ऊरू जानुनी च सकृदेव वर्णयति–

करीन्द्राणां [1]शुण्डान् कनककदलीकाण्डपटली-
मुभाभ्यामूरुभ्यामुभयमपि[2] निर्जित्य भवति[3]।
सुवृत्ताभ्यां पत्यु: प्रणतिकठिनाभ्यां गिरिसुते
[4]विधिज्ञे जानुभ्यां [5]विबुधकरकुम्भद्वयमसि[6]।। ८२।।

Karīndrāṇāṁ śuṇḍān kanaka-kadalī-kāṇḍa-paṭalīm
ubhābhyām ūrubhyām ubhayam api nirijitya bhavati/
Su-vṛttābhyāṁ patyuḥ praṇati-kaṭhinābhyāṁ girisute
vidhijñe jānubhyāṁ vibudha-kari-kumbha-dvayam asi//

Translation : O Daughter of the Mountain! having surpassed alike the trunks of lordly elephants and the clusters of golden plantain-stumps with Thy two thighs, Thou hast likewise surpassed the pair of frontal globes of the divine elephant with

1. शुण्डा: ; शुण्डां।
2. उभयमसि।
3. भवती।
4. विजिग्ये।
5. विविध।
6. द्वयमपि।

Thy pair of perfectly round knees, hardened by (constant) prostration before Thy Lord.

करीन्द्राणां गजेन्द्राणां, **शुण्डान्** करदण्डान्, शुण्डाशब्दस्य पुल्लिङ्गताप्यस्ति इति रक्षितमतम्। **कनककदलीकाण्डपटलीं** सुवर्णरम्भास्तम्भसंहतिम्, **उभाभ्यामूरुभ्यां उभयं** करिकररम्भास्तम्भात्मकम्, **अपि निर्जित्य** विजित्य, **भवति!** त्वं, सुवृत्ताभ्यां: शोभनाभ्यां, वर्तुलाभ्यां **पत्युः** परमेश्वरस्य, **प्रणतिकठिनाभ्यां** प्रणतिभिः कठिनाभ्यां प्रणतिदशायां जान्वोः भूमिस्पर्शादित्यर्थः। **गिरिसुते!** हिमाद्रितनये, **विधिज्ञे!** विधिं वेदार्थं जानातीति विधिज्ञा सर्वज्ञेत्यर्थः। यद्वा–वेदार्थानुष्ठात्री। अत एव पत्युर्नमस्कारः प्रतिदनं वैध इति कृतः न तु तस्याधिक्यानुरोधादिति नर्मवचनम्। तस्याः संबुद्धिः। **जानुभ्यां विबुधकरिकुम्भद्वयं** दिग्दन्तिकुम्भस्थलद्वितयम्, **असि** भवसि।

अत्रेत्थं पदयोजना–हे विधिज्ञे! गिरिसुते! भवति! करीन्द्राणां शुण्डान् कनककदलीकाण्डपटलीं उभाभ्यामूरुभ्यां उभयमपि निर्जित्य सुवृत्ताभ्यां पत्युः प्रणतिकठिनाभ्यां जानुभ्यां विबुधकरिकुम्भद्वयमपि निर्जित्य असि वर्तसे स्फुरसीति यावत्।।

अत्र भवच्छब्दयोगेऽपि असीति मध्यमपुरुष एव भवति, तस्य संबोधनमात्रपरत्वात्। अत्रेदं तत्त्वम्–भवच्छब्दो द्विविधः संबोध्यपरः संबोधनमात्रपरश्चेति। सम्बोध्यपरत्वे भवच्छब्दस्य युष्मदर्थत्वाभावात् 'युष्मद्युपपदे इत्यादिना प्राप्त्यभावात् शेषे प्रथम एव तद्योगे।' यथा–[1]**'सूते जगन्ति भवती भवती बिभर्ति जागर्ति तत्क्षयकृते भवती भवानि'** इत्यादि। यदा–संबोधनमात्रपरत्वं भवच्छब्दस्य तदा युष्मदर्थत्वात् मध्यमपुरुषः स्यादेव। यथा 'भवति भिक्षां देहि' इति। तत्र संबोधनमात्रपरत्वेऽपि ङीप्प्रत्ययः गौरादौ भवतेः प्रातिपदिकस्य पाठात् सिद्धः। अत एव रक्षित आह–'भवतु प्रातिपादिकसामर्थ्यात् स्त्रीलिङ्ग एव भवच्छब्दस्य संबोधनमात्रपरत्वम्' इति। अयमाशयः–भवच्छब्दस्य सर्वनामसु 'भवतु' इति प्रातिपादिकग्रहणात् 'उगितश्च' इति ङीप् सिद्ध एवेति अत्र गौरादौ पठितस्य भवच्छब्दस्य वैयर्थ्यात् स्त्रीत्व एव संबोधनमात्रपरत्वमिति ज्ञापयतीति।।

नन्वेवं रक्षितेनैव "युष्मदस्मदोः स्त्रीपुन्नपुंसकेषु तुल्यलिङ्गत्वं, संबोधनमात्रपरत्वात् युष्मदस्मदोः, एकद्विबहुत्वपरत्वं तु संबोध्यलक्षणतया[2]। न च लिङ्गलक्षणा, आकांक्षाभावात्" इत्युक्तम्। तद्वद्भवच्छब्दस्याप्यलिङ्गत्वं प्राप्नोतीति। मैवं, दत्तोत्तरत्वादित्यलमतिविस्तरेण। यत्तु 'त्वामस्मि वच्मि विदुषाम्' इति श्लोकव्याख्यानावसरे काव्यप्रकाशिकाटीकाकारेण भास्करेणोक्तं तदमूलमिति नोपन्यस्य दूषितम्।।

अत्रोपमालङ्कारस्स्पष्ट एव।।८२।।

---

1. चर्चास्तवः, श्लो० ४। 2. लक्षणया।

Notes : The divine elephant—Airāvata, Indra's elephant. It is usual to compare the thighs of a woman to the trunk of an elephant as well as to the stump of a plantain tree.

[1]पराजेतुं रुद्रं द्विगुणशरगर्भौ गिरिसुते
निषङ्गौ जङ्घे ते विषमविशिखो[2] बाढमकृत[3]।
यदग्रे [4]दृश्यन्ते दश[5]शरफलाः पादयुगली-
नखाग्रच्छद्मानः [6]सुरमकुटशाणै[7]कनिशिताः।।८३।।

Parājetuṁ rudraṁ dvi-guṇa-śara-garbhau giri-sute
niṣaṅgau jaṅghe te viṣama-viśikho bāḍham akṛta/
Yad-agre dṛśyante daśa śara-phalāḥ pāda-yugalī-
nakhāgrac-chadmānaḥ sura-makuṭa-śāṇaikniśitāḥ//

Translation : O Daughter of the Mountain! to vanquish Rudra (in battle) Viṣama-viśikha has forsooth turned Thy two shanks into two quivers, encasing twice the number of arrows, and over their crests are revealed the ten arrow-heads in the form of toe-nails on Thy pair of feet, exclusively sharpened over the whet-stones of the crowns of the gods.

पराजेतुं तिरस्कर्तुं, **रुद्रं** हरं, **द्विगुणशरगर्भौ** द्विगुणीकृताः शराः पञ्चबाणाः गर्भे ययोस्तौ। **गिरिसुते!** पार्वति! **निषङ्गौ** तूणीरौ, जङ्घे जङ्घाकाण्डौ, **ते** तव, **विषमविशिखः** पञ्चबाणः, **बाढं** ध्रुवं, **अकृत** कृतवान्। **यदग्रे** ययोः निषङ्गयोरग्रे, **दृश्यन्ते**। **दशशरफलाः** दशानां शराणां द्विगुणितानां पञ्चानामित्यर्थः तेषां फलाः अयोमुखानि, **पादयुगलीनखाग्रच्छद्मानः** पादयोः प्रपदयोः युगली द्वितयं तस्या नखाग्राणां दशानां छद्म व्याजो येषां ते, **सुरमकुटशाणैकनिशिताः** सुराणाम् इन्द्रादीनां मकुटेष्वेव शाणेषु एकनिशिताः मुख्यतया उत्तेजिताः।।

अत्रेत्थं पदयोजना–हे गिरिसुते! विषमविशिख. रुद्रं पराजेतुं द्विगुणशरगर्भौ निषङ्गौ **ते** जङ्घे अकृत बाढम्। यदग्रे पादयुगलीनखाग्रच्छद्मानः सुरमकुटशाणैकनिशिताः दशशरफला दृश्यन्ते।।

1. पुरां जेतुं।
2. विषयविशिखो।
3. गाढमकृत।
4. लक्ष्यन्ते।
5. शितशरफला।
6. सुरमकुट।
7. शाणौघनिशिताः।

अत्र उत्प्रेक्षालङ्कारः, जङ्घयोः तूणीरतया संभावनात्। अपह्नवालङ्कारश्च, नखाग्राणां फलत्वेनापह्नवात्। अनयोस्संसृष्टिः, अपृथक्स्थित्या प्रयोज्यप्रयोजकभावावगतेः। विषमविशिखो बाढमकृतेत्यत्र अतिशयोक्तिरलङ्कारः, साधारणब्रह्मसृष्टिव्यतिरिक्तत्वेन प्रतीतेः। एतच्च पूर्वमेव स्पष्टीकृतं '**कुचौ सद्यः स्विद्यत्**'[1] [2]इति श्लोकव्याख्यानावसरे। अलङ्कारेण अलङ्कारध्वनिरपि, द्विगुणशरगर्भौ दशशरफला इति पदद्वयेन पादाङ्गुलीनां शराणां च अभेदाध्यवसायप्रतीतेरित्यलम्।। ८३।।

Notes : *Viṣama-viśikha*—literally one having an odd number of arrows, *viz.*, five, *i.e.*, Manmatha, the god of love. *Twice the number*—*viz.*, ten, each toe-nail being compared to an arrow-head, protruding from the quiver. *Whet-stones*—the crowns of the gods, as they come into contact with the Devī's feet, while they prostrate themselves before her, are so many whet-stones.

श्रुतीनां मूर्धानो दधति तव यौ शेखरतया
ममाप्येतौ मातः शिरसि दयया[3] धेहि चरणौ।
ययोः पाद्यं पाथः पशुपतिजटाजूटतटिनी
ययोर्लाक्षालक्ष्मी[4]रुरुणहरिचूडामणिरुचिः ।।८४।।

Śrutīnāṁ mūrdhāno dadhati tava yau śekharatayā
mamāpy etau mātaḥ śirasi dayayā dhehi caraṇau/
Yayoḥ pādyaṁ pāthaḥ paśu-pati-jaṭā-jūṭa-taṭinī
yayor lākṣā-lakṣmīr aruṇa-hari-cūḍā-maṇi-ruciḥ//

Translation : O Mother! pray place those feet of Thine, in the plenitude of Thy mercy, on my head, feet which the foremost parts of the Vedas wear as a crest-bud, the water washing which (feet) forms the river (Ganges) flowing over the matted-hair of Paśupati, and the beautiful lac-dye over which (feet) is the lustre of the red crest-jewel of Hari.

श्रुतीनां निगमानां, **मूर्धानः** शिरांसि वेदान्ता इत्यर्थः। **दधति** धारयन्ति प्रतिपादयन्तीत्यर्थः। **तव** भवत्याः, **यौ** चरणौ पादौ, **शेखरतया** उत्तंसतया। यद्वा–श्रुतीनां श्रुतिवधूनां मूर्धानः श्रुतयः भगवतीपादाब्जं उत्तंसयन्ति। यथोक्तम्–श्रुतिवाक्यं शक्तिं प्रति वसिष्ठेन–

---

1. ८० श्लो०।
2. इत्यादिश्लोकद्वय।
3. कृपया।
4. ररुणतरचूडा ; ररुणहरचूडा।

नमो देव्यै महालक्ष्म्यै श्रियै सिद्ध्यै नमो नमः।
ब्रह्मविष्णुमहेशानवेदकैः पूजिताङ्घ्रये।।

वेदकैरित्यत्र वेदानां कैः शिरोभिरिति।

नमस्त्रिपुरसुन्दर्यै शिवायै विश्वमूर्तये।

इत्यादि।

एवं स्तुता महादेवी श्रुतिभिः प्रीतमानसा।
प्राह ताः प्रति तादृग्भिः वचोभिरमरेश्वरी।।

इत्यादि वसिष्ठसंहितायाम्। **ममापि एतौ** चरणौ, **मातः!** जननि! **शिरसि** मूर्धनि, **दयया** कृपया कृपाविष्टचित्तेनेत्यर्थः। **धेहि** निधेहि। **चरणौ** पादौ, **ययोः** चरणयोः सम्बन्धि, **पाद्यं पाथः** पादनिर्णेजनजलम्। यद्यपि पाद्यमित्युक्ते पादसम्बन्धः प्रतीयते तथापि पाद्यमित्युक्ते पादप्रक्षालनार्हं पाद्यमित्यर्हतामात्रप्रतीतौ विशेषाकारेण ययोरित्यस्यान्वय इति न पौनरुक्त्यम्। **पशुपतिजटाजूटतटिनी** पशुपतेः शिवस्य जटाजूटे कपर्दे तटिनी गङ्गा, **ययोः** चरणयोः, **लाक्षालक्ष्मीः** लाक्षारसकान्तिः, **अरुणहरिचूडामणिरुचिः** अरुणश्चासौ हरिचूडामणिश्च कौस्तुभः तस्य रुचिः रक्तिमा।।

अयमर्थः– प्रणयकोपशान्तये प्रणतस्य पशुपतेः जटाजूटवर्तिनी गङ्गा पादाग्रवर्तिनी आसीदिति गङ्गायाः पाद्यजलत्वं कथितम्। प्रतिदिनं सायंप्रातः सेवार्थं नमस्कुर्वाणस्य विष्णोः मकुटघटितकौस्तुभमणेः श्वेतवर्णस्य लाक्षारसप्रसादजन्या अरुणिमेति ध्येयम्।।

अत्रेत्थं पदयोजना–हे जननि! तव यौ चरणौ श्रुतीनां मूर्धानः शेखरतया दधति। हे मातः! एतौ चरणौ ममापि शिरसि दयया धेहि। ययोः पाद्यं पाथः पशपुतिजटाजूटतटिनी ययोः लाक्षालक्ष्मीः अरुणहरिचूडामणिरुचिः।।

एतदुक्तं भवति–भगवत्याः पादाम्बुजद्वितयस्य वेदमूर्धनि सदाशिवमूर्धनि विष्णुमूर्धन्येव सञ्चार इति मूर्धसञ्चारस्वाभाव्यमस्ति। अतो मम मूर्धन्यपि सञ्चरतु पादाम्बुजमिति प्रार्थनासामञ्जस्यमिति कवेरभिप्रायः। यद्वा–प्रपञ्चजनयित्र्याः सादाख्यायाः प्रपञ्चान्तःपातिनः हरिविरिञ्चिपशुपतिवेदान्ताः पादाम्बुजं शिरसि धारयन्ति तन्निर्णेजनजलेन पवित्रितगात्राः तन्महिम्ना तत्तदधिकारान् भजन्ति इति युज्यत एवेति।।

अत्र रूपकालङ्कारः स्पष्टः।। ८४।।

Notes : The sanctity, as well as the beauty of the Devī's feet, is described here.

[1]नमोवाकं ब्रूमो नयनरमणीयाय पदयो–
स्तवास्मै द्वन्द्वाय स्फुटरुचिरसालक्तकवते।
असूयत्यत्यन्तं[2] यदभिहननाय[3] स्पृहयते
पशूनामीशानः प्रमदवनकङ्केलितरवे।। ८५।।

Namo-vākaṁ brūmo nayana-ramaṇīyāya padayos
tavāsmai dvandvāya sphuṭa-ruci-rasālaktaka-vate/
Asūyaty atyantaṁ yad-abhihananāya spṛhayate
paśūnām īśānaḥ pramada-vana-kaṅkeli-tarave//

Translation : Our salutations we respectfully tender to this Thy pair of feet, ravishingly beautiful, distinctly bright with the lac-dye freshly painted over them. The Lord of Paśus grows extremely jealous of the Kaṅkeli tree in (Thy) pleasure-garden, which ardently aspires to be kicked by them (Thy pair of feet).

नमोवाकं नम इति वाक्यम्। नमोवाकशब्दो निपातनात्साधुः। ब्रूमः वदामः, नमस्कुर्म इत्यर्थः। **नयनरमणीयाय** नेत्रयोः प्रियकराय, **पदयोः** चरणयोः, **तव अस्मै** परिदृश्यमानाय, **द्वन्द्वाय** युग्माय, **स्फुटरुचिरसालक्तकवते** स्फुटरुचये स्फुरत्प्रभाय रसालक्तकवते सार्द्रालक्तकाय, विशेषणसमासः। **असूयति** ईर्ष्यति। **अत्यन्तं** नितरां, **यदभिहननाय** येन पदयुगेन अभिहननं ताडनं तस्मै, अभिहननं न सहत इत्यर्थः। अशोकश्चरणाहतिव्यक्तपुष्प इति दोहदकौतुके। **स्पृहयते** स्पृहां **कुर्वते, पशूनामीशानः** पशुपतिः, **प्रमदवनकङ्केलितरवे** प्रमदवनं उद्यानवनं तत्र कङ्केलितरुरशोकः तस्मै असूयति ईर्ष्यति। उभयत्र 'क्रुधद्रुह' इत्यादिना 'स्पृहेरीप्सितः' इत्यनेन च संप्रदाने चतुर्थी।।

अत्रेत्थं पदयोजना–हे भगवति! तव नयनरमणीयाय स्फुटरुचिरसालक्तकवते पदयोरस्मै द्वन्द्वाय नमोवाकं ब्रूमः। पशूनामीशानः यदभिहननाय स्पृहयते प्रमदवन-कङ्केलितरवे अत्यन्तं असूयति।।

प्रणयकलहसमये अनुग्रहात्मा पादाघातो न कस्यापि संभाव्यत [4]इति अचेतनवस्तु-ऽनोपि कङ्केलितरोः कथं स्यादिति तत्रैवासूया नान्यत्रेति भावः। अनेनात्यन्तं पातिव्रत्यं पार्वत्याः प्रतिपादितम्। एतादृशं पातिव्रत्यं लक्ष्मीसरस्वत्योर्नास्तीति ध्वन्यते।।

---

1. नमोवाचं ; नमो वा किं।
2. असूयत्यत्यर्थं।
3. तदभिहननाय।
4. इत्युच्यते। तेन तस्यापि कङ्केलितरोः (पा०)।

अत्रातिशयोक्तिरलङ्कारः, पशुपतेरीर्ष्ययाऽसंबन्धेऽपि संबन्धकथनादभेदाध्यवसायप्रतीतेः।। ८५।।

Notes : Jealous of the Kaṅkeli—the Kaṅkeli is a tree which, according to tradition, when barren, blossoms only when kicked by the tender feet of women of the highest class, known as Padminīs. Śiva is represented here as envying the barren Kaṅkeli tree in the Devī's garden, for the exclusive privilege, which it enjoys, of receiving kicks, from its mistress's feet. In other words, he wishes very much that some of them be administered to himself.

मृषा कृत्वा गोत्रस्खलनमथ[1] वैलक्ष्यनमितं
ललाटे भर्तारं चरणकमले[2] ताडयति ते।
चिरादन्तःशल्यं दहनकृतमुन्मूलितवता[3]
तुलाकोटिक्वाणैः [4]किलिकिलितमीशानरिपुणा।। ८६।।

Mṛṣā kṛtvā gotra-skhalanam atha vailakṣya-namitaṁ
lalāṭe bhartāraṁ caraṇa-kamale tāḍayati te/
Cirād antaḥ-śalyaṁ dahana-kṛtam unmūlitavatā
tulā-koṭi-kvāṇaiḥ kili-kilitam īśāna-ripuṇā//

Translation : O Devī! When Thy lotus-like foot kicked, on the forehead, Thy husband, who, having frivolously blundered in calling (Thee by a wrong) name, was in consequence bent with shame; through the jingling of (Thy) anklets, there was an acclamation of triumph, as it were, from Īśāna's foe, who thus had his vengeance, generated by (his) being burnt to ashes and rankling for a long time, wreaked.

मृषा अकस्मादेव, **कृत्वा गोत्रस्खलनं** गोत्रस्य स्खलनं नाम नायिकायामनुरागं प्रकटयतस्तत्समीप एव प्रमादात् नायिकान्तराविष्टचित्तस्य तन्नामोच्चारणम्। **अथ** गोत्रस्खलनानन्तरं, **वैलक्ष्यनमितं** वैलक्ष्येण इति कर्तव्यतामौढ्येन नमितम्। अत्र नमितमिति वैलक्ष्यप्राधान्यात् वैलक्ष्येणैव नमितः न तु स्वयं वैलक्ष्यान्नमितः। अत्युत्कृष्टं वैलक्ष्यमासीदिति नमितशब्दं प्रयुञ्जानस्य भावः। **ललाटे** निटिलप्रदेशे, **भर्तारं** पशुपतिं,

---

1. गोत्रस्खलितमथ।
2. चरणकमलं ; चरणयुगले।
3. दहनकृतमुन्मीलिवता ; ......मुत्कीलितवता।
4. किंलकिलितमीशानरिपुणा।

चरणकमले पादाम्बुजे, **ताडयति** घ्नति सति चरणकमलेन भर्तुर्ललाटं ताडितवत्यां भवत्यामित्यर्थः। ललाटताडनं भर्तृपर्यन्तं गच्छतीति भर्तारं ताडयतीत्युक्तिराञ्जसीति एतादृशप्रयोगाः महाकविशिक्षावशादायाताः सहृदयहृदयाह्लादकाः। **ते** तव, **चिरात्** चिरकालमनुस्यूतं, **अन्तश्शल्यं** हृदयशल्यं, वैरमित्यर्थः। **दहनकृतं** नयनाग्निना प्लोषणकृतं, **उन्मूलितवता तुलाकोटिक्वाणैः** तुला नूपुरं तस्य कोटयः अग्राणि, तैरन्तर्गता मणयः क्षुद्रघण्टयदयः लक्ष्यन्ते, तेषां क्वाणैः शिञ्जितैः। **किलिकिलितम्** किलिकिलेत्यनुकरणं विजयिनः सुप्रसिद्धम्। किलिकिलिरवः कृत इत्यर्थः। **ईशानरिपुणा** मन्मथेन। मन्मथस्य ईशानं प्रति रिपुत्वं तदा सिद्धमिति भावः।।

अत्रेत्थं पदयोजना–हे भगवति! मृषा गोत्रस्खलनं कृत्वा अथ वैलक्ष्यनमितं भर्तारं ते चरणकमले ललाटे ताडयति सति ईशानरिपुणा चिरात् दहनकृतम् अन्तःशल्यम् उन्मूलितवता तुलाकोटिक्वाणैः किलिकिलितम्।।

अत्रातिशयोक्तिरलङ्कारः, तुलाकोटिक्वाणानां किलिकिलितध्वनित्वेनाध्यवसानात् भेदे अभेदनिबन्धनातिशयोक्तिः।। ८६ ।।

Notes : The poet creates, out of his imagination, an amorous interval, wherein Śiva is represented as being found out by his spouse, when, in jest, he calls her by a wrong name, the implication being that the Devī scents therein his amour with some other woman and punishes him therefore with a kick. Manmatha, who was only waiting for an opportunity for venting his spleen on his enemy Śiva, by seeing him lowered in esteem, uses the jingling of the anklet as a sign of his triumph over Śiva. It may also be noted that, in this stanza, the poet creates an opportunity cleverly enough for the Lord to receive the kick he so much longed for, as shown in the previous stanza, by creating a situation as depicted here, *viz.*, the blunder of using a wrong name.

हिमानीहन्तव्यं हिमगिरिनिवासैकचतुरौ[1]
निशायां निद्राणं निशि च परभागे च[2] विशदौ[3]।

---

1. हिमगिरितटक्रान्तिरुचिरा ; हिमगिरितटक्रान्तिचतुरौ ; हिमगिरितटक्रान्तिरुचिरौ।
2. निशि चरमभागे च ; निशि च परभागेण। 'निशिच परभागे च'–this *pāṭha* is accepted by most of the commentators. But the commentator Lakṣmīdhara has accepted. ....'निशि चरमभागे च' *pāṭha.*
3. रुचिरौ।

[1]वरं लक्ष्मीपात्रं श्रियमतिसृजन्तौ[2] समयिनां[3]
सरोजं त्वत्पादौ जननि जयतश्चित्रमिह[4] किम्।।८७।।

Himānī-hantavyaṁ hima-giri-nivāsaika-caturau
niśāyāṁ nidrāṇaṁ niśi ca para-bhāge ca viśadau/
Varaṁ lakṣmī-pātraṁ śriyam atisṛjantau samayināṁ
sarojaṁ tvat-pādau janani jayataś citram iha kim//

Translation : O Mother! what (is here to) wonder at, if Thy two feet, quite adapted to abide in the snow-capped mountain, bright all through night and its counterpart (the day) and lavishing their grace on their devotees, have outdone the lotus-flower, which easily blights with snow-fall, sleeps during night and only slightly attains Lakṣmī's grace?

हिमानीहन्तव्यं हिमान्या हिमसंहत्या हन्तव्यं नाशितव्यं, **हिमगिरिनिवासैकचतुरौ** सर्वदा हिमगिरावेव वसन्तावित्यर्थः। **निशायां** शर्वर्यां, **निद्राणं** मुकुलितं, **निशि चरमभागे च विशदौ** प्रसन्नौ, चेतनाशक्तेः तत्रैवोत्पत्तेरिति भावः। चकारात् दिवापि प्रसन्नावित्यर्थः। **वरम्** ईप्सितं, **लक्ष्मीपात्रं** लक्ष्म्या अधिष्ठितमित्यर्थः। **श्रियं** लक्ष्मीम्, **अतिसृजन्तौ** उत्पादयन्तौ, **समयिनां** स्वभक्तानाम्, समयस्वरूपं '**तवाधारे मूले**'[5] इति श्लोके निरूपितम्। **सरोजं** कमलं कर्मभूतं, **त्वत्पादौ जननि!** हे मातः! **जयतः** विजयेते। **चित्रम्** आश्चर्यम्, इह अस्मिन्नर्थे, **किं** न किमपीत्यर्थः।

अत्रेत्थं पदयोजना–हे जननि! हिमगिरिनिवासैकचतुरौ निशिचरमभागो च विशदौ समयिनां श्रियमतिसृजन्तौ त्वत्पादौ हिमानीहन्तव्यं निशायां निद्राणं वरं लक्ष्मीपात्रं सरोजं जयतः; इह किं चित्रं, आधिक्यस्य स्फुटत्वादित्यर्थः।।

अत्र व्यतिरेकालङ्कारः स्फुटः।।८७।।

Notes : It is usal for poets to compare the Devī's feet to the lotus flower. It this stanza the poet tries to show the fallacy as it were, lurking in such a comparison, as it is only in one respect, and that too only slightly, that such resemblance can hold good. *Lakṣmī's grace*—the grace of the Devī's feet, *i.e.*, red colour and that too

1. परं।
2. श्रियमपि सृजन्तौ ; श्रियमपिदिशन्तौ।
3. प्रणयिनाम्।
4. हसतश्चित्रमिह।
5. ४७ श्लोक।

slightly, during only a part of the day, *i.e.*, during daylight, when the lotus is in bloom.

पदं ते [1]कीर्तीनां प्रपदमपदं देवि विपदां
कथं नीतं सद्भिः कठिनकमठीकर्परतुलाम्[2]।
कथं[3] वा बाहुभ्यामुपयमनकाले पुरभिदा
यदादाय न्यस्तं दृषदि दयमानेन मनसा[4]।।८८।।

Padaṁ te kīrtīnāṁ prapadam a-padaṁ devi vipadāṁ
kathaṁ nītaṁ sadbhiḥ kaṭhina-kamaṭhī-karpara-tulām/
Kathaṁ vā bāhubhyām upayamana-kāle pura-bhidā
yad ādāya nyastaṁ dṛṣadi dayamānena manasā.//

Translation : O Goddess! how is it that the fore-part of Thy foot, which is the seat of all fame, which cannot be touched by danger (of any kind), and which was somehow lifted at the time of (Thy) marriage by the vanquisher of the (three) Puras, with a soft heart, and placed on a stone, has been made a peer of the hard tortoise-shell by great poets?

पदं स्थानं ; **ते** तव, **कीर्तीनां** यशसां, **प्रपदं** पादाग्रं, **अपदम्** अस्थानं, **देवि!** द्योतनशीले! भगवति! **विपदाम्** आपदां, **कथं** कथङ्कारं, **नीतं** प्रापितं, **सद्भिः** कवीन्द्रैः **कठिनकमठीकर्परतुलां** कठिनस्य कमठीकर्परस्य कूर्मपृष्ठकपालस्य तुलां, **कथं वा** कथंकृत्वा, **बाहुभ्यां** हस्ताभ्यां, **उपयमनकाले** विवाहसमये, **पुरभिदा** सदाशिवेन, **यत् पदम् आदाय** गृहीत्वा, **न्यस्तं** क्षिप्तं, **दृषदि** उपलाधारभूता शिला दृषत्, उपलं हरिद्रादिद्रव्यस्य पेषणिका शिला। तदाधारभूता शिला दृषत्। सा विवाहसमये अश्मस्थापनानुष्ठानार्थं पात्रत्वेन प्रयुक्ता। तस्यां दृषदि **दयमानेन** दयावता, **मनसा।** दयां विहायातिमृदुलं पादाम्बुजं दृषदि कथं स्थापितं शम्भुना। अमृतस्यन्दिनीभिः वाग्विलासैः कवीश्वराः कमठपृष्ठेन तुल्यतया कथम्? एतदुभयमयुक्तमित्यर्थः।।

अत्रेत्थं पदयोजना–हे दवि! कीर्तीनां पदं विपदामपदं ते प्रपदं सद्भिः कठिनकमठीकर्परतुलां कथं नीतम्? दयमानेन मनसा पुरभिदा उपयमनकाले बाहुभ्यां यदादाय कथं वा दृषदि न्यस्तम्?

---

1. कान्तीनां।
2. कठिनकमठीनां पदतुलाम् ; कठिनकमठीखर्परतुलाम्।
3. कथं स्वाबाहुभ्यामुपनयनकाले ; कथं चिद्बाहु......; कथं वा हस्ताभ्यां।
4. वपुषा।

अत्रानन्वयालङ्कारो ध्वन्यते, सदृशान्तरनिषेधात् असदृशस्य पादाम्बुजवस्तुनः स्वयमेव स्वस्य तुल्यमिति प्रतीतेः।।८८।।

Notes : Here the poet calls into question the propriety of comparing the forepart of the Devī's foot, which has become reputed as the bestower of the ends and aims of existence and as warding off all danger, to a hard tortoise-shell, which does little credit to the artistic skill of great poets. There is also a reading "*Kathaṁ vā, etc.*", when the meaning would be : "How did Śiva manage to life, *etc.*?" implying thereby that Śiva was light-hearted enough to do the wrong thing by placing the Devī's soft feet on a hard piece of flint. Kaivalyāśrama remarks in his gloss on this stanza: "This Stanza is not in accord with Śaṅkarācārya's Saṁpradāya, as it is not found either in the Malaiyālam manuscript or in the South Indian manuscripts." But Arthur Avalon, in his Introduction to his edition of Ānandalaharī, quotes this remark and applies it to stanza 99, apparently by mistake.

नखैर्नाकस्त्रीणां करकमलसङ्कोचशशिभि-
स्तरूणां दिव्यानां हसत इव ते चण्डि चरणौ।
फलानि स्वःस्थेभ्यः[1] किसलयकराग्रेण [2]ददतां
दरिद्रेभ्यो भद्रां श्रियमनिशमह्नाय ददतौ।।८९।।

Nakhair nāka-strīṇāṁ kara-kamala-saṅkoca-śaśibhis
tarūṇāṁ divyānāṁ hasata iva te caṇḍi caraṇau/
Phalāni svaḥ-sthebhyaḥ kīsalaya-karāgreṇa dadatāṁ
daridrebhyo bhadrāṁ śriyam aniśam ahnāya dadatau//

Translation : O Caṇḍī! Thy two feet, which lavish plenty of wealth at all time and at once, on the poor, laugh as it were with their toe-nails, which resemble (so many) moons causing the closing of the lotus-like hands of celestial women, at the Kalpaka trees which give their fruits exclusively to the denizens of the celestial world, with their finger-like sprouts.

नखैः नखरैः, **नाकस्त्रीणां** सुराङ्गनानां शच्यादीनां, **करकमलसङ्कोचशशिभिः** करा एव कमलानि तेषां सङ्कोचे मुकुलीभावे शशिनः चन्द्रात्मकाः पाददर्शनवेलायां नखकान्तयः चन्द्रकिरणा इव तत्करान् मुकुलयन्ति अञ्जलिसन्धानं कारयन्ति। **तरूणां**

1. स्वस्थेभ्यः।
2. दधतां।

वृक्षाणां **दिव्यानां** दिवि भवानां, **हसतः**। तरूणां हसत इति कर्मणि षष्ठी। हसन्तौ **इव ते** तव, **चण्डि!** भगवति! **चरणौ फलानि स्वस्थेभ्यः** स्वर्गस्थेभ्य एव न तु दरिद्रेभ्य इति विशेषणवशात्प्रतीयते। **किसलयकराग्रेण** किसलया एव कराः तेषामग्रं तेन, **ददतां** दिशतां, **दरिद्रेभ्यो** दीनेभ्यश्च, **भद्राम्** अमन्दां, **श्रियं** लक्ष्मीं, **अनिशं** सर्वदा, **अह्नाय** शीघ्रं, **ददतौ**।।

अयमर्थः—कल्पवृक्षाः किसलयकरैः स्वस्थेभ्य एव आशानुसारेण शनैः शनैः फलं ददति। ते पादाम्बुजं तु स्वस्थेभ्यो दरिद्रेभ्यश्च शीघ्रं भद्रां श्रियं ददातीति व्यतिरेकः।।

अत्रेत्थं पदयोजना—हे चण्डि! किसलयकराग्रेण स्वस्थेभ्यः एव फलानि ददतां दिव्यानां तरूणां दरिद्रेभ्यो भद्रां श्रियं अनिशमह्नाय ददतौ ते चरणौ नाकस्त्रीणां करकमलसङ्कोचशशिभिः नखैः हसत इव।।

अत्र व्यतिरेकालङ्कारः स्फुट एव। स च स्वस्थेभ्य इत्यत्र श्लेषानुप्राणित इत्यनुसन्धेयम्।। ८९ ।।

Notes : The Devī's feet, which have the quality of bestowing plenty on the needy at all times and at once, are made by the poet to laugh at Kalpaka trees, which, notwithstanding their much talked of pretensions as regards granting boons to all, after all grant the desires of people above want (the *Svasthas*). There is a play on the word '*Svasthas*', which means (1) who are above want, and (2) who are celestial. Again, the crescent-like toe-nails, which are so many moons, extort the homage of celestial women, as their hands, which resemble the lotus-flower, are forced to be closed in veneration, on their approaching the Devī's feet, which contain many moons.

***ददाने दीनेभ्यः श्रियमनिशमाशाऽनुसदृशी-[1]**
ममन्दं सौन्दर्यप्रकरमकरन्दं[2] विकिरति।
तवास्मिन्मन्दारस्तबकसुभगे यातु चरणे
निमज्जन्मज्जीवः करणचरणः[3] षट्चरणताम्।। ९० ।।

Dadāne dīnebhyaḥ śriyam aniśam āśā-'nusadṛśīm
a-mandaṁ saundarya-prakara-makarandaṁ vikirati/

---

1. मात्मानुसदृशी ; मीशानसदृशीं।
2. स्तबकमकरन्दं।
3. करणचरणैः।

* In the Saurastra Edn. (1961) this verse 90 is read as verse No. 29.

Tavāsmin mandāra-stabaka-su-bhage yātu caraṇe
nimajjan maj-jīvaḥ karaṇa-caraṇaḥ ṣaṭ-caraṇatām//

Translation : May my soul attain the quality of a six-footed (bee), with the (six) senses as its feet, by immersing in this, Thy foot, which is ever giving to the helpless, wealth in proportion to their desire, scattering abundant honey in the form of a flood of beauty, and which is auspicious as a cluster of Mandāra flowers.

ददाने ददति, **दीनेभ्यो** दरिद्रेभ्यः, **श्रियं** लक्ष्मीं, **अनिशम् आशानुसदृशीं** वाञ्छानुरूपाम्, **अमन्दम्** अधिकं, **सौन्दर्यप्रकरमकरन्दं** सौन्दर्यस्य लावण्यस्य प्रकरः समूह एव मकरन्दः पुष्परसः तं, **विकिरति** क्षिपति, **तव** भवत्याः, **अस्मिन्** दृश्यमाने, **मन्दारस्तबकसुभगे** कल्पवृक्षगुच्छसौभाग्यवति, **यातु** प्राप्नुयात्। **चरणे** पादाब्जे, **निमज्जन्** नितरां मज्जनं कुर्वन्, **मज्जीवः** अहं चासौ जीवश्च मज्जीवः, **करणचरणः** करणानि पञ्चेन्द्रियाणि मनष्षष्ठानि तान्येव चरणा यस्य सः **षट्चरणतां** भ्रमरत्वम्।।

अत्रेत्थं पदयोजना–हे भगवति! दीनेभ्यः आशानुसदृशीं श्रियम् अनिशं ददाने अमन्दं सौन्दर्यप्रकरमकरन्दं विकिरति मन्दारस्तबकसुभगे अस्मिन् तव चरणे करणचरणः मज्जीवः निमज्जन् षट्चरणतां यातु।।

अत्रातिशयोक्तिरलङ्कारः, चरणस्य कमलत्वेन निगीर्याध्यवसानात्। मन्दारस्तबक-सुभग इत्यत्र उपमालङ्कारः। अनयोः संसृष्टिः। करणचरण इत्यत्र रूपकं करणानां चरणत्वेन[1] रूपणात्। मज्जीवष्षट्चरणतां यात्वित्यत्र परिणामालङ्कारः स्पष्टः। अनयोरङ्गाङ्गिभावेन सङ्करः। सौन्दर्यप्रकरमकरन्दं विकिरतीत्यत्र रूपकं निगीर्याध्यवसाने निमित्तम्। अत एव नैकदेशरूपकम्, अवयवानां प्रतिपादनात्। करणचरणष्षट्चरणतां यात्विति फलत्वेनोद्देशात् अवयवत्वं तस्य। अतोऽस्मिन् चरण इति आरोपविषतया चरणमुपादाय कमलमारोप्यमाणबुद्ध्या निगीर्णमिति सम्यक्। एवं परिणामातिशययोः सङ्कर एव न तु संसृष्टिरिति ध्येयम्।। ९०।।

Notes : In this stanza the poet compares the Devī's feet to a cluster of Mandāra flowers, in point of auspiciousness, scattering of honey and beauty and the bestowing of wealth on the needy, and the soul of the votary possessed of the six senses to a six-footed bee. The underlying idea is : The votary prays that his mind be ever absorbed in meditating on the Devī's feet.

---

1. आरोपणात्।

पदन्यासक्रीडापरिचयमिवारब्धुमनस-[1]
श्चरन्तस्ते[2] खेलं [3]भवनकलहंसा न जहति।
[4]स्वविक्षेपे शिक्षां सुभगमणिमञ्जीररणित-
च्छलादाचक्षाणं चरणकमलं[5] चारुचरिते[6]।।९१।।

Pada-nyāsa-krīḍā-paricayam ivārabdhu-manasaś
carantas te khelaṁ bhavana-kala-haṁsā na jahati/
Sva-vikṣepe śikṣāṁ subhaga-maṇi-mañjīra-raṇitac
chalād ācakṣāṇaṁ caraṇa-kamalaṁ cāru-carite//

Translation : O Goddess with a stately carriage! Thy household swans, frolicking as if prone to practise the balancing of their steps, do not leave off Thy lotus-like foot, which imparts instruction in its own art (of balancing steps) as it were, by the tinkling of the beautiful anklet (filled) with gems.

पदन्यासक्रीडापरिचयं पदयोर्न्यासः तस्मिन् क्रीडा विनोदः तस्य परिचयमिव अभ्यासमिव। इवशब्दः संभावनावचनः नूनमित्यर्थः। **आरब्धुमनसः** संपादयितुकामाः, **स्खलन्तः** स्खलद्गतयः, **ते** तव, **खेलं** खेलनं विलासं सञ्चारं, **भवनकलहंसाः** भवने परिपोषिताः कलहंसाः हंसविशेषाः, **न जहति** न परित्यजन्ति त्वदनुसरणं न कदाचिदपि त्यजन्तीत्यर्थः। **अतः** कारणात्, **तेषां** कलहंसानां, **शिक्षां** खेलनशिक्षां, **सुभगमणिमञ्जीररणितच्छलात्** मणिमञ्जीरो मणिप्रधाननूपुरः स चासौ सुभगः रम्यतरः। यद्वा—सुभगैः मणिभिः पद्मरागादिभिः युक्तः, तस्य मञ्जीरस्य रणितानां शिञ्जितानां छलात् व्याजात्। **आचक्षाणम्** उपदिशत्, **चरणकमलं** पादाम्बुजं, **चारुचरिते!** शोभनगमने!

अत्रेत्थं पदयोजना–हे चारुचरिते! पदन्यासक्रीडापरिचयम् आरब्धुमनसः भवन-कलहंसाः स्खलन्तः ते खेलं न जहति ; अतः चरणकमलं सुभगमणिमञ्जीररणितच्छलात् तेषां शिक्षाम् आचक्षाणमिव।।

अत्रोत्प्रेक्षालङ्कारः–मञ्जीररणितानां शिक्षावचनात्मतया संभावनात्। पूर्वार्धे

1. लब्धु।
2. स्खलन्तस्ते ; चलन्त्यास्ते।
3. भुवन ; शरण।
4. अतस्तेषां ; सुविक्षेपे।
5. चरणयुगलं।
6. चारुचरितम्।

अतिशयोक्तिः, भवनकलहंसानां स्वाभाविके पोषकजनानुसरणे पदन्यासक्रीडा-परिचयार्थत्वेन अध्यवसानात् असंबन्धे संबन्धनिबन्धनातिशयोक्तिः। उभयोरङ्गाङ्गिभावेन सङ्करः।। ९१ ।।

Notes : The Devī's beautiful gait is represented by the poet as imparting instruction to her household swans, who themselves have a graceful gait.

एवं मकुट्यदिपादान्तं वर्णयित्वा पुनः स्वरूपं प्रस्तौति–

[1]गतास्ते मञ्चत्वं दुहिणहरिरुद्रेश्वरभृतः[2]
[3]शिवः स्वच्छच्छायाघटितकपटप्रच्छदपटः[4]।
त्वदीयानां भासां [5]प्रतिफलनरागारुणतया
शरीरी शृङ्गारो रस इव दृशां दोग्धि कुतुकम्।। ९२ ।।

Gatās te mañcatvaṁ druhiṇa-hari-rudreśvara-bhṛtaḥ
śivaḥ svacchac-chāyā-ghaṭita-kapaṭa-pracchada-paṭaḥ/
Tvadīyānāṁ bhāsāṁ pratiphalana-rāgāruṇatayā
śarīrī śṛṅgāro rasa iva dṛśāṁ dogdhi kutukam//

Translation : Thy servants, Druhiṇa, Hari, Rudra and Īśvara, have become Thy cot. Śiva with His imaginary bedsheet of a transparent hue, (Himself) tinged red with Thy lustre reflected therein, yields pleasure to Thine eyes, assuming as it were the form of erotic sentiment incarnate.

गताः प्राप्ताः, **ते** तव, **मञ्चत्वं** खट्वारूपत्वं **दुहिणहरिरुद्रेश्वरभृतः** दुहिणो ब्रह्मा हरिर्विष्णुः रुद्रः ईश्वरः, एते अधिकारपुरुषाः महेश्वरतत्त्वान्तर्गताः ते च ते भृतश्च। क्विबन्तोऽयं शब्दः बहुवचनान्तः। भृतो भृतकाः विशेषणसमासः। तेषां कामरूपाणां अत्यन्तसन्निकृष्टसेवार्थं मञ्चस्य पादचतुष्टयरूपतायुज्यत एव। **शिवः** शिवशब्दो व्याख्यातः शिवतत्त्वात्मक एवाधिकारिपुरुषः। **यद्वा**–सदाशिवतत्त्वम्। **स्वच्छच्छाया-घटितकपटप्रच्छदपटः** स्वच्छा चासौ छाया च स्वच्छच्छाया, कान्तिः सैव घटितः कपटप्रच्छदपटः शुभ्रकान्तिरेव वस्त्रात्मनावस्थित इत्यर्थः। **त्वदीयानां** भवत्सम्बन्धिनीनां,

---

1. गतस्ते।
2. रुद्रेश्वरधृतः।
3. शिवस्वच्छ।
4. प्रच्छदपटम्।
5. प्रतिफलनभावारुणतया ; प्रतिफलनलाभारुणतया ; प्रतिफलनलाभादरुणितः।

भासां कान्तीनां, **प्रतिफलनररागारुणतया** प्रतिफलनेन यो रागः रक्तिमा सङ्क्रान्तः तेनारुणो रक्तवर्णः तस्य भावस्तत्ता तया। **शरीरी** मूर्तः, **शृङ्गारः** शृङ्गाराख्यो **रस इव**। शृङ्गाररसः रक्तवर्ण इति महाकविप्रसिद्धिः। इवशब्दः संभावनायाम्। **दृशां** भवद्वीक्षणानां, **दोग्धि** दुग्धे प्रसूते करोतीति यावत्, **कुतुकम्** आनन्दम्।।

अत्रेत्थं पदयोजना–हे भगवति! ते मञ्चत्वं द्रुहिणहरिरुद्रेश्वरभृतः गताः ; शिवः स्वच्छच्छायाघटितकपटप्रच्छदपटः सन् त्वदीयानां भासां प्रतिफलनरागारुणतया शरीरी शृङ्गारो रस इव दृशां कुतुकं दोग्धि।।

अत्रेदमनुसन्धेयम्–आधारस्वाधिष्ठानमणिपूरानाहतविशुद्ध्याज्ञाचक्रात्मकं षट्चक्रसदनं पृथिव्यग्निजलवायुगगनमनस्तत्त्वाधिष्ठानं एकादशेन्द्रियाधिष्ठानं च। एवम् आज्ञाचक्रान्ते एकविंशतितत्त्वान्यधिष्ठितानि तदात्मनावस्थितानि। तव उपरि मायाशुद्धविद्यामहेश्वरसदाशिवात्मकतत्त्वचतुष्टयं ब्रह्मग्रन्थ्यनन्तरभाविचतुर्द्वारात्मक-भूपुरत्रितयात्मक श्रीचक्रद्वारचतुष्टये स्थितम्। प्रागादिद्वारदेशेषु मायादीनि चत्वारि तत्त्वानि। तान्येव मञ्चस्य चतुष्पदानि। शुद्धविद्यायाः सदाशिवतत्त्वाभिनिवेशात् तच्छायापत्त्या सहस्रकमलान्तर्गतशिवः सदाशिवात्मा अनुरागवशात् शुद्धविद्यायाः संवलनात् तादात्म्यं प्रतीयते। सहस्रकमलान्तस्थितस्य चतुर्द्वारात्मकस्य कर्णिकारूपस्य श्रीचक्रस्य मध्यवर्तिचतुरश्रात्मकबैन्दवापरपर्यायसरघाशब्दवाच्यसुधासिन्धौ शिवशक्त्योर्मेलन-मिति। अवशिष्टं सर्वं '**सुधासिन्धोर्मध्ये**' [1]इति श्लोकव्याख्यानावसरे कथितम्।।

अत्र तद्गुणालङ्कारानुप्राणित उत्प्रेक्षालङ्कारः, शिवस्यातिधवलस्य कामेश्वरीतनु-कान्त्या ताद्गुण्यात् शरीरी शृङ्गारो रस इवेत्युत्प्रेक्षणादिति।। ९२।।

Notes : *Druhiṇa, Hari, Rudra, Īśvara*—the four agents inherent in the Sadā-śiva-tattva. The six Cakra-mansions commencing from the *Mūlādhāra* and ending with the Tattvas *Ājñā,* representing respectively Earth, Fire, Water, Air and Ether in their subtle and gross forms, and Manas, as also the ten organs of sense, contain the twenty-one Tattvas. Thus, these twenty-one Tattvas are contained in and constitute the six Cakras. The four Tattvas standing above them, *viz.,* Māyā, Śuddha-vidyā Maheśvara and Sadāśiva, take their rest on the four doors of the triad of quadrangles, known as *Bhūpura,* in their order commencing from the door facing the East, on the other side of the Brahma-granthi. The four Tattvas so situated are the four legs of thecot. As Śuddha-vidyā bears affinity

1. ८मः श्लोकः।

to Sadā-śiva, the latter is overshadowed by the former and on that account becomes identical with it. Śiva and the Śakti have their conjunction in the *Baindava-sthāna,* otherwise described as 'Sudhā-sindhu' and 'Saraghā', in the middle of the Śrī-cakra with the four doors, of the form of the pericarp of the *Sahasra-dala-kamala.*

अराला केशेषु प्रकृतिसरला[1] मन्दहसिते
शिरीषाभा [2]गात्रे दृषदिव कठोरा कुचतटे।
भृशं तन्वी मध्ये [3]पृथुरपि वरारोहविषये
जगत्त्रातुं शंभोर्जयति करुणा काचिदरुणा।। १३।।

Arālā keśeṣu prakṛti-saralā manda-hasite
śirīṣābhā gātre dṛṣad iva kaṭhorā kuca-taṭe/
Bhṛśaṁ tanvī madhye pṛthur api varāroha-viṣaye
jagat trātuṁ śaṁbhor jayati karuṇā kā cid aruṇā//

Tanslation : The transcendent Aruṇā, Śiva's Grace incarnate, curly in Her hair, artless in Her gentle smile Śirīṣa-like in Her frame, hard like stone in the region of Her breasts, extremely slim in Her waist, and prodigious in the region of Her lips, excels in Her Glory for the welfare of the world.

अराला वक्रा, **केशेषु** नान्यत्रेत्यर्थः। **प्रकृतिसरला** प्रकृत्या स्वभावेन सरला ऋज्वी, **मन्दहसिते** मन्दस्मिते, **शिरीषाभा** शिरीषकुसुमाभा अतिमृद्वीत्यर्थः। **चित्ते** अतःकरणे, **दृषदुपलशोभा** [4]दृषदि य उपलः पेषणिका दृषदुपल इति पूर्वमेवोक्तं तस्येव शोभा यस्याः सा। **कुचतटे** स्तनतटे, **भृशं** अत्यर्थं, **तन्वी** कृशा, **मध्ये** वलग्ने, **पृथुः** स्थूला, **उरसिजारोहविषये** स्तनविषये नितम्बविषये च। विषयशब्दः स्थलवाची। **जगत्** प्रपञ्चं, **त्रातुं** रक्षितुं, **शम्भोः** सदाशिवस्य, **जयति** अहमेवेति स्फुरतीत्यर्थः। **करुणा** कृपात्मिका, **काचित्** अनिर्वाच्या, **अरुणा** अरुणाख्या शक्तिः। यद्वा—अरुणवर्णा काचित् करुणा कृपा करुणाया आरुण्यारोपात् मूर्ता करुणेव भातीति वाक्यार्थः। अरुणाख्या शक्तिरर्थादवगता।।

अत्रेत्थं पदयोजना—शंभोः काचित् केशेषु अराला मन्दहसिते प्रकृतिसरला चित्ते शिरीषाभा कुचतटे दृषदुपलशोभा मध्ये भृशं तन्वी उरसिजारोहविषये पृथुः अरुणा करुणा जगत् त्रातुं जयति।।

---

1. प्रकृतिरसिका।
2. चित्ते दृषदुपलशोभा।
3. पृथुरुरसिजारोहविषये।
4. दृषदिवोपल इव कुचतटे स्तनप्रदेशे कठोरा।

अत्र कामेश्वर्या: अरुणाकरुणाशब्दाभ्यां निगीर्याध्यवसानात् अतिशयोक्ति:।। ९३।।

Note : *Aruṇā*—the Devī, as Kāmeśvarī is referred to.

कलङ्कः कस्तूरी रजनिकरबिम्बं जलमयं[1]
कलाभिः कर्पूरैर्मरकतकरण्डं निबिडितम्[2]।
[3]अतस्त्वद्भोगेन प्रतिदिनमिदं[4] रिक्तकुहरं
विधिर्भूयो भूयो निबिडयति नूनं तव कृते।। ९४।।

Kalaṅkaḥ kastūrī rajani-kara-bimbaṁ jala-mayaṁ
kalābhiḥ karpūrair marakata-karaṇḍaṁ nibiḍitaṁ/
Atas tvad-bhogena prati-dinam idaṁ rikta-kuharaṁ
vidhir bhūyo bhūyo nibiḍayati nūnaṁ tava kṛte//

Translation : The (Moon's) dark spot is the musk ; the watery disc of the Moon is the canister of emerald, replete with the (lumps of) camphor (called) the digits of the Moon. Hence, *Vidhi* verily fills the empty (canister) depleted by Thy use, every day and over again, on Thy account.

कलङ्कः लाञ्छनं, **कस्तूरी** मृगनाभि: **रजनिकरबिम्बं** चन्द्रबिम्बं, **जलमयम्।** स्वार्थे मयट्। पन्नीरमित्यर्थ:। **कलाभिः** कलात्मकै:, **कर्पूरैः** सह **मरकतकरण्डं** मरकतमणिना रचितम्। मरकतशब्दो वर्णव्यत्ययेन मकरशब्दादुत्पन्न: मकरात् मकरत:। मकरवक्त्राज्जातं मकरतमिति भोजराज:। करण्डं **निबिडितम्** अन्त: पूरितम्। **अतः त्वद्भोगेन** तव देव्या: उपभोगेनानुभवेन कस्तूरीपन्नीरकर्पूराणाम् अनुभवेन, **प्रतिदिनं** दिनेदिने **इदं** परिदृश्यमानमिन्दुमण्डलं, **रिक्तकुहरं** शून्यान्तरं, **विधिः** ब्रह्मा, **भूयोभूयः** प्रतिदिनं **निबिडयति** पूरयति। **नूनं तव कृते** तुभ्यमित्यर्थ:।

अर्थे कृते च तादर्थ्ये निपातद्वयमीरितम्।
इति कृतेशब्दस्तादर्थ्ये निपातित: तद्योगे षष्ठ्येव।।

अत्रेत्थं पदयोजना–हे भगवति! कलङ्क: कस्तूरी रजनिकरबिम्बं जलमयं कलाभि: कर्पूरै: निबिडितं मरकतकरण्डम्। अत: इदं प्रतिदिनं त्वद्भोगेन रिक्तकुहरं विधि: भूयोभूय: तव कृते निबिडयति नूनम्।

---

1. जडमयं।
2. निविभृतम्।
3. पुनस्त्वद्भोगेन ; अतस्तद्भोगेन।
4. प्रतिकलमिदं।

अत्रातिशयोक्तिरलङ्कारः, मरकतकरण्डत्वेन चन्द्रमण्डलस्याध्यवसानात्। यद्वा–अपह्नवालङ्कारः, अयं कलङ्को न भवति अपि तु कस्तूरीः ; इदं रजनिकरबिम्बं न भवति किन्तु बहिःप्रतिफलितमन्तर्गतं पन्नीरम् ; इमाः कलाः न भवन्ति अपि तु कर्पूररजः; इदमिन्दुमण्डलम् अन्तस्थितद्रव्यप्रतिफलनवशात् पीतवर्णं प्रतीयते, वस्तुतस्तु श्वेतवर्णमेवेत्याद्यवस्थापह्नवमालायाः प्रतीतेः। उत्प्रेक्षालङ्कारश्च ; प्रतिपदादिदिनेषु वृद्धिक्षयवतः चन्द्रमसः कस्तूर्यादिद्रव्यव्ययप्रवेशाभ्यां ईषद्रिक्तत्वसंपूर्णत्वयो-स्सम्भावनात्। अतः अनयोरनुसृष्टिः अङ्गाङ्गिभावेन पृथक्स्थित्या अवस्थानात्।। ९४।।

Notes : The Moon is here compared to an emerald-canister containing musk and refined camphor for the daily use of the Devī. As the supply is exhausted every day, it is being replenished by Brahman, the Devī's servant, then and there. To bring about this effect the poet has artfully pitched upon the Moon with its waxing and waning as the Devī's toilet-canister and made the bright white *kalās* (digits) of the Moon serve the purpose of the white crystals of refined camphor. The waning and waxing processes of the Moon in the design of Nature complete the picture of the supply the being exhausted and replenished daily, the Devī's day consisting of an entire lunar month.

पुरारातेरन्तःपुरमसि ततस्त्वच्चरणयोः
सपर्यामर्यादा तरलकरणानामसुलभा।
तथा[1] ह्येते नीताः शतमखमुखाः सिद्धिमतुलां
तव द्वारोपान्तस्थितिभिरणिमाऽऽद्याभिरमरा[2]ः।। ९५।।

Purārāter antaḥ-puram asi tatas tvac-caraṇayoḥ
saparyā-maryādā tarala-karaṇānām asulabhā/
Tathā hy ete nītāḥ śata-makha-mukhāḥ siddhim a-tulāṁ
tava dvāropānta-sthitibhir aṇimā-" dyābhiramarāḥ//

Translation : Thou art the harem of the foe of the (three) Puras. Therefore, the privilege of adoring Thy feet is unattainable by the fickle-minded. Hence, it is that these gods, with Śatamakha as their leader, have been reduced to a status equal to that of the psychic powers, Aṇimā and others, standing near Thy doorway.

---

1. तथाऽप्येते।
2. अणिमाद्याभिरमराः।

पुरारातेः पुरान्तकस्य, **अन्तःपुरं** अवरोधः पट्टमहिषीति यावत्। **असि** भवसि। **ततः** तस्मात्कारणात्, **त्वच्चरणयोः** तव पादयोः, **सपर्यामर्यादा** पूजाप्रकारः, **तरलकरणानां** चञ्चलचित्तानाम्, **असुलभा** दुर्लभा। "अन्तःपुरप्रवेशः चञ्चलचित्तानां नास्तीति प्रसिद्धम्। अतो निश्चलचित्तैस्तु सौविदल्लैः प्रवेष्टव्यम्" इति नीतिवाक्यामृते। निर्मलचित्तैरेव सुधाम्भोधिमध्यस्थितायाः पादाम्बुजसेवा ज्ञायते नान्यैरित्यर्थः। **तथा, हि**ः प्रसिद्धौ। **एते नीताः शतमखमुखाः** इन्द्रमुख्याः सुरगुणाः **सिद्धिं** संसिद्धिम्, **अतुलां** असदृशीं, **तव** भवत्याः **द्वारोपान्तस्थितिभिः** द्वारसमीपे स्थितयो यासां ताभिः। **अणिमाद्याभिः** अणिमाप्रमुखाभिः सिद्धिभिः सह **अमराः** निर्जराः।।

अत्रेत्थं पदयोजना–हे भगवति! पुरारातेरन्तःपुरमसि। ततस्त्वच्चरणयोस्सपर्यामर्यादा तरलकरणानामसुलभा। तथा हि—एते शतमखमुखाः अमराः तव द्वारोपान्तस्थितिभिः अणिमाद्याभिः सह अतुलां सिद्धिं नीताः।

यथा तव द्वारोपान्तमेव अणिमादिसिद्धयस्सेवन्ते एवमिन्द्रादयोऽपि। इयांस्तु विशेषः–अणिमाद्यष्टसिद्धीनां द्वारपालकत्वेन सर्वदा तत्र वासः स्वभावसिद्धः। इन्द्रदीनां तु तरलकरणत्वात् अन्तःपुरप्रवेशानर्हत्वात् दौवारिकानुमत्या द्वारदेशेऽवस्थानं सिद्धिशब्दार्थः इति तात्पर्यम्।। ९५ ।।

Notes : Unattainable by the fickle-minded—not even the gods dare disturb the privacy of the Devī's home and face the Vanquisher of Pura-s there. How then can poor mortals even think of making an attempt to have a Darśana of the Lord and his Lady in their bed-chamber? *Śata-makha*—the performer of a hundred sacrifices, *i.e.,* Indra. The successful completion of a hundred sacrifices is believed to be rewarded with Indra's crown, according to tradition. Indra and other gods, by merely standing at the doorway of the harem, are credited with attaining psychic powers.

कलत्रं वैधात्रं कति कति भजन्ते न कवयः
श्रियो देव्याः को वा न भवति पतिः कैरपि धनैः।
महादेवं हित्वा तव सति सतीनामचरमे
कुचाभ्यामासङ्गः[1] कुरवकतरोरप्यसुलभः।। ९६ ।।

Kalatraṁ vaidhātraṁ kati kati bhajante na kavayaḥ
śriyo devyāḥ ko vā na bhavati patiḥ kair api dhanaiḥ/
Mahā-devaṁ hitvā tava sati satīnām acarame
kucābhyām āsaṅgaḥ kuravaka-tator apy asulabhaḥ//

---

1. कुचाभ्यामाभोगः।

Translation : O Ideal of chastity! how many poets have not courted the wife of Vidhātṛ? Who does not become the lord of Śrī-devī (the goddess of wealth) by (commanding) whatever (little) wealth? O foremost amongst the chaste! saving the Great Lord (Mahādeva), the embrace of Thy breast is unattainable even by the Kuravaka tree.

कश्मलात्त्रायत इति **कलत्रं पत्नी।** कश्मलं नरकं मध्यवर्णलोप: पृषोदरादित्वात्साधु:। कलत्रं कश्मलात् त्रायत इति रक्षित:। वैधात्रं विधातृसम्बन्धि। विधातृशब्दस्य 'तस्येदम्' इत्यणि कृते संबन्धमात्रपरत्वे तद्विशेषजिज्ञासायां कलत्रशब्दस्यान्वय इति। धातु: कलत्रमित्युक्ते तु संबन्धमात्रे निहिता षष्ठी सबन्धिन्येव पर्यवस्यतीति साक्षादन्वय इति भाव:। अतो नायं प्रयोगो दोषावह:। वैधात्रं कलत्रं सरस्वतीं **कतिकति भजन्ते** सेवन्ते। **न कवय:** के वा कवयो न भजन्ते सर्वेऽपि भजन्त इत्यर्थ:। **श्रियो देव्या:** लक्ष्म्या:, **को वा न भवति पति:** [1]**कैरपि धनै:। महादेवं** सदाशिवं, **हित्वा तव** भवत्या:, **सति!** पतिव्रते! **सतीनां** पतिव्रतानां, **अचरमे!** अग्रगण्ये! **कुचाभ्याम् आसङ्ग:** आलिङ्ग:, **कुरवकतरोरपि असुलभ:** सुलभो न भवति। कुचालिङ्गनं दोहदत्वेनापि कुरवकतरोरचेतनस्यापि न सम्भवति, किमु वक्तव्यं पुरुषान्तर इति पातिव्रत्यं वाचामगोचरमिति भाव:।।

अत्रेत्थं पदयोजना—हे सति! वैधात्रं कलत्रं कतिकति कवय: न भजन्ते। श्रियो देव्या: कैरपि धनै: को वा पति: न भवति। हे सतीनामचरमे! महादेवं हित्वा तव कुचाभ्यामासङ्ग: कुरवकतरोरप्यसुलभ:।।

अयमर्थ:—ये मन्त्रजपाद्यासादितसारस्वता: ते सरस्वतीवल्लभा इति गीयन्ते। ये धनधान्याश्वगजादिसमृद्धिमन्त: ते लक्ष्मीपतय: इति गीयन्ते। पार्वतीपतिस्तु महादेव एवेति पातिव्रत्यमहिमा अवाङ्मनसगोचर इति।। ९६।।

Notes : The wife of Vidhātṛ—the wife of Brahman, *i.e.*, Sarasvatī, the goddes of learning, at whose command is the gift of poesy and whose favour is therefore courted by poets.

Śrī-devī—Lakṣmī, the goddess of wealth. *Wealth*—in the form of hoards of precious metals, gems, coins, grains, elephants, horses and other emblems of prosperity. Even the possession of a little of one or more of the above evokes praise of the owner, as a Lakṣmīpati, lord of wealth. The vein of levity assumed by the poet in his

1. अधिपतिरित्यधिक:।

references to Sarasvatī and Lakṣmī as fickle-minded is for the purpose of heightening the effect of the Devī's chastity. Even the inaminate Kuravaka tree is denied the pleasure of the Devī's embrace, to be cured of its barrenness.

गिरामाहुर्देवीं द्रुहिणगृहिणीमागमविदो
हरेः पत्नीं पद्मां हरसहचरीमद्रितनयाम्।
तुरीया काऽपि[1] त्वं दुरधिगमनिःसीममहिमा
[2]महामाया विश्वं भ्रमयसि परब्रह्ममहिषि।।१७।।

Girām āhur devīṁ druhiṇa-gṛhiṇīm āgama-vido
hareḥ patnīṁ padmāṁ hara-sahacarīm adri-tanayām/
Turīyā kā 'pi tvaṁ dur-adhigama-niḥ-sīma-mahimā
mahā-mayā viśvaṁ bhramayasi para-brahmamahiṣi//

Translation : O Queen of the Para-brahman! the knowers of the Āgamas call only Thee as the goddess of letters who is the wife of Druhiṇa; they call only Thee as Padmā who is the wife of Hari; they call only Thee the partner of Hara, the daughter of the Mountain; while Thou perplexest the world, as the transcendent fourth entity unattainable, and with Thy boundless splendour, as the Great Illusory Being and the fountain of all chastity.

गिरां वाचाम्, **आहुः** कथयन्ति। **देवीम्** अधिदेवतां **द्रुहिणगृहिणीं** ब्रह्मणः पत्नीं, **आगमविदः** आगमरहस्यवेदिनः, **हरेः** विष्णोः, **पत्नीं** जायां, **पद्मां** पद्मालयां **हरसहचरीं** शंभुपत्नीम् **अद्रितनयां** पार्वतीम्। **तुरीया** चतुर्थी, **कापि** अनिर्वाच्या, **त्वं दुरधिगमनिस्सीममहिमा** दुःखेन अधिगन्तुं शक्यः स चासौ निस्सीमो महिमा यस्याः सा, देशतः कालतो वस्तुतश्चापरिच्छेद्येत्यर्थः। **महामाया** शुद्धविद्यान्तर्गतं मायातत्त्वं, **विश्वं** प्रपञ्चं, **भ्रमयसि** विवर्तयसीति विवर्तं ब्रह्मधर्मं मायायामतिदिशति। **परब्रह्ममहिषि** परब्रह्मणः सदाशिवस्य महिषि! तथा च श्रूयते –'**ह्रीश्च ते लक्ष्मीश्च पत्न्यौ**'[3] इति पुरुषसूक्ते। ह्रीः भुवनेश्वरी लक्ष्मीः श्रीविद्या उभे ब्रह्मणस्ते पत्न्यौ। अत्र तयोर्मध्ये श्रीविद्यायाः प्राधान्यं, श्रीविद्यायां भुवनेश्वर्या अन्तर्भावात्। भुवनेश्वर्यां न श्रीविद्याया अन्तर्भाव इति चन्द्रकलाप्राधान्येन सैव महिषीति ध्येयम्।।

1. कापि।
2. महामाये विश्वं।
3. तै०आ० ३.१३।

अत्रेत्थं पदयोजना–हे परब्रह्ममहिषि! आगमविद: त्वामेव द्रुहिणगृहिणीं गिरां देवीमाहु: ; त्वामेव हरे: पत्नीं पद्मामाहु:, त्वामेव हरसहचरीं अद्रितनयामाहु:, त्वं तुरीया कापि दुरधिगमनिस्सीममहिमा महामाया सती विश्वं भ्रमयसि।।

अयमर्थ:—एकामेव भगवतीं नानानामभि: गृणन्त्यागमविद: परब्रह्ममहिषी श्रीविद्यापरनामधेया चन्द्रकला एकैवेति।। ९७।।

Note : Here the manifold purpose served by the Devī, and the various aspects in which she is worshipped by her diverse followers, are referred to.

कदा काले मात: कथय कलितालक्तकरसं
पिबेयं विद्यार्थी तव चरणनिर्णेजनजलम्।
प्रकृत्या मूकानामपि च कविताकारणतया
[1]**कदा धत्ते वाणी**[2]**मुखकमलताम्बूलरसताम्**[3]।। ९८।।

Kadā kāle mātaḥ kathaya kalitālaktaka-rasaṁ
pibeyaṁ vidyārthī tava caraṇa-nirṇejana-jalam/
Prakṛtyā mūkānām api ca kavitā-kāraṇatayā
Kadā dhatte vāṇī-mukha-kamala-tāmbūla-rasa-tām//

Translation : O Mother! pray tell (me), when shall I, who am eagerly desirous of (imbibing) wisdom, drink the water which has cleansed Thy feet and is (thereby) rendered red with the lac-dye; water, which assumes the quality of the chewed betel-juice, (spat out) of the mouth of Vāṇī, through enabling even deaf-mutes to become poets.

कदा काले जन्मप्रभृत्यवसानपर्यन्त इति शेष:। **मात:!** जननि! **कथय** सम्यगुपदिश। **कलितालक्तकरसं** कलितं उपदिग्धम् अलक्तकरसं लक्षारसं यावकं वा। स्त्रीणां पादाधरोष्ठरञ्जनार्थं अलक्तकद्रवं उपदिहन्ति सैरन्ध्र्य:। **पिबेयं** प्रार्थनायां लङ्। **विद्यार्थी** विद्या: अर्थयत इति विद्यार्थी। यद्वा—अर्थ: प्रयोजनमस्य अर्थी विद्याभि: अर्थीति। अत्र रक्षित आह–'**अर्थशब्दान्मत्वर्थे**[4] **इनिप्रत्यय:**' इति। अत एव '**तेनार्थवान् लोभपराङ्मुखेन**' इति कालिदासेन मतुबेव प्रयुक्त:। माघे–

1. यदादत्ते।
2. वार्णी।
3. ताम्बूलरसनानाम् ; ताम्बूलरचनाम्।
4. शब्दात् भावार्थे।

'नितान्तमर्थिनः' इति णिनिरेव। 'अर्थी समर्थी विद्वान्' इत्यादावपि णिनिरेव। अत एव पूर्वव्याख्यैव समीचीना। **तव** भवत्याः, **चरणनिर्णेजनजलं** चरणयोः पादयोः निर्णेजनजलं पाद्योदकं, **प्रकृत्या** स्वभावेन **मूकानां, अपि** विरोधे, चकारश्शङ्काच्छेदे, **कविताकारणतया** कवितायाः हेतुतया, **कदा धत्ते वाणीमुखकमलताम्बूलरसतां** वाण्याः सरस्वत्याः मुखकमले यस्ताम्बूलरसः तस्य भावस्तत्ता ताम्।।

अयं भावः-भगवतीपादारविन्दनिर्णेजनजलं सालक्तकं कविताहेतुः कवीश्वरस्य वदने स्थितं सरस्वतीताम्बूलरस इव प्रत्यक्षं भाति। स तु कवीश्वरः पुंभावमापन्ना सरस्वतीवाभातीति।।

अत्रेत्थं पदयोजना-हे मातः! तव कलितासक्तकरसं चरणनिर्णेजनजलं विद्यार्थी अहं कदा काले पिबेयं कथय। तच्च प्रकृत्या मूकानां अनेडमूकानां वक्तुं श्रोतुं अशिक्षितानामपि च कविताकारणतया वाणीमुखकमलताम्बूलरसतां कदा धत्ते।।

अत्रेदमनुसन्धेयम्-भगत्पादैः अनेडमूकेभ्यः लघुचर्चास्तोत्रद्वयं हस्तमस्तकसंयोग-महिम्ना अवाचि। तन्महिम्ना भगवती पादारविन्दनिर्णेजनजलं तन्मुखे दत्तवती। तन्निर्णेजनजलं पुनः प्रार्थयत्याचार्यः। अनेन सामीप्यमुक्तिरुदिता। तद्विशेषानुत्तरश्लोके विवरिष्यामः। चरणनिर्णेजनजलमिति वदता समयिमतमेवोक्तं, कौलमते भुजगाकारेणैव देव्या अवस्थानात् चरणनिर्णेजनजलस्याभावात्। सहस्रकमल एव चरणनिर्णेजन-जलमिति पूर्वमेव बहुधा प्रपञ्चितम्। अत एव-

सुधाधारासारैश्चरणयुगलान्तर्विगलितैः
प्रपञ्चं सिञ्चन्ती पुनरपि रसाम्नायमहसः।।[1]

इतीदमर्धं समयमतप्रतिपादकम्।

अवाप्य स्वां भूमिं भुजगनिभमध्युष्टवलयं
स्वमात्मानं कृत्वा स्वपिषि कुलकुण्डे कुहरिणि।।[1]

इतीदमर्धं कौलमतप्रतिपादकमिति विवेकः।।

अत्रोत्प्रेक्षालङ्कारः, चरणनिर्णेजनालक्तकरसस्य सरस्वतीताम्बूलरसत्वेनाध्यव-सानात्। समयिनः साक्षात्सरस्वतीस्वरूपत्वेनाध्यवसानाच्च उत्प्रेक्षातिशयोक्त्योः सङ्करः।। ९८।।

Notes : Here the marvellous qualities possessed by the

1. दशमः श्लोकः।
2. शास्त्रभेद।

washings of the Devī's feet in inducing even deaf-mutes of burst into hymns of praise of the Devī are indicated. *Quality of the chewed betel*—instances of devotees of the Goddess of Learning blossoming into great poets by chewing the chewed betel-and-nut spat out of her mouth, or otherwise winning her favour, are not wanting according to tradition, *e.g.*, Kālidāsa the great lyric poet, Mūka, the author of the Mūka-pañcaśatī, *etc.* This stanza is said to refer to the seeker in quest of *Sāmīpya mukti*, liberation attained by proximity. Lakṣmīdhara is of the opinion that this stanza extols the Samaya doctrine of worshipping the Devī in the *Sahasrāra*, the washings of whose feet are coveted by the seeker, and that the Kaula form of worship is not indicated, as in that case it cannot be maintained that the Devī in the form of the Kuṇḍalinī in the hollow of the *Mūlādhāra* has Caraṇas. He also seeks the support of stanza 10 to strengthen his contention, and says that the former half of that stanza refers to the Samaya form and the latter half to the Kaula form of worshipping the Devī.

प्रक्रान्तां स्तुतिं उपसंहरन् षट्कमलभेद[2]सिद्धान्तं निर्दिशति–

सरस्वत्या लक्ष्म्या विधिहरिसपत्नो[1] विहरते
रतेः पातिव्रत्यं शिथिलयति रम्येण वपुषा।
चिरं जीवन्नेव[2] क्षपितपशुपाशव्यतिकरः
[3]परानन्दाभिख्यं रसयति रसं [4]त्वद्भजनवान्।। ९९।।

Sarasvatyā lakṣmyā vidhi-hari-sapatno viharate
rateḥ pāti-vratyaṁ śithilayati ramyeṇa vapuṣā/
Ciraṁ jīvann eva kṣapita-paśupāśa-vyatikaraḥ
parānandābhikhyaṁ rasayati rasaṁ tvad-bha-jana-vān//

Translation : Thy devotee diverts himself with Sarasvatī and Lakṣmī, (*i.e*, becomes enlightened and opulent), and thus excites the jealousy of Vidhi and Hari, (their husbands); shatters Rati's chastity with his beautiful frame; and, endowed with long life, tastes the sweetness of what is called exquisite Bliss, bereft of the ignorance incidental to mortals.

---

1. विधिहरिसपत्न्या।
2. चिरं जीवनैष।
3. परब्रह्माभिख्यं।
4. त्वद्भजितवान् ; त्वद्भजनभाक् ; त्वद्भजनतः।

सरस्वत्या भारत्या, **लक्ष्म्या** पद्मालयया, **विधिहरिसपत्नः**—यथाक्रममिति शेषः। सरस्वतीपतित्वेन विधिः ब्रह्मणः सपत्नः असूयास्पदम्, लक्ष्मीपतित्वेन हरेः असूयास्पदमित्यर्थः। **विहरते** विहरमाणः, **रतेः** काममहिष्याः, **पातिव्रत्यं** पतिव्रताधर्मं पुरुषान्तरासंपर्करूपं, **शिथिलयति,** मन्मथाकारतया रतेः मन्मथभ्रान्तिं जनयन् सम्भोगेच्छां जनयतीति भावः। **रम्येण** अतिसुन्दरेण, **वपुषा** शरीरेण, तादात्म्यबुद्ध्येति यावत्। एवं सादाख्यायाः कलायाः उपासकस्य ऐहिकफलमुक्त्वा आमुष्मिकमप्याह—**चिरंजीवन्नेव** नित्यजीवनस्सन्। सावयवद्रव्यस्य नित्यत्वं पशुपाशव्यतिकरक्षपणहेतुकम्। अत्र केवलव्यतिरेकि अनुमानं साधनत्वेन प्रयोज्यम्—सावयवं यत् क्षपितपशुपाशव्यतिकरं न भवति, तन्नित्यं न भवति, यथा पश्वादि, इति जीवन्मुक्तिसिद्धिः। सावयवाः कपिलादयः, मार्कण्डेयादयो नित्यसिद्धाः, अतः अन्वयव्यतिरेकि वा भवतु सावयवस्य नित्यतायां साधनम्। **एवं** नित्यजीवनः सन् **क्षपितपशुपाशव्यतिकरः** क्षपितः विनष्टः पशुपाशयोः व्यतिकरः। पशुः जीवः, इन्द्रियैः प्रपञ्चं पश्यतीति। यद्वा—बन्धने इत्यस्माद्धातोः पशुः अविद्याबद्धो जीवः, पाशः अविद्या। एतच्च श्रूयते—

अदितिः पाशं प्र मुमोक्त्वेतन्नमः
पशुभ्यः पशुपतये करोमि॥[1]

अस्यार्थः—अदितिः आदित्यमण्डलान्तर्गता बैन्दवी शक्तिः। पाशं अविद्याकृतं बन्धं प्रमुमोक्तु प्रकर्षेण अत्यन्तं मोचयतु। एतत् नमः नमस्कारं पशुपतये करोमि। पशुभ्य इति तादर्थ्ये चतुर्थी। तदर्थत्वं निवृत्तिः। पशुत्वनिवृत्त्यर्थम्। अयमर्थः—अदितिः पशुपतिना सदाशिवेन युक्ता पाशविमोचनं करोत्विति। पशुशब्दस्य जीववाचित्वं तैत्तिरीयके सौम्यकाण्डे **'तेषामसुराणाम्'**[2] इत्यनुवाके तेषामसुराणामित्यारभ्य **'तस्मादुद्रः पशूनामधिपतिः'** [2]इत्यन्तेन प्रतिपादितम्। अतः पशुपाशौ जीवाविद्ये, तयोर्व्यतिकरः संबन्धः, स च क्षपितः विदलितपशुपाशसंबन्धः सदाशिवतत्त्वात्मनाऽवस्थितः, **परानन्दाभिख्यं** परानन्दात्मिका अभिख्या ज्योतिर्यस्य सः तं परानन्दाभिख्यं ज्योतीरूपं, **रसयति** आस्वादयति **रसं, सुखं, त्वद्भजनवान्** त्वद्भक्तः—तव भजनं सेवा॥

अत्रेत्थं पदयोजना—हे भगवति! त्वद्भजनवान् सरस्वत्या लक्ष्म्या विधिहरिसपत्नः सन् विहरते। रम्येण वपुषा रतेः पातिव्रत्यं शिथिलयति। क्षपितपशुपाशव्यतिकरः चिरंजीवन्नेव परानन्दाभिख्यं रसं रसयति॥

---

1. तै०सं० ३ १-४।
2. तै०सं० ६-१-३।

अत्रेदमनुसन्धेयम्–जीवन्मुक्तानां अविद्यानिवृत्तावपि कुलालचक्रभ्रमणन्योयेन देहसंबन्धः। यथोक्तं षष्टितन्त्रे सप्तत्याम्–

सम्यज्ज्ञानाधिगमाद्धर्मादीनामकारणप्राप्तौ।
तिष्ठति संस्कारवशाच्चक्रभ्रमवद्धृतशरीरः।। इति।।

अत्र त्वद्भजनवानित्यत्र द्विविधं भजनं–षट्चक्रसेवात्मकं धारणात्मकं च। आद्यं निरूप्यते–आधारस्वाधिष्ठाने तामिस्रलोकत्वात् नोपास्ये। मणिपूरप्रभृतिसहस्रकमलपर्यन्तं पञ्च चक्राणि पूज्यानीति। तत्र मणिपूरकपूजापराणां सार्ष्टिरूपा मुक्तिः। सार्ष्टिर्नाम देव्याः पुरसमीपे पुरान्तरं निर्माय सेवां कुर्वाणस्य अवस्थितिः। संवित्कमलपूजारतानां सालोक्यमुक्तिः। सालोक्यं नाम देव्याः पट्टणे निवासः। विशुद्धिचक्रोपासकानां सामीप्यमुक्तिः। सामीप्यं नाम अङ्गसेवकत्वम्। आज्ञाचक्रोपासकनां सारूप्यमुक्तिः। सारूप्यं नाम समानरूपत्वम्। पृथग्देहधारित्वेनेति सायुज्याद्भेदः। एतत् चतुर्विधं गौणं बाह्यदुःखातिवर्तित्वमात्रात् मुक्तिरिति व्यपदिश्यते। परं तु सायुज्यात्मिकैव शाश्वती मुक्तिः सहस्रकमलोपासकानामेवेति। अत एव परानन्दाभिख्यं रसं यथायोग्यं त्वद्भजनवान् रसयति इति।।

अत्रेदं मततत्त्वम्–षट्कमलभेदमते सुखस्वरूपैव मुक्तिः। सुखं तु लौकिकदृष्टान्तेन स्त्रीसंभोगात्मिकै(त्मकमे)व। लोकेऽपि स्त्रीसम्मेलनात् परं सुखं नास्ति। एवमत्यन्तदुःखोच्छेदानन्तरं सायुज्यसंसिद्धौ शिवशक्तिसम्पुटान्तर्भावात् तदात्मिकैव मुक्तिरिति।

तदयमत्र निष्कर्षः–पूर्वं मूलाधारादिषट्चक्राणां त्रिकोणाष्टकोणदशारद्वितयमन्वश्र-शिवचक्रात्मना तादात्म्यं प्रतिपादितम्। एतदेव नादबिन्द्वोरैक्यम्। तथा हि–नादो नाम श्रीचक्रम्। बिन्दुर्नाम षट्कमलगहनं वक्ष्यते। तयोरैक्यं नाम आधारचक्रं चतुर्दल, तत्कर्णिका त्रिकोणात्मिका ; स्वाधिष्ठानं षड्दलं, तत्कर्णिका अष्टकोणात्मिका ; मणिपूरं दशदलं पद्मं, तत्कर्णिका दशकोणात्मिका; अनाहतं द्वादशदलं, तत्कर्णिका द्वितीयदशकोणात्मिकैव ; विशुद्धिचक्रं षोडशदलं, तत्कर्णिका चतुर्दशकोणात्मिका; एतावत्पर्यन्तं शक्तिचक्रैक्यम्। आज्ञाचक्रं द्विदलं, अष्टकोणमेकत्र षोडशकोणमपरत्रेति द्विधा भिन्ना कर्णिका। अयं भावः–[1]द्विधा भिन्नं चतुरश्रप्रकृतिकं शिवचक्रचतुष्टयात्मकं आधारस्वाधिष्ठानात्मकं चेति प्रपञ्चितम्। वृत्तत्रयं स्वाधिष्ठानान्ते एकं वृत्तं रुद्रग्रन्थ्यात्मकं; अनाहतान्ते एकं विष्णुग्रन्थ्यात्मकं, आज्ञाचक्रान्ते एकं ब्रह्मग्रन्थ्यात्मकम्। तत उपरि

1. द्विदलाद्भिन्नम्।
2. त्रितयोपेतं पुरत्रयम्।

चतुर्द्वारोपेतं भूपुर[2]त्रितयं द्वारेषु चतुर्षु सोपानयुक्तम्। तच्च सहस्रदलकर्णिका। तस्य कमलस्य दलानि सहस्रम्। बैन्दवस्थानं चतुर्द्वारोपेतं कर्णिकामध्ये। एवं प्रासादन्यायेन श्रीचक्रस्य कमलानां चैक्यमनुसन्धेयम्। एतच्च नादबिन्द्वैक्यं गुह्यात् गुह्यतमं शिष्यानुग्रहात् उपदिष्टम्।।

अस्मिन् षट्चक्रे पञ्चाशत्कलानामन्तर्भावः कथितः। चन्द्रखण्डे स्वराः, सूर्यखण्डे स्पर्शाः, अग्निखण्डे अन्तस्थाः ऊष्माणश्च हकारवर्जिताः, हकारळकारौ बैन्दवे, क्षकारस्सर्वत्रेति [1]"**सवित्रीभिः**' इति श्लोकेन प्रागेव प्रतिपादितम्। मूलाधारादिदलेषु कलानाम् अन्तर्भावः प्रागेव प्रतिपादितः। कलानां तिथ्यात्मकत्वं, नित्यानां कलात्मकत्वं, कलानां मूलमन्त्रगतपञ्चदशाक्षरात्मकत्वं, पञ्चदशाक्षराणां त्रिखण्डत्वं, त्रिखण्डस्य सोमसूर्यानलात्मकत्वं, सोमसूर्यानलानां ग्रन्थित्रयात्मकत्वं, ग्रन्थित्रयस्य मन्त्रगतह्रीङ्कारत्रयात्मकत्वं, ह्रीङ्कारस्य भुवनेश्वरीमन्त्रत्वं, भुवनेश्वरीमन्त्रस्य मूलमन्त्रान्तर्गतत्वं मूलमन्त्रस्य चक्रेणैक्यं, तच्चक्रनवकस्य मूलाधारादिषट्चक्रेषु ब्रह्मग्रन्थ्यादित्रिकेऽपि सहस्रकमलकर्णिकादौ तादात्म्यम्। एतदेव कलानादयोरैक्यं नाम।।

अयमत्र निष्कर्षः–नादेन बिन्दोरैक्यं, बिन्दुना कलायाः ऐक्यं, कलायाश्च नादेनैक्यम्, एवं त्रितयं; कलया बिन्दोरैक्यं, कलया नादस्यैक्यं, श्रीविद्यया पञ्चकस्यैक्यमिति षड्विधत्वमैक्यस्येति परमरहस्यं गुरूपदेशवशात् ज्ञेयम्। एवं षोढैक्यं भगवत्याः सपर्येति सम्यगुपवर्णितम्। षोढैक्यानुसन्धानानन्तरं दशभुजा भगवती श्रीविद्या मणिपूरे प्रत्यक्षं परिदृश्यमाना सपर्यया सन्निधेयेति ऐक्यानुसन्धानमेव सपर्येति वदतो ममाशयः इति विज्ञेयम्।

अधुना बिन्दुस्वरूपं प्रपञ्च्यते–बिन्दुरिति मूलाधारादिचक्रषट्कम्। बिन्दुः जगदुत्पत्तिलयहेतुः शिवस्य शक्तिविशेषः। स च एक एव सहस्रकमलान्तचतुर्द्वारात्मककर्णिकामध्यगतचतुष्कोणात्मकं शक्तितत्त्वम्। तन्मध्यगतशिवतत्त्वं नादं इत्युच्यते। स चतुर्विध इति प्रागेवोक्तम्। उभयोः शक्तिशिवयोः शब्दार्थरूपत्वात् कलात्मकत्वं उभयसाधारणम्। अतश्च मेलनं नादबिन्दुकलातीतमिति समयमतरहस्यम्। स च बिन्दुः दशधा भिद्यते। यथोक्तम्–

> दशधा भिद्यते बिन्दुरेक एव परात्मकः।
> चतुर्धाऽऽधारकमले षोढाऽधिष्ठानपङ्कजे।।
> उभयाकाररूपत्वादितरेषां तदात्मता। इति।।

अस्यार्थः–एक एव बिन्दुः मूलाधारकमलगतचतुर्दलेषु चतुर्धा, स्वाधिष्ठानपद्मगत–

1. १७ श्लोक।

षड्दलेषु षोढा, एवं दशधा भिद्यते। अयं भावः–मूलाधारं चतुष्पत्रं सरसिजं, स्वाधिष्ठानं षड्दलं, मणिपूरं दशदलं, अनाहतपद्मं द्वादशदलं, विशुद्धिपद्मं षोडशदलं, आज्ञाचक्रं द्विदलमिति सर्वयोगशास्त्रसिद्धम्। अत्र आधारपद्मस्य दलचतुष्टयं बिन्दुचतुष्टयात्मकम्। ते च बिन्दवो मनोबुद्ध्यहङ्कारचित्ताख्याः प्रकृत्यात्मकाः जगन्निर्माणहेतव इति सर्वयोगशास्त्रसिद्धम्। स्वाधिष्ठानपद्मगतषड्दलानां कामक्रोधलोभमोहमदमात्सर्यात्मकाः षड्बिन्दवः। अत एव ते संहृतिबिन्दव इत्याहुः। तदुक्तं भगवता पतञ्जलिना–'स्वाधिष्ठाने संहारः षड्बिन्दुकृतः' इति। एवं दश बिन्दवः कमलद्वयदलात्मकाः। मणिपूरं मूलाधारस्वाधिष्ठानात्मकमिति कृत्वा दशदलम्। अनाहतचक्रे मणिपूरप्रकृतिकं दशदलं, पूर्वकमलद्वयप्राकृतिकं दलद्वयं द्वादशदलं अनाहतपद्मम्। विशुद्धिपद्मं तु अनाहत-चक्रप्रकृतिकं द्वादशदलम्, आधारप्रकृतिकं चतुर्दलम्, एवं षोडशदलम्। तथा मणिपूरप्रकृतिकं दशदलं स्वाधिष्ठानप्रकृतिकं षड्दलमिति षोडशदलम्। आज्ञाचक्रं तु आधारस्वाधिष्ठानात्मकमिति द्विदलम्। एवं मणिपूरप्रभृति आज्ञान्तानि चत्वारि कमलानि मूलाधारस्वाधिष्ठानप्रकृतिकानि। अत एव मूलाधारद्विके उत्तरकमलचतुष्कमन्तर्भूतमिति एकस्यैव बिन्दोः दशधात्वं नान्यथेति सिद्धम्।।

यद्यपि कौलानां द्विकानुसन्धानात् षट्कमलानुसन्धानफलं सेत्स्यति, तथापि षड्विधैक्यानुसन्धानाभावात् कुलमार्ग एवेति न देव्या मणिपूरे सान्निध्यं, पञ्चविधमुक्ति-युक्त्यभावश्च, नादबिन्दुकलातीतत्वमप्यसंभाव्यमेव कौलमते इति। समयिनां तु कार्यभूतचतुष्कानुसन्धानादेव कारणभूतकमलद्वयानुसंधानफलं सेत्स्यतीति। अत एव पञ्चविधसाम्यसिद्धौ समयसमयिभावः प्रत्यक्षं परिदृश्यते समयसमयिनोः समयिनां सेवकानामिति भगवत्पादमततत्त्वम्।।

एवं भजनशब्दार्थं प्रतिपाद्य प्रकारान्तरेण भजनशब्दार्थो निरूप्यतेयदाहुः भगवत्पादाः **'धारणापरिज्ञानान्मुक्तिः'** इति। अस्यार्थः–धारणाः षष्ट्युत्तरत्रिशतसङ्ख्याकाः। धारणा नाम वायोः कमलेषु नादकलाभ्यां निरोधः। स च षट्कमलेषु षोढा सप्तमे कमले समयशब्दाभिलप्येन सार्धं सप्तविधः। एकैकस्मिन् कमले पञ्चाशदिति षष्ट्युत्तरत्रिशतं धारणाः। ताश्च पृथक् नादबिन्दुकलाभिस्सार्धं मेलनप्रकारैरनन्ता धारणा गुरूपदेशवशादवगन्तव्याः। धारणानां फलं आधारादिचक्रषट्के यथाक्रमं मतिस्मृतिबुद्धि-प्रज्ञामेधाप्रतिभासंविद्रूपं दिङ्मात्रं दर्शितम्। अधिकं तु सुभगोदये चरणागमे च सप्रपञ्चं बहुधा प्रतिपादितं तत एवावधार्यं ग्रन्थविस्तरभयान्नोपवर्णितमिहेति। अत एव काळिदासभगवत्पादैः कुलसमयमतभेदप्रतिपादकश्लोकेन सकलजननीस्तोत्रे कथितम्। यथा–

चतुष्पत्रान्तष्षड्दलपुटभगान्तस्त्रिवलय-
स्फुरद्विद्युद्वह्निद्युमणिनियुताभद्युतिलते।।

षडश्रं भित्त्वाऽऽदौ दशदलमथ द्वादशदलं
कलाश्रं च द्व्यक्षं गतवति नमस्ते गिरिसुते।।

अस्यार्थः-चतुष्पत्रं आधारकमलं अन्तः अन्तस्स्थितं अन्तर्भूतमित्यर्थः, यस्मिन् तत्। स्वाधिष्ठानमिति बहुव्रीहिः, न तु तत्पुरुषः, उत्तरस्य पूर्वस्मिन्नन्तंर्भावायोगात्। 'षडश्रं भित्त्वाऽऽदौ' इत्युत्तरवाक्यानन्वयाच्च बहुव्रीहिरेव। चतुष्पत्रान्तश्च तत् षड्दलं स्वाधिष्ठानं च चतुष्पत्रान्तष्षड्दलम्। तस्य पुटभगाः पुटात्मकाः सम्पुटात्मकाः तत्प्रकृतिका इति यावत्, ते च ते भगाः त्रिकोणानि। मणिपूरप्रभृति चतुश्चक्रस्य मूलाधारप्रकृतिकत्वस्योक्तत्वात् तेषां त्रिकोणात्मकत्वम्। 'त्रिकोणे बैन्दवं श्लिष्टं अष्टारेऽष्टदलाम्बुजम्' इत्यत्र सम्यङ्निर्णीतम्। पुटभगानां अन्तः मध्ये। त्रिवलयं ग्रन्थित्रयं स्वाधिष्ठानानाहताज्ञान्तेषु अग्निसूर्यचन्द्रात्मकरुद्रग्रन्थिविष्णुग्रन्थिब्रह्मग्रन्थिपर्यायत्वेन स्थितमित्यर्थः। तत्र स्फुरत् स्फुरन्ती। 'स्त्रियाः पुंवद्भाषितपुंस्कादनूङ्समानाधिकरणे' इत्यादिना पुंवद्भावः। विद्युतः सौदामिन्याः वह्नेः अग्नेः द्युमणेस्सूर्यस्य। नियुतशब्दः अगाणेयां सङ्ख्यां लक्षयति। तस्येवाभा यस्यास्सा, सा च सा द्युतिलता, नित्या तद्विल्ली स्थिरसौदामिनीति यावत्। तस्याः सम्बुद्धिः। आज्ञाचक्रान्ते ब्रह्मग्रन्थिभेदनसमये विद्युन्नियुताभा, स्वाधिष्ठानान्ते रुद्रग्रन्थिभेदनसमये वह्निनियुताभा, अनाहचक्रान्ते विष्णुग्रन्थिभेदनसमये द्युमणिनियुताभा इति विवेकः। षडश्रं मूलाधारगर्भितं स्वाधिष्ठानं आदौ भित्त्वा अथ तदनन्तरं दशदलं मणिपूरं भित्त्वा द्वादशदलं अनाहतचक्रं भित्त्वा कलाश्रं विशुद्धिचक्रं भित्त्वा द्व्यश्रं आज्ञाचक्रं भित्त्वा गतवति सहस्रकमलमिति शेषः। हे गिरिसुते! हिमाचलतनये! ते नमः।।

अत्र चतुष्पत्रं मूलाधारं स्वाधिष्ठाने अन्तर्भूतं कौलाः उपासत इति प्रागेव प्रतिपादितम्। समयिनस्तु स्वाधिष्ठानं भित्त्वा मणिपूरं प्रविष्टायाः देव्याः उपासनं कुर्वन्तीति समयमततत्त्वं च प्रतिपादितम्! अत्रेदमुपह्वरं-षट्कमलेषु भूतपञ्चकं तादात्म्येनावतिष्ठते। तच्च पिण्डण्डब्रह्माण्डयोरैक्यानुसन्धानमहिम्ना षट्कमलानुसन्धानमहिम्ना पञ्चविधसाम्यानु-सन्धानमहिम्ना षड्विधैक्यानुसन्धानमहिम्ना पिण्डाण्डं ब्रह्माण्डवदवभासत इति सर्वयोगशास्त्र रहस्यम्। अत एव योगिना चतुर्विधैक्यानुसन्धानं कर्तव्यमेव। तथा च श्रूयते-

पिण्डब्रह्माण्डयोरैक्यं लिङ्गसूत्रात्मनोरपि।
स्वापाव्याकृतयोरैक्यं क्षेत्रज्ञपरमात्मनोः।

अयमर्थः-पिण्डाण्डब्रह्माण्डयोरैक्यं ज्ञातव्यम्। तदनन्तरं लिङ्गात्मसूत्रात्मनोरैक्यम् अवगन्तव्यम्। लिङ्गात्मा लिङ्गशरीरं एकादशेन्द्रियगणः तन्मात्रापञ्चकं षोडशकं

लिङ्गशरीरम्। सूत्रात्मा ब्रह्माण्डावच्छिन्नो वायुः लिङ्गशरीरस्य अर्चिरादिमार्गप्रापकः। तयोरैक्यमवगन्तव्यम्। स्वापाव्याकृतयोः-स्वापः सुषुप्त्यवस्थापन्नः साक्षी प्राज्ञः अव्याकृतः अविद्याशबलितं ब्रह्म तयोरैक्यम्। क्षेत्रज्ञः जीवः, परमात्मा ब्रह्मस्वरूपं, तयोरैक्यं ज्ञातव्यम्। एवं संप्रदायरहस्यसंक्षेपः। विस्तरस्तु सुभगोदये शारीरके ज्ञातव्यः। अस्मिन् श्लोके सौन्दर्यलहर्या यावत्प्रमेयजातं समयसिद्धान्तरहस्यत्वेन कौलसिद्धान्त-रहस्यत्वेन न प्रतिपादितमस्माभिः संक्षेपतः तत्सर्वं सूक्ष्मदृशा महात्मभिरनुसन्धेयमिति सर्वमनवद्यम्।। ९९।।

Notes : *Shatters*—fascinates and thus renders her devotion to her lord inconstant. Taking this stanza as the penultimate one of the work, Lakṣmīdhara says that this stanza indicates the worshipper's piercing through the six *Cakras* in order to reach the *Sahasrāra*. In substantiation of this veiw he proceeds thus : The *Jīvanmukta* continues to function in the body out of sheer *Vāsanā*, even after the removal of ignorance, even as the potter's wheel continues to whirl after the pot has been brought into shape completely. The *Bhajana* indicated in the last line is of two kinds : by the worshipping of the six *Cakras* and by Dhāraṇā. As regards the former, the first two *Cakras*, being in a region of darkness, are unworthy of being worshipped. The other five *Cakras*, including the *Sahasrāra*, alone are to be taken into account. Worshippers of the *Maṇi-pūra* attain the liberation known as Sārṣṭi, which consists is raising a city by the side of the Devī's city and abiding there, ever engaged in her service. Worshippers of the *An-āhata* attain liberation of the Sālokya type. Sālokya is residence in the Devī's city. Worshippers of the *Viśuddhi* attain liberation of the Sāmīpya type. Sāmīpya consists in ministering to the comforts of the Devī. Worshippers of the *Ājñā* attain liberation of the Sārūpaya type. Sārūpya consists in attaining similarity of form with the Devī, which, however, being distinct and separate, is not Sāyujya. The aforesaid four types of liberation are known as *Gauṇa* or accessory, for the reason that external torments alone are warded off in these types. Worshippers of the *Sahasrāra* alone have the privilege of attaining liberation of the Sāyujya type, wherein even internal torments vanish, and which is therefore the ideal type of perpetual liberation referred to in the last line of the stanza.

After getting over all sorts of difficulties, the votary renders himself fit for attaining Sāyujya. When Sāyujya is reached he merges into the conjoint forms of Śiva and the Śakti. This is *Kaivalya*.

The identity of the six *Cakras* of the body, *viz.*, the *Mūlādhāra* and others, with the six *Cakras*, of the *Śrī-cakra, viz.*, the *Trikoṇa* and others, has already been dealt with. The same also establishes the identity of the *Nāda* with the *Bindu*. The *Nāda* is the *Śrī-cakra*. The *Bindu*, as will be shown presently, is the group of six lotuses. The *Mūlādhāra* is of four petals. Its pericarp is the *Trikoṇa*. The *Svādhiṣṭhāna* is of six petals. Its pericarp is the *Aṣṭa-koṇa*. The *Maṇipūra* is of ten petals. Its pericarp is the *Antar-daśāra*. The *An-āhata* is of twelve petals. Its pericarp is the *Bahirdaśāra*. The *Viśuddhi* is of sixteen petals. Its pericarp is the *Catur-daśa-koṇa*. Thus, far the identity of the *Śakti-cakras* with the five Cakras of the body. The *Ājñā* is of two petals. Its pericarp is of two phases : the *Aṣṭadala-padma* is of one phase and the *Ṣoḍaśadala-padma* of the other phase. Of the three circles, one is of the character of the Rudra-granthi at the end of the *Svādhiṣṭhāna*, another is of the character of the Viṣṇu-granthi at the end of the *An-āhata*, and the third is of the character of the Brahma-granthi at the end of the *Ājñā-cakra*. Above these, the three quadrilaterals with the four doors have flights of steps of the four doors. This *Bhū-gṛha* is the pericarp of the *Sahasradala-padma*. There are a thousand petals to this lotus. The *Baindava-sthāna* is in the middle of the pericarp with the four doors. In this manner the identity of the *Śrī-cakra* with the *Kamalas* serving as palaces for the Devī may be seen. This identity, known as that of the *Nāda* with the *Bindu*, should be preserved as a profound secret and has to be divulged only by the Guru for the benefit of the disciple.

The inhering of the fifty *Kalās* in the six *Cakras* has already been dealt with. The vowels inhere in the lunar Khaṇḍa, the five Vargas from *Ka* to *Ma* in the solar Khaṇḍa, the rest excluding *Ha* and *La* in the Agni-khaṇḍa, and *Ha* and *La* in the *Baindava*, while *Kṣa* inheres in all. The inhering of the *Kalās* in the petals of the *Mūlādhāra* and other *Cakras* has likewise been already dealt with. From the above will be clearly seen the *Tithi*-character of the *Kalās*, the *Kalā*-character of the Nityās, the character of the *Kalās* as inhering in the fifteen letters of the *Mūla-mantra* the fifteen letters being of the character of the three Khaṇḍas, the three Khaṇḍas being of the Moon, Sun and Fire, the latter being of the character of the three Granthis, the three Granthis being of the character of the three *Hrīṁ-s* of the Mantra, the *Hrīṁ* being of the character of the Bhuvaneśvarī-mantra, the Bhuvaneśvarī-mantra being of the character of being included in the *Mūla-mantra*, the identity of the *Mūla-mantra* with the *Śrī-*

cakra, the nine *Cakras* of the same being identical with the six *Cakras* and the three Granthis as well as the pericarp of the thousand-petalled lotus of the human body. This alone establishes the identity of the *Kalā* with the *Nāda*.

With the *Nāda* is the *Bindu* identical, the *Kalā* with the *Bindu*, the *Kalā* with the *Nāda*, the *Bindu* with the *Kalā*, the *Nāda* with the *Kalā* and all these five with the *Śrī-vidyā*. The five-fold nature of this identity should be understood from the precept of the Guru. Thus the six kinds of identity form the worship of the Devī. This means that the Goddess, *viz.*, the *Śrī-vidyā* with her ten forearms manifesting herself directly in the *Maṇi-pūra*, should be propitiated with the formalities of worship.

Now is described the real form of the *Bindu*. The *Bindu* is made up of the five *Cakras* commencing from the *Mūlādhāra*. It is the cause of the creation and the dissolution of the world and is the power wielded by Śiva. That alone is the Śakti-tattva of the character of the quadrilateral which is in the middle of the pericarp with four doors of the one-thousand-petalled lotus. The Śiva-tattva in the middle of this is the *Nāda*. Its four-fold character has already been explained. As both the Śakti and Śiva are of the form of the Śabda (word) and *Artha* (its significance), the character of the *Kalā* is common to them. Therefore, their union transcends the *Nāda*, *Bindu* and *Kalā*. This is the secret of the Samaya doctrine.

This *Bindu* is divided into ten divisions, each one occupying the four petals of the *Mūlādhāra* and the six petals of the *Svādhiṣṭāna*. The four divisions of the *Bindu*, on the four petals of the *Mūlādhāra*, are *Manas*, *Buddhi*, *Ahaṁkāra* and *Citta* of the character of matter, which are the cause of the creation of the universe. The six divisions of the *Bindu* on the six petals of the *Svādhiṣṭhāna* are *Kāma* (lust), *Krodha* (anger); *Lobha* (covetousness), *Moha* (delusion), *Mada* (infatuation) and *Mātsara* (spite).

The *Maṇi-pūra* os of ten petals because of its being made up of the characteristics of the *Mūlādhāra* and the *Svādhiṣṭhāna*. Of the twelve petals of the *An-āhata*, ten are of the character of the *maṇi-pūra* and the two remaining petals represent the *Mūlādhāra* and the *Svādhiṣṭhāna*. Of the sixteen petals of the *Viśuddhi*, twelve represent the *An-āhata* and four the *Mūlādhāra*, or ten of them represent the petals of the *Maṇi-pūra* and six the petals of the *Svādhiṣṭhāna*. The two petals of the *Ājñā* represent the two *Cakras* of the *Mūlādhāra* and the *Svādhiṣṭhāna.* Thus the four *Cakras* beginning from the *Maṇi-pūra* and ending with the *Ājñā* are based on the *Mūlādhāra* and the *Svādhiṣṭhāna.* As the four other *Cakras* inhere in the two *Cakras,* the *Mūlādhāra* and the *Svādhiṣṭhāna,* the ten-fold character of the One *Bindu* becomes established.

Even though the Kaula-s, by restricting their worship only to the first two *Cakras,* profess to attain the full fruits of worship, still, as the worship through the six identities is entirely absent in their form of worship, they cannot obtain the fruits of the several stages of the Samaya form of worship. The Samayins, on the other hand, even though they restrict their worship to the four *Cakras* above the first two, in effect attain the full fruits of the worship of all the six *Cakras.*

As for the other way of worship by Dhāraṇās; Dhāraṇā is the restraining of the vital air in the six *Cakras* by means of the *Nāda* and the *Kalā.* There are six kinds of Dhāraṇās, one in each of the six *Cakras,* and if the *Sahasrāra* is also included, the kinds of Dhāraṇās will be seven in all. At the rate of fity Dhāraṇās in each *Cakra,* the total number will be 7×50=350. These, when severally combined with the *Nāda, Bindu* and *Kalā* and formed into permutations, will become infinite in number, and further light should be sought from the Guru thereon. The fruits of the Dhāraṇās as generated in the six *Cakras* are in order—*Mati, Smṛti, Buddhi, Prajñā, Medhā,* and *Pratibhā* (various grades of intellect). For further details reference is made by Lakṣmīdhara to works such as the Subhagodaya, the Caraṇāgama, *etc.*

Reference has already been made to the Kaula practice of worship of the four-petalled *Mūlādhāra* inhering in the *Svādhiṣṭhāna,* as also to the doctrine of the Samayīns, in accordance with which they worship the Devī that has reached the *Maṇipūra,* after bursting through the *Svādhiṣṭhāna.* One other point that may be noted in this connection is that the five Elements along with the *Manas* are established as identical with the six lotuses. Meditation on the identity of the Microcosm with the Macrocosm, the identity of the six lotuses, of the five kinds of similarities and the six kinds of identities, exercises so great an influence as to make the Microcosm manifest itself as the Macrocosm. This is the secret underlying all Śāstras bearing on Yoga, which enjoin on the Yogin to have recourse to the practice of such meditation with a view to his successful accomplishment of Yoga. This is also endorsed by the Śruti, which says: "(The Yogin should meditate on) the identity of the Microcosm with the Macrocosm, like-wise of the *Liṅga* with the Sūtrātman, of the sleeping with the unmanifested states, and of the *Kṣetra-jña* with the Paramātman."

प्रदीपज्वालाभिर्दिवसकरनीराजनविधिः
सुधासूते[1]श्चन्द्रोप्पलजललवैरर्घ्यरचना[2] ।
स्वकीयैरम्भोभिः सलिलनिधिसौहित्यकरणं
त्वदीयाभिर्वाग्भिस्तव[3] जननि वाचां स्तुतिरियम्।।१००।।

Pradīpa-jvālābhir divasa-kara-nīrājana-vidhiḥ
sudhā-sūteś candroppala-jala-lavair arghya-racanā/
Svakīyair ambhobhiḥ salila-nidhī-sauhitya-karaṇaṁ
tvadīyābhir vāgbhis tava janani vācāṁ stutir iyam//

Translation : O Mother of diction! composing this hymn (in praise) of Thee, in words originating from Thee, is very much like adoring the Sun by waving a light (before him), offering, the Moon, drops of water (flowing out) of a moon-stone, and pleasing the Ocean by (pouring) water into it.

प्रदीपस्य करदीपिकायाः, **ज्वालाभिः** कीलाभिः, **दिवसकरस्य** सूर्यस्य, **नीराजनविधिः** नीराजनकृत्यम्, **सुधासूतेः** चन्द्रस्य, **चन्द्रोपलजललवैः** चन्द्रोपलानां चन्द्रकान्तानां जललवैः निष्यन्दैः, **अर्घ्यरचना। स्वकीयैः** आत्मसंबन्धिभिः, एतत्स्वकीयपदं प्रदीपज्वालाभिरित्यादौ व्यत्ययेनान्वेति स्वकीयाभिरिति। **अम्भोभिः** जलैः, **सलिलनिधिसौहित्यकरणं** समुद्रस्य तृप्तिहेतुः तर्पणविशेषः। **त्वदीयाभिः** त्वदुत्पन्नैः त्वत्स्वरूपैः **वाग्भिः** वाक्यसंदर्भैः **तव** भवत्याः, **जननि!** मातः! सवित्रीत्यर्थः। **वाचां** वाक्यप्रपञ्चस्य **स्तुतिरियम्।**

अत्रेत्थं पदयोजना– हे वाचां जननि! यथा स्वकीयाभिः प्रदीपज्वालाभिः दिवसकरनीराजनविधिः, यथा स्वकीयैश्चन्द्रोपलजललवैः सुधासूतेरर्घ्यरचना भवति, यथा स्वकीयैरम्भोभिः सलिलनिधिसौहित्यकरणं भवति, तथा त्वदीयाभिः वाग्भिरेव तवेयं स्तुतिः।।

---

1. सुधासूनोश्चन्द्रोपल।
2. रर्घ्यघटना।
3. त्वदीयाभिर्वाग्भिर्मम।

अत्र इयं स्तुतिरिति यदा पूर्वोक्तप्रदीपज्वालादिवाक्यप्रतिपादितार्थसाम्यपरामर्शः तदा प्रतिवस्तूपमालङ्कारः, उपमानोपमेययोर्वस्तुप्रतिवस्तुभावेनान्वयात्। यदा इयं स्तुतिरिति स्वरूपमात्रं परामृश्यते तदा भिन्नवाक्यत्वेन बिम्बप्रतिबिम्बाक्षेपात् दृष्टान्तालङ्कारः। एवं प्रतिवस्तूपमादृष्टान्तालङ्कारयोः अन्वयभेदेन प्रतीयमानत्वात् वाक्यद्वयाश्रयणात् संसृष्टिरेवेति ध्येयम्।।

अस्मिन् सौन्दर्यलहरीश्लोकशतक '**समानीतः पद्भ्यां**'[1] इति '**समुद्भूतस्थूलस्तनभरम्**'[2] इति '**निधे नित्यस्मेरे**'[3] इति श्लोकत्रयं वर्तते। तत्तु भगवत्पादरचितं न भवति केनचित्प्रक्षिप्तमिति न व्याख्यातम्। श्लोकशतकमेव व्याख्यातम्।। १००।।

इति श्रीलोल्लकुलसंप्रदायप्रवर्तकभ्रमराम्बिकावरप्रसादसमुल्लसितमहासारस्वतभट्टलोल्लपतिग्रन्थविवरणकर्तृ श्रीमहोपाध्यायमहादेवाचार्यसप्तमेन साहित्यपारिजातस्मृतिकल्पतरुप्रबन्धप्रबन्धृलक्ष्मीधरार्यषष्ठेन भरतार्णवपोताख्यसाहित्यमीमांसाग्रन्थद्वयप्रणेतृविरिञ्चिमिश्रपञ्चमेन मीमांसाद्वयजीवातुनिर्मातृपुरुषोत्तममहोपाध्यायनप्त्रा प्राभाकरामृतवाहिनीप्रभावलीखण्डनाद्यनेकप्रबन्धसन्दर्भप्रवर्तकबिरुदपदमहोपाध्यायलक्ष्मणार्यपौत्रेण नयविवेकदीपिकाप्रबन्धसंविधातृमहोपाध्यायविद्वत्सार्वभौमनूतनव्यासाद्यनेकविरुदाङ्कितश्रीविश्वनाथभट्टारकतनयेन अधीतदशशतनयेन पार्वतीगर्भशुक्तिमुक्तारत्नेन बहूकृतधीचिरत्नेन लोल्लकुलकलशाम्बुधिसुधांशुना यशःप्रांशुना हरितगोत्रकल्पशाखिना आपस्तम्बशाखिना षड्दर्शनीपारदृश्वना प्रतिपक्षवृक्षजञ्झामातरिश्वना भ्रमराम्बिकाप्रसादसमासादितप्रतिभाविशेषेण भुवि शेषेण निखिलयामलतन्त्रार्णवावगाहनरुद्रेण आश्रयीकृतगजपतिवीररुद्रेण नीलगिरिसुन्दरचरणारविन्दचञ्चरीकेण वाणीसहचरीकेण सरस्वतीविलासाद्यनेकस्मृतिनिबन्धनलक्ष्मीधराद्यनेकसाहित्यनिबन्धननयविवेकभूषणाद्यनकेगुरुमतनिबन्धनयोगदीपिकाद्यनेकपातञ्जलमतनिबन्धनमहानिबन्धनाख्यमानवधर्मशास्त्रटीकाकर्णावतंससबर्हावतंसाद्यनेककाव्यकल्पकेन आश्रितजनकल्पकेन निग्रहानुग्रहकौशिकेन श्रीमहोपाध्यायलक्ष्मीधरदेशिकेन कृतेयं लक्ष्मीधराख्या सौन्दर्यलहरीस्तुतिव्याख्या।।

अनया सन्तुष्टा भवती भगवती भवानी।।

---

1. अयं 'अराला केशेषु' इत्यनन्तरं पठ्यते।
2. अयं 'गिरिमाहुः' इत्यनन्तरं पठयते।
3. अयं 'सरस्वत्या' इत्यनन्तरं पठ्यते। इमे श्लोकाः प्रथमानुबन्धस्यान्तिमे भागे निर्दिष्टाः।।

Notes : The poet here says that his attempt at composing this work is very much like "carrying coals to Newcastle", if one more simile may be used to explain his several similes. Kaivalyāśrama's gloss deals with all the 100 stanzas. He is however of opinion that stanza 88 is an inerpolation.

त्रयः श्लोका अधिकतयोपलभ्यन्ते कासुचित् व्याख्यामातृकासु। लक्ष्मीधराचार्याः तेषां शंकरभगवत्पादकर्तृकत्वं नाभ्युपयन्ति। तथापि प्रामाणिकैरन्यैर्व्याख्यातत्वात्, भगवत्पादकर्तृकत्वेनाभिहितत्वाच्च, ते श्लोका अत्रोपलब्धाभिर्व्याख्याभिः सह प्रकाश्यन्ते।

श्रीभगवत्या वदनप्रतिबिम्बमहिमानं प्रस्तौति–

समानीतः [1]पद्भ्यां [2]मणिमुकुरतामम्बरमणिः
भया[3]दास्यादन्तः स्तिमितकिरणश्रेणिमसृणः[4]।
दधाति [5]त्वद्वक्त्रप्रतिफलनमश्रान्तविकचं
निरातङ्कं चन्द्रान्निजहृदयपङ्केरुहमिव[6] ।। १०१ ।।

Samānītaḥ padbhyāṁ maṇi-mukuratām ambara-maṇiḥ
bhyād āsyād antaḥ stimita-kiraṇa-śreṇi-masṛṇaḥ/
Dadhāti tvad-vaktra-pratiphalanam aśrānta-vikacaṁ
nir-ātaṅkaṁ candrān nija-hṛdaya-paṅke-ruham iva//

Translation : The Sun, having attined the position of a mirror (cut out) of crystal for Thy feet, rendered him with his beams withdrawn for fear of (burning) Thy face, reflects Thy face, as it were, *viz.*, his own heart-lotus, which, by no means troubled by the Moon, is ever in bloom.

सौभाग्यवर्धनीव्याख्या : समानीत इति। मणिमुकुरतां पद्भ्यां, मणिमयादर्शरूपां लक्ष्मीं शोभां, समानीतः; प्राप्तः अम्बरमणिः अस्य भयात् अन्तःस्तिमितकिरणश्रेणिमसृणः, स्वकिरणसंपर्कात् जगदम्बिकावदनस्य ग्लानिर्भविष्यतीति भयात् अन्तः संकुचितकिरणश्रेणिभिः मसृणः चिक्कणः सन्, त्वद्वक्त्रप्रतिफलनं दधाति। किमिव? अश्रान्तविकचम्; अनवरतविकस्वरम्, चन्द्रान्निरातङ्कम्; अम्लानं, निजहृदयपङ्केरुहमिव ; दर्पणीभूते दिनमणौ तव वदनं प्रतिबिम्बितम्, तस्य हृदयकमलायत इति भावः। समानीतः पद्भ्यामिति क्वचित्पाठः।

1. पद्माम्।
2. पद्मामणि।
3. भयादस्य स्निग्धस्तिमित ; भयादस्यान्तः स्तिमित।
4. मसृणं।
5. त्वद्वक्त्रं प्रतिफलनविश्रान्त ; त्वद्वक्त्रं प्रतिफलितविश्रान्ति।
6. भुवः।

तव चरणाभ्यां मुकुरतां समानीतः। तादर्थ्ये चतुर्थी। तव चरणार्थं मुकुरुतां प्राप्त इत्यर्थः। तव चरणप्रतिफलयोग्योऽयं वदनप्रतिबिम्बधारणे का शक्तिरस्य? तथापि तव चरणकरुणया वदनप्रतिबिम्बं दधानेति भावः।। १०१ ।।

Notes : According to Lakṣmīdhara stanzas 101, 102 and 103 are inerpolations. Hence, they have not been dealt with in his gloss. *The position of a mirror for Thy feet*—standing there as he does, for Pādasevā, the Sun being worthy of only such a position and not of facing Thee and directly serving the purpose of a mirror for thy face. *By no means troubled by the Moon*— as the presence of the Moon would not have the effect of closing its petals, it being overshadowed by the presence of the Devī. Lotuses generally bloom in sunlight and close their petals at nightfall. But the heart-lotus of the Sun, in the presence of the Devī, would be ever in bloom and thus resemble the Devī's lotus-like face in a way. There is the implication that the face of the Devī, reflected in the mirror of the Sun, causes an imprint of it, as it were, to appear in the heart of the Sun, which is all the while meditating upon the Devī.

अथ श्रीदेव्युपासनाया सारूप्यरूपकफलमाह–

समुद्भूतस्थूलस्तनभरमुरश्चारु हसितं
कटाक्षे कंदर्पाः[1] कतिचन कदम्बद्युतिवपुः।
हरस्य त्वद्भ्रान्तिं मनसि जनयन्ति[2] स्म विमला
[4]भवत्या ये भक्ताः परिणतिरमीषामियमुमे।। १०२ ।।

Samudbhūta-sthūla-stana-bharam uraś cāru hasitaṁ
kaṭākṣe kaṁdarpāḥ kati cana kadamba-dyuti vapuḥ/
Harasya tvad-bhrāntiṁ manasi janayanti sma vimalā
bhavatyā ye bhaktāḥ pariṇatir amīṣām iyam ume//

Translation : O Umā! a chest bearing well-developed breasts, a charming smile, a side-glance emitting Cupids as it were, a Kadamba-like frame, all these (conspire) together to create in Hara's mind a delusive impression, if it were Thou. Whoever are Thy faultless devotees, this is their consummation.

---

1. कटाक्षव्याक्षेपः।
2. जनयन्ती सुवदने ; जनयामास मदनो ; जनयन्तः समतुलां ; जनयन्त; सुवदने।
3. भवत्याम्।

सौभाग्यवर्धनीव्याख्या–

समुद्भूतेति। हे उमे! भवत्या ये भक्ताः विमलाः मनोवाक्कायकर्मभिः भवच्चरणोपासनपराः दम्भादिदोषरहिताः एतेषां, इयं परिणतिः उपसनायाः परिणामः, सा का? समुद्भूतस्थूलस्तनभरम् उरः, चारुहसितं, कटाक्षे कन्दर्पाः, कटाक्षविक्षेपेण बहव उज्जीविता भवन्तीति भावः। कदम्बद्युतिवपुः ; रोमाञ्चकञ्चुकितं वपुः, महादेवावलोकनसमुद्भूतसात्विकभाव इति रहस्यम्। मनसि त्वद्भ्रान्तिं जनयति, एवंरूपा परिणतिर्भवति। त्वत्सारूप्यं प्राप्य तवैव संनिधौ सख्य इव वर्तमानाः त्वमिव महादेवस्य मनसि भान्ति। अनेन पूर्वोक्ताया भावनायाः फलमहिमा प्रतिपादितः। अत्र भ्रान्तिमानलङ्कारः।। १०२।।

Notes : The implication is that all devotees of the Devī, by constantly meditating on her form, themselves develop a similar form, as constant believing is seeing, seeing develops into knowing, and knowing is becoming.

स्वकृतस्तुतिं निगमयति–

निधे नित्यस्मेरे[1] निरवधिगुणे नीतिनिपुणे
निराघाटज्ञाने[2] निय[3]मपरचित्तैकनिलये।
नियत्या निर्मुक्ते निखिलनिगमान्तस्तुतपदे[4]
निरातङ्के नित्ये निगमय[5] ममापि स्तुतिमिमाम्।। १०३।।

Nidhe nitya-smere nir-avadhi-guṇe nīti-nipuṇe
nir-āghāṭa-jñāne niyama-para-cittaika-nilaye/
Niyatyā nirmukte nikhila-nigamānta-stuta-pade
nir-ātaṅke nitye nigamaya mamāpi stutim imāṁ//

Translation : O Treasure-mine! ever smiling, possessed of boundless qualities, proficient in holding the scales even, uninterrupted fountain of Wisdom, ever abiding in well-controlled minds, by no means bound to conventions, with feet glorified by all the Upaniṣads, void of risks and eternal, hallow this laudatory composition of even mine (Thy humble devotee).

1. नित्यंस्मेरे।
2. निराघातज्ञाने।
3. नियतपरिवित्तैकनिलये।
4. स्तुतिपदे।
5. निशमय।

सौभाग्यवर्धनीव्याख्या–

निधे इति। निधीयते जगदस्यामिति निधिः, हे निधे! जगदाधारभूते; तथा च मार्कण्डेये–"आधारभूता जगतस्त्वमेका" इति। नित्यस्मेरे! सर्वदानन्दनिर्भरोन्मेष-लसद्वदने। ननु जगदाधारभूता इति पूर्वं प्रतिपादितम्। अधुना नित्यस्मेरे इत्युच्यते। स्मेरता शरीरधर्मः जगदाधारभूता शक्तिरशरीरा। अत्र पूर्वोत्तरसंबोधनयोः परस्परं विरोध इत्यत आह–निरवधिगुण इति। निरवधिगुणे! निरवधयः असंख्यातशक्तिविलासाः गुणाः यस्याः भक्तानुग्रहशरीरायाः। स्मेरा अचिन्त्यरूपाधारशक्तिरशरीरेति न विरोधः। यदि भक्तानुग्रहाय शरीरपरिग्रहस्तर्हि भक्तेषु तारतम्यं कुतः? कश्चिद्राजा, कश्चित्प्रभुः कश्चिद्दरिद्रः, कश्चिद्विरक्त इत्यत आह—नीतिनिपुणे इति। नीतिनिपुणे! नीतौ निपुणा। यादृशो यस्यानुग्रह उचितः अनाद्यविद्यासंवलिततत्कर्मानुबद्धः तादृगनुग्रहः। तर्हि कर्मपारतन्त्र्यं भगवत्याः, न तु स्वातन्त्र्यमित्यस्मदादिवत्सा जातेत्यत्राह–निराघाटज्ञान इति। आघाटः इयत्तापरिमाणघटना, निराघाटः अखण्डः तादृशसंविदुल्लासरूपे। अस्याः सान्निध्यवशात् तत्तच्छक्तिसमवायेन तत्तत्कर्मानुग्रहो भवतीत्यर्थः। एतादृशी कथमुपास्या भवति? ध्यानादिभिराकलितुमयोग्यत्वादित्यत आह–नियमेति। नियमपरचित्तैकनिलये! ये जपपूजाध्यानादिनियमैरुपासते, तेषां चित्तैकनिलये! तेषां चित्ते आविर्भूय प्रकाशत इत्यर्थः। तर्हि भगवत्याः नियमपरचित्तैकनिलयं प्रकाशमानता नान्यत्रेति नियतिपरतन्त्रता जाता इत्यत आह—नियत्येति। नियत्या निर्मुक्ते! लीलया नियमपरचित्ते प्रकाशते न तु नियतिपरतन्त्रतया! यथा कल्पद्रुमः सर्वसाधारणोऽपि सेवापराणां फलदाता, नान्येषां, यथा वा सूर्यः जलादौ निर्मले वस्तुनि प्रतिबिम्बते, नान्यत्र, तेन न सूर्यस्य नियतिपारतन्त्र्यं तथेति भावः। एतस्या देवतायाः सद्भावे किं प्रमाणमित्यत आह—निखिलेति। निखिलनिगमान्तस्तुतपदे! निगमान्ता वेदान्ता उपनिषदः, ताभिरुपलक्षितपदे ; उपनिषदः प्रमाणमित्यर्थः। केन प्रकारेण स्तुतपदा? तमेव प्रकारमाह—निरातङ्के इति। निरातङ्के नित्ये! तथा च श्रुतिः "**अभयमक्षरममितमनणवस्थूलमविकारं केवलं चिन्मात्रमयं ब्रह्म**" इति। एवंप्रकारेण स्तुते इति। निगमय ममापि स्तुतिमिमां; निगमय-निगमीकुरु। तत्करोतीत्यर्थे णिच्। वेदमिव सर्वसंप्रतिपन्नां कुरु। यथा वाल्मीकिव्यासादीनां वाचः स्मृतिपुराणेतिहासादयः निगमवत् सर्वसंप्रतिपन्नास्त्वया कृताः, तथा ममापीयं स्तुतिः निगमीक्रियतामित्यर्थः। तथाच कौर्मे भगवत्या वचनं हिमवन्तं प्रति–

वेदरूपा पराशक्तिर्मम लोके प्रवर्तते।
तयाधिष्ठानि कर्माणि कुर्वन्ति सुरसत्तमाः।।
देवर्षयो राजर्षयो व्यासादिमुनयस्तथा।
तैः प्रणीतानि सर्वाणि कल्पसूत्रमुखानि वै।।

धर्मशास्त्रपुराणानि सेतिहासस्मृतीनि च।
ज्ञेयानि वेदवत्तानि नात्र कार्या विचारणा।।

इति। अत्र बहुकारणेषु एकक्रियायोगात् मालादीपकालंकारः।।

Notes : This stanza is commented upon by Kāmeśvara-sūri, which indicates that is inds a place in his manuscript and has been recognized by him as part of the work. The poet characterizes the Devī as a Treasure-mine and gives us some specimens of the gems it contains, without forcing us to the necessity of delving deeply into it. Mark the alliteration.

अनुबन्धः-१

सौन्दर्यलहरीस्थश्लोकानां बीजाक्षरयुतयन्त्रपूजापुरश्चरण-नैवेद्यफलानि

अनुष्ठानप्रकारः

श्रीत्रिपुरसुन्दर्यै नमः

विनियोगः– अस्य श्रीसौन्दर्यलहरीस्तोत्रस्य गोविन्दः ऋषिः। अनुष्टुप् छन्दः। श्रीमहात्रिपुरसुन्दरी देवता। शिवः शक्त्या युक्त इति बजीम्। सुधासिन्धोर्मध्ये इति शक्तिः। जपो जल्पः शिल्पमिति कीलकम्। श्रीललितामहात्रिपुरसुन्दरीप्रीत्यर्थे जपे विनियोगः।

करन्यासः–ह्रां अङ्गुष्ठाभ्यां नमः; ह्रीं तर्जनीभ्यां स्वाहा; ह्रूं मध्यमाभ्यां वषट्; ह्रैं अनामिकाभ्यां हुं; ह्रौं कनिष्ठिकाभ्यां वौषट्; ह्रः करतलकरपृष्ठाभ्यां फट्।

अङ्गन्यासः–ह्रां हृदयाय नमः; ह्रीं शिरसे स्वाहा; ह्रूं शिखायै वौषट् ; ह्रैं कवचाय हुं; ह्रौं नेत्रत्रयाय वौषट्; ह्रः अस्त्राय फट्।।

ध्यानम्

लौहित्यनिर्जितजपाकुसुमानुरागां
पाशाङ्कुशे धनुरिषूनपि धारयन्तीम्।
ताम्रेक्षणामरुणमाल्यविशेषभूषां
ताम्बूलपूरितमुखीं त्रिपुरां नमामि।।

पञ्चोपचारः–लं पृथिव्यात्मने गन्धं कल्पयामि; हं आकाशात्मने पुष्पं कल्पयामि; यं वाय्वात्मने धूपं कल्पयामि; रं वह्न्यात्मने दीपं कल्पयामि; वं जलात्मने नैवेद्यं कल्पयामि।। ॐ।।

सौन्दर्यलहरीस्तोत्रपारायणोपयोगि-करन्यास-अङ्गन्यास-ध्यानादीनां सर्वेषामपि श्लोकानां च क्रमशः बीजाक्षरयुतयन्त्रपूजापुरश्चरणनैवेद्यफलानां विवरणम्।

श्लोकः-१

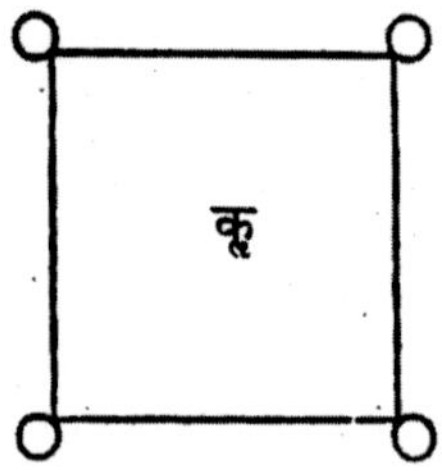

(i) यन्त्रमिदं तण्डुलपिष्टेन स्थण्डिले विलिख्य घृतदीपसंस्थापनपूर्वकं द्वादश दिनानि संपूज्य प्रत्यहं श्लोकमिमं सहस्रमावर्तयेत्। अनेन सकलकार्यजयः।

(ii) इदमेव यन्त्रं हेमपट्टतले विलिख्य पूर्वाभिमुखो द्वादश दिनानि संपूज्य श्लोकमिमं प्रतिदिनं सहस्रमावर्त्यं कण्ठे धारयेत्। अनेन सकलाभिवृद्धिः। उभयत्र नैवेद्यं त्रिमधुरम्। त्रिमधुरं नाम गुडनारिकेलकदलीफलानां मिश्रणेन संपादितं द्रव्यम्।

श्लोकः-२

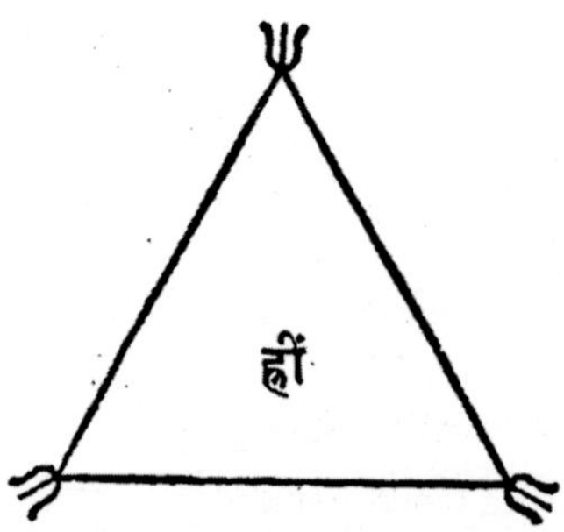

यन्त्रमिदं स्पर्णपट्टे विलिख्य, उत्तराभिमुखः पञ्चपञ्चाशद्दिनानि संपूज्य श्लोकमिमं प्रतिवासरं सहस्रमावर्त्य धारयेत्। अनेन सर्वलोकवश्यता प्रकृतिजयश्च। नैवेद्यं क्षीरपायसम्।

श्लोकः-३

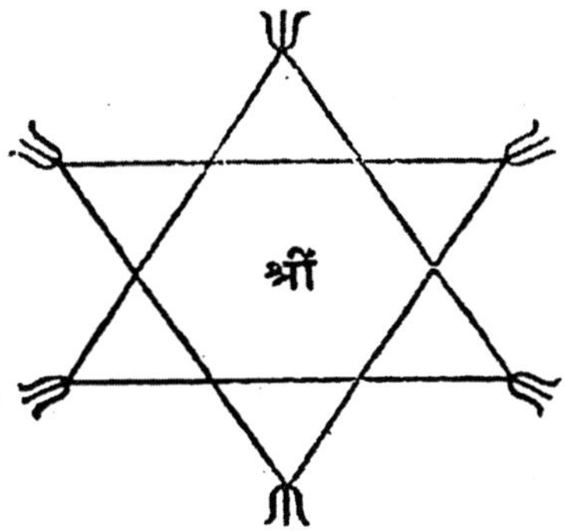

(i) इदं यन्त्रं कनकपट्टतले विलिख्य ईशानाभिमुखः पञ्चदश दिनानि संपूज्य श्लोकमिमं प्रत्यहं सहस्रमावर्त्य धारयेत्। अनेन सर्वैश्वर्यविद्ये भवतः।

(ii) इदमेव यन्त्रं चतुःपञ्चाशद्दिनानि पूर्ववदभ्यर्च्य प्रतिवासरं श्लोकमिमं द्विसहस्रमावर्त्य साधयेत्। साधको वेदविद्भवेत्। उभयत्र नैवेद्यम्–माषापूपः।

श्लोकः-४

(i) यंत्रमिदं रजतपट्टे विलिख्य पूर्वाभिमुखः षोडश दिनान्यभ्यर्च्य श्लोकमिमं प्रतिदिनं सहस्रमावर्त्य धारयेत्। फलम्–साम्राज्यसिद्धिः।

(ii) इदमेव यन्त्रं षट्त्रिंशद्दिनानि पूर्ववदभ्यर्च्य श्लोकमिमं प्रत्यहं सहस्रमावर्तयेत्। अनेन साधकं दारिद्र्यरोगादयो न बाधन्ते। उभयत्र नैवेद्यम्–हरिद्रान्नम्। अत्र केरलभाषापुस्तके श्रीमिति बीजाक्षरं दृश्यते।

श्लोकः-५

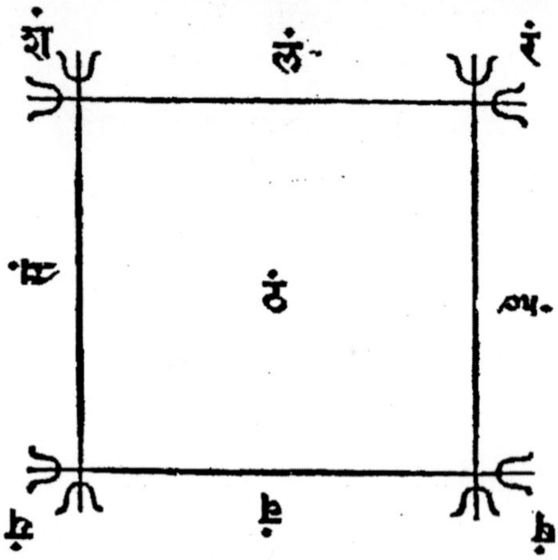

इदं यन्त्रं ताम्रपट्टे विलिख्य वायव्याभिमुखोऽष्टौ दिनानिसंपूज्य प्रत्यहं श्लोकमिमं द्विसहस्रमावर्त्य शिरसि धारयेत्। फलं सकलजनसंमोहनं स्त्रीणां पुरुषवश्यता च। नैवैद्यम्–गुडपायसम्।

श्लोकः-६

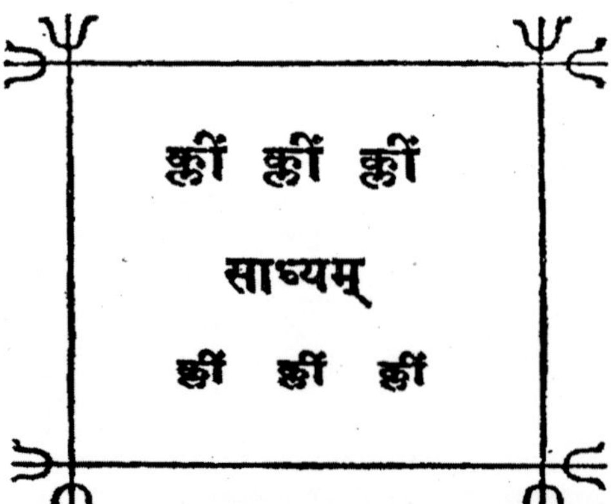

यन्त्रमिदं कनकपट्टतले विलिख्य पूर्वाभिमुखः एकविंशतिदिनानि समाराध्य पद्यमिदं प्रतिदिनं पञ्चशतमावर्त्य धारयेत्। फलम्–साधकस्य षण्डत्वनिवृत्त्या पुत्रावाप्तिः। नैवेद्यम्–इक्षुखण्डः।

श्लोकः-७

यन्त्रमिदं हाटकपट्टे विलिख्य पूर्वाभिमुखः पञ्चचत्त्वारिंशद्दिनानि समभ्यर्च्य श्लोकमिमं प्रतिवासरं सहस्रमावर्त्य शिरसि धारयेत्। भस्म वाऽभिमन्त्र्य धारयेत्। अनेन शत्रुजयः। नैवेद्यं क्षीरपायसम्।

श्लोकः-८

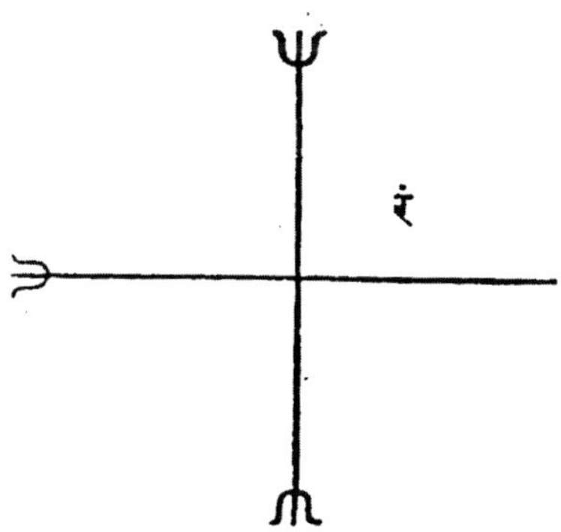

यन्त्रमिदं रक्तचन्दनखण्डे निर्माय द्वादश दिनानि रक्तपुष्पैरभ्यर्च्य पद्यमिदं प्रत्यहं द्विशतोत्तरसहस्रमावर्त्य धारयेत्। फलं कारागृहनिवृत्तिः सकलकार्यजयश्च। नैवेद्यं कृष्णमरीचः।

श्लोकः-९

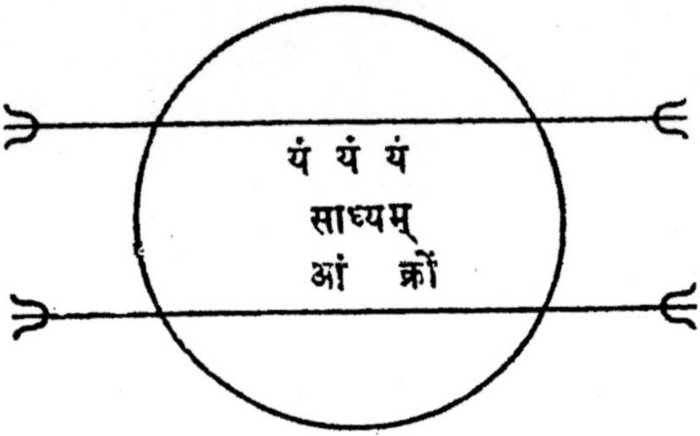

(i) यन्त्रमिदं कनकपट्टे विलिख्य दश दिनान्यभ्यर्च्य प्रत्यहं श्लोकमिमं सहस्रमावर्तयेत्। फलम्–देशान्तरगतस्य क्षिप्रागमनम्।

(ii) इदमेव यन्त्रं गन्धचोलिकयालिप्य पञ्चचत्वारिंशद्दिनानि समाराध्य पद्यमिदं प्रतिवासरं सहस्रमावर्तयेत्। अनेन साधकः पञ्चभूतानि जयिष्यति। उभयत्र नैवेद्यं क्षीरपायसम्।

श्लोकः-१०

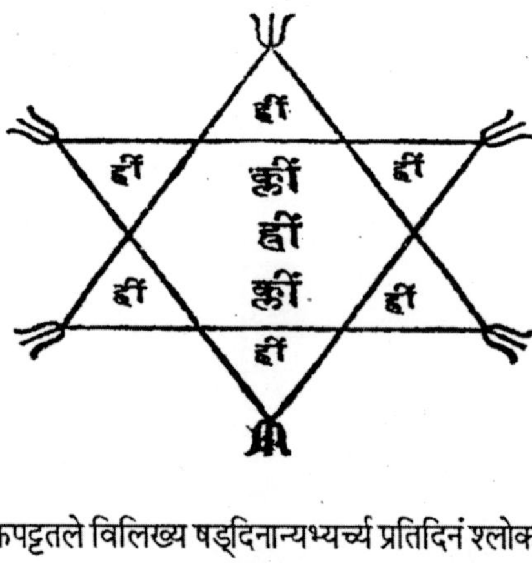

इदं यन्त्रं हाटकपट्टतले विलिख्य षड्दिनान्यभ्यर्च्य प्रतिदिनं श्लोकमिमं सहस्रमावर्त्य रक्तक्षौमतन्तौ निबध्य धारयेत्। फलम्–वृष्यं स्त्रीणां रजोदर्शनं च। नैवेद्यम्–कदलीफलम्।

श्लोकः-११

इदं यन्त्रं कनकपट्टतले विलिख्य एकाशीतिदिनानि संपूज्य श्लोकमिममनुदिनं सहस्रमावर्त्य धारयेत्। नवनीतं वाऽभिमन्त्र्य सेवयेत्। अनेन वन्ध्यादोषो निवर्तते। नैवेद्यम्–गुडपायसम्।

श्लोकः-१२

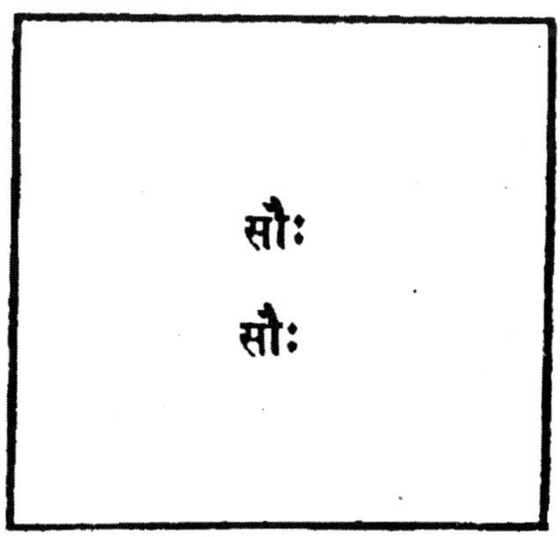

यन्त्रमिदं जले विलिख्य पञ्चचत्वारिंशद्दिनान्यभ्यर्च्य जलं स्पृष्ट्वा श्लोकमिमं प्रत्यहं सहस्रमावर्त्य पिबेत्। अनेन मूकोऽपि कविर्भवेत्, वशित्वं सिध्येत्। नैवेद्यम् मधु।

श्लोकः-१३

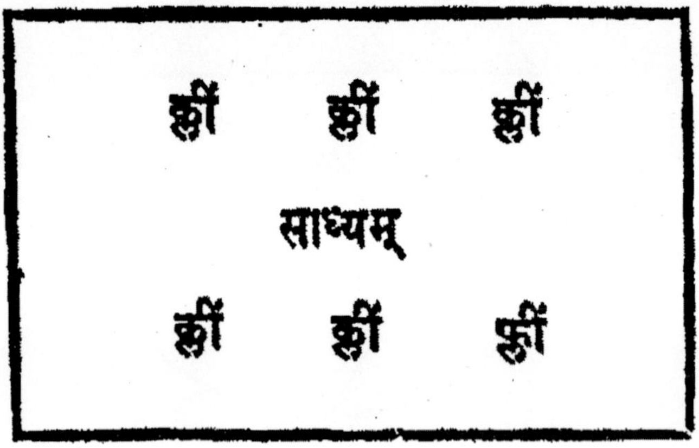

इदं यन्त्रे हेमपट्टे विलिख्य षड्दिनानि समाराध्य श्लोकमिममनुदिनं सहस्रमावर्त्य धारयेत्। फलं स्त्रीवश्यता। नैवेद्यम्-त्रिमधुरम्।

श्लोकः-१४

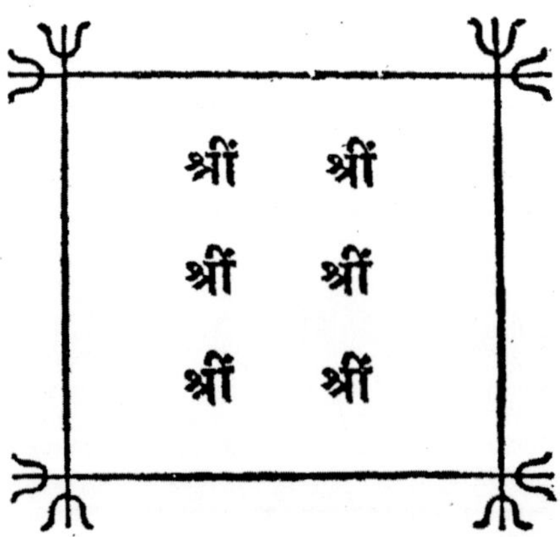

यन्त्रमिदं हाटकपट्टतले विलिख्य पञ्चचत्वारिंशद्दिनान्यभ्यर्च्य श्लोकमिमं प्रतिवासरं सहस्रमावर्त्य धारयेत्। अनेन वसन्तादिरोगाः दुर्भिक्षं च न बाधेत। नैवेद्यं क्षीरपायसम्।

श्लोकः-१५

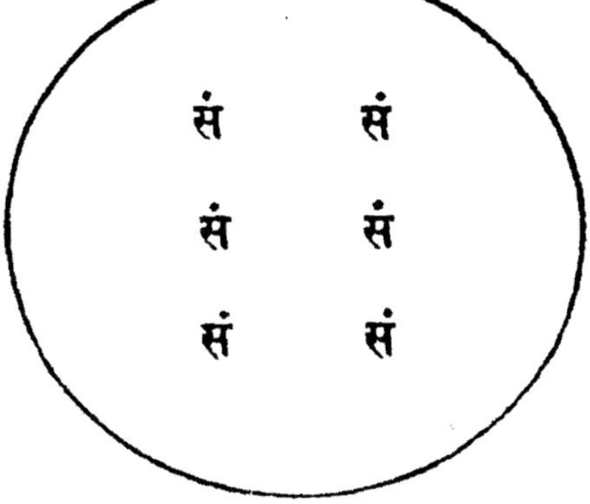

(i) यन्त्रमिदं सुवर्णपट्टे विलिख्य एकचत्वारिंशद्दिनानि संपूज्य श्लोकमिमं प्रत्यहं सहस्रमावर्त्य धारयेत्। अनेन साधकः कविर्विज्ञान च भवेत्।

(ii) इदमेव यन्त्रं जले विलिख्य पूर्ववत्संपूज्य जप्त्वा पिबेत्। फलं पूर्ववत्। उभयत्र नैवेद्यं मधु कदलीफलं शर्करा च।

श्लोकः-१६

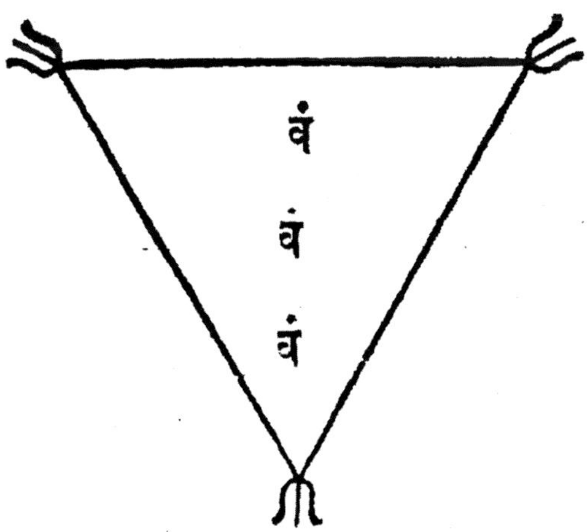

यन्त्रमिदं हेमपट्टतले विलिख्य एकचत्वारिंशदहानि समाराध्य श्लोकमिममनुदिनं सहस्रमावर्स्य धारयेत्। फलं वेदशास्त्रादिज्ञानम्। नैवेद्यं मधु।

श्लोकः-१७

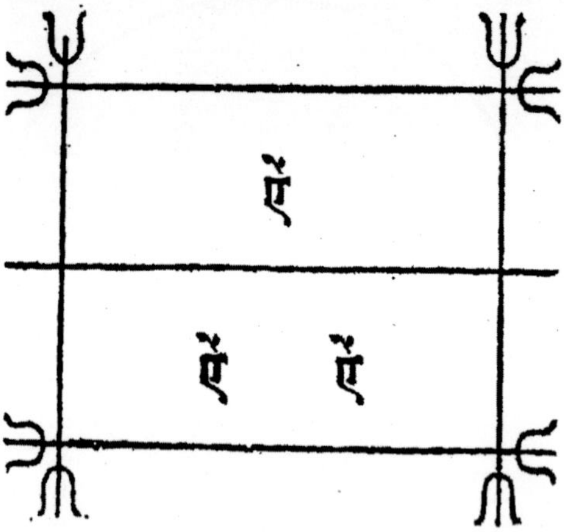

इदं यन्त्रं हाटकपट्टे विलिख्य एकनवतिदिनान्यभ्यर्च्य श्लोकमिममनुदिनं सहस्त्रमावर्त्य धारयेत्। अनेन साधकः सकलकलाकोविदो भवेत्। नैवेद्यं मधु कदलीफलं क्षीरं शर्करा खण्डशर्करा च।

श्लोकः-१८

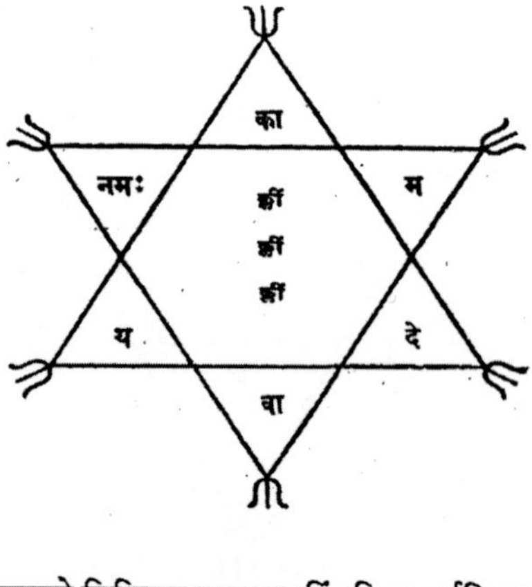

यन्त्रमिदं सुवर्णपट्टतले विलिख्य पञ्चचत्वारिंशद्दिनान्यर्चयित्वा प्रत्यहं श्लोकमिमं सहस्त्रमावर्त्य धारयेत्। चन्दनं कुङ्कुमं पुष्पं वाऽभिमन्त्र्य दद्यात् फलं–सकलप्राणिवश्यता। नैवेद्यं क्षीरपायसं ताम्बूलं च।

श्लोकः-१९

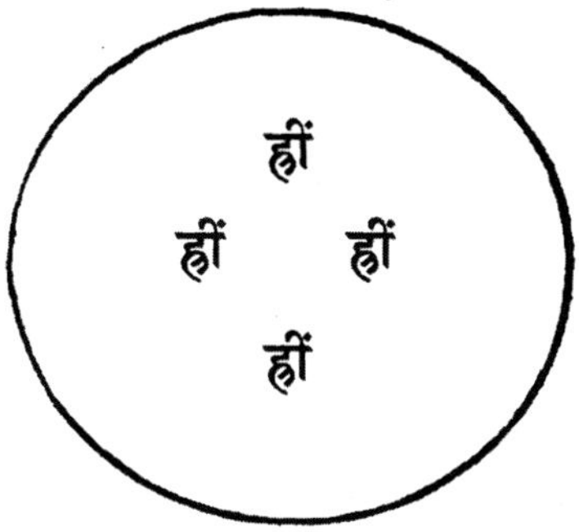

इदं यन्त्रं हेमपट्टतले विलिख्य पञ्चविंशतिदिनान्याराध्य श्लोकमिमं प्रतिवासरं द्विशताधिकसहस्रमावर्त्य धारयेत्। चन्दनं पुष्पं भस्म कुङ्कुमं वाऽभिमन्त्र्य धारयेत्। अनेन सकलराजराक्षसमृगस्त्रीवश्यता भवति। नैवेद्यं क्षीरं मधु कदलीफलं च।

श्लोकः-२०

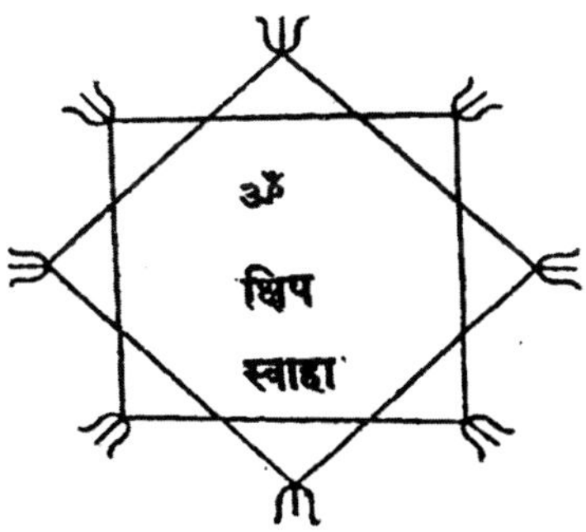

(i) यन्त्रमिदं भस्मनि विलिख्य श्लोकमिमं सहस्रमावर्त्य तद्भस्म दद्यात्। अनेन विषनिवृत्तिर्भवति। इदं भस्म सर्पे लग्नं चेत् मुह्यात्। ज्वरश्च निवर्तेत।

(ii) इममेव श्लोकं पञ्चचत्वारिंशद्दिनानि प्रत्यहं द्विसहस्रमावर्त्य साधयेत्। अनेन साधकस्य कदापि विषभीतिर्न जायते।

(iii) इदमेव यन्त्रं मयूरताम्रेण पुन्नागताम्रेण वा मिश्रितसुवर्णपट्टतले विलिख्य श्लोकमिमं पूर्ववत्संसाध्य तद्यन्त्रमङ्गुलीयकं कृत्वा धारयेत्। तद्धस्तेन सर्पदष्टे जले प्रोक्षिते विषनिवृत्तिर्भवति।

श्लोकः-२१

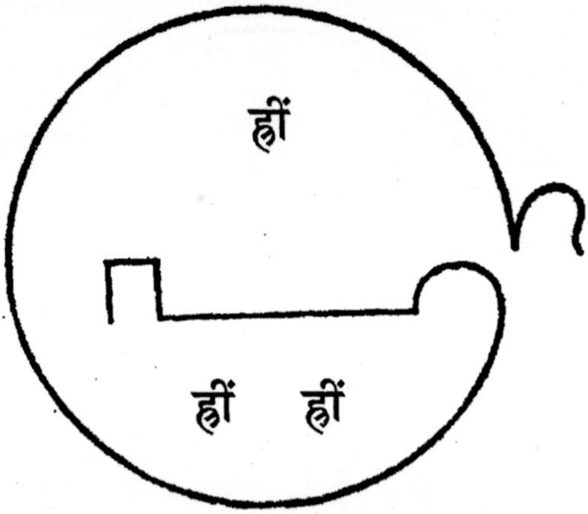

यन्त्रमिदं स्वर्णपट्टे रजतपट्टे ताम्रपट्टे वा विलिख्य पञ्चचत्वारिंशदहानि पूजयित्वा श्लोकमिममनुदिनं सहस्रमावर्त्य धारयेत्। अनेन सकलजनविरोधनाशः वश्यता च। नैवेद्यं कदलीफलं मधु गुडं च।

श्लोकः-२२

चक्रमिदं सुवर्णपट्टतले विलिख्य कस्मिंश्चित्पुण्यतीर्थे क्षेत्रे देवीसन्निधौ वा उपविश्य पञ्चचत्वारिंशदहानि संपूज्य श्लोकमिममहरहस्सहस्रमावर्त्य साधयेत्। अनेन ऐहिकसर्वाभीष्टसिद्धिः सकलैश्वर्यप्राप्तिः साम्राज्यावाप्तिश्च भवति। नैवेद्यं मधु त्रिमधुरं दधि क्षीरं चित्रान्नं च।

श्लोकः-२३

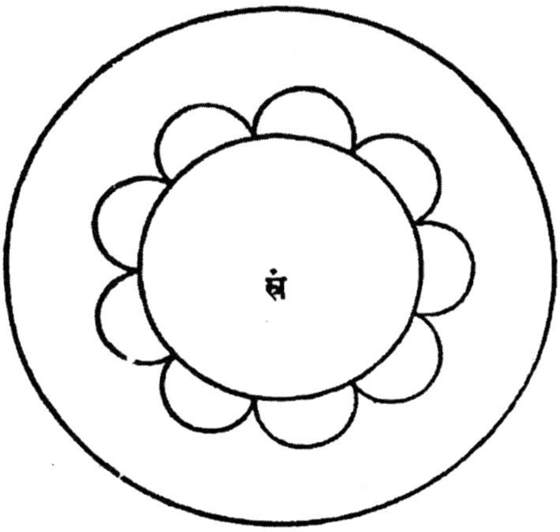

यन्त्रमिदं हेमपट्टे विलिख्य गृहे संस्थाप्य त्रिंशद्दिनान्यभ्यर्च्य प्रत्यहं श्लोकमिमं त्रिसहस्रमावर्तयेत्। फलं सर्वापन्निवृत्तिः ऋणमोचनं भूतप्रेतशमनं च भवति। नैवेद्यं क्षीरपायसम्।

श्लोकः-२४

न	शि	य	मः	वा
य	मः	वा	न	शि
वा	न	शि	य	मः
शि	य	मः	वा	न
मः	वा	न	शि	य

शिवयन्त्रमिदं हाटकपट्टतले विलिख्य त्रिंशद्दिनानि सम्पूज्य श्लोकमिममहरहस्सहस्रमावर्त्य धारयेत्। फलम्–भूतप्रेतपिशाचास्मारादिनिवारणम्। नैवेद्यम् मधु माषापूप तिलपिष्टं च।

श्लोकः-२५

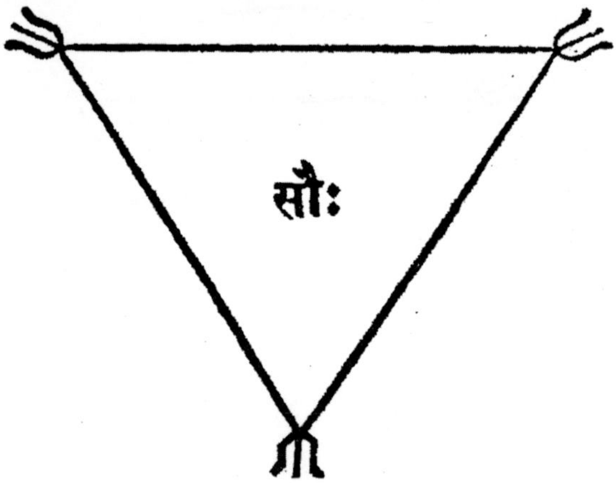

इदं यन्त्रं हेमपट्टतले विलिख्य पञ्चचत्वारिंशद्दिनान्यभ्यर्च्य श्लोकमिमं सहस्रमावर्त्य धारयेत्। फलम्–राजकीयाधिकारः उत्कृष्टपदवीलाभश्च। नैवेद्यम्–मधु।

श्लोकः-२६

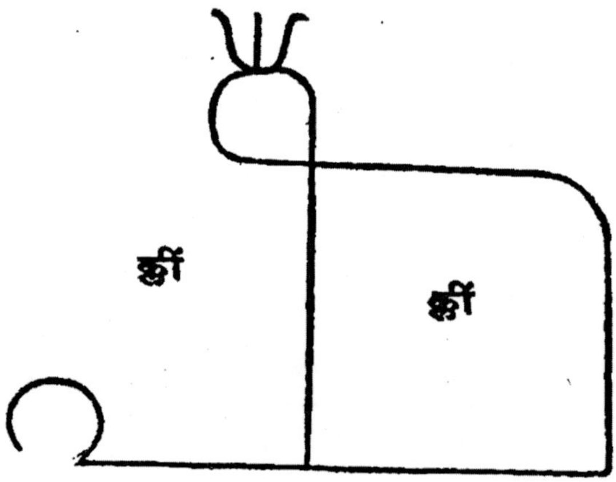

(i) यन्त्रमिदं सुवर्णपट्टतले विलिख्यार्चयित्वामावास्यायां श्लोकमिमं सहस्रमावर्त्य धारयेत्। फलम्–सर्वसिद्धिः।

(ii) इदमेव यन्त्रं षड्दिनानि पूजयित्वाऽनुदिनं श्लोकमिमं सहस्रमावर्तयेत्। अनेन शत्रुजयो भवति। उभयत्र नैवेद्यम्–गुडपायसम्।

श्लोकः-२७

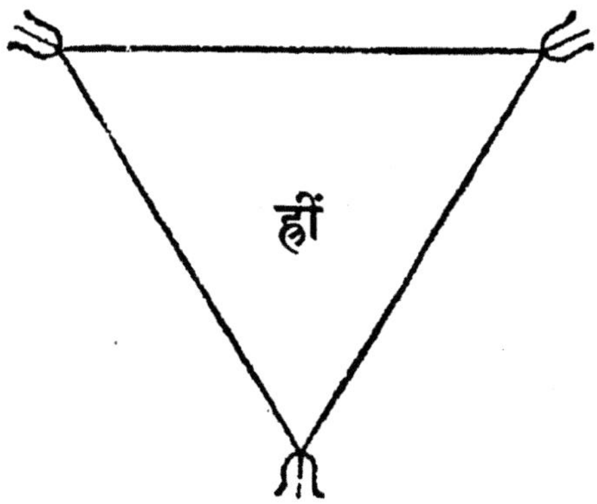

इदं यन्त्रं हेमपट्टे लिखित्वा पञ्चचत्वारिंशदहानि पूजयित्वा श्लोकमिममहरहः सहस्रमावर्त्य धारयेत्। फलम्-मन्त्रसिद्धिः देवीदर्शनं आत्मज्ञानं च। नैवेद्यं गुडपायसम्।

श्लोकः-२८

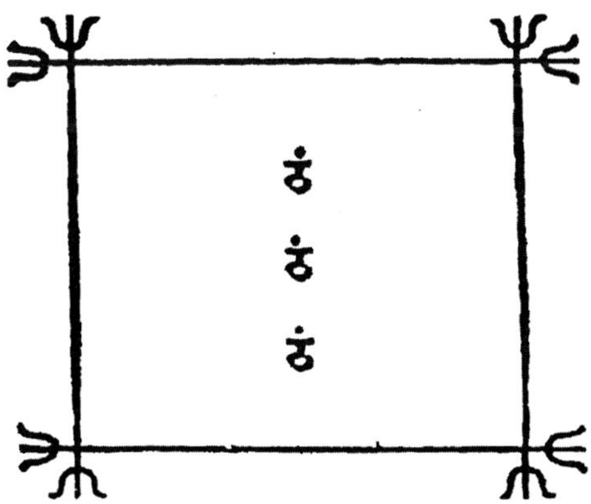

यन्त्रमिदं हाटकपट्टे विलिख्य पञ्चचत्वारिंशद्दिनानि समाराध्य प्रत्यहं श्लोकमिमं सहस्रमावर्त्य धारयेत्। फलं-स्त्रीणां सकलकार्यसिद्धिः पुरुषाणामपमृत्युनिवारणं च। नैवेद्यम्-क्षीरपायसं त्रिमधुरं ताम्बूलं च।

श्लोकः-२९

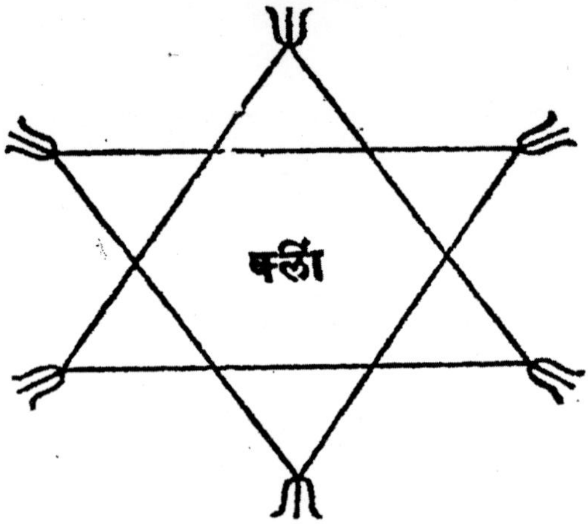

इदं यन्त्रं हेमपट्टे विलिख्य पञ्चचत्वारिंशद्दिनान्यर्चयित्वा-श्लोकमिमं प्रतिवासरं सहस्रमावर्त्य धारयेत्। फलम्-दुष्टान् मूर्खांश्च सतः कृत्वा स्ववशीकरणम्। नैवेद्यम्-मधु माषापूपश्च।

श्लोकः-३०

यन्त्रमिदं कनकपट्टतले विलिख्य षण्णवतिदिनानि समाराध्य श्लोकमिममहरहस्सहस्रमावर्त्य धारयेत्। फलम्-अणिमाद्यष्टसिद्धिः परकायप्रवेश अग्निस्तम्भनं च। नैवेद्यम्-मधु त्रिमधुरं ताम्बूलं च।

श्लोकः-३१

चक्रमिदं हाटकपट्टे विलिख्य पञ्चचत्वारिंशदहान्यर्चयित्वा हस्ते निधाय श्लोकमिममनुदिनं सहस्रमावर्तयेत्। अनेन सकलजनवश्यं राजवश्यं च भवेत्। नैवेद्यम्–मधु क्षीरं च।

श्लोकः-३२

इदं यन्त्रं स्वर्णपट्टतले विलिख्य पञ्चचत्वारिंशद्दिनानि संपूज्य प्रत्यहं श्लोकमिमं सहस्रमावर्त्य धारयेत्। फलम्–सकलविद्यासिद्धिः रसायनसिद्धिश्च। नैवेद्यं दध्यन्नं माषापूपश्च। (अत्र केरलभाषापुस्तके यमिति बीजाक्षरं न दृश्यते।)

श्लोकः-३३

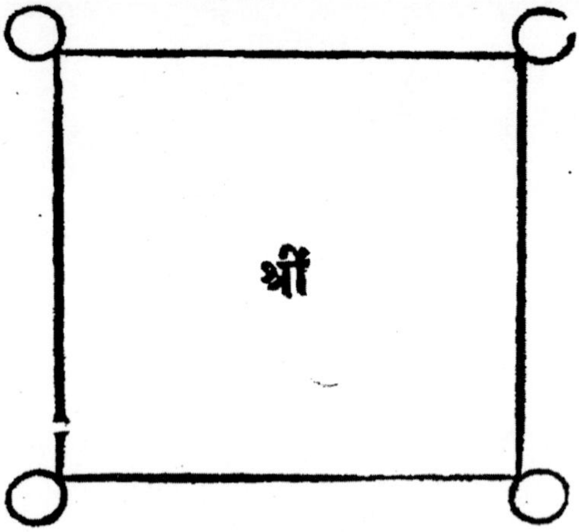

यन्त्रमिदं कनकपट्टतले विलिख्य तत्र रौप्यकं निधाय पञ्चचत्वारिंशद्दिनानि संपूज्य श्लोकमिममनुदिनं सहस्रमावर्तयेत्। फलम्-भूरिधनावाप्तिः। नैवेद्यं मुद्गान्नं मधु।

श्लोकः-३४

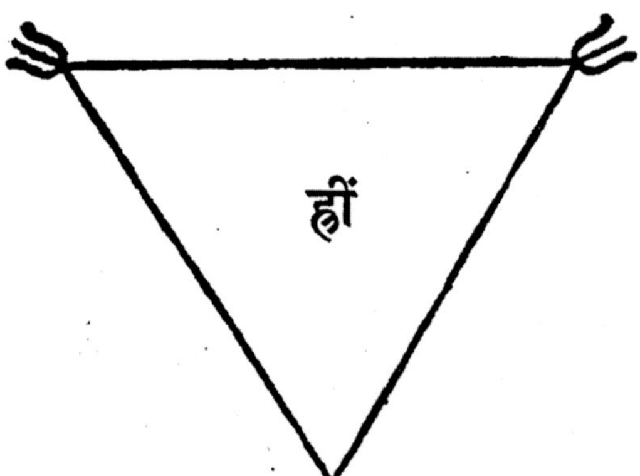

यन्त्रमिदं हेमपट्टे विलिख्य पञ्चचत्वारिंशदहान्यभ्यर्च पद्यमिदं प्रत्यहं सहस्रवारं जप्त्वा धारयेत्। अनेन साधकः महाबुद्धिमान् भवेत्। नैवेद्यम्-मधु।

श्लोकः-३५

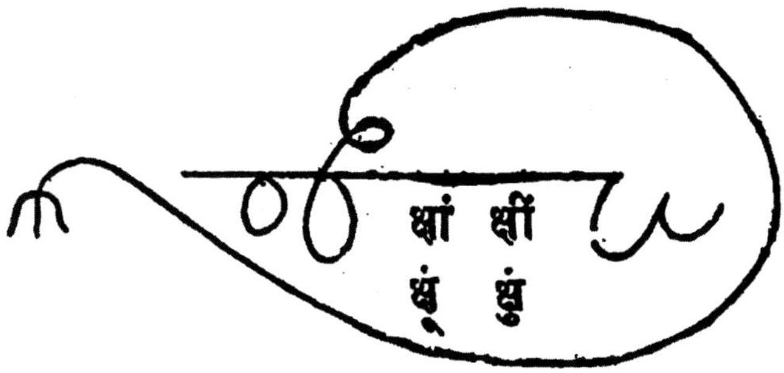

इदं यन्त्रं स्वर्णपट्टतले विलिख्य पञ्चचत्वारिंशद्दिनान्यभ्यर्च्य श्लोकमिमं प्रतिवासरं सहस्रमावर्त्य धारयित्वा हरीतकीमभिमन्त्र्य सेवयेत्। अनेन क्षयरोगो निवर्तते। नैवेद्यम्-मधु क्षीरपायसं च।

श्लोकः-३६

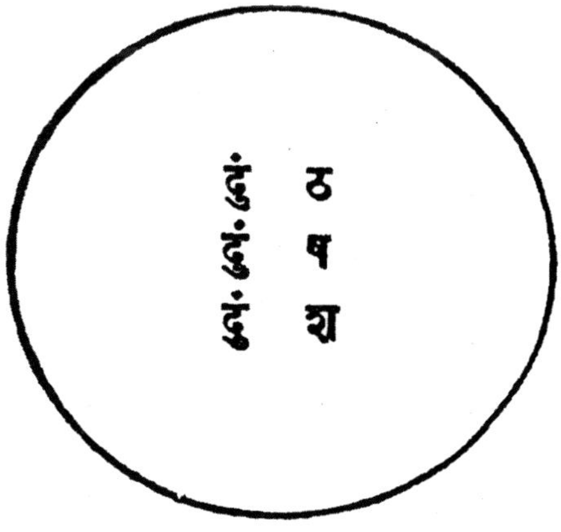

यन्त्रमिदं कनकपट्टे विलिख्य पञ्चचत्वारिंशदाहान्यर्चयित्वा पद्यमिदमहरहः सहस्रवारं जप्त्वा धारयेत् रोगशान्तये जलं वाऽभिमन्त्र्य पाययेत्। फलं नानाविधकठिन-रोगनिवृत्तिः नैवेद्यम्-मधु माषापूपश्च।

श्लोकः-३७

इदं यन्त्रं जातरूपपट्टे विलिख्यार्चयित्वा पद्यमिदं पञ्चसहस्रमावर्त्य धारयेत्। जलं वाभिमन्त्र्य पिबेत्। फलं-ब्रह्मरक्षोबाधानिवृत्तिः। नैवेद्यम्-गुडपायसं नारिकेलफलं कदलीफलं च।

श्लोकः-३८

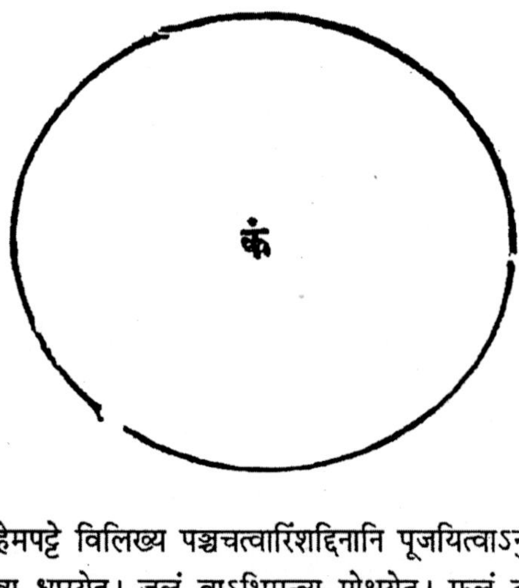

यन्त्रमिदं हेमपट्टे विलिख्य पञ्चचत्वारिंशद्दिनानि पूजयित्वाऽनुदिनं श्लोकमिमं सहस्रवारं जप्त्वा धारयेत्। जलं वाऽभिमन्त्र्य प्रोक्षयेत्। फलं बालारिष्टनिवृत्तिः। नैवेद्यम्-११माषापूपाः ताम्बूलं नारीकेलफलं कदलीफलं च।

श्लोकः-३९

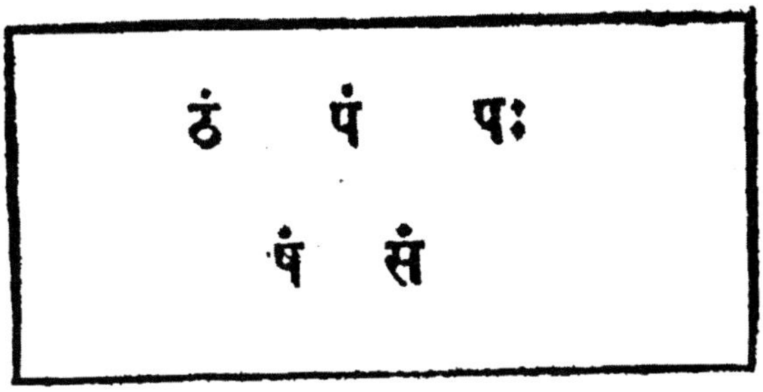

यन्त्रमिदं कनकपट्टतले विलिख्य द्वादशदिनान्यभ्यर्च्य प्रत्यहं श्लोकमिममष्टोत्तर-शतमावर्त्य धारयेत्। अनेन दुस्स्वप्नं शाम्यति। नैवेद्यम्–क्षीरं क्षीरपायसं मधु च।

श्लोकः-४०

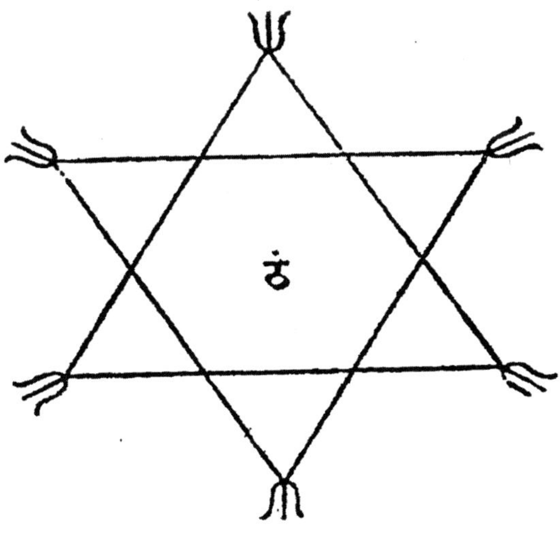

इदं यन्त्रं हेमपट्टे विलिख्य पञ्चचत्वारिंशदहान्यर्चयित्वा पद्यमिदमनुदिनं सहस्रमाव-र्त्योपधाने निक्षिप्य शयीत। फलम्–इष्टार्थस्य स्वप्ने दर्शनम्। नैवेद्यम्–मधु क्षीरपायसं ताम्बूलं च।

श्लोकः-४१

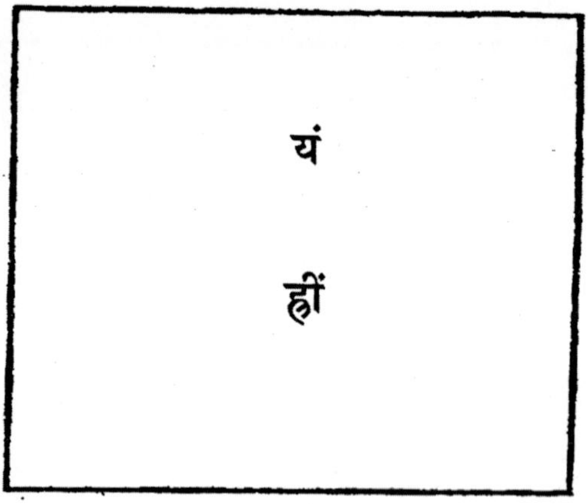

यन्त्रमिदं हेमपट्टतले विलिख्य त्रिंशदहानि पूजयित्वा पद्यमिदमहरहश्चतुस्सहस्र-मावर्त्य धारयेत्। फलम्–सकलोदररोगनिवृत्तिः नैवेद्यम्–मधु।

श्लोकः-४२

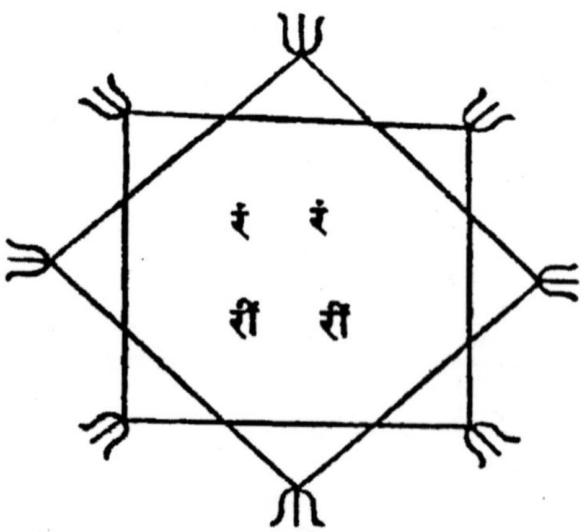

इदं यन्त्रं स्वर्णपट्टे विलिख्य पञ्चचत्वारिंशद्दिनानि समाराध्य श्लोकमिममनुदिनं सहस्रवारं जप्त्वा धारयेत्। अनेन महोदरव्याधिर्नश्यति। नैवेद्यम्–शर्करा।

श्लोकः-४३

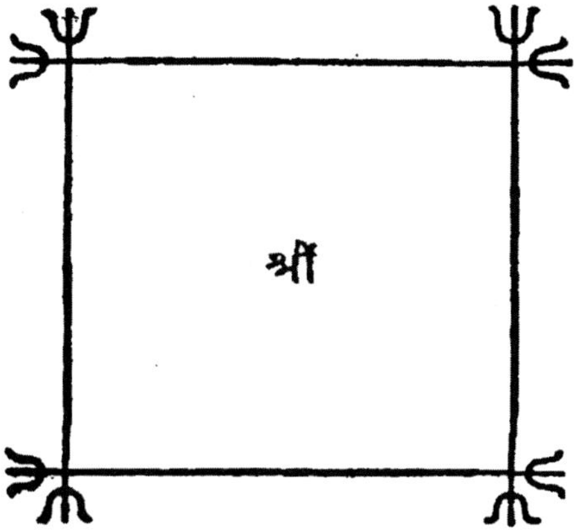

यन्त्रमिदं हाटकपट्टे विलिख्य चत्वारिंशदहान्यभ्यर्च्य पद्यमिदमनुदिनं त्रिसहस्रमावर्त्याङ्गुलीयकं कृत्वा धारयेत्। फलम्-सकलजनवश्यता। नैवेद्यम्-मधु।

श्लोकः-४४

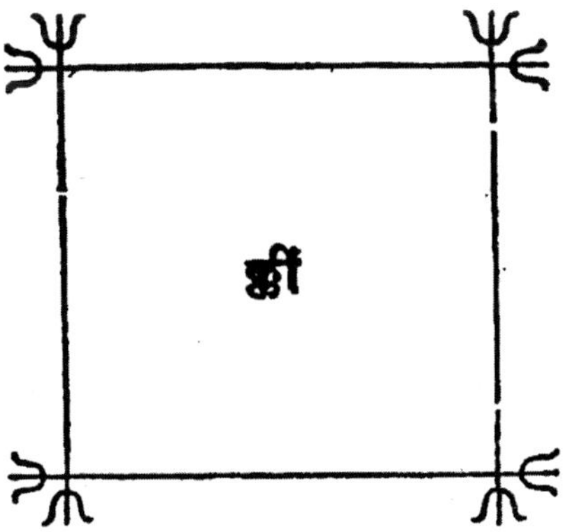

यन्त्रमिदं कनकपट्टतले विलिख्य द्वादशाहान्यर्चयित्वा श्लोकमिमं प्रतिवासरं सहस्रमावर्त्य धारयेत्। कुङ्कुमं हरिद्राचूर्णं वाऽभिमन्त्र्य तिलकं धारयेत्। अनेन वश्यता बाधानिवृत्तिश्च भवेत्। नैवेद्यम्-गुडपायसम्।

श्लोकः-४५

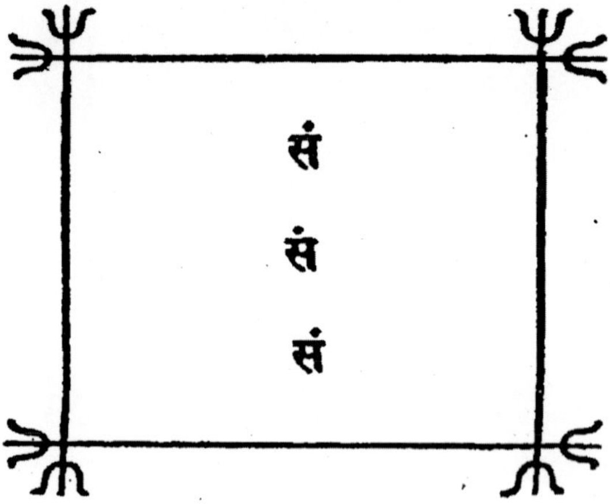

इदं यन्त्रं स्वर्णपट्टतले विलिख्य चत्वारिंशदहानि समाराध्य पद्यमिदमनुदिनं सहस्रवारं जप्त्वा धारयेत्। फलम्–वाक्सिद्धिः। नैवेद्यम्–त्रिमधुरं मधु च।

श्लोकः-४६

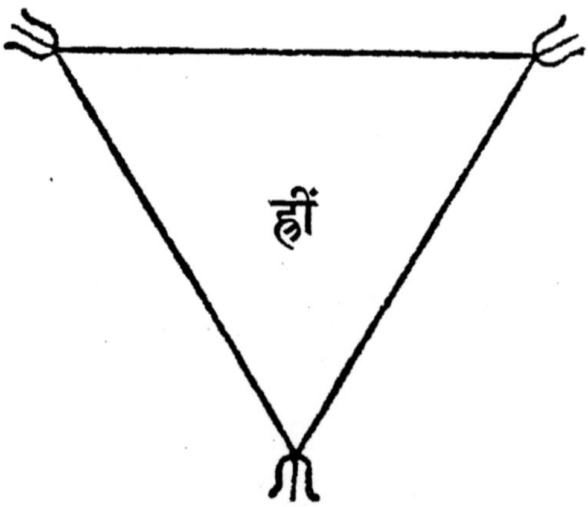

यन्त्रमिदं कनकपट्टतले विलिख्य पञ्चचत्वारिंशद्दिनानि संपूज्य प्रत्यहं श्लोकमिमं सहस्रमावर्त्य धारयेत्। अनेन भर्तृसमागमो गर्भधारणं च भवति। नैवेद्यम्–क्षीरपायसं, मधु च।

श्लोकः-४७

ह्रीं
ह्रीं
ह्रीं

(i) इदं सुवर्णपट्टे विलिख्य पञ्चविंशतिदिनानि संपूज्य पद्यमिदमनुदिनं सप्तसहस्रमावर्त्य धारयेत्। अनेन देवता वशमेष्यति।

(ii) भस्म वाऽभिमन्त्र्य धारयेत्। फलम्-सकलवश्यता। उभयत्र नैवेद्यम्-नारिकेलफलं कदलीफलं मधु च।

श्लोकः-४८

बु	शु	च
गु	र	कु
रा	श	के

यन्त्रमिदं कनकपट्टतले विलिख्य एकोनविंशतिदिनानि समाराध्य श्लोकमिमं सहस्रवारं जप्त्वा धारयेत्। अनेन नवग्रहदोषशान्तिर्भवति। नैवेद्यम्-चित्रान्नं कदलीफलं मधु च।

श्लोकः-४९

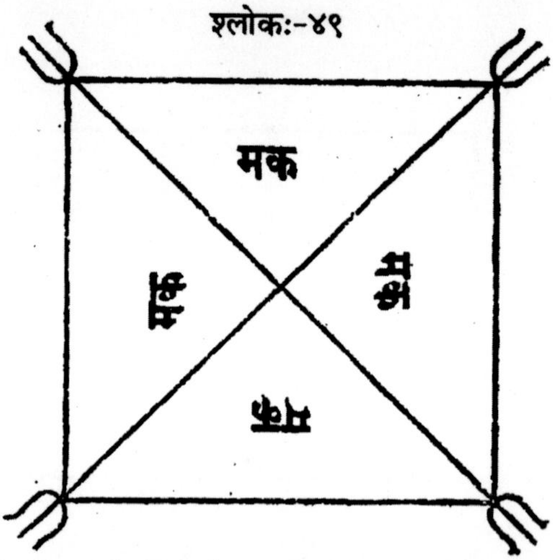

यन्त्रमिदं हरिद्राखण्डे लिखित्वा पञ्चविंशतिदिनान्यभ्यर्च्य श्लोकमिममहरहस्सहस्रमावर्त्य हरिद्राखण्डमग्नौ दग्ध्वा तत्तैलेन पिष्ट्वा पञ्चदशवर्षीयस्य मार्जालदृशो बालकस्य हस्तेन अक्ष्णोर्लेपयित्वा पश्यतो निधिदर्शनं भवति। नैवेद्यम्-मुद्गान्नं मधु च।

श्लोकः-५०

इदं यन्त्रं कनकपट्टतले विलिख्य चत्वार्यहान्यर्चयित्वा पद्यमनुदिनं सहस्रवारं जप्त्वा धारयेत्। जलं वाभिमन्त्र्य सेवेत। एवं कृते मसूरिका न समागमिष्यति। नैवेद्यम्-शर्करा खण्डशर्करा गुडं कदलीफलं मधु नारिकेलं च।

श्लोकः-५१

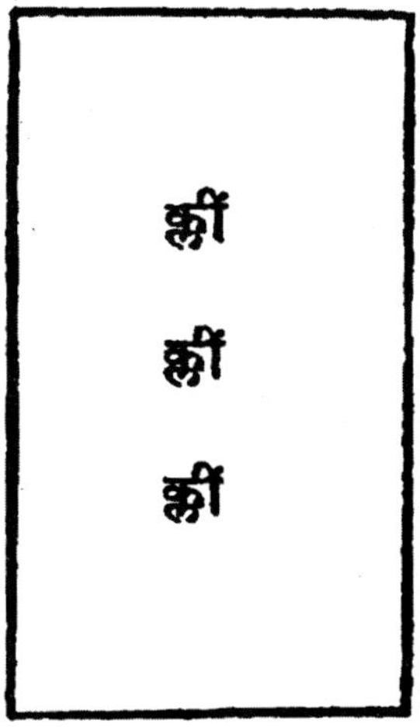

यन्त्रमिदं सुवर्णपट्टे विलिख्य, पञ्चचत्वारिंशदहानि संपूज्य प्रत्यहं श्लोकमिमं सहस्रवारं जप्त्वा धारयेत्। चन्दने वा विलिख्य पूर्ववत्पूजादिकं कृत्वा तिलकं धारयेत्। फलम्–सर्वजनवश्यता। नैवेद्यम्–माषापूपः मधु च।

श्लोकः-५२

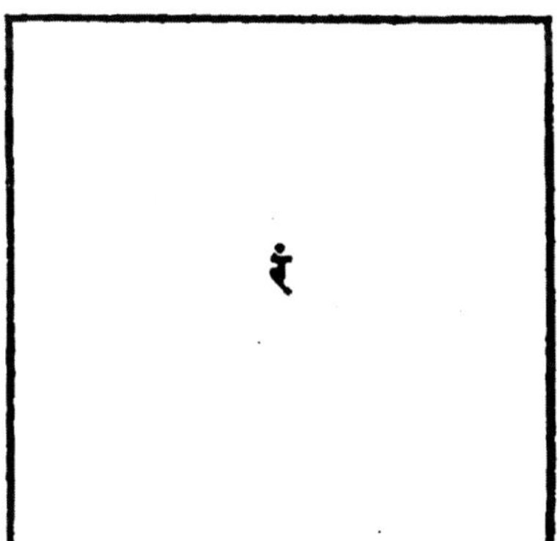

इदं यन्त्रं कलकपट्टतले विलिख्य पञ्चचत्वारिंशदहानि समाराध्य श्लोकमिममनुदिनं सहस्रमावर्त्य धारयेत्। फलम्–कर्णरोगशमनं नेत्ररोगनिवृत्तिश्च। नैवेद्यम्–तिलान्नं क्षीरपायसं च।

श्लोकः-५३

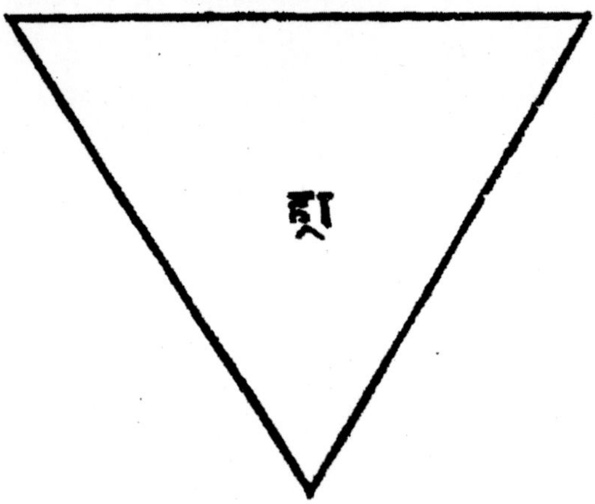

यन्त्रमिदं स्वर्णपट्टे विलिख्य भूमौ संस्थाप्य तत्र दीपं निधाय श्लोकमिमं त्रिसहस्रमावर्तयेत्। अनुकूलतायां दीपं उज्ज्वलेत् न चेत्प्रातिकूल्यम्। नैवेद्यम्–गुडपूपः माषापूपः क्षीरपायसं च।

श्लोकः-५४

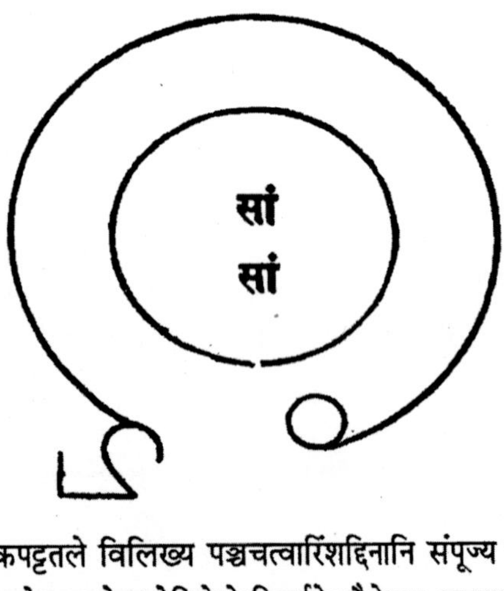

यन्त्रमिदं कनकपट्टतले विलिख्य पञ्चचत्वारिंशद्दिनानि संपूज्य पद्यमिदमनुदिनं सहस्रवारं जप्त्वा धारयेत्। अनेन योनिरोगो निवर्तते। नैवेद्यम्–गुडपायसम्।

श्लोकः-५५

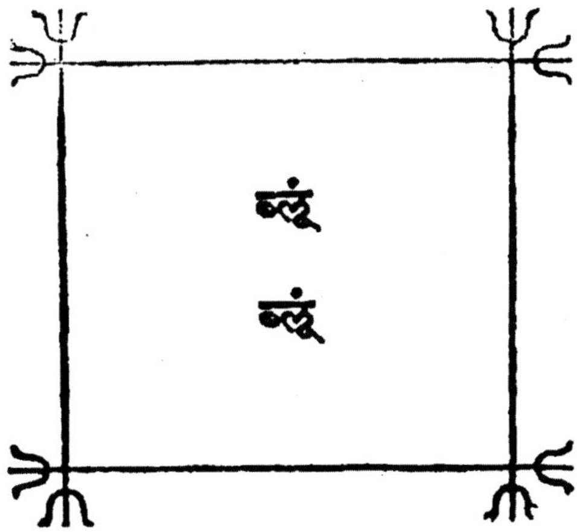

इदं यन्त्रं हाटकपट्टे विलिख्य पद्यमिदं सहस्रवारं जप्त्वा धारयेत्। कलिद्रुमफलं वाऽभिमन्त्र्य बध्नीयात्। अनेनाण्डव्याधिश्शाम्यति। नैवेद्यं कदलीफलं क्षीरपायसं मधु ताम्बूलं च। (अत्र केरलभाषापुस्तके "बंला संला" इति बीजाक्षरभेदो दृश्यते)।

श्लोकः-५६

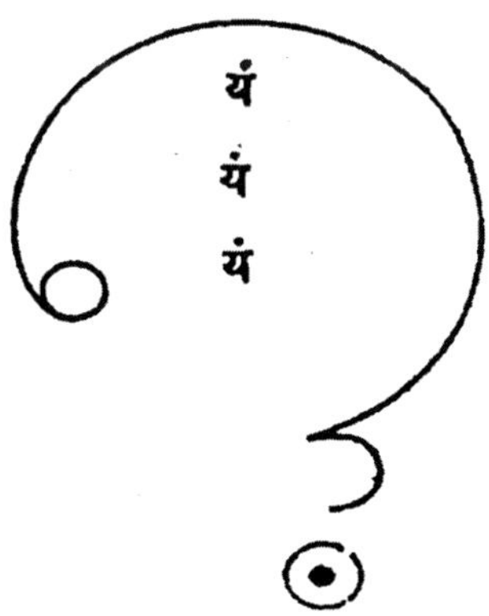

यन्त्रमिदं जातरूपपट्टतले मकरमत्स्यदन्ते वा लिखित्वा पञ्चचत्वारिंशदहान्यभ्यर्च्य श्लोकमिमं प्रत्यहं विंशतिसहस्रमावर्त्य स्वस्मिन्निवेशयेत्। अनेन द्वारपालको धावेत्। मुद्रितं कवाटं स्वयमुद्घाटयेत्। वृष्टिश्च भवेत्। नैवेद्यम्–मधु।

श्लोकः-५७

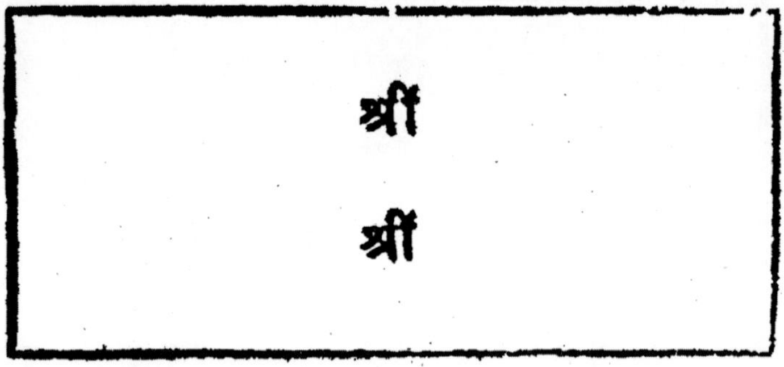

इदं यन्त्रं हेमपट्टे विलिख्य षडहान्यभ्यर्च्य पद्यमिदमनुदिनं सहस्रमावर्त्य धारयेत्। साधको बहुभाग्यवान् भवेत्। नैवेद्यम्–क्षीरपायसं मधु च।

श्लोकः-५८

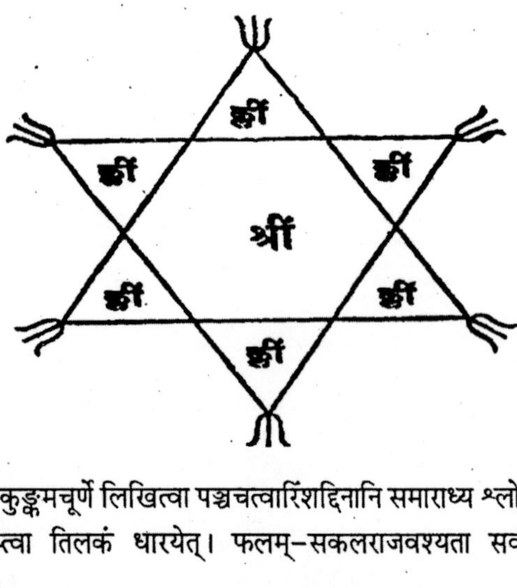

यन्त्रमिदं कुङ्कमचूर्णे लिखित्वा पञ्चचत्वारिंशद्दिनानि समाराध्य श्लोकमिममनुदिनं सहस्रवारं जप्त्वा तिलकं धारयेत्। फलम्–सकलराजवश्यता सर्वव्याधिहृतिश्च। नैवेद्यम्–मधु।

श्लोकः-५९

इदं यन्त्रं स्वर्णपट्टतले विलिख्य पञ्चचत्वारिंशद्दिनानि संपूज्य पद्यमिदमनुदिनं सहस्रमावर्त्य धारयेत्। फलम्-सकलजनवश्यता। नैवेद्यम्-गुडोदनं मधु च।

श्लोकः-६०

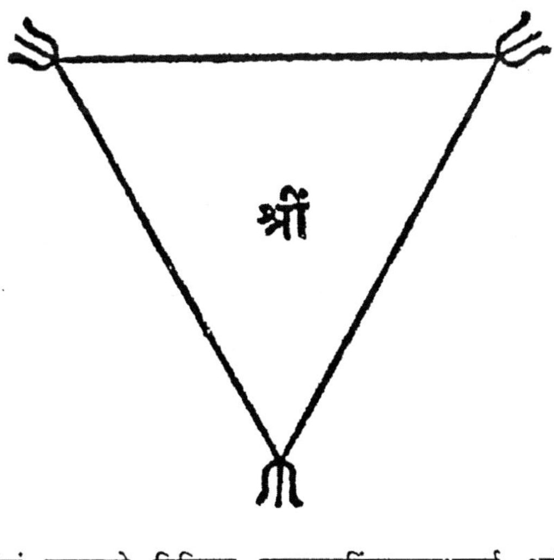

यन्त्रमिदं हाटकपट्टे विलिख्य पञ्चचत्वारिंशदहान्यभ्यर्च्य श्लोकमिममह-रहस्सहस्रमावर्त्य धारयेत्। अनेन साधकः सकलविद्यामाप्नुयात्। नैवेद्यं मधु क्षीरपायसं च।

श्लोकः-६१

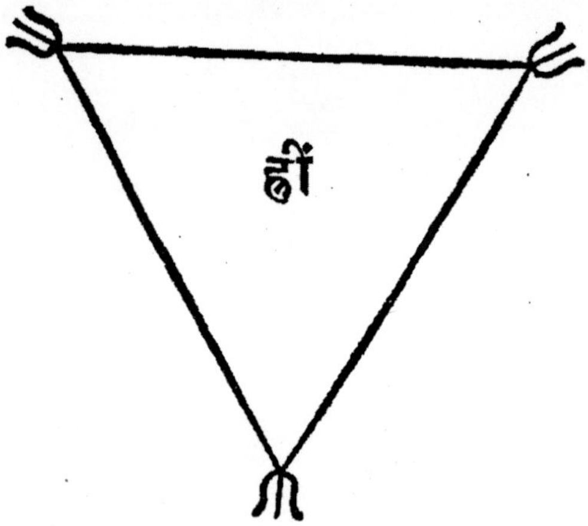

इदं यन्त्रं कनकपट्टे विलिख्याष्टौ दिनानि समाराध्य पद्यमिदमनुदिनं द्वादशसहस्र-मावर्त्य स्त्रीणामाभरणे निक्षिपेत्। अनेन सकलपुरुषवश्यता भवेत्। नैवेद्यम्–नारिकेलफलं कदलीफलं मधु च।

श्लोकः-६२

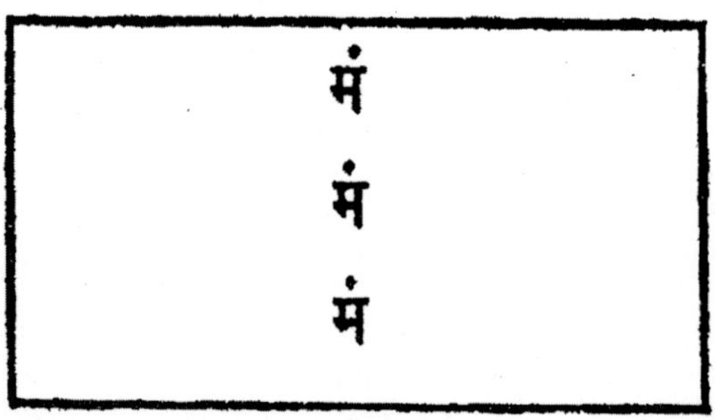

यन्त्रमिदं हेमपट्टतले लिखित्वाष्टौ दिनानि संपूज्य श्लोकमिमं प्रत्यहमष्टसहस्रवारं जप्त्वा रात्रौ निद्राविहीनस्य समीपे स्थापितं चेत् स निद्रां लभते। नैवेद्यम्–माषापूपः मधु च।

श्लोकः-६३

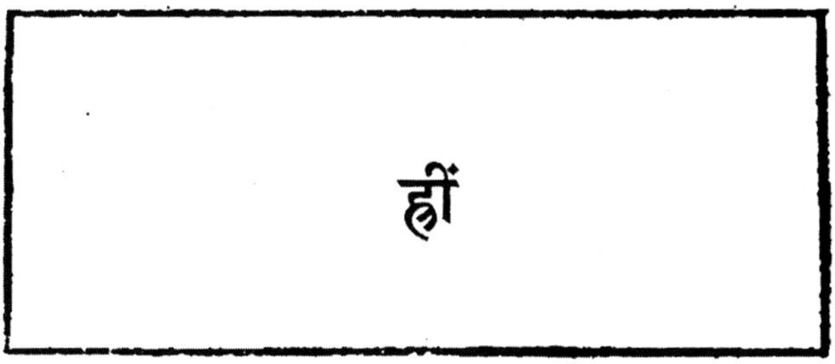

यन्त्रमिदं हाटकपट्टतले विलिख्य त्रिंशद्दिनान्याराध्य पद्यमिदमनुदिनं त्रिंशत्सहस्रवारं जप्त्वा धारयेत्। अनेन सर्वोऽपि यथोक्तमाचरेत्। नैवेद्यम्–नारिकेलफलम्। (केरलभाषा-पुस्तके यन्त्रमिदं न दृश्यते।)

श्लोकः-६४

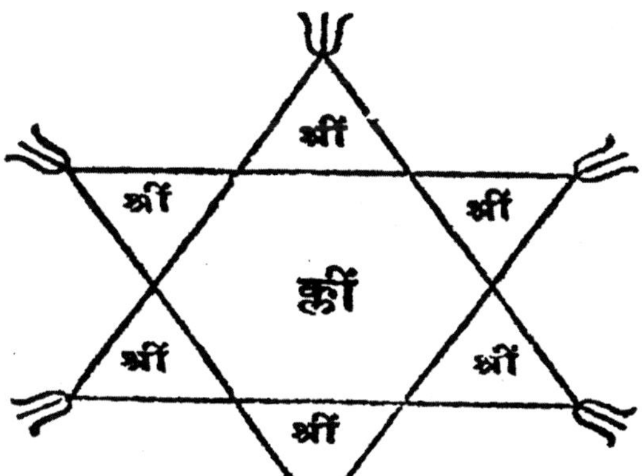

इदं यन्त्रं कुङ्कुमे विरच्याष्टावहानि पूजयित्वा प्रत्यहं श्लोकमिममयुतवारं जप्त्वा धारयेत्। फलम्–सकलजनवश्यता। नैवेद्यम्–गुडपायसं मधु च।

श्लोकः-६५

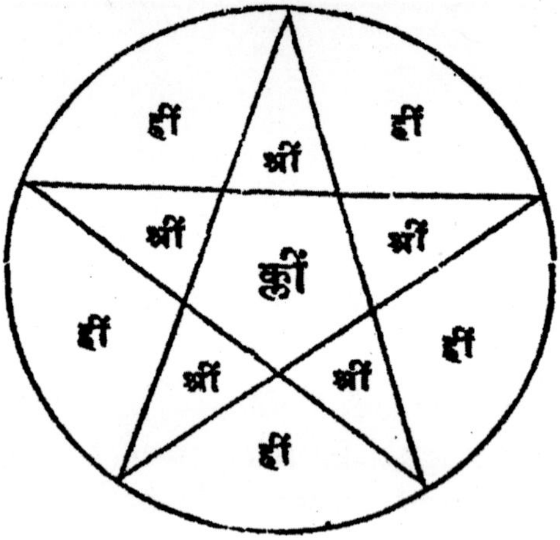

यन्त्रमिदं हेमपट्टतले विलिख्य गुग्गुलेन धूपयित्वा पञ्चचत्वारिंशद्दिनानि रक्तपुष्पैः श्रीचक्रवदभ्यर्च्य श्लोकमिमं प्रतिवासरं सहस्रमावर्त्य धारयेत्। अनेन सर्वोऽपि स्ववशगो भवेत्। नैवेद्यम्–मधु।

श्लोकः-६६

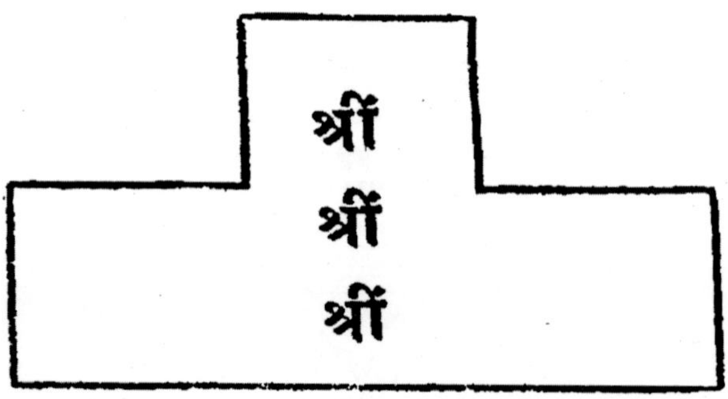

इदं यन्त्रं कनकपट्टतले लिखित्वा पञ्चचत्वारिंशद्दिनानि समाराध्य पद्यमिदमनुदिनं सहस्रवारं जप्त्वा धारयेत्। अनेन साधकः वीणादिसङ्गीतविद्याकुशलो भवेत्। नैवेद्यम्–गुडपायसं मधु च।

श्लोकः-६७

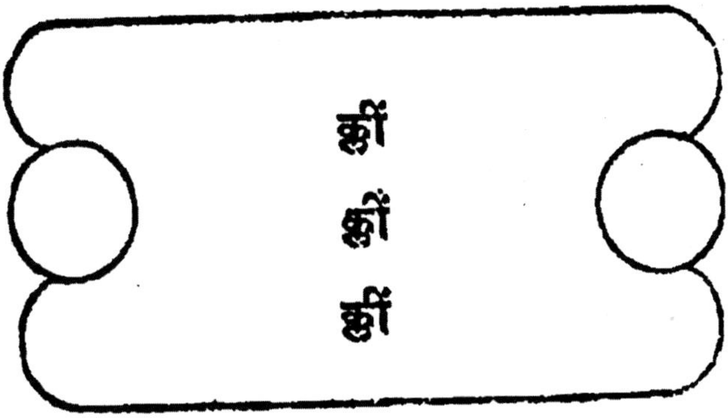

यन्त्रमिदं स्वर्णपट्टतले विलिख्य पत्न्या साकं पञ्चचत्वारिंशदहानि समाराध्य पद्यमिदमनुदिनं सहस्रमावर्त्य धारयेत्। फलम्-सकलस्त्रीवश्यता। नैवेद्यम्-मधु क्षीरपायसं ताम्बूलं च।

श्लोकः-६८

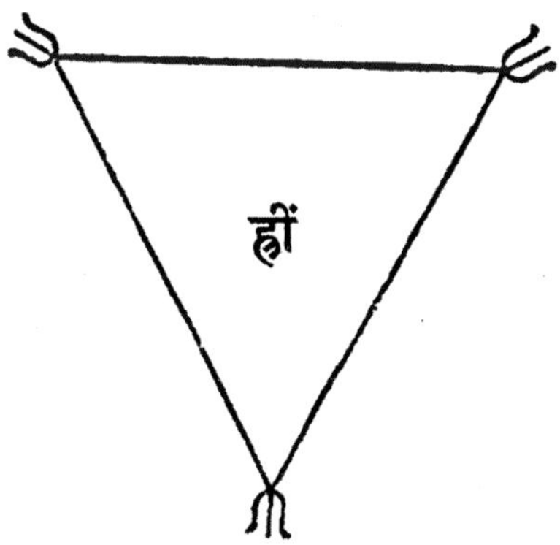

इदं यन्त्रं कुंकुमे विलिख्य पञ्चचत्वारिंशद्दिनानि श्रीचक्रवदभ्यर्च्य प्रत्यहं श्लोकमिमं सहस्रवारं जप्त्वा धारयेत्। फलं सकलराजवश्यता। नैवेद्यम्-मधु तांबूलं च। (केरल-भाषापुस्तके यन्त्रमिदं नास्ति)।

श्लोकः-६९

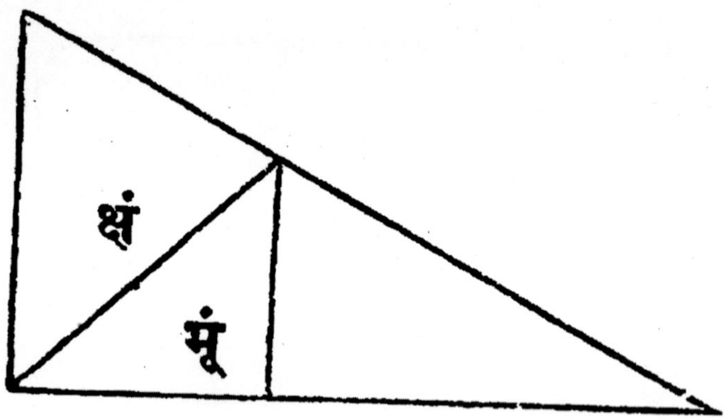

यन्त्रमिदं स्वर्णपट्टतले लिखित्वा पञ्चचत्वारिंशद्दिनानि समाराध्य प्रत्यहं श्लोकमिमं सहस्रमावर्त्य साधयेत्। चम्पकपुष्पमभिमन्त्र्याभिलषितस्त्रियै दद्यात्। सा वशमेष्यति। नैवेद्यम्–मधु। (केरलभाषापुस्तके यन्त्रमिदं न दृश्यते।)

श्लोकः-७०

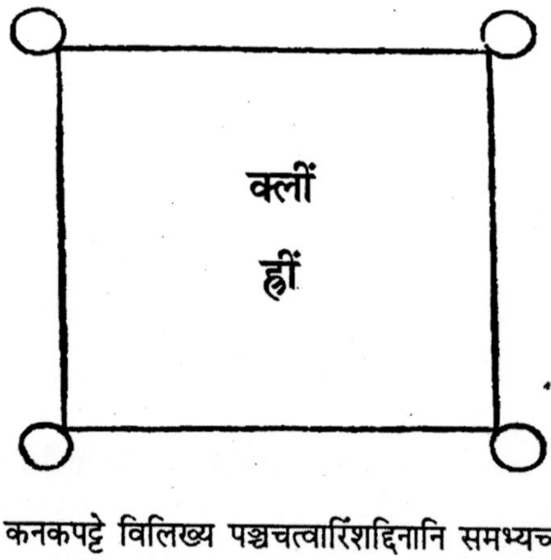

इदं यन्त्रं कनकपट्टे विलिख्य पञ्चचत्वारिंशद्दिनानि समभ्यर्च्य पद्यमिदमनुदिनं सहस्रवारं जप्त्वा धारयेत्। फलं सकलपुरुषवश्यता। नैवेद्यं नारिकेलफलं मधु च।

श्लोकः-७१

यन्त्रमिदं हाटकपट्टतले विलिख्य पञ्चचत्वारिंशद्दिनानि पूजयित्वा वटवृक्षे उपविश्य पद्यमिदमनुदिनं द्वादशसहस्रमावर्त्य साधयेत्। अनेन यक्षिणी वशमेष्यति। नैवेद्यं मधु।

श्लोकः-७२

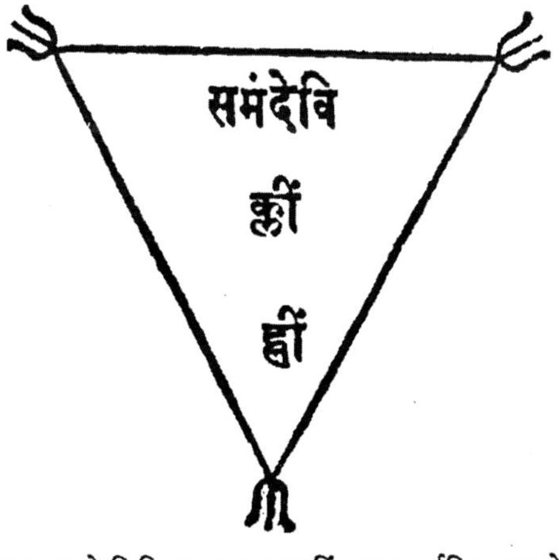

इदं यन्त्रं कनकपट्टतले विलिख्य पञ्चचत्वारिंशदहान्यर्चयित्वा श्लोकमिमं प्रत्यहं सहस्रमावर्त्यं धारयेत्। एवं कृते साधकः रात्रौ यत्र कुत्र वा गन्तुं शक्नुयात्। भयलेशोऽपि नास्ति। नैवेद्यम्–मधु।

श्लोकः-७३

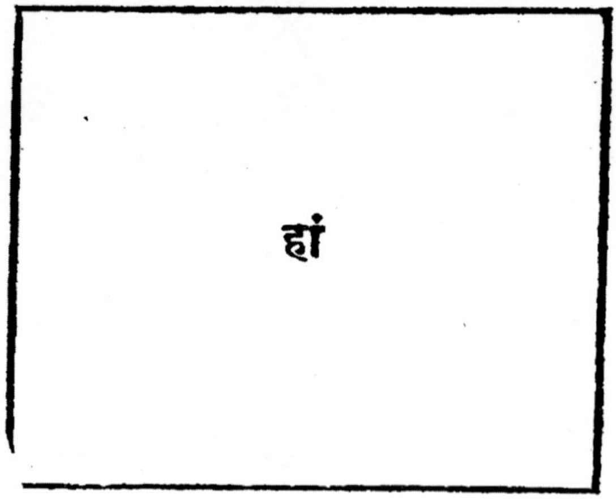

इदं यन्त्रं कनकपट्टे विलिख्य सप्तदिनान्यभ्यर्च्य पद्यमिदमनुदिनं सहस्रवारं जप्त्वा धारयेत्। फलं–स्त्रीणां स्तन्याभावे स्तन्यप्राप्तिः, धेनूनां स्थगितस्य पयसो बहिर्निस्सरणं च। नैवेद्यम्–मधु क्षीरं च।

श्लोकः-७४

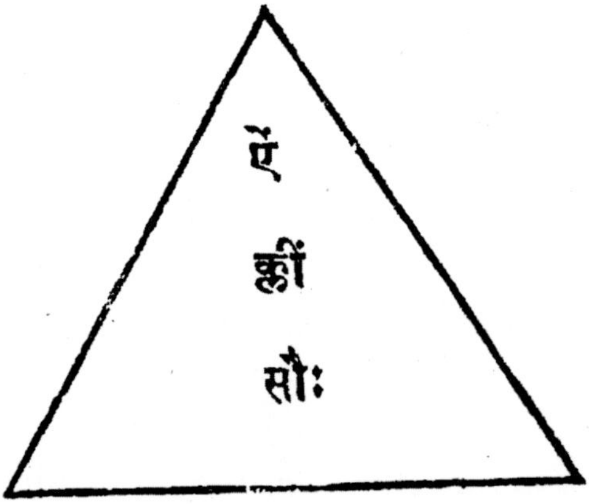

यन्त्रमिदं हेमपट्टतले विलिख्य देवसन्निधौ पञ्चचत्वारिंशदहानि समाराध्य श्लोकमिमं प्रतिवासरमष्टोत्तरशतमावर्त्य धारयेत्। अनेन साधकः कीर्तिमाप्नुयात्। नैवेद्यम्–क्षीरपायसं मधु च।

श्लोकः-७५

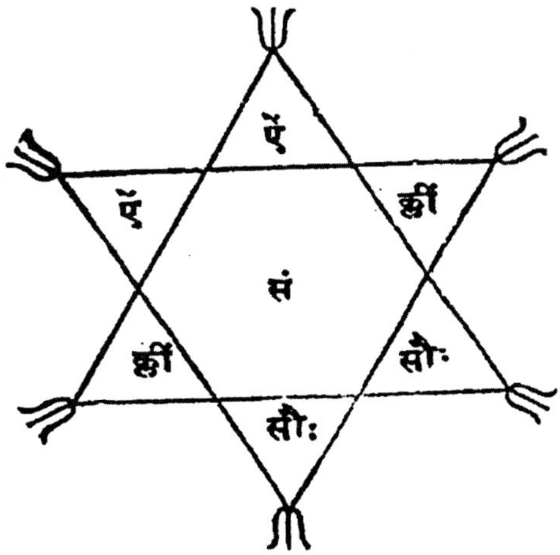

इदं यन्त्रं हाटकपट्टतले विलिख्य त्रीणि दिनान्याराध्य श्लोकमिमं प्रत्यहं सहस्रवारं जप्त्वा धारयेत्। अनेन साधकः कविर्भवेत्। नैवेद्यम्–कदलीफलं मधु च।

श्लोकः-७६

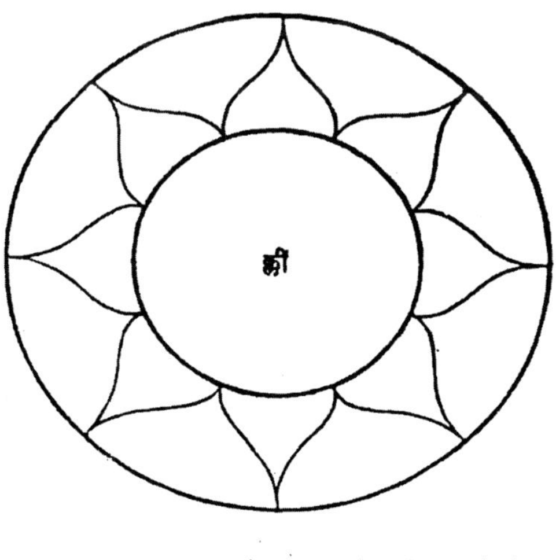

यन्त्रमिदं स्वर्णपट्टतले लिखित्वाऽष्टौ दिनान्यर्च्य पद्यमिदमनुदिनं द्वादशसहस्रमावर्त्य धारयेत्। फलं सकलजनवश्यता। नैवेद्यं नारिकेलफलं कदलीफलं दध्यन्नं मधु च।

श्लोकः-७७

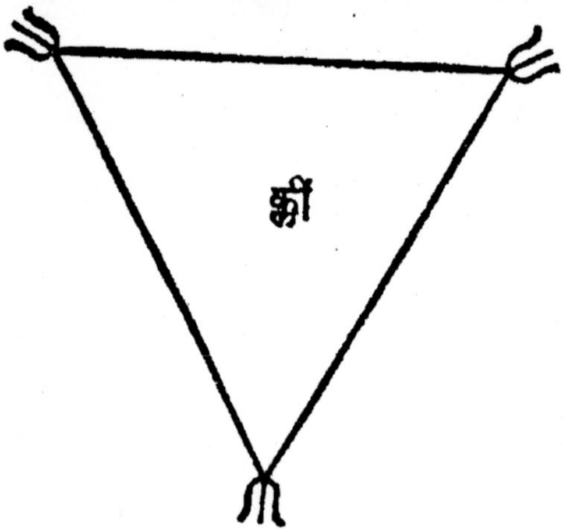

कपिलागोघृतमर्दितरक्तोत्पलेङ्गाले यन्त्रमिदं श्लोकं च विलिख्य दश दिनानि संपूज्य श्लोकमिममनुदिनं द्विसहस्रमावर्त्य तिलकं धारयेत्। फलम्-राजवश्यता। नैवेद्यम्-कदलीफलं मधु च।

श्लोकः-७८

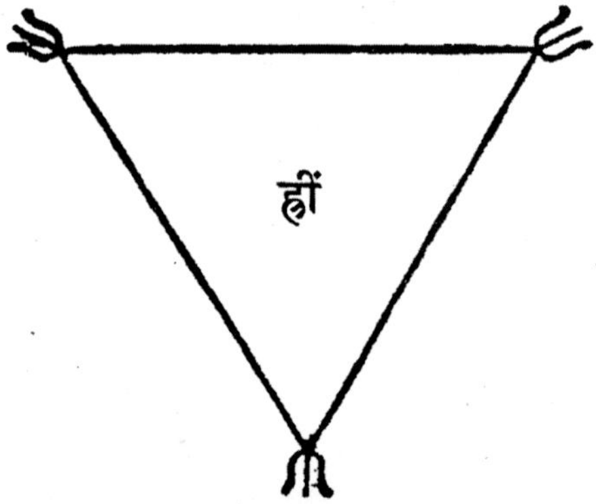

रक्तचन्दनं पत्रीराख्यपुष्पद्रवेण पिष्ट्वा गन्धचेलिकामिश्रिते तस्मिन् यन्त्रमिदं विरच्य चत्वारिंशद्दिनानि संपूज्य पद्यमिदमनुदिनमष्टोत्तरशतमावर्त्य ललाटे धारयेत्, अनेन सकलराजवश्यता भवेत्। नैवेद्यम्-मधु माषापूपश्च।

श्लोकः-७९

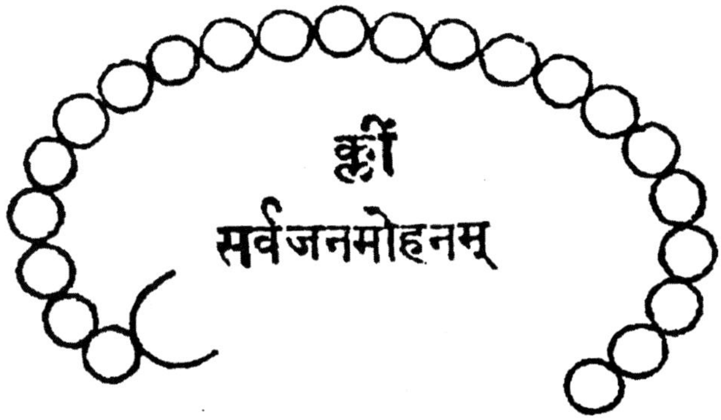

यन्त्रमिदं हेमपट्टे विलिख्य पञ्चचत्वारिंशद्दिनान्यभ्यर्च्य पद्यमिदं प्रत्यहं सहस्रवारं जप्त्वा धारयेत्। साधकः इन्द्रजालविद्यानिपुणो भवेत्। नैवेद्यम्-मधु क्षीर पायसं च।

श्लोकः-८०

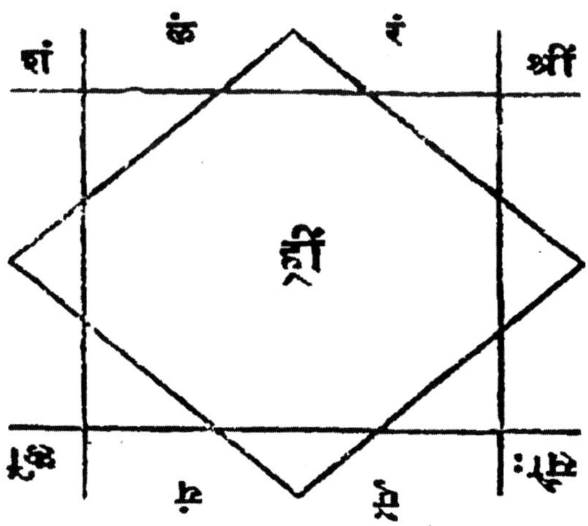

इदं यन्त्रं कनकपट्टतले लिखित्वा प्रथमपुष्पिण्या योनौ संस्थाप्य पञ्चदिनान्यर्चयित्वा पद्यमिदमनुदिनं सहस्रमावर्त्य हस्ते निबध्य तिलकं धारयेत्। अनेन साधकः इन्द्रजालं दर्शयितुं समर्थो भवेत्। नैवेद्यम्-मधु।

श्लोकः-८१

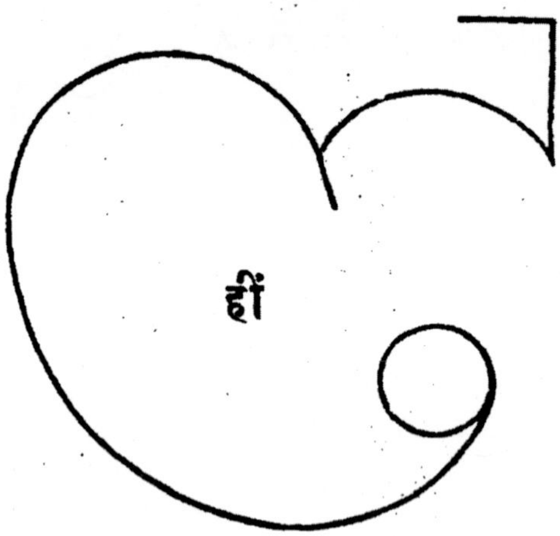

यन्त्रमिदं हाटकपट्टतले लिखित्वाऽऽग्नेयाभिमुखः षोडश दिनानि समाराध्य प्रत्यहं श्लोकमिमं सहस्रमावर्त्य साधयेत्। अनेन अग्निस्तम्भनं कर्तुं शक्यते। नैवेद्यम्–गुडपायसं मधु माषापूपश्च।

श्लोकः-८२

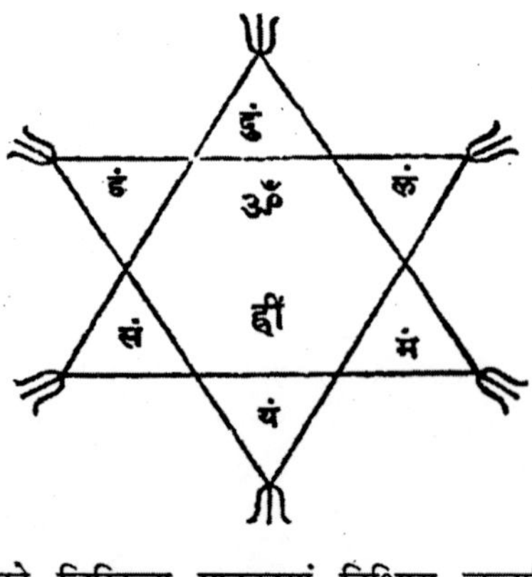

इदं यन्त्रं भूर्जपत्रे लिखित्वा पादुकायां निक्षिप्य चत्वारिंशदहानि संपूज्य पद्यमिदमनुदिनं सहस्रवारं जप्त्वा तत्पादुकां धारयेत्। अनेन साधको जले चरितुं समर्थो भवेत्। नैवेद्यम्–नारिकेलफलं कदलीफलं मधु च।

श्लोकः-८३

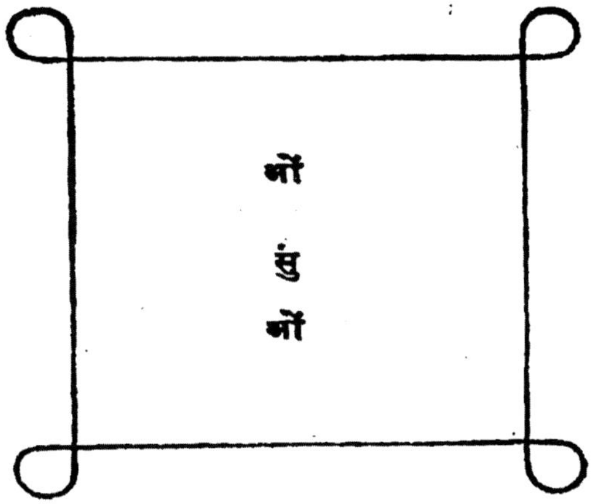

यन्त्रमिदं कनकपट्टे विलिख्य द्वादशदिनानि जपाकुसुमैरभ्यर्च्य पद्यमिदमहरहस्सहस्रमावर्त्य धारयेत्। फलम्–गजतुरगसैन्यस्तम्भनम्। नैवेद्यम्–गुडपायसं मधु च।

श्लोकः-८४

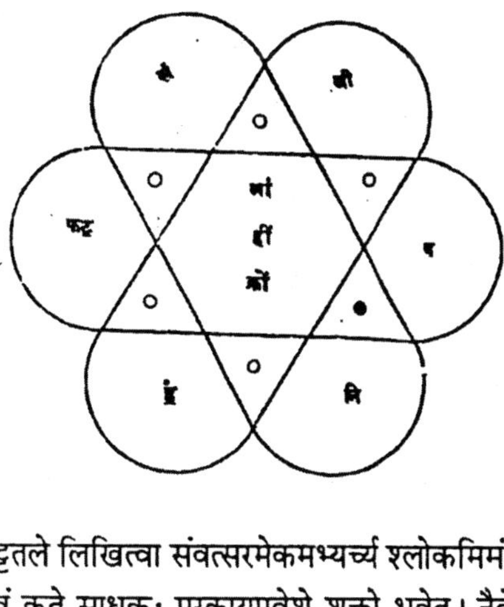

इदं यन्त्रं हेमपट्टतले लिखित्वा संवत्सरमेकमभ्यर्च्य श्लोकमिमं प्रत्यहं सहस्रवारं जप्त्वा धारयेत्। एवं कृते साधकः परकायप्रवेशे शक्तो भवेत्। नैवेद्यम्–क्षीरपायसं चित्रान्नं मधु च।

श्लोकः-८५

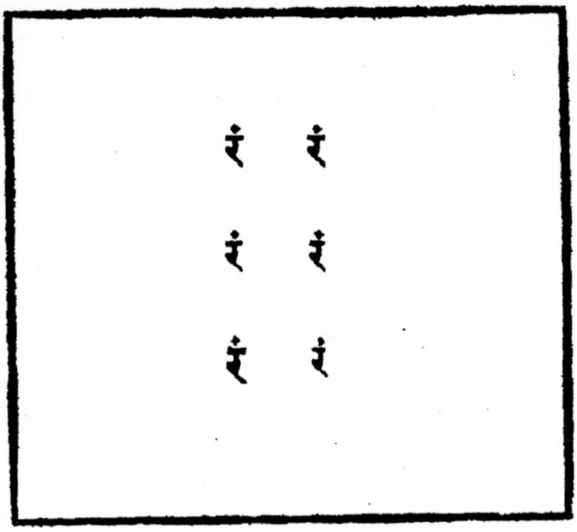

यन्त्रमिदं स्वर्णपट्टतले लिखित्वा द्वादशाहानि रक्तपुष्पैः संपूज्य पद्यमिदमनुदिनं सस्रमावर्त्य धारयेत्। अनेन भूतबाधानिवृत्तिः। नैवेद्यम्–गुडोदकं कदलीफलं च।

श्लोकः-८६

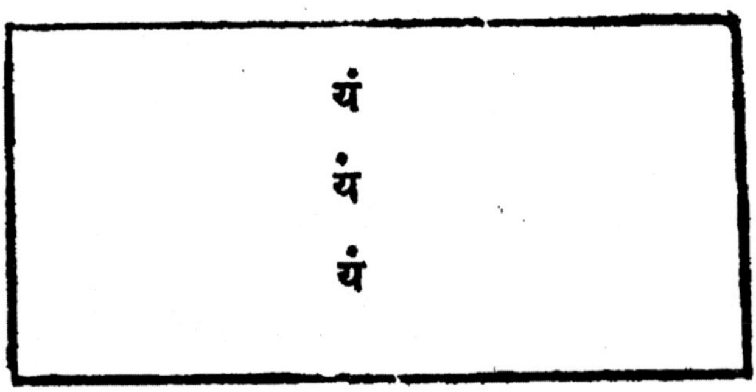

इदं यन्त्रं हाटकपट्टे विलिख्यः एकविंशतिदिनानि संपूज्य प्रत्यहं श्लोकमिमं सहस्रमावर्त्य धारयेत्। कलशोदकमभिमन्त्र्याभिषिञ्चेत्। अनेन समस्तपिशाचबाधाः निवृत्तिः। नैवेद्यं क्षीरपायसं नारिकेलफलं कदलीफलं मधु च।

श्लोकः-८७

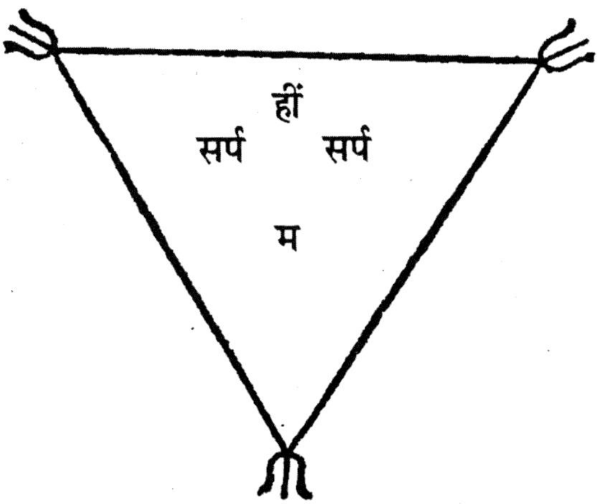

यन्त्रमिदं श्मशानभस्मनि विरच्य दशदिनान्याराध्य पद्यमिदमहरहः सहस्रमावर्त्य साधयेत्। साधक; सर्पानयने समर्थो भवेत्। नैवेद्यम्–क्षीरपायसं मधु कदलीफलं नारिकेलफलं च।

श्लोकः-८८

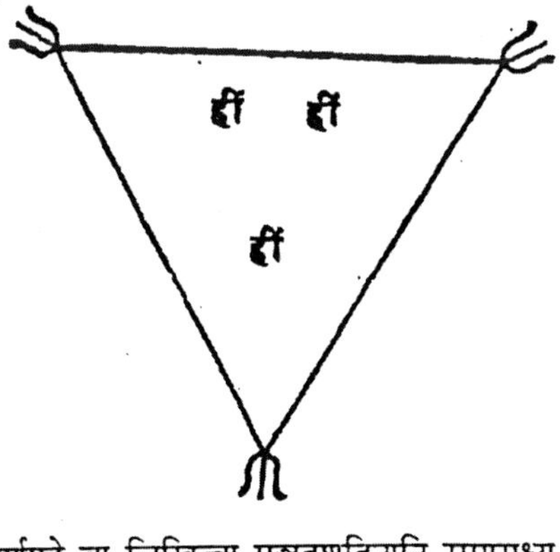

इदं यन्त्रं स्वर्णपट्टे वा लिखित्वा पञ्चदशदिनानि समाराध्य श्लोकमिमं प्रत्यहं सहस्रवारं जप्त्वा धारयेत्। साधकः मृगानयने प्रभवति। नैवेद्यम्–गुडपायसं नारिकेलफलं कदलीफलं च।

श्लोकः-८९

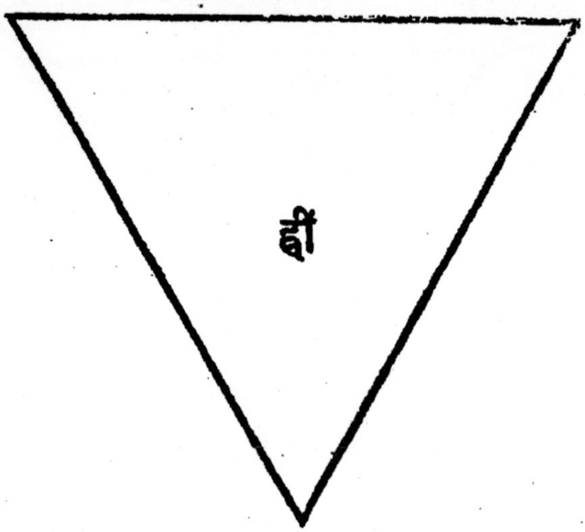

यन्त्रमिदं हाटकपट्टतले लिखित्वा त्रिंशदहान्यर्चयित्वा पद्यमिदमनुदिनं सहस्रमावर्त्य धारयेत्। फलम्–सर्वरोगशमनम्। नैवेद्यम्–गुडपायसं मधु च।

श्लोकः-९०

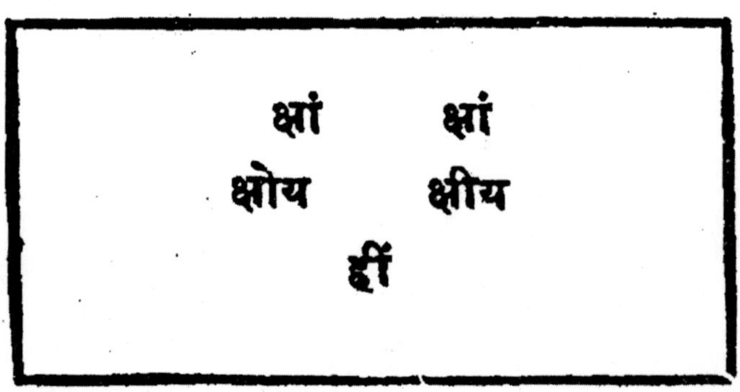

इदं यन्त्रं हाटकपट्टे लिखित्वा पञ्चदशाहान्यभ्यर्च्च श्लोकमिममहरहस्सहस्रमावर्त्य धारयेत्। फलम्–क्षुद्रबाधानिवृत्तिः नैवेद्यम्–क्षीरपायसं मधु च।

श्लोकः-११

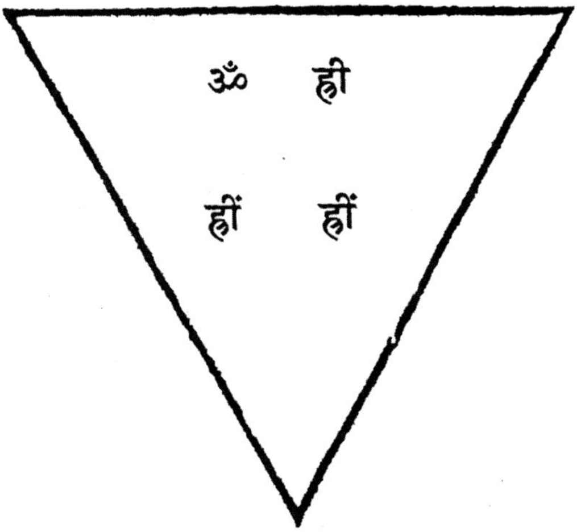

यन्त्रमिदं पद्यं च कनकपट्टतले लिखित्वा पञ्चविंशत्यहानि समाराध्य पद्यमिदमनुदिनं सहस्रवारं जप्त्वा धारयेत्। साधकस्य भूलाभो धनलाभश्च भवति। नैवेद्यम्–क्षीरपायसम्।

श्लोकः-१२

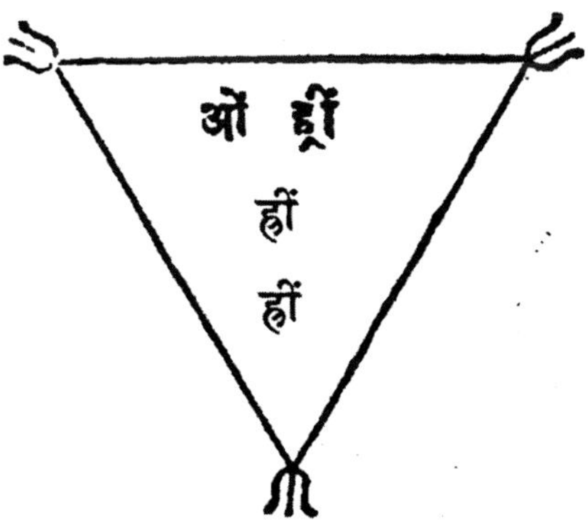

इदं यन्त्रं सुवर्णपट्टे विलिख्य पञ्चविंशतिदिनान्यभ्यर्च्य प्रत्यहं श्लोकमिमं सहस्रमावर्त्य धारयेत्। अनेन साधको राज्यं लभते। नैवेद्यम्–चित्रान्नं क्षीरं क्षीरपायसं ताम्बूलं च।

श्लोकः-१३

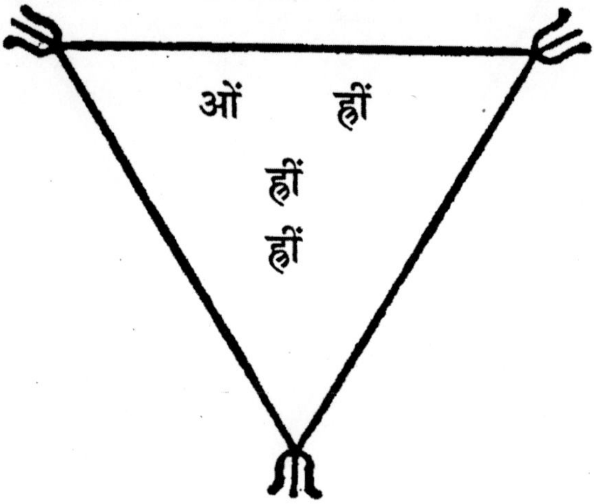

यन्त्रमिदं हेमपट्टतले विलिख्य पञ्चविंशतिदिनानि पूजयित्वा पद्यमिदमनुदिनं सहस्रमावर्त्य धारयेत्। अनेन सकलाभीष्टसिद्धिर्भवति। नैवेद्यम्–मधु।

श्लोकः-१४

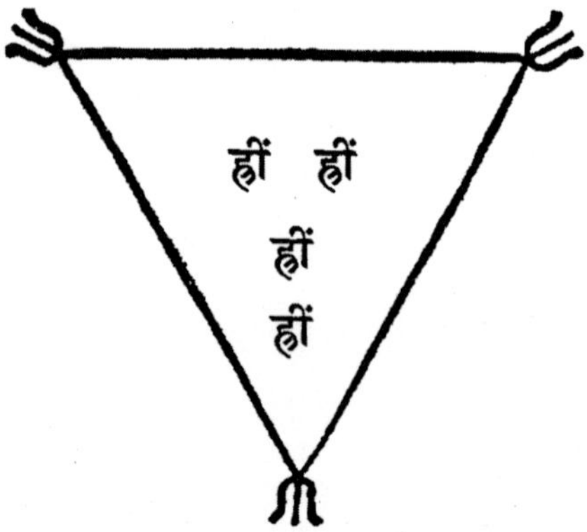

इदं यन्त्रं हाटकपट्टे लिखित्वा पञ्चविंशत्याहान्यभ्यर्च्य श्लोकमिमं प्रतिवासरं सहस्रमावर्तयेत्। फलम्–इष्टार्थसिद्धिः। नैवेद्यम्–मुद्गान्नं नारिकेलफलं कदलीफलं च।

श्लोकः-९५

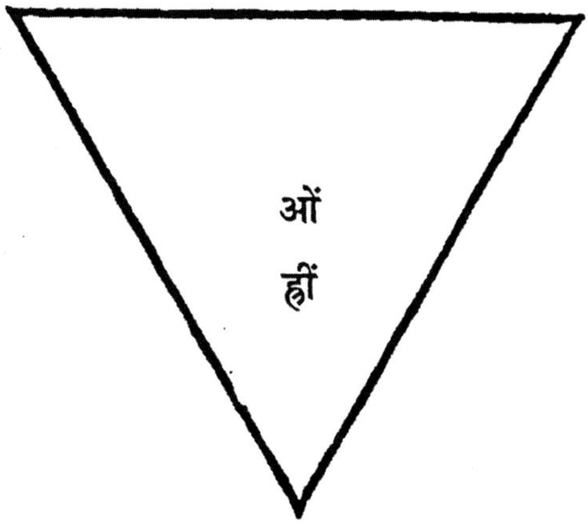

यन्त्रमिदं कनकपट्टतले विलिख्य तिलतैले निक्षिप्य त्र्यहमाराध्य पद्यमिदमनुदिन-मष्टोत्तरशतमावर्त्य तत्तैलं व्रणे विलिम्पेत्। फलम्–सद्योव्रणविरोपणम्। नैवेद्यम्–तिलान्नं गुडं च।

श्लोकः-९६

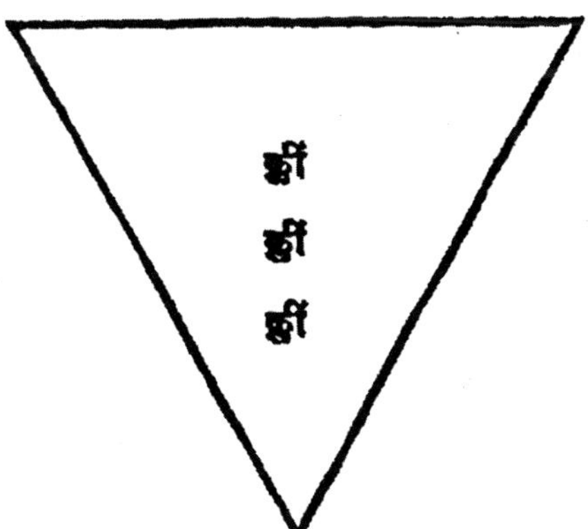

इदं यन्त्रं श्वेतार्कक्षीरेण धारणयोग्ये कस्मिंश्चिद्वस्तुनि लिखित्वाऽष्टौ दिनानि संपूज्य श्लोकमिमं प्रत्यहं सहस्रवारं जप्त्वा धारयेत्। साधको विद्यावान् भवेत्। नैवेद्यम्–मधु क्षीरपायसं च।

श्लोकः-१७

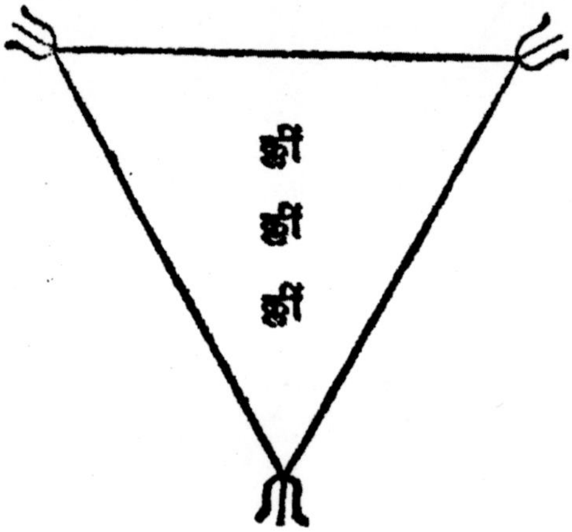

यन्त्रमिदं स्वर्णपट्टे ताम्रपट्टे वा लिखित्वाऽष्ट दिनानि समाराध्य श्लोकमिममहरहःसहस्रमावर्त्य धारयेत्। साधको दृढकायो भवेत्। नैवेद्यम्–शाल्यन्नं मधु च।

श्लोकः-१८

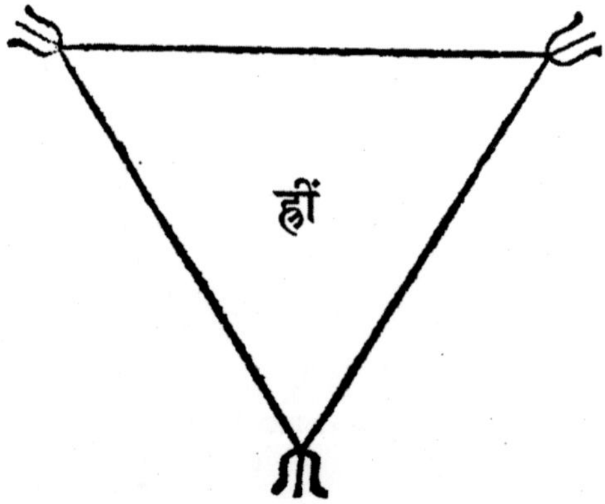

इदं यन्त्रं कनकपट्टतले विलिख्य षोडशदिनान्यर्चयित्वा पद्यमिदमनुदिनं सहस्रवारं जप्त्वा धारयेत्। अनेन स्त्रीणां गर्भधारणं पुरुषणां बहुवृष्यता च भवेत्। नैवेद्यं मधु।

श्लोकः-९९

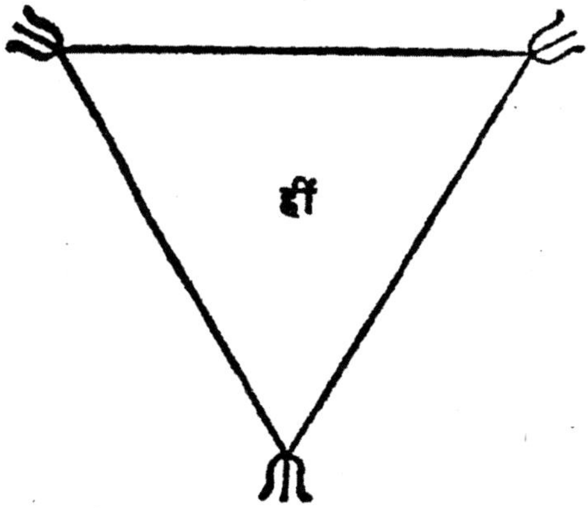

यन्त्रमिदं हेमपट्टे लिखित्वा षोडश दिनान्यभ्यर्च्य प्रत्यहं श्लोकमिमं सहस्रमावर्त्य धारयेत्। अनेन साधकः शूरो भवेत्। नैवेद्यम्–त्रिमधुरं माषा मधु च।

श्लोकः-१००

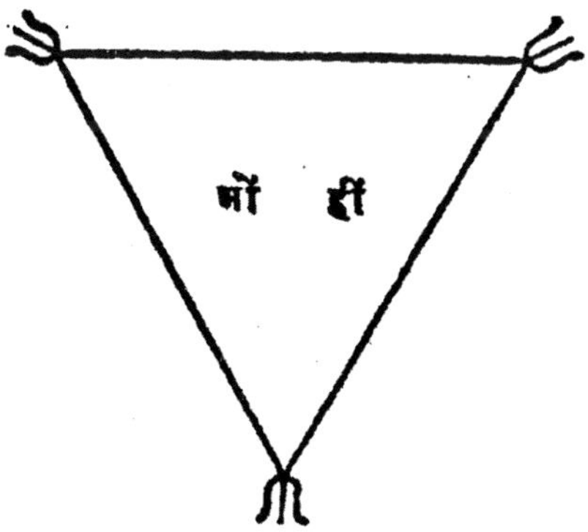

इदं यन्त्रं स्वर्णपट्टतले विलिख्य षोडश दिनान्याराध्य श्लोकमिमं प्रतिवासरं सहस्रमावर्त्य धारयेत्। अनेन सकलकार्यसिद्धिर्भवेत्। नैवेद्यम्–नारिकेलफलं कदलीफलं च।

शं भूयात्

।। श्रीमहात्रिपुरसुन्दरीचरणारबिन्दापर्णमस्तु ।।

Practical Application *(Prayoga)* of *Saundaryalaharī* Verses

The *Saundaryalaharī* contains 103 verses. Here, in this list the practical Application of one-hundred verses is given. The *prayoga* or *Practical Application* given in this section has been drawn on a very careful study of the different Tāntric texts. The worship as prescribed is to be done each day as also recital of the same upto the prescribed number of times. In the preceding pages the figure of *Yantra* for each verse (*i.e.* one hundred *yantras*) has been mentioned in a systematic order for the benefit of Śrīvidyā *sādhakas* and true lovers of Tantra Vidyā.

Bibliography

Original (Sanskrit) Texts :

Ānandalaharī of Śaṅkarācārya, ed. with the commentaries of Raghavabhaṭṭa, Bhāskararāya and Lakṣmīdhara, Mumbai.

Īśvara Pratyabhijñā Vimarśinī, edite by Mukundaram Shastri, Vols. I-II, Srinagar, 1918 *et seq.*

Upadeśasāhasrī, ed. with Comm. & Eng. tr. by Dr. N.C. Panda, Bhartiya Kala Prakashan, Delhi, 2007.

Tantrāloka of Abhinavagupta, ed. with Comm. of Jayaratha and Śivopādhyāya by Mukundarama Sastri, Vol. I-XII, Srinagar, 1918 *et. seq.*

Pratyabhijñā Hṛdaya of Kṣemarāja, ed. by J.C. Chatterji, Srinagar, 1911.

Śiva Sūtra with Vimarśinī Comm. of Kṣemarāja, ed. by J.C. Chatterji, Srinagar, 1911.

Saundaryalaharī with several commentaries, ed. by A. Kuppusvami, Tiruchirapalli, 1976.

________ with Tipura Sanskrit Comm. by Acharya Shricharanatirth Maharaj, published by Sri Bhuvaneswari Peetha, Gondala, Saurashtra, 1961.

_________ed. by N.S. Venkaranathacharya, Oriental Research Institute, Uni. of Mysore, Mysore, 1969.

______by S. S. Sastri & T.R.S. Ayyangar, the Theosophical Publishing House, Madras, 1948.

_______by V.K. Subramanian, Motilal Banarsidass, Delhi, 1980.

_______by Swami Tapasyananda, Sri Ramakrishna Math, Chennai, 1987.

_______ed. with Hindi Translation by Sri 108 Swami Vishnu Tirtha, Tihiri, Gadwal, 3rd reprint, 1970.

General Books :

Bagche, P.C.; *Studies in the Tantras,* Vol. I-II, Calcutta, 1939.

Kaviraj, Gopinath; *Bhartiya Saṃskṛti Aur Sādhanā,* Vol. I-II (in Hindi), Patna, Bihar, 1957.

Pandeya, K.C. ; *Abhinavagupta : An Historical and Philosophical Study,* Chowkhamba Prakashan, Varanasi, 1929.

Sen Sharma, D.B. ; *Aspects of Tantra Yoga,* India Books, Varanasi, 2007.

Woodroffe, J.; *Principles of Tantra,* Vol. I-II, Channai.

Woodroffe, J.; *Śakti and Śākta,* Channai.

Index to Verses

Pāda Index

Glossary

Āditya : Lit. means: Sun or *sūrya*. In the *śāstras* it is mentioned that Ādityas are twelve in number, viz. 1. Dhātṛ, 2. Mitra, 3. Aryaman, 4. Rudra, 5. Varuṇa, 6. Sūrya, 7. Bhaga, 8. Vivasvat, 9. Pūṣan, 10. Savitṛ, 11. Tvaṣṭṛ and 12. Viṣṇu.

Ānanda: Lit. means: happiness, joy, delight, pleasure, etc. *Ānanda* or Bliss is the nature of *Śakti* and it is also the essential nature of Paramaśiva along with *cit*. It is the state of *mukti* or *mokṣa* or *nirvāṇa* in which the self becomes free from all fetters. In Indian Philosophical contexts, *ānanda* or Bliss is a characteristic of the Brahman, others being *sat* and *cit* are too known its characteristics.

Aṇu or *paramāṇu :* Both the terms are synonymous and denote an atom, i.e. an indivisible particle of matter.

Bhairava: Lit. means: terrible, frightful, horrible, formidable, etc. The letter *'bha'* of this word indicates *bharaṇa* or maintenance of the world, and *'va'* indicates *vamana* or projection of the world. Thus, Bhairava is one who brings about the *sṛṣṭi, sthiti* and *saṁhāra* of the universe. He is Lord Śiva who is known as Bhairava. A Tāntric *sādhaka* may consider himself as a Bhairava.

Bhūta : Lit. means: being, existing, gross physical element, etc. *Bhūta is* primarily the concept of creature with both idea of being or originated and becoming or in process. It is an entity which 'was produced' a creature, living or insentient. The term refers to the whole process of evolution and to particular stages at the same time. There are five *bhūtas* (elements), viz. earth, water, fire, air and space. These are also known as *mahābhūtas*.

Caitanya: Absolute Consciousness characterized by *svātantrya,* absolute autonomy and knowledge *(jñāna)* and activity *(kriyā).*

Citi: It means the Absolute Consciousness, i.e. consciousness in its Initial and unconditioned state. The consciousness-power of the Absolute brings about the world process. It is also known as *cit.*

Citta: 'The empirical mind'. The limited individual consciousness, the psychological status of the individual is known as *Citta.*

Dīkṣā : Lit. means consecration for a religious ceremony, initiation in general. *Dīkṣā* is of two kinds, viz. Vedic and Tāntric. In order to lead a religious life as prescribed by the Vedas and texts of Vedic tradition, a formal initiation is required, but it is not as important as in the case of Tāntric *sādhanā,* in which it is an essential precondition. Abhinavagupta defines *dīkṣā* as 'a process of imparting real knowledge *(jñāna)* and a preceptorial instruction which removes the bondage of *pāśa.* Such kind of benediction and benevolent act is known as *dīkṣā* :

dīyate jñāna sadbhāvaḥ kṣīyate paśuvāsanā/
dāna kṣapaṇasaṁyuktā dīkṣā teneha kīrtitā.// (Tantrāloka).

According to the Śāradā Tilaka, 'that which gives spiritual knowledge *(divya jñāna)* and brings the annihilation of baset propensities *(pāpa)* are verily the initiation *(dīkṣā).* The Kulārṇava Tantra presents a detailed analysis of different categories of initiation. It speaks about seven kinds of *dīkṣā, viz. kriyā, varṇa, kalā, sparśa, vāk, dṛk,* and *mānasa.* According to the Rudrayāmala, *dīkṣā* is of three types, viz. *āṇavī, śāktī, śāmbhavī.*

Hence, *dīkṣā* is a spiritual enrolment to carry on scientific research with the self. It is not a religious anointment but an esoteric discipline. It is not a faith but an inner conviction. It is not ritualistic ostentation but a mystic necessity. However, in Tāntric *sādhanā* the evil deeds are purified through *dīkṣā.*

Guru: A teacher or a preceptor who teaches the essential truth is known as *guru.* Guru may be said to be the power of Divine Grace. That power of Grace affording a favourable opportunity to the aspirant is the means to unraveling of the secret of the *mantra.* The word *guru is* often used in the sense of any elderly person, male or female, who is entitled to get respect. The parents and *ācāryas* are often regarded as the three highest *gurus.* According to the Manusmṛti (2.141-42), *guru* is one who performs the *saṁskāras* and imparts Vedic education. *Guru* is the pivot of Tāntric *sādhanā,* the one who dispels darkness. The Śiva-sūtra (2.6) says: *'gurupāyaḥ."* It means, the *guru* who has attained self-realization can alone help the aspirant for acquiring it. The Mālinīvijaya Tantra (II.10) also says: *'sa gurumatsamaḥ prokto mantravīryaprakāśakaḥ.'* Here, Lord Śiva is addressing Pārvatī as: "One who knows all the principles in their essentials, being able to throw light on the virility or efficiency of *mantras,* is a real *guru* like me." Hence, it is said that *'gṛṇāti upadiśati tāttvikamarthamiti guruḥ.'*

Īśvara: Lit. means : God. The word *īśvara* is derived from the root *is-* 'to rule, be master of', with the suffix *varac* according to the Aṣṭādhyāyī (3.2.175). The Nirukta (3.12) says: *'īśvaraḥ sarveṣāmindriyāṇāṁ gopāyitātmā', i.e. īśvara* is treated here as the soul. The Vedas believe in *Īśvara.* The Cārvāka, Bauddha, Jaina, Sāṁkhya and Mīmāṁsā darśanas do not believe in God. But, on the other hand Nyāya, Vaiśeṣika, Yoga, Vedānta, *darśanas* believe in *īśvara* (God).

Jīva: Lit. means : a bonded being, *paśu, aṇu, puruṣa, etc.* The term is also used to denote' individual self or soul'. The Buddhists reduce it to a stream of thought or a series of cognitions. The Nyāya-vaiśeṣikas hold it as a unique substance, to which all cognitions, feelings and conations belong as attributes. The Mīmāṁsaka says that it is a substance which has the capability of consciousness. *Jīva* remains under the control of *māyā* and seeks for liberation through the performance of various auspicious deeds, sacrifices, *vratas*, serious meditation and regular practice of *yogic sādhanās*.

Kālī: Lit. means: 'the Black one'. Goddess Kālī is one of the most popular deities, worshipped mainly by the Hindus. In the Devīmāhātmya section of Mārkaṇḍeya Purāṇa (VII.5ff.) it is stated that She merged from the forehead of the Divine Mother who became black with anger as the demons headed by Caṇḍa and Muṇḍa came to attack her. Kālī came out with a big hideous face and a dreadful appearance. More or less fearful forms of the deity with the name Mahākālī or Bhadrakālī are described in the works like the Kāraṇāgama, Bhaviṣya Purāṇa, Devī Purāṇa, etc. Kālī is generally considered in twelve aspects or forms. The twelve Kālīs as presented by Abhinavagupta, a great scholar of Kashmir Śaivism, are: (1) Sṛṣṭi Kālī, (2) Rakta Kālī, (3) Sthitināśa Kālī, (4) Yama Kālī, (5) Saṁhāra Kālī, (6) Mṛtyu Kālī, (7) Bhadra Kālī, (8) Mārtaṇḍa Kālī, (9) Paramārka Kālī, (10) Kālāgnirudra Kālī, (11) Mahākāla Kālī, (12) Mahābhairavaghora-Chaḍḍakālī. Kālī or Parāśakti or Parāsaṁvid or Universal Consciousness, always manifests powers of *sṛṣṭi, sthiti* and *saṁhāra*.

Linga: Lit. means: a mark, sign, token, an emblem, a badge, symbol, a distinguishing mark, characteristic, etc. From etymological sense *liṅga* is that by which mark, one being or word is cognized whether one is male, female, eunuch or masculine, feminine, neuter. The commentator of Amarakośa, Rāmāśramī comments on the term as *'liṅgayate anena, ligi gatau halaśca iti ghañ.'* The Ajitāgama (Kriyāpāda, III. 17cd-18ab) defines liṅga as: *'layaṁ gacchanti bhūtāni saṁhāre nikhilāni ca nirgacchanti yataścāpiliṅgokistena hetunā.'* The Tantrāloka (V.113-114) also says: *'atra viśvamidaṁ līnam atrāntaḥsthaṁ ca gamyate'*—it is from the liṅga the universe comes into being and dissolves in it. Generally, *liṅga* has been a popular object of worship in India started from prehistoric to modern period. The Āgamic tradition uses the term *liṅga* mostly in the sense of arch-symbol and a formal representative of Lord Śiva. The Kūrma Purāṇa describes about the origin of *liṅga* and its worship. The Liṅga Purāṇa also speaks about the Śivaliṅga and its symbolical components. It also praises the style of worshipping *liṅga* along with its pedestal. The Vāmana Purāṇa lauds several holy places where ancient *liṅgas* are established. There are twelve *(dvādaśa) jyotirliṅgas* of Lord Śiva being worshipped in India since ancient times.

Mala: Lit. means: dross, dirt, impurity, dust, any impure Matter, etc According to Kashmir Śaivism, *mala* is that which covers and conceals the real nature of the Divine Consciousness. It is a limiting condition which hampers the free expression of the spirit. It is of three types, viz. *āṇava mala, māyīya mala* and *kārma mala*. Āṇava mala is the primary limiting condition which reduces the universal consciousness to an *aṇu* or the empirical individual. Māyīya mala is the limiting condition brought about by *Māyā* that gives to the soul its gross and subtle body. *Kārma mala* is the limiting condition brought about by the *vāsanās* under the influence of desire. It is the force of those *vāsanās* that carries the *jīva* from one life to another.

Maṇḍala: Lit. means: round, circular. The Amarakośa defines the term *Maṇḍala:* as: *'cakravalaṁ to maṇḍalam* (1.3.6), *bimbo'strī manḍḍalaṁ triṣu* (1.3.15) and *pariveṣastu paridhirūpasūryaka, maṇḍale* (1.3.32).' It means, a sensible horizon, a circle or ring, disc of the sun or moon and halo. In the Taittirīya Saṁhitā (V.3. 9.2) *'maṇḍaleṣṭakā'* is used to denote circular bricks. The Bṛhadāraṇyaka Upaniṣad (V.5.2) refers to the person in the orb *Maṇḍala:* of the, sun *(etasmin maṇḍale puruṣa)*. In the later Vedic and Sanskrit Literature *Maṇḍala* is used to mean a circular diagram or figure drawn on any altar and *pūjā* ritual. In Śulbasūtras also it specifically refers the squaring of a circle *(caturaśraṁ maṇḍalam*–Āpastamba Śulbasūtra, 3.2-3). *Maṇḍala* worship is very popular and even important in Tāntric rituals. In Śaivite tradition various *maṇḍalas* are worshipped in different months. Several *maṇḍalas* are described in the Śāradā Tilaka, Pauṣkara Saṁhitā and other Tāntric texts. The Buddhist Tantras also describe *maṇḍalas, e.g. Sarvatobhadra* etc. Now a days *Maṇḍala* worship is a common feature in any *pūjā* rituals.

Mantra: It is a sacred or mystic formula for recitation. The word *mantra is* composed of two letters *'man'* and *'tra'*. *Man* implies *mananāt* (by pondering), and *'tra'* implies *'trāyate* (protects). Hence, *mantra* means that which protect or save by pondering. Yāska says: *mantra mananāt* (Nirukta, VII.12) which means Vedic verses are derived from the root *man-*, 'to think'.The Kulārṇava Tantra says *'mantra'* is so called since it saves from all dangers, as the aspirant thereby is led to ponder over God of immeasurable refulgence that is the only principle in the world. The Śāradā Tilaka (6.3) divides *mantras* into three categories, viz. the male *mantra*, female *mantra* and neuter *mantra*. The masculine *mantras* end in *'hum'* and *'phaṭ'*, female with *'svāhā'* and neuter *mantra* with *'namaḥ'*. Purāṇas and some Smṛtis prescribe short *mantras* of five, six, eight, twelve, thirteen. and more syllables as very efficacious for securing all objects. The best Vedic *mantra* is the Gāyatrī (Ṛgveda, 111.62. 10). The Atharvaveda (XIX.71.1) calls it Vedamātā. The Tāntric works (rituals) have their own sacred *mantras*, but they also employ Vedic *mantras*, e.g. *'tryambakaṁ yajāmahe sugandhim'...* (ṚV 7.59.12) is addressed to Rudra, but is known as *mahā-mṛtyuñjaya mantra* or *mṛtasañjīvanī mantra* in Tāntric works and is prescribed for purifying the mind in the Mahānirvāṇa Tantra (8.243). Similarly, the Gāyatrī *mantra* is employed by the Tāntrikas (vide Śāradā Tilaka, XXI.108 and Prapañcasāra Tantra, which devotes two chapters, i.e. 19 & 30 for explaining *praṇava mantra* or *oṁkāra)*. The Mahānirvāṇa Tantra (III.14-37) recommends that *'om sac-cid-ekaṁ brahma'* is the best of *mantras*, that those who perform the *pūjā & upāsanā* of the Highest *Brahma* or Supreme Lord, are in need of no other *sādhanā* and that by the mere perfection of that sacred *mantra* the individual self merges in Brahma. The Buddhist Tantras also claimed ti show the way to the attainment of various worldly objects and even Nirvāṇa through the *mantras.*

Māyā: Generally, it means deceit, jugglery, witchcraft, fraud, trick, etc. The Amarakośa (2.10.11) records the term in the sense of magic *(indrajāla)* and Kṣīrasvāmin comments on this as: *'mātyasyāṁ viśvaṁ māyā.'* According to the Abhidharmakośa Bhāṣya (V.49), *māyā is* used in the sense of magic which deceives others *(parvañcanā māyā).* The term is very frequently used in the Ṛgveda in the sense of magic *(māyābhiraśvinā yuvam-* ṚV V.78.6; *indromāyābhiḥ pururūpa īyate--ṚV* 6.47.18). According to Śaṅkara the world is called *māyā,* because of its unreality. *So, māyā* is the root of every creation. But different philosophical schools develop different thoughts on this concept of *māyā.* According to Kashmir Śaivism, Parama Śiva have two forms of Śakti--Cit Śakti and Māyā Śakti. They may be called Vidyā-māyā and Avidyā-māyā. The nature of Vidyā-māyā is to help in the attainment of Parama Śiva with her power of *hlādinī* and *saṁvita.* It accelerates the process of evolution. Whereas *avidyā-māyā* brings about the crudification of self. It creates the phenomenal world. With the power of her *āvaraṇa* and *vikṣepa* it obscures, limits and blinds the Self. But these two powers or functions of Śiva are not independent and separable. *Māyā* creates five principles or powers known as *kañcukas,* which limit the knowledge and power of the Universal Self. These five *kañcukas* are: *kalā, (aśuddha) vidyā, rāga, niyati & kāla.* It is with these sheaths that *māyā* enwraps *puruṣa.* The microcosm goes into deep slumber and forgets his Divine nature and origin.

Mokṣa: Lit. means: salvation, liberation, emancipation, release, *nirvāṇa, mukti, apavarga,* etc. It is the last of the four goals of a human being *(puruṣārtha),* the remaining three being righteousness *(dharma)*, material well-being *(artha)*, and sexual pleasure *(kāma)*. The Amarakośa (1.5.6) records the term *mokṣa* as a synonym of *mukti* along with other terms like: *kaivalya, nirvāṇa, śreyas, niḥśreyas, amṛta* and *apavarga*. Kṣīrasvāmin comments on the same as: *mokṣaḥ pāśebhyaḥ ātmanaḥ pṛthakbhāvaḥ*--free from the bindings of one's self. The Laghu Yoga-Vāsiṣṭha (6.1.9) defines the term as: *aśeṣeṇa parityāgo vāsanānāṁ ya uttamaḥ, mokṣa ityucyate*, i.e. abandonment of all sorts of desires *(vāsanās)* is the best means of liberation. Hence, to be freed from all sorts of sufferings is known as *mokṣa*. It is rightly defined by Śabdakalpadruma as: *'mokṣyate duḥkhamanena.'* This is the main subject of discussion in all the Indian philosophical systems. The Vedānta, Sāṁkhya Yoga, Nyāya-vaiśeṣika, Mīmāṁsā, Bauddha, Jaina, Kashmir Śaiva Darśana, etc.have treated it according to their own philosophical thought.

Mudrā: Lit. means: a seal, an instrument for sealing or stamping; a stamp, print, mark, impression; an image, a sign; name of certain positions of fingers practiced in devotion or religious worship. Generally, it is known as posture of the body, especially of hands needed for *yogic* exercise and spiritual attainment. It is called *mudrā* (root *mud-* 'to rejoice', 'to please', with the suffix *rak* and *tāp)*, because it gives the bliss of spiritual consciousness. The derivative meaning of the term *mudrā* is: *'mudaṁ harṣaṁ rāti dadāti iti mudrā'*--it gives delight in the heart. *Mudrās* like Abhaya, Varada, Dharmacakra, Bhūmisparsa, Namaskāra, etc. are commonly found in iconic representation symbolizing the quality associated with the deity. The Haṭhayoga Pradīpikā devotes a complete chapter on *mudrās*. Some of which are: Mahāmudrā, Mahāvedha, Khecarī, Mahābandha, Uḍḍīyyānabandha, Mūlabandha, Jālandharabandha, etc. However, the scholars explain *mudrā* in different ways denoting mystic pose of the hand', manual signs indicative of various ideas', finger signs', hand poses adopted during meditation or exposition.

Nāda: Lit. means: loud roar, shout, cry and sounding in general. The Amarakośa (1.6.22) refers it as a synonym of *śabda*. The Nighaṇṭu (III.16.9) records it as a synonym of *stoṭa*, i.e. 'one who praises'. However, most of the related words of *nāda* bear the etymological sense of the verbal root nad- 'to sound' or 'to praise'. In the Tāntric literature *nāda* is related with creation. When the Supreme Being or Parama Śiva begins to manifest itself in creation, its first vibration or the primordial sound is known as *nāda*, which is actually the manifestation of the consciousness of the Supreme Being revealed as sound. The Divine pleasure of this union, i.e. Śiva - Śakti is called *nāda*, As the supreme seed, the primeval sound *nāda* abides in all living beings.

Nirguṇa: The term *guṇa* means quality, virtue, cord, etc., while *nirguṇa* which is opposite to *saguṇa*, means having no cord or string or without good qualities or virtues, bad, worthless, vicious, etc. The term *nirguṇa* appears several times in the Upaniṣads in the sense of devoid of all qualities or properties. Basically the terms *saguṇa* and *nirguṇa* are associated with Brahman, viz. *Saguṇa* Brahman & *Nirguṇa* Brahman. *Nirguṇa* Brahman is unqualified Absolute. The best method of describing it, therefore, is by negative terms (*neti-neti*). The concept of *Nirguṇa* is found in the Upaniṣads, Epics, Purāṇas and other texts of Indian tradition. In the Śvetāśvatara Upaniṣad (VI. 11), Brahman or God is described as omnipotent, omniscient, omnipresent, an observer and devoid of all qualities. Hence, *Nirguṇa* devoid of (*guṇas*) qualities is an attribute of Brahman, and without which Brahman cannot be defined in the Upaniṣadic texts.

Parama Śiva : He is known as the Supreme or the Absolute of Tāntric Philosophy. Parama Śiva is the *pūrṇa-ahantā*, self-luminous and pure-consciousness. The *pūrṇa-ahantā* is the essence of ParamaŚiva. He is also known as the Supreme Reality. Besides, He is of the nature of Bliss and complete in Himself. He holds in Himself the un-manifested universe as an idea. That reality out of which thirty-six *tattvas* evolve and into which all of them get absorbed. At the same time, He transcends the Universe. He is the transcendental Reality, Pure Intelligence as well as the one all-including Supreme Experience. Hence, Parama Śiva is both transcendent and immanent. He is Truth, Consciousness and Bliss.

Paśu: The empirical individual bound by ignorance (*avidyā*) or spiritual nescience is known as *paśu*. Abhinavagupta explains it in his Paramārthasāra (verse 16) as: '*māyāparigrahavaśād bodho malinaḥ pumān paśurbhavati.*' *Puruṣa* is the finite subject who takes a finite individual I-consciousness, having limited power to know and to do, as his self. Having lost his finiteness, he is known as '*aṇu*', a finite being. He sees that everything and everyone as different from him. Such viewpoint of diversity and such finitude are the main impurities of such individual I consciousness, which being fastened by the chains of ignorance and finitude, is known as *paśu*, a bonded being.

Pīṭha: Lit. means: a seat, a chair, stool or shrine of a deity (usually a goddess). In the Amarakośa (2.6.138) the term is recorded as a synonym of *āsana* to mean 'seat' or more specifically a chair or stool. At present the term is mostly focused on the senses of the seat of a deity, an altar, a pedestal, a religious seat, or throne of the *āśramas*. Various holy *pīṭhas* of Goddess Śakti are famous in India. Tantracūḍāmaṇi records a list of 51 *pīṭhas*, widely known as holy resorts of Śakti origin of which is associated with Dakṣayajña legend describing the falling of 51 pieces cut-off from the body of Satī. Each *pīṭha* is supposed to contain a limb of *Devī* Satī, a presiding goddess and her Bhairava. Some of the famous Śakti *pīṭhas* are: Varanasi, Kañcī, Kāmākhyā, Kurukshetra, Ujjayinī, Hiṅgulā, Jvālāmukhī, etc. There are also some minor *pīṭhas*, known as *upapīṭhas*. The Hevajra Tantra and Kalikāpurāṇa enumerate four *pīṭhas*, viz. Jālandhara, Oḍiyāna, Pūrṇagiri, and Kāmarūpa. The Devī Bhāgavata Purāṇa records 108 *pīṭhas*. A complete list of 108 Śakti *pīṭhas* along with the 108 names of the goddess is formed for the first time in the Matsya Purāṇa (13.25-53). The Tāntric and Purāṇic texts have elaborately discussed various Śakti *pīṭhas* and its religious importance.

Prajñā: It stands for perfect knowledge, which liberates an individual mind from the miseries and torments of life and removes the veil of ignorance.

Prāṇa: Lit. means: breathe. It is derived from the root *pṛ-* 'to fill, to nourish, to satiate. The term *prāṇa* is traditionally derived from the conjunction of *pra-an* + *ac* (cf. *ānīdavātaṁ svadhayā tadekam*–Ṛgveda X.129.2), which means 'breathing forth' and *prāṇiti jīvati*, means breathes properly and goes on living. The root *an-*, 'to breathe' , with the suffix kvip means one who breaths. *Prāṇa* is defined in the Chāndogya Upaniṣad (1.3.3) as: *'yad vai prāṇiti sa prāṇaḥ'*--that which breaths, is truly breath. In the narrow sense prang denotes one of the vital airs of which five are usually distinguished, viz. *prāṇa, apāna, vyāna, udāna,* and *samāna*. *Prāṇa* is brahman. It is an all-conditioning, yet inscrutable agent. This is said in the Kena Upaniṣad (1.9) as: *'yatprāṇena na prāṇiti yena prāṇaḥ praṇīyate, tadeva brahma tvaṁ viddhi.'* In accordance with the Upaniṣads, Abhinavagupta in his Tantrāloka states that the vital energy is basically one, but it assumes the five specific modes, viz. *prāṇa, apāna,* etc.

Pratyabhijñā: It is a name of Kashmir Śaivism, i.e. Śaiva system of Kashmir. *Prati+abhi+jñā* = *Pratyabhijñā. Prati* means *pratipam,* i.e. contrary, in other words though known, now appearing as forgotten through delusion. *Abhi* means facing, i.e. close at hand. *Jñā* means illumination or knowledge. Hence, *pratyabhijñā* means re-cognition of the real self. Since the term means recognition it refers to the way of realizing the soul's identity with Lord Śiva.

Rāga : means mental desire, such as: greed, passion, *etc.*, which lead one to bondage and *Saṁsāra.*

Śakti : Lit. means: energy, power, especially the creative energy that generates and continues to activate the universe. The term *Śakti* is derived from the root *śak-* 'to be able', 'to be powerful', with the suffix *ktin.* Kṣīrasvāmin, the commentator of the Amarakośa comments on the term as: *śakyate anayā jetuṃ Śakti.* The derivative sense of *Śakti* is 'that through which it is possible to conquer or through which something can be conquered *(śakyate jetum ābhiḥ śaktyaḥ).* The Aṣṭādhyāyī of Pāṇini (3.2.129), uses the term *Śakti* in sense of capability. The primordial female principle or the power of the Supreme Being is treated *Śakti* through the manifestation of the universe is affected. *Parāśakti* is conceived as female principle. It is the energy of Lord Śiva and regarded as the instrumental cause of creation. Besides, Śakti is symbolically represented as the spouse of Śiva and hence, She is the immanent principle of Śiva. Devoid of Śakti, Śiva would be insentient *(jaḍa)* and consequently, as good as 'dead' *(śava).* Śiva knows Himself only through His Great Śakti She is also the power of freedom of the Lord. Śakti has been addressed as *janani, mātri* and *ambā.* Generally, Śakti or Devī is identified with Vidyāmāyā. With the help of Vidyāmāyā, *jīva* proceeds towards spiritual sublimity. Śakti or Devī helps *jīva* in moving towards Paramaśiva. Without the help of Śakti it is not possible for the *jīva* to attain the Supreme Oneness with Paramaśiva.

Śaṅkara: This is another name of Śiva. *'Sam karoti iti Śaṁkaraḥ',* i.e. one who brings about happiness and welfare is known as Śaṅkara.

Śānti: Lit. means: peace, tranquility, etc. The term *śānti* (fem.) is a mufti-dimensional concept in the Vedic, Purāṇic, Tāntric & Buddhist Literature. It is a word of current usage in the sense of peace or calmness of mind, absence of passion, averting of pain, quiet, etc. It is derived from the root *Sam-* 'to be appeared', 'to kill', 'to stop', etc. Kṣīrasvāmi, the commentator of Amarakośa (3.2.3) says: *'kāmakrodhādyabhāva śānti'*—absence of lust, anger, etc. is known as *śānti.* The indeclinable particle *śam* means welfare, happiness, prosperity, and it is also used in the sense of peace, quiet, etc. Though the word *śānti* does not occur in the Ṛgveda, but *'śam'* occurs several times in this text. Similarly, in the Vājasaneyi Saṁhitā also *'śum'* occurs a number of times. The word *śānti'* is occurred many a times in the Taittirīya Saṁhitā (6.1.7.7-8, 6.2.2, 6.3.5, etc.) as well as in the Atharvaveda (XIX.9.14). In the Upaniṣads, the word *śānti* is used in the sense of 'peace'. According to Atharvaveda Pariśiṣṭa (LXX.10.4), *śānti* does not occur / happen on account of the following reasons :

apūjanāttu pūjyasya tathāpūjyasya pūjanāt /
antaḥkaraṇadoṣācca hetoḥ śāntirnajāyate //

It means, persons those who are not honouring one who is honourable, honouring one who is not honourable, and keep blemishes in the mind. So, due to these reasons the peace desiring people never get peace in their life time. The Gītā uses the words *śānti* and *nirvāṇa* to indicate the Bliss of the person who abides in God *(śāntiṁ nirvāṇa paramām* ...). According to the Viṣṇusahasranāma Bhāyṣa (75), Brahman is known as *śānti* as those who have abandoned all attachments find peace in Him. The Agni Purāṇa (263.7-8) describes eighteen *śāntis.* The Kūrma Purāṇa (I.12.66) describes *śānti* as a goddess, whereas it is known as *parva* as mentioned in the Mahābhārata, i.e. *Śānti parva.* In Buddhism, *nirvāṇa* is known as the best *śānti* (peace). The Dhammapada rightly says: *'natthi śānti paramaṁ sukham'*--there is no Bliss, which surpasses the perfect peace. The Nārada Bhakti Sūtra (VI.1.60) records that love is the nature of peace and it is of the nature of Supreme Bliss.

Sāvitrī : This was one of the most important philosophical doctrines of the Ṛgveda, in which the creative principle is symbolized as Savitā, the impeller of all and his energy as Sāvitrī. Savitā and Sāvitrī are known as an inseparable pair. Sūrya is the great deity, Savitā and his energy is Sāvitrī which he is radiating through out the space and each one of the living organisms in the plant, animal and human kingdoms is receiving that Sāvitrī or solar light. In the Sāvitrī Upaniṣad nine Savitā-Sāvitrī pairs are enumerated as:

	Savitā	**Sāvitrī**
1.	Agni	Pṛthvī
2.	Varuṇa	Āpaḥ
3.	Vāyu	Ākāśa
4.	Yajña	Chandāṁsi
5.	Stanayitnu	Vidut
6.	Āditya	Dyauḥ
7.	Manas	Vāk
8.	Puruṣa	Strī

The above (list) is almost similar in the Jaiminīya Upaniṣad Brahmaṇa, Ch. 4, Tāṇḍya 28, which shows that the doctrine of Sāvitrī Vidyā was specially featured in the Sāmaveda tradition. The Gopatha Brāhmaṇa (1.1.53) is also explains in detail the Sāvitrī doctrine and records twelve pairs of Savitā -Sāvitrī.

Siddhis: Super-natural powers attained through the practice of *yoga*. These *siddhis* are eight in number, viz. *aṇimā, laghimā, mahimā, garimā, prāpti, prākāmya, vaśitva,* and a s *īśitva.*

Śraddhā: Lit. means: trust, faith, belief and confidence. Belief in divine revelation or religious faith is known as *śraddhā*. It is very much extolled in Vedic literature and occurs in the Indian religious tradition as an essential element in the making of the truthful man. *Śrat* is *satyam* and the faculty which accepts truth as its cardinal virtue is called *Śraddhā (śraddhīyate asmat iti śraddhā).*

Śrī: Goddess Lakṣmī, the deity and consort of Lord Viṣṇu, who embodies the qualities of prosperity and beauty. She is worshipped especially by the Vaiṣṇavas as inseparable from Viṣṇu.

Tryambaka: Lit. means Lord Śiva The word *ambaka* is understood as the eye, and Śiva is therefore represented as the deity with three eyes and hence called Virūpākṣa. The three eyes are are taken to be Sūrya, Candra, and Agni corresponding to the triadic conceptions employed in the Vedic cosmogony. Śiva's *Śakti* Māheśvarī is also represented as the Goddess with three eyes both in sculpture and painting. Agni is also called *Tryambaka* because of his three births on the three different levels of manifestation (Ṛ̣V X.45.1), each birth requiring one mother.

Vidyā: Lit. means: knowledge (from the root *vid-* 'to know') learning, lore, science, etc. *Vidyā* is stated to be fourteen, i.e. the four Vedas, six *aṅgas* (Vedāṅgas), Dharmaśāstra, Mīmāṃsā, Tarka or Nyāya and the Purāṇas. As knowledge, *vidyā* is of two kinds, viz. *parāvidyā* (spiritual knowledge) and *aparāvidyā* (material knowledge).

Viriñci : Lit. means Brahmā. It is the same as Viriñcā. Both the words denote Brahman, the creator of this whole world/ universe.

Vrata: Lit. means a religious act of devotion or austerity, a vow in general. It is an observance of pious act like fasting on a particular sacred day. In the sense of religious observance the Āpastamba Śrautasūtra *(vratam upaiti*-IV.2.6), the Kātyāyana Śrautasūtra *(vratopeta*-2.1.11), and the Baudhāyana Śrauta-Sūtra (I.1), which includes abstinence from certain things like: *māṣa* (beans), *māṁsa* (flesh) and sexual intercourse. One has to follow certain prescribed rules while observing a particular *vrata*. *Vrata* also means rituals intended for certain purposes. These are regional and local in character, performed specially by the women folk for averting diseases and calamities, for progeny and prosperity and for other practical purposes of life. The majority of the *vratas* are supposed to produce tangible results. Their performer is endowed with a beautiful form, and he/she gets immense fortune, subdues the enemy, and is rendered free from all earthly calamities including various diseases. In short, all conceivable temporal Bliss can be obtained through *vratas*.

Yantra: Lit. means : restraint, curb, check, bind, fasten, force, etc. The term *yantra is* derived from the root *yam-*, 'to control'. Besides, it also denotes a fetter, band, tie and rain. In the Ṛgveda, (X.149.1) it is used in the sense of bend or fetter. In the Aṣṭāṅgahṛdaya (Sūtrasthāna XXV.3-28), *yantra* is described as instruments of different types of. According to the Sūryasiddhānta (XIII.19-24), various *yantras* were used for measuring time, like: *chāyā-yantra, kapāla-yantra, toya-yantra*, etc. The Mayamata, as an archaeological text, used *yantra* in the sense of a device and machine as: *jala-yantra*. In the Tantric point of view, *yantra* means an amulet, i.e. a mystical or astronomical diagram used as an amulet. This diagram is engraved or drawn on metal, paper, stone, wood or other materials which are worshiped in the same manner as an image. The *yantra* worship is an essential feature of Tāntric *sādhanā* and it is also a mystic process of awakening the Divine Power.

Yoni : Lit. means: womb, uterus, vulva, the female organ of generation (cf. *jīvo mṛtasya carati svadhābhiramartyor martyenā sayoniḥ*--Ṛgveda, 1.164.30cd). The term is derived from the root *ya-* 'to unite, to yoke, to push or to worship' towards, etc. Brahman is the *yoni* (main source) of everything. *Yoni* signifies the causal factor that produces a particular class of beings. In the Bhagavad Gītā, Lord Śrī Krisṇa says that His womb is the great sustainer where He places the seed of creation (*mama yonirmahad Brahma tasmin garbhaṁ dadhāmyaham*—XIV.3).

General Index

C

R

S

T